The Communicator's Commentary

Psalms 73-150

THE COMMUNICATOR'S COMMENTARY SERIES
OLD TESTAMENT

I   *Genesis* by D. Stuart Briscoe

II   *Exodus* by Maxie D. Dunnam

III *Leviticus* by Gary W. Demarest

IV   *Numbers* by James Philip

V   *Deuteronomy* by John C. Maxwell

VI   *Joshua* by John A. Huffman, Jr.

VII *Judges, Ruth* by David Jackman

VIII *1, 2 Samuel* by Kenneth L. Chafin

IX   *1, 2 Kings* by Russell H. Dilday

X   *1, 2 Chronicles* by Leslie C. Allen

XI   *Ezra, Nehemiah, Esther* by Robert M. Norris

XII *Job* by David L. McKenna

XIII *Psalms 1–72* by Donald M. Williams

XIV *Psalms 73–150* by Donald M. Williams

XV   *Proverbs, Ecclesiastes, Song of Solomon* by David A. Hubbard

XVI *Isaiah* by David L. McKenna

XVII *Jeremiah, Lamentations* by John Guest

XVIII *Ezekiel* by Douglas Stuart

XIX *Daniel* by Sinclair B. Ferguson

XX   *Hosea, Joel, Amos, Obadiah, Jonah, Micah* by Lloyd J. Ogilvie

XXI *Nahum, Habakkuk, Zephaniah, Haggai, Zechariah, Malachi* by Lloyd J. Ogilvie

Lloyd J. Ogilvie

—————— General Editor ——————

The Communicator's Commentary

Psalms 73-150

Donald M. Williams

WORD BOOKS, PUBLISHER • DALLAS, TEXAS

Library of Congress Cataloging in Publication Data
Main entry under title:

The Communicator's commentary.
   Bibliography: p.
   Contents: OT14. Psalms 73–150 / by Donald M. Williams
   1. Bible. O.T.—Commentaries.   I. Ogilvie, Lloyd
John.   II. Williams, Donald M., 19–.
BS1151.2.C66   1986   221.7'7   86–11138
ISBN 0–8499–0420–X (v. OT14)

Printed in the United States of America

5 6 7 8 9 9 AGF 9 8 7 6 5

To
Bob and Nancy Hunt
Lifelong friends,
Coworkers in the gospel

Contents

Editor's Preface		11
Author's Preface		17

73	Caught between Theory and Practice	19
74	When the Roof Falls In	29
75	In His Time . . .	38
76	God Is Awesome!	44
77	When the Lights Go Out	49
78	Pass It On	56
79	A Present Grief	73
80	Prayer for Revival	80
81	The Best Is Yet to Come	89
82	When Lady Justice Loses Her Blindfold	95
83	Call to Battle!	101
84	Homesickness	108
85	Recovery	115
86	God of the Gaps	121
87	The City of God	129
88	In Death's Shadow	133
89	When Experience Contradicts Theology	140
90	A Light at the End of the Tunnel	158
91	Dwelling in the Secret Place	165
92	Who Really Prospers?	173
93	Stability in the Storm	179
94	True Liberation Theology	183
95	Sing to the Lord!	190
96	Sing to the Lord a New Song!	195
97	The Lord Reigns!	201
98	Sing a Song of Salvation	207
99	He Is Holy!	211

100 Make a Joyful Shout   216
101 The State of the Union   220
102 Prayer in Pain   225
103 Mercy over All   233
104 God's Care for Creation   241
105 Claim the Covenant!   251
106 Depravity, Destruction, and Deliverance   261
107 Riotous Renewal   274
108 A Combination of Psalms 57:7–11 and 60:5–12   288
109 How to Pray When Falsely Accused   290
110 Whose Son Is the Messiah?   299
111 The Works of the Lord   305
112 God's Blessing upon the Righteous   311
113 The What and Why of Worship   317
114 What Makes God's People Special?   322
115 What to Say When Unbelievers Scoff   326
116 When Death Doesn't Get through the Door   333
117 Praise for the Instant Generation   340
118 Mercy! Mercy! Mercy!   342
119 The Word of God   352
120 How to Deal with Liars   399
121 When the Going Gets Tough   403
122 The Joy of Jerusalem   407
123 Waiting for God's Mercy   411
124 Gratitude for God's Mercy   414
125 Clearing the Moral Air   418
126 Homecoming!   422
127 God's Energy or Our Vanity   426
128 The Blessing of a Healthy Fear of God   429
129 A Curse upon Our Enemies   434
130 When Guilt Overwhelms Us   438
131 How to Get Ready for God   442
132 God's Rule and Realm   445
133 Dwelling in Unity   451
134 How to Have a "Good Night"   455
135 Know the God You Worship   458
136 Blest Be the Tie That Binds   464
137 No Song in Exile   471
138 Why Worship?   476

139	God's Intimacy with Us	480
140	Prayer for Deliverance	489
141	Praying against the Deeds of the Wicked	494
142	Abandoned by All but God	498
143	Big Prayer: Answer Me, Deliver Me, Revive Me	502
144	Battle and Blessing	507
145	Praising God the King	514
146	Where to Get a Good Return on Your Investment	521
147	One of a Kind	525
148	Total Worship	531
149	A New Song	535
150	Praise the Lord!	539

Editor's Preface

God has called all of His people to be communicators. Everyone who is in Christ is called into ministry. As ministers of "the manifold grace of God," all of us—clergy and laity—are commissioned with the challenge to communicate our faith to individuals and groups, classes and congregations.

The Bible, God's Word, is the objective basis of the truth of His love and power that we seek to communicate. In response to the urgent, expressed needs of pastors, teachers, Bible study leaders, church school teachers, small group enablers, and individual Christians, the Communicator's Commentary is offered as a penetrating search of the Scriptures of the Old and New Testament to enable vital personal and practical communication of the abundant life.

Many current commentaries and Bible study guides provide only some aspects of a communicator's needs. Some offer in-depth scholarship but no application to daily life. Others are so popular in approach that biblical roots are left unexplained. Few offer impelling illustrations that open windows for the reader to see the exciting application for today's struggles. And most of all, seldom have the expositors given the valuable outlines of passages so needed to help the preacher or teacher in his or her busy life to prepare for communicating the Word to congregations or classes.

This Communicator's Commentary series brings all of these elements together. The authors are scholar-preachers and teachers outstanding in their ability to make the Scriptures come alive for individuals and groups. They are noted for bringing together excellence in biblical scholarship, knowledge of the original Hebrew and Greek, sensitivity to people's needs, vivid illustrative material from biblical, classical, and contemporary sources, and lucid communication by the use of clear outlines of thought. Each has been selected to contribute to this series because of his Spirit-empowered ability to help people live in the skins of biblical characters and provide a "you-are-there" intensity to the drama of events of the Bible which have so much to say about our relationships and responsibilities today.

The design for the Communicator's Commentary gives the reader an overall outline of each book of the Bible. Following the introduction, which reveals the author's approach and salient background on the book, each chapter of the commentary provides the Scripture to be exposited. The New King James Bible has been chosen for the Communicator's Commentary because it combines with integrity the beauty of language, underlying Hebrew and Greek textual basis, and thought-flow of the 1611 King James Version, while replacing obsolete verb forms and other archaisms with their everyday contemporary counterparts for greater readability. Reverence for God is preserved in the capitalization of all pronouns referring to the Father, Son, or Holy Spirit. Readers who are more comfortable with another translation can readily find the parallel passage by means of the chapter and verse reference at the end of each passage being exposited. The paragraphs of exposition combine fresh insights to the Scripture, application, rich illustrative material, and innovative ways of utilizing the vibrant truth for his or her own life and for the challenge of communicating it with vigor and vitality.

It has been gratifying to me as editor of this series to receive enthusiastic progress reports from each contributor. As they worked, all were gripped with new truths from the Scripture—God-given insights into passages, previously not written in the literature of biblical explanation. A prime objective of this series is for each user to find the same awareness: that God speaks with newness through the Scriptures when we approach them with a ready mind and a willingness to communicate what He has given; that God delights to give communicators of His Word "I-never-saw-that-in-that-verse-before" intellectual insights so that our listeners and readers can have "I-never-realized-all-that-was-in-that-verse" spiritual experiences.

The thrust of the commentary series unequivocally affirms that God speaks through the Scriptures today to engender faith, enable adventuresome living of the abundant life, and establish the basis of obedient discipleship. The Bible, the unique Word of God, is unlimited as a resource for Christians in communicating our hope to others. It is our weapon in the battle for truth, the guide for ministry, and the irresistible force for introducing others to God.

A biblically rooted communication of the Gospel holds in unity and oneness what divergent movements have wrought asunder. This commentary series courageously presents personal faith, caring for individuals, and social responsibility as essential, inseparable dimensions of biblical Christianity. It seeks to present the quadrilateral Gospel in its fullness which calls us to unreserved commitment to Christ, unrestricted self-esteem in His grace, unqualified love for others in personal evangelism, and undying efforts to work for justice and righteousness in a sick and suffering world.

A growing renaissance in the church today is being led by clergy and laity who are biblically rooted, Christ-centered, and Holy Spirit-empowered. They have dared to listen to people's most urgent questions and deepest needs and then to God as He speaks through the Bible. Biblical preaching is the secret of growing churches. Bible study classes and small groups are equipping the laity for ministry in the world. Dynamic Christians are finding that daily study of God's Word allows the Spirit to do in them what He wishes to communicate through them to others. These days are the most exciting time since Pentecost. The Communicator's Commentary is offered to be a primary resource of new life for this renaissance.

It has been very encouraging to receive the enthusiastic responses of pastors and teachers to the twelve New Testament volumes of the Communicator's Commentary series. The letters from communicators on the firing line in pulpits, classes, study groups, and Bible fellowship clusters across the nation, as well as the reviews of scholars and publication analysts, have indicated that we have been on target in meeting a need for a distinctly different kind of commentary on the Scriptures, a commentary that is primarily aimed at helping interpreters of the Bible to equip the laity for ministry.

This positive response has led the publisher to press on with an additional twenty-one volumes covering the books of the Old Testament. These new volumes rest upon the same goals and guidelines that undergird the New Testament volumes. Scholar-preachers with facility in Hebrew as well as vivid contemporary exposition have been selected as authors. The purpose throughout is to aid the preacher and teacher in the challenge and adventure of Old Testament exposition in communication. In each volume you will meet Yahweh, the "I AM" Lord who is Creator, Sustainer, and Redeemer in the unfolding drama of His call and care of Israel. He is the Lord who acts, intervenes, judges, and presses His people into the immense challenges and privileges of being a chosen people, a holy nation. And in the descriptive exposition of each passage, the implications of the ultimate revelation of Yahweh in Jesus Christ, His Son, our Lord, are carefully spelled out to maintain unity and oneness in the preaching and teaching of the Gospel.

This volume completes the commentary on the Psalms by Dr. Donald Williams. Odds are good that you are already familiar with Don from his outstanding first volume on the Psalms. Everything I said about his work there pertains here as well. Once more, this scholar-pastor has served us well with his exceptional combination of penetrating scholarship, in-depth application, and illuminating illustration.

In reading this manuscript, I have been impressed again with three extraordinary aspects of Don's work. First of all, he focuses our attention upon the actual text of each psalm. Words, phrases, sentences, and paragraphs are carefully exegeted. Although you don't need to know Hebrew to use this commentary, you will appreciate Don's thorough study of the original language. This commentary will guide you into a clear understanding of what the psalmist actually intended to communicate many centuries ago.

Second, although Don excels as a biblical historian, I am struck by his ability to set each psalm within a modern context. As an astute observer of contemporary culture, he enables the historical text to speak with relevance to our world. He allows the psalms to address both personal and social concerns. This is what good communication of Scripture is all about—thorough study of the text combined with insightful application to our time of history.

Third, I am impressed with Don's passion for worship. In his introduction to the first volume, he promised to connect the psalms with the renewal in worship that we are experiencing throughout the church today. Don has kept his promise! He has shown us how the psalms teach us to worship God with vigor and intimacy. His own fervor for God-directed adoration encourages us to praise with power.

Don's pastoral adventure has taken a new turn since the publication of the first volume. In the preface to that commentary I mentioned some of the roles that he has played since his days at Princeton Seminary: graduate student at Columbia University, college pastor at

Hollywood Presbyterian, evangelist on the streets of Hollywood, college and seminary professor, nationally recognized speaker, author of many books, senior pastor, and radio communicator. Now Don has begun a fresh chapter in his life by planting a church in north San Diego county. As always, he evinces a heart devoted to church renewal in leading the Coast Vineyard.

Don is a pioneer in the faith—breaking new ground, ever on the edge of some exciting project, always taking risks for the sake of God's Kingdom. Thus it comes as no surprise that a sense of adventure permeates this commentary. You will experience the psalms as they come alive through the life and teaching of Don Williams.

With the publication of this volume, we complete an outstanding segment of the Communicator's Commentary. I commend to you both volumes on Psalms. Together they lead us into personal and corporate renewal.

LLOYD OGILVIE

Author's Preface

This volume is the continuation of my commentary on the Psalms. While it can stand alone, it presupposes the Introduction, critical notes, and bibliography that have already appeared in *Psalms 1–72,* which is volume 13 in the Old Testament set of the Communicator's Commentary series. The reader is referred to that volume for the background to this work.

My special thanks again to Lloyd Ogilvie for his gracious invitation to participate in this series and his patience with me in seeing it to completion. Also may I express my appreciation to Mark Roberts of Hollywood Presbyterian Church and to Ernie Owen of Word Books and his staff who have helped to bring this volume into the light of day. Finally, my wife Kathryn accepted my long hours in the study and encouraged me. My deep love to her and thanks for her prayers.

CHAPTER SEVENTY-THREE

Caught between Theory and Practice

Psalm 73

The Bible asserts that God rewards the righteous and punishes the wicked. What happens, however, when this "theory" is challenged by practice? Too often we see the wicked prospering. Dictators strut across the stage of history raping and pillaging like barbarians. Financial empires are built on the backs of the poor and hungry. As in the TV soap operas, villains seem to win in the end, leaving honest and upright people in the dust. Where then is the goodness of God when Job is covered with boils?

Recently my parents, who are now in their early eighties, both recovered from major illnesses. My mother had a kidney removed, and my father suffered months of pain from a bad fall. Only a week before their long awaited visit to my home, while climbing the stairs to their house, my mother fell backwards upon my father and they both crashed over together. Talk about adding insult to injury! Here are two good pious older people thrown into great pain and discouragement entering a second year as invalids. This example could be multiplied a thousandfold.

Not only do the righteous suffer with apparent injustices, the unrighteous also, as we have noted, seem to get away unscathed. For every deposed strong man like Ferdinand Marcos of the Philippines, scores more remain untouched. How much of the world today lives under oppressive rulers? Over a third of our planet is dominated by communist governments. Democracies in the Middle East, Africa, and South and Central America are few and far between. Moreover, the church in many parts of the world is a suffering church. Over 300,000 Christians were martyred last year for their faith. Where is

God's protection in these wounds? Why do the church's prayers seem to go unanswered so often?

The psalmist here confesses God's goodness to the pure in heart (v. 1). Nevertheless, his experience is to the contrary when he sees the prosperity of the wicked (v. 3). They escape harm living prideful violent lives (vv. 4–6). They overflow with abundance (v. 7) and speak against the heavens (v. 9). The godly, however, know plague and chastening (v. 14). This contradiction is only resolved when the psalmist goes into God's sanctuary to understand the end of the wicked (v. 17). There he learns of divine judgment to come (vv. 18–20) and the foolishness of questioning God's will (vv. 21–24). Glory will be his; all he has is God alone in heaven and on earth (v. 25). Since the wicked will perish (v. 27), therefore, to trust in God is ultimate security (v. 28). History finds its meaning not within its own relative flow but "beyond history," eschatologically, at the throne of God. In light of this end, the psalmist can now live in peace.

Psalm 73 is attributed to Asaph. Ezra identifies him as the ancestor of the temple singers (Ezra 2:41), and Chronicles places him in Solomon's time as a chief musician (2 Chron. 5:12). Thus this psalm could come from him or from a guild of temple singers called by his name. Commentators classify Psalm 73 as a psalm of trust or thanksgiving with clear wisdom motifs (see vv. 22–24). The thought moves from the opening complaint (vv. 1–3), to a commentary on that complaint (vv. 4–9), to a confession of confusion (vv. 10–14), to resulting clarity (vv. 15–17), to God's ultimate condemnation (vv. 18–20), and to the psalmist's final confidence (vv. 21–26). It concludes in a witness to God's trustworthiness (vv. 27-28).

COMPLAINT

73:1 Truly God *is* good to Israel,
     To such as are pure in heart.
   2 But as for me, my feet had almost stumbled;
     My steps had nearly slipped.
   3 For I *was* envious of the boastful,
     When I saw the prosperity of the wicked.
                                    Ps. 73:1-3

In verse 1 the psalmist begins with a traditional affirmation of faith: *"Truly God is good to Israel."* The word *truly* suggests that even as he starts to meditate on the contradiction between the experiences of the godly and the ungodly there will be a resolution. This psalm will demonstrate that this confession is true—God *is* good to Israel. The word *good* signifies all of God's graciousness and blessing to His people. In the context here it includes the gifts of God's presence, God's power, God's wisdom (v. 23), and God's ultimate purpose: "And afterward [You] receive me into glory" (v. 24).

The parallel member in verse 1 defines Israel more specifically as those who are *"pure in heart."* In Ps. 24:4 the pure in heart is the person who has not worshiped idols or dealt dishonestly, "sworn deceitfully." His heart is open and clear toward Yahweh. Furthermore, Jesus promises that the pure in heart will see God (Matt. 5:8). Israel, therefore, is to be pure before God in singlehearted devotion. To His people then, He is good.

This positive confession, however, immediately evokes a negative admission in verses 2–3. The psalmist almost stumbled and slipped in his walk before God (contrast the fate of the wicked in v. 18). Now the real issue surfaces. What has happened, contradicting his traditional theology? The psalmist was *"envious of the boastful"* because, simply, the wicked prospered (v. 3). Thus the problem is twofold. The psalmist's heart is bad, he is envious in himself, and events seem to contradict his confession of faith: the boastful, the wicked prosper. The *wicked* here are criminals who violate God's law. Nevertheless, they experience *prosperity,* meaning "well-being," which includes "health" or "wholeness."

In this context then, these questions haunt us. What are we to do with the suffering of the saints and the success of the sinners? How are we to understand God's goodness when violent, oppressive people run off with the world? How can we believe that God is good to the pure in heart when they get it in the neck and the wicked live in peace and prosperity? If we haven't asked these questions, our hearts must be closed or we are living in massive denial.

COMMENTARY

73:4 For *there are* no pangs in their death,
But their strength *is* firm.

> 5 They *are* not in trouble *as other* men,
>   Nor are they plagued like *other* men.
> 6 Therefore pride serves as their necklace;
>   Violence covers them *like* a garment.
> 7 Their eyes bulge with abundance;
>   They have more than heart could wish.
> 8 They scoff and speak wickedly *concerning*
>   oppression;
>   They speak loftily.
> 9 They set their mouth against the heavens,
>   And their tongue walks through the earth.
>
> *Ps. 73:4–9*

To make his complaint clear, the psalmist now offers an exposition on the prosperity of the wicked. He does not want us (or God!) to miss the force of his argument.

First, the wicked die peacefully. They do not have *pangs* or trauma in death. To "lie down" in peace is a sign of blessing (see Gen. 15:15). Second, *"their strength is firm,"* or literally, "fat." Here "fat" is also a sign of blessing (see Gen. 45:18). Third, they do not know *"trouble"* or "labor" or plague (v. 5). In other words, they avoid toil and illness. As a result, they are adorned in a chain of *"pride"* and a garment of *"violence"* (v. 6). They exalt themselves and live without restraint, their adornment reflecting their true character. Moreover, like some Mafia godfather, their *"eyes bulge with abundance"* or "fatness" and their hearts are full to overflowing (v. 7). This composite picture proves that the wicked have everything and lack nothing. For the Hebrew mind, they are exactly where the righteous should be since the blessing of God comes with physical and material bounty (see Gen. 17:6–8). The only difference would be that the righteous would have humility rather than arrogance, knowing that all this blessing comes from God. This, of course, is not true of the wicked. The psalmist continues in verse 8 that they scoff or, literally, "speak with evil oppression" and use lofty speech. This prideful discourse is against God Himself: *"They set their mouth against the heavens"* (v. 9). They are like the builders of the tower of Babel (Gen. 11:1ff.). They also plague the earth with their pride as their tongue *walks* or "strides" across the planet spewing lies and propaganda.

Many a modern dictator in his prime would illustrate this passage. Not only do the world's "great" amass huge fortunes, and exude physical and mental strength (like the Pharaohs) from pictures and statues bigger than life, they also employ pride and violence as instruments of power. Moreover, in the Marxist world they attack heaven in order to control earth. Some even attempt to deny death. Thus Lenin "lives" embalmed in his Moscow tomb witnessing to a timeless, materialistic immortality.

CONFUSION

> 73:10 Therefore his people return here,
> And waters of a full *cup* are drained by them.
> 11 And they say, "How does God know?
> And is there knowledge in the Most High?"
> 12 Behold, these *are* the ungodly,
> Who are always at ease;
> They increase *in* riches.
> 13 Surely I have cleansed my heart *in* vain,
> And washed my hands in innocence.
> 14 For all day long I have been plagued,
> And chastened every morning.
>
> *Ps. 73:10–14*

The next section of this psalm describes the arrogance of the wicked and their followers (vv. 10–12). This is then contrasted by the psalmist's brokenness and futility (vv. 13–14). It begins in verse 10 with those belonging to the wicked, "*his people,*" returning and draining or drinking the "*waters of a full cup,*" or the "waters of abundance." Thus they also share in the material blessings of their evil leaders (see v. 7). With such good fortune they join the functional unbelief of the wicked (see v. 9). They ask in disdain, "'*How does God know?*'" Where is knowledge in the "*Most High*" (for this title, see Gen. 14:18)? If God is holy and powerful and sees the hearts and actions of men, they assert, how can they now live as they do and get away with it? Either God is not God, or there is no justice and relativism reigns. For this reason, it doesn't matter what you do. Furthermore, since the ungodly are "*at ease*" and "*increase in riches*" (v. 12), they are the pragmatic answer to those who claim that God is good to the "pure in heart" (v. 1). He isn't. Experience says He is good to the wicked. What kind of God then is this?

What kind of God allows syndicated crime to control a vast empire of pornography and gambling? What kind of God allows drug dealers to live like kings? What kind of God keeps the world in fear of terrorists? What kind of God lets an atheistic ideology enslave masses of people? In light of this canvas of human evil and its benefits, why be righteous? Why be faithful? The psalmist now turns to his own situation in verse 13. Since the wicked prosper, why should he lament his sins? What is the functional purpose of repentance? Why be open to God? What good does it do? Now the psalmist parallels his inner disposition with his outer action: he has washed his *"hands in innocence"*; that is, he has engaged in purification naively. The reason for this futility is given in verse 14: *"For all the day long* ['continually'] *I have been plagued* ['struck, stricken'].*" This seems to indicate some illness or chronic affliction. He continues: *"And chastened every morning."* The noun *chasten* means either "rebuke" or "correction." Since the intention here seems to be more than educational, the meaning of "chastened" as "rebuked" would be a better parallel to *"plagued."* While the wicked prosper, the psalmist is plagued and rebuked. Following his traditional theology, however, that "God is good," he suffers from punishment and seeks to have it lifted by repentance and cleansing—but to no avail. Here is his crisis. His theology is not functional.

Again and again, I have been thrown into the crisis of bad theology. I once believed that certain spiritual gifts were not for today. Then I experienced those very gifts. I was also taught once by a famous pastor that Jesus would return in the early 1980s, and He didn't. Then I was told that God doesn't heal people miraculously today, but later I experienced His healing in my life. In light of this, what should we do when our traditional theology goes into crisis? To this the psalmist now turns.

CLARITY

73:15 If I had said, "I will speak thus,"
          Behold, I would have been untrue to the
               generation of Your children.
     16 When I thought *how* to understand this,
          It *was* too painful for me—

17 Until I went into the sanctuary of God;
   Then I understood their end.

                                        Ps. 73:15–17

The whole thrust of the complaint that begins in verse 3 is now brought into question. Here is the turning point. If the psalmist followed the empirical evidence of the wicked, he would have been *"untrue"* to (or *"betrayed"*) God's people, the *"generation of Your children."* Since to reject God's people is to reject God, he would have broken from the family of faith, the God of Abraham, Isaac, and Jacob (Exod. 3:16). Now, however, he must surrender his reason and his worldly observations. He cannot *"understand* ["know"] *this,"* that is, achieve a reconciliation between theory and practice, by his own effort. It is too *"painful,"* or *"troubling."*

What is the alternative? Beyond reason is revelation. Or, as Luther says more radically, our reason must die with Christ in order to be resurrected into a new life of faith. The psalmist now goes into God's sanctuary ("sanctuaries," the plural is intensive, meaning the Jerusalem temple). Here, in the context of worship, God speaks. His revelation does not concern the present success of the wicked, but their *"end"* or "final lot." When we know how the novel ends, we understand the plot. Contradictory clues now make sense.

CONDEMNATION

73:18 Surely You set them in slippery places;
      You cast them down to destruction.
   19 Oh, how they are *brought* to desolation, as in a
      moment!
      They are utterly consumed with terrors.
   20 As a dream when *one* awakes,
      So, Lord, when You awake,
      You shall despise their image.

                                        Ps. 73:18–20

Rather than seeing the success of the wicked, God shows the psalmist their horrible end. While he thought that he was slipping (see v. 2), it was really the wicked who were on *"slippery places,"* since they will be *"cast down"* to *"destruction,"* literally, to "deceptive ground." In other words, their foundation is insecure. They are building on the sand, and the storms will level them (see Matt. 7:24–27). Moreover, this catastrophe will happen *in a moment* (v. 19): "Here today, gone tomorrow." Then the wicked will be *utterly consumed* or literally, "they have been completed"; "they have been ended." But what are the *"terrors"* that bring this about? One possibility is human evil; another is demonic attack (see Job 18:14). Whatever the means of their destruction, however, the ultimate cause is divine judgment. Thus in verse 20 it is God who *"wakes up"*; that is, He now acts and despises either the image of the wicked or the image of their idols.

The message is clear. Death will reveal the true condition of those who *"speak loftily"* and *"set their mouth against the heavens"* (vv. 8–9). God, not humankind, has the last word. It is in His temple where the ultimate truth will be told. Likewise, today, if we don't hear the truth in our churches, where will we hear it? Understanding comes in submission to His word and will.

CONFIDENCE

73:21 Thus my heart was grieved,
       And I was vexed in my mind.
   22 I *was* so foolish and ignorant;
       I was *like* a beast before You.
   23 Nevertheless I *am* continually with You;
       You hold *me* by my right hand.
   24 You will guide me with Your counsel,
       And afterward receive me to glory.
   25 Whom have I in heaven *but You?*
       And *there is* none upon earth *that* I desire
          besides You.
   26 My flesh and my heart fail;
       But God *is* the strength of my heart and my
          portion forever.
                                        Ps. 73:21–26

The psalmist now experiences his own humiliation and brokenness. His *"heart"* ("intellect") and *"mind"* (literally, "kidneys," the seat of emotion), that is, his whole self, are *"grieved"* ("soured, embittered") and *"vexed"* ("pierced"). He is like a dumb cow before God's revelation (v. 22). Likewise, when Paul preaches the gospel of Christ crucified, God makes "foolish the wisdom of this world" (1 Cor. 1:20). His ways are not our ways, and His thoughts are not our thoughts (Isa. 55:9).

Nevertheless, God does not treat the psalmist according to his own feelings. Rather, as he is with the Lord, he is held by His right hand (see Ps. 63:8), receiving protection. He is also guided by divine *"counsel,"* receiving direction. And he will find his end in *"glory,"* receiving exaltation. All of this is in sharp contrast to the wicked whose future is destruction (see v. 18). In the final end, *"eschatologically,"* theory and practice become one.

Before the ultimate issues of life and death, the psalmist recognizes that all that he has is God (vv. 25–26). Heaven is heaven because God is there. As the old retired pastor said at my grandmother's funeral, "I don't know much about heaven. But heaven is where Jesus is and that's enough." Earth also finds its meaning in the presence of God: *"There is none upon earth that I desire besides You."* The verb *desire* means "to delight in, to have pleasure in." God is the object of the psalmist's passion. Although his humanity (*"my flesh and my heart"*) fails or has been *"consumed"* or *"spent,"* it is God who is his *"strength"* (literally, "the rock of my heart") and *"portion* ['share', "provision," that is, "life"] *forever."* Thus he is held in both time and eternity by the eternal God who alone satisfies. As Peter replied to Jesus when asked if he too would follow the offended crowd and go away: "Lord, to whom shall we go? You have the words of eternal life" (John 6:68).

CONCLUSION

73:27 For indeed, those who are far from You shall
          perish;
       You have destroyed all those who desert You
          for harlotry.
   28 But it is good for me to draw near to God;
       I have put my trust in the Lord GOD,
       That I may declare all Your works.
                                          Ps. 73:27–28

The psalmist brings his meditation to a close with a summary of his thesis. Regardless of how good people look, regardless of their health, their power, their success, even their "peace" in this world, they will all *"perish"* apart from God. They will perish because God is their life, and to be separated from Him is to die. They will also perish because of divine judgment. Those who desert God for *"harlotry"* are *"destroyed"* ("cut off," v. 27). Their "harlotry" here probably represents their idolatry, or spiritual adultery. This is a common theme in Hosea: "The land has committed great harlotry / By departing from the Lord" (1:2, see 2:8). In their death God will prove Himself to be God. In their judgment the theory that sin brings punishment will become practice. Even though there may not be manifest justice in this life, God will yet prove Himself just before all humankind, and He Himself will close the gulf between theory and practice (see Rev. 20:11–15).

In light of this, the psalmist concludes that it is *"good,"* that is, morally and spiritually right, for him to draw near to God (v. 28). Since God has the last word, he puts his *"trust"* (literally, "sets his refuge") in Him. The consequence of this, finally, is witness: now he declares all of God's works. This comprehensive statement suggests that he is witnessing to the totality of what God has done for him and for Israel. This psalm, which opens Book Three of the Psalter (Psalms 73–89), is an eloquent record of this witness. Here he rests his case and so do we. Since death is certain and only God stands beyond the grave, the day will come when God Himself will bridge the gulf between the theory of His justice and the practice of justice in this life. Therefore, in light of His final resolution, it is good to draw near to Him now, to rest in Him and then to speak of what He has done.

CHAPTER SEVENTY-FOUR

When the Roof Falls In

Psalm 74

With our psychological and sociological "depth" we tend to look upon human history as ambiguous. While philosophers such as Marx have tried to unlock its laws, assuming that it moves in some rational way, we tend to be more modest. No longer do we even engage in moralizing about "just wars" or "human rights" transcending time and space. Content with our confusion, we splash about in the soup of relativity. This is, in a phrase from the seventeenth century, our "climate of opinion." Having surrendered the quest for meaning, we simply focus on the "facts" (Carl Becker). This pragmatism masks our despair. Life becomes an immediate stream of experiences and events with no beginning, no ending, and no transcendent judgment or purpose. Personal and historical catastrophe are shrugged off as further documentation for this ambiguity. Who can understand an earthquake in Mexico City or a reactor meltdown in the Soviet Union?

This "climate of opinion" receives a jolt, however, when we turn to Psalm 74. Here, in the context of national disaster, which includes the destruction of the temple (vv. 3–8) and the dispersion of Israel (vv. 19–21), we are greeted with a surprising conclusion. Such a holocaust does not mean that history is "bunk" (Henry Ford). Such a holocaust means that God is angry (v. 1). There is a moral order after all, and God is to be known in judgment as well as in redemption. This means that life is no neutral zone where the will of God is inoperative. Rather, life is a battle zone where the will of God and the will of human beings (and the devil himself) are in continual conflict. Thus Israel experiences not God's indifference or her own ambiguity, but she feels God's judgment when the roof falls in. As Augustine puts it, if we reject God's mercy we are only left with His wrath.

This psalm, like Psalm 73, is attributed to Asaph, the chief musician of Solomon's time (2 Chron. 5:12). If its setting is the destruction of the temple, its composition would be after 586 B.C. "Asaph" would indicate a guild of temple singers called by his name. Commentators identify this psalm as a corporate lament. The thought moves from the experience of God's rejection and Israel's response (vv. 1–2), to a call to action (vv. 3–11), to a confession of faith (vv. 12–17), to an appeal for God's response (vv. 18–21) and concludes with a call for vindication (vv. 22–23).

DIVINE REJECTION; HUMAN RESPONSE

74:1 O God, why have You cast *us* off forever?
     Why does Your anger smoke against the sheep
          of Your pasture?
   2 Remember Your congregation, *which* You have
          purchased of old,
     The tribe of Your inheritance, *which* You have
          redeemed—
     This Mount Zion where You have dwelt.
                                        Ps. 74:1–2

Verse 1 begins with a cry of despair. It asks the age-old question: Why? The psalmist's experience is that God has rejected His people *"forever."* This is final and eternal. Yet, as the thought progresses it is clear that he hopes for restoration. Nevertheless, the devastation is so awesome that it at least feels like forever. As Jesus showed from His cross, in the deepest moments of depression, however, our cry to God is still the link to life (cf. Ps. 22:1). Thus this prayer was not only spoken; it was treasured and transmitted.

Next, the parallel thought to rejection focuses on the *"anger"* of God. The word for anger signifies the sound of snorting made through the nose (cf. Ps. 18:15). God's enraged nose blows smoke at Israel, *"the sheep of Your pasture."* Note the contrast between God's violent wrath (like a roaring predator) and His helpless, meek flock of sheep (see Pss. 23:1–4; 100:3).

After challenging God's rejection with his "why?" the psalmist immediately responds by calling Yahweh to remember His people in verse 2. They are a *"purchased congregation,"* and a *"redeemed tribe."* They are bound in a covenant with Him (see v. 20). As a *"congregation"* Israel was gathered by the divine call in the Exodus, and as a *"tribe"* she became God's own people, His *"inheritance,"* bearing His name down through the generations. All of this happened by divine intervention. He *"purchased"* ("acquired") Israel by an act of redemption, setting former slaves free from Pharaoh's "house of bondage" (Exod. 20:2). They were given the Promised Land and built God's house there on Mount Zion in Jerusalem. It is as if verse 2 cries out, "Remember Your people and remember Your place."

What does the psalmist do when the roof falls in? First, he asks God, "Why?" and, second, he reminds Him of the commitment that He has made to His people who are now under His judgment. The hope is that as God remembers His covenant, He may remember them with favor once again.

CALL TO ACTION

74:3 Lift up Your feet to the perpetual desolations.
    The enemy has damaged everything in the
      sanctuary.
  4 Your enemies roar in the midst of Your
      meeting place;
    They set up their banners *for* signs.
  5 They seem like men who lift up
    Axes among the thick trees.
  6 And now they break down its carved work, all
      at once,
    With axes and hammers.
  7 They have set fire to Your sanctuary;
    They have defiled the dwelling place of Your
      name to the ground.
  8 They said in their hearts,
    "Let us destroy them altogether."
    They have burned up all the meeting places of
      God in the land.
  9 We do not see our signs;
    There is no longer any prophet;

> Nor *is there* any among us who knows how
> long.
> 10 O God, how long will the adversary reproach?
> Will the enemy blaspheme Your name forever?
> 11 Why do You withdraw Your hand, even Your
> right hand?
> *Take it* out of Your bosom and destroy *them.*
>   Ps. 74:3–11

The psalmist now exhorts God to intervene. He invites Him to walk back (*"lift up Your feet"*) to the burned city of Jerusalem and its devastated temple where He has dwelt in the past. Verses 3–8 provide a graphic picture of destruction. Clearly the psalmist's hope is to awaken God's anger toward Israel's enemies and rekindle His compassion toward His people by this description. But what is God to see?

First, the city is in ruins, *"perpetual desolations"* (v. 3). This suggests that the actual conquest of Jerusalem was some time ago. Second, the *"sanctuary"* ("holy place") also is in ruins. Third, God's *"enemies roar"* ("boast"?) in the *"meeting place."* It is now occupied territory where their *"banners"* (probably military standards) are set up as a sign of victory over Yahweh. Fourth, the temple has been plundered, with its wooden carvings destroyed (vv. 5–6, cf. Jer. 52:17ff.). Fifth, it has been burned (v. 7, see Jer. 52:13). Sixth, it has been totally *"defiled* ['polluted'] *to the ground"* (v. 7). Notice throughout these verses the stress on God's ownership. It is His mountain (v. 2), His meeting place (v. 4), and His sanctuary where His name (His presence) dwells (v. 7). Verse 8 brings this description to a close. God's enemies *"said in their hearts,"* that is, they *"thought and intended"* to put all the *"meeting places,"* or better, "the whole temple" (taking the plural noun as an intensive) to the torch. This horror is what God is to see when He returns to Jerusalem.

Next, in verses 9–11 the psalmist recounts what he sees, or, better, what he doesn't see. To begin with, there are no *"signs."* Commentators are divided on the meaning of this word. In the larger context, this may be a reference to military standards (see v. 4). In the immediate context, however, it may refer to the symbols of faith now taken from the temple or to prophetic oracles or omens. It could also indicate attesting signs that accompany the prophetic word, that is miracles (see Deut. 18:22). In favor of this, there is the next point: there is also no prophet. God's voice is silent (a *"sign"* of judgment).

There are no works of God and no words from God. This explains the consequences in verse 10. Since in the biblical world-view the prophet gives God's will for both the present ("forthtell") and the future ("foretell"), the absence of a prophet means that no one knows the time or length of the adversary's *"reproach"* ("taunt") and blasphemy. No wonder, when God's salvation is given in Christ, as the messianic age breaks in, the gift of the living voice of prophecy is restored (see Acts 21:10–11; 1 Cor. 14:1). These living words continue to be a part of the Holy Spirit's gifts to us as the church is being renewed today. For example, a close friend of mine was taken prisoner by corrupt police in a foreign country. His distraught wife, fearing for his life, came to church the next day after hearing the news. She sat silently through the service weeping softly. As she was then crossing the parking lot to go home, a young man whom she had never met rushed up to her saying, "I've never had anything like this happen to me and I feel really strange, but does 'He's all right' mean anything to you?" To be sure, this prophetic word did, and her husband was safely home in two days. As a postscript to this story, while she was in church her husband was praying at that very time, "Lord, let my wife know that I'm all right." That our God still speaks today is an essential sign that He is the living God in our midst.

Here, however, the judgment of God is seen not only in His silence, but also in His inactivity. The psalmist cries because God's *"right hand,"* the hand of power and authority (see Exod. 15:6), the hand of battle, has been withdrawn. Next, this cry is followed by a call to action: *"Take it out of Your bosom and destroy them"* (v. 11). It is as if the psalmist says to God, "Show Your hand." We can certainly identify with this longing when we see a disintegrating world and an apathetic and corrupt church. We, too, long for God to act once again, to hurl back our enemies, the hosts of Satan's kingdom, and restore the fortunes of His church, reviving her with the power of a new Pentecost.

HUMAN CONFESSION

74:12 For God *is* my King from of old,
Working salvation in the midst of the earth.

13 You divided the sea by Your strength;
   You broke the heads of the sea serpents in the
      waters.
14 You broke the heads of Leviathan in pieces,
   And gave him *as* food to the people inhabiting
      the wilderness.
15 You broke open the fountain and the flood;
   You dried up mighty rivers.
16 The day *is* Yours, the night also *is* Yours;
   You have prepared the light and the sun.
17 You have set all the borders of the earth;
   You have made summer and winter.

Ps. 74:12–17

The psalmist confesses his faith in Yahweh in verse 12 and addresses Him in prayer in verses 13–17, reminding Him of His former mighty deeds. First, God is his *"King."* Note the personal possessive pronoun *my,* witnessing to a vital, intimate submission. Throughout the Old Testament it is asserted that God is the true King over His people (cf. 1 Sam. 8:7). Thus human kings only reign under His sovereignty (Ps. 2:6). As King, Yahweh is Israel's leader in battle. He works *"salvation"* ("deliverances," the plural indicates fullness) on this earth. This means that since our God makes history, He cannot be confined to some mythological, "upper story" in the clouds, never touching our earth (Francis Schaeffer). So Moses sings, "Who is like You, O Lord, among the gods? / Who is like You, glorious in holiness, / Fearful in praises, doing wonders?" (Exod. 15:11).

As the psalmist has shown God the devastations of Jerusalem (vv. 3–8), so now, starting with verse 13, he shows Him His former mighty deeds. First, God split the sea, destroying *"the sea serpents"* and the *"heads of Leviathan"* (see Ps. 104:26; Leviathan is a serpent-like monster). We see that the themes from both creation and redemption (the Exodus) appear in these verses. Behind these great water-beasts lies the whole cosmology of the ancient world, especially the Babylonian creation epic where order results from Marduk's conquering the chaos of the waters (Tiamat). This is especially powerful since it is Babylon who has defeated Judah and destroyed Jerusalem. The psalmist asserts that chaos has been conquered, not by the gods of Babylon but by Yahweh. While the psalmist in no way embraces the pagan myths, he "breaks" them for his poetic and historical purpose (Brevard Childs). Here there is also an implicit appeal for Yahweh to conquer chaos again by restoring Israel's fortunes. So we read in Isa. 51:9: "Awake, awake, put on strength / O arm of the Lord! . . . Are You not the arm that cut Rahab [perhaps a name for chaos] / And wounded the serpent?" We must also remember that in parting the Red Sea Yahweh destroyed the chaos of Egypt's chariots (Exod. 15:8–10). What God does in ordering creation, He also does in redeeming His people. Giving Leviathan *as food to the people inhabiting the wilderness* combines the manna in the wilderness theme with creation myth allusions (v. 14).

Next, the God who rules the waters breaks them open, *the fountain* ["springs," singular, collective] *and the flood* ["streams"]." He not only releases the waters, He also dries them up as in the Exodus (v. 15; see Exod. 14:16). He rules the day and night, *the light* ("moon"?) and *the sun* (v. 16; Gen. 1:14). He establishes *the borders* [continents or political boundaries, Gen. 1:9] *of the earth* and summer (dry) and winter (rainy), the two seasons of Israel (v. 17). Thus all of God's creation and "holy" history (*Heilsgeschichte*) witness to His rule. In contrast to the modern mind, there is no ambiguous relativity here. Indeed, God is King, working salvation (v. 12).

APPEAL FOR RESPONSE

74:18 Remember this, *that* the enemy has reproached,
     O LORD,
    And *that* a foolish people has blasphemed
     Your name.
19 Oh, do not deliver the life of Your turtledove
     to the wild beast!
    Do not forget the life of Your poor forever.
20 Have respect to the covenant;
    For the dark places of the earth are full of the
     haunts of cruelty.
21 Oh, do not let the oppressed return ashamed!
    Let the poor and needy praise Your name.
                  Ps. 74:18–21

Having confessed his faith in Yahweh as King and having recalled all of God's saving acts, the psalmist now invites Him to respond.

The heart of this appeal is to the divine memory. God is faced with blasphemers (v. 18). He must have compassion on His poor (v. 19). But there is His covenant (v. 20), and if God responds He will receive the worship due to Him (v. 21).

The beginning of this appeal is the reminder of what the enemy has done. God has been *"reproached"*; His name is *"blasphemed"* (see v. 10) by a *"foolish people."* The word *foolish* designates a people with no ethical and spiritual reality, that is, idolaters. As this people berates Israel for her destruction, Yahweh, too, is berated as a weak, minor god. As the dwelling place for God's name is defiled, God is defiled too (see v. 7). Certainly the psalmist's intention is to turn God's wrath (v. 1) from Israel to Babylon. How can God put up with a people who curse Him?

Next, the psalmist asks God not to turn His people, His *"turtle-dove"* (literally, "the soul [or life] of His turtledove") over to a *"wild beast."* The bird image may come from the sacrificial system—Israel is being sacrificed to a beast (see Lev. 1:14)—or it may simply be a term of affection and humility. Because of the following parallel member, it is probably the latter. Now the psalmist appeals to God not to forget the life of "[His] *poor."* The poor here include the humble, afflicted, weak, and pious. In this appeal he touches the heart of God, which is on their side (cf. Ps. 72:12; Isa. 61:1; Matt. 5:3). The contrast is clearly made in verses 18 and 19. God must choose between a blaspheming beast and His turtledove, His pious poor.

What other grounds does Israel have in dealing with God, along with this spiritual appeal? The answer is the covenant (v. 20). God must be true to His own Word; He is the covenant-keeping God who has bound Himself to His people by His treaty. As they repent they must be restored. Apart from the operation of the covenant, there will only be *"the dark places of the earth* [or, "land," that is, Israel] *full of the habitations* ["pastures"] *of cruelty* ["violence"]." In light of the New Testament this means that without God's kingdom, God's order and authority, operating there will only be Satan's kingdom of darkness and disorder or violence (see Col. 1:13; Eph. 2:1–3).

If God will restore His people, they (*"the oppressed"*) will not *"return"* (or "turn") to Him ashamed. On the contrary they (*"the poor and needy"*) will *"praise"* God's *"name"* once again. Their deliverance will evoke worship, public boasting in God. This is the clincher argument. God calls a people to Himself to be worshipers (John 4:23). This is the goal of salvation (2 Cor. 4:15).

Throughout verses 18–21 the psalmist refuses to capitulate to the present wrath of God (v. 1) or to indulge in the modern "climate of opinion" about historical ambiguity. Darkness and violence threaten (v. 20), but when God restores His covenant with His people, the light will shine again, exploding in praise to Yahweh's name.

CALL TO VINDICATION

74:22 Arise, O God, plead Your own cause;
Remember how the foolish man reproaches
You daily.
23 Do not forget the voice of Your enemies;
The tumult of those who rise up against You
increases continually.

Ps. 74:22–23

The psalmist has made His case. It is up to God to act. The call in verse 22 for Him to *arise* is the call for Him to stand up from His throne and execute judgment. We read in Ps. 7:6: "Arise, O Lord, in Your anger; / Lift Yourself up because of the rage of my enemies; / Rise up for me to the judgment / You have commanded!"

As God lifts His wrath from Israel He will *"plead"* His *"own cause"*; that is, in vindicating His people He vindicates Himself, since they are called by His name (see v. 2). It is His cause that is ultimately at stake. This is the doctrine of grace. Salvation is God's work. If His people languish in their sin under His wrath forever, it is sin that wins rather than the triumphant, militant, pursuing love of God. In Christ, however, we know that nothing can ultimately separate us from that love (Rom. 8:37–39).

Once again, God is to remember the continual (*"daily"*) reproach of the *"foolish"* (vain, idolatrous; see v. 18) *"man."* His enemies' voices are raised, not in praise (v. 21) but in *"tumult"* ("noise"), as they rebel against Him, and this offensive cacophony *"increases continually"* or *"is going up continually."*

The choice is clear. Either God will keep His wrath upon Israel and receive the "noise" of the nations, or He will turn His wrath upon them and receive the praises of His people. It is for His sake, it is for His glory, that the psalmist calls upon Him to act.

Likewise, when the roof falls in upon us, we are not to despair and indulge in the nihilism of the age. Rather, we are to pray. In Jesus we know that beyond God's judgment is His grace. Here is our covenant, sealed in the Savior's blood, and as God restores His church we too will praise Him.

CHAPTER SEVENTY-FIVE

In His Time . . .

Psalm 75

Today we are a terribly verbal culture. We know little of what it means to wait in silence before God (Ps. 62:1). Our churches are busy. Our devotions are busy. The mass media fill our lives with music and talk. Our "ghetto-blasters" and Walkmen take sounds everywhere. We cannot even be put on hold on a telephone or ride an elevator without some tune providing "background" music. No wonder we never hear the voice of the Lord. Even if our world-view allows for God to speak, in practice we shut Him out. He never has a chance. To add insult to injury, we complain that God never says anything to us, and we look with jealousy upon those who give Him their silence. We call them "mystics" or specially gifted. Here, however, in Psalm 75, we have a model prayer for God hearing, speaking, and acting "in His time." He is sovereign. We cannot force His hand. We must wait for Him, but we must *wait* indeed!

Traditionally, we view prophecy as God's Word to us and the psalms as our words to Him. Nevertheless, the Psalter is laced with God's responses to prayer through His revealed Word (see, e.g., Pss. 2:6; 4:2). The psalms witness to the "dialogical" faith of the Bible (Martin Buber). They show us that prayer is active communication with the living God from both sides; speaking and listening are essential to the life of faith.

In the context of worship, the psalmist hears God's Word, which centers on the judgment of the wicked and the exaltation of the righteous.

Authorship of this psalm is attributed to Asaph, a chief musician in Solomon's temple (2 Chron. 5:12). It may come from him or from a guild of singers named after him. Commentators identify the form as a hymn of praise, or a mixed form of praise and prophecy or a prophetic liturgy. It seems unnecessary to speak of mixed forms, however, when God addresses those who address Him. This lies at the heart of Israel's faith. Thus a "hymn of praise" seems adequate. The thought moves from our worship (v. 1), to God's Word (vv. 2–5), to our response (vv. 6–9) and ends with God's response (v. 10).

OUR WORSHIP

75:1 We give thanks to You, O God, we give thanks!
For Your wondrous works declare *that* Your
name is near.

Ps. 75:1

Verse 1 begins with an acclamation of praise to God. The repetition of the word *"thanks"* makes the opening dramatic and intensive. The basis for this worship is given: God's *"wondrous works,"* namely His "surpassing, extraordinary acts" or His "interventions," *"declare"* that His name, that is, that He Himself, is near. Obviously some clear act, some miracle, has triggered this psalm. When Jesus commands Peter to haul in a catch of fish, the disciple falls at His feet in fear and wonder (Luke 5:8). Here it is not Jesus' word but His work in providing the catch that breaks him. Again, after Jesus casts a demon out of a man in the synagogue at Capernaum the crowd is amazed (Mark 1:27). Later Thomas worships the risen Christ when shown His wounds (John 20:27–28). This cannot be stressed enough. True worship is offered when God's nearness, God's presence, is communicated by His actions. The church goes into revival when the power of God comes upon it. This is an *event* that reveals the living God in our midst.

GOD'S WORD

75:2 "When I choose the proper time,
       I will judge uprightly.
    3 The earth and all its inhabitants are dissolved;
       I set up its pillars firmly. Selah
    4 "I said to the boastful, 'Do not deal
          boastfully,'
       And to the wicked, 'Do not lift up the horn.
    5 Do not lift up your horn on high;
       Do *not* speak with a stiff neck.'"

Ps. 75:2–5

The mighty intervention of God breaks us and breaks us open to praise Him. Now, with awestruck hearts we are ready to receive His Word. In this context God speaks. It is unnecessary to attribute this Word to an official prophet or temple oracle. God does not limit His speaking to professionals (cf. Amos 1:1). What does He say?

First of all, God is the Lord of time (v. 2). He alone chooses when to act. He is sovereign, and we are subject to His agenda; He is not subject to ours. In every area of ministry this can cause us a certain frustration. Many pray for years for the conversion of a loved one. However, healing comes in God's time, not ours, with death the ultimate healing prior to Jesus' return (Francis MacNutt). Revival cannot be produced by programs or techniques. God's work is His work, and we must wait for Him while praying diligently. As Jesus told the disciples: "It is not for you to know times or seasons which the Father has put in His own authority" (Acts 1:7). As we look to God rather than to ourselves then, we are taught lessons of His lordship and we grow in faith and character. Paul writes of Abraham, "He did not waver at the promise of God [for a son] through unbelief, but was strengthened in faith, giving glory to God, and being fully convinced that what He had promised He was also able to perform" (Rom. 4:20–21). No wonder Abraham is the archetypal man of faith! He trusted God for His time.

Second, God declares Himself to be the *upright* ("straight, just") judge (v. 2). When He is ready He will execute His disposition. Is this an immediate judgment or the final, eschatological end? Probably the latter since God elaborates in verse 3 that the whole *"earth"* and *"all its inhabitants are dissolved* ["melt away"]." Peter says, "But the day of the Lord will come as a thief in the night, in which the heavens will pass away with a great noise, and the elements will melt with fervent heat; both the earth and the works that are in it will be burned up" (2 Pet. 3:10). This is followed by the recreation of all things, the new heaven and the new earth (Rev. 21:1). Verse 3 continues: *"I set up its pillars"* (the earth's foundations, see 1 Sam. 2:8) firmly, or literally, "I regulate [or adjust] her pillars." After judgment the foundations are restored in the consummated kingdom of God (see 1 Cor. 15:24–25). This will be God's final "wondrous work" (see v. 1).

In light of the coming judgment, God addresses the *"boastful"* and the *"wicked"* in verses 4–5. Biblical ethics are always based upon apocalyptic, the sense of the final end. But what does He say?

First, God warns the *"boastful: Do not deal boastfully* [or "be boastful"]." The boastful are those who glory in themselves rather than in God. God says through Jeremiah, "Let not the wise man glory in his wisdom, / Let not the mighty man glory in his might, / Nor let the rich man glory in his riches; / But let him who glories glory in this, / That he understands and knows Me" (Jer. 9:23–24).

Second, God addresses the *"wicked"* ("criminals, lawbreakers," see Ps. 1:1): *"Do not lift up the horn."* The *"horn"* is a symbol of power (Ps. 18:2). As God warns through Isaiah: "For the day of the Lord of hosts / Shall come upon everything proud and lofty, / Upon everything lifted up— / And it shall be brought low—" (Isa. 2:12; see Luke 1:51–52). God adds: *"Do not speak with a stiff* ["arrogant"] *neck,"* that is, an unbending neck. Later in the psalm the reason for this warning will be fully given: "All the horns of the wicked / I will also cut off" (v. 10). This is the final judgment, sure to come. In this age, however, the awesome sense of the end issues in a warning designed to bring us to repentance. In God's stern words there is yet grace.

OUR RESPONSE

75:6 For exaltation *comes* neither from the east
Nor from the west nor from the south.
7 But God *is* the Judge:
He puts down one,
And exalts another.
8 For in the hand of the LORD *there is* a cup,
And the wine is red;
It is fully mixed, and He pours it out;
Surely its dregs shall all the wicked of the
earth
Drain *and* drink down.
9 But I will declare forever,
I will sing praises to the God of Jacob.

Ps. 75:6–9

The psalmist now meditates upon the Word of God (vv. 2–5), which he has received as he worships (v. 1). This gives us a clue as to our own spiritual growth. When we hear God speak in public worship services, we must not race out for "coffee hour" or "greeting visitors." It is time to quietly weigh what He has said. A dear friend of mine was converted by a neighbor in Brooklyn, New York, years ago. She then found her spiritual home in a Baptist church but always sat near the door so that she could slip away after hearing the Word preached. She refused to have God's address to her stolen by human chatter. No wonder that now, late in life, "Mom," as she is called, is rock-solid in her faith and one of the most vibrant witnesses to Christ in our community as she sits each day behind her cash register in a local coffee shop.

What does the psalmist receive in his meditation? His first thought is that *"exaltation"* doesn't come from a geographical location, neither *"east," "west,"* nor *"south"* (literally, "the wilderness"); it does not originate on this planet. His second thought is that exaltation comes from God. He is the *"judge"* (see v. 2). He *"puts down one"* and *"exalts another"* (v. 7). It is before Him that we stand or fall. To the wicked He gives the cup of judgment or destiny (see Ps. 11:6; Mark 10:38). This cup is held in His hand, since He is sovereign. Moreover, it is *"fully mixed"*; it is ready to be drunk, and it will be drained completely.

42

In light of these awesome realities, the psalmist *"will declare* ['tell, confess'] *forever"* (v. 9). The content of his witness, as we have seen, embraces Yahweh as Judge (v. 7). Such witness leads to worship. Thus he will also *"sing praises* ['make music'] *to the God of Jacob,"* that is "Israel" (see Exod. 19:3; Isa. 2:5–6). Likewise, when the heavenly host sees the Lamb upon His throne, they too break out in songs of triumph (Rev. 5:8–14).

GOD'S RESPONSE

75:10 "All the horns of the wicked I will also cut off,
But the horns of the righteous shall be
exalted."

Ps. 75:10

God now has the last word. He will destroy the *"wicked"* (see v. 4). Their *"horns,"* their power (see vv. 4–5), will be *"cut off,"* terminated. However, the horns of the *"righteous,"* those who live in the covenant and who obey Torah (the law), will be exalted. Their godly power will be magnified on the day of judgment.

As we too face the coming resolution of all things before God, we must recognize that there are only two alternatives, two ways (see Psalm 1). We will either be exalted or put down. We will either be among the righteous or among the wicked. Certainly this prepares us for the gospel. As we wait before the Lord He will act, doing His *"wondrous works,"* and He will speak His wondrous word. But how can we be sure of this? The answer lies in the Incarnation: Here and here alone the word of God became fully the work of God as the Word became flesh and dwelt among us (John 1:14). Thus Christ, the righteous One, makes us righteous (Phil. 3:8–9). As He is exalted we will be exalted (Rom. 8:32). His power, His horn, is our power (Rom. 8:11). We too can sing our praises to the "God of Jacob." He will judge uprightly "in His time" (v. 2).

CHAPTER SEVENTY-SIX

God Is Awesome!

Psalm 76

Most people have a hard time dealing with the wrath of God. It is a subject to be avoided. For some, to speak of God's wrath is to project our "shadow side" on the Almighty (C. G. Jung). This makes God into the devil. For others, God's wrath is a childhood memory of emotional preaching describing the fires of hell. These people need healing from this fear of dangling like a spider over the flames. Still, for others, God's wrath projects a legalistic, "policeman" image, which keeps them in line and prohibits them from ever knowing God's unconditional love. For most, however, God's wrath is a vestige of the past, a medieval image from which they have been delivered. If they have any real belief at all, it is belief in a good-time God who certainly loves all and, therefore, could punish none. This God is even less than Santa Claus because even he "sees you when you're sleeping and knows when you're awake," and "he knows whether you've been bad or good, so be good for goodness' sake." The good-time God, however, doesn't care whether you've been bad or good. There is no moral to the song about him.

In Psalm 76, however, the living God is a God of power who has real enemies and who destroys them (vv. 3–6). He is to be feared because He gets angry (v. 7) and arises in judgment to deliver the oppressed (v. 9). Therefore, it is crucial that vows made to Him be kept (v. 11). Otherwise, the rulers will only know His just retribution (v. 12). The specific descriptions of battle (vv. 3–6, 12) suggest that a military triumph is the occasion for the psalm's composition. However much our world-view may reject this warning about God's wrath, our own present history suggests that we should take it seriously and re-examine whether we really know the true and living God.

As with the previous psalms in Book Three (Psalms 73–75), this psalm is attributed to Asaph (see the comments on him in the introduction to Psalm 73). Commentators identify the literary type here as a hymn of victory. The thought moves from a confession of who God is (vv. 1–2), to a prayer praising His power (vv. 4–6), to a prayer praising His wrath (vv. 7–9) and ends with a conclusion of confidence and warning (vv. 10–12).

WHO GOD IS

> 76:1 In Judah God *is* known;
>   His name *is* great in Israel.
>   2 In Salem also is His tabernacle,
>   And His dwelling place in Zion.
>   3 There He broke the arrows of the bow,
>   The shield and sword of battle.   Selah
>
> *Ps. 76:1–3*

Verses 1–2 identify the God who is revealing Himself in His wrath. In verse 1 He is defined by His relationships, His people. He is known *"in Judah."* Judah (the Southern Kingdom) "knows" (lives in intimate relationship with and experience of) God. His *"name* [presence] *is great* ["magnified"] *in Israel* [the Northern Kingdom]." Here God's greatness is seen in His deeds. Ps. 86:10 confesses, "For You are great, and do wondrous things; / You alone are God."

Along with His relationships, God is also defined by His place. In *"Salem"* (Jerusalem, see Gen. 14:18) is His tabernacle, for He dwells there on Mount Zion (v. 2, see 2 Sam. 6:17; Ps. 2:6). Finally, God is also defined by His works. It was in Jerusalem that He defeated His enemies, destroying the weapons of war, the *"arrows"* (literally, "the flames" or "fiery derts of the bow"), the *"shield,"* and the *"sword"* (v. 3). This final description leads us into the direct confession of God's greatness in battle in verses 4–9.

PRAYER: PRAISE TO GOD'S POWER

> 76:4 You *are* more glorious and excellent
>   *Than* the mountains of prey.

5 The stouthearted were plundered;
  They have sunk into their sleep;
  And none of the mighty men have found the
     use of their hands.
6 At Your rebuke, O God of Jacob,
  Both the chariot and horse were cast into a
     dead sleep.

Ps. 76:4–6

The psalmist now directly addresses God. He praises Him as more glorious or "O Glorious One," literally, "O Lighted One." His glory manifests itself to the eye as light (compare 1 John 1:5). In the tabernacle in the wilderness God showed His presence as glory, cloud, and fire (Exod. 40:34–38; Isa. 4:5). Light is numinous, a sign of the holy God who is other than we are (R. Otto; see Isa. 9:2). Moreover, God is *more excellent* ("majestic") than *the mountains of prey* (or "everlasting mountains"). Regardless of whether the mountains are loaded with game or enduring and eternal, God is greater. His glory and His excellence are seen in His mighty deeds in battle. The *stouthearted,* the *mighty men* (warriors, see 2 Sam. 23:8), the *chariot,* and the *horse* have all been destroyed: *they have sunk into their sleep* (v. 5); they were cast into *a dead sleep* (v. 6; for death as sleep, see Acts 7:60; 1 Thess. 4:13). Also in death, the mighty men have been unable to use their hands (v. 5). God's glory has been made known in the defeat of these warriors. He plundered them, taking their spoils as a result of victory (v. 5). As the God of Jacob (see Ps. 75:9) He uttered His rebuke, His mighty Word, and they were destroyed (see Jer. 1:9–10). No wonder He is more glorious and excellent (v. 4). We stand in awe of Him as we survey the silent battlefield littered with corpses, dead horses, and broken chariots. This God is not to be trifled with. He is omnipotent.

PRAYER: PRAISE TO GOD'S WRATH

76:7 You, Yourself, *are* to be feared;
     And who may stand in Your presence
     When once You are angry?
   8 You caused judgment to be heard from heaven;
     The earth feared and was still,

> 9 When God arose to judgment,
>   To deliver all the oppressed of the
>   earth.   Selah
>
> *Ps. 76:7-9*

As the smoke and dust of battle clear, displaying the horror of death, the psalmist responds with a proper sense of fear. This he addresses to God, speaking literally: "You are terrible ('cause astonishment, awe') You." The reason for this fear or even horror is then given: when God is angry no one can stand in His presence (before His face). For *anger* see Ps. 74:1.

We must beware of excessively personifying God's wrath, however; His anger is not simply an emotional outburst. It is a manifestation of His *"judgment"* which is transcendent and absolute. Thus it is *"heard from heaven"* ("the heavens," plural of fullness, v. 8). When such divine intervention is executed, the earth responds in fearful silence. God speaks. There is nothing more to be said.

Verse 9 tells us the motive for God's righteous wrath. God *"arose* [stood up from His throne to go into battle] *to judgment* ["for justice"] *to deliver* [or "save"] *all the oppressed* ["poor, afflicted, pious"]." These are the people of *"the earth,"* or, better *"the land"* (of Israel).

Over against the oppressor, God comes and executes His active wrath, His justice, by defeating Israel's enemies in battle and delivering the pious poor. He always sides with the oppressed, and His judgment is certain. God intervenes with His kingdom, and His will is now done on earth as it is in heaven (see Matt. 6:10). God's wrath is experienced as blessing for it fulfills our longing for His moral order to be actualized.

CONCLUSION: CONFIDENCE AND WARNING

> 76:10 Surely the wrath of man shall praise You;
>   With the remainder of wrath You shall gird
>   Yourself.
>   11 Make vows to the LORD your God, and pay
>   *them;*
>   Let all who are around Him bring presents to
>   Him who ought to be feared.

12 He shall cut off the spirit of princes;
He is awesome to the kings of the earth.

Ps. 76:10–12

God is sovereign in all of His works; as He executes His judgments even the wrath of man praises Him. In destroying Israel's enemies who bring their wrath upon His people, He is praised. God uses even the evil intention of our hearts for His glory. We find this supremely in the cross where God's grace is greater than our sin. At the deepest point of our rebellion, He is redeeming the world.

Moreover, beyond stopping the *"wrath of man"* in battle, God is able to triumph over all further wrath. He wears it like a garment or trophy. We can have confidence in His ultimate victory over sin, Satan, and death.

In light of this, what is to be our response? We are to make our *"vows"* to God and *"pay them"* (v. 11). Vows are usually promises made in times of trouble. They must be fulfilled since God is the righteous God who holds us accountable for all that we offer to Him. Furthermore, *"all who are around Him,"* namely, the nations, must bring their *"presents"* ("homages") for He *"ought to be feared."* God *"shall cut off* ["kill"] *the spirit* ["self"] *of princes"* and *"He is awesome* ["terrible"] *to the kings of the earth."* All nations and their rulers must bow before Him and submit to His judgment.

How then are we to understand the wrath of God? It is real. It is moral. It is directed against those who oppress God's pious poor. Our cry for justice will be satisfied by Him (rather than by our political manipulations). He is awesome, and we are called to responsibility before Him. The pride of man, the rulers of the nations, will be broken by Him.

There is also one further word. In Christ, God takes His own wrath upon Himself. The judgment we deserve is borne by the sinless Son of God. In Him "the enmity" between God and humankind has been put to death (Eph. 2:16). The gospel is a message of peace. Where it spreads, the wrath of God is lifted and the war is over. This makes our God incredibly awesome.

CHAPTER SEVENTY-SEVEN

When the Lights Go Out

Psalm 77

A good friend of mine was chronically depressed throughout most of his life. Because he had lived this way from childhood, he didn't actually know his condition. He thought that this was the way life was. Finally some bizarre behavior brought him into therapy, and his depression was diagnosed. For him, a major part of his cure came from proper medication. Today he would tell us that through these "medical means" he experienced the miracle of God's healing. Greater healing, far beyond the depression itself, also lay ahead for him and his marriage. But where does depression come from? For many depression comes from loss. It is introverted anger experienced as grief. Death, illness, divorce, unemployment, moving to another city, abuses of various kinds, the withdrawal of love—all of these and more can trigger depression. When it comes many retreat and withdraw into themselves. They refuse to be around people. They stop eating. They want to sleep excessively. They become physically ill. In extreme cases they want to die. Oftentimes, unknown to us, depression has spiritual roots. People feel distant from God. "He must hate me," they think. Moral failure creates guilt, resulting in spiritual dryness and abandonment. As is often true on a human level, people feel the loss of God's love. They suppose, "He could never forgive me." Intimacy with the Heavenly Father is replaced by self-hatred, and Satan is there to take advantage of our situation.

In Psalm 77 the psalmist is experiencing "the dark night of the soul." He is having his "day of trouble," and there is no comfort for him (v. 2). Complaint leads to a sense of being "overwhelmed" (v. 3). He is so troubled that silence descends upon him (v. 4). At the center of his despair is the sense of God's rejection: "Will the Lord cast off forever?" (v. 7). This could refer both to the psalmist and to God's people Israel. How then does he cope with these feelings and how can we do the same? Psalm 77 provides the answer in this prayer and meditation.

The authorship of this psalm is ascribed to Asaph (see the introduction to Psalm 73 and 2 Chron. 5:12). Its origins may lie in the Northern Kingdom (see the references to Jacob and Joseph, Northern tribes, in v. 15). The psalm is an individual lament that includes hymnodic and confessional elements (vv. 13–20). The thought moves from a cry to God (v. 1–3), to human consternation (vv. 4–6), to the question of divine rejection (vv. 7–9), to the memory of redemption (vv. 10–15) and ends with a confession of Creation/Exodus themes (vv. 16–20).

CRY TO GOD

77:1 I cried out to God with my voice—
To God with my voice;
And He gave ear to me.
2 In the day of my trouble I sought the Lord;
My hand was stretched out in the night
without ceasing;
My soul refused to be comforted.
3 I remembered God, and was troubled;
I complained, and my spirit was
overwhelmed.   Selah

Ps. 77:1–3

Verse 1 arrests us. The psalmist cries out ("calls," even "clamors" or "shouts") to God. He prays out loud, *"with my voice."* This thought is repeated for emphasis: *"To God with my voice."*

The next thought gives us immediate assurance. All is not lost. God *"gave ear to me."* In the midst of the darkness there is a glimmer of light. No wonder the psalmist continues his prayer.

The context of this cry is given in verse 2. It is a *"day of my trouble"* ("distress," literally, "constriction," plural intensive). This day probably includes some national as well as personal disaster (military defeat?). Thus the psalmist sought the Lord. The verb can indicate going to the sanctuary to receive God's oracle (see v. 13). Moreover, his "body language" communicated his anguish. His hand was out-stretched in supplication (cf. 1 Kings 8:22) through the night *"without ceasing"* (literally, "and was not numb"; that is, the blood kept flowing). Also his *"soul"* refused comfort. His whole self is consumed in anguish.

Moreover, thinking of God makes the psalmist *"troubled"* ("moan"). This is undoubtedly because of his memory of God's mighty acts in the past (see vv. 10–20). He *"complained"* ("meditated," "pondered") and his spirit ("self") *"was overwhelmed"* ("fainted"). While the psalmist knows that God hears him, the lights have gone out, and all that he experiences as he prays is sorrow and grief. Here is a broken man.

There are some today who teach that a Spirit-filled Christian should always experience health, prosperity, and happiness. What they seem to advocate at times is a state of virtual denial and call it "faith." While God is still in the healing business, He never promises in this fallen world dominated by the devil to protect us from all loss, suffering, and grief. He does, however, promise to take us through. Thus Jesus agonized in Gethsemane (Luke 22:39ff.), and Paul suffered continual calamity as Christ's apostle (2 Cor. 11:22ff.). As he tells the Philippians: this is God's grace in Christ, "not only to believe in Him, but also to suffer [persecution] for His sake" (Phil. 1:29).

HUMAN CONSTERNATION

77:4 You hold my eyelids *open;*
　　　 I am so troubled that I cannot speak.
　　 5 I have considered the days of old,
　　　 The years of ancient times.
　　 6 I call to remembrance my song in the night;
　　　 I meditate within my heart,
　　　 And my spirit makes diligent search.
　　　　　　　　　　　　　　　　 Ps. 77:4–6

Verse 4 continues the theme of verses 1–3. Here the psalmist describes his wakefulness. He can't close his eyes. Then in his trouble (literally, "being hit or struck") he *"cannot speak."* His mood swings from yelling in anger (v. 1) to depressed silence.

Now mute, the psalmist allows his mind to return to former days, *"the days of old, the years of ancient times."* He remembers his past joy, his *"song in the night"* where he rejoiced in the darkness. As he meditates (see v. 3) with his *"heart"* ('mind'), his spirit searches to understand God's ways.

At this point we begin to see the resources for breaking depression beyond the sheer act of prayer itself. The silence is good. The psalmist now quits complaining and his mind begins to work. He taps into his memory. In the past he has sung in the night. The darkness has been penetrated before. His mind begins to actively search for God. This leads us to the battery of questions in verses 7–9 as the psalmist turns from himself ('I') to God ('He').

DIVINE REJECTION?

77:7 Will the Lord cast off forever?
And will He be favorable no more?
8 Has His mercy ceased forever?
Has *His* promise failed forevermore?
9 Has God forgotten to be gracious?
Has He in anger shut up His tender
mercies?   Selah

Ps. 77:7–9

The first question centers on whether God's rejection is permanent. It may be viewed as rhetorical, implying, "of course not." Next, His covenant-character comes into view. Will God no longer be *"favorable"*? Will He have no *"mercy"* ('covenant-love')? Has His *"promise"* ('word,' 'oracle of salvation') to His people failed? Has He *"forgotten to be gracious"*? Has His *"anger"* ('wrath') extinguished His *"tender mercies"* ('compassion')? Note the stress on finality: *"forever, no more"* (v. 7), *"forever, forevermore"* (literally, 'from generation to generation,' v. 8). All of these questions paint the real hope of the psalmist. Whatever the tragedy may be that has caused his depression, he now turns to the Lord in prayer (v. 1), knowing that God's mercy is greater than His wrath and the psalmist's sin. This is the light that dawns. God has made a covenant with Israel and granted promises in His Word that He can be held to. So Moses intercedes in the wilderness: "Pardon the iniquity of this people, I pray, according to the greatness of Your mercy, just as You have forgiven this people, from Egypt even until now." Then Yahweh responds, "I have pardoned, according to your word" (Num. 14:19–20).

THE MEMORY OF REDEMPTION

77:10 And I said, "This *is* my anguish;
    But I will remember the years of the right hand
        of the Most High."
   11 I will remember the works of the LORD;
    Surely I will remember Your wonders of old.
   12 I will also meditate on all Your work,
    And talk of Your deeds.
   13 Your way, O God, *is* in the sanctuary;
    Who *is* so great a God as *our* God?
   14 You *are* the God who does wonders;
    You have declared Your strength among the
        peoples.
   15 You have with *Your* arm redeemed Your
        people,
    The sons of Jacob and Joseph.   Selah
                                        Ps. 77:10–15

In verse 12 the psalmist identifies his *"anguish"* (literally, *"wound"*). To what, however, does this refer? Probably, in the immediate context, it comes from his memory of God's covenant-love (see vv. 7–9). Verse 12 literally translates: "And I said, 'My sickness is this—the years of the right hand of the Most High.'" To be in God's right hand would be to experience His power and His protection (see Exod. 15:6), His redemption. Now, in its absence, there is only anguish. For God as "Most High" see Gen. 14:18–20.

The psalmist continues that he remembers God's *"works"* ("deeds") and *"wonders"* ("extraordinary acts," that is, "miracles") in verse 11. The distinction is probably between God's saving acts and, more strongly, His mighty, direct interventions. This is what it means to be in God's right hand. Here Israel experiences His mighty works. For us, now that Jesus is at the right hand of the Father (Eph. 1:20), we too dwell there (Eph. 2:6) and receive His saving works and mighty interventions in our lives. Our prayers are answered in His name (John 16:24) and demons are expelled by that same authority (Acts 16:18).

The psalmist continues in verse 12 that he will *"meditate"* ("speak," "murmur") on all of God's *"work"* and talk of His *"deeds."* Where then is God's work and way to be known? The answer is given in verse 13: *"the sanctuary"* ("the Holy Place," cf. Isa. 6:1–13). To know God's way, we must seek His face. His will is revealed where His law is proclaimed and worship is offered. With this thought in mind the psalmist confesses or exclaims his faith: *"Who is so great a God as our God?"* The answer, of course, is no one. God is "wholly other." He is incomparable. As Ps. 95:3 puts it: "For the Lord is the great God, / And the great King above all gods." How then are we to know the greatness of Yahweh? The answer is given in verses 14–15.

First, our God works *"wonders"* ("miracles," see v. 11). He intervenes directly and dramatically in our lives. Thus His *"strength"* ("might") is *"declared"* ("made known experientially") to the nations as He acts: "You have a mighty arm; / Strong is Your hand, and high is Your right hand" (Ps. 89:13). With His mighty *"arm"* He *"redeemed"* ("bought back") His people, *"the sons of Jacob and Joseph"* (v. 15). The reference throughout this section is to the Exodus. Moses sings, "Who is like You, O Lord, among the gods? / Who is like You, glorious in holiness, / Fearful in praises, doing wonders? / You stretched out Your right hand; / The earth swallowed them. / You in Your mercy led forth / The people whom You redeemed" (Exod. 15:11–13). The mention of the sons of Jacob and Joseph here either refers to all of Israel or specially designates the Northern Kingdom (see Amos 5:6).

In sum, God is the redeemer. He is the living God who performs signs and wonders. In His rejection of the psalmist there is a great grief and *"anguish"* (v. 10). If we have no expectations for God's work, we won't be disappointed. If we expect God, however, to act, to save, to deliver, to heal, to empower, when He is silent there is a real crisis. A close friend of mine has a clear gift of healing. For a period of time God withdrew that gift and he couldn't fake it; he was a broken man. He cried out to the Lord, saying that he could not continue to minister. Then God restored the gift at a special moment. Through the period of darkness, however, he knew exactly what the psalmist experienced here. When we know God's presence and power, we also know His absence and silence as well.

CONFESSION OF FAITH

77:16 The waters saw You, O God;
    The waters saw You, they were afraid;
    The depths also trembled.
  17 The clouds poured out water;
    The skies sent out a sound;
    Your arrows also flashed about.
  18 The voice of Your thunder *was* in the
      whirlwind;
    The lightnings lit up the world;
    The earth trembled and shook.
  19 Your way *was* in the sea,
    Your path in the great waters,
    And Your footsteps were not known.
  20 You led Your people like a flock
    By the hand of Moses and Aaron.

Ps. 77:16–20

Now, having recalled God's mighty acts, the psalmist addresses Him in a recital of His work in history. This is a liturgy containing Creation/Exodus themes.

Verses 16–18 describe the tumult of nature. Here the psalmist mentions *"the waters"* (of the Exodus or primeval chaos, see Ps. 74:13–14), *"the depths," "the clouds," "the skies,"* rain, lightning (*"Your arrows . . . flashed,"* v. 17), thunder, the whirlwind, and earthquakes (*"the earth trembled and shook,"* v. 18). But why this upheaval? Because God is revealed: *"The waters saw You, O God,"* and they respond in fear (literally, "whirling or writhing," as a woman in labor). Creation then is awed before almighty God. While this drama may contain motifs of the divine ordering of the watery chaos (Gen. 1:2), here the description becomes a prelude to the Exodus. Thus in verse 19 the psalmist continues that God's *"way"* (see v. 13), *"God's path,"* is through the sea, but His footsteps ("footprints") were not known. It was by Moses and Aaron (Exod. 3:14–16) then that God's flock crossed over from Egypt on dry land (v. 20, see Exodus 14). It is well for us to remember that only in the Incarnation are God's footprints finally seen as the Word became flesh and dwelt among us (John 1:14).

What spiritual resources do we see here for dealing with depression? What is available for us beyond proper medication and professional counseling? First, prayer. Second, the memory of past joys in the night. Third, the confession of who God is as the gracious covenant-keeping God. Fourth, a return to God's sanctuary. Fifth, the recollection of God's power, His right hand, and His supernatural interventions in history and our lives. What God has done before, He will do again. This will hold us when the lights go out.

CHAPTER SEVENTY-EIGHT

Pass It On

Psalm 78

God's people have always made a substantial commitment to bringing up the next generation in the "nurture and admonition of the Lord" (Eph. 6:4). Throughout the Old Testament there is a continual exhortation to teach the faith to those coming along behind. Thus in the Passover liturgy children are expected to ask the meaning of the meal, and proper answers are provided for them (see Exod. 13:8). Likewise, the Book of Proverbs contains instruction from a father and a mother to their son (Prov. 1:8). In a sense, the whole existence of the Bible witnesses to God's commitment to the future. The generations that come after His mighty acts must know about them and learn from them. After the first, great commandment to love God with all that we are, we immediately read: "And these words which I command you today shall be in your heart. You shall teach them diligently to your children" (Deut. 6:6–7). While the Sunday school is a relatively modern invention, bringing up children in the faith is as old as Cain and Abel. For the Bible, nurturing first began with the example and instruction of the parents and the extended family in the home. Instruction also took place in the shrines scattered about the Holy Land during the period of the Judges and later at the Jerusalem temple. This was followed by the establishment of synagogues, rabbinic schools, and separated communities of instruction like monastic Qumran by the Dead Sea. This psalm then is a teaching psalm designed to give guidance to the next generation. What shall we teach our children? A major Old Testament answer is given here.

Psalm 78 contains instruction in law (Torah, "revelation," vv. 1 and 5), parable, dark sayings (v. 2), testimony (v. 5), and commandments (v. 7). It concentrates upon a long recital of Israel's history, centering in the Exodus. Through it all there is a lesson to be learned: when Israel is faithless, God is faithful. He judges sin, yet His mercy triumphs. Therefore, we must be like those who take God at His Word and not be among the unbelieving, rebellious fathers who died in the wilderness (see vv. 8, 17, 31, 32–33, 36–37, 40–42, 56–57). This psalm provides a hermeneutical principle for biblical interpretation. There is a moral order to history as God reveals Himself in judgment and redemption. This is what we must learn and pass on to our children.

Psalm 78 is attributed to Asaph (see the introduction to Psalm 73 and 2 Chron. 5:12). It is, as we have suggested, a teaching psalm in the form of a hymn. Since the temple still stands (v. 69), its date must be pre-exilic. The thought moves from a call to receive instruction (vv. 1–4), to the divine commission and purpose for that instruction (vv. 5–8), to a warning about the children of Ephraim (vv. 9–11), to God's redemption and Israel's rebellion (vv. 12–20), to God's provision and judgment (vv. 21–33), to Israel's repentance and God's compassion (vv. 34–39), to Israel's rebellion and God's judgment and mercy (vv. 40–55), to Israel's rebellion and God's wrath (vv. 56–64), to God's judgment against His enemies (vv. 65–66) and concludes with God's sovereignty in election (vv. 67–72).

CALL TO RECEIVE INSTRUCTION

78:1 Give ear, O my people, *to* my law;
    Incline your ears to the words of my mouth.

> 2 I will open my mouth in a parable;
> I will utter dark sayings of old,
> 3 Which we have heard and known,
> And our fathers have told us.
> 4 We will not hide *them* from their children,
> Telling to the generation to come the praises of
> the LORD,
> And His strength and His wonderful works
> that He has done.
>
> *Ps. 78:1–4*

Verse 1 begins with a call to instruction. Israel, *"my people,"* is to hear the psalmist's *"law"* ("revelation") and listen to his *"words."* Thus the recitation is oral. The form here is typical of wisdom teachers (cf. Ps. 49:1–4; Prov. 4:1). The psalmist will also offer a *"parable"* ("instruction," see Ps. 49:4) and *"dark sayings of old"* (v. 2). The dark sayings may also be "parables" or "riddles." They come with the authority of the past, *"of old,"* and bring revelation. Thus they are dark to autonomous reason.

The instruction here is not creative. Israel does not value what modern scholarship values, namely, a fresh contribution to human knowledge. Rather, this instruction stands in a chain of tradition. It has been *"heard and known"* ("experienced") from the fathers. It is incumbent that the chain not be broken: *"the generation to come"* is told the *"praises of the Lord"* (v. 4). These are offered as a response to God's *"strength"* ("might") and *"wonderful works"* ("surpassing, extraordinary acts," that is, "miracles"). As Claus Westermann argues, praise is our reaction to God's act. It is evoked by an event (see *Praise and Lament in the Psalms*), which here is God's strength revealed in His intervention, His *"wonderful works."* What we can expect throughout the remainder of this psalm is the recitation of these works. Their purpose is clear: the work of God is for the worship of God. Confronted by His acts we are to fall down before Him in adoration and praise.

THE DIVINE BASIS AND PURPOSE
FOR INSTRUCTION

> 78:5 For He established a testimony in Jacob,
> And appointed a law in Israel,
> Which He commanded our fathers,

That they should make them known to their
children;
6 That the generation to come might know *them*,
The children *who* would be born,
That they may arise and declare *them* to their
children,
7 That they may set their hope in God,
And not forget the works of God,
But keep His commandments;
8 And may not be like their fathers,
A stubborn and rebellious generation,
A generation *that* did not set its heart aright,
And whose spirit was not faithful to God.
Ps. 78:5–8

What is the authority for the psalmist's teaching? Is antiquity, a
chain of tradition, enough? Hardly. Thus in verse 5 he offers his basis
in divine revelation. His law (v. 1) reflects God's law (v. 5), because
God *"established a testimony in Jacob."* *Jacob* designates Israel as a spiritual reality since this patriarch experienced God as deliverer in his
dealings with his brother Esau (Gen. 33:4) and in Egypt (Genesis 46).
The *"testimony"* is defined as *"His law in Israel"* in the parallel member
("synonymous parallelism," see the *Introduction, Psalms 1–72,* Communicator's Commentary, Old Testament, no. 13). This *"law"* (Torah,
"revelation") comes from God to the fathers and is then to be given to
their children. They, in turn, will *"know"* ("experience") it and *"arise"*
("erect," "set up the law") and *"declare"* it to the next generation (v. 6).
Here we see that in verses 5–6 revelation leads to communication.

But what is the purpose for this teaching? The answer is given positively in verse 7 and negatively in verse 8. First, positively, the teaching creates *"hope in God,"* revealing the living God who keeps His
covenant and redeems His people (see, e.g., vv. 12–16). Second, it
reminds Israel of God's *"works"* ("saving deeds"), protecting her from
forgetting Him. Third, it leads to obedience. Consequently, Israel
keeps God's *"commandments."* These are the good results of godly
instruction. Negatively, in verse 8, this instruction will come as a
warning, so that God's people won't be *"like their fathers,"* namely, a
generation who was *"stubborn,"* *"rebellious,"* not setting *"its heart
right"* ("whose heart was not fixed"), *"whose spirit was not faithful* ["steadfast"] *to God."* As this psalm unfolds, these positive and

negative purposes will be fulfilled. We will be encouraged by God's mighty works and warned by the rebellious fathers and those who followed them. Here then is teaching by historical memory and example. This same style of teaching is employed by Luke in the history that he recounts in the Book of Acts (Martin Hengel).

A WARNING FROM EPHRAIM'S CHILDREN

78:9 The children of Ephraim, *being* armed *and*
    carrying bows,
    Turned back in the day of battle.
10 They did not keep the covenant of God;
    They refused to walk in His law,
11 And forgot His works
    And His wonders that He had shown them.
                             Ps. 78:9–11

As the psalmist prepares to exposit history according to his purposes, he pauses for a comment about Ephraim's children, who ran from battle. It is possible that we have a note here from "current events," around the time of composition, that vividly illustrates the warnings in verse 8. If this is true, these few verses would exert tremendous power on the first hearers of this psalm. They may also be a later insertion that would serve the same function, updating the psalm for the present.

In verse 9 the children of Ephraim (the second son of Joseph, Gen. 41:50–52), who were a part of northern Israel, went to war armed but turned back in the day of battle. Their flight was a consequence of disobedience to God's covenant, their breaking of His law (v. 10), and their mindlessness (or disregard) about His works and His wonders ("miracles") that they had seen (in the Exodus and in their own experience, see v. 12 and Ps. 77:14). Thus they were like the fathers "whose spirit was not faithful to God" (v. 8). This picture serves as a negative example and exhortation: Don't be like them!

GOD'S REDEMPTION AND ISRAEL'S REBELLION

78:12 Marvelous things He did in the sight of their
    fathers,
    In the land of Egypt, *in* the field of Zoan.

13 He divided the sea and caused them to pass
      through;
    And He made the waters stand up like a heap.
14 In the daytime also He led them with the
      cloud,
    And all the night with a light of fire.
15 He split the rocks in the wilderness,
    And gave *them* drink in abundance like the
      depths.
16 He also brought streams out of the rock,
    And caused waters to run down like rivers.
17 But they sinned even more against Him
    By rebelling against the Most High in the
      wilderness.
18 And they tested God in their heart
    By asking for the food of their fancy.
19 Yes, they spoke against God:
    They said, "Can God prepare a table in the
      wilderness?
20 Behold, He struck the rock,
    So that the waters gushed out,
    And the streams overflowed.
    Can He give bread also?
    Can He provide meat for His people?"

Ps. 78:12–20

After his excursus on the children of Ephraim, the psalmist turns
to the exposition of his thesis in verses 7–8. History is to teach us to
hope in God, to remember His works, and to obey His commandments and not be like the rebellious fathers.

Consider first, then, the work of God. In the presence of the fathers of Israel, God performed *"marvelous things"* ("a wonder, a miracle," see v. 4) through the plagues (Exodus 7–12). This took place in
time and space, in Egypt; *"in the field of Zoan"* (a city in the eastern
Nile Delta, see Isa. 17:11; mentioned in Exod. 1:11 as the store-city
Raamses). Moreover, Yahweh split the Red Sea and marched Israel
through as the waters stood up *"like a heap"* (v. 13, see Exod. 14:21–
22). Next, He provided His presence and guidance with a pillar of
cloud by day and a pillar of fire by night (v. 14, see Exod. 13:21).
Furthermore, He gave Israel water to drink from the cleft rock in
"abundance" (v. 15, see Exod. 17:6) and *"caused waters to run down like*

rivers" (v. 16, see Num. 20:10ff.). Here the wonders of God are seen in judgment, redemption, guidance, and provision. Israel's every need has been supplied by the Lord. Certainly this memory should build hope and encourage obedience.

In the midst of these miracles, however, Israel did just the opposite. Thus the fathers *"sinned"* ("missed the mark") all the more, *"rebelling against the Most High* [see Gen. 14:18–24] *in the wilderness"* (v. 17). They *"tested* ["tried"] *God in their hearts"* (the center of thought and volition), demanding *"food of their fancy"* (*nepeš*, "soul" or "appetite," or "lust"). They were like the Jews who demanded a sign from Jesus in the midst of His miraculous ministry (Luke 11:29ff.). The cynicism and evil of their hearts is revealed in verse 19 when the fathers ask if God is able to *"prepare a table in the wilderness."* Yes, they saw the water, but that isn't enough. What about bread? What about meat (v. 20)? Those who seek the gifts rather than the giver are never satisfied. Those who focus on the miracle rather than on the miracle-worker never believe. All of God's benefits are meant to bring us to Him. But in our sinful, hard hearts we refuse to believe and demand that God jump over the higher spiritual and material hurdles that we erect. This is why the Pharisees could never accept Jesus' signs. They denied His miracles because they denied Him. If they had accepted His mighty works as from God, they would have been forced to abandon their law-scrolls and fall at His feet. Israel had the same problem in the wilderness. She constantly wanted to go back to Egypt's safety and worship the golden calf of her own making. Thus she fought the very wondrous works of God, demanding more and better proofs. Submission, no. Rebellion, yes. This was the battle of the wilderness. It is no surprise that a generation died there.

GOD'S PROVISION AND JUDGMENT

> 78:21 Therefore the LORD heard *this* and was furious;
> So a fire was kindled against Jacob,
> And anger also came up against Israel,
> 22 Because they did not believe in God,
> And did not trust in His salvation.
> 23 Yet He had commanded the clouds above,
> And opened the doors of heaven,

24 Had rained down manna on them to eat,
And given them of the bread of heaven.
25 Men ate angels' food;
He sent them food to the full.
26 He caused an east wind to blow in the
heavens;
And by His power He brought in the south
wind.
27 He also rained meat on them like the dust,
Feathered fowl like the sand of the seas;
28 And He let *them* fall in the midst of their
camp,
All around their dwellings.
29 So they ate and were well filled,
For He gave them their own desire.
30 They were not deprived of their craving;
But while their food *was* still in their mouths,
31 The wrath of God came against them,
And slew the stoutest of them,
And struck down the choice *men* of Israel.
32 In spite of this they still sinned,
And did not believe in His wondrous works.
33 Therefore their days He consumed in futility,
And their years in fear.

Ps. 78:21–33

God now responds to Israel's test (v. 18). His wrath is kindled, on the one hand, and His provision pours forth, on the other.

To begin with, the Lord is *"furious"* (see vv. 59 and 62). His wrath, like a fire, blazes *"against Jacob," "against Israel"* (see v. 5). For example, we read in Num. 11:1, "Now when the people complained, it displeased the Lord, for the Lord heard it, and His anger was aroused. So the fire of the Lord burned among them, and consumed some in the outskirts of the camp."

The reason for God's wrath is Israel's unbelief. To *"believe"* is not merely to assent to propositions about God; rather, it is to throw ourselves upon Him, abandoning all other support or hope. Moreover, in verse 22 Israel *"did not trust* ["become secure"] *in His salvation* ["deliverance"]." No wonder God felt used and rejected. Nevertheless, the psalmist goes on to relate His provision for His people. Here grace is abounding, greater than our sin (see Rom.

63

5:20). Thus from the open *"doors of heaven"* God *"rained down manna"* (v. 24, Exod. 16:4). This is *"the bread* ["corn," "grain"] *of heaven," "angels' food"* that was sent for satisfaction (v. 25). Speculations about the nature and substance of this manna continue. For the Bible it is a supernatural food that was provided for six days each week (a double portion came before the Sabbath, Exod. 16:5) until Israel entered the Promised Land (see Josh. 5:12). Thus it is one of God's wonders (v. 12).

Moreover, God also met the people's demand for meat (see v. 20). By a great *"east wind"* and the *"south wind,"* that is, a southeast wind, *"feathered fowl"* rained like *"dust," "like the sand of the seas"* (vv. 26–27). This, of course, refers to the quail in Exod. 16:12–13. The birds came, not by "Mother Nature," but by God's *"power"* (v. 26).

Furthermore, as the quail came and Israel's desires were fully met, God's judgment fell, *"while the food was still in their mouths"* (v. 30). Thus Num. 12:33 records, "But while the meat was still between their teeth, before it was chewed, the wrath of the Lord was aroused against the people, and the Lord struck the people with a very great plague" (Num. 12:33). The cause of this wrath, as we have seen, was Israel's testing or trying God, an act of unbelief (v. 18). It was as if God said, "All right, I'll grant your wish," and then destroyed His people before they were able to enjoy His gift. As they got the meat in their mouths, their lives were taken, even the best of the lot, *"the stoutest," "the choice men of Israel"* (v. 31).

Despite God's supernatural provision and His awesome judgments, Israel *"still sinned,"* that is, she refused to *"believe"* ("trust") in God's *"wondrous works"* ("miracles," plural for fullness). Here we learn that miracles cannot compel faith. Even the Egyptian sorcerers can do them (Exod. 7:11). Once again, we must ask, "Do we believe in the miracle or in the God of the miracle?" When we know the living God, then we will welcome His supernatural visitations in our lives.

Here God's judgment is just. He consumed in futility (literally, "like a breath," "a vapor") the wilderness generation of the Exodus (v. 33). Similar to Donner's party, snowbound in the high Sierras of California, they never reached their goal, the Promised Land. Thus their years ended in fear ("dismay," "terror"). No wonder we are taught not to be like these fathers who were stubborn and rebellious and who were not faithful to God (see v. 8).

ISRAEL'S REPENTANCE AND GOD'S COMPASSION

78:34 When He slew them, then they sought Him;
　　　And they returned and sought earnestly for
　　　　God.
　35 Then they remembered that God *was* their
　　　　rock,
　　　And the Most High God their Redeemer.
　36 Nevertheless they flattered Him with their
　　　　mouth,
　　　And they lied to Him with their tongue;
　37 For their heart was not steadfast with Him,
　　　Nor were they faithful in His covenant.
　38 But He, *being* full of compassion, forgave *their*
　　　　inequity,
　　　And did not destroy *them.*
　　　Yes, many a time He turned His anger away,
　　　And did not stir up all His wrath;
　39 For He remembered that they *were but* flesh,
　　　A breath that passes away and does not come
　　　　again.

Ps. 78:34-39

In this section Israel's spiritual life moves from judgment to repentance and then ends with God's forgiveness. Such a pattern is familiar throughout the Bible and our personal experience as well.

In verse 34 God's wrath is not a theological concept. It is an event: *"He slew them."* (Likewise, grace is also an event.) Israel's response is self-protective; *then they sought Him.* The verb *seek* means to seek after God in the temple and in worship or to consult an oracle. The thought here is repeated for emphasis: they *"returned"* ("turned back," repented") and, literally, "sought God early" (that is, quickly). Certainly, this is "fox-hole" religion. It is promises in the cancer-ward; airplane prayers in turbulent weather. Israel seeks God now to avoid punishment.

Moreover, in the crisis clarity returned; "Hanging wonderfully concentrates the mind" (Samuel Johnson). Now Israel remembers that God, *"the Most High God"* (see v. 17), is her *"rock"* and her *"redeemer"* (v. 35). As her *"rock"* He is both her security and protection: "He only is my rock and my salvation; / He is my defense; / I shall not be greatly moved" (Ps. 62:2). As her *redeemer* He purchases Israel from bondage, delivering her from her enemies (see Exod. 15:13 and 16). Now we would certainly believe that all would change, but the next two verses and our own experience do not bear this out.

With the pressure off, God's people become deceptive (v. 36). They flatter Him, treating Him as dishonestly as they would each other. Their tongues lie, manifesting fickle hearts that are not *faithful* ["steadfast"] *in His covenant*" (v. 37, cf. v. 8). Thus they employ a smokescreen of ritual and worship, thinking that God will be impressed as they continue their rebellion. God similarly speaks through Isaiah, "I have nourished and brought up children, / And they have rebelled against Me; / The ox knows its owner / And the donkey its master's crib; / But Israel does not know" (Isa. 1:2–3). Then He commands, "Bring no more futile sacrifices. . . . I cannot endure iniquity and the sacred meeting" (Isa. 1:13).

Beyond God's judgment, however, is His mercy, and His wrath is again and again overcome by His love. It is this that ultimately sends Jesus to the cross, the sinless One dying the sinner's death. Thus the psalmist continues, *"But He being full of compassion* ["tender mercy"] *forgave* ["covered"] *their iniquity* ["guilt"]." This forgiveness lifts the judgment: *"God did not destroy them"* (v. 38). What this meant for God is now suggested. "He *turned His anger away,"* or, literally, "returned His anger (to Himself)." Furthermore, He refused to *"arouse all His wrath."* Make no mistake. It is still there and operative. God, however, simply holds back. If all His wrath were to be unleashed, who would be left? Nevertheless, this reserve will not always be. The day will come when the age of grace has passed. As the cosmos collapses, the whole world will seek to hide in the caves and the rocks, calling, "Fall on us and hide us from the face of Him who sits on the throne and from the wrath of the Lamb! For the great day of His wrath has come, and who is able to stand?" (Rev. 6:16–17).

Now, however, God continues to have compassion upon us. So the psalmist notes in verse 39 that God remembered that Israel was *"but flesh,"* a fleeting *"breath"* that *"does not come again* ["return"]." Thus Isaiah says that "all flesh is grass" (40:6), and James reminds us that our life is a "vapor that appears for a little time and then vanishes away" (4:14).

ISRAEL'S REBELLION AND GOD'S
JUDGMENT AND MERCY

78:40 How often they provoked Him in the wilderness,
And grieved Him in the desert!

41 Yes, again and again they tempted God,
And limited the Holy One of Israel.

42 They did not remember His power:
The day when He redeemed them from the
enemy,

43 When He worked His signs in Egypt,
And His wonders in the field of Zoan;

44 Turned their rivers into blood,
And their streams, that they could not drink.

45 He sent swarms of flies among them, which
devoured them,
And frogs, which destroyed them.

46 He also gave their crops to the caterpillar,
And their labor to the locust.

47 He destroyed their vines with hail,
And their sycamore trees with frost.

48 He also gave up their cattle to the hail,
And their flocks to fiery lightning.

49 He cast on them the fierceness of His anger,
Wrath, indignation, and trouble,
By sending angels of destruction *among them*.

50 He made a path for His anger;
He did not spare their soul from death,
But gave their life over to the plague,

51 And destroyed all the firstborn in Egypt,
The first of *their* strength in the tents of Ham.

52 But He made His own people go forth like
sheep,
And guided them in the wilderness like a
flock;

53 And He led them on safely, so that they did
not fear;
But the sea overwhelmed their enemies.

54 And He brought them to His holy border,
This mountain *which* His right hand had
acquired.

> 55 He also drove out the nations before them,
> Allotted them an inheritance by survey,
> And made the tribes of Israel dwell in their
>   tents.
>
> *Ps. 78:40–55*

At this point, we would think that Israel has learned her lesson, but, sadly, this is not true. (We can also imagine the psalmist exhorting us to learn the lesson that the wilderness generation forgot.) Thus the narration of sin, judgment, and mercy continues.

To begin with, now the psalmist sums up Israel's hard heart in verse 40. Again and again God's people *"provoked"* ("rebelled against") Him and *"grieved"* Him or, "caused Him pain" as they wandered (cf. v. 17). Moreover, they *"tempted,"* or better, "tried" or "tested" God (see v. 18) and *"limited* [or probably "grieved"] *the Holy One of Israel."* As the Holy One, God is separate, absolutely other. He is, in Karl Barth's phrase, the "unknown God." Thus Barth writes, "We suppose that we know what we are saying when we say 'God.' We assign to Him the highest place in our world; and in so doing we place Him fundamentally on one line with ourselves and with things. . . . We assume that we are able to arrange our relation to Him as we arrange our other relationships. We press ourselves into proximity with Him. . . . We dare to deck ourselves out as His companions, patrons, advisors, and commissioners. We confound time with eternity. This is the *ungodliness* of our relation to God. . . . Secretly we are ourselves the masters in this relationship. We are not concerned with God, but with our own requirements, to which God must adjust Himself. . . . And so, when we set God upon the throne of the world, we mean by God ourselves" (*The Epistle to the Romans,* on 1:18). Isn't this Israel in the wilderness? Isn't this Everyman?

This reduction of God, this denial of the *"Holy One of Israel"* results, in part, from forgetting *"His power"* (literally, "hand," "action"), which was seen when He *"redeemed"* ("ransomed") Israel *"from the enemy"* (v. 42). Deliverance was accomplished by God's *"signs"* ("miracles," see Exod. 4:7–9) and *"wonders in Egypt, in Zoan"* (see v. 12). What then were these signs? Verses 44–51 now summarize the plagues cataloged in Exodus 7–12. The order, however, is changed and the list is incomplete. First, the *"rivers"* (plural of fullness? The

Nile?) were turned to blood (v. 44; Exod. 7:14–25). Second, *"flies . . . devoured them"* (v. 45; Exod. 8:20–32). Third, *"frogs . . . destroyed them"* (v. 45; Exod. 8:1–15). Fourth, the *"caterpillar"* and *"locust"* ate the crops (v. 46; Exod. 10:1–20). Fifth, there were *"hail"* and *"frost"* (vv. 47–48; Exod. 9:18–26). Sixth, and finally, there was the death of the firstborn (vv. 49–51; Exod. 11:1–12:30). This final plague consummates the exposition of God's wrath. Thus the psalmist speaks of *"the fierceness* ["heat"] *of His* [God's] *anger," "wrath"* ("rage"), *"indignation," "trouble," "angels of destruction"* (v. 49, see Exod. 12:23), *"death,"* and *"the plague"* (v. 50). All of this is poured out on the firstborn as God *"made* ["leveled"] *a path for His anger"* (v. 50). His wrath found its target like a laser-guided "smart" bomb. What was the result? *"All the firstborn in Egypt"* were *"destroyed,"* namely *"the first* [issue] *of their strength in the tents of Ham"* (that is, "Egypt," see Gen. 10:6–12; Ps. 105:23). Nevertheless, while the power of God was manifested in judgment upon Egypt, it was also manifested in the redemption of Israel (see v. 42). To this theme the psalmist now turns in verses 52–55.

The God who pours vengeance upon Egypt now becomes Israel's shepherd. He is sovereign: He *"made His own people go forth."* Furthermore, *"He guided them"* (v. 52). Israel is never left on her own as God liberates and leads. He protected His people: *"He led them on safely,"* and they were relieved of their *"fear"* ("dread, fear of judgment"). Instead, it was the Egyptians who were drowned in the sea (v. 53).

The goal of the Exodus, however, was the Promised Land. God brought Israel to *"His holy border,"* that is, "the Holy Land." The conquest is symbolized by the *"mountain which His right hand* [the hand of power, Exod. 15:6] *had acquired"* (v. 54). This mountain is either mountainous Canaan or Zion. In the immediate context it is probably more general than Zion, since Jerusalem was only conquered later by David (see 2 Sam. 5:6ff.). Next, God expelled the other nations before Israel (see Joshua 6–12), established their tribal inheritances (Joshua 13–21) and made them settle down *"in their tents"* (v. 55).

Throughout this narrative of God's judgment and redemption, the psalmist's purpose is clear. While the wilderness generation did not remember God's power and sinned, we will be better instructed (v. 42). As we see the signs and wonders of the living God, we will

hope in Him and obey Him (v. 7). Paul holds that all of this ultimately is for us as the church. Consequently, after Paul recalls God's
mercy and Israel's rebellion, he concludes, "Now all these things
happened to them as examples, and they were written for our admonition, on whom the ends of the ages have come (1 Cor. 10:11).

ISRAEL'S REBELLION AND GOD'S WRATH

> 78:56 Yet they tested and provoked the Most High
> God,
> And did not keep His testimonies,
> 57 But turned back and acted unfaithfully like
> their fathers;
> They were turned aside like a deceitful bow.
> 58 For they provoked Him to anger with their
> high places,
> And moved Him to jealousy with their carved
> images.
> 59 When God heard *this*, He was furious,
> And greatly abhorred Israel,
> 60 So that He forsook the tabernacle of Shiloh,
> The tent He had placed among men,
> 61 And delivered His strength into captivity,
> And His glory into the enemy's hand.
> 62 He also gave His people over to the sword,
> And was furious with His inheritance.
> 63 The fire consumed their young men,
> And their maidens were not given in marriage.
> 64 Their priests fell by the sword,
> And their widows made no lamentation.
>
> *Ps. 78:56–64*

The bitter history of Israel's sin continues, however, in the Promised Land. Despite all that God had done, the next generations repeated the cycle of the wilderness. They too *tested* ["tried," vv. 18,
41] *and provoked* ["rebelled against," vv. 8, 17] *the Most High God*
[for "Most High" see vv. 17 and 35]." Their sin manifested itself
in disobedience: "*they . . . did not keep* ["preserve, protect"] *His testimonies.*" Rather, they "*turned back*" ("backslid"), "*acted unfaith-
fully*" ("treacherously"), and "*were turned aside* ["overturned"] *like a*

deceitful bow," that is, a bow that fails the one who trusts it. While being in the Promised Land, they became the objects of God's wrath as He cast them aside. But why was this so?

God's anger came against idolatrous Israel for her *"high places"* and *"carved images"* (Baals), that is, her pagan shrines and gods (v. 58). Since our God is a *"jealous God,"* He demands our exclusive allegiance. Syncretism is sin. Thus He complains, "My people ask counsel from their wooden idols. . . . They offer sacrifices on the mountaintops, / And burn incense on the hills" (Hos. 4:12–13). This is spiritual adultery. So God became *"furious"* as He *"greatly abhorred* ['utterly rejected'] *Israel"* (v. 59). He abandons the *"tabernacle of Shiloh,"* the "tent of meeting" for the twelve tribes, which was destroyed by the Philistines in 1050 B.C. (see v. 60, 1 Sam. 1:3, 9; Jer. 7:12). Moreover, the Ark of the Covenant (*"His strength,"* *"His glory,"* see Exod. 37:1–9) is captured (v. 61, see 1 Sam. 4:11). Since God is *"furious"* (see v. 21) with *"His inheritance"* (Israel), His people are slaughtered in battle (v. 62), the *"maidens"* are left husbandless, the priests are also killed and their *"widows made no lamentation;"* that is, the disaster was so great that no proper mourning was possible (vv. 63–64). To provoke God is to provoke His judgment.

GOD'S JUDGMENT AGAINST HIS ENEMIES

> 78:65 Then the Lord awoke as from sleep,
>   Like a mighty man who shouts because of
>   wine.
>   66 And He beat back His enemies;
>   He put them to a perpetual reproach
>
> Ps. 78:65–66

God is righteous. Since He is sovereign, He uses pagan nations as the rod of His anger against Israel. His judgments on Egypt, however, show that He will not allow those nations in turn to go unpunished. Thus the psalmist boldly shows the Lord here as a *"mighty man,"* a warrior, who awakes and goes on a wine-inspired rampage, literally, "shouting for joy because of wine" (v. 65). He beats back his enemies and makes them a *"reproach"* ('taunt') forever (v. 66). Their name and memory are scorned (cf. Pss. 69:19–20 and 71:13).

GOD'S SOVEREIGNTY IN ELECTION

78:67 Moreover He rejected the tent of Joseph,
        And did not choose the tribe of Ephraim,
   68 But chose the tribe of Judah,
        Mount Zion which He loved.
   69 And He built His sanctuary like the heights,
        Like the earth which He has established
        forever.
   70 He also chose David His servant,
        And took him from the sheepfolds;
   71 From following the ewes that had young He
        brought him,
        To shepherd Jacob His people,
        And Israel His inheritance.
   72 So he shepherded them according to the
        integrity of his heart,
        And guided them by the skillfulness of his
        hands.
                                          Ps. 78:67–72

God's sovereignty now brings this teaching psalm to its proper conclusion. Down through history He chooses one and rejects another (for example, Esau and Jacob, see Rom. 9:13). Thus *"the tent of Joseph"* (the sanctuary at Shiloh, see v. 60) and *"the tribe of Ephraim"* are set aside (v. 67). *"Judah,"* however, and *"Mount Zion"* are chosen (v. 68). Here in Jerusalem the temple (*"sanctuary"*) is built *"like the heights"* or *"exalted places,"* that is, patterned on heaven (cf. Heb. 9:23–24). It is also as permanent as the earth, *"which He has established forever"* (v. 69). This promise is ultimately fulfilled in the New Jerusalem that comes down from heaven, where *"the tabernacle of God is with men"* (Rev. 21:3).

Likewise, David is also chosen to be God's *"servant"* (cf. Isa. 44:1–5; 49:3; 52:13). He goes from shepherding sheep to shepherding *"Israel His [God's] inheritance"* (vv. 70–71, see v. 62). Thus David cared for God's people as the shepherd-king *"according to the integrity of his heart."* This contrasts clearly with the fathers, the generation *"that did not set its heart aright, / And whose spirit was not faithful to God"* (v. 8). With the praise of David the psalm concludes. The teaching is done. The lesson is over.

What, we may ask, have we learned? First, we are now an instructed generation. The chain of tradition continues (v. 4). Second, we know the works and the wonders of God in judgment and redemption (vv. 34–35). Third, since God is God we will obey His commandments (v. 7). Fourth, we will learn from the wilderness generation, remember God's power and not try Him by our rebellion (vv. 41–42). Fifth, God is sovereign in all things. Thus we have no claim upon Him (vv. 67–68).

"Those who fail to learn from history are bound to repeat it." The living God does not change. What He did with Israel He will do with us. History moves in the mystery of God's judgments as He carries out His redemptive purpose in our world today. Judgment begins with the house of God (1 Pet. 4:17). Since God is not mocked, what we sow we reap (Gal. 6:7). As we study this psalm, we are to hope in God and not forget His works (v. 7). Our responsibility is to those who follow. We must "pass it on" to the next generation.

CHAPTER SEVENTY-NINE

A Present Grief

Psalm 79

The destruction of the church in times of decay brings reproach upon the Head of the church. It is easy for the world to look at divisive denominations, prideful and power-hungry clergy, and materialistic church members indifferent to the injustice and suffering of the world and blame Jesus. Where is He, anyway? Is He uninvolved? Aloof? Absent?

Certainly before the Reformation it seemed that God had abandoned His people. Again, in the eighteenth century, when deism and gin had eroded the moral and spiritual life of England, the church was the subject of mockery. As Bishop Stephen Neil says of Jesus, "Invulnerable in His person, but vulnerable because of His friends." Looking at the church is always grounds for accusing its Lord. This must be a part of Christ's present sufferings (see Col. 1:24).

Israel, too, brought reproach to the name of Yahweh. Especially in times of national disaster, it was easy to say, "Weak people, weak God." There were always those nationalistic prophets who smugly assumed that God would never destroy His temple (His "house") because He "needed" a place to dwell on the earth, and He "needed" a people to praise Him; otherwise, His name and memory would vanish (contrast Jer. 7:1–15). John the Baptist challenged this theology, asserting that God could raise up children to Abraham from stones (Luke 3:8). In this psalm the ultimate fear has been realized. Jerusalem is in ruins, littered with corpses (vv. 1–2). The surrounding nations laugh (v. 4). But what does this mean? Is God weak or indifferent? Hardly. It is His wrath that is upon His people (vv. 5–6). In light of this the psalmist pleads for God's mercy to return to Israel and for His vengeance to come upon her enemies (vv. 6–12). When this happens worship and praise will again be given Him (v. 13), and His name will be glorified.

The author of Psalm 79 is identified as Asaph (see the introduction to Psalm 73). Its date is clearly after the destruction of Jerusalem in 586 B.C. Its literary form is a lament. The plural throughout suggests that it was used in corporate worship. The thought moves from Israel's destruction (vv. 1–4) to a call for God's intervention (vv. 5–12) and concludes with a promise of worship (v. 13).

ISRAEL'S DESTRUCTION

79:1 O God, the nations have come into Your
          inheritance;
      Your holy temple they have defiled;
      They have laid Jerusalem in heaps.
  2 The dead bodies of Your servants

They have given *as* food for the birds of the
heavens,
The flesh of Your saints to the beasts of the
earth.
3 Their blood they have shed like water all
around Jerusalem,
And *there was* no one to bury *them.*
4 We have become a reproach to our neighbors,
A scorn and derision to those who are around
us.

Ps. 79:1–4

Verse 1 establishes the crisis and historical setting of the psalm;
God is informed that the *"nations"* ("Gentiles") have come into His
"inheritance," which here refers not to His people but to His land
("property," see Deut. 4:21). This generalization is now made specific:
the *"temple"* is defiled and Jerusalem is laid *"in heaps."* Thus the temple is no longer *"holy"* ("separated") because it has been penetrated
by unclean Gentiles and destroyed. Moreover, Jerusalem is a ruin
(Jer. 52:13–14). Beyond physical destruction is human destruction.
God's *"servants"* (He is the King to whom Israel has submitted, see
Deut. 6:13) are dead (v. 2). The bodies of His *"saints"* ("pious," loyal
to the covenant) lie unburied, exposed to birds and beasts (fulfilling
the curse in Deut. 28:26). This is especially offensive since burial
of the dead is a godly duty. Even the priests who normally cannot
touch dead bodies are allowed to do so in the case of their relatives
in order to assure proper interment (Lev. 21:1–3). Thus the thought
is emphasized in verse 3: Jerusalem is drenched in blood like water,
"and there was no one to bury them [the saints]."

This massive destruction in turn evokes taunts from Israel's
"neighbors" (v. 4). This includes *"reproach"* ("scorn"), *"mocking,"* and
"derision." So, after defeat in battle, Ps. 44:13–14 laments: "You make
us a reproach to our neighbors, / A scorn and a derision to those all
around us. / You make us a byword among the nations, / A shaking
of the head among the peoples" (this fulfills the curse in Deut. 28:37).

Such is Israel's dark hour, her present grief. Her land lies prostrate, and her neighbors mock her. How does the psalmist deal with
this national disaster?

CALL FOR INTERVENTION

79:5 How long, LORD?
    Will You be angry forever?
    Will Your jealously burn like fire?
  6 Pour out Your wrath on the nations that do not
       know You,
    And on the kingdoms that do not call on Your
       name.
  7 For they have devoured Jacob,
    And laid waste his dwelling place.
  8 Oh, do not remember former iniquities against
       us!
    Let Your tender mercies come speedily to meet
       us,
    For we have been brought very low.
  9 Help us, O God of our salvation,
    For the glory of Your name;
    And deliver us, and provide atonement for our
       sins,
    For Your name's sake!
 10 Why should the nations say,
    "Where *is* their God?"
    Let there be known among the nations in our
       sight
    The avenging of the blood of Your servants
       which has been shed.
 11 Let the groaning of the prisoner come before
       You;
    According to the greatness of Your power
    Preserve those who are appointed to die;
 12 And return to our neighbors sevenfold into
       their bosom
    Their reproach with which they have
       reproached You, O Lord.

Ps. 79:5–12

Perhaps to our surprise, as the psalmist surveys the landscape cratered like the moon, he does not conclude that God's hand has been taken from His people. On the contrary, His hand is there, and it is a hand of judgment. Furthermore, he does not become cynical and skeptical, indulging in practical atheism. He does not announce,

"God is dead." Neither does he reevaluate his theology and begin to limit God ("after all He is in process just like we are") as many theologians do today. No, the psalmist simply sees Israel's destruction as the consequence of God's kingdom, God's moral order and authority, which endures. God is angry with Israel and His wrath is upon her.

In verse 5 the psalmist asks about the duration of God's *"anger"*: will it be *"forever"*? In the parallel question he asks if God's *"jealousy"* will *"burn like fire."* This assumes the exclusive covenant that Yahweh has with Israel and His jealousy when that covenant is broken. Furthermore, this also assumes that idolatry lies behind His destruction of Israel. He is jealous because she has gone after other gods. Thus God commands and warns: "You shall not go after other gods, the gods of the peoples who are all around you (for the Lord your God is a jealous God among you), lest the anger of the Lord your God be aroused against you and destroy you from the face of the earth" (Deut. 6:14-15).

Now the psalmist entreats the Lord to turn His wrath from Israel to the pagan nations ("Gentiles") *"that do not know You,"* that is, those nations who have not received God's Word (v. 6). Paul later describes the Gentiles as alienated "from the life of God, because of the ignorance that is in them" (Eph. 4:18), and as "having no hope and without God in the world" (Eph. 2:12). These are the *"kingdoms that do not call on"* God's *"name"*; that is, they do not worship Him. This contrasts with Israel who blesses God's "holy name" (Ps. 103:1). They deserve God's wrath (cf. Rom. 1:18) because they do not fulfill the first commandment (Exod. 20:3). Moreover, they have not only denied God, but they have destroyed His people; *"they have devoured"* ("eaten") Jacob (see Ps. 78:5) and *"laid waste* ["devastated," "ravaged"] *his dwelling place."*

Next, after the judgment of the Gentiles, the psalmist asks the Lord to change His relationship with Israel. First, he wants Him to *"not remember former iniquities,"* or literally, "the iniquities of our forefathers." If we follow the NKJV and render this phrase "former iniquities," then this generation is the cause of judgment. If, however, we translate literally using "forefathers," then this generation bears the consequences of past rebellion. Second, after God forgets Israel's sin, the psalmist wants Him to restore His *"tender mercies"* (plural intensive), or send them *"speedily,"* because Israel is *"brought very low."* Thus God's people are "on their backs." Forgiveness and mercy lie at the heart of his request.

The call for action is direct: *"Help us"* (v. 9). Who is to help? The *"God of our salvation"* ("deliverance"), that's who. Hope for an answer is not because God's people are low but because of the *"glory"* ("praise") of God's *"name."* When God acts He will vindicate His name before the nations that blaspheme Him. Again, the psalmist crys out for two things: deliverance and *"atonement for our sins."* The verb *deliver* literally means to snatch the prey out of an animal's mouth. Here he wants Israel to be pulled out of the devouring crunch of the enemy (cf. v. 7). *Atonement* means to "cover," "propitiate." He asks that God's people's sins be removed or covered by God. This is salvation indeed: deliverance from the enemy and deliverance from sin and the wrath of God. Again, the motive is "for Your name's sake." In His mercy God glorifies Himself. For the Christian this cry for salvation has been fulfilled by Jesus Christ. It is He who snatches us from the devil (who seeks us like a lion, 1 Pet. 5:8) and covers our sins with His atoning blood (Rom. 3:25).

When God acts, He will be glorified before the whole world. Thus the psalmist asks why the nations should get away with assuming God's absence (or impotence, v. 10). He cries out for the peoples *"in our sight"* (Israel's neighbors, see v. 4) to experience the *"avenging* ["revenging"] *of the blood of Your servants"* (see v. 2), namely, the innocent who died with the guilty when Jerusalem was destroyed. Here God will prove Himself to be God when His retributive justice destroys those who have destroyed His people. For the psalmist there is no contradiction between God judging Israel through pagan armies and His judging them personally. All are guilty before God. In His sovereignty He may use a Pharaoh or a Nebuchadnezzar as a hammer of His justice, but this in no way vindicates them as righteous or absolves them from the punishment that is sure to come.

Now in verse 11 the psalmist gives an emotional appeal for God to act. First, he pictures the prisoner of war groaning under the oppressor's yoke. He wants God to hear (or *"let . . . come before* [Your face]") that *"groaning"* ("lamentation," cf. Exod. 2:24). Second, he sees those *"appointed to die"* ("the sons of death") and asks that God preserve them *"according to the greatness of* [His] *power"* ("arm," Ps. 71:18). He beseeches God to act and set the captives free.

This is followed by a curse in verse 12. The psalmist asks that the mocking neighbors around Israel receive *"sevenfold* ["fully," seven being the perfect number] *into their bosom* [the fold of the garment at the breast, see Exod. 4:6]" the very reproaches with which they have reproached Israel. These taunts are summarized in verse 10 when the nations say: *"'Where is their God?'"* When Yahweh acts their gods will vanish from the scene, and their reproaches will boomerang upon them, hitting them fully in the chest.

The call for God's intervention in verses 5–12 is a call for God to forgive the past, have compassion on the prisoners, destroy the nations that do not know Him, and lift the reproach of those who claim His absence as His judgment rather than His presence in His wrath. In light of the weakness of the church today, can we not own this Psalm as our own? We too need God's forgiveness, God's atonement for our sins and those of our forefathers. We too need the Lord to hear the cry of the prisoners, those bound in Satan's darkness and the darkness of their own compromised theology. We too need God to glorify His name and vindicate Himself against those false idols who blaspheme Him and reproach Him and His Son.

PROMISE OF WORSHIP

79:13 So we, Your people and sheep of Your pasture,
  Will give You thanks forever;
  We will show forth Your praise to all
   generations.

           Ps. 79:13

When God acts again for Israel's sake, thanks and praise will be the result. Here the psalmist employs common images as he promises a renewal in worship. Israel is God's people and the sheep of His pasture (land). We read in Ps. 100:3: "Know that the Lord, He is God; / It is He who has made us, and not we ourselves; / We are His people and the sheep of His pasture." Restored into relationship with Him, there will be *"thanks forever"* (perpetual thanks) and *"praise"* (public witness to God's mighty works) from generation to generation. When renewal and revival come this is always the result, an explosion of heartfelt, genuine worship. I have seen this happen again and again as people in their sorrow and shame come to Christ for forgiveness and freedom. The present grief becomes a past grief and a distant memory. The tears are wiped away as joy is experienced and expressed in the presence of the living God.

CHAPTER EIGHTY

Prayer for Revival

Psalm 80

In his book on American revivalists, *The Spiritual Awakeners,* Keith J. Hardman identifies five phases of God's working. First, revival is usually preceded by a time of spiritual depression, apathy, and gross sin. Second, a small group of God's people becomes conscious of its sins and backslidden condition, repents, and longs for a new outpouring of God's grace. Third, leaders arise with prophetic insights into the causes and remedies for the current problems. A new revelation of God's holiness stimulates a striving after that holiness by God's people. Fourth, the awakening occurs, which may both renew the church and evangelize those outside. Fifth, the awakening may be God's preparation to strengthen His people for future challenges or trials.

In our own time certainly the first three phases have occurred in this country. We are in a time of great spiritual depression that is the consequence of a whole world-view shift to relativism. As Arthur M. Schlesinger, Jr., writes, "The acceleration of change compels us to perceive life as motion, not as order; the universe not as complete, but as unfinished." This has resulted in moral anarchy, producing a long list of abuses including abortion, drug addiction, child abuse, incest, white-collar crime, divorce, sexual exploitation, pornography, and the idealization of greed, lust, materialism, homosexuality, and violence. At the same time, there are pockets of people across the land who are deeply moved by God's Spirit to pray and work for revival. Among them there is a growing expectation that we are entering a new era of awakening. There are also new prophetic voices being heard in the land, such as John Wimber and Francis MacNutt. These voices refuse to minimize the sins of the culture and the church for the safety of public approval. Moreover, they are moving in the power of the Spirit, sparking the awakening of God's people wherever they go.

In Psalm 80 we have Israel in the midst of Hardman's five phases of God's working. Clearly a time of gross sin and apathy has characterized her life. This, however, is not directly stated here because judgment has fallen. God is angry (vv. 4 and 16). Israel's "hedges" or fences are broken down, and the land is ravaged, burned, and uprooted (v. 16). Now a time of repentance has come. The people are praying (v. 4). They are calling for restoration (vv. 3, 7, 19) and revival (v. 18). They are weeping over their condition (v. 5). They cry to God to return, to see, and to visit them once again (v. 14). Here is prayer for revival.

Similar to all of the psalms from 73 to 83, Psalm 80 is attributed to Asaph (see the introduction to Psalm 73). It is composed as a lament in a formal, liturgical style (see the refrains in vv. 3, 7, and 19). The mention of Ephraim, Benjamin, and Manasseh may indicate an origin in the Northern Kingdom just prior to its fall in 721 B.C., since these tribes can still be identified. The thought moves from the petition to God to listen and save (vv. 1–2), to the refrain (vv. 3), to the complaint: How long? (vv. 4–6(1)), to the refrain (v. 7), to the reminder of God's past acts (vv. 8–11), to the complaint: Why? (vv. 12–13), to the call for God to return (vv. 14–18) and ends with a final refrain (v. 19).

PETITION TO GOD: LISTEN AND SAVE

80:1 Give ear, O Shepherd of Israel,
    You who lead Joseph like a flock;

> You who dwell *between* the cherubim, shine
>   forth!
> 2 Before Ephraim, Benjamin, and Manasseh,
>   Stir up Your strength,
>   And come *and* save us!
>
> *Ps. 80:1–2*

God is called in verse 1 to hear this prayer: *"Give ear."* He is identified as Israel's *"shepherd"* (see Ps. 23:1). Thus He is her true King (Ezek. 34:11ff.) and leads *"Joseph* [probably all Israel, see Ps. 77:15] *like a flock"* (cf. Pss. 79:13; 100:3). Lest He be made too familiar, however, He also dwells in glory *"between the cherubim,"* the angelic beings who guard His throne (see Exod. 25:18–20). From there the psalmist entreats: *"shine forth* ['appear']!" This revelation will mean redemption. The petition continues in verse 2 for God to arouse (*"stir up"*) His strength, *"come"* and *"save* ['rescue,' 'deliver'] *us."* This is to take place before *"Ephraim, Benjamin, and Manasseh,"* the tribal mid-section of Palestine. The geography suggests that this psalm's origin was during Assyria's siege of Samaria (2 Kings 17:5ff.). The cry here is for God to make a move. The psalmist knows Yahweh as the living God who intervenes directly in history, in the life of His people. As He stirs up His strength, Israel's enemies will be defeated. God will come and visit His people with salvation.

REFRAIN

> 80:3 Restore us, O God;
>   Cause Your face to shine,
>   And we shall be saved!
>
> *Ps. 80:3*

The theme of this psalm is now given in the refrain repeated three times (vv. 3, 7, 19). The call *"restore us"* means "return us." It is the cry to be restored into a right relationship with God Himself, which will then restore Israel's fortunes. To be restored means to see God's face shining. When He is angry, He turns His gaze away. When He is gracious, He returns His gaze to us. Thus Aaron pronounces a benediction upon Israel: "The Lord bless you and keep you; / The

Lord make His face shine upon you; / And be gracious to you; / The Lord lift up His countenance upon you, / And give you peace" (Num. 6:24–26). God's shining face is salvation: *"And we shall be saved."* This is the answer to the petition in verse 2, "Come and save us!" When God looks upon us, lifting His wrath, no enemy can stand. At its heart revival is nothing less than the manifest presence of God. The great turning point for the Evangelical Awakening in eighteenth-century England came when God encountered its leaders, empowering them with His Holy Spirit. John Wesley records this event in his journal dated January 1, 1739:

> Mr. Hall, Hinching, Ingham, Whitefield, Hutching and my brother Charles were present at our love feast in Fetter Lane with about sixty of our brethren. About three in the morning as we were continuing instant in prayer the power of God came mightly upon us, insomuch that many cried out for exulting joy and many fell to the ground. As soon as we were recovered a little from the awe and amazement at the presence of His Majesty, we broke out with one voice, "We praise Thee O God, we acknowledge Thee to be Lord."

Here is the shining face of God.

COMPLAINT: HOW LONG?

80:4 O LORD God of hosts,
   How long will You be angry
   Against the prayer of Your people?
 5 You have fed them with the bread of tears,
   And given them tears to drink in great
      measure.
 6 You have made us a strife to our neighbors,
   And our enemies laugh among themselves.
                               Ps. 80:4–6

God is identified now as *"Lord God of hosts."* The hosts are His angelic armies and messengers who do His will (see Ps. 103:20–21). In asking for divine intervention the psalmist stresses God's power in battle.

The question addressed is the duration of God's *"anger"* (literally, His "smoking") against the prayer of Israel. This prayer would be a lamentation, covering the petitions of Psalm 80. God's people have poured out their tears, which have become their *"bread"* and *"drink,"* the very food by which they live (v. 5). They also come in *"great measure"* (literally, a "third," a part of an ephah?). The psalmist sees God as the source of this massive bitterness. His wrath has caused the pain.

Beyond God's anger and Israel's tears is the ridicule of her neighbors and enemies (v. 6). Again God, in His judgment, is the source of this distress: *"You have made us . . . ."* For the nations bordering Israel, she has become a *"strife"* ("contention"). Her judgment throws them into confusion and discord over her: "weak people; weak God." Moreover, her enemies, such as Assyria, *"laugh* ["mock"] *among themselves"* over Israel's weakness and deride her in her defeat.

The question of this section is how long will this go on? How long will God's wrath be upon His people? How long will Israel weep and the pagans around her argue and scorn her name?

These same questions plague us in the absence of revival. When God turns us over to our sin, this is a sign that His wrath is upon us (Rom. 1:18ff.). Moreover, when judgment begins "at the house of God" (1 Pet. 4:17), it is a time for weeping. In fact, when God's mercy over sin is given to a godly remnant, tears may well become their "daily bread." When there is some taste of God's mercy, the tears may well increase. Thus George Whitefield, the great Anglican evangelist of the eighteenth-century revival recounts in his journal of November 5, 1740 that while he was preaching with Gilbert Tennant, the Presbyterian revivalist and educator, a man cried out: "He is come! He is come!" Whitefield continues, "[that the man] could scarce sustain the manifestation of Jesus to his soul. But having heard the crying of others for the like favor [this] obliged me to stop, and I prayed over them as I saw their agonies and distress increase." Whitefield goes on, "At length we sang an hymn and then retired to the house, where the man that received Christ continued praising and speaking of Him until near midnight. My own soul was so full that I retired and wept before the Lord, and had a deep sense of my own vileness and the sovereignty and greatness of God's everlasting love."

In the absence of revival, the "neighbors" of Christ, those looking at Him, like the neighbors of Israel, see a powerless, defeated church and are in confusion while His enemies laugh and scorn His name.

REFRAIN

80:7 Restore us, O God of hosts;
     Cause Your face to shine,
     And we shall be saved!

Ps. 80:7

Such observations bring us to cry out again for God's restoration, God's shining face, and God's salvation. The only difference between this verse and verse 3 is the addition to God's name of the descriptive *"of hosts"* (see v. 4). The hosts denote God's warrior angels who gather before His throne. Here is an implied call to arms, a summons for God to join in the battle for Israel's sake. This indeed is the answer to our woes. This is revival.

THE REMINDER OF GOD'S PAST ACTS

80:8 You have brought a vine out of Egypt;
     You have cast out the nations, and planted it.
  9 You prepared *room* for it,
     And caused it to take deep root,
     And it filled the land.
 10 The hills were covered with its shadow,
     And the mighty cedars with its boughs.
 11 She sent out her boughs to the Sea,
     And her branches to the River.

Ps. 80:8–11

Using the extended metaphor of a vine, the psalmist recalls redemptive history, reminding God of what He has done in the past for His people.

To begin with God brought Israel out of Egypt as a *"vine"* (always grape bearing). The symbolism suggests that as this plant was treasured for its fruit, so is Israel. The vine often represents God's people (see Ezek. 17:6ff.; Hos. 10:1, 14:7; Jer. 2:21, 6:9) and becomes a metaphor for Jesus and His relationship with His disciples (John 15:1ff.).

After the Exodus, God expelled the nations in the Promised Land and planted Israel in their place (v. 8). Moreover, He prepared the soil as the vine-dresser (see John 15:1) and saw that His plant was deeply rooted (literally, "You have rooted its roots"). It then filled the land (v. 10, see all of Judges, 1 and 2 Samuel). Even the cedars (literally, "the cedars of God") were covered with the vine (or, "the boughs of the vine were as the cedars of God"). Here the cedars represent that which is "high and lifted up" (Isa. 2:13). Israel, however, is higher. Her kingdom, *"her boughs,"* also extended to *"the Sea"* (the Mediterranean Sea) and to *"the River"* (the Euphrates, see Deut. 11:24).

We see that the past glory of God's people intensifies the psalmist's present anguish even as periods of great awakening make our own churches look so threadbare.

COMPLAINT: WHY?

80:12 Why have You broken down her hedges,
So that all who pass by the way pluck her
fruit?
13 The boar out of the woods uproots it,
And the wild beast of the field devours it.
Ps. 80:12–13

This complaint can be taken in two ways. The first is that the psalmist cannot understand God's judgment. The second is that while the psalmist can accept God's original judgment, he now questions why His wrath continues. In the context, the second interpretation seems more likely (compare vv. 4–6). Thus the *"broken . . . hedges"* ("fences") allow outsiders to take the vine's fruit (v. 12). Moreover, a wild *"boar"* (unclean animal, Lev. 11:7, Assyria?) *"uproots"* ("tears away") the vine, and the *"wild beast"* feeds. Such is the catastrophe that has come upon God's people (see v. 6). But why does it continue? Is it not time for God to intervene?

CALL FOR GOD TO RETURN

80:14 Return, we beseech You, O God of hosts;
Look down from heaven and see,
And visit this vine
   15 And the vineyard which Your right hand has
planted,
And the branch *that* You made strong for
Yourself.
   16 *It is* burned with fire, *it is* cut down;
They perish at the rebuke of Your
countenance.
   17 Let Your hand be upon the man of Your right
hand,
Upon the son of man *whom* You made strong
for Yourself.
   18 Then we will not turn back from You;
Revive us, and we will call upon Your name.
                                               Ps. 80:14–18

God is now addressed as the commander of angelic armies, the *"God of hosts."* The psalmist crys out for Him to *"return"* ("turn"), that is, to turn His face back upon His people. He is to *"look down from heaven"* (He is the exalted Lord), *"see,"* and *"visit* ['attend to'] *this vine* [Israel]" and its *"vineyard"* ("stock"), planted by His right hand, the hand of authority and power (Exod. 15:6). The next phrase in verse 15, *"And the branch which You made strong for Yourself,"* literally translates, "And upon the son whom You have strengthened for Yourself." This is probably a variant of verse 17b and therefore a corruption of the text.

The vine needing God's attention is defined in verse 16 as *"burned with fire"* (the fire of wrath, see v. 4), and *"cut down"* (compare vv. 12–13). The cause of this is the *"rebuke"* (see Pss. 76:6, 104:7) of God's *"countenance"* ("face"). Israel perished when separated from God.

Now in verses 17–18, the call for action is repeated. The psalmist asks for God's hand to be upon Israel again. This includes both the king or Messiah, *"the man of Your right hand"* (see Ps. 110:1; Eph. 1:20; Heb. 1:13), and the people personified as the *"son of man"* (this too could be messianic, see Dan. 7:13–14) who God has *"made strong"* ("secured") for Himself. This petition is ultimately fulfilled in Christ, who comes to Israel as the "man of God's right hand" to revive His people and accomplish their salvation. In praying this prayer as His church, we ask for a fresh visitation from the risen Lord while we await His return and the final consummation.

Once God acts, the promise in verse 18 will be secure. God's people will not turn from Him. This, however, must be His work: *"Revive us"* (*"Give us life,"* *"Make us alive"*). The consequence of revival is worship: *"and we will call upon Your name."*

REFRAIN

80:19 Restore us, O LORD God of hosts;
       Cause Your face to shine,
       And we shall be saved!

Ps. 80:19

The final refrain repeats verse 7 with one addition. God is also called Yahweh, *"Lord."* The psalm closes with this theme: God must restore His people by turning the light of His face upon them. In this renewed relationship they will be saved.

D. Martyn Lloyd-Jones asks why the church in the English-speaking world has experienced no great revival in the twentieth century. His answer is that the church has accommodated itself to the modern scientific world-view. Up until this century, when the church was weak, sinful, and apathetic, a remnant of godly people got down upon their knees, repenting and beseeching God to send a revival. Now, however, since we have embraced the technological society, when the church is weak, sinful, and apathetic, rather than humbling ourselves and crying out to God, we organize an evangelistic crusade. Genuine revival, however, cannot be accomplished by our energy and technique. It is God's alone to give. Thus in our crisis we must call out to the Lord: *"Restore us."* *"Cause Your face to shine."* Send the power, send the Spirit, manifest the glory, *"and we shall be saved!"*

CHAPTER EIGHTY-ONE

The Best Is Yet to Come

Psalm 81

We worship and God speaks. This is to be the structure of our life with Him. Thus Paul promises that when we offer our bodies to God as living sacrifices in worship, He will transform our minds and we will prove (or "approve") His will: good, acceptable, and perfect (Rom. 12:1–2). That will is revealed as a result of worship.

It is certainly true that historically we have structured our corporate church-life accordingly. Typically, on Sundays we worship, sing hymns, pray, and give our "offerings" and then hear the Word of God in a sermon or homily. At this point are we merely expecting good advice, theological and Biblical insight, inspirational thoughts, or are we expecting God personally to address us? Will we go away from worship with a word from the Lord?

More recently, I have grown to expect that word. I am dissatisfied if God does not speak to me. He is not a dumb idol. As I preach I am listening for the "word within the Word." I am looking for a moment when the Spirit will anoint me with a special message that He wants to thrust home apart from solid biblical and theological exposition. In my devotional life also I am listening as well as speaking. I can pray with David: "I waited patiently for the Lord; / And He inclined to me, / And heard my cry" (Ps. 40:1). And again, "Truly my soul silently waits for God; / From Him comes my salvation" (Ps. 62:1). Here in Psalm 81 Israel worships (vv. 1–5), and God speaks (vv. 6–16). As God's people open their hearts to Him in praise, He reminds them of His past deeds and recalls them to an exclusive submission to Himself. If they will respond, judgment will be lifted and the blessing of God will return in great bounty.

The authorship of this psalm is given to Asaph (see the introduction to Psalm 73). Its structure contains both an exhortation to worship and a prophetic or divine oracle in response. Commentators identify the form as a prophetic liturgy, which may be delivered in the context of a major feast (v. 3). The references to the New Moon and full moon probably indicate the Feast of Tabernacles as its immediate setting (v. 3). The Hebrew calendar was composed of lunar months, which began when the thin crescent was first visible at sunset with the full moon coming midmonth. Thus Tabernacles was heralded on the first day of the seventh month (*Tishri*) with the Feast of Trumpets (see Num. 29:1ff.), and, following the Day of Atonement on the tenth, began itself on the fifteenth when the moon was full and lasted for seven days (see v. 3, Num. 29:12ff.). The thought here moves from Israel's call to worship (vv. 1–5), to God's response in redemption (vv. 6–7), to a call to faithfulness (vv. 8–10), to His judgment on unfaithfulness (vv. 11–12) and concludes with promises yet to be fulfilled (vv. 13–16).

ISRAEL'S CALL TO WORSHIP

81:1 Sing aloud to God our strength;
　　　Make a joyful shout to the God of Jacob.
　　2 Raise a song and strike the timbrel,
　　　The pleasant harp with the lute.
　　3 Blow the trumpet at the time of the New
　　　　Moon,
　　　At the full moon, on our solemn feast day.
　　4 For this *is* a statute for Israel,
　　　A law of the God of Jacob.
　　5 This He established in Joseph *as* a testimony,
　　　When He went throughout the land of Egypt,
　　　Where I heard a language I did not understand.
　　　　　　　　　　　　　　　　　　Ps. 81:1–5

Verse 1 summons God's people to praise. Their worship is to be robust, like troops rejoicing over victory in battle. A good analogy would be the shouts of winning fans at the Super Bowl when the final gun sounds. Israel is to *"sing aloud* [express public joy, *"give a ringing cry"] to God"* who is her *"strength"* ("might," realized in His mighty acts). This worship is to include *"a joyful shout* ["blast, war-cry, shout in triumph," see Pss. 47:1; 66:1] *to the God of Jacob,*" namely, the God who is her deliverer (see Exod. 19:3–4).

After defining what is to be done in verse 1, there is a brief elaboration on how it is to be done in verse 2: singing is to be accompanied by *"timbrel"* (a woman's instrument used in dancing), *"harp"* (stringed lyre), and *"lute"* (a guitar with a bulging, resonance-body at the lower end). This worship is not random. It is ordered and filled with song.

Next, the *"trumpet"* (ram's horn) is to be sounded, probably marking the Feast of Trumpets. This inaugurates the seventh month of the year and prepares for the Feast of Tabernacles to follow *"at the full moon"* (v. 3, see the introduction). Moreover, these celebrations are grounded in revelation. They are God's *"statute"* ("decree") and *"law"* ("ordinance") and therefore to be carried out (v. 4).

The festivals, however, are not to be performed in blind obedience merely because God says to do them. They are a *"testimony established* ["set"] *in Joseph* [God's whole people, see Ps. 80:1]," which witnesses to the Exodus, *"when He went throughout* ["over" or "against," with plagues?] *the land of Egypt."*

The final clause of verse 5 can be taken in two ways. It either refers to the unknown language of Egypt (so NKJV) or it refers to the psalmist's prophetic inspiration to follow. If the latter is true, it is a transition to verses 6–16 and translates literally, "A lip ("speech, language") which I knew not I shall hear."

This call to worship is a call to hearty praise in the context of the festivals that are established as a testimony to God's delivering His people from Egypt. The central festival here is probably Tabernacles (v. 3), the harvest festival, which also remembers Israel's wandering in the wilderness, living in booths, and God's provision there day by day. Thus the natural cycle of sowing and reaping is submitted to the mighty acts of God in delivering Israel from bondage in Egypt. Eschatological (or teleological) history gives meaning and purpose to the calendar, using it to witness to God's special revelation in redeeming His people. This is a time for shouting joyfully indeed!

GOD'S RESPONSE: REDEMPTION

81:6 "I removed his shoulder from the burden;
          His hands were freed from the baskets.

> 7 You called in trouble, and I delivered you;
>   I answered you in the secret place of thunder;
>   I tested you at the waters of Meribah." Selah
>
> *Ps. 81:6–7*

As Israel worships, God now speaks directly. Here is "dialogical faith" (Martin Buber). God responds, declaring that He lifted Israel's burden, delivered His people from bondage, spoke to them, and tested them in the wilderness. All of this is a part of God's saving work toward us who believe. First of all, there is the burden lifted. Israel's shoulder is freed from the weight of slave city-building. Moreover, the *"baskets,"* carrying clay and straw for bricks, are dropped. This liberation points to Jesus, who bids the weary and heavy-laden to come to Him for rest (Matt. 11:28). Second, God responds to Israel's cry *"in trouble"* ("distress, constriction") and delivers ("rescues," see Ps. 50:15) her (v. 7). Israel is not only set free; she is also brought out. Again Jesus delivers us from the devil, the penalty and power of sin and the wrath to come (Col. 1:13; Rom. 8:1, 6; 1 Thess. 1:10). Third, God speaks to Israel, answering her, *"in the secret place of thunder,"* giving her His law. This is probably a reference to Sinai (Exod. 20:18ff.). Likewise, Jesus reveals the Father to us and shows us His will (John 14:9, 15–16). Fourth, God proves ("tests, examines") Israel *at the waters of Meribah* (see Exod. 17:1–7). While she tries to test Him there, complaining for lack of water, it is really God who tests her, revealing her contentious, ungrateful heart. As we walk with Jesus through the suffering of this life, we too are tested and purified by Him. Paul writes, "tribulation produces character; and character hope. Now hope does not disappoint, because the love of God has been poured out in our hearts by the Holy Spirit who was given to us" (Rom. 5:3–5). As God speaks, therefore, He lifts our burdens, delivers us from sin, answers our cry with His word, and proves our faith. Here is redemption.

GOD'S RESPONSE: CALL TO FAITHFULNESS

> 81:8 "Hear, O My people, and I will admonish you!
>   O Israel, if you will listen to Me!
>   9 There shall be no foreign god among you;
>   Nor shall you worship any foreign god.

> 10 I *am* the LORD your God,
>   Who brought you out of the land of Egypt;
>   Open your mouth wide, and I will fill it."
>
> > Ps. 81:8–10

Next, God calls Israel to put down her idols. Knowing that He is at the heart of the matter, He is emphatic in verse 8: *"Hear* [šāmaʿ] *O my people* [compare Deut 6:4, "Hear O Israel"] . . . *if you will listen to* [šāmaʿ] *Me!"* What then will God do? He will *"admonish"* ("enjoin solemnly" or "witness against") Israel. The warning that follows implies that, indeed, idols have crept in. Thus we hear the command not even to permit a *"foreign god"* in the land (*"among you"*), much less to worship it (v. 9). And why is this? It is because Yahweh has redeemed Israel *"out of the land of Egypt"* (v. 10). She is exclusively His (see Exod. 20:1–3). Moreover, it is Yahweh who will fill Israel's mouth, that is, satisfy her. Therefore, God concludes, *"open your mouth wide"* (compare v. 16). This is always our temptation, to allow something to sneak into our hearts and replace the living God. 1 John concludes, "Little children, keep yourselves from idols. Amen" (5:21). Calvin comments, "The human mind is a permanent factory of idols." These verses are for us.

GOD'S RESPONSE: JUDGMENT ON UNFAITHFULNESS

> 81:11 "But My people would not heed My voice,
>   And Israel would *have* none of Me.
>   12 So I gave them over to their own stubborn heart,
>   To walk in their own counsels."
>
> > Ps. 81:11–12

God speaks (v. 7), but Israel refuses to *"heed"* ("hear"). Like a rejected lover, He concludes that His people *"would have none of Me,"* or "yield to Me." What is the result? Yahweh gives them up to their own hard hearts ("the stubbornness of their heart"). Since they have refused His way, they will have to walk in their own (v. 12). All they will hear is their own voice chattering. This is God's passive wrath as He lets them go their own way. So Paul writes, "For the wrath of God is revealed from heaven against all ungodliness and unrighteousness of men. . . . Therefore God also gave them up to uncleanness, in the lusts of their hearts, to dishonor their bodies among themselves" (Rom. 1:18, 24; cf. Ps. 5:10). There is no greater judgment upon those who have heard God's voice than silence, abandonment. Moreover, why should He speak when we refuse to hear?

GOD'S RESPONSE: PROMISES
YET TO BE FULFILLED

> 81:13 "Oh, that My people would listen to Me,
>   That Israel would walk in My ways!
>   14 I would soon subdue their enemies,
>   And turn My hand against their adversaries.
>   15 The haters of the LORD would pretend
>   submission to Him,
>   But their fate would endure forever.
>   16 He would have fed them also with the finest
>   of wheat;
>   And with honey from the rock I would have
>   satisfied you."
>
> *Ps. 81:13–16*

God now cries out, perhaps in pain and longing, for Israel to listen to His word and walk in His ways. This is a summary of the life of faith. By faith we hear God's voice and by faith we obey Him. Thus Jesus tells us, "If anyone loves Me, he will keep My word; and My Father will love him, and We will come to him and make our home with him" (John 14:23).

If Israel then would so respond, God promises to reverse her fortunes. He would *"soon subdue"* (or "humble") her *"enemies,"* turning His *"hand"* (see Exod. 15:6) against them (v. 14). These *"haters of the Lord would pretend submission"* or, better, "will cringe to Him in fear" and *"their fate* ["time"] *would endure* ["shall be"] *forever."* After such deliverance, which is an eternal Exodus (cf. vv. 6–7), God would then provide for His people. Now, rather than manna, there is *"the finest* ["the fatness," i.e., fullness] *of wheat."* Rather than water from the rock, now *"honey"* flows (see Deut. 32:13). If Israel will open her mouth to God, He will fill it indeed (v. 10). There could be no greater promise: *"I would have satisfied you"* (v. 16).

In these final promises we see what salvation is. On the negative side we are saved *from* sin, Satan, and death. On the positive side we are saved *for* all of the goodness and blessing of God. Jesus Himself is this blessing to us. So He promises, "Whoever eats My flesh and drinks My blood has eternal life, and I will raise him up at the last day. For My flesh is food indeed, and My blood is drink indeed" (John 6:54–55). Indeed, the best is yet to come!

CHAPTER EIGHTY-TWO

When Lady Justice Loses Her Blindfold

Psalm 82

The ideal for justice, even in our age of relativity, is impartiality. All are held to be equal under the law. Likewise, the violation of the law should bring just punishment. According to this understanding the law is held to be an absolute standard by which society is organized and community in this fallen world is made possible. At the same time, we make distinctions between absolute law given, for example, in the Constitution and relative law, which applies and interprets that law. This legislation allows us change in response to changing conditions. Moreover, the very fact that even the Constitution must be reinterpreted in new situations and for new generations, and also the fact that it can be amended, opens the door to relativity and human corruption. Consequently schools of interpretation arise, and labels like "conservative" and "liberal" follow. In our culture the whole theory of the law is up for grabs today. Many secularists see no enduring moral and legal structure for society at all. They become "functionalists," holding that the law is simply the majority opinion of any given society at any given time. For traditionalists, however, the law in our culture has a religious basis and, therefore, reflects the Judeo-Christian heritage that lies behind it. For Christians and orthodox Jews the relative laws of our society are only just in so far as they reflect the revealed law of God given in the Bible. There is an absolute, transcendent, unchanging law upon which the moral order of humanity is to be based. This view makes actions such as Hitler's genocide a crime against humanity as a whole, or, better, a crime against God's law, to which humanity is ultimately responsible.

The longing for justice in our hearts and our offense at injustice show that we are not simply random creatures swimming in the soup of relativity (C. S. Lewis). No, our cry for a just universe and our demand for order reflect the reality of that transcendent order held in the hand of God. Here then in Psalm 82 there is a cry for "Lady Justice" to put her blindfold of impartiality back on and for God to establish justice in the earth (v. 8).

This psalm is bracketed with God's judging "the gods" (v. 1) and "the earth" (v. 8). Between the opening and closing verses there is an extended oracle or prophetic word of judgment (vv. 2–7). Clearly injustice rules the day (v. 2) and as a result "all the foundations of the earth are unstable" (v. 5). Thus God will judge the judges: "But you shall die like men" (v. 7).

Psalm 82 is attributed to Asaph (see the introduction to Psalm 73). Commentators hold it to be a didactic psalm or a hymn or a lament over injustice. The crucial question of interpretation involves the meaning of gods (ʾelohîm) in verses 1 and 6. These may be fallen angels ("principalities and powers," Eph. 6:12) who rule over the nations unjustly (hidden behind their idols), or they may be human judges ("mighty ones") who are "gods" because they exercise divine justice, having received the word of God. Thus they are not gods by nature but have a god-like function in bringing justice to the world and in judging human life. This would best account for Jesus' use of this psalm to confound His opponents who charge

Him with blasphemy because He claims to be the Son of God. In John 10:33–36 He argues that since God calls those to whom the word of God came (on Sinai) gods, the Jews should not be offended by His being the Son of God. He has been sent into the world by the Father (the argument is from the lesser to the greater). This reflects the rabbinical teaching that when Israel received the law she became divine and then lost this position by worshiping the golden calf (see C. K. Barrett, *The Gospel according to John,* ad loc). Thus we will take the view that the "gods" here are human judges who judge unjustly (v. 2). This makes the most sense of the call to justice (vv. 3–4). Moreover, God would not call upon fallen angels to free the poor and needy from the wicked (v. 4). Thus the judgment "you shall die like men" doesn't imply that the "gods" are not men, but merely means that regardless of their position and authority they have a human fate awaiting them.

The thought in this psalm moves from the announcement that God is judge (v. 1), to His charge and exhortation of the judges (vv. 2–4), to the consequences of injustice (v. 5), to the judgment of the judges (vv. 6–7) and concludes with an appeal for God to judge (v. 8).

GOD IS JUDGE

82:1 God stands in the congregation of the mighty;
He judges among the gods.

Ps. 82:1

Verse 1 announces that God *"stands in the congregation* ['assembly'] *of the mighty,"* or "the congregation of God (*'ēl*)." The setting is judgment: *"He judges among* ['in the midst of'] *the gods* [*'elohīm*]." As noted above, we take these gods to be human judges executing divine justice, the "mighty ones." Thus *'elohīm* (plural) is rendered "judges" in legal settings in Exod. 21:6 and 22:8–9. As noted above, these judges execute godlike functions in bringing judgment and justice to God's people. Also they bear the law, divine revelation, and thus do what only God can do. As Jesus says, they are the ones to whom the word of God has come (John 10:35). Now, however, God judges the judges.

GOD'S CHARGE AND EXHORTATION

> 82:2 How long will you judge unjustly,
>   And show partiality to the wicked?   Selah
>   3 Defend the poor and fatherless;
>   Do justice to the afflicted and needy.
>   4 Deliver the poor and needy;
>   Free *them* from the hand of the wicked.
>
> Ps. 82:2–4

Having called His court into session, God now addresses the judges. He accuses them of judging *"unjustly"* by asking how long they will show *"partiality to the wicked,"* or, literally, "lift up the faces of the wicked ("lawbreakers"). In contrast to our human counts, the absolute standard of justice is not in doubt here. These judges, however, have refused to apply it properly. Thus, they have favored the wicked, perhaps being bribed to do so. As Camus notes, the magistrates wear white wigs in order to mask their injustice.

God now exhorts these judges to change in verses 3–4. Since He *"watches over the strangers; / [and] relieves the fatherless and widow"* (Ps. 146:9), He expects them to do the same. Thus they are to *"defend* ["judge justly"] *the poor* ["the weak"] *and fatherless"* (see Isa. 1:17). As God warns Israel, "I will not turn away its punishment, / Because they sell the righteous for silver, / And the poor for a pair of sandals" (Amos 2:6).

Moreover, the judges are to *"do justice* [render help] *to the afflicted* ["poor, pious"] *and needy* ["destitute"]." In doing this, they are acting on God's behalf, in His place. They are ʾelohîm. Thus when the messianic King comes, He will bear God's own justice and righteousness to the poor and needy (see Ps. 72:1–4; Luke 6:20).

Next, the judges are to intervene by delivering *"the poor* ["the weak," v. 3] *and needy"* from *"the hand* [power] *of the wicked* [see v. 2, "law-breakers, criminals"]." The verbs are strong: *"deliver"* ("bring into security, cause to escape"), and *"free"* ("rescue, snatch prey from an animal's mouth"). Here is active justice changing the social environment. Here are judges not merely upholding the law of God; they are obeying the law of God. For the Bible, God's justice, is both to be *defended* and *done*. Thus when Jesus enters into His public ministry He not only attacks the unjustice of the Sabbath tradition, He also heals on the Sabbath (Luke 6:6–11). There must be for these judges (and for us) no separation between theory and practice. As injustice is exposed, justice must be pursued.

One tragedy in the separation of the "personal" gospel from the "social" gospel has been evangelical indifference to social justice and the surrender of prophetic passion to liberal theology. This was not true of the great revivalists of past generations such as Wesley and Finney, who held the two sides of the same coin together. The call to social justice forces us to test our own selfishness, greed, apathy, and escapism from the wounds of our generation. It also forces us to admit that God's kingdom order, which is breaking in upon us, embraces all of life.

THE CONSEQUENCES OF INJUSTICE

82:5 They do not know, nor do they understand;
They walk about in darkness;
All the foundations of the earth are unstable.
Ps. 82:5

When the judges are unjust, the poor and afflicted, God's "little people," *do not know* (by experience) or *understand* ("discern"). They *walk* [live morally] *in darkness.* It is both the hearing and doing of God's law that bring light. Justice must be modeled and experienced. Otherwise, it becomes a remote concept, distorted by the injustice of the world. This breeds skepticism, cynicism, and despair. In our modern world it also breeds dictatorships, where the law of God is replaced by the will of the leader. The ultimate consequences of this are that *all the foundations of the earth are unstable* ["shall be moved"]. Moral order becomes Jell-O. Thus we build on sand and are carried away (Matt. 7:24ff.). This breakdown has vast psychological as well as sociological consequences as personality structure collapses under confusion. Life goes out of control, producing guilt and emptiness. No wonder that in the Korean prisoner of war camps Christians who had a strong sense of self were segregated as being too hard to brainwash into the communist ideology. Moreover, the loss of justice, with all of its personal and social impact, also prepares for the final injustice, the coming of Antichrist to the world, defined by Paul as the "lawless one" (2 Thess. 2:8).

THE JUDGMENT OF THE JUDGES

82:6 I said, "You *are* gods,
     And all of you *are* children of the Most High.
   7 But you shall die like men,
     And fall like one of the princes."

Ps. 82:6–7

God now addresses the *ʾelohīm*, the mighty judges, emphatically:
"I said." First, He gives them their identity: *"You are gods."* Executing
God's justice puts them in His place. Only the King could have a
higher office as God's son and messianic forerunner (see Ps. 2:7). In
the parallel clause they are also identified as *"children ['sons'] of the
Most High"* (v. 6; see Gen. 14:18ff.). This phrase is unique here to the
Old Testament. Again, the judges are sons by appointment, not by
nature, since they are called to execute God's will and character.
This concept is based on the calling in Israel of faithful sons to execute the will and character of their father.

Second, after recalling their exalted identity, God establishes
their destiny. Regardless of how godlike they may be, they will die
like men (v. 7). Their destiny (and God's judgment) makes them
very human. Moreover, they will *"fall like one of the princes."* The
verb here can refer to violent death and be figurative for going to
ruin or perishing. Thus the princes of Israel who are exalted in
station or office also perish. This will be their destiny under divine
judgment. It is never a bad thing to remember our mortality and be
humbled.

APPEAL FOR GOD'S JUDGMENT

82:8 Arise, O God, judge the earth;
     For You shall inherit all nations.

Ps. 82:8

The psalmist now returns (see v. 1) with a final call after God's
prophetic word has been spoken. He asks God to arise, that is, to get
up from His throne and execute judgment. The call is for God to do
what the unjust judges refuse to do: judge the earth. As we have
seen, this means not only for God to uphold His law but also to

establish right relationships, to bring in His kingdom, a just society, a righteous order.

The call is eschatological and universal: God is to *"judge the earth, for* [He] *shall inherit* ["take possession of"] *all nations."* Thus this call is only fulfilled by Jesus, the Messiah. It is He who comes to establish justice in the earth (Rev. 20:11–15) and to Him belong all of its nations (Phil. 2:9–11).

What then can we say in conclusion? First, God is our final judge. All justice, all law, must be submitted to Him. This is even true in our age of relativism. Second, human judges are called to be just and to do justice. They are accountable to God when they misappropriate even the relative justice of this fallen world. They also have a god-like position, holding the issues of life and death in their hands. Thus they must not show partiality. Third, without justice the order of life collapses. Fourth, we now know that final justice is in the hands of Jesus Christ. He will judge the earth and inherit the nations. Even in our courts today we swear testimony on a Bible, admitting that there is a divine law beyond human law and that one day we will all stand before the Final Judge.

CHAPTER EIGHTY-THREE

Call to Battle!

Psalm 83

A single enemy is one thing. A confederacy is another. It is much harder to fight a war on several fronts. For example, when Hitler attacked the Soviet Union, he stranded his armies in North Africa, who were facing the English and the Americans there. Because of this, after the defeat of Rommel and his "Afrika Korps," the allies were able to invade Italy and land later at Normandy on the western coast of France. Germany was overextended, being forced to supply several armies at once. The end of World War II was not in doubt when the allies coordinated their military strategy. Likewise, the modern state of Israel has always been exposed on the northern, eastern, and southern flanks. She has balanced herself between the various powers surrounding her, signing a peace treaty with Egypt, committing troops in Lebanon while supporting "Christian" forces there, and keeping Jordan calm. This has allowed her major military energy to be directed toward Syria, the most threatening immediate enemy among the Arab states. The greatest blow to Israel would be a united Arab world. Their internal divisions keep her relatively secure.

In the ancient world Israel was also surrounded by enemies. Her historical fate was balanced between Egypt to the southwest and Assyria (and Babylon) to the northeast. During the period of the monarchy, the smaller states around her could only hope for victory in accord with the larger, distant empires. In Psalm 83 this accord has been reached. In the roll call of Israel's enemies allied against her (vv. 6–8) the real scare is in verse 8: "Assyria also has joined with them." The resulting call to battle is a call for God to fight for His people. The psalmist hopes that past victories will become present once again (vv. 9–12), and that God will be exalted over all the earth (v. 18). For the psalmist, a conspiracy against Israel is a conspiracy against God (v. 5). He must, therefore, rise up and destroy it.

It is not undue spiritualization to note that the church also is faced with a confederacy of evil. Our enemies, Satan, his fallen angelic hosts, and his historical, human operatives would seek to destroy all true Christians because of a violent hatred for God and His Son, Jesus. As we study this psalm we can keep in mind relevant application to our own spiritual warfare in this world.

The authorship of Psalm 83 is given to Asaph (see the introduction to Psalm 73). Commentators identify its form as a national lament caused by an immediate threat of invasion. The mention of Assyria would put the date between the ninth and seventh centuries B.C. The thought moves from the crisis exposed (vv. 1–4) to the confederacy identified (vv. 5–8) and concludes with a call for battle (vv. 9–18).

THE CRISIS EXPOSED

83:1 Do not keep silent, O God!
　　Do not hold Your peace,
　　And do not be still, O God!
　2 For behold, Your enemies make a tumult;
　　And those who hate You have lifted up their
　　　head.
　3 They have taken crafty counsel against Your
　　　people,
　　And consulted together against Your sheltered
　　　ones.
　4 They have said, "Come, and let us cut them off
　　　from *being* a nation,
　　That the name of Israel may be remembered
　　　no more."

Ps. 83:1–4

The opening appeal in verse 1 is emphatic. It translates literally, "O God, let there not be silence (quiet, inactivity) to You, do not be silent (speechless, dumb), do not be still (undisturbed), O God." The double address and the repetition of the verbs make the point clear. The psalmist pleads for God's attention and action. He wants to stir Him up.

The reasons for arousing God are now given in verses 2–4. First, His enemies are active. They *"make a tumult"* ("murmur, growl") and *"have lifted up their head"* (in pride or rebellion, v. 2). It is as if we can hear their armies assembling for battle with the clank of gear and the babble of voices. Second, these enemies *"have taken crafty counsel"* (or, "craftily devised a secret") against Israel by *"consulting together"* (v. 3). The secret would include both their confederacy (see vv. 5–8) and battle plan. Israel is defined as God's *"hidden ones"* (or "treasured ones, saints"). They are the apple of His eye and belong to Him. Third, these enemies' goal is the destruction of Israel (v. 4). They want to cut off God's people and blot out their name in order that it might be remembered no more. Here is the demand for total victory, a holy war against Israel. This final point clinches the argument. Certainly now God has to arise to meet this threat to Israel's existence. He must be true to His covenant.

As noted above, the church today faces a similar battle. Satan and his forces make a tumult and have rebelled against God. They are involved in a cosmic conspiracy to defeat His armies. Like Israel's enemies, they plan our destruction. Now we must call upon God to act. As in Psalm 83 He is our only hope.

CONFEDERACY IDENTIFIED

> 83:5 For they have consulted together with one
>   consent;
>   They form a confederacy against You;
>   6 The tents of Edom and the Ishmaelites;
>   Moab and the Hagrites;
>   7 Gebal, Ammon, and Amalek;
>   Philistia with the inhabitants of Tyre;
>   8 Assyria also has joined with them;
>   They have helped the children of Lot.   Selah
>   Ps. 83:5–8

The consultation in verse 3 is now more clearly defined. The enemies have *"consulted together with one consent,"* or to paraphrase the thought, "they have put their minds together." Thus they have come up with a *"confederacy* ["covenant"] *against You"* (v. 5, note the identification of Yahweh with His people). To touch them is to touch Him. For this reason, as Paul persecutes the church he persecutes Jesus (Acts 9:4–5).

Now the members of this war-covenant are listed in verses 6–8. Ten nations are identified. Since the immediate historical setting cannot be established from the Old Testament, this has led to speculation that the list is cultic, typical, or exaggerated for poetic reasons. The fact may be, however, that this crisis event is not contained in our present historical books and, nevertheless, really happened. For example, perhaps the war was never fought and thus escaped the record. Who, then, are these nations?

First, there is *"Edom,"* occupied by Esau's descendents, bordering on Judah's south. Next, there are the nomadic *"Ishmaelites,"* descendents of Abraham and Hagar. In Judges 8:24 they are identified with the Midianites. Then there are the *"Hagarites"* (also related to Abraham?), dwelling east of the Jordan beyond Gilead (v. 6; 1 Chron. 5:10). Furthermore, there is *"Gebal,"* south of the Dead Sea in Edom.

This is followed by *"Ammon,"* Lot's son associated with his other son Moab, a state east of the Jordan. Then there are nomadic *"Amalek,"* dwelling south of Judah, and *"Philistia"* on Israel's and Judah's western border. Next, there is *"Tyre,"* a Phoenician city on the coast north of Israel (v. 7). Finally, the Assyrian Empire has been drawn in, backing the *"children* ['sons'] *of Lot"* (Moab and Ammon, v. 8).

Thus God's people are surrounded by nations, cities, and tribes who have joined in a covenant to destroy them. Here is an ominous threat. Here is probable battle on several fronts. This is the crisis that evokes the call for God to act (see v. 1).

Likewise, the church is faced with a battle-covenant engaging the forces of Satan and the kingdoms of this world who do his bidding (see Matt. 4:8). The enemy employs everything he can to defeat us. We are surrounded by a hostile world that continually beams false goals, values, and assumptions at us. We too must fight on many fronts. There is the battle for the mind, the will, the heart, the body. Every part of us can be oppressed by demonic attack. There is also the battle for the church, its unity and purity. Jesus teaches us to pray, "Deliver us from the evil one [the devil]" (Matt. 6:13).

CALL FOR BATTLE

83:9 Deal with them as *with* Midian,
As *with* Sisera,
As *with* Jabin at the Brook Kishon,
10 Who perished at En Dor,
Who became *as* refuse on the earth.
11 Make their nobles like Oreb and like Zeeb,
Yes, all their princes like Zebah and Zalmunna,
12 Who said, "Let us take for ourselves
The pastures of God for a possession."
13 O my God, make them like the whirling dust;
Like the chaff before the wind!
14 As the fire burns the woods,
And as the flame sets the mountains on fire,
15 So pursue them with Your tempest,
And frighten them with Your storm.
16 Fill their faces with shame,
That they may seek Your name, O LORD.

17 Let them be confounded and dismayed
forever;
Yes, let them be put to shame and perish,
18 That they may know that You, whose name
alone *is* the LORD,
Are the Most High over all the earth.
Ps. 83:9–18

Now the psalmist calls for God to intervene. Verses 9–12 use past history and verses 13–15 use images from nature as the basis for this appeal. Then verses 16–18 bring the psalm to its conclusion: God must act to vindicate His name as *"Most High over all the earth"* (v. 18).

To begin with, God is reminded of His past victories and asked to act again. He is to deal with His enemies as He dealt with *"Midian."* The psalmist refers to Gideon's rout of this nomadic people by three hundred valiant men who frightened them into self-destruction (Judges 7). Then there were General Sisera and his king, *"Jabin,"* Canaanite leaders, defeated by the prophetess Deborah and Barak at the *"Brook Kishon"* (on the plain of Esdraelon, v. 9, Judg. 4:7). This was in the area of *"Endor"* where the corpses littered the earth as *"refuse"* ("dung," v. 10), unburied as a sign of judgment (see Ps. 79:3). The psalmist asks God to do the same to this confederacy. Similarly, He is to make their nobles like the two Midianite leaders *"Oreb"* and *"Zeeb,"* who were killed by the men of Ephraim (Judg. 7:25), and their princes like the Midianite kings *"Zebah"* and *"Zalmunna,"* who were killed by Gideon (Judg. 8:21). These enemy leaders who will be destroyed exercise blatant self-will as they desire *"the pastures of God"* (v. 12). No wonder God should act again as He did in the time of the Judges.

Starting in verse 13, the psalmist turns from history to nature. Employing storm images, he again calls upon God to act. At the same time, he is intensely personal: *"O my God, . . ."* First, he asks that these enemies become like *"whirling dust"* or a dust storm and be blown away as nothing. Second, he wants them to be like *"chaff"* when it is separated from the wheat and carried off by the wind (v. 13; cf. Ps. 1:4). Third, he wants God to pursue these enemies as *"fire"* that *"burns the woods"* and *"the flame"* (volcanic? lightning?) that *"sets the mountains on fire"* (v. 14). As they experience God's *"tempest,"* His *"storm"* ("whirlwind," v. 15), it will be like the fire of His wrath. Here the psalmist may actually expect God's intervention through nature, or he still may be speaking metaphorically.

What will be the consequences of God's intervention? Israel's enemies will be broken, their faces filled *"with shame"* ("disgrace"). As Isaiah promises, "For the day of the Lord of hosts, / Shall come upon everything proud and lofty, / Upon everything lifted up— / And it shall be brought low" (Isa. 2:12). Then they will turn to God and *"seek Your name* [presence], *O Lord"* (v. 16). Judgment will bring, for some, redemption, as they admit that Israel's God is the living God. Most, however, will fall. The psalmist, therefore, asks that these enemies be *"confounded"* ("ashamed"), *"dismayed"* ("troubled"), *"put to shame and perish"* ("vanish, be destroyed"). Also this is to be final, *"forever"* (v. 17).

The destruction of this evil confederacy will prove that Yahweh is God. Psalm 83 concludes that the results will be revelatory: *"that* [they] *may know* [by experiencing what God has done] *that You, whose name alone is the Lord* [Yahweh], / *are the Most High* [supreme] *over all the earth"* (v. 18). It is God's work, His supernatural intervention, that proves that His name is true. As Jesus says, "Believe Me that I am in the Father and the Father in Me, or else believe Me for the sake of the works themselves" (John 14:11).

As we have already suggested, we too are locked in a spiritual battle against our enemies in this world. But how can we triumph over them? We can't. Jesus has and can. We must call upon Him to go into battle for us. Like the psalmist of old, we can take heart in His past victories. We can thrill at great missionary advances. We can praise God for defeating Satan in the lives of a C. S. Lewis, a Karl Barth, a Billy Graham, a Diana Ross, a Bob Dylan. We can look at great revivals of the past and pray, "Lord, do it again." We can also look at all of the sin and evil in our world, such as the drug traffic and child pornography, and pray, *"Make them like the whirling dust; Like the chaff before the wind"* (v. 13).

We long for God to vindicate His name on this earth. Thus we pray, "Thy kingdom come . . ."

CHAPTER EIGHTY-FOUR

Homesickness

Psalm 84

In the ancient world the pagan gods had their palaces or temples where they lived. Their images could be seen and worshiped there. Thus their followers or citizens (in the case of the state gods) would go to these houses to visit them. Their priests cared for them and made certain that proper worship was offered in their temples on behalf of the people. For example, Athena lived in Athens and Artemus lived in Ephesus. In turn, Yahweh lived in Jerusalem. Here, however, the analogy between Israel's God and the pagan gods breaks down. One major difference, to be sure, is the absence of any image for Yahweh in His temple. This is strictly prohibited in the Old Testament (see Exod. 20:4–5). Thus, Yahweh didn't really live in Jerusalem. While He granted the gift of His presence in the temple, that presence could be removed. Moreover, as Solomon says upon dedicating the Jerusalem temple, "But will God indeed dwell on the earth? Behold, heaven and the heaven of the heavens cannot contain You. How much less this temple which I have built!" (1 Kings 8:27). Thus in the Old Testament there is no idolatry of place allowed.

Nevertheless, good Jews prayed facing Jerusalem (Dan. 6:10), and Jesus called the temple "My Father's house" (John 2:16). To go to the temple, therefore, is to seek the presence of God. While it cannot contain Him, it is a place where He can be found. Moreover, the temple is a copy of heaven itself where all who believe will be finally home forever. Thus the earthly sanctuary reflects the heavenly sanctuary where Jesus went after making the final sacrifice upon the cross for our sins (Heb. 9:11–12). Although the Jerusalem temple has now been destroyed in judgment (Mark 13:1–2) and our bodies are God's temple where His Spirit dwells on earth (1 Cor. 6:9), one day we will go to be with Jesus and be fully home, in His house forever

(John 14:2-3). It is in this context then that we should read Psalm 84.

Here the psalmist longs for God's house, delights in God's house, and blesses the pilgrimage to God's house. He lovingly describes its courts (vv. 2, 10) and its altars (v. 3). He would rather be a "doorkeeper" there than dwell in the "tents of wickedness" (v. 10). But the temple is not an end. It is a means to the end of being in the very presence of God. Thus his longing for God's house becomes a longing for God. This is his *summum bonum*.

This psalm is attributed to the "sons of Korah," who were probably a family of temple singers (see *Introduction, Psalms 1–72*, Communicator's Commentary, Old Testament, no. 13). Its form is mixed, containing elements of a hymn, a lamentation, and wisdom teaching ("Blessed . . . ," vv. 4–5). The references to the king (v. 9) makes it pre-exilic in origin. The thought moves from praise and longing for God's house (vv. 1–2), to a blessing upon those dwelling there (vv. 3–4), to a blessing upon those coming there (vv. 5–7), to a prayer for the (messianic) King and concludes with a meditation (vv. 10–11) and a final blessing (v. 12).

PRAISE AND LONGING FOR GOD'S HOUSE

84:1 How lovely *is* Your tabernacle,
   O LORD of hosts!
   2 My soul longs, yes, even faints
   For the courts of the LORD;
   My heart and my flesh cry out for the living
      God.

Ps. 84:1-2

In verse 1 the psalmist addresses the mighty God over all the angels, "*O Lord of Hosts*" (see Ps. 103:20–21). He speaks with fervor of His "*tabernacle*" (literally, "tabernacles," plural for fullness); it is "*lovely*" ("beloved"). His "*soul longs* ["yearns"], *yes, even faints* ["has been consumed, languishes, is spent"]" for God's "*courts*" where the pilgrims gather (v. 2, see 1 Kings 6). It is almost as if the temple is a person and the psalmist a passionate lover.

This longing for the temple is a longing for the God who dwells there. The psalmist's "*heart and . . . flesh cry out for the living God.*"

In verse 2 his whole being, his *"soul"* ("self"), his *"heart"* ("mind"), and his *"flesh"* ("humanity") are engaged. The verb *cry out* means to "shout or give a ringing cry." There is no reserve here. His prayer is vocal and boisterous. Moreover, it is not the ground of being or nature's god that captures the psalmist's passion: it is the *"living God,"* the God who sees, hears, and acts (see v. 11).

There is no doubt that Jesus could pray this prayer. He loved the temple, His Father's house. Thus He was grieved at its abuse and longed for its purity and holiness (John 2:13ff.). At the same time, He spoke harsh words of judgment upon it and knew that His resurrection body would be the living temple through which we would have access to the Father (John 2:21–22). The Christian too can pray this prayer, although the temple now lies in ruins covered with a huge Muslim mosque, The Dome of the Rock. The *"courts of the Lord"* for us, as the Book of Hebrews indicates, are heavenly courts, and our deepest desire is to be there (cf. Phil. 1:23).

A Blessing upon Those Dwelling in God's House

84:3 Even the sparrow has found a home,
      And the swallow a nest for herself,
      Where she may lay her young—
      Even Your altars, O LORD of hosts,
      My King and my God.
  4 Blessed *are* those who dwell in Your house;
      They will still be praising You.   Selah
                        Ps. 84:3–4

Now the psalmist meditates upon the birds who have found their security in the temple (v. 3). Even the little, humble *"sparrow"* is there along with the *"swallow"* who nests and raises her young. They are near the *"altars,"* the altar of burnt offering in front of the temple (Exod. 27:1–8; 2 Kings 16:14) and the altar of incense in front of the Holy of Holies, the innermost shrine (Exod. 30:1–10). As the psalmist thinks of the altars where sacrifices are offered and incense rises to God, he exclaims in worship: *"O Lord of Hosts, / My King and my God."* Here he acknowledges, first, that God rules all things, even the hosts of heaven (see v. 1). Second, this God who rules all is his own King (ruler) and his personal God (*"my God"*). No wonder he cries out for the living God (v. 2).

Now in verse 4 the psalmist blesses those who dwell in God's house. The noun *Blessed* is in the plural, expressing fullness (see Ps. 1:1, "fully happy, rewarded"). The objects of this blessing would be the temple staff and those who find their life in the temple in worship (including the birds). The blessing then leads to praise: *"They will still be praising You,"* namely, making their public, confessional witness of Yahweh. Their homesickness is over and they are lost (or found) in worship.

God's blessing and the response of praise are not merely reserved for this life. They characterize heaven too. There the redeemed *"shall see [God's] . . . face, and His name shall be on their foreheads. . . . And they shall reign forever and ever"* (Rev. 22:4–5). All of creation will worship God and the Lamb upon His throne (Rev. 5:8–14).

BLESSING UPON THE PILGRIMAGE
TO GOD'S HOUSE

84:5 Blessed *is* the man whose strength *is* in You,
    Whose heart *is* set on pilgrimage.
  6 *As they* pass through the Valley of Baca,
    They make it a spring;
    The rain also covers it with pools.
  7 They go from strength to strength;
    Each one appears before God in Zion.

Ps. 84:5–7

To be in the temple is to experience God's blessing. To be on the road there is to be similarly blessed. The same full blessing (*"Blessed"*—plural, see v. 4) is given to the man *"whose strength"* ("might") is in the Lord and who therefore sets his heart *"on pilgrimage"* (v. 5). As the travelers journey to Jerusalem, they pass through the *"Valley of Baca"* (presently unknown to us) and find springs and *"rain"* ("early rain," falling from the last of October to the first of December) creating *"pools"* (v. 6). This natural irrigation, which refreshes them along the way (cf. Isa. 43:20–21), points to the spiritual refreshing that will come in God's house. Thus they go from *"strength to strength"* (the phrase is used of mighty men of valor, warriors). Their journey, rather than wearying them, exhilarates them because of God's grace in transit and the goal before them. For this reason they gain in strength as they go, until each one *"appears before God in Zion"* (v. 7; for Zion see Ps. 2:6). In light of this they could certainly pray with Ps. 42:1–2: "As the deer pants for the water brooks, / So pants my soul for You, O God. / My soul thirsts for God, for the living God."

PRAYER FOR THE (MESSIANIC) KING

84:8 O LORD God of hosts, hear my prayer;
        Give ear, O God of Jacob!   Selah
    9 O God, behold our shield,
        And look upon the face of Your anointed.
                                                    Ps. 84:8–9

Perhaps in these verses we have now arrived at the temple where prayers are offered for the king. At the same time, there is a deeper sense in which these prayers are calling upon God to look at His Son, the anointed ("Messiah"). It is implied that God is to have favor upon us as He has favor upon Him. Behind this, in part, is the theology: "As with king, so with people."

God then is addressed in verse 9. He is Yahweh, the God of Israel and also the God of all the heavenly hosts (see v. 1). This is the one who is to hear this prayer by giving His ear (attention) to it. He is also the *"God of Jacob,"* namely the God who delivers His people as He did Jacob (see Ps. 81:1). With this elaborate (and liturgical) address, God is now called upon to *"behold our shield,"* which in the parallel clause is the King-Messiah. The *"shield"* here is a round, small, defensive armament (see Ps. 3:3). The King protects God's people as the shield protects a warrior. The King-Messiah is also God's *"anointed"* (māšēaḥ). This anointing, ceremonially with oil, separates kings from the people and endows them with the divine authority of their office (for Saul see 1 Sam. 10:1; for David see 1 Sam. 16:13, where David is also anointed by the Spirit of God). The psalmist then

asks God to *"look upon the face"* of His anointed. To look at His face is
to show favor, to look with grace.

This prayer for grace for the King, as we have noted, will also
bring grace to the people. Moreover, we now know in Christ, our
Messiah-King, that as God looks at Him, He is our shield, our protection, because we are in Him. As God sees the face of His anointed
Son so He sees us. We pray in His name, and our prayers are heard
and answered (1 John 2:1). Therefore, we come to God with boldness through His anointed, beloved Son (see Ps. 2:6–7), and all that
is His is ours.

MEDITATION

84:10 For a day in Your courts *is* better than a
        thousand.
        I would rather be a doorkeeper in the house of
        my God
        Than dwell in the tents of wickedness.
   11 For the LORD God *is* a sun and shield;
        The LORD will give grace and glory;
        No good *thing* will He withhold
        From those who walk uprightly.

Ps. 84:10–11

The psalmist now reflects on the joy of being in God's house
(v. 10), delighting in who He is and what He gives (v. 11). To be in
God's courts (see v. 2) *"for a day"* is better *"than a thousand"* (days
elsewhere). Thus it is the quality of life before God, rather than the
quantity of life, that fulfills us. For this reason, to be a *"doorkeeper,"*
or, literally, "to be at the threshold in the house of . . . God" as a
supplicant is better than dwelling in the *"tents of wickedness"* ("law-
lessness"). Even to be at the edge of the temple is better than a permanent, secure place among the godless (v. 10). Why is this so? The
answer is given in verse 11: it is because of God Himself.

It is not the beauty of the place that attracts the psalmist but the
beauty of the person. God is *"a sun and shield."* While the Old Testament normally avoids identifying God with the sun because of pagan
(especially Egyptian) religion, John sees the face of Jesus shining as

the sun at full strength (Rev. 1:16). The sun in this psalm suggests the glory of God's person. God is also our shield, our protector (see v. 9). He gives to us from who He is, full of *"grace and glory."* As David prays, "But You, O Lord, are a shield for me, My glory" (Ps. 3:3). With His love upon us and His glory about us, we are assured that He will not withhold any *"good"* from us if we *"walk uprightly"* ("soundly, with integrity").

The sequence in verse 11 is important. First, there is God Himself, *"a sun and shield."* Second, there is what God gives, *"grace and glory."* Third, there is who we are to be, walking *"uprightly."* To walk this walk, however, we must know this God and receive His gifts. Only by His grace can we be among those who obey Him.

No wonder that the psalmist longs for God's house (v. 2) and delights to be there, even on the fringe (v. 10). It is there that God reveals Himself (see Isa. 6:1ff.), and it is there that His grace and glory come down.

For us that grace and glory are given in Jesus, the Word made flesh. As John says, He has dwelt, or literally "tabernacled," among us, and we have beheld His glory, "the glory as of the only begotten of the Father, full of grace and truth" (John 1:14). Here is our temple. We meet God in the face of the Son; "He who has seen Me has seen the Father" (John 14:9).

As the church is being renewed today, Jesus' grace and glory are especially being experienced in worship. Like Israel of old, as we gather in His name and direct our sustained praises to Him (not just about Him), His Spirit descends and His presence is manifest in our midst. Jesus is here, and we are saved, healed, and delivered from our enemies.

FINAL BLESSING

84:12 O LORD of hosts,
　　　Blessed *is* the man who trusts in You!
　　　　　　　　　　　　　　　　　　Ps. 84:12

Addressing God, the *Lord of hosts* (see vv. 1, 3, 8), the psalmist promises blessing (in the plural, see vv. 4 and 5) upon the person who *trusts* ("feels secure, unconcerned") in Him. The verb "trusts" comes from a root meaning "to lie down." Thus the person who trusts in the Lord throws his weight upon Him and rests in Him. To go to the temple is to find our whole selves, soul, heart, and flesh, refreshed by the living God (v. 2). Here, like the sparrow and swallow, is our true dwelling place. Our homesickness is over. We are safe at last.

A young student from UCLA was dying of cancer at home. As his mother would go into his room where he was heavily sedated, she would ask, "Dennis, are you here?" He would then answer, "Yes, Mother, I'm here." On the day of his death, however, he responded to her question, "No, Mother, I'm going home."

Over his bed in his now empty room stands this saying:

> I hear you, Christian,
> Riotous, joyful, unafraid,
> For you hear a song
> From the other side of death.

CHAPTER EIGHTY-FIVE

Recovery

Psalm 85

Many of us live between memory and hope. We recall what God has done in the past with gratitude, and we hope that He will do it again. This makes present sorrow and discouragement bearable. A dear friend of mine recently lost her husband to cancer. Now in her grief she is sustained with a flood of memories from the past, which bring her joy. She also must face living out the rest of her life in this world knowing that the Lord will be there each step of the way as she is sustained by her hope of reunion beyond the grave. Many questions will be answered later. How will she adjust to her new single life? Will she ever remarry? How should she restructure her finances? Should she sell her house? How can she relate to her children without leaning excessively upon them? How will her needs for intimacy be met? In working through these issues she is held by the hope that the God who worked in the past will work in the future. The day will come when her depression will lift and the sun will break through the overcast again. A neighbor of mine lost his wife to cancer and relayed that it took him two years to heal emotionally. What can we do in the meantime? This is the issue before us in this psalm.

Clearly Israel has experienced a great loss. She knows that God's wrath is upon her (vv. 4–5). This is probably reflected in military defeat. Yet the psalmist recalls that God brought His people out of captivity before (v. 1) and forgave them, removing His wrath (vv. 2–3). Thus he is bold to ask Him to do it again (vv. 6–7). God will speak peace beyond the noise of battle (v. 8) and restore His glory to the land (v. 9). Then His righteousness will rule, and Israel will once more be blessed (vv. 11–12).

The authorship of this psalm is attributed to the sons of Korah (see the introduction to Psalm 84). Commentators describe it as a national lament, which contains both Israel's intercession and God's response. If verses 1–3 refer to the return from exile, the date would be postexilic. The thought moves from God's past mercy (vv. 1–3), to God's present wrath (vv. 4–7), to God's peace (vv. 8–9) and concludes with confidence in God's righteousness (vv. 10–13).

GOD'S PAST MERCY

85:1 Lord, You have been favorable to Your land;
   You have brought back the captivity of Jacob.
 2 You have forgiven the iniquity of Your people;
   You have covered all their sin.   Selah
 3 You have taken away all Your wrath;
   You have turned from the fierceness of Your
      anger.

                                        Ps. 85:1–3

In verses 1–3 God is addressed directly. He is identified as "Yahweh," the personal God of Israel, who has *"been favorable"* ("pleased with") His land (v. 1). This favor is seen in restoring Jacob (designating Israel as delivered by God, see Exod. 19:3; Ps. 20:1) from *"captivity."* Thus, although the historical setting is indistinct, we may suppose that God's people have returned from Babylon as they did from Egypt. This return is a sign of mercy. *"Iniquity"* ("guilt") is *"forgiven"* ("lifted" and removed) and *"sin"* ("missing the mark") is covered (vv. 2; cf. Isa. 40:2). Throughout the Bible, God's judgment (here, the Exile?) is always a result of His righteousness and our moral failure. For this reason there will never be restoration, revival, or reunion apart from forgiveness. This makes the cross where Jesus was sacrificed central to our faith: "Behold! The Lamb of God who takes away the sin of the world!" (John 1:29). Now we can come home to God.

When restoration occurs, based on forgiveness, this means that God's wrath is lifted. Thus the psalmist continues in verse 3 that His *"wrath"* is *"taken away,"* or, literally, "gathered in." The word *wrath* here denotes overflowing rage (see Ps. 90:9, 11). Moreover, in the parallel clause, God has *"turned from the fierceness of [His] . . . anger"* or, literally, "from the heat of [His] anger." As He restores His people He removes their sin and rescinds His wrath. Here is mercy indeed.

All of this, as we have suggested, is fulfilled in Christ. He breaks us free from Satan's captivity, cancels our sin, and takes God's judgment upon Himself. How then can we deal with our present depression and darkness? The first thing to do is to remember the past light, remember what Jesus has done. As Paul says, all the promises of God are "yes" in Him (2 Cor. 1:20). We must rivet our minds to this truth.

GOD'S PRESENT WRATH

85:4 Restore us, O God of our salvation,
  And cause Your anger toward us to cease.
 5 Will You be angry with us forever?
  Will You prolong Your anger to all
   generations?

> 6 Will You not revive us again,
>   That Your people may rejoice in You?
> 7 Show us Your mercy, LORD,
>   And grant us Your salvation.
>
> *Ps. 85:4–7*

The issue is not the past, however; the issue is the present. God's wrath has returned because Israel has sinned again. The period after the exile was dreary (cf. Ezra 9:10). Now the psalmist prays: *"Restore* ["turn"] *us."* God is addressed as the *"God of our salvation"* ("deliverance"). The focus continues to be on His *"anger"* (see v. 3). Note the emphasis: *"Your anger . . . Will You be angry . . . Will You prolong* ["draw out"] *Your anger . . . ?"*

There are two problems: the fact of God's wrath and its duration. It seems as if it continues *"forever, to all generations"* (v. 5). Since God is the "God of our salvation," however, He can *"restore"* His people (v. 4) and *"revive"* them ("restore them to life") again (v. 6).

It is important that there are only two options: either God's wrath or God's life. Both come from Him. Israel cannot work up repentance and thus somehow deserve divine mercy. God must do the work. All that we can do is ask Him for it. These truths emphasize His sovereign grace. They also lift the responsibility from us for our salvation and place it back upon Him where it belongs. We cannot save people or heal people or give them spiritual gifts or fill them with the Holy Spirit. All that we can do is pray. The work of restoration and revival (giving life) is God's work because He alone is the source of life.

Thus in depression and darkness we must remember the past (vv. 1–3) and then pray in the present (vv. 4–7). This opens us up to a new work, which God, in His time, will do. And what are the consequences? God's people will *"rejoice"* ("be glad") in Him. Such an act of God is celebrated by worship.

I recently prayed for a woman with a long history of drug problems. She also was deeply depressed and chronically suicidal. She and I both suspected that she was also subject to demonic attack. While we were praying she began to experience tremendous anxiety and identified an evil spirit manifesting itself in her. As I took authority over the spirit and ordered it out of her in Jesus' name, her trembling and anxiety immediately broke. She felt the release and joy covered her face. Spontaneously she said, "Praise the Lord." As she felt life again, she fulfilled the result clause in verse 6: "That Your people may rejoice in You."

Now the psalmist completes his petition in verse 7, asking God to *"show"* His *"mercy"* ("covenant-love") to Israel. She will see this as He grants her His *"salvation"* ("deliverance"). As He lifts His wrath, revives His people, and gives them joy in His presence, they will know that He is trustworthy, true to His covenant, and the God who saves by intervening in their lives.

GOD'S PEACE

85:8 I will hear what God the LORD will speak,
    For He will speak peace
    To His people and to His saints;
    But let them not turn back to folly.
  9 Surely His salvation *is* near to those who fear
     Him,
    That glory may dwell in our land.

                            Ps. 85:8–9

Here the psalmist becomes personal: *"I will hear, . . ."* Having addressed God in a cry for help for the nation (vv. 4–7), he now listens. Prayer is a two-way street. What God says is *"peace"* ("wholeness"). This is an all-encompassing word of salvation (cf. Eph. 2:15) addressed through the psalmist to God's *"people,"* namely, to His *"saints"* ("kind, pious").

This promise of salvation is immediately followed by an exhortation not to *"turn back to folly"* ("stupidity," v. 8). Grace must never create presumption. We are to *"fear"* ("have awe before") God. As we do so, *"salvation is near"* ("nearby," as near as God is, see vv. 4, 7). With God's deliverance, His *"glory"* comes; that is, the very presence of God dwells among His people (see Exod. 33:14–23). Beyond the gifts of God is God Himself. His peace and salvation point to His glory. It is His glory, evoking our praise, however, that is enduring and fulfilling. As Jesus prays before the cross, "And now, O Father, glorify Me together with Yourself, with the glory which I had with You before the world was" (John 17:5). Whatever our darkness may be, the prayer for God's glory will not go unanswered. The sun will break through the clouds again.

CONFIDENCE IN GOD'S RIGHTEOUSNESS

85:10 Mercy and truth have met together;
      Righteousness and peace have kissed.
   11 Truth shall spring out of the earth,
      And righteousness shall look down from
         heaven.
   12 Yes, the LORD will give *what is* good;
      And our land will yield its increase.
   13 Righteousness will go before Him,
      And shall make His footsteps *our* pathway.
                                             Ps. 85:10–13

The final verses of this psalm are confessional and prophetic. Key aspects of God's character are personified: *"mercy"* ("covenant-love," see v. 7) and *"truth"* ("trustworthiness") meet, and *"righteousness"* ("covenant faithfulness") and *"peace"* ("wholeness," see v. 8) kiss (v. 10). *"Truth"* springs from the earth like a plant, and *"righteousness"* peers from heaven like an angel (v. 11). Finally, *"righteousness"* precedes God like a guide as Israel follows in His footsteps (v. 13).

What these verses express is the union of God's saving grace (mercy and peace) on the one hand and His kingdom order and trustworthiness (truth and righteousness) on the other hand. In the ultimate resolution of all things, when God restores and revives His people (vv. 4–6), law and gospel, demand and gift, are fused into one by His grace. We are pointed to Jesus who bears all of these attributes in His own person. As Luther puts it, God's holiness and God's love kiss in the cross.

God's harmonious character is reflected in His blessing upon the earth. As truth springs forth and heavenly righteousness approves (v. 11), God gives His goodness (rain?) to a land, which *"will yield its increase"* (v. 12).

The key word in verses 10–13, repeated three times, is *"righteousness."* The word signifies right relationships and the terms that keep them. In various contexts the word can mean anything from salvation or victory to righteous help and healing. Whatever keeps God's covenant operative in accord with His character is righteous.

Here then God's righteousness, which we have paraphrased as *"covenant faithfulness,"* is united to peace (v. 10). Thus righteousness brings peace or "wholeness" to God's people. Furthermore, right-eousness is divine; it comes from heaven as God's gift and measures and judges the earth (v. 11). Finally, God works and acts in right-eousness. He is true to Himself. For this reason the psalmist can say boldly that righteousness even goes before God and either makes *"His footsteps our pathway"* (v. 13), or, literally, "makes a way for His footsteps." God lives and acts righteously because He is righteous. No wonder Abraham can intercede for Sodom and Gomorrah asking, "Shall not the Judge of all the earth do right?" (Gen. 18:25).

In the midst of the darkness the psalmist is held by a great vision. God's mercy and righteousness will triumph, and the earth will be blessed again. Here is hope for the future, based on God's faithful-ness in the past (vv. 1–3) and the confidence that prayer will be answered. God will act in the future. This is the road to recovery.

CHAPTER EIGHTY-SIX

God of the Gaps

Psalm 86

Certain apologetic systems use God merely to fill in the missing links of the "gaps" in our overall picture of reality. They suppose that life today can largely be understood without Him. In their view, God creates everything with a "big bang" and then withdraws. Or, after millions of years He only acts in order to insert Adam into the evolu-tionary scheme.

Again, when we need a miracle in our lives, God may perform one, but then we go on without Him. History, as well as nature, moves by immanent causes creating immanent effects, and only in such major events as the Exodus or the Incarnation does the "God of the gaps" act directly. What this theory is supposed to account for is the naturalistic life that we lead. At the same time it is to keep us open for God to work when a gap appears. Most people don't live "in the middle of a miracle" (James Mallory). Thus their world-view largely rejects the supernatural. The problem, of course, with all of this is that it denies God's active control over us and pushes Him out to the margins of our lives. Dietrich Bonhoeffer speculated about a "religionless" Christianity, which would restore God to the center stage once again by effectively denying the supernatural (in *Letters and Papers from Prison*). The options now seem clear. Either we reformulate the faith and encourage its radical secularization by identifying God with all of the natural process of life and thus avoid a "gap theology," or we embrace a radical supernatural world-view and admit that all of nature and history are one big gap, dependent upon Him. In this view, God is continually breaking through an indeterminate natural order that, under His control and His surprises, is our daily bread.

Apart from the world-view issue, there is also the human issue when God seems distant from our lives. In our sin or unbelief we may block Him from an active involvement with us. Then, when we find ourselves in a "foxhole" we suddenly cry out for divine intervention, expecting a "foxhole" God to answer. Rather than nurturing a vital experience of God that prepares us for the crunch, we expect God to be at our beck and call because the crunch has come. Thus we perpetuate the gap theology because we want to run our own lives. In this secret rebellion we are only willing to submit to God's control when some catastrophe puts us out of control.

Clearly Psalm 86 reflects a crisis and addresses this problem of the gap. A day of trouble has dawned (v. 7), the proud have risen up against the psalmist, and a mob seeks his life (v. 14). Here is a gap. At the same time, God has delivered his soul "from depths of Sheol" (v. 13). He has helped him and comforted him (v. 17). The psalmist turns instinctively to prayer, crying "all day long" (v. 3). He is "poor and needy" (v. 1). He is also God's servant (vv. 2, 4, 16) who is teachable, and who fears His name (v. 11). So he prays in the crisis, because he knows the God who answers prayer (v. 7). There is no God like the living God who does His works (v. 8), great and wondrous things (v. 10). The psalmist not only asks for mercy and strength; he also asks for a sign to confound his enemies (vv. 16–17). Rather than God being the God of the gaps, all of life is a gap in which God is God: "For you are great, and do wondrous things; / You alone are God" (v. 10).

The authorship of Psalm 86 is traditionally given to David. Since there are no compelling reasons to deny this, we will follow it here. The form of the psalm is an individual lament. Its thought moves from a cry to God for mercy (vv. 1–7), to a confession of God's uniqueness (vv. 8–10), to submission to God (vv. 11–13), to a complaint before God (vv. 14–15) and ends with a call for resolution (vv. 16–17).

CRY FOR MERCY

86:1 Bow down Your ear, O LORD, hear me;
  For I *am* poor and needy.
  2 Preserve my life, for I *am* holy;
   You are my God;
   Save Your servant who trusts in You!
  3 Be merciful to me, O Lord,
   For I cry to You all day long.
  4 Rejoice the soul of Your servant,
   For to You, O Lord, I lift up my soul.
  5 For You, Lord, *are* good, and ready to forgive,
   And abundant in mercy to all those who call
    upon You.
  6 Give ear, O LORD, to my prayer;
   And attend to the voice of my supplications.
  7 In the day of my trouble I will call upon You,
   For You will answer me.

Ps. 86:1–7

Verse 1 opens with a cry to the God who is both transcendent and immanent. Although He stands beyond history, He is active in history. Because God is transcendent, He must *"bow down"* His ear. Because God is immanent, however, He has an ear to bow down and can hear David as he prays.

David must ask God to condescend to him not just because He is exalted but because he himself is *"poor and needy."* This is his good fortune, since it is exactly the *"poor and needy"* for whom Yahweh has special care (see Isa. 3:13–15; Amos 5:11; Ps. 72:4, 12–13).

Moreover, his life is in danger. Therefore, he calls upon God to *"preserve"* ("keep, guard") it (v. 2). The basis for his request is now given. David is *"holy,"* which means that he is separated from the world and bound by the covenant. Yahweh is his personal God: *"my God."* David is His *"servant,"* submitted to His divine lordship and kingship. As God's servant he can expect Him to *"save"* ("deliver") him because he *"trusts"* ("finds security") in Him for all things. It would be an evil king who would not protect His serf or vassal.

The call for help continues in verse 3 as a cry for *"mercy"* ("grace"). David's hope lies in his persistence; he cries *"all day long."* The tenacity of his prayer does not force God to be merciful. It does prove David's trust and need, however. Jesus tells us that a man who knocks at his neighbor's door at midnight gets bread "because of his persistence" (Luke 11:8).

Next, David asks God, *"Rejoice the soul of Your servant"* (v. 4). As He hears his prayer, keeps his life, saves him, and shows mercy upon him, David will worship Him. David's *"soul"* or *"self"* will *"rejoice"* ("be glad"). He lifts up his soul to the Lord with the expectation of that gladness to come.

In prayer David comes to the God who is *"good"* or "kind" in verse 5. God's goodness and grace are closely connected: "For the Lord is good; / His mercy is everlasting" (Ps. 100:5). After confessing that God is good, David immediately thinks of His readiness *"to forgive"* ("pardon"), with *"abundant mercy"* ("covenant-love") for all who call upon Him. We see now that David is bound in the covenant ("holy," v. 2) with the covenant God (v. 5). This frames his reality and his prayer.

After rehearsing who God is and who David is in verse 1–5, David now returns to direct address: *"Give ear, O Lord . . ."* (v. 6; cf. v. 1). His prayer is oral (*"attend to the voice"*) and is identified as *"supplications"* (requests for favor). These supplications will include both prayers for David's discipleship (v. 11) and deliverance from his enemies (vv. 16–17). The urgency of this psalm is expressed by the phrase *"in the day of my trouble"* ("distress, restriction") in verse 7. Thus David prays in the crisis. He calls and God will answer.

What we see in these verses is no absent God of the gaps. Rather, we see the covenant God, bound to David, ready to give ear to his prayer and shower him with *"abundant mercy"* when he calls (v. 5). In the *"day of . . . trouble"* there will be an answer (v. 7), and when we find ourselves in the same covenant relationship, we can expect the same answer. God is God, yesterday, today, and forever.

Confession of God's Uniqueness

> 86:8 Among the gods *there is* none like You, O Lord;
>   Nor *are there any works* like Your works.
> 9 All nations whom You have made
>   Shall come and worship before You, O Lord,
>   And shall glorify Your name.
> 10 For You *are* great, and do wondrous things;
>   You alone *are* God.
>
> *Ps. 86:8–10*

Having called upon God to act on his behalf, David makes his own confession to the Lord. The key to this passage lies in verse 10 where God is *"great"* and does *"wondrous things"* or *"extraordinary acts."* Not only is God's covenant heart committed to David, but David knows Him as the mighty God who (as in the Exodus) pours out His judgments upon His enemies and leads His people in triumph. Thus David knows not only the presence of the Lord but also the power of the Lord.

There are no gods like God: *"You, O Lord"* (ʾadōnāi). The idols shrink to nothing because the God of Israel is unique in His *"works"* (v. 8). These actions cover a broad range (see Ps. 100:3). They include His creation of the nations (see Deut. 26:19), which will come and *"worship"* ("bow down", see Ps. 95:6) and *"glorify"* ("praise") His *"name"* (see Isa. 2:2–4).

David's assurance for this final, eschatological triumph is the present action of God. He is *"great"* because He does *"wondrous things"* (that is, miracles, see Exod. 15:11). This means, as David says, that *"You alone are God"* (v. 10). Notice here that the specialness of Yahweh is seen in what He does, not merely in what He says. He is no God of the gaps. He creates the nations and He performs great acts because He is great. What He does reflects who He is. For this reason, Jesus comes both to bear the word of the Father and to do the work of the Father (John 14:10–11). To separate the word

125

from the work is to create abstractions. The living God speaks and acts and expects us not only to hear His word but to do His word as well (Matt. 7:24).

In my own pilgrimage I have come to see that God speaks to us, but He also wants to work through us. Thus Jesus' agenda for ministry, preaching to the poor, releasing the captives, giving sight to the blind, and liberating the oppressed (Luke 4:18), is to be ours. Only when we do what Jesus does can we claim to be His disciples. As Dietrich Bonhoeffer says, when Jesus called His disciples to follow Him, they did not stand up in their boats and recite the Apostles' Creed. They dropped everything and went after Him! Can we do less?

SUBMISSION TO GOD

86:11 Teach me Your way, O LORD;
    I will walk in Your truth;
    Unite my heart to fear Your name.
   12 I will praise You, O Lord my God, with all my
        heart,
    And I will glorify Your name forevermore.
   13 For great *is* Your mercy toward me,
    And You have delivered my soul from the
        depths of Sheol.
                                        Ps. 86:11–13

David now asks God to instruct him so that he may obey Him (v. 11) and worship Him (v. 12). The basis for this is His intervention in his life (v. 13). Thus God redeems us in order to disciple us.

The *"way"* of God (v. 11) is the path that He wants us to take. It embraces all of life. David will *"walk"* it in God's *"truth"* ("trustworthiness"). Instruction is not merely for information; it is for obedience. This obedience, however, is not grim. As David asks God: *"Unite* ["make single"] *my heart* [versus a divided heart] *to fear* ["be in awe of"] *Your name* [that is, Your presence]." When God unites my heart, obeying Him is my joy.

Such *"fear"* evokes worship in verse 12. This includes *"praise"* with all of David's faculties, *"all my heart,"* and means glorifying God's name (His presence and character revealed in His acts) *"forevermore."* Since God is eternal, He is to be eternally praised.

But why this explosion of worship? The answer is given now in verse 13. It is because of God's great *"mercy"* ("covenant-love," see v. 5). This mercy is revealed as David's *"soul"* ("self") is *"delivered"* ("snatched") *"from the depths of Sheol."* *Sheol* is the dwelling place of the dead in the lowest parts of the earth (see Ps. 30:3; 139:8). When death reached out for David, God pulled him back.

A dear friend of mine overdosed on cocaine. As he lay dying, he was aware that his spirit was leaving his body. Suddenly Jesus appeared to him and said, "It's not your time. Go back." He returned to his body, snatched from the jaws of Sheol. No wonder, like David, he is worshiping God today.

COMPLAINT BEFORE GOD

> 86:14 O God, the proud have risen against me,
>   And a mob of violent *men* have sought my life,
>   And have not set You before them.
>   15 But You, O Lord, *are* a God full of compassion,
>   and gracious,
>   Longsuffering and abundant in mercy and
>   truth.
>
> *Ps. 86:14–15*

Having called upon God for His mercy (vv. 1–7), having confessed His faith in God (vv. 8–10), and having submitted himself to God (vv. 11–13), David is now ready to become specific about his crisis. He is facing an insurrection. *"The proud"* have revolted—*"risen against me"* (v. 14). They are a *"mob"* ("congregation") of *"violent men"* ("terror striking") who seek to kill him. Since they do not worship God (*"set You before them"*), they are free to attack His king.

In countering this revolt, David turns to the Lord in verse 15: *"But You"* (His God) are *"full of compassion"* ("merciful and gracious"), *"longsuffering"* (literally, "slow of anger"), and full of *"mercy"* ("covenant-love," vv. 5, 13) and *"truth"* ("trustworthiness," v. 11). When chaos sets in, it is God who is certain and consistent. David rests in who He is.

CALL FOR RESOLUTION

86:16 Oh, turn to me, and have mercy on me!
    Give Your strength to Your servant,
    And save the son of Your maidservant.
  17 Show me a sign for good,
    That those who hate me may see *it* and be
      ashamed,
    Because You, LORD, have helped me and
      comforted me.

Ps. 86:16–17

With his enemies attacking (v. 16) and his confidence in God secure (v. 15), David calls for divine intervention. *"Oh, turn to me,"* means for God to turn His face toward David in grace. Thus He will *"have mercy"* upon him (see vv. 3, 15).

Next, David asks God to give him what He alone has: *"Your strength"* ("might"). Thus Jesus' disciples needed Pentecost, not just Calvary, for ministry (see Acts 2:1ff.). After grace comes power. This strength to fight will mean salvation or deliverance. In calling his mother a *"maidservant"* he identifies her as a "slave born in the house," that is, a slave of God forever.

God's mercy, strength, and salvation will be accompanied by *"a sign* ["omen, miracle"] *for good"* (v. 17). David's enemies (*"those who hate me"*) will see this intervention of God and *"be ashamed"* ("confounded"). They will know that God has *"helped"* him by delivering him and has *"comforted"* him with His presence.

What we have here is no natural order occasionally interrupted by the "God of the gaps." What we have instead is the living God who has created all things (vv. 8–9), who is true to His covenant (v. 5), who hears prayer (v. 1, 6), who performs mighty miracles (v. 10, 17), who instructs in His ways (v. 11), who abounds in mercy (vv. 3, 13, 15, 16) and who, thus, is the object of praise and worship (v. 12). Life is not to be lived in hope of God's occasional intervention. Life is to be lived in the presence of the living God, where every day holds the promise of His surprise. The present adventure of my Christian life is to know exactly this, and to drive out the unbelief and secularization of my heart, denouncing the "God of the gaps" as an idol created by the modern mind.

CHAPTER EIGHTY-SEVEN

The City of God

Psalm 87

Augustine, Bishop of Hippo, saw the Goths, led by Alaric in A.D. 410, sack Rome, the city, as he said, that was "ruled by its lust of rule." This passing show and the pagan accusation that the Eternal City fell because the Christians had offended her gods, led him to write *The City of God*, which was to become the most important book in Western civilization for a thousand years. In it Augustine pursued this theme of "The glorious city of God," that city now seen by faith, which one day will "dwell in the fixed stability of its eternal seat" and obtain "final victory and perfect peace." To see this city, Augustine said, he must persuade the proud to become humble. Only then will they be raised "by divine grace, above all earthly dignities that totter on this shifting scene."

Similarly, Psalm 87 celebrates Zion, God's city, where His foundation is laid (v. 1). Glorious things are spoken of her (v. 3). She is established by the "Most High Himself" (v. 5). The cities of this world (v. 4) pale into insignificance in comparison to Zion where the Lord registers those who are born there (v. 6). Here worship finds its source, as Zion's singers and instrumentalists say, "all my springs are in you" (v. 7).

The authorship of this psalm is attributed to "the sons of Korah" (see the introduction to Psalm 73). Its form is mixed with a hymn of praise, an oracle, and a meditation. Verse 7 suggests that it may have been used in processional or festival worship in the temple. Commentators hold that the reference to Gentile cities in verse 4 may either add a missionary note as the nations come to Zion, or make the psalm post-Exilic as the despised Jews return home. It may also merely contrast the greatness of being born in Zion with being born elsewhere, since Zion is established by God and He records His native-born (v. 5). The thought moves from praise to Zion (vv. 1–3), to the birth records of the nations (v. 4), to the birth records of Zion (vv. 5–6) and concludes with the source of worship (v. 7).

PRAISE TO ZION

87:1 His foundation *is* in the holy mountains.
   2 The LORD loves the gates of Zion
      More than all the dwellings of Jacob.
   3 Glorious things are spoken of you,
      O city of God!   Selah

Ps. 87:1–3

In verse 1 the psalmist sees that God's *"foundation"* is in *"the holy mountains."* The basis for His Kingdom and His house (temple) is laid there. The mountains are *"holy"* ("separated") because the God who dwells in them is holy (Isa. 6:3). Moreover, these mountains become an eschatological sign for the final triumph of God's Kingdom. Thus Isaiah promises: "Now it shall come to pass in the latter days / That the mountain of the Lord's house / Shall be established on the top of the mountains, / And shall be exalted above the hills; / And all nations shall flow to it" (Isa. 2:2).

Zion is the apple of God's eye; He loves her *"gates"* (v. 2; for Zion see Ps. 2:6). Since the gates protect the city, the psalmist sees God's love as resting upon them, granting security. Furthermore, His care for His city is more than all the *"dwellings"* ("tabernacles," other places of worship?) *"of Jacob."* Here *Jacob* represents all of Israel redeemed from bondage (Exod. 19:3).

The *"city of God"* has *"glorious things"* spoken of her because of Yahweh's presence and love. The *"glorious things"* are the praises offered concerning Zion. For example in Ps. 48:2 we read: "Beautiful in elevation, / The joy of the whole earth, / Is Mount Zion on the sides of the north, / The city of the great King." The praise of God's city also points forward to the New Jerusalem, the bride of Christ, which will come down from heaven and in which the eternal presence of God will dwell (Rev. 21:2).

BIRTH RECORDS OF THE NATIONS

87:4 "I will make mention of Rahab and Babylon to
those who know Me;
Behold, O Philistia and Tyre, with Ethiopia:
'This *one* was born there.'"

Ps. 87:4

God now speaks a prophetic word. First, He identifies *"Rahab,"* a mythological creature of chaos who signifies Egypt (Isa. 30:7), lying at one end of the Fertile Crescent. Next, He identifies Babylon lying at the other end. In between are Philistia on the coast, Tyre to the north, and Ethiopia to the southwest. But to whom does God speak? The answer is *"to those who know me."* But who are these people? They could be the Gentiles who are coming to know God in the latter days (Isa. 2:2), or the Jews dispersed among the Gentiles, or the Jews in Zion. Probably God is telling the Jews that He is keeping a register of the Gentiles as He sees each one and notes: *"This one was born there."* He knows their origin and race. As Charles Spurgeon says, "He oversees all and overlooks none." God is the God of the Gentiles as well as the Jews. Their cities are in His hands, but beyond them stands the City of God.

BIRTH RECORDS OF ZION

87:5 And of Zion it will be said,
"This *one* and that *one* were born in her;
And the Most High Himself shall establish
her."
6 The LORD will record,
When He registers the peoples:
"This *one* was born there."   Selah

Ps. 87:5-6

Now we have a clear contrast between the pagan cities and God's city. In a meditation containing another prophetic word, the psalmist notes that God also keeps the records of His people saying, literally, "a man and a man (one man after another) was born in her [Zion]"

(v. 5). Each one is recorded and registered with the same notation given the Gentiles in verse 4: "This one was born there" (v. 6).

But what is the difference between these cities? The answer is given in verse 5. Zion is established by *the most High Himself,*" the God above all gods (see Gen. 14:18). To belong to Zion is to come to the mountain founded and loved by Him. It is for this reason that the nations will come to Jerusalem and the law will go forth from her (Isa. 2:2–3).

The contrast between the Gentile cities and Zion gives the Jews gratitude in belonging to God's own city. At the same time, the celebration of the greatness of Zion (vv. 1–3) would trigger a longing in Gentile hearts to belong to Zion also. There is an implicit missionary message here.

SOURCE OF WORSHIP

87:7 Both the singers and the players on instruments
    say,
   "All my springs *are* in you."
                                        Ps. 87:7

The *"singers"* and the instrumentalists ("pipeplayers" or "dancers") bear their witness as the psalm ends. They find their *"springs"* in Zion. The *"springs"* are metaphorical for life; they represent lifegiving water (cf. Isa. 41:18). In John's Gospel Jesus promises that when the Holy Spirit comes rivers of living water will flow from us (John 7:38–39). To be in Zion is to be refreshed for the joyous worship that we are to give to God.

The City of God is both our origin and our destiny. Regardless of where we are born, we must find Jerusalem as our mother, our true city. Only Zion is established by God. As Augustine saw, all earthly cities will fade and fail. God's city, however, endures. Glorious things are spoken of her because God Himself establishes her.

In our pilgrimage through this life, as people and things slip through our fingers, we long for security and stability, we long to go home at last. This is the longing for God's Kingdom; this is the longing for that eternal Zion, heaven itself. "For here we have no continuing city, but we seek the one to come" (Heb. 13:14).

CHAPTER EIGHTY-EIGHT

In Death's Shadow

Psalm 88

It is hard for us to accept life in this world without any final resolution. Something inside of us demands justice now. We want criminals apprehended. We want terrorists captured. We want victims vindicated. Yet, the reality of death stands before both sinner and saint. Since death is not a part of God's original design, its existence alone shows us that there must be a final resolution beyond our time and history. Since Jesus has conquered death, it is His resurrection that gives us the assurance that such a resolution will be accomplished. In the meantime, we may have to suffer and wait.

For the Christian, however, there is light in the darkness. The Kingdom has come and is coming. Jesus promises us His presence up to and through death. His Spirit abides with us, and we now have the assurance that when we repent God's wrath is lifted from us and placed upon our Savior. Suffering, rather than punitive, is a result of Satan's attack and the fallenness of this world. Nevertheless, there are occasional warnings in the New Testament that if we lapse into conscious sin we cannot escape some form of judgment. There is a moral order to the universe, and we cannot break that order without suffering the consequences. As Paul warns the Galatians: "Do not be deceived, God is not mocked; for whatever a man sows, that he will also reap. For he who sows to his flesh will of the flesh reap corruption, but he who sows to the Spirit will of the Spirit reap everlasting life" (Gal. 6:7–8). God's intention is to chasten us to repentance rather than to crush us in His wrath (see 1 Cor. 11:32).

For the Old Testament, final resolution was yet to come. In prophecy and type (such as the sacrificial system) the preparation was made, but the puzzle was only complete when Jesus Himself assembled the Messianic pieces. In the meantime, physical illness was seen as judgment due to sin. It was experienced as the heavy hand of God's wrath. This appears clearly in Psalm 88.

This psalm comes from a man ground down by an acute illness that pushes him resolutely toward death (vv. 3–7). In this sorry state he is abandoned by friends who hold that he is also abandoned by God (vv. 8, 18). Sick, depressed, and alone, he still prays. He cries out "day and night" (v. 1). He calls "daily" and stretches out his hands to the Lord (v. 9). In the morning he prays again (v. 13). Surprisingly, the psalm ends without resolution (contrast Psalms 22 and 28). There may be a lesson here for us, however. The psalmist's resolution is in the act of praying itself. Rejected though he is, he still cries out to the God of his salvation (v. 1).

Psalm 88 is attributed to the "sons of Korah" (see the introduction to Psalm 73). Commentators identify it as an individual lament. The thought moves from ceaseless prayer (vv. 1–2), to ceaseless troubles (vv. 3–5), to ceaseless wrath (vv. 6–9a), to ceaseless prayer "at the brink" (vv. 9b–12) and concludes with ceaseless rejection in silence and suffering (vv. 13–18).

CEASELESS PRAYER

> 88:1 LORD, God of my salvation,
>   I have cried out day and night before You.
>   2 Let my prayer come before You;
>   Incline Your ear to my cry.
>
> *Ps. 88:1–2*

In verse 1 God is addressed as Yahweh, the personal God of Israel, and is identified as the *"God of my salvation"* ("deliverance"). This is reason enough to pray. The psalmist knows God as his Savior. Whatever else may be said, he is anchored in the God who saves His people. No wonder that he can pour out the bitter agony of his soul before God. To know God as our Savior is to know just enough. We can come to Him without pretense and tell Him who we really are.

Next, the psalmist expresses his continual prayer. He barrages God. Like Jacob the psalmist will not let God go until God blesses him (see Gen. 32:26). Thus he cries out ("clamors") *"day and night."*

This perseverance in prayer is partially because of who God is. He delights in those who continually seek Him. He honors those who will argue with Him on behalf of their cause. Abraham bargained with God for Sodom (Gen. 18:16), and Jesus commended the man who prayed until the answer came (Luke 11:8). The psalmist, however, also pursues God because of the catastrophe upon him. As his life "draws near to the grave" (v. 3), he has nowhere else to go.

Having identified the God to whom he prays and having expressed his intensity, the psalmist now asks Yahweh to accept his prayer. He wants it to come before God as a petition comes to a king, and he asks that God's ear be turned toward his *cry* (v. 2). The verb is intense. It means a "ringing cry," a "loud summons." The psalmist shouts and moans before the Lord.

CEASELESS TROUBLES

88:3 For my soul is full of troubles,
    And my life draws near to the grave.
  4 I am counted with those who go down to the
        pit;
    I am like a man *who has* no strength,
  5 Adrift among the dead,
    Like the slain who lie in the grave,
    Whom You remember no more,
    And who are cut off from Your hand.
                                        Ps. 88:3–5

Now the psalmist turns to his complaint. He begins with the diagnosis of his own ills. To begin with, his *"soul"* or "self" is filled with *"troubles."* The noun includes "distress, injury, misery, calamity." This overwhelming sorrow has brought him to the brink of death itself. His *"life draws near to the grave,"* or literally to Sheol, the abode of the dead. The etymology of this word is uncertain. It may mean a place of inquiry (necromancy) or a hollow place (hell). Or it may have mythological connections to the underworld.

Others agree that the psalmist is terminal; he is *"counted with those who go down to the pit"* (v. 4). The *"pit"* is the grave, the entrance to the abode of the dead. His symptoms are clear. The psalmist has lost his *"strength"* (or "help"; that is, he is powerless). He is *"adrift,"* or "free," *"among the dead"* like those wounded in battle *"who lie* [down] *in the grave"* (v. 5).

As a dead man, the psalmist is nothing. He is among those forgotten by God, *"cut off"* from His hand (v. 5). To be severed from God is to be severed from life. This stands in clear contrast to Jesus' promise to His disciples, "I give them eternal life, and they shall never perish; neither shall anyone snatch them out of My hand" (John 10:28). Indeed, the psalmist is experiencing "the dark night of the soul."

CEASELESS WRATH

88:6 You have laid me in the lowest pit,
In darkness, in the depths.
7 Your wrath lies heavy upon me,
And You have afflicted *me* with all Your
waves.   Selah
8 You have put away my acquaintances far
from me;
You have made me an abomination to them;
I am shut up, and I cannot get out;
9a My eye wastes away because of affliction.
Ps. 88:6–9a

The sense of God's rejection expressed in verse 5 is now given full treatment. It is God who has brought the psalmist to the edge of death, placing him in the grave, the *"lowest pit"* (cf. v. 4). He is in deep darkness, or, literally "in the deeps" ("the depths of the sea," Ps. 107:24). These death images all symbolize the distress that is upon him.

Behind this despair lies the wrath of God (v. 7). The psalmist does not identify the cause of the divine displeasure, only the consequences. This wrath *"lies heavy"* or "rests" upon him, coming in waves. It includes not only separation (see v. 5) but affliction. God's moral judgment is active and punitive. Similarly, Paul sees a future day where there will be "indignation and wrath, tribulation and anguish, on every soul of man who does evil" (Rom. 2:8–9). This is also experienced presently, as God gives us over to our sin (Rom. 1:24). The good news of the gospel, however, is that Jesus has taken God's wrath from us (Eph. 2:3, 15), and there is now no condemnation for those who are in Him (Rom. 8:1).

Separated from God and under His judgment, the psalmist is also separated from his *"acquaintances"* or companions (v. 8). God has made him an *"abomination"* to them. This could refer to a sickness that has made him ritually unclean or to their moral rejection of him because his illness comes as a result of sin and judgment (compare John 9:2).

How then is he and how does he feel? He is *"shut up,"* either in physical and emotional distress, or in confinement or imprisonment, or both. He is also trapped; he *"cannot get out"* (v. 8). This confinement is permanent, a "sickness unto death" (Kierkegaard). His eye *"wastes away"* or "grows dim." Since, as Jesus says, the eye is the lamp of the body, a dark eye reveals a body "full of darkness" (Matt. 6:23).

The thought progresses in verses 3–9 from mental and physical pain to divine and human rejection. Here is a picture of total despair. It is as if we hear the cry of dereliction as Jesus hangs on the cross.

CEASELESS PRAYER

> 88:9b LORD, I have called daily upon You;
> I have stretched out my hands to You.
> 10 Will You work wonders for the dead?
> Shall the dead arise *and* praise You?   Selah
> 11 Shall Your lovingkindness be declared in the
> grave?
> *Or* Your faithfulness in the place of
> destruction?
> 12 Shall Your wonders be known in the dark?
> And Your righteousness in the land of
> forgetfulness?
>
> *Ps. 88:9b–12*

The theme of constant prayer that begins this psalm is reintroduced. Again God is addressed by His personal name, "Yahweh." The psalmist reminds the Lord that he has *"called* ["cried aloud"] *daily"* to Him. His hands have been stretched out in supplication (see 1 Kings 8:22). His body language is consistent with his need and desire.

With this established, a shotgun of rhetorical questions are addressed to God in verses 10–12. It is as if the psalmist is bargaining with Him. Since, for him, death is the end (the resurrection of the dead not having yet been revealed), it is his task to convince God to heal and deliver him. After all, it is in God's best interest to keep him alive. Why is this so?

First, there are no *"wonders"* or miracles for the dead. Only the living can be the objects of divine intervention and power. That Jesus' ministry included raising the dead meant that the final, eschatological Kingdom had broken in upon God's people. Up until then the dead were dead. Second, the dead will not rise up and praise God. If He wants worshipers, He should keep the psalmist alive (v. 10). Third, there is no witness to Yahweh from the grave. No one there will declare His *"lovingkindness"* ("covenant-love") or His *"faithfulness"* (v. 11). Fourth, in the *"dark,"* in the *"land of forgetfulness,"* God's *"wonders,"* His mighty acts (see v. 10), and His *"righteousness"* will not be *"known"* (or experienced, v. 12). For all of these reasons, the Lord should answer the psalmist's prayers with healing and deliverance. Implied, of course, is the promise that if God does perform a miracle, worship and witness will be his response. His expectation for God's mighty intervention places him at the heart of Israel's covenant experience of the living God (see Exodus 15). No wonder he pours out his soul in persevering prayer. He doesn't give up on God even though he fears that God has given up on him.

I have experienced dark times in my own walk with the Lord. One season brought intense emotional pain when my marriage was threatened. Another period came when I was rejected by coworkers who were near and dear to me. What kept me going and ultimately brought me through those times was prayer, continual, abiding prayer, like the psalmist engages in here.

CEASELESS REJECTION

88:13 But to You I have cried out, O LORD,
    And in the morning my prayer comes before
    You.

14 LORD, why do You cast off my soul?
   Why do You hide Your face from me?
15 I *have been* afflicted and ready to die from *my*
      youth;
   I suffer Your terrors;
   I am distraught.
16 Your fierce wrath has gone over me;
   Your terrors have cut me off.
17 They came around me all day long like water;
   They engulfed me altogether.
18 Loved one and friend You have put far from
      me,
   And my acquaintances into darkness.

                                        Ps. 88:13–18

The psalmist reinforces his supplication by reminding Yahweh that he prays to Him. (The verb in verse 13, *cried out,* means "to cry out for help.") Furthermore, he prays *"in the morning"*; he begins his day seeking God's face (cf. v. 1). Nevertheless, he is greeted with silence. Thus he asks: *"Lord, why do you cast off my soul?"* His deepest pain is God's absence as His face is turned from him in rejection and displeasure (cf. Ps. 22:1–2).

This affliction has been longstanding. It has been going on since the psalmist was a youth (v. 15). God's *"terrors"* have made him *"distraught"* (the verb appears only here, and its meaning is uncertain), and His *"fierce wrath"* (plural for fullness) has gone over him like the Egyptian plagues. Furthermore, God's *"terrors"* ("alarms") have metaphorically cut him off or annihilated him (v. 16). These afflictions have come like Noah's flood and *"engulfed"* him *"altogether"* (v. 17). Finally, he is rejected by the community: his *"loved one,"* his *"friend"* ("neighbor"), and his *"acquaintances"* ("companions," see v. 8). It is God who has taken them away. With this sorrowful observation the psalm abruptly ends.

As we conclude our study, we may well ask, why is there no resolution here? Why is there no confession of faith? Why is there no cry of confidence? Why is there no healing? As we have previously suggested, it may be that prayer itself is enough. In Mark's Gospel, Jesus only prays from the cross, "My God, my God, why have You forsaken me?" (Mark 15:34). Even our sense of abandonment takes place before God. A further observation, however, is in order. This prayer was incorporated into the Psalter and is thus a prayer for us. Since it does not end in resolution, God's answer is still open. It is a prayer for the sick, not for the healed. In our darkness, in our anguish we too can pray this psalm. The promise is that God will hear and answer. The resolution lies in His sovereign hand. Moreover, this "incomplete" psalm demands the gospel to complete it. Jesus is the lamb of God who has taken away the sin of the world (John 1:29). It is by His stripes that we are healed (Isa. 53:5).

CHAPTER EIGHTY-NINE

When Experience Contradicts Theology

Psalm 89

Thomas Kuhn describes the history of scientific inquiry as a process of establishing models or paradigms that explain observed phenomena satisfactorily. These paradigms include law, theory, application, and instrumentation and become coherent traditions of scientific research (*The Structure of Scientific Revolutions*, p. 10). The more exact the paradigms become, however, the more "anomalies" tend to appear: that is, embarrassing facts that don't fit the paradigms. For example, is light a transverse wave motion, as was universally held up until fifty years ago? Or is light a photon exhibiting aspects of both waves and particles? We know today that the latter answer is true because exacting research forced the older model or paradigm to be abandoned. Thus, although we resist change and will even deny anomalies or explain them by our old categories, their persistence will finally force a change in our paradigm, a modification in our world-view, a modification in the way we perceive reality itself.

What is true for science is also true for theology. For example, the Jews expected a conquering Messiah who would be their political, warrior-king. Jesus refused to fit this paradigm. For the earliest church there was a paradigm shift from the old Jewish model when the resurrected Lord demonstrated that His crucifixion was an integral part of God's plan of salvation, accomplished now through humiliation, suffering, and death (see Luke 24:44–46). More currently for much of the church, God's supernatural power to heal directly through prayer has been isolated to a few saints or denied altogether, being consigned to the Apostolic Age. This paradigm, however, has again been challenged by an increasing number of witnesses to God's direct healing through prayer today (see, for example, John Wimber, *Power Healing*). This in turn is creating a world-view crisis for many Christians who have denied God's direct intervention in this way because of their commitment to the so-called modern scientific world-view.

Psalm 89 witnesses to a paradigm crisis. The operative theology concerning God's promise to David and his heirs is no longer functional. Rather than the monarchy enduring with growing power and splendor (see v. 4), it is "cast off and abhorred" (v. 38). Actual historical experience is forcing a paradigm shift of major proportions. The King's sword has been turned back (v. 43), and his throne is "cast . . . down to the ground" (v. 44). Chaos follows military and political defeat. Thus the psalmist cries out: Where is God and where are His promises?

The first half of the psalm rehearses the covenant made with David (vv. 1–37). The second half shows that experience now contradicts that covenant (vv. 38–52). Out of the upheaval, however, the door is opened for a new paradigm, and the biblical resolution lies beyond this psalm in the new covenant that God will establish with His people (Jer. 31:31).

The authorship of Psalm 89 is attributed to "Elham the Ezrahite," a wise man and a contemporary of Solomon (1 Kings 4:31). Commentators, however, place its composition in a variety of times and places, such as after the fall of Samaria, or after the fall of Jerusalem. Others see it as liturgical rather than historical in nature. Therefore, it may be either an individual lament, even of the king himself (see vv. 47, 50), or a national (or cultic) lament for the king. We prefer to see it as an individual lament, probably after the fall of Jerusalem (586 B.C.) when the Davidic monarchy was dethroned and Jehoiachin was taken to Babylon by Nebuchadnezzar (see vv. 39, 44; 2 Kings 24:15). The thought moves from a vow to worship (vv. 1–2), to the word of God (vv. 3–4), to witness-worship (vv. 5–18), to a vision of the covenant with David (vv. 19–29), to a vision of the covenant with David's sons (vv. 30–37), to the contradiction of the vision (vv. 38–45) and concludes with questions and complaints (vv. 46–51). The psalm ends with a blessing in verse 52, which closes the third book of the Psalter (see our *Introduction* in *Psalms 1–72*, Communicator's Commentary, Old Testament, no. 13, 20).

A VOW TO WORSHIP

89:1 I will sing of the mercies of the LORD forever;
With my mouth will I make known Your
faithfulness to all generations.
2 For I have said, "Mercy shall be built up
forever;
Your faithfulness You shall establish in the
very heavens."

Ps. 89:1–2

Verse 1 introduces us immediately to the covenant in its broader sense, based upon God's character. The psalmist vows to sing of Yahweh's *"mercies,"* His covenant-love revealed in His many acts, and His *"faithfulness,"* His trustworthiness (in covenant-keeping, v. 1). The *"mercies of the Lord"* will be sung about continually, *"forever,"* and throughout Israel's history, *"to all generations."* That the psalmist is singing indicates his praiseful worship: there is joy in contemplating God's promises and commitment to His people. Worship is also for witness and instruction. Thus the promise to pass on who God is to those yet to come is fulfilled in writing this psalm.

142

How often individual worship and witness in our hymns have become the treasure for the future. Who would remember Charles Wesley apart from his ringing gift of praise?

The vow to sing in verse 1 is based upon the confession in verse 2, *"For I have said . . ."* The content of this confession continues the double theme of *"mercy"* and *"faithfulness."* Mercy will be *"built up forever."* No wonder the psalmist will also sing of it (v. 1). The verb *built up* means to be "established" or "made permanent." God's mercy does not grow; it stands. The psalmist will be able always to trust His covenant (but contrast v. 39, which reveals the paradigm crisis). At the same time, *"faithfulness"* is established ("fixed," "made firm") by God Himself *"in the very heavens"*; that is, it is grounded in that realm where God Himself dwells (cf. 1 Kings 8:27; Matt. 6:9). Mercy and faithfulness, therefore, are eternal and transcendent. They endure when all else fails.

THE WORD OF GOD

89:3 'I have made a covenant with My chosen,
I have sworn to My servant David:
4 'Your seed I will establish forever,
And build up your throne to all
generations.'" Selah

Ps. 89:3–4

God now speaks. These verses may contain a prophetic, living word, or they may cite a previous word now a part of the tradition (written or oral). The word declares God's *"covenant"* with His *"chosen,"* His *"servant David"* (v. 3). The meaning of *covenant (berit)* probably comes from its association with an Akkadian word rendered "to clasp," "to fetter." Thus the covenant is a bond between two parties. The phrase *"I have made a covenant"* translates literally 'I have cut a covenant." The idea of cutting is likely derived from the covenant ceremony where an animal was cut in two (Gen. 15:9). Israel knew two types of covenants. The first was the obligatory type based on the model of the suzerain-vassal treaty and given through Moses. The second was the promissory type modeled on the royal grant and given to Abraham (the land) and David (the house or dynasty). This covenant was unconditional and made with those who loyally served their masters. Here, the covenant with David comes simply by grace. David is chosen by God although he is the least of his brothers (v. 3, see 1 Sam. 16:10–13). He is now God's *"servant,"* bound to Yahweh, the great King over all, as a vassal king was bound to a great suzerain (see 2 Samuel 7). When God elects David unconditionally, He also gives him an unconditional promise that follows the Near Eastern covenant form. He validates His covenant with an oath that stands through eternity: *"Your seed I will establish forever"* (v. 4). God will be able to fulfill this promise since His faithfulness is secured in the heavens (v. 2). Moreover, David's *"throne"* or authority and rule will be built up ("made permanent") *"to all generations"* (v. 4). Again, this is based on God's "mercy" or covenant-love, which is "built up forever" (v. 2).

Clearly the oracle in verses 3–4 reflects God's promise made to David through Nathan the prophet: "And your house and your kingdom shall be established forever before you. Your throne shall be established forever" (2 Sam. 7:16). The psalmist sings of God's mercies because they have become concrete in David and in the enduring promise given to him. It is exactly this promise that provokes a later crisis (vv. 38–51), because of, in Thomas Kuhn's thought, an anomaly that doesn't fit the old paradigm. In other words, what happens when God's word is heard, "Your seed I will establish forever," and then the monarchy is destroyed?

WITNESS-WORSHIP

89:5 And the heavens will praise Your wonders, O
　　　Lord;
　　　Your faithfulness also in the assembly of the
　　　saints.
　6 For who in the heavens can be compared to
　　　the Lord?
　　　Who among the sons of the mighty can be
　　　likened to the Lord?
　7 God is greatly to be feared in the assembly of
　　　the saints,
　　　And to be held in reverence by all *those*
　　　around Him.

8 O LORD God of hosts,
  Who *is* mighty like You, O LORD?
  Your faithfulness also surrounds You.
9 You rule the raging of the sea;
  When its waves rise, You still them.
10 You have broken Rahab in pieces, as one who
     is slain;
  You have scattered Your enemies with Your
     mighty arm.
11 The heavens *are* Yours, the earth also *is* Yours;
  The world and all its fullness, You have
     founded them.
12 The north and the south, You have created
     them;
  Tabor and Hermon rejoice in Your name.
13 You have a mighty arm;
  Strong is Your hand, *and* high is Your right
     hand.
14 Righteousness and justice *are* the foundation
     of Your throne;
  Mercy and truth go before Your face.
15 Blessed *are* the people who know the joyful
     sound!
  They walk, O LORD, in the light of Your
     countenance.
16 In Your name they rejoice all day long,
  And in Your righteousness they are exalted.
17 For You *are* the glory of their strength,
  And in Your favor our horn is exalted.
18 For our shield *belongs* to the LORD,
  And our king to the Holy One of Israel.

Ps. 89:5–18

The psalmist addresses God in verse 5 and verses 8–18 and meditates upon His uniqueness in verses 6–7. In a continuation of witness and worship, the vow to "sing of the mercies of the Lord forever," given in verse 1, occurs.

In verse 5 worship begins in heaven. *"The heavens,"* which would include the angels, *"will praise* ['give thanks, confess'] *Your wonders, O Lord."* These *"wonders"* signify the surpassing, extraordinary acts of God (see Exod. 15:11). God's *"faithfulness"* ("trustworthiness," see

vv. 1–2) is celebrated *"in the congregation of the saints"* or "the assembly of the holy ones," that is, among the heavenly beings (cf. Pss. 82:1; 103:20). As we have seen in verse 2, this faithfulness is established "in the very heavens." Yahweh is worshiped for His dramatic interventions and for His consistent care. Both facts are true of Him and are to be experienced by us. Jesus both calms the storm with a command (Matt. 8:23–27) and teaches that God consistently makes the rain fall on the just and the unjust (Matt. 5:45).

Having witnessed to heavenly worship, the psalmist meditates upon Yahweh's uniqueness (vv. 6–7). Verse 6 contains two rhetorical questions, both demanding the response "No one." The first asks who among *"the heavens"* (literally, "in the sky") can be compared to Yahweh? The answer is that no sun or planet is equal to Him. The second asks who *"among the sons of the mighty can be likened to the Lord?"* The phrase *"sons of the mighty"* literally translates as "the sons of gods" (see Ps. 29:1). Again, the answer is that no divine being is comparable to the Lord. Thus in verse 7 the psalmist asserts that God is *"greatly"* to *"be feared"* and *"to be held in reverence"* ("great and terrible") in heaven, among *"the assembly"* ["counsel"] *of the saints"* or "holy ones" (see v. 5). All of those heavenly beings gathered around Him in His court are to have a sense of awe and even dread or terror before His numinous holiness (R. Otto). Only "God is God" (Karl Barth).

In verse 8 the psalmist returns to addressing God directly as the *"Lord God of hosts"* (that is, the God of the heavenly army; see Ps. 24:8–10). The question of "who . . . can be compared to the Lord" now becomes *"Who is mighty like You, O Lord?"* Again, the implied answer is "No one." God's uniqueness is asserted in His *"faithfulness"* (see vv. 1, 2, 5). This "trustworthiness" is seen as He rules the raging sea (or "the pride of the sea") by calming its surging waves (v. 9). Again, He has slain *"Rahab,"* the dragon, sea-monster (v. 10; see Isa. 51:9), which can signify Egypt (Isa. 30:7), and He has dispersed His enemies with His *"mighty arm"* (compare Exod. 15:6). Yahweh is sovereign over all the chaos of nature and history.

God is confessed as the Creator, in verses 11–12, and the Redeemer, starting in verse 13. *"The heavens"* and *"the earth"* belong to Him. This includes everything in the world, *"all its fullness,"* since *"You have founded* ["established," see Ps. 24:2] *them"* (v. 11). A part of that fullness is *"the north and the south."* These compass points are represented by Mount *"Tabor"* to the south, on the edge of the plain of Jezreel, and Mount *"Hermon"* to the north, in Lebanon (v. 12). Both rejoice in the name of Yahweh. But God is not only worshiped as the Creator; He is also worshiped as the Redeemer. With this the psalmist begins a description of Yahweh, which includes His arm, His right hand (v. 13), His throne, His face (v. 14), His countenance (v. 15), and His name (v. 16).

God is known in His relationships. Israel is introduced in verse 15 as blessed because she knows *"the joyful sound."* She also walks before the Lord (v. 15), rejoices in His name, is exalted in His righteousness (v. 16), and receives her strength, horn (v. 17), shield, and king from Him (v. 18).

Let us look at how God is described. He has a *"mighty* ['strong, valiant'] *arm"* (see v. 10) and a *"strong"* and *"high . . . right hand"* (v. 13). Here, of course, God is the God of battle: "Your right hand, O Lord, has become glorious in power; Your right hand, O Lord, has dashed the enemy in pieces" (Exod. 15:6). Yahweh is "The Lord strong and mighty, the Lord mighty in battle" (Ps. 24:8). No wonder the angels marvel at His *"wonders"* (v. 5).

God also reigns on His throne; He is the mighty King (v. 14). As we have suggested in our discussion of the covenant, David is only a vassal-king under the sovereignty of the great suzerain. God's throne (authority, rule), however, is not capricious. It is founded on *"righteousness and justice."* "Righteousness" for Israel is defined by the covenant obligation to obey the law. "Justice" or "judgment" is exercised by God based on His righteousness. God's throne or rule defines the moral order, holds us accountable, and judges us accordingly. Based on this, Paul speaks of a "day of wrath" where there will be the "revelation of the righteous judgment of God, who 'will render to each one according to his deeds'" (Rom. 2:5-6).

Moreover, *"mercy* ['covenant-love," see vv. 1-2] *and truth* ['trustworthiness'] *go before* ['meet," "are in front of'] *Your face."* To see God's face, to be face to face with Him, is to see this mercy and truth (cf. John 1:14).

Now, perhaps overwhelmed by God's character and conscious that God has revealed Himself to Israel, the psalmist responds: *"Blessed* [plural for fullness, see Ps. 1:1] *are the people who know the joyful sound"* (v. 15). This sound is the "festal shout." It includes a war-cry in battle, the signal for a march, and the shout of triumph over enemies. When uttered in worship, it celebrates God's victory over all things and here is the only valid response to God's revelation given in verses 11–14 (see Pss. 47:1ff.; 66:1ff.). Thus the people who know this *"walk, O Lord, in the light of Your countenance."* God's face is turned toward them, and the light of His covenant-love and truth is upon them (see v. 14; Ps. 4:6). They also rejoice ("exult") in God's *"name,"* which reveals His relationship with them and actualizes His presence and authority (see Exod. 3:13–14). This worship goes on *"all the day long,"* that is, continually. As a result, *"in Your righteousness"* (see v. 14) *"they are exalted"* ("lifted up," "raised up").

Notice the anticipation of the gospel. Israel is exalted in God's righteousness, not her own. This ultimately is fulfilled in the gift of righteousness given through faith in Jesus (see Phil. 3:9). The reasons for this joyful worship and walk before the Lord are now given in verses 17–18.

First, God is *"the glory of their strength."* The word *glory* here denotes beauty and can be used of festal garments. Israel's strength manifests the glory or the beauty of God. Since she belongs to Him and finds her life in Him, He is seen in her triumphs. Next, it is by God's favor that Israel's *"horn is exalted"* (v. 17). The *horn* here is a synonym for "strength" and may represent the king (cf. v. 24; see Ps. 132:17). Finally, verse 18 describes Israel's shield (protection) and king either as belonging to God or as being God Himself. If the preposition (*L*ᶜ) is an emphatic *lāmed,* then the verse will read: "For our shield indeed [is] the Lord, / And our king indeed the Holy One of Israel." If the horn in verse 17 is the king, then the confession in verse 18 that Yahweh Himself is the ultimate king makes sense both in the progression of thought and in the covenant theology of Israel (see v. 3).

The witness-worship of this extensive passage comes to its proper climax. God is praised by the heavenly beings; no one is like Him. He is the Creator and Redeemer. He is the King of Israel.

A VISION OF THE COVENANT WITH DAVID

89:19 Then You spoke in a vision to Your holy one,
And said: "I have given help to *one who is*
mighty;
I have exalted one chosen from the people.

20 I have found My servant David;
   With My holy oil I have anointed him,
21 With whom My hand shall be established;
   Also My arm shall strengthen him.
22 The enemy shall not outwit him,
   Nor the son of wickedness afflict him.
23 I will beat down his foes before his face,
   And plague those who hate him.
24 "But My faithfulness and My mercy *shall be*
    with him,
   And in My name his horn shall be exalted.
25 Also I will set his hand over the sea,
   And his right hand over the rivers.
26 He shall cry to Me, 'You *are* my Father,
   My God, and the rock of my salvation.'
27 Also I will make him *My* firstborn,
   The highest of the kings of the earth.
28 My mercy I will keep for him forever,
   And My covenant shall stand firm with him.
29 His seed also I will make *to endure* forever,
   And his throne as the days of heaven."

Ps. 89:19–29

The prophetic word of God given by a vision is now revealed. This word comes through a picture, which the prophet sees and then speaks. In 2 Sam. 7:17, after the covenant promise of David's house, kingdom, and throne being established forever, we read, "According to all these words and according to all this vision, so Nathan the prophet spoke to David." The *"holy one"* (or *"ones,"* see NKJV footnote) probably refers to Nathan or, if it is plural, to the prophets through whom this word was continually confirmed.

First, then, God gives *"help* ['succor", or "sets help upon"] *to one who is mighty* ["valiant", often used of a warrior]" and exalts him as He chooses him *"from the people"* (v. 19). In verse 20 the mighty one is identified as David, God's *"servant"* (see v. 3; 1 Sam. 16:1–13). As a servant, David is only a vassal-king under divine authority. Next, David is anointed with *"holy oil,"* which is closely identified with the Holy Spirit: "Then Samuel took the horn of oil and anointed him [David] in the midst of his brothers; and the Spirit of the Lord came upon David from that day forward" (1 Sam. 16:13). This is the help

God gives (see v. 19). In God's anointed there is also a foreshadowing here of the messianic hope (see Luke 4:18).

David, as God's representative to the people, will establish the Lord's *"hand"* (authority and power, see v. 13). In turn, he will also be strengthened by God's *"arm"* (v. 21). Thus he only exercises divine authority by divine power. This, of course, means doom to his adversaries. As a result, *"the enemy shall not outwit* ['deceive'] *him"*; that is, his strategies will not triumph in battle. Moreover, *"the son of wickedness"* ("iniquity", "injustice") will be unable to afflict him. This could be a reference to Satan (cf. Ezek. 28:14–15, where "wickedness" is found in "the anointed cherub" who was perfect in all his ways). Thus no natural or supernatural evil will overcome him. God promises in verse 23 that He *"will beat down* ['crush'] *his foes before his face / and plague* ['strike down'] *those who hate him."*

The theme of victory continues in verses 24–25, where God promises to give David His *"faithfulness"* and *"mercy"* ("covenant-love"; compare vv. 1–2) and *"in* [His] . . . *name"* (authority) exalt his *"horn"* ("strength," see v. 17). His *"hand"* (power) will be *"over the sea"* and *"the rivers."* This probably refers to the Mediterranean Sea and the Tigris or the Euphrates, which would be the ideal extent of David's kingdom.

David is also granted a unique relationship with God. He will call to Him, *"You are my Father"* (v. 26), and God will make him His *"firstborn"* (v. 27). As Jeremias points out, the deity as father is a familiar mythological idea in the ancient Near East (*The Central Message of the New Testament*, chap. 1). Likewise, since the king represents his people, he enjoys a special share of divine dignity, power, and irrevocable authority. In the Old Testament, however, God is only spoken of as Father fourteen times, and His fatherhood is related to Israel alone, His firstborn, chosen out of all peoples (Deut. 14:1f.). This choice is grounded not in mythology but in the Exodus (Hos. 11:1). The king, as the representative of the people, is also addressed as God's firstborn (v. 27). Likewise, in his enthronement he steps into the role of mediator between God and Israel (see Ps. 2:7).

Thus David addresses God as *"Father"* and *"the rock of my salvation"* (v. 26; see Ps. 62:2). As the *"rock"* God is his strength, security, and fortress. God's response, as we have seen, is to make David His *"firstborn"* and to exalt him over all the *"kings of the earth"* (cf. Psalm 2). This verse is pregnant with messianic overtones. These promises are now sealed with oaths in verses 27–28 (cf. vv. 3–4). God's *"mercy"* ("covenant-love") will always be his. The *"covenant"* stands (v. 28). David's seed (dynasty) will be *"forever / And his throne* [rule] *as the days of heaven."* This means that his rule will be as enduring as heaven itself.

Here, in an extended oracle, we have God's unconditional covenant with David. God has chosen, anointed, and strengthened him. David will defeat all of his enemies by God's power. His kingdom will be extensive, and he will enjoy a special relationship with God as father. Moreover, he will be exalted over all other kings, and his dynasty will endure forever.

A VISION OF THE COVENANT WITH
DAVID'S SONS

89:30 "If his sons forsake My law
 And do not walk in My judgments,
 31 If they break My statutes
 And do not keep My commandments,
 32 Then I will punish their transgression with the
  rod,
 And their iniquity with stripes.
 33 Nevertheless My lovingkindness I will not
  utterly take from him,
 Nor allow My faithfulness to fail.
 34 My covenant I will not break,
 Nor alter the word that has gone out of My
  lips.
 35 Once I have sworn by My holiness;
 I will not lie to David:
 36 His seed shall endure forever,
 And his throne as the sun before Me;
 37 It shall be established forever like the moon,
 Even *like* the faithful witness in the
  sky." Selah

Ps. 89:30–37

The single vision given in verse 19 continues. Now, however, it is applied to David's seed or dynasty (see v. 29). The question here is to what extent it does apply, especially if David's sons violate the covenant made with him. The answer, in sum, is that the covenant stands, although those who violate it will be punished.

Thus verses 30–31 ask about the fate of the sons who *forsake* God's *"law,"* do not *"walk"* in (obey) His *"judgments"* (*"ordinances"*), *"break"* His *"statutes,"* and violate His *"commandments."* These several clauses are in synonymous parallelism, all expressing disobedience to the covenant-will of God.

The consequences of such rebellion are given in verse 32: the disobedient will be punished. *"Transgression,"* rebellion against God's authority, will receive the *"rod,"* a club used in battle. *"Iniquity"* will receive *"stripes,"* inflicted by the whip. This sin, as we have seen, is the violation of the covenant law. The history of the Davidic monarchy is, over all, a sad commentary on this warning (see 1 and 2 Kings). Too often the word is heard, "He also did evil in the sight of the Lord . . ." (see 2 Kings 15:9; 24:19).

Regardless of the sin and the sinner, however, God's *"lovingkindness"* (*"covenant-love"*) stands (v. 33). It is based upon His unconditional promise to David and his house "forever" (vv. 4, 29). Despite the present king, God promises: *"My lovingkindness I will not utterly take from him."* God's *"faithfulness"* (*"trustworthiness"*) will not *"fail"* (*"be false"*). God's character is established in His *"covenant"* (see v. 3), which He *"will not break"* (*"violate,"* v. 34). Moreover, the oath that accompanies the covenant is a word from God's lips that cannot be altered (v. 34; cf. Isa. 40:8; 55:11). When God swears by His *"holiness,"* by that which makes Him unique, He *"will not lie to David"* (v. 35). The promise that his seed (dynasty) will endure forever stands (vv. 4, 29). His *"throne"* (rule, kingdom) will be just as permanent as the *"sun"* and the *"moon"* before the Lord (vv. 36–37). These heavenly bodies are faithful witnesses to God's enduring covenant (v. 37).

What we find in the prophetic vision in verses 19–37 is the covenant made with David concerning himself and his house. It cannot be stressed too strongly that this is not merely a theological discourse. This is a divine word (vv. 19, 34–35), and God will not lie to David (v. 35). What happens when Israel's historical experience contradicts this covenant promise? What happens when an anomaly appears in this theological paradigm? Has the covenant failed? Has God lied after all? To this we now turn.

THE CONTRADICTION OF THE VISION

89:38 But You have cast off and abhorred,
You have been furious with Your anointed.
39 You have renounced the covenant of Your
servant;
You have profaned his crown *by casting it* to
the ground.
40 You have broken down all his hedges;
You have brought his strongholds to ruin.
41 All who pass by the way plunder him;
He is a reproach to his neighbors.
42 You have exalted the right hand of his
adversaries;
You have made all his enemies rejoice.
43 You have also turned back the edge of his
sword,
And have not sustained him in the battle.
44 You have made his glory cease,
And cast his throne down to the ground.
45 The days of his youth You have shortened;
You have covered him with shame.   Selah
Ps. 89:38–45

Now, in an abrupt transition, the crisis is joined. The very Davidic monarchy that God promised would endure forever has collapsed, and God stands accused by the psalmist.

Verse 38 brings the issue before us: God's *"anointed"* (see v. 20) has been *"cast off* ["rejected"] *and abhorred* ["despised"]." Moreover, God has been *"furious"* with him in His wrath. This is more than personal judgment in verse 39, however: *"You have renounced the covenant of your servant"* (the king, see vv. 3, 20). Not only has an individual been rejected; the whole structure of God's relationship with David's house has been broken. The *"crown"* has been cast *"to the ground,"* or, literally, "You have profaned (defiled) his crown to the earth." In Jer. 13:18–19 the collapse of the crown is identified with the Babylonian exile. This is probably the meaning here also.

This destruction of David's house has been the result of a great invasion. In verse 40 the *"hedges"* ("walls," "defenses") have been broken down and the *"strongholds"* ruined. With the overpowering of these fortifications there has been a resulting plunder. The king is plundered as the kingdom is plundered (see *"him"* in v. 41). This, in turn, brings reproach upon David's house from the surrounding peoples, such as Edom to the east of the Jordan (v. 41; cf. Pss. 31:11; 79:4).

Furthermore, in this defeat and destruction it is the *"right hand"* (power) of David's *"adversaries"* that is now exalted rather than his horn and his right hand (v. 42; cf. vv. 24–25). This has happened because *"the edge* [literally *"rock,"* figure for strength] *of his sword* [his army]*"* has been *"turned back,"* and God has *"not sustained him in the battle"* (v. 43). Note the violence done here to the covenant promise: *"*I will beat down his foes before his face, / And plague those who hate him*"* (v. 23).

As a result of this massive rout, the king's *"glory"* ("brightness") ceases with *"his throne"* cast *"down to the ground"* (v. 44; see v. 39). God has also shortened *"the days of his youth"*; either the defeat has aged him or he has died. If the setting for this is the Babylonian conquest, it could refer to Zedekiah, who came to the throne at twenty-one years of age and reigned for eleven years. He then was taken captive to Babylon, and his house ended: "they killed the sons of Zedekiah before his eyes, put out the eyes of Zedekiah, bound him with bronze fetters, and took him to Babylon" (2 Kings 25:7). As the psalmist concludes: *"You have covered him with shame"* (v. 45). The garment that manifests his heart is deep humiliation. "The loftiness of man shall be bowed down, / And the haughtiness of men shall be brought low; / The Lord alone will be exalted in that day" (Isa. 2:17).

Two observations need to be made at this point. History shows us that God has broken His unconditional covenant with David and his house. This is the anomaly that challenges the former paradigm that the kingdom would always stand. At the same time, it is God, not history, that has done this. He is still the sovereign Lord of all: *"But you have cast off and abhorred, / You have been furious with Your anointed"* (v. 38). Out of this crisis we may believe that a new paradigm will emerge, taking into account both the unconditional covenant and its renunciation by the Lord. This observation, of course, drives us toward the New Testament.

QUESTIONS AND COMPLAINTS

89:46 How long, LORD?
Will You hide Yourself forever?
Will Your wrath burn like fire?
47 Remember how short my time is;
For what futility have You created all the
children of men?
48 What man can live and not see death?
Can he deliver his life from the power of the
grave? Selah
49 Lord, where *are* Your former lovingkindnesses,
Which You swore to David in Your truth?
50 Remember, Lord, the reproach of Your
servants—
How I bear in my bosom *the reproach of* all the
many peoples,
51 With which Your enemies have reproached, O
LORD,
With which they have reproached the
footsteps of Your anointed.

Ps. 89:46–51

With the full contradiction before him, the psalmist cries out, *"How long, Lord?"* Indeed, how long? We too know that cry. We pray for someone, and they are not converted. Yet we are promised that God answers prayer. We see someone come to Christ, and they "fall away." Yet we are promised that no one can pluck them out of Jesus' hand (John 10:28). We ask God to heal someone, and they continue to be sick. Yet we are promised that God heals all our diseases (Ps. 103:3).

Israel in her destruction and defeat is experiencing God's rejection. It is as if He has turned away; His face is hidden (v. 46). Will it be forever? This is not a Job-like experience of God's absence; God is very present, but He is present in His *"wrath"* ("hot displeasure"), which burns *"like fire."* God consumes His people like a desert wind, like the Santa Anas, which push forest fires across Southern California in the dry days of summer. In fact, Jerusalem lies in smoking ruins—not by the torches of Babylon, however, but by the wrath of God.

Now the psalmist appeals to his own mortality. He calls upon the Lord to *"remember"* the brevity of his life: *"how short my time is,"* or literally, "Remember with regard to me what the age is" (v. 47). It is, as Paul says, "This present evil age" (Gal. 1:4). The personal pronoun may indicate that the king is speaking here. This would make him the author of this psalm. His thought now moves from the particular to the universal. What about all human beings? Are they simply created for futility ("vanity")? Is there no stability, assurance, or meaning? Is God a nihilist after all? Then, death consumes us. It is our universal condition and destiny (v. 48). The rhetorical question *"What man can live and not see death?"* is followed by a synonymous, parallel thought: No one can *"deliver his life* ["soul," "self"] *from the power of the grave* [or, literally, "the hand of Sheol"; for *hand* see vv. 13 and 25]."

Here we have the human condition summed up: God's wrath; our brevity and mortality (cf. Eph. 2:1–2). If God is not gracious, if He does not intervene, we are just a part of a cosmic joke. Moreover, the joke is all the more absurd in light of God's promises to David and His mighty acts in the past. Must the paradigm of His covenant be abandoned? Has history destroyed it?

In verse 49, the psalmist cries out to God: *"Lord, where are Your former lovingkindnesses"* ("covenant mercies," plural; see v. 1). Where is the covenant that He sealed with oaths, swearing *"to David"* in His *"truth"* ("faithfulness"; see v. 1, cf. vv. 19–37)? It is as if the psalmist says to God, "Remember who You are by what You have done!"

Next, he follows this appeal with, "Remember who we are!" Israel is a people under *"reproach"* from her enemies (v. 50; see v. 41). The personal, *"How I bear in my bosom* ["breast," "chest"] *the reproach of all the many peoples,"* may again be the king speaking as he represents Israel to the nations in his humiliation. Verse 50 continues the theme of reproach. It is labored, thrusting home by repetition the dirge with which this psalm closes: *"With which Your enemies* [note not just Israel's] *have reproached, O Lord, / With which they have reproached the footsteps of Your anointed* [the king as he is taken in shame to Babylon; cf. v. 20]." With this the psalm proper ends. The paradigm of God's covenant with David is broken. The monarchy is destroyed. We are left with the anomaly of the exile. The resolution and rebuilding of the old paradigm lies beyond Psalm 89, and at the same time, this psalm demands it and prepares for it. God is true. His covenant-love endures. His word stands (v. 34). He will not lie to David (v. 35). At the same time, Israel cannot presume upon God. Sin will be punished, and God can even destroy the monarchy in order to resurrect it in His time and to His glory.

This, of course, happens when the Son of God comes into the world—from the house of David (see Matt. 1:1–20; Rom. 1:3). He inherits all of the covenant promises given to the King and His heirs (vv. 19–37). It is Jesus who by His death lifts the wrath of God from Israel (and from the nations; see 1 Thess. 1:9), and it is Jesus who is "declared to be the Son of God with power, according to the Spirit of holiness, by the resurrection from the dead" (Rom. 1:4). It is Jesus who reestablishes God's Kingdom forever and fulfills every promise in Psalm 89: "I will not lie to David; / His seed shall endure forever, / And his throne as the sun before Me" (vv. 35–36). In the anomaly of judgment upon Israel, God forces a paradigm shift that will only be fulfilled when Jesus enters the world. Thus this psalm forces the crisis; it is all true and resolved in the miracle of God's Son: "'For My thoughts are not your thoughts . . . ,' says the Lord" (Isa. 55:8). From this we too take heart. God has the freedom to break our paradigms, even about Himself, because He will rebuild them with His miracles and prove in our experience to be the living God who brings resurrection out of death. We cannot put Him in a box. At the same time, in surprising ways, He will prove Himself faithful to His word.

I must add my own personal witness here. I was brought up in traditional evangelicalism which denied that the power and "charismatic" gifts of the Spirit are for today. I was told that a second filling or baptism of the Spirit added something to the finished work of Christ. Then, in the mid-1970s I experienced an overwhelming empowering of the Spirit as I prayed alone on a hillside in Glendale, California. It was as if the Spirit welled up inside of me, like the living water that Jesus promised in John 7:38–39, and came down upon me in a mighty baptism or anointing. I experienced such joy that I began to speak out in an unknown (to me) language of praise and worship.

In this moment God forced an anomaly upon me, breaking my paradigm of what He can and cannot do. Rather than adding something to Jesus, Jesus added something to me and recovered for my ministry and experience several key passages of the New Testament. I would never be the same again because that day God broke the box which I had put Him in. This is the God who inspired Psalm 89 and then fulfilled it in the coming of Jesus, Son of David, Son of God.

BLESSING

89:52 Blessed *be* the LORD forevermore!
      Amen and Amen.

Ps. 89:52

This verse is a scribal addition, which ends Book Three of the Psalms (see Pss. 40:13; 106:48; *Introduction, Psalms 1–72,* Communicator's Commentary, Old Testament, no. 13, 20). It appropriately points us to the God who is to be praised even when our paradigms are broken.

CHAPTER NINETY

A Light at the End of the Tunnel

Psalm 90

In the 1960s the United States became increasingly mired down in Vietnam as its military forces swelled to nearly 500,000 men strong. The public became numb to daily body counts and fire-fights on the evening news. As national distaste for this war grew, the presidency of Lyndon Johnson became a casualty along with close to 50,000 GIs. General Westmoreland, however, continued his optimistic reports and promised that there was a "light at the end of the tunnel." As it turned out, the light was our pulling out of the war and all of Vietnam coming under communist rule. This, of course, was not the light that the general had imagined or had hoped for.

In the darkness, political and military leaders have always looked for some light. Hitler hoped for a secret weapon to reverse his fortunes. Nixon thought that tape erasures and silence would salvage his White House years. How many cancer patients look for a miracle drug or diet to reverse years of bodily abuse?

Psalm 90 deals with the reality of the dark tunnel we all face. Human life is fragile, like grass (v. 5). God's response to sin is wrathful anger, and it is consuming (vv. 7–8). Our years are a burden: "We finish our lives like a sigh" (v. 9). Where is the light? It is there because beyond God's judgment stands His mercy (vv. 13–14). There is a gladness that comes from the grace of God (vv. 14–15), and God will place upon our passing work the mark of eternity (v. 17). Thus the only real light is God's light. Human promises fail because humans fail. History is littered with broken treaties and broken lives. We must look beyond time to eternity, and this is where Psalm 90 begins and ends: "Even from everlasting to everlasting, You are God" (v. 2).

Tradition gives this psalm (alone in the Psalter) to Moses, the leader-legislator who delivered Israel from Egypt. Its specific internal content, however, does not reflect specific Exodus motifs. Neither does it reflect the longevity of Moses, who lived to be 120 years old (Deut. 34:7; contrast v. 10). Thus, we will leave the issue of authorship open. Commentators identify Psalm 90 as a communal lament, although it also has the elements of a hymn (vv. 1–2) and, therefore, is more of a mixed type. It contains wisdom language as well (v. 12). The occasion for its composition is divine affliction (vv. 15, 7–12). The thought moves from God as the eternal God (vv. 1–2), to man as finite man (vv. 3–6), to God angry with our sin (vv. 7–12) and concludes that God will be merciful in our need (vv. 13–17). We have before us one of the greatest prayers of Israel, which begins the fourth book of the Psalms (see *Introduction, Psalms 1–72,* Communicator's Commentary, Old Testament, no. 13, 20).

GOD IS THE ETERNAL GOD

90:1 LORD, You have been our dwelling place in all
    generations.
  2 Before the mountains were brought forth,
    Or ever You had formed the earth and the
    world,
    Even from everlasting to everlasting, You *are*
    God.

Ps. 90:1–2

In verse 1 the psalmist addresses God directly: *"Lord [ˀadōnāi], You
have been our dwelling place* ["refuge"] *in all generations."* Here a great
foundational reality is confessed. Throughout her history, God has
been home to Israel. He is like a house, filled with comfort and
security. It is not the Promised Land or ever the temple that lets
God's people be at home, but God Himself. Like the prodigal in
Jesus' parable, to go home is to go home to the "waiting Father"
(Helmut Thielicke; see Luke 15:11ff.). This is the experience of generation after generation.

God, however, preexists His creation in verse 2. Even without
Israel, He would still be God. He is no tribal deity since He exists
before *"the mountains were brought forth"* ("birthed"), or even before
He *"had formed* [literally, "to writhe in travail," "to bear"] *the earth
and the world"* (see Gen. 1:1; cf. Col. 1:16). Thus *"from everlasting to
everlasting"* ("age to age," "continually") the psalmist confesses, *"You
are God [ˀel]."*

Among twentieth-century theologians, it was Karl Barth who in-
sisted that "God is God." By this he meant that the god that the church
reveres is no *god* at all. This god is simply a construction of the modern mind and is, therefore, an idol. It is the secret way in which we
have enthroned ourselves. Thus that which is called god is in truth
humanity itself. (For example, the liberal says, "God cannot perform
miracles," or in its dispensational form the church says, "God does not
perform miracles today," telling God what He can and cannot do). If,
however, Psalm 90 is true, then God is God because He is the Creator
who has given the universe being. The life of the creation is always
derivative from Him. There can never be a confusion between God
and humankind. We have no independent existence, and since we
cannot create ourselves, we must submit to "God is God."

MAN IS FINITE MAN

90:3 You turn man to destruction,
And say, "Return, O children of men."
4 For a thousand years in Your sight
Are like yesterday when it is past,
And *like* a watch in the night.
5 You carry them away *like* a flood;
They are like a sleep.
In the morning they are like grass *which* grows
up:
6 In the morning it flourishes and grows up;
In the evening it is cut down and withers.

Ps. 90:3–6

From the confession of God as the center of Israel's security and as the eternal Creator, the psalmist now turns to man (generic, "human beings"). Thus we must always see ourselves in the light of God. To reverse the equation (as Calvin proposed was possible) can lead to theological ruin, because it puts us in danger of recreating God in our own image. In the light of who God is, the problem of man is now properly expounded in verses 3–12. The thesis is immediately given in verse 3: God *"turns [šûb] man to destruction ["crushing"]"* and, at the same time, calls him to *"return [šûb]"* or "repent."

The first sign of *"destruction"* or "crushing" is our mortality (vv. 4–6). The second sign is God's wrath against us, His "No" (vv. 7–12). There is a light at the end of the tunnel, however, because the last word is God's mercy toward us, His "Yes" (vv. 13–17). This is the content behind the call to repent.

The context in which we are turned to destruction, or crushed into dust, is the sweep of time (v. 4). For God, a millennium is *"like yesterday when it is past."* As Peter puts it, "with the Lord one day is as a thousand years, and a thousand years as one day" (2 Pet. 3:8). Again, a thousand years is *"like a watch in the night"* (four hours); it is nothing from the vantage point of eternity. Within this panorama of time, the psalmist's life speeds away, carried *"like a flood"* (v. 5). Furthermore, people are *"like a sleep,"* they are gone overnight. Or to change the metaphor, in verse 6 they are *"like grass,"* which, after a rain, springs up in the morning, *"flourishes and grows up,"* and is *"cut down"* and dead by nightfall. The deception lies in the flourishing, because even then, when the grass looks its best, the day is close to ending. Thus Isaiah says, "All flesh is grass . . . [and] the grass withers" (Isa. 40:6–7).

I was in a museum in Germany's *Schwartzwald* years ago. There I saw one of the earliest clocks ever made. On its face was carved a couple embracing, a banker with a money sack, and a priest with his prayer book. Over the face was the grim reaper who swung his scythe as the clock ticked. Inscribed in German were these words, *Alle sind mein,* "Everything is mine." As the psalmist says, "You turn man to destruction" (v. 3).

GOD IS ANGRY WITH OUR SIN

90:7 For we have been consumed by Your anger,
And by Your wrath we are terrified.
  8 You have set our iniquities before You,
Our secret *sins* in the light of Your
countenance.
  9 For all our days have passed away in Your
wrath;
We finish our years like a sigh.
10 The days of our lives *are* seventy years;
And if by reason of strength *they are* eighty
years,
Yet their boast *is* only labor and sorrow;
For it is soon cut off, and we fly away.
11 Who knows the power of Your anger?
For as the fear of You, *so is* Your wrath.
12 So teach *us* to number our days,
That we may gain a heart of wisdom.
Ps. 90:7–12

If the first sign of our destruction is our mortality, then, as we have noted, the second sign is God's wrath. Thus, the psalmist continues in verse 7 that Israel has *"been consumed* [figuratively, "destroyed"] *by Your anger."* The root of the noun *anger* is "nose." When God is angry He snorts like a wild horse (see Ps. 18:15). The psalmist continues, *"And by Your wrath we are terrified."* This terror is Israel's response to the impending judgment of God. In the Old Testament God's wrath is seen in His plagues on Egypt, in drought and famine, and in avenging enemy armies. Since He is the Lord of history, He uses the nations as the rod of His anger (see Isa. 10:5).

Israel's terror is also related to her sin, which is now addressed in verse 8. God's wrath is always His moral response to disobedience (cf. Rom. 1:17ff.). Thus the psalmist continues, *"You have set our iniquities* ['guilt'] *before You."* God not only judges public, moral violations of His will. He also addresses the sins of the heart. He sees *"our secret sins"* (cf. Matt. 5:21ff.). They stand in *"the light"* of God's *"countenance"* (literally, "face"). Here they are exposed. Even the sins that we have blocked out or denied are revealed. God's light dispels all of our darkness.

Moreover, God's wrath is not merely a particular response to a particular sin. Israel lives in a season of wrath. The psalmist laments in verse 9: *"For all our days have passed away* ['declined'] *in Your wrath,"* and he concludes, *"We finish* ['complete,' 'end'] *our years like a sigh* ['moan,' 'groan']." This *"sigh"* is both a sigh of grief and a final fleeting sound, a last breath.

The shortness of life is asserted in verse 10 (contrast v. 2). Here the human life-span can go to *"seventy years,"* or even to *"eighty, if by reason of strength,"* which in our culture would include a low-cholesterol diet and jogging. Yet, the psalmist continues with some cynicism, "Why the effort?" The years *"boast . . . only labor"* ('trouble'; cf. the curse in Gen. 3:17–19) and *"sorrow."* Then death comes. We are *"soon cut off"* and *"fly away."* We are terminal, however, not merely because of our mortality. We are terminal because of God's wrath. The psalmist asks, *"who knows* ['experiences'] *the power* ['strength'] *of Your anger?"* The implied answer is, "No one." We continue to sin and whistle in the dark. But the *"fear of You"* (the fear due to God) is due because of His *"wrath,"* and it is this wrath, as we have seen, that turns us *"to destruction"* (v. 3).

The moral, reminiscent of Proverbs, is given in verse 12. All of this meditation on our mortality (vv. 3–6) and God's wrath against sin (vv. 7–11) is designed for our instruction. The psalmist asks God to *"teach us to number our days,"* or literally, "Make us to know the number of our days." By keeping track of the calendar we will know the truth of the psalm's teachings, and we won't engage in some infantile fantasy about our omnipotence and immortality (Freud). This will give us *"a heart* ['mind'] *of wisdom."* All of this, as we have seen, is predicated upon letting God be God. We understand our days and receive wisdom as His light shines upon us.

GOD WILL BE MERCIFUL IN OUR NEED

90:13 Return, O LORD!
How long?
And have compassion on Your servants.
14 Oh, satisfy us early with Your mercy,
That we may rejoice and be glad all our days!
15 Make us glad according to the days *in which*
You have afflicted us,
The years *in which* we have seen evil.
16 Let Your work appear to Your servants,
And Your glory to their children.
17 And let the beauty of the LORD our God be
upon us,
And establish the work of our hands for us;
Yes, establish the work of our hands.

Ps. 90:13–17

The psalmist implores the Lord to *"return"* ("turn") in verse 13. As God has called Israel to repent of her sin (v. 3), so the psalmist calls upon the Lord to repent of His wrath (see v. 7; cf. Gen. 6:6; Exod. 32:14). This bold cry is immediately followed by the question, *"How long?"* The season of wrath must end. God's "No" must be lifted. The burden is too great to be borne any longer.

The call to *"return,"* is followed by a call for *"compassion."* As the sovereign King, God is to have pity on His *"servants"* (Israel).

This *"compassion"* will include *"mercy"* ("covenant-love") and bring satisfaction (v. 14). The psalmist asks for it *"early"* ("in the morning"). In other words, "Bring it now." The results will be that Israel will *"rejoice* ["give a ringing cry"] *and be glad* ["exult"] *all our days."* This outburst of worship, based on God's love restored, will give Him glory and praise.

Moreover, the psalmist asks that God will now make His people *"glad"* (see v. 14) to the same extent in which He *"afflicted"* ("humbled") them through the years in which they saw *"evil"* (v. 15; cf. v. 9). He also asks in verse 16 for God's *"work"* to *"appear"* or "be

164

seen" by His *"servants"* (Israel; see v. 13). This *"work"* will be the comprehensive grace of God in their midst. Furthermore, he requests that the next generation see God's *"glory"* ("majesty," evoking praise). As Israel's children are blessed, she is blessed.

This psalm ends with the call for *"the beauty* ['favor'] *of the Lord* [Yahweh] *our God"* to be upon His people in verse 17. This favor, ultimately, is the favor of His presence. This gives the basis for the emphatically repeated final request: *"And establish* ['make firm," "secure'] *the work of our hands for us."* Israel will only prosper in the presence of the Lord. As she builds upon Him, her work will endure. As Paul puts it, "Therefore, my beloved brethren, be steadfast, immovable, always abounding in the work of the Lord, knowing that your labor is not in vain in the Lord" (1 Cor. 15:58).

If God turns from His wrath and returns to His people, they will receive His covenant-love, His mercy, His work, His glory, and His beauty. In Him their work will be secured, and God will be God. This is the light at the end of the tunnel, and in Jesus, this light is for us (John 8:12). All other lights are at best temporary and at worst false.

CHAPTER NINETY-ONE

Dwelling in the Secret Place

Psalm 91

This is both a triumphant and a troubling psalm. It is triumphant because it guarantees that God will be our guard and guide through the evils of this life. It is troubling because it seems to be based on an unworkable theology: a theology of glory. What about suffering? What about the martyrs? What about the cross? What about children with Down's syndrome? What about Christians who pray for healing only to hear silence?

As a pastor I have had to deal with the whole range of human experience. On the streets of Hollywood in the 1960s I found prostitutes, drag-queens, runaways, drug addicts, and every conceivable diagnostic disorder. Trying to minister to these people brought me a combination of joy and sorrow both then and now. Some of the converts from that time have become mature in their faith, but many others are far from Christ today.

To change the scene, as a pastor, I have married hundreds of couples over the years. They come, in most part, smiling to the altar, faces glowing, reflecting their love and hope for the future. Few of these many marriages, however, have survived unscathed. Many have ended in divorce with children torn between their parents' conflicts. Some barely survive. Others have gone through deep waters, later to emerge with health and vitality. But how can this psalm of triumph be applied to all of these people equally?

The fact that our victory in this world is so partial forces us to look more deeply at Psalm 91. We must also remember that Satan distorted this very text by using verses 11–12 to tempt Jesus to destroy Himself by leaping from the temple (Matt. 4:5–7). One irony, as we shall see, is that this psalm is directed against demonic assault.

If Psalm 91 is unqualified in its application to all believers, then it seems contradicted by much of our experience. It is not unqualified, however. It is addressed only to those who dwell "in the secret place of the Most High" and confess God as their "refuge and fortress" (v. 1). It is these who will be protected in the midst of the battle. Neither "the terror by night" nor "the arrow that flies by day" will touch them (v. 5). God's angels will be their guards (v. 11), and even wild beasts will be under their command (v. 13). Prayers will be answered by God's presence and protection (v. 15), and the result will be salvation in all of its fullness (v. 16). The issue of this psalm becomes then, "How may we journey into these promises and see them fulfilled in our experience?"

There is no tradition of authorship associated with Psalm 91. Commentators describe its mixed form as a wisdom poem (vv. 1–13) followed by a word from God (vv. 14–16). It may be associated with the temple liturgy, where instruction in divine protection leads to God's personal response in the form of an oracle. The thought moves from the confession of God's protection (vv. 1–2) to confidence in deliverance (vv. 3–13) and concludes with God's word of salvation (vv. 14–16).

CONFESSION: GOD'S PROTECTION

91:1 He who dwells in the secret place of the Most
       High
     Shall abide under the shadow of the Almighty.
  2 I will say of the LORD, *"He is* my refuge and
       my fortress;
     My God, in Him I will trust."

Ps. 91:1–2

Verse 1 answers the question, "To whom does this psalm apply?" The promise of victory, which is its theme, is for the person who *"dwells in the secret place of the Most High"* (see Gen. 14:19–20 for this name of God). It is for no one else. The verb *to dwell* means "to remain, stay, tarry, endure, have one's abode." It suggests continuance and permanence.

Jesus identifies His disciples as those who "abide" or "dwell" in Him through eating His flesh and drinking His blood (John 6:56). They also dwell in His word (John 8:31). Above all else, they dwell in *Him* as branches dwell or abide in the vine (John 15:7–8). This abiding life, to live and remain in Jesus, is the New Testament counterpart to "dwelling in the secret place of the Most High." But what is that *"secret place?"* It is a "covering," a "hiding-place," a "shelter." It can refer to the temple (Ps. 27:5), but only because God's presence is there (Ps. 31:20).

This secret place is the intimacy of God's presence; it is our secure communion with Him. By dwelling or living in the surrender of unceasing worship and prayer (see 1 Thess. 5:16–17), we are like Moses, who was put in the cleft of the rock and covered with God's hand while His glory passed by (Exod. 33:22).

God's presence in verse 1 leads to His protection. The person who dwells in the secret place *"shall abide* ["lodge"] *under the shadow of the*

Almighty." The metaphor is that of a mother hen who gathers her chicks under her feathers. David prays, "Hide me under the shadow of Your wings, from the wicked who oppress me" (Ps. 17:8–9).

In response to God's promise in verse 1, the psalmist now gives his confession in verse 2. He will say to Yahweh, *"He is my refuge and my fortress,"* or, better, in direct address: "God, my refuge and my fortress." The imagery here is military; God is his defensive position against all enemies. Moreover, He is personal, *My God.* The psalmist concludes, *"in Him I will trust"* ("feel secure, be unconcerned").

The theme of this psalm is now clearly established; God will give complete security and victory to the person who dwells in Him and puts his trust in Him. Intimacy and faith will bear this fruit in our lives.

CONFIDENCE FOR DELIVERANCE

91:3 Surely He shall deliver you from the snare of
      the fowler
     And from the perilous pestilence.
  4 He shall cover you with His feathers,
     And under His wings you shall take refuge;
     His truth *shall be your* shield and buckler.
  5 You shall not be afraid of the terror by night,
     Nor of the arrow *that* flies by day,
  6 *Nor* of the pestilence *that* walks in darkness,
     Nor of the destruction *that* lays waste at
      noonday.
  7 A thousand may fall at your side,
     And ten thousand at your right hand;
     But it shall not come near you.
  8 Only with your eyes shall you look,
     And see the reward of the wicked.
  9 Because you have made the LORD, *who is* my
      refuge,
     Even the Most High, your dwelling place,
 10 No evil shall befall you,
     Nor shall any plague come near your dwelling;
 11 For He shall give His angels charge over you,
     To keep you in all your ways.

12 In *their* hands they shall bear you up,
   Lest you dash your foot against a stone.
13 You shall tread upon the lion and the cobra,
   The young lion and the serpent you shall
      trample underfoot.

Ps. 91:3–13

In verses 3–13, we have an extended exposition of what God will do for the person dwelling in Him. While he will experience suffering and evil in this fallen world, he will also know divine protection and deliverance.

In verse 3 the psalmist asserts, *"Surely He shall deliver* ['snatch or tear away'] *you from the snare* [trap or net] *of the fowler."* The person dwelling in God will never be a caged or eaten bird. Furthermore, God will deliver him *"from the perilous pestilence."* (The noun *pestilence* means a lethal disease; Exod. 9:15; Num. 14:12.) As we have seen, God will cover the psalmist with His *"feathers,"* hiding him *"under His wings"* (see v. 1; Ps. 61:4). Here he will *"take refuge."*

On the surface, the psalmist may be describing deliverance from human adversity. But in light of verses 5–6 (see comments below), it is probable that he has a darker enemy in mind. The fowler and the *"perilous pestilence"* become demonic agents of spiritual and physical assault. Paul warns new converts about falling "into reproach and the snare of the devil" (1 Tim. 3:7). Behind much disease stands supernatural evil. So Jesus heals a bent woman whom Satan bound for eighteen years (Luke 13:16).

In the midst of verse 4 the metaphor shifts to military equipment. The person dwelling in God's "secret place" will have *"His truth"* as a *"shield"* and *"buckler."* This shield is large, protecting the whole body. The word rendered *buckler* appears only here in the Old Testament. It probably means a round shield. The two pieces of armor illustrate the full (and double) protection offered by God's truth. In the New Testament truth is a weapon against the devil. Jesus exposes Satan with His word as He declares Himself to be the light of the world (John 8:12ff.), and Paul instructs us to wear the "whole armor of God," which includes the truth of the gospel in several aspects, "that you may be able to stand against the wiles of the devil" (Eph. 6:11).

The results of this protection are sketched in verses 5–6. The person dwelling in God's secret place will not be afraid of *"the terror* ['dread'] *by night"* (v. 5). While this could refer to a surprise military attack, it probably indicates demonic assault. (A psychologist friend of mine experienced such an attack when she awakened from a nap after midnight in a room where several clients involved in the occult had been counseled. After rebuking the demons in Jesus' name, she was able to go back to sleep.) Furthermore, the person dwelling in God's secret place will not fear the *"arrow that flies by day."* While this may have a human context, it may also be a metaphor for demonic assault coming like fiery darts (see Eph. 6:16).

In verse 6 the person hidden in God need not fear *"the pestilence that walks in darkness."* Here, in contrast to verse 3, the pestilence is qualified. It stalks at night, having a demonic character. Finally, this person is free from *"the destruction that lays waste at noonday,"* which may well represent supernatural assaults in broad daylight. From all of this human and demonic activity, the person "dwelling in the secret place of the Most High" is protected.

The promise of God's care is expressed physically in verses 7–8. While vast numbers of people are falling all around, a *"thousand . . . at your side, / And ten thousand at your right hand, it* [the plague, battle casualties, demonic conquest?] *shall not come near you"* (v. 7). The protected person walks through this holocaust of evil untouched. Moreover, he will also see the *"wicked"* ("hostile enemies," "lawbreakers") get their just reward (v. 8). In the New Testament Jesus and the early church saw God's power overcoming the works of Satan; demons were cast out as the authority of God's Kingdom was manifest. When the seventy returned to Jesus from their mission, they reported, "Lord, even the demons are subject to us in Your name." And He responded, "I saw Satan fall like lightning from heaven" (Luke 10:17–18).

Why this victory over evil? The answer is given in verses 9–13. The foundation is laid in verse 9, which repeats the promise and confession of verses 1–2. The protected person prospers because the Lord is his *"refuge"* (see v. 2) and the *"Most High"* (see v. 1) his *"habitation"* ("lair," "dwelling place"). There, living in God's presence (v. 10), *"No evil* ['distress', calamity'] *shall befall you."* Moreover, no *"plague"* ("scourge") will *"come near your dwelling"* ("tent"). His family and possessions will be safe as well. By dwelling in the

Lord, armed with His truth, we cannot be touched by Satan or his minions of evil. He cannot penetrate that secret place, near to God's heart. He cannot gain an advantage over those of us who are now held in Jesus' hand.

To be under God's shadow (v. 1), covered with His feathers (v. 4), means also to have angelic aid. God sends His supernatural messengers to have *charge over you, / To keep* ["guard," "preserve"] *you in all your ways*" (v. 11). These angels are Elisha's chariots of fire filling the mountains around us with protection against our enemies (see 2 Kings 6:17). More than once, close personal friends of mine, whose mature Christian walk I respect, have reported to me that as I have gotten up to preach the platform is filled with angels.

This angelic care is complete. These guardians bear up the protected person *"in their hands"* so that he will not even *"dash"* his *"foot against a stone"* (v. 12). Moreover, he will experience victory over all evil: treading upon *"the lion and the cobra,"* and (in parallel) trampling *"the young lion"* and *"the serpent"* (v. 13).

In the disputed ending to Mark's Gospel, Jesus promises His evangelists, "They will take up serpents; and if they drink anything deadly, it will by no means hurt them" (Mark 16:18). Paul also promises, "And the God of peace will crush Satan under your feet shortly" (Rom. 16:20). As we indicated above, the fact that the devil took these verses in this psalm and used them to tempt Jesus is ironic since this same psalm promises complete protection from malignant, supernatural evil. At the same time, that Jesus refuted the temptation and walked through untouched proves that the promises of verses 3–4 for deliverance and protection are true (see Matt. 4:1–11).

GOD'S WORD OF SALVATION

91:14 "Because he has set his love upon Me, therefore
I will deliver him;
I will set him on high, because he has known
My name.
 15 He shall call upon Me, and I will answer him;
I *will be* with him in trouble;
I will deliver him and honor him.

16 With long life I will satisfy him,
And show him My salvation."

Ps. 91:14–16

God now speaks from His "secret place" in verse 14. Because the
person who dwells there loves Him, or *"has set His love upon Him,"*
He will *"deliver him"* ("cause him to escape [all evil]"). God will be
faithful to His beloved. No demonic presence can stand before Him.
Moreover, the Lord will *"set him on high"* ("securely exalt him," see
Ps. 69:29) because he has known His name; that is, he has had an
intimate relationship with Him (cf. Exod. 3:13–14).

Out of this intimacy he will experience vital prayer: *"He will call
upon Me, and I will answer him"* (v. 15). So Jesus promises His disciples, "If you abide (dwell) in Me, and My words abide in you, you will
ask what you desire, and it shall be done for you" (John 15:7). God
will also grant His presence and protection: *"I will be with him
in trouble* ["distress"] / *I will deliver him."* Moreover, he will *"honor*
["glorify"] *him,"* give him *"long life"* (a sign of blessing), and *"show
him"* (that is, "have him experience") His *"salvation"* ("deliverance").

Here is the divine response to the person who dwells and lives in
intimacy with the Lord. He knows God's presence ("on high"), God's
power ("I will answer him"), God's protection ("I will deliver him"),
and God's provision ("I will satisfy him"). This is salvation!

For those of us who experience so much brokenness in this world,
Psalm 91 can either be a mockery or a call and a hope. If we long
for and desire greatly to be intimate with God, He promises to be
intimate with us. The road to intimacy lies in self-disclosure (John
Wimber). As we disclose ourselves to God, He will disclose Himself
to us, and Satan will be locked out of our hearts as God's Kingdom
reigns there. This is what it means to dwell in the secret place, to be
hidden and covered by the Almighty.

CHAPTER NINETY-TWO

Who Really Prospers?

Psalm 92

Throughout the Bible the question of the wicked who prosper haunts us. Justice in this world seems often so remote and relative. It is only in the presence of God that this issue can be dealt with adequately. Rather than offering a comprehensive exposition of the subject, however, the Scriptures give us a series of insights that come in particular times and places. For example, the wicked may prosper because they live under no moral restraint. They are then free to plunder widows and manipulate the courts. Their prosperity is a sign of sin, rather than a sign of God's favor upon them. In other cases, the wicked may prosper because they have sold their souls to the devil. Since he is the god of this world, and controls the kingdoms of this world, such an unholy alliance may bring in incredible wealth for a season. A current example of this is the drug traffic today. As James Mills points out in his book *The Underground Empire,* supplying illegal drugs is the largest growth industry in the world. Its annual revenues exceed half a trillion dollars. He writes, "The international narcotics industry is, in fact, not an industry at all, but an empire. Sovereign, proud, expansionist, this Underground Empire . . . never fails to present a solid front to the world at large. It has become today as ruthlessly acquisitive and exploitative as any nineteenth-century imperial kingdom. . . . Aggressive and violent by nature, the Underground Empire maintains its own armies, diplomats, intelligence services, banks, merchant fleets, and airlines. It seeks to extend its dominance by any means, from clandestine subversion to open warfare" (p. 3). Those who align themselves with this empire may prosper unbelievably, for a season.

In Psalm 92 the question of the wicked and their prosperity is raised once again (vv. 6–7). This issue is placed in the context of worship of the righteous (vv. 8–15). The authorship of this psalm is unknown. In its form it is a hymn that contains a personal statement of worship (vv. 1–4) and is resolved in the destiny of the wicked and the destiny of the righteous (vv. 8–15). The authorship of this psalm is unknown. In its form it is a hymn that contains a personal statement of worship (v. 4) and witness (vv. 10–11). The writer has enemies who remain undefined. They, however, receive divine judgment. The thought moves from our worship (vv. 1–4) to God's works (vv. 5–11) and ends with our witness (vv. 12–15).

OUR WORSHIP

> 92:1 *It is* good to give thanks to the LORD,
> And to sing praises to Your name, O Most
> High;
> 2 To declare Your lovingkindness in the
> morning,
> And Your faithfulness every night,
> 3 On an instrument of ten strings,
> On the lute,
> And on the harp,
> With harmonious sound.
> 4 For You, LORD, have made me glad through
> Your work;
> I will triumph in the works of Your hands.
> *Ps. 92:1–4*

Verse 1 begins with an affirmation of worship: *"It is good* [fulfilling and right] *to give thanks to the Lord."* This thanksgiving manifests itself in singing *"praises"* to God's *"name."* To begin with, God is worshiped as God; He is worshiped for who He is. His name is, first, *"the Lord,"* Yahweh. This is His personal name, which He revealed to Moses in the Exodus (see Exod. 3:14). He is also worshiped as *"O Most High [ʿelêyôn]."* He is the God above all gods and the God of the nations. This is expressed in Melchizedek's blessing of Abraham: *"Blessed be Abram of God Most High, / Possessor of heaven and earth"* (Gen. 14:19). Thus our God is both personal and transcendent: praise and singing are His due.

Having told us what to do in verse 1, the psalmist now tells us when to do it in verse 2. We are to bracket our day with worship, to speak of

God's *lovingkindness* ["covenant-love"] *in the morning"* and His *"faithfulness* ["trustworthiness"] *every night."* Here are two central characteristics of God (cf. Psalm 89). As we begin our day we are to praise Him for His "covenant-love," which binds us to Himself. It is this love that gives us the security and stability to face the hours ahead. We know that we are held by Him, close to His heart and, as Paul puts it, nothing "shall be able to separate us from the love of God which is in Christ Jesus our Lord" (Rom. 8:39). As we end our day we are to praise God for His *"faithfulness."* Indeed, He has brought us through another day, and He has proven Himself to be trustworthy.

But how are we to worship? This is now addressed in verse 3. We are to sing accompanied by an instrument of ten strings, *"the lute,"* and *"the harp / with harmonious sound,"* or, literally, "upon a meditation with the harp." Such singing enhances our praise.

Why do we worship? The psalmist answers this in verse 4: *"For You, Lord, have made me glad through Your work."* This *work* indicates all that God does, especially in salvation (Ps. 74:12). He continues that he will *"triumph* [literally, "shout for joy," "give a ringing cry"] *in the works of Your* [God's] *hands."* In the context, these works include the destruction of the psalmist's enemies (vv. 8–11). No wonder he shouts for joy.

In these verses we are called to worship. It is good to worship the Lord (v. 1). We are created to do so, and if we don't worship Him, we will worship some idol. True worship has its heart in praise. We are to present our songs to the Lord as we adore Him: "Therefore by Him [Jesus] let us continually offer the sacrifice of praise to God, that is, the fruit of our lips, giving thanks to His name" (Heb. 13:15).

Our worship is also to be confessional. We witness to God's love and faithfulness, and it is to be continual, day and night (v. 2). As God works, we worship. We are to live in expectation of His interventions. Thus we will shout with joy when we see Him act. Where the church is being renewed today, she is being renewed in worship. She is shouting for joy as God is moving mightily in her midst.

GOD'S WORKS

92:5 O LORD, how great are Your works!
Your thoughts are very deep.

6 A senseless man does not know,
   Nor does a fool understand this.
7 When the wicked spring up like grass,
   And when all the workers of iniquity flourish,
   It is that they may be destroyed forever.
8 But You, LORD, *are* on high forevermore.
9 For behold, Your enemies, O LORD,
   For behold, Your enemies shall perish;
   All the workers of iniquity shall be scattered.
10 But my horn You have exalted like a wild ox;
   I have been anointed with fresh oil.
11 My eye also has seen *my desire* on my enemies;
   My ears hear *my desire* on the wicked
   Who rise up against me.

Ps. 92:5–11

Having spoken in verse 4 of God's works that cause him joy, the psalmist now offers a meditation upon those works, especially as they relate to the issue of this psalm, the prosperity of the wicked. He begins by praising God: *"O Lord, how great are Your works!"* This is immediately applied to the *"thoughts"* ("devices," "plans") of God that *"are very deep"* (v. 5), namely, beyond unaided human comprehension. As God says through Isaiah, "For as the heavens are higher than the earth, / So are My ways higher than your ways, / And My thoughts than your thoughts" (Isa. 55:9). No wonder *"a senseless* ["brutish"] *man does not know,"* and a *"fool"* ("stupid fellow") does not *"understand this"* (v. 6; see Prov. 1:22). Apart from revelation we lie in darkness. As Paul puts it, "the natural man does not receive the things of the Spirit of God, for they are foolishness to him" (1 Cor. 2:14).

What are God's deep thoughts that the foolish cannot comprehend? They are given in verse 7. Although the *"wicked* ["lawbreakers"] *spring up like grass"* and the *"workers of iniquity* [those who scheme together; see Ps. 28:3] *flourish* [literally, "flower"]," this is not for their blessing but for their curse: *"It is that they may be destroyed forever."* Like flowers, they are grown to be plucked, and they pass away. In a similar vein, Paul tells us that God lets sin run its course, only to self-destruct. This is the reality of His passive wrath as He gives us over to our sin prior to His Day of Wrath (see Rom. 1:17ff.).

It is as if God lets us exalt ourselves in our pride, so that He can then humble us and exalt Himself as righteous (see Isa. 2:12–22).

As opposed to the evil workers who flourish for a moment by their own devices, God is *"on high forevermore"* (v. 8). They are lifted up unrighteously. God is lifted up righteously. They endure for a moment. He endures forever. In verse 9 the psalmist calls upon the Lord: *"For behold* ['lo!" interjection], *Your enemies, O Lord."* The emphatic, repeated clause almost becomes a curse: *"For behold, Your enemies shall perish* ["be destroyed"]*"* and the *"workers of iniquity* [see v. 7] *shall be scattered* ["separated," "dispersed"]*."* They will be separated from both God and His people (cf. Psalm 1).

While God's enemies prosper only to fall, the psalmist prospers to stand. Thus in verse 10 his *"horn"* ("strength," see Ps. 89:24) is *"exalted like a wild ox."* He has been renewed by the Lord. He has also been *"anointed with fresh oil."* This could represent a fresh filling of God's Spirit (cf. 1 Sam. 16:13). He sees God's judgment upon his enemies and hears his desire against *"the wicked / Who rise up against me"* fulfilled (v. 11). The assertion that the wicked will be destroyed (v. 7) is vindicated. God does dethrone Watergate burglars, stock market manipulators, and haughty dictators even in this life. Therefore, we are to shout with joy over God's works (v. 4). He brings down His enemies, even as they flourish (v. 7). Their season of glory is fleeting, and we are not to be taken in by it. At the same time, God renews His own. The final victory belongs to them (v. 10).

OUR WITNESS

92:12 The righteous shall flourish like a palm tree,
    He shall grow like a cedar in Lebanon.
  13 Those who are planted in the house of the
      LORD
    Shall flourish in the courts of our God.
  14 They shall still bear fruit in old age;
    They shall be fresh and flourishing,
  15 To declare that the LORD is upright;
    He is my rock, and *there is* no unrighteousness
      in Him.

                                  Ps. 92:12–15

The psalmist witnesses to the destiny of the righteous in verses 12–15. Using an agricultural simile, they are like a tree (v. 12) planted in the temple (v. 13), with a lifetime of fruitfulness (v. 14) confessing the justice of God (v. 15).

In verse 12 *"the righteous* [the one who keeps the covenant] *shall flourish* ["be fruitful"] *like a palm tree* ["date palm"]." He will also have the strength and height of *"a cedar in Lebanon"* (found in the area north of Israel; cf. Isa. 2:13). As these fruitful, strong trees are *"planted in the house of the Lord,"* that is, in the temple in Jerusalem (v. 13), they will *"flourish"* (see v. 12; cf. Ps. 1:3). The presence of God, the worship of God, the sacrifices to God, the word of God, and the people of God will all be a part of this fruitfulness. There will even be *"fruit in old age / They shall be fresh and flourishing,"* or *"*fat*"* (v. 14).

Such fruitfulness is expressed in witness in verse 15. These trees of the Lord declare that Yahweh *"is upright"* ("straight," "just"). Their confession is also personal: *"my rock* [strength]," in whom *"there is no unrighteousness* ["iniquity"]."

The question of who really prospers is answered. While the unrighteous may be fruitful for a season, their success is deceptive. Like a flower, they flourish only to be cut off forever. The wise person will see through this facade and trust in God's righteousness and judgment. It will surely come (v. 9).

The person who truly prospers is planted in Yahweh and His house. He worships Him and sees His works (v. 4). His life is fruitful even to old age (v. 14). Thus our prosperity is not to be found in this fleeting world; it is to be found in knowing the living God and being *"planted in the house of the Lord"* (v. 13).

CHAPTER NINETY-THREE

Stability in the Storm

Psalm 93

A house in the block below us was recently moved. Sliced in two and jacked up from its foundation, this little landmark was hauled off in the early morning hours. My neighbor remarked at how unnerving it all was. The house had looked so permanent; it was a part of our common landscape. Now, suddenly it was gone, extracted like a rotten tooth. Here is a little parable of life. So often people and things seem enduring, and then are "gone with the wind."

We all face being destabilized not merely by one crisis, but by many: going to college, moving, taking a job, getting married, having children, buying a house, letting children go, dealing with death. Moreover, all of these crises take their psychic toll upon us. Where can we find stability? Is there an anchor to hold us? What can we count on when all else fails?

Psalm 93 addresses the crisis of change. In the midst of the chaos of this world, there is one fixed point: the living God. His Kingdom is eternal (v. 2). He establishes the world in Himself (v. 1), and He reigns above the floods (v. 4). His testimonies are certain, and the holiness of His house is forever (v. 5). We must look beyond the flux of this life and see His glory. Since He cannot be moved, we cannot be moved either.

Commentators see this psalm as a hymn of praise. Its date and author are unknown. It is possible that it was employed in the temple (v. 5) during a ceremony celebrating God's reign (Enthronement Ceremony?). The thought moves from stability in God's reign (vv. 1–2), to stability in the storm (vv. 3–4), to stability in God's word and house (v. 5).

STABILITY IN GOD'S REIGN

93:1 The LORD reigns, He is clothed with majesty;
The LORD is clothed,
He has girded Himself with strength.
Surely the world is established, so that it
cannot be moved.
2 Your throne *is* established from of old;
You *are* from everlasting.

Ps. 93:1–2

Verse 1 opens with the joyous proclamation: *"The Lord* [Yahweh] *reigns."* There could be no shorter or more powerful confession. Its New Testament equivalent lies in 1 Cor. 12:3, "Jesus is Lord." That Yahweh reigns is at the heart of the Old Testament. It is He who has delivered Israel from Pharaoh's kingdom. As the Warrior-King, He brought His people under His rule. He also takes His vassal-servants to His own land (see Exod. 15:3ff.). He makes a treaty with them at Sinai, giving them His law to govern their life in this world (Exod. 20:1). He sits invisibly enthroned in Israel on the mercy seat of the Ark of the Covenant (Exod. 25:21–22). Thus when Israel asks for a human king, she is not rejecting the final judge, Samuel, but God from being King over her (1 Sam. 8:7). Yahweh, however, still reigns through the monarchy as His mediator. When Messiah comes, He will restore His direct rule in Israel (Psalm 2).

The psalmist, after confessing God as King, describes His apparel: *"He is clothed with majesty* ["exaltation"]," but His royal robe is not some flattering garment; it is His power: *"He has girded Himself with strength* ["might"]." This, of course, is seen as God creates, upholds, and rules the world. Listen to Moses sing of God's power: "I will sing to the Lord / For He has triumphed gloriously! / The horse and its rider / He has thrown into the sea! / The Lord is my strength and song, / And He has become my salvation" (Exod. 15:1–2). The power of God is not merely a doctrine; it is an event, an experience of deliverance.

Next, God's strength is seen in His establishing the world *"so that it cannot be moved."* This probably refers to creation. Ps. 104:5 speaks of God as "You who laid the foundations of the earth, / So that it should not be moved forever." The earth, however, has no autonomous existence. It is established because God is established. Therefore, the psalmist quickly adds in verse 2: *"Your throne is established* ["fixed," "securely determined"] *from old."* The throne of God represents the kingship and rule of God. This rule is *"from old"* because God is *"from everlasting."* Thus the world is established in the eternal God. He reigns as King (v. 1) and manifests this reign through His faithful preservation of this planet and His powerful interventions in our lives.

A young teenage girl for whom we had prayed lay dying of leukemia. During the final hours of life, she had a vision of Jesus coming to her. She told us that He was coming "to take me home." Her life was being quickly spent in time, but it was held in eternity. Her "going home" faith lifted us all to praise as she died.

STABILITY IN THE STORM

93:3 The floods have lifted up, O LORD,
   The floods have lifted up their voice;
   The floods lift up their waves.
  4 The LORD on high *is* mightier
   Than the noise of many waters,
   Than the mighty waves of the sea.

Ps. 93:3–4

The psalmist now introduces the figure of the *"floods"* ("rivers"), which *"have lifted up"* in rebellion against God (v. 3). The next phrase adds the metaphor of their *"voice."* Thus they represent more than natural chaos. Moreover, they lift *"up* [imperfect tense, "will lift up," eschatological?] *their waves* ["crushing," "pounding"]" as they batter the order of this world and threaten our life here.

A few years ago I had a very personal experience of this watery attack. I had gone swimming in the ocean near our home, and as I turned my back a wave threw me into the sand headfirst. I staggered out of the water in shock with my neck wrenched and my right arm useless. Months of immobility and pain lay ahead for me as I learned again that God alone is my security.

Over against all of this confusion stands the Lord. He is *"the Lord on high"* (transcendent) whose "throne is established from of old" and who is *"from everlasting"* (v. 2). He is *"mightier than the noise* ["voices," see v. 3] *of many waters."* When Jesus speaks to the storm, "Be still!" (Mark 4:39, literally, "be muzzled," which suggests a demonic attack, compare Mark 1:25 where the same verb is used), His voice commands the voices of the waves. Indeed, God is mightier *"than the mighty waves of the sea"* (v. 4).

STABILITY IN GOD'S WORD
AND HOUSE

93:5 Your testimonies are very sure;
Holiness adorns Your house,
O LORD, forever.

Ps. 93:5

As in verse 2, now the psalmist addresses the Lord directly. He confesses that God's *"testimonies"* ("decrees"), that is, His covenant promises and demands, *"are very sure"* ("steadfast," "trustworthy"). We can throw our weight upon them. They stand; the world does not (Isa. 40:8). Moreover, *"holiness"* [moral and ritual purity, "separateness"] *adorns* [God's] *house,"* that is, the Jerusalem temple (1 Kings 8:13) *"forever."* It is holy because the God who dwells there is holy (1 Kings 8:6, 10–11). For us, the eternal holiness of God's house refers to the risen body of Jesus (John 2:21–22) through which we have access into heaven itself (Heb. 9:24). Here is our ultimate stability in the storm, the risen, reigning Lord. Let the crisis come and go! We cannot be moved.

CHAPTER NINETY-FOUR

True Liberation Theology

Psalm 94

In the context of grinding poverty and an entrenched aristocracy in Latin America, radical theologians have called for a revolutionary faith that seeks to wed Marxism and Christianity. Taking major themes from the Exodus, they see God on the side of the poor and redemption accomplished through a violent attack on modern pharaohs. Whenever oppressive dictatorships are being overthrown, it is supposed, there is the hand of God. No salvation is possible apart from challenging the economic power-base that holds the masses in bondage. Thus the church must enter into this struggle and divest itself from defending the status quo and its own comfortable life in this world.

While there is much truth in the critique of oppressive social structures offered by the Liberation theologians, this attempt to blend biblical faith and Marxism fails on several counts. First, the assumption that by changing social structures we can change people is invalid. Too often political revolutions merely replace one oppressor with another. Yesterday's czar becomes today's politburo. Second, the understanding of evil is too shallow. Satan is the god of this world, and all humanity is bound in original sin. No wonder revolutions simply enthrone a new generation of egotists under demonic rule. Third, the source of redemption is shifted from the cross to political action, and salvation is equated with our violence rather than with Christ's sacrifice. Once again, a new theology claims salvation is attained not by God's grace but by our historical effort as we take destiny into our own hands.

One major point of the Liberation theologians, however, is valid. That is, that evil is not only personal; it is political, corporate, and institutional. While the human heart must be changed by the gospel, society also must be changed. The whole fortress of Satan must be sieged, including his supernatural principalities and powers that determine so much of our life in this world (see Eph. 6:10–20). In Psalm 94 we find true Liberation Theology because the psalmist knows both personal and institutional evil. He speaks of the proud, the wicked, and the workers of iniquity (vv. 2–4). But he sees these people in their corporate sin of injustice against the widow, the stranger, and the fatherless (vv. 6–7). Consequently he witnesses "the throne of iniquity," which "devises evil by law" (v. 20). Only God can overturn this evil (v. 17). No human revolution or resolution is enough.

The author of Psalm 94 is anonymous. Commentators identify it as an individual or national lament. It carries both prophetic and wisdom motifs. The thought moves from a call for judgment (vv. 1–3), to the indictment of the wicked (vv. 4–7), to a call for wisdom (vv. 8–11), to a blessing upon the teachable (vv. 12–15), to God's presence as protection (vv. 16–19) and concludes that God's judgment is final (vv. 20–23).

CALL FOR JUDGMENT

> 94:1 LORD God, to whom vengeance belongs—
>   O God, to whom vengeance belongs, shine
>   forth!
>   2 Rise up, O Judge of the earth;
>   Render punishment to the proud.
>   3 LORD, how long will the wicked,
>   How long will the wicked triumph?
>
> *Ps. 94:1–3*

Verse 1 addresses God directly. He is called (literally) "O God of Vengeances" (plural of fullness, that is, ultimate, final vengeance). God's *"vengeance"* includes His vindication of the righteous (vv. 16–17) and His punishment of the wicked (v. 23). The psalmist, using repetition for emphasis, next asks "O God of Vengeances" to *"shine forth"* ("beam out"). This image probably refers to God's shining with the fire of judgment (see Ps. 50:2–3). In verse 2 the psalmist calls God *"O Judge of the earth"* and asks Him to *"rise up"* (from His throne) to execute His judgment, the *"punishment"* ("recompense") of *"the proud"* (those who rebel, see Isa. 2:12). These proud are described in verse 4 as those who "speak insolent things" and "boast in themselves." They also do insolent things by breaking "in pieces Your people" (v. 5). As we shall see, in their boldness they thumb their noses at God (v. 7).

After calling upon God to act, the psalmist complains of His delay by asking (with repetition for emphasis): *"How long will the wicked* ["lawbreakers"] *triumph* ["exult"]?" Certainly, as we see the evil of this world, we can join this cry. Millions live in grinding poverty, famine stalks deforested lands, innocent babies are aborted, and addicts nod out on the streets of our cities. Indeed, how long *will* the wicked triumph?

THE INDICTMENT OF THE WICKED

94:4 They utter speech, *and* speak insolent things;
    All the workers of iniquity boast in
      themselves.
  5 They break in pieces Your people, O LORD,
    And afflict Your heritage.
  6 They slay the widow and the stranger,
    And murder the fatherless.
  7 Yet they say, "The LORD does not see,
    Nor does the God of Jacob understand."
                    Ps. 94:4-7

Who exactly are these wicked who triumph? The psalmist now answers in some detail. In the first place, they are guilty of speaking *"insolent things,"* or "they speak arrogancy." These *"workers of iniquity* [those who haughtily use words as weapons] *boast in themselves."* This is practical or functional atheism; we either boast in the Lord or boast in ourselves. This is why salvation is God's gift alone, "lest anyone should boast" (Eph. 2:9).

In the second place, they are engaged in corporate evil. The psalmist continues in verse 5: *"They break in pieces* ["crush"] *Your people, O Lord."* Israel is ground down by them. Moreover, they *"afflict* ["bow down," "humiliate"] *Your heritage."* This *"heritage"* could be the land of Canaan (Judg. 20:6), but in the context it refers to Israel (cf. Isa. 47:6).

The specifics of this indictment are given in verse 6. The wicked *"slay the widow and the stranger* ["sojourner"]*"* and *"murder"* orphans. Rather than protecting the poor, they destroy them, using the legal system to do it (v. 20). This is clear disobedience to God's law (see Exod. 22:22; 23:9; Lev. 19:9, 15, 33–34). The Lord says to His people, "Learn to do good; / Seek justice, / Reprove the oppressor; / Defend the fatherless, / Plead for the widow" (Isa. 1:17; see James 1:27).

This *"murder,"* these acts of violence (whether literal or metaphorical), toward the defenseless poor occur because of the denial of God in verse 7. The wicked claim that He *"does not see."* Like the eyes of any blind idol, His eyes are closed to what they do. Furthermore, *"the God of Jacob"* (spiritual Israel, Israel of the promise; compare Rom. 9:10–13) does not *"understand"* ("observe," "consider"). Thus when God is dethroned as judge, we are enthroned, and the result is a reign of terror.

A CALL FOR WISDOM

94:8 Understand, you senseless among the people;
     And *you* fools, when will you be wise?
  9 He who planted the ear, shall He not hear?
     He who formed the eye, shall He not see?
 10 He who instructs the nations, shall He not
     correct,
     He who teaches man knowledge?
 11 The LORD knows the thoughts of man,
     That they *are* futile.
                             Ps. 94:8–11

Although the wicked claim that God does not *"understand"* in verse 7, it is really they who do not *"understand"* in verse 8. Thus they are addressed as *"senseless"* ("brutish") and *"fools,"* those, according to Prov. 1:22, who "hate knowledge." The psalmist, however, gives an evangelical call to a whole change in perception, asking, *"When will you be wise* ["prudent," "have insight"]*?"*

First, the argument from the lesser to the greater is made in verse 9. Certainly the God who created (*"planted"*) our ears must be able to hear. The God who created (*"formed"*) our eyes must be able to see. Does God give us faculties that He Himself does not possess? Absurd!

Second, won't the God who *"instructs the nations,"* the one who *"teaches man knowledge,"* *"correct"* ("judge") Israel (v. 10)? Certainly He will not give more to all men (Ps. 19:1–4; Rom. 1:18ff.) than He gives to His covenant people.

Indeed, God hears, sees, and speaks ("teaches") because He *"knows the thoughts* ["devices," "plans"] *of men,"* which are *"futile"* ("vanity"). These empty thoughts reflect the idols that pollute our minds without the truth of God, creating a spiritual bondage over us (see Jer. 51:17–18). Thus the claims of the wicked that God does not see and understand (v. 7) are the claims of the senseless and the fools (v. 8). They reveal the futility of their thoughts when separated from God (v. 11).

BLESSING UPON THE TEACHABLE

> 94:12 Blessed *is* the man whom You instruct, O LORD,
> And teach out of Your law,
> 13 That You may give him rest from the days of
> adversity,
> Until the pit is dug for the wicked.
> 14 For the LORD will not cast off His people,
> Nor will He forsake His inheritance.
> 15 But judgment will return to righteousness,
> And all the upright in heart will follow it.
> *Ps. 94:12–15*

In contrast to the foolish, the psalmist announces a blessing for those instructed by the Lord. The word *blessed* is in the plural ("Full blessings"; see Ps. 1:1). This happy person is taught *"out of"* God's *"law."* The truth of divine revelation displaces the futile thoughts of his own mind (see v. 11). Similarly, in Ps. 1:2 the blessed man finds "his delight . . . in the law of the Lord." As Paul says, Israel's special grace is found in having the "oracles of God" (Rom. 3:2). Note that God Himself is to be our teacher (see 1 John 2:27).

The results of such instruction are now given. First, God will grant *"rest from the days of adversity."* This rest indicates a quietness or peace that comes from the fulfillment of God's promises given in His law. While we may now be experiencing *days of adversity* ("evil"), they will not last. Deliverance will come. Then *the pit* ("grave") will be *dug for the wicked* ("law breakers," see v. 3).

The assurance of this future salvation is now elaborated upon in verses 14–15. Indeed, Yahweh *will not cast off* ["abandon"] *His people, / Nor will He forsake His inheritance* (see v. 5). He will be true to His covenant. As a consequence, *"judgment* [or, better, "justice"] *will return to righteousness,"* that is, what is right or normal (ṣedeq). No longer will "the throne of iniquity" devise "evil by law" (v. 20), since justice will be expected and executed (contrast vv. 5–6). *"All the upright* ["straightforward"] *in heart will follow it."* Their own integrity will respond to the reestablishment of a just society.

Here is the promise that God will not only deal with personal evil, but also with corporate, institutional evil. His promise is nothing less than a just society under His reign, the Kingdom of God.

GOD'S PRESENCE AS PROTECTION

> 94:16 Who will rise up for me against the evildoers?
> Who will stand up for me against the workers
> of iniquity?
> 17 Unless the LORD *had been* my help,
> My soul would soon have settled in silence.
> 18 If I say, "My foot slips,"
> Your mercy, O LORD, will hold me up.
> 19 In the multitude of my anxieties within me,
> Your comforts delight my soul.
>   *Ps. 94:16–19*

The psalmist now turns from his future hope given in God's law to his present pain and asks *"who will rise up"* and protect him against *"the evildoers"* and *"the workers of iniquity"* (see v. 4). The answer, of course, is Yahweh Himself (v. 17). If He had not been his *"help"* ("succor," "assistance"), he *"would soon have settled in silence"*; that is, he would have been dead (see Ps. 115:17). But even if his *"foot slips,"* God is there in His *"mercy"* ("covenant-love") to hold him up (v. 18). The psalmist concludes, *"In the multitude of my anxieties* ["disquieting thoughts"] *within me, / Your comforts* ["consolation," plural intensive] *delight my soul* [me]."

These comforts come, to be sure, from the law of God (v. 12), but more than that, they come from the presence of God (v. 17). As He keeps His covenant (v. 18), our anxieties are put to rest.

GOD'S JUDGMENT IS FINAL

94:20 Shall the throne of iniquity, which devises evil
          by law,
        Have fellowship with You?
    21 They gather together against the life of the
          righteous,
        And condemn innocent blood.
    22 But the LORD has been my defense,
        And my God the rock of my refuge.
    23 He has brought on them their own iniquity,
        And shall cut them off in their own
          wickedness;
        The LORD our God shall cut them off.

Ps. 94:20–23

The full institutionalization of evil is disclosed in verse 20. The *"throne of iniquity"* (literally, *"destructions"*), the monarchy, or, more probably, the tribunal of justice *"devises evil* ["trouble," "mischief"] *by law."* But in doing so it is cut off from Yahweh (see v. 23). Its lawless *"justice"* is executed as the righteous are attacked and *"innocent blood"* is condemned (v. 21; see v. 6). In the midst of this "reign of terror," however, the psalmist knows Yahweh as his *"defense"* ("high place") and *"the rock of my refuge,"* that is, his fortress and the security in battle (v. 22). The *"iniquity"* of the unjust will come back upon them, and they shall be *"cut . . . off in their own wickedness* ["evil"]; / *The Lord our God shall cut them off."* This final, solemn repetition assures their fate. As the wicked execute the innocent unjustly, so they too will be executed justly by the living God.

In this psalm is true Liberation Theology. It is based on God's justice, and it is realized when God Himself, rather than our imminent historical forces, rises up to judge the earth (v. 2). The corporate structures of evil (v. 20) will be destroyed, and their pragmatic atheism (v. 7) will be found empty. Now is the time to receive divine instruction (v. 12) in the confidence that God will not abandon those who belong to Him (v. 14). Moreover, even in this age God defends the righteous against evildoers (v. 16) and upholds His covenant-love (v. 18). Finally, He Himself will come and resolve the injustice of our present history. Beyond this psalm, however, we know that this is all true because Jesus, the Son of God, has broken "the throne of iniquity" (v. 20) by defeating the devil and all of his works (1 John 3:8). This same Jesus will also return and consummate His Kingdom. Then His vengeance will shine forth, and His inheritance will be restored in a corporate world of justice for the upright in heart (v. 15).

CHAPTER NINETY-FIVE

Sing to the Lord!

Psalm 95

At the heart of my spiritual renewal there has been a renewal in worship. To be candid, for a good part of my Christian life I have been bored in church. What passes as worship has been stiff, formal, predictable, and routine. At times great hymns have inspired and instructed me and choirs singing Handel or Bach have lifted me, but these have been the exceptions rather than the rule. Moreover, as I have just implied, my worship orientation has been with *my* feelings and experiences. In college I had great aesthetic flights in the university chapel with its gothic arches and the organ cutting like a laser. For me, however, this became a short-lived substitute for the real thing—the Holy Spirit's ministry in my life and my ministry before the Lord in worship.

In 1983 I attended an evening service of the Vineyard Church in Anaheim Hills, California. That night I experienced worship which was, for me, "state of the art." Under the leadership of the pastor,

John Wimber, this church has become a dynamic center for the Holy Spirit and one of the keys to this has been a renewal in worship.

As I gathered there for my first time with about two thousand others, I noticed several things. The first was that the congregation sang for about forty minutes, uninterrupted. The second was that no hymnals or song sheets were provided because almost everyone knew the songs from memory. The third was that the songs were simple, and virtually all of them were addressed directly to either the Father, the Son, or the Holy Spirit, or all three persons of the Trinity. The fourth was that the faces and body language of the worshipers freely expressed their feelings, and the fifth was that the instrumental accompaniment was contemporary: electric guitar, bass, drums, and keyboard. This worship group, however, was not in place to "cheerlead" the congregation. They too were engaged with the whole church in worshiping the Lord. As the service progressed I was deeply moved, and although I knew few of the songs, I was able to sing along with most of them because of their simplicity. The high point for me that evening was that through the worship my mind and heart were drawn to the Lord Himself.

In Psalm 95 we are told the what, the why, and the how, of worship. Worship is directed not to ourselves but to God (v. 1), with thanksgiving as our proper mode of entrance into His presence (v. 2). The content of our worship is God Himself, our King, Creator (vv. 3–5), and Shepherd (v. 7). The act of worship means surrender and submission (v. 6). Israel's wilderness history stands as a warning against our hard, disobedient hearts (vv. 7d–11). In worship we will be softened again and again.

Commentators describe this psalm as a prophetic hymn because of the exhortation in verses 7d–11. Its date and author are unknown. It is likely that it was written for the temple liturgy (see vv. 2, 6), but it may be associated with a particular festival such as Tabernacles (see Lev. 23:33ff.). The thought moves from worship (vv. 1–7c) to warning (vv. 7d–11).

WORSHIP

95:1 Oh come, let us sing to the LORD!
     Let us shout joyfully to the Rock of our
     salvation.

2 Let us come before His presence with
    thanksgiving;
  Let us shout joyfully to Him with psalms.
3 For the LORD *is* the great God,
  And the great King above all gods.
4 In His hand *are* the deep places of the earth;
  The heights of the hills *are* His also.
5 The sea *is* His, for He made it;
  And His hands formed the dry *land.*
6 Oh come, let us worship and bow down;
  Let us kneel before the LORD our Maker.
7 For He *is* our God,
  And we *are* the people of His pasture,
  And the Sheep of His hand.

Ps. 95:1–7c

Verse 1 is both an invitation and an exhortation and tells us the what
of worship: *"Oh come, let us sing to the Lord!"* The verb *sing* means "to
sing aloud," "to shout," "to give a ringing cry." Here it expresses joy
in praise of Yahweh. Jeremiah, prophesying Israel's return from exile, sees the redeemed coming and singing ("shouting") "in the height
of Zion" (Jer. 31:12). For Isaiah, when the dead are raised they
"awake and sing (shout)" (Isa. 26:19). This is the cry of those delivered from exile and death. No wonder the psalmist continues, *"Let us
shout joyfully* [that is, "shout in triumph over enemies"] *to the Rock of
our salvation."* Yahweh is the *"Rock,"* the fortress, the secure refuge
where we are delivered.

Parallel to the opening of verse 1, in verse 2 we are exhorted
to come *"before His presence* [literally, "face"] *with thanksgiving*
["praise"]." The vehicles for this boisterous worship, (*"shout joyfully,"*
see v. 1) are *"psalms"* or "songs." Verse 3 explains why we worship
God our Rock in verse 1: *"For the Lord is the great God."* The adjec-
tive *great* separates Yahweh from all other gods (note the definite
article). So Solomon speaks of the temple: "And the temple which I
build will be great, for our God is greater than all gods" (2 Chron.
2:5). The same thought also appears in Ps. 86:10, "For You are great,
and do wondrous things; / You alone are God."

In verse 3 Yahweh is also *"the great King above all gods."* He is the
great monarch who rules all other "gods" (demonic powers manifesting themselves in idols; see Deut. 32:16–17). As such He also rules

history. Even Cyrus, the Persian king, is His anointed (Isa. 45:1).

This great King is the Creator and Sustainer of all things (vv. 4–5). The *"deep places of the earth"* (the underworld, Phil. 2:10) are in *"His hand"* and the *"heights of the hills are His also"* (v. 4). Furthermore, the *sea* (often representing chaos, see Ps. 93:3–4) is His, created by Him (Gen. 1:10), *"and His hands formed the dry land"* (v. 5; Genesis 1:9). The metaphor of God's hands stresses His immensity in relationship to creation. His hands also communicate His power and control (Exod. 15:6). Jesus says of His sheep, *"neither shall anyone snatch them out of My hand"* (John 10:28).

This meditation on the Creator leads to a new exhortation in verse 6, where we are told how to worship: *"Oh come, let us worship and bow down: / Let us kneel before the Lord our Maker."* *Worship* means to prostrate oneself in surrender and submission to a superior. Thus Moses met God, *"and bowed his head toward the earth, and worshiped"* (Exod. 34:8). Likewise to *bow down* is to assume a posture of supplication. As Ps. 72:9 says, *"Those who dwell in the wilderness will bow before Him."* Furthermore, to *kneel* represents our humility before God, the proper position of the creation confronted by the Creator: *"Our Maker."*

Here then a crucial point is made. Our worship is not centered in what we get out of church (edification or inspiration). Our worship is centered in what we give to God. Worship is the turning of our lives over to Him, nothing less. A service of worship, therefore, is a service of surrender. This reality, if expressed, will deliver us from much of the self-centered so-called worship of the modern church.

The basis for submission is given in verse 7. We worship because God is *"our God."* We belong to Him as Creator (v. 6). More than this, however, He is our Redeemer. He is personal, *"our God."* Thus *"we are the people of His pasture, / And the sheep of His hand."* The picture here is God as the shepherd of Israel (see Psalm 23) and God who feeds His people in His pasture and protects them by His hand (see Ps. 100:3). God as shepherd receives its ultimate expression when Jesus declares Himself to be the "Good Shepherd" who lays down His life for the sheep (John 10:11).

In verses 1–7c we have the what, why, and how of worship. The *what* is that we are to "sing to the Lord," "shout joyfully," and come before Him "with thanksgiving." The *why* for such praises is that He is "The Rock of our salvation," "the great God," "the great King above

all gods," "our Maker," "our God and we are the sheep of His hand."
The *how* is in our submission and surrender to Him. In this we offer
our bodies as living sacrifices—this is our "reasonable service [of
worship]" (Rom. 12:1).

WARNING

95:7 Today, if you will hear His voice:
  8 "Do not harden your hearts, as in the
      rebellion,
    As *in* the day of trial in the wilderness,
  9 When your fathers tested Me;
    They tried Me, though they saw My work.
 10 For forty years I was grieved with *that*
     generation,
    And said, 'It *is* a people who go astray in their
    hearts,
    And they do not know My ways.'
 11 So I swore in My wrath,
    'They shall not enter My rest.'"

Ps. 95:7d–11

What will keep us from worship as surrender? Simply, hard hearts.
Thus the psalmist hears Yahweh recall the Exodus tradition as appro-
priate warning. The introduction in verse 7d calls us to immediacy,
"Listen now": *Today* (see Deut. 5:3; 6:6). This word is a living word!

The Lord Himself speaks in verse 8. He warns us, as we have seen,
of hardening our *"hearts, as in the rebellion* [literally, "Meribah," "the
place of contention"], / *As in the day of trial* [literally, "Massah,"
"tempted"]." This refers to Israel's doubting God's presence in the Exodus and His subsequent provision of water from the rock. Exod. 17:7
concludes, "So he [Moses] called the name of the place Massah and
Meribah, because of the contention of the children of Israel, and because they tempted the Lord, saying, 'Is the Lord among us or not?'"

The Lord declares in verse 9 that the *"fathers* [ancestors] *tested*
["tempted," see Exod. 17:2]" Him, and *"proved"* ("tried") Him, as He
says, *"though they saw my work"* (in judgment and redemption, see Ps.
44:1ff.). This testing out of unbelief brought Yahweh grief for forty
years *"with that generation . . . who go astray in their hearts"* (literally, "a nation of wandering heart"), not knowing (or experiencing)

His *"ways"* (moral will). The forty years, of course, guaranteed that this generation would die outside the Promised Land (see Num. 14:23). Thus God *"swore"* (an oath) in His *"wrath"* ("anger"): *"'They shall not enter My rest* [Canaan].'"

As we have seen, this warning is for us now: "Today" (v. 7d). God's voice still speaks. In Heb. 3:7–11 this same exhortation, attributed to the Holy Spirit, is cited. Hebrews concludes, "Beware, brethren, lest there be in any of you an evil heart of unbelief in departing from the living God; but exhort one another daily, while it is called 'Today,' lest any of you be hardened through the deceitfulness of sin" (Heb. 3:12–13).

The answer for our hardness of heart is hearing the voice of God. This comes to us in the context of joyful worship, which is the expression of our submission to the living God, our Rock, our King, and our Creator.

As I noted above, when I experienced worship at the Vineyard, expressed in sustained, direct singing to the Lord, my hard heart was melted. The word of God cut through like a knife. Then my own renewal began.

CHAPTER NINETY-SIX

Sing to the Lord a New Song!

Psalm 96

Some years ago a friend of mine, Scott Watt, recounted being at the Vineyard in Santa Monica, California. The time of singing in a remarkable worship service became so intense that the pastor, before delivering his sermon, gave a call for people to come forward and receive Christ. The response was overwhelming, because at this moment worship had become witness. The sheer abandon of the people, and the high note of praise, became convicting. The presence and power of God were in their midst, and nonbelievers had to respond to such a manifestation of glory. This sense of worship as witness also lies at the heart of Psalm 96.

In the previous psalm (Psalm 95) worship is directed to God, coming from the heart of His people, Israel. Another note, however, appears in Psalm 96. Worship is not merely for the sake of Yahweh and His people; it is also for the sake of the nations. Thus a new song is sung to the Lord (v. 1) as His salvation and glory are declared "among the nations" (v. 3). It is now the "kindreds of the kindreds of the peoples" who are to worship Him (v. 7) as they proclaim, "The Lord reigns" (v. 10). Since God rules over all the earth, He will judge all of its peoples (v. 13). Worship is a weapon in the advancement of God's Kingdom, as He claims all creation for Himself.

While the author of this psalm is unidentified in the Psalter, 1 Chron. 16:7 attributes it to David when he brought the Ark to Jerusalem. Thus 1 Chron. 16:23–33 parallels Ps. 96:1–13. Commentators describe the form as a hymn celebrating Yahweh's kingship over all the earth. Several themes, such as the new song, the denunciation of the idols, and the exaltation of God's reign connect this psalm to sections of Isaiah 40–66, making it missionary and eschatological. The thought moves from a call to worship God as Savior (vv. 1–5) to a call to worship God as King (vv. 7–13).

WORSHIP GOD AS SAVIOR

96:1 Oh, sing to the LORD a new song!
      Sing to the LORD, all the earth.
   2 Sing to the LORD, bless His name;
      Proclaim the good news of His salvation from
         day to day.
   3 Declare His glory among the nations,
      His wonders among all peoples.
   4 For the LORD *is* great and greatly to be praised;
      He *is* to be feared above all gods.

5 For all the gods of the peoples *are* idols,
   But the LORD made the heavens.
6 Honor and majesty *are* before Him;
   Strength and beauty *are* in His sanctuary.

Ps. 96:1–6

In verse 1 the nations are to join the singing to Yahweh, who is the God of *"all the earth."* But *what* are they to sing? The answer is a *"new song"* in response to His saving work (compare v. 2). Similarly, in Isa. 42:9 God declares "new things" that will come to pass (including the redemption of Israel from bondage, Isa. 43:19–21). The exhortation follows, "Sing to the Lord a new song, / And His praise from the ends of the earth" (Isa. 42:10).

This call to sing to the Lord is repeated in verse 2 with the addition: *"bless* ['give praise to'] *His name"* (which signifies His authority and His personal presence). Worship, however, turns to witness: *"Proclaim the good news of His salvation from day to day* [that is, continually]." The verb rendered "proclaim the good news" (*bāśar*) means "to bear good tidings, to herald, or to preach," and in Isa. 40:9 its object is the coming of Yahweh to redeem His people. Here, this message of "God's gladness" (George Buttrick) centers in His *"salvation"* ("help, deliverance"); it is gospel and must be announced. In the New Testament, when the authorities seek to silence the apostles, they reply, "we cannot but speak the things which we have seen and heard" (Acts 4:20).

In verse 3 the proclamation of God's saving work includes both *"His glory"* and *"His wonders."* His *"glory"* (literally, "heavy") is the heaviness of a warrior returning from battle weighted down with the spoils of victory. His *"wonders"* are His supernatural works by which He redeems His people (see Exod. 15:11). God's glory and wonders show us the reality of His salvation. He goes into battle and intervenes on our behalf. This finds its fulfillment in Jesus Christ, who manifests the glory of God and does the work of God (John 3:36). The Bible celebrates His salvation with a new song, in which the elders and the living creatures sing to the Lamb because they have been redeemed by His blood (Rev. 5:9).

In these opening verses, the "new song" is our response to salvation. When we receive God's grace, we shout for joy, and immediately our worship turns to witness. An illustration of this comes from the ministry of Peter Cartright, the nineteenth-century circuit-riding Methodist evangelist, who once preached at a conference led by a very proper seminary student. When Cartright gave the invitation, a huge man with monstrous, ape-like arms came forward and, after throwing himself down, began to pray. He was a sinner, and he told God so loudly. At this point the seminary student rushed over and said, "Compose yourself, brother, compose yourself." But Cartright pushed him aside, slapped the penitent on the back and said, "Pray on, brother; there's no composure in hell where you're going." Finally the man broke through to God, leaped to his feet, and with a howl of delight hugged the seminary student. He picked the student up, and went dancing around, praising God at the top of his voice. Indeed, for him worship became witness.

Having told us what we are to do in verses 1–3, the psalmist tells us why we are to do it in verses 4–6. Our new song is based upon our *"great"* ("mighty") God who is *"greatly to be praised"* (v. 4; cf. Ps. 95:3). Our worship should be appropriate to its object. If our hymns are sung by rote and our prayers are mumbled, this tells us much about the God we think we are addressing. He is a fantasy of our imagination, a distant "first cause," or an absentee landlord. Yahweh, however, deserves better: great worship is deserved by a great God. Moreover, He is *"to be feared above all gods."* This fear includes a sense of awe before His supreme, almighty power. Other gods are not to be compared with Him because they are *"idols"* (v. 5). *"The peoples"* have created them, but our God *"created the heavens"* in which He dwells. When we gaze into a star-filled sky or see the sun setting into the ocean, we have some sense of God's glory.

In verse 6 the psalmist personifies *"honor"* ("splendor") and *"majesty."* They become God's kingly attendants, standing *"before Him"* (literally, "before His face"). They are then joined by *"strength"* ("might") and *"beauty"* ("glory"). All are in Yahweh's *"sanctuary,"* either the earthly tabernacle, or temple, or heaven itself where He reigns (see 1 Kings 8:27). These glorious figures are appropriate to the Lord who is great (v. 4), who covers Himself *"with light as with a garment"* (Ps. 104:2). They manifest the splendor of His presence.

God is great. He is great in His salvation, what He does. He is great in who He is, surrounded by glory inexpressible. We give our new song to Him, and in our worship, expressed in glad praise, the nations will hear our witness.

WORSHIP GOD AS KING

96:7 Give to the LORD, O families of the peoples,
Give to the LORD glory and strength.
  8 Give to the LORD the glory *due* His name;
Bring an offering, and come into His courts.
  9 Oh, worship the LORD in the beauty of
    holiness!
Tremble before Him, all the earth.
10 Say among the nations, "The LORD reigns;
The world also is firmly established,
It shall not be moved;
He shall judge the peoples righteously."
11 Let the heavens rejoice, and let the earth be
    glad;
Let the sea roar, and all its fullness;
12 Let the field be joyful, and all that *is* in it.
Then all the trees of the woods will rejoice
    before the LORD.
13 For He is coming, for He is coming to judge
    the earth.
He shall judge the world with righteousness,
And the peoples with His truth.

Ps. 96:7-13

Now we are confronted by a new call to worship in verses 7–9, which parallel verses 1–3. Here the psalmist exhorts us to give *"glory and strength"* to the Lord. All the *"kindreds* ["families"] *of the peoples,"* that is, all the families or tribes of the earth, are to join us. In this call for the universal worship of Yahweh, we hear the missionary heartbeat of this psalm.

What are we to offer to God in worship? The psalmist responds in verse 8: *"Give to the Lord the glory due His name"* (see Ps. 29:2). This glory is the praise of our hearts when we see His majesty, His beauty, His "heaviness" because of victory in battle (see v. 3). Since God's name is above every other name, and since He is our Redeemer and our Creator, His name alone is to be glorified. As He says in Isa. 42:8: "I am the Lord, that is My name; / And My glory I will not give to another."

As we come to the Lord, we are to *"bring an offering, and come into His courts."* This offering is the tribute brought to Yahweh by the nations. In Rev. 21:24 we read of the New Jerusalem, "And the nations of those who are saved shall walk in its light, and the kings of the earth bring their glory and honor into it." The entrance into God's courts by the "kindreds of the peoples" (v. 7) also indicates that the Gentiles have access into the very presence of God.

Finally, in verse 9 those who *"worship* ["surrender, bow down," see Ps. 95:6] *the Lord"* are to worship *"in the beauty of holiness."* They are to be holy as He is holy (1 Pet. 1:16). Notice that holiness is beautiful. All the stain of sin is gone. While holiness here implies ritual purity, there is more involved. For us, this holiness is now ours in Christ. As Paul says, Jesus cleanses the church "that He might present it to Himself a glorious church, not having spot or wrinkle or any such thing, but that it should be holy and without blemish" (Eph. 5:27). Our holiness, which is His gift and work, never is a ground for presumption. Thus the whole earth is to *"tremble* ["be pained"] *before Him,"* for He is the great and glorious God. Fear is a proper response when we are confronted by His numinous otherness (R. Otto).

Once again, in verse 10 worship turns to witness. The "kindreds of the peoples" (v. 7) now proclaim *"among the nations, 'The Lord reigns'"* or "Yahweh reigns" (see Ps. 93:1). This confession challenges all other gods, all other rulers and authorities. There is only one King. The line is drawn. The decision must be made: submission or destruction.

Since Yahweh reigns, *"the world is also firmly established."* The powers of chaos cannot overcome His creation, which He continues to uphold "by the word of His power" (Heb. 1:3). *"It shall not be moved."* Moreover, as King, Yahweh not only rules; He also judges. He establishes the order of His Kingdom and holds us accountable to it. Therefore, *"He shall judge the peoples righteously* ["with equity"]." This judgment is present both in His rule now and in His final judgment to come (see v. 13).

How then should the creation react to this good news that Yahweh reigns? The only adequate response is joy, because the reigning King is also our Savior (see vv. 2–3), and His judgment will be righteous and true (v. 13). Thus in verse 11 the psalmist calls upon the heavens, created by God (v. 5), to *"rejoice"* ("to take pleasure in, to exult"). The earth also is to *"be glad"* and *"the sea roar, and all its fullness"* (its waves? fish?).

In verse 12 the psalmist calls upon *"the field"* and its animals, *"all that is in it,"* to be *"joyful,"* and the trees in return will *"rejoice* ["give a ringing cry"] *before the Lord."* Why this poem of praise? The answer is given in verse 13. The God who redeems and reigns *"is coming,"* and He will *"judge the earth." "Righteousness,"* the covenant obligations given in the law, and *"truth"* ("trustworthiness") will be His standard. In that day all of those who know Him and worship Him throughout the earth will be vindicated as His reign is fully manifested.

The "new song" of this psalm embraces all the nations as the object of God's salvation, God's reign, and God's just judgment. Here is a missionary psalm, painting a wide canvas, which finds its consummation in the Son of God who accomplishes salvation, who reigns now at God's right hand, and who will return to judge the nations. We must sing and say among the nations, "The Lord reigns" (v. 10) because "Jesus is Lord" (1 Cor. 12:3).

CHAPTER NINETY-SEVEN

The Lord Reigns!

Psalm 97

It is hard for us to grasp the meaning of God's reign. With the passing of political power from the king to the people and with the elective process, which moves parties in and out of office, we no longer have a sense of stable, enduring, absolute authority centered in one person. It is common for us to think of God as our partner rather than as our Lord. It is easier for us to think that we choose to belong to Him rather than that He chooses to belong to us.

In England the symbols of an absolute monarchy are sustained, even though the power behind them has been lost. Citizens of Great

Britain are subjects of the Queen. The Bobbies in London wear E.R.II on their hats; they serve under the reign of Elizabeth II. England is her realm. To open Parliament she sits on her throne reading the ruling party's address. In the United States, however, presidents are elected by the people and pass in and out of office with limited terms. But God is more like England's monarch than like our president. He is a benevolent dictator—and dictator He is! God creates all things, orders all things, and rules all things. Even though He grants us limited freedom, He will use that very freedom for His own glory and ultimate purpose. He calls us not only to salvation but to submission. When Jesus opened His ministry in Galilee, He announced that "the Kingdom of God," that is, God's reign, God's rule, is "at hand," breaking in upon us. This was followed by the severe call: "repent and believe in the gospel" (Mark 1:15). In the words of Ian Thomas, Jesus didn't come to take sides; He came to take over.

Psalm 97 both confesses and comments upon God's reign. The great vision of the exalted King results in a series of exhortations: "Let the earth rejoice" (v. 1); "Let all be put to shame who serve carved images"; "Worship Him, all you gods" (v. 7); "You who love the Lord, hate evil!" (v. 10); and "Rejoice in the Lord, you righteous" (v. 12). This psalm serves as a corrective to our distorted vision, corrupted by our culture. Only when we see God for who He really is will we also see ourselves secure and stable under His eternal rule.

The author of this psalm is unknown. Commentators see it as one of the enthronement psalms proclaiming Yahweh's reign (see v. 1). It is written in hymnic form. The thought moves from the confession that the Lord reigns (vv. 1–6) to the exhortation that defines our proper response to this one great fact (vv. 7–12).

CONFESSION: THE LORD'S REIGN

97:1 The LORD reigns;
    Let the earth rejoice;
    Let the multitude of isles be glad!
2 Clouds and darkness surround Him;
    Righteousness and justice *are* the foundation
        of His throne.
3 A fire goes before Him,
    And burns up His enemies round about.

4 His lightnings light the world;
   The earth sees and trembles.
5 The mountains melt like wax at the presence
      of the LORD,
   At the presence of the Lord of the whole
      earth.
6 The heavens declare His righteousness,
   And all the peoples see His glory.

Ps. 97:1-6

Verse 1 opens with the assertion: *"The Lord reigns"* (see Pss. 93:1; 96:10). It is Yahweh who is enthroned in Israel. He delivers His people from Egypt as the Warrior-King. He makes His covenant with them as an emperor or suzerain would with a vassal state. While He accommodates Himself to their demand for an earthly king, He promises, one day, to reestablish His rightful, direct reign again over Israel: "Behold, the Lord God shall come with a strong hand, / And His arm shall rule for Him; / Behold, His reward is with Him, / And His work before Him" (Isa. 40:10).

This announcement that Yahweh reigns is immediately followed by a call to respond: *"Let the earth rejoice."* Not only Israel is to worship the Lord; the whole earth is to be joyful at the news that God is King. The parallel exhortation, *"Let the multitude of isles* [or *"seacoasts"] be glad* ["take pleasure in, exult"]," may refer to the coasts around Israel or to the farthest extent of the earth. In Isaiah the promise of God's messianic servant embraces the Gentiles: "the coastlands shall wait for His law" (Isa. 42:4), and He will be "a light to the Gentiles" (Isa. 42:6). The reign of Yahweh is to evoke worship from the whole earth. He made it, and He comes for it. The particularism of Israel is always for the sake of the universalism of God Himself.

In verses 2–6 we have a description of what it means for Yahweh to reign. In this theophany is the necessary corrective to our blurred, secular vision.

First of all, in verse 2, God's face is hidden. He veils His majesty as *"clouds and darkness surround Him."* On Sinai when God came down, there were "thunderings and lightnings, and a thick cloud" (Exod. 19:16). Not even Moses could see His face and live (Exod. 33:20).

Second, God is seated on His throne as the exalted ruler with *"righteousness"* (covenant order) and *"justice"* (covenant judgment) as

203

"the foundation." The community of earth will be ruled by God's law. This makes life here possible as evil is restrained and the oppressed are defended (cf Ps. 72:2).

Third, God deals with His opposition (v. 3). The *"fire"* of judgment *"burns up His enemies round about."* This was certainly true for Israel in the Exodus and in the conquest of the Promised Land. When God's people, however, became His enemies through idolatry and immorality, the fire was turned against them. It is important to remember that the national destiny of Israel is never synonymous with the moral will of God. John the Baptist cried, "Brood of vipers! Who warned you to flee from the wrath to come?" (Luke 3:7), and then added, "every tree which does not bear good fruit is cut down and thrown into the fire" (Luke 3:9).

Fourth, God manifests His glory through His *"lightnings,"* which cause the earth to see and tremble (v. 4; see Ps. 77:18). Lightning reveals Yahweh's power in the thunderstorm and brings His awesome presence near. Trembling is our appropriate response to such a display. Moreover, in verse 5 the *"mountains melt like wax at the presence of the Lord."* God is the fire that dissolves them (cf. Heb. 12:29). In 2 Pet. 3:10 we read that on the day of the Lord, "The elements will melt with fervent heat; both the earth and the works that are in it will be burned up." This, indeed, is the judgment of the one God, *"the Lord of the whole earth."*

Fifth, the heavens above *"declare"* ("have shown") God's *"righteousness,"* His covenant faithfulness to the earth. We only know of this righteousness by revelation. In response, *"all the peoples,"* the whole earth, see *"His glory."* This is the glory that God manifests through His mighty work of redemption: "Arise, shine; / For your light has come! / And the glory of the Lord is risen upon you" (Isa. 60:1). "And we beheld His glory, the glory as of the only begotten of the Father, full of grace and truth" (John 1:14).

Now the confession: *"The Lord reigns"* (v. 1), is filled with content. God reigns in heaven, surrounded with majesty. He reigns in righteousness and executes His judgments against His enemies. The world is shocked before His presence as He claims the whole earth for Himself. As the heavens announce His righteousness, He shows the earth the glory of His salvation. No wonder the earth is to rejoice and the isles are called to *"be glad"* (v. 1).

EXHORTATION: PROPER RESPONSE

97:7 Let all be put to shame who serve carved
    images,
    Who boast of idols.
    Worship Him, all *you* gods.
  8 Zion hears and is glad,
    And the daughters of Judah rejoice
    Because of Your judgments, O LORD.
  9 For You, LORD, *are* most high above all the
    earth;
    You are exalted far above all gods.
10 You who love the LORD, hate evil!
    He preserves the souls of His saints;
    He delivers them out of the hand of the
    wicked.
11 Light is sown for the righteous,
    And gladness for the upright in heart.
12 Rejoice in the LORD, you righteous,
    And give thanks at the remembrance of His
    holy name.

Ps. 97:7–12

The false gods and those who worship them are addressed in verse 7. First, those *"who serve* [that is, serve in worship] *carved images and boast of idols"* are to be *"put to shame"* ("disappointed," "disconcerted"). Their shame comes from the impotence of their idols before Yahweh. Isaiah asks, "Who would form a god or cast a graven image / That profits him nothing? / Surely all his companions would be ashamed" (Isa. 44:10–11). Second, the idols themselves must bow before Yahweh: *"Worship* ["bow down to"] *Him, all you gods."* If the idols are nothing, their worship of Yahweh is merely poetic as they are destroyed by Him. However, since demons mask themselves behind the idols, they may be the object of this call (see 1 Cor. 10:19–22).

While the idolaters are ashamed in verse 7, Zion, God's mountain in Jerusalem, *"hears and is glad"* ("exalts," v. 8). God's reign vindicates His people. Likewise, *"the daughters of Judah rejoice."* This joy comes from God's *"judgments"* against His enemies, since, as we have seen, "righteousness and justice are the foundation of His throne" (v. 2).

As the idols are cast down, God is seen to be *"most high above all the earth"* (v. 9). In this state He is *"exalted far above all gods."* Isaiah asks, "To whom will you liken God? / Or what likeness will you compare to Him?" (Isa. 40:18). The answer, of course, is that He is incomparable. The living God stands alone, judged by no one and judging all. He is both His own standard and ours. No wonder Zion rejoices. Zion knows the true and real God.

Such joy before God is shown to have moral consequences. To *"love the Lord"* means to *"hate evil"* ("distress, injury, calamity"). This appears in the form of exhortation in verse 10. At the same time, God takes care of His own: *"He preserves* ["keeps"] *the souls of His saints* [the "pious"]*"* by delivering them *"out of the hand of* [power of] *the wicked* ["lawbreakers"]*."* As the saints hate evil, God hates the evildoers.

The negative of deliverance from evil in verse 10 is now made positive in verse 11. *"Light,"* which includes revelation and salvation (cf. John 1:5; 1 John 1:5, 7), *"is sown for the righteous,"* namely, for those who keep the covenant. *"Gladness"* ("exultation") is also sown *"for the upright in heart."* Based upon this, the final exhortation in verse 12 calls for a response to grace: *"Rejoice in the Lord, you righteous."* This is the fruit of the sowing. Thanks is also to be given *"at the remembrance* ["memorial"] *of His Holy Name,"* or, "His holiness."

The exhortations in verses 7–12 are addressed to both idolaters and to the faithful. Since God reigns (vv. 1–6), the idols must fall. There is no debate. There is no election to be held. Also, since God reigns, evil must go. As the light of God's salvation is sown, there will be a harvest of joy. What we believe now in faith when we confess, "The Lord reigns," we will see in fact. As the heavenly voice says to John, "Behold, the tabernacle of God is with men, and He will dwell with them, and they shall be His people, and God Himself will be with them and be their God" (Rev. 21:3).

CHAPTER NINETY-EIGHT

Sing a Song of Salvation

Psalm 98

Momentous events need to be celebrated. I recall as a young boy going to downtown Los Angeles on the evening of Japan's surrender ending World War II. The streets were jammed with delirious people. Sailors embraced every girl they could find. Horns honked. Confetti flew. Some were drunk; all were happy. This was America's shining moment.

Great art and great music also mark turning points in human life. Who can miss the grandeur and pathos of Tchaikovsky's *1812* Overture, reflecting Napoleon's defeat at the gates of Moscow? Or who can remain seated as Handel's *Messiah* climaxes in the "Hallelujah Chorus"?

Church history also shows us that every great revival has produced new songs. Suddenly an awakened people breaks traditional forms, giving vent to their praise. This was true in the Reformation, in the Wesleyan awakening, and in the gospel music of Moody and Sankey. So in our century Pentecostalism, the charismatic movement, and the Jesus movement have all brought new worship music into the life of the church. In Psalm 98 God's marvelous works prompt the call for a new song.

Israel has experienced "marvelous things." God has acted and gained "the victory" (v. 1). Israel has experienced salvation because God has remembered His covenant (vv. 2–3). The earth is called to join in the singing with accompanying instruments and joyful shouts (vv. 4–6). Finally, all of creation must add its praise because God is coming to judge the earth and bring in His final resolution (vv. 7–9).

The author of this psalm is unknown. Commentators identify its form as a hymn of praise. A possible setting is the return of Israel from the exile, although more probably it reflects an actual battle in which God has triumphed (see v. 1). The thought moves from the call for a new song (vv. 1–3) to instruction in how to sing (vv. 4–6) and concludes with an invitation for the earth to join in because God is coming to judge (vv. 7–9).

A NEW SONG

98:1 Oh, sing to the LORD a new song!
For He has done marvelous things;
His right hand and His holy arm have gained
Him the victory.
2 The LORD has made known His salvation;
His righteousness He has revealed in the sight
of the nations.
3 He has remembered His mercy and His
faithfulness to the house of Israel;
All the ends of the earth have seen the
salvation of our God.

Ps. 98:1–3

Verse 1 sets the theme: a *"new song"* is to be sung to the Lord (see Ps. 96:1). The reasons for this immediately follow. God has *"done marvelous things."* The word rendered "marvelous things" denotes God's direct, supernatural intervention in the life of His people. These wonders are the result of God's *"right hand and His holy arm"* gaining the victory. These parts of the divine anatomy symbolize God's power and authority in battle. Moses in the Exodus sings, "Your right hand, O Lord, has become glorious in power; / Your right hand, O Lord, has dashed the enemy in pieces" (Exod. 15:6).

The Lord's victory means Israel's *"salvation"* ("deliverance") in verse 2. By God's action this salvation has been made known. God's *"righteousness,"* His covenant-faithfulness, which has bound Him to Israel, has also been *"openly shown in the sight of the nations."* Divine action has come because Yahweh *"remembered His mercy* ["covenant-love"] *and His faithfulness* ["trustworthiness"] *to the house of Israel"* (v. 3). In other words, God has kept His promise to His people and lived up to His covenant character. This divine intervention has also revealed God's salvation to *"all the ends of the earth."* The nations have seen what God has done for Israel.

No wonder the old songs are no longer appropriate! Such new intervention by Yahweh demands new music and new worship. This outbreak of joy must find its own form. The lid has been blown off, and the saints are dancing in the aisles.

A dear friend of mine, Vern Bullock, was converted in my living room some years ago. Having dropped out of society during the Vietnam War, he was hitchhiking across California with a knapsack, a guitar, and a puppy. Somehow he came to my door at the height of the Jesus movement and was led to Christ by my roommates as they studied John 3 together and talked about the new birth. Since Vern was a talented musician, after he accepted Christ, there was an explosion of new music within him. By the next evening he was in a coffeehouse in Hollywood singing about the Lord. God did a new work in Vern and gave him a new song as a result.

HOW TO SING

98:4 Shout joyfully to the LORD, all the earth;
    Break forth in song, rejoice, and sing praises.
  5 Sing to the LORD with the harp,
    With the harp and the sound of a psalm,
  6 With trumpets and the sound of a horn;
    Shout joyfully before the LORD, the King.

Ps. 98:4–6

The earth's music must be appropriate for the momentous event that it celebrates. Thus the psalmist instructs us in our response to God's act. To begin with, we are to *"shout joyfully to the Lord"* (vv. 4, 6). The meaning of the verb includes shouting a war cry, shouting in triumph over enemies, and shouting in worship. In Ps. 47:1 we read, "Oh, clap your hands, all you peoples! / Shout to God with the voice of triumph!" This joyful cry is to be made by *"all the earth,"* since all have "seen the salvation of our God" (v. 3).

In the next parallel member in verse 4, the shouting is to turn to song: *"Break forth in song, rejoice* ["give a ringing cry"], *and sing praises* ["sing psalms"]." This singing is also to be accompanied. The *"harp"* mentioned in verse 5 is an instrument of three to twelve strings. The *"trumpets"* in verse 6 were straight cylinders made of metal. The horn is the ram's horn or shophar. All of this music is to be presented *before the Lord, the King.* The final phrase in verse 6 repeats the thought of the opening phrase of verse 4: a joyful shout is to be made. All of this music is fit for royalty because God is King over Israel and over the whole earth (see Ps. 97:1).

THE EARTH JOINS IN

98:7 Let the sea roar, and all its fullness,
     The world and those who dwell in it;
  8 Let the rivers clap *their* hands;
     Let the hills be joyful together before the
       LORD,
  9 For He is coming to judge the earth.
     With righteousness He shall judge the world,
     And the peoples with equity.
Ps. 98:7–9

Here the psalmist exhorts all the earth to join in joyful worship. The sea is to roar *"and all its fullness"* (waves? fish? see Ps. 96:11). The world is also to join *"and those who dwell in it,"* including both humankind and the animals.

In verse 8, the *"rivers"* ("floods") are to *"clap their hands"* in praise before Yahweh. The *"hills"* also join in joy *"before the Lord."* Creation is personified in order to express the totality of the earth celebrating God's salvation (cf. Isa. 11:6–9; Rom. 8:21). Salvation, however, is greater than God's victory for Israel. The creation rejoices because God is *"coming to judge the earth"* (see Ps. 96:13). This judgment will be with *"righteousness"* (covenant-faithfulness) and *"equity"* ("fairness"). In describing God's final resolution, this verse anticipates the messianic kingdom. Beyond human celebration with the new song, in that day, all of creation will salute God's final Kingdom order.

That God intervenes in the penultimate, in order to deliver us from our enemies, means that God will intervene in the ultimate. Since the Kingdom has come in Jesus' first coming, we can be sure that the Kingdom will be consummated in His return. Then our new song will blend into the chorus of a renewed heaven and a renewed earth.

CHAPTER NINETY-NINE

He Is Holy!

Psalm 99

That God is holy receives little pulpit or pew attention today. In this anxious age, we want a God who makes us feel secure. In our isolation and alienation, we want a God who accepts us. We are also interested in a God who will build our self-esteem and forgive our sins. But we would rather avoid holiness with its themes of moral absolutes.

There are at least two reasons that we no longer have the luxury of this head-in-the-sand approach to holiness, however. The first is that, whether we like it or not, God is holy and ultimately we will have to deal with Him as He is. The second is that our moral malaise is tearing our nation apart. A recent edition of *Time* magazine featured this question on its cover: "What ever happened to ethics?" The subtitle read, "Assaulted by sleaze, scandals and hypocrisy, America searches for its moral bearings." Inside, *Time* quoted church historian Martin Marty, who sees a "widespread sense of moral disarray." Furthermore, Bryn Mawr political scientist Stephen Salkever notes that there once "*was* a traditional language of public discourse, based partly on biblical sources and partly on republican sources." This, however, has fallen into disuse, and now we have no common moral *lingua franca*. *Time* fails to note that the passing of a common language signifies the passing of a common world-view. The result is the chaos of moral relativity.

How can our moral landmarks be recovered? The answer lies in revival. Only out of an intense spiritual awakening can the ethical foundation be relaid and the spiritual energy be restored that will make those ethics work. But what is the key to revival? On the personal level it is sustained prayer, and on the theological level it includes a new sense of the holiness of God. This leads us to Psalm 99.

In this meditation on the greatness of the Lord's reign (v. 1), the call for us to worship Him climaxes in the statement "He is holy" (v. 3). Next, God's justice brings this exhortation: "Exalt the Lord our God, / And worship at His footstool; / For He is holy" (v. 5). Moreover, a holy God produces holy men. Moses, Aaron, and Samuel are role models for us (vv. 6–7). God answered them and forgave transgressions because "the Lord our God is holy" (v. 9).

Commentators describe this psalm as one of the enthronement psalms because of the opening statement, "The Lord reigns" (cf. Pss. 93:1; 96:10; 97:1). Its style is mixed, containing both hymnic elements and direct address to Yahweh (vv. 3, 4, 8). Its date and author are unknown. The thought moves from God's reign in holiness (vv. 1–3) to God's justice in holiness (vv. 6–7) and concludes with God's forgiveness (vv. 8–9).

GOD REIGNS IN HOLINESS

> 99:1 The LORD reigns;
>   Let the peoples tremble!
>   He dwells *between* the cherubim;
>   Let the earth be moved!
> 2 The LORD *is* great in Zion,
>   And He *is* high above all the peoples.
> 3 Let them praise Your great and awesome
>   name—
>   He *is* holy.
>
> *Ps. 99:1–3*

Verse 1 begins with triumphant proclamation: *"The Lord reigns."* God is sovereign over all. He is the great and mighty King (see Ps. 98:6). Because of His majesty, the exhortation follows: *"Let the peoples tremble."* When Isaiah sees the Lord seated on His throne, he cries out "Woe is me. . . !" (Isa. 6:5). The psalmist tells us that God *"dwells between the cherubim"* (cf. Ps. 80:1). The cherubim are angelic beings. They first appear in the Old Testament when God sends them to guard Eden after the Fall (Gen. 3:24). Later, when the Ark of the

Covenant is constructed during the Exodus, two cherubim are placed over the mercy seat, covering it with their wings (Exod. 25:19–20). They guard the portable throne of God where He is invisibly seated (1 Sam. 4:4). This symbolizes the fact that God dwells between the cherubim in heaven (Isa. 37:16). The awesomeness of the God who has these beings in His court leads to the next exhortation: *"Let the earth be moved!"* A quaking people and a quaking earth respond rightly to the reign of God.

The sense of God's majesty, which leads to trembling, prepares us for the next response. With a proper humility and fear before the Lord, we are to know that *"the Lord is great in Zion,"* God's mountain in Jerusalem (v. 2; see Pss. 2:6; 48:1–3). His greatness means that *"He is high above all the peoples."* This, of course, signifies that He reigns over all the inhabited earth. As Amos warns, God judges Damascus, Gaza, Tyre, Edom, Ammon, and Moab as well as Judah and Israel (Amos 1–2). Through Isaiah God calls the Persian King, Cyrus, *"His anointed"* (Isa. 45:1).

Because the Lord is over all, He is to be worshiped by all. So the psalmist now asks, *"Let them praise Your great"* and *"awesome* ['terrible'] *name."* Notice that this is a prayer. Only God can bring the nations to worship Him. Today He is doing this through the gospel.

The reign of God, the majesty of God among the cherubim, and the greatness of God and His name are sealed by a final phrase: *"He is holy"* (v. 3). The word *holy* means separate or distinct. There is no other being like God; He stands alone. As creatures and as sinners we are separated from Him. God's holiness also includes His moral purity. When we see God's glory, we know that we have fallen short and stand under His judgment (Rom. 3:23). Thus the Lord reigns. He reigns in holiness. This is the sure foundation upon which to build our lives.

GOD'S HOLINESS IS JUST

99:4 The King's strength also loves justice;
You have established equity;
You have executed justice and righteousness in
Jacob.

5 Exalt the LORD our God,
  And worship at His footstool—
  He *is* holy.

Ps. 99:4–5

The thesis for the next section appears poetically, *"The King's strength also loves justice"* (v. 4). This thought may be paraphrased: "The power of God is always related to justice." This means, of course, that God is never arbitrary. He always acts in relation to His moral character.

From this thesis the psalmist offers a commentary using direct address to the Lord: *"You have established equity"* ("straightforwardness"). God is fair. He continues, *"You have executed justice and righteousness in Jacob."* Jacob signifies Israel as a religious people, delivered from Egypt in the Exodus (see Ps. 20:1). With justice and righteousness, God is true to His covenant law.

The meditation on God's justice leads to another call to worship in verse 5: *"Exalt the Lord our God."* His exaltation means our humiliation. Thus the psalmist continues, *"And worship* ["bow down"] *at His footstool."* Notice that our faces are at His feet. Now the risen, reigning Christ is seated in heaven with God having "put all things under His feet" (Eph. 1:22). This meditation on God's justice concludes with the same affirmation given concerning His reign: *"For He is holy."* The Lord's justice and righteousness are absolute. This both separates Him from us and gives Him authority over us. Moreover, His holiness manifests His moral perfection. Knowing this God, then, will deliver us from our present moral chaos and reestablish His divine order in our human relationships in this world.

GOD'S LEADERS

99:6 Moses and Aaron were among His priests,
     And Samuel was among those who called
        upon His name;
     They called upon the LORD, and He answered
        them.

> 7 He spoke to them in the cloudy pillar;
>   They kept His testimonies and the ordinance
>   He gave them.

> *Ps. 99:6–7*

How can we approach this holy and just God? Moses, Aaron, and Samuel are presented as men who did exactly that. The key thought of verses 6–7 is that *"they called upon the Lord, and He answered them."*

First are Moses and his brother Aaron. Both are identified here as *"priests"* (v. 6). While Aaron was the first high priest of Israel (see Exodus 28–29), Moses carried out priestly functions. He sealed the covenant between God and Israel in blood (Exod. 24:6); He anointed the tabernacle and its priests (Exod. 40:9ff.); and he continually interceded for Israel. Samuel, as the last of the judges, was known as a prophet in Israel (1 Sam. 3:20). The common experience of their lives, as we have seen, is that these three men experienced answered prayer. The answers came as God addressed them: *"He spoke to them in the cloudy pillar"* (v. 7). This refers specifically to Moses and Aaron, who were led by *"a pillar of cloud"* in their wilderness wanderings (Exod. 13:21).

As their response to God, these men *"kept* ["preserved," "protected"] *His testimonies and the ordinance He gave them."* In other words, they upheld His law. Thus the holy God had holy men through whom He led His people. God expects nothing less than this for us today. As Peter writes, "be sober . . . as obedient children, not conforming yourselves to the former lusts, as in your ignorance; but as He who called you is holy, you also be holy in all your conduct, because it is written, 'Be holy, for I am holy.'" (1 Pet. 1:13–16).

GOD FORGIVES

> 99:8 You answered them, O LORD our God;
>   You were to them God-Who-Forgives,
>   Though You took vengeance on their deeds.
> 9 Exalt the LORD our God,
>   And worship at His holy hill;
>   For the LORD our God *is* holy.

> *Ps. 99:8–9*

Returning to addressing God directly, the psalmist reminds Him again that He *"answered them."* This refers back to Moses, Aaron, and Samuel (see v. 6). Moreover, *"You were to them God-Who-Forgives"* (as a name of God), or "You were a forgiving God to them." Here the "them" may refer to the sins of the three men, or it may refer to Israel's sins, which were forgiven through their intercession (see, for example, Moses' prayer during the fire of the Lord, Num. 11:1–2). While God forgives, He also *"took vengeance on their deeds."* Thus the wilderness generation, including Moses, failed to enter the Promised Land. The Mosaic covenant is conditional: obedience brings blessing. Disobedience brings judgment (see Deuteronomy 28). God forgives, but He is still the holy God (see vv. 4–5). It is only in the finished work of Christ that the curse is lifted from us (Gal. 3:13–14).

The psalmist's meditation on God's forgiveness and judgment leads to a final call to worship. Verse 9 closely parallels verse 5: *"Exalt* ['lift up," in praise] *the Lord our God."* However, rather than worshiping at His footstool, we are to worship *"at His holy hill"* (Zion, see v. 2). And why are we to worship? The answer is: *"For the Lord our God* [notice the expanded designation of God in the conclusion; cf. vv. 3, 5] *is holy."* He is the God who is "wholly other." He reigns (v. 1). He judges (v. 4). He answers (v. 6). He forgives (v. 8).

When we come again to this God, our moral foundation will be secure, and the "winter of our discontent" will pass.

CHAPTER ONE HUNDRED

Make a Joyful Shout

Psalm 100

Some years ago A. W. Tozer described worship as "the missing jewel in the church." As God is renewing His church today, however,

He is renewing our worship. The Vineyard in Anaheim, California, under the leadership of John Wimber, has especially been in the forefront of this renewal. In fact, this church was born out of worship. As John's wife Carol describes it, "We began worship with nothing but a sense of calling from the Lord to a deeper relationship with Him." As this group, which was then a small house fellowship, sang together, something became clear. As Carol says, "We began to see a difference between songs about Jesus and songs to Jesus." It was the songs to Jesus that created intimacy with Him. Carol continues, "About that time we realized our worship blessed God, that it was for God alone and not just a vehicle of preparation for the pastor's sermon. This was an exciting revelation. After learning about the central place of worship in our meetings, there were many instances in which all we did was worship God for an hour or two."

Psalm 100 is a jewel for worship in the Psalter. It is a literary masterpiece singing with spiritual vitality. Through this psalm we are called into God's presence based upon the revelation of who He is. This psalm also makes our worship an end in itself, rather than the means to another end, such as our own inspiration. The heart of worship is expressed in verse 4: "Be thankful to Him, and bless His name."

Commentators describe Psalm 100 as a hymn that may have served in a festival procession: "Enter into His gates with thanksgiving, / And into His courts with praise" (v. 4). Its date and author are unknown. The thought moves from praise in God's presence (vv. 1–3) to praise in God's palace (vv. 4–5).

PRAISE IN GOD'S PRESENCE

100:1 Make a joyful shout to the LORD, all you lands!
    2 Serve the LORD with gladness;
      Come before His presence with singing.
    3 Know that the LORD, He *is* God;
      It is He *who* has made us, and not we
        ourselves;
      We are His people and the sheep of His
        pasture.

Ps. 100:1–3

Verse 1 summons us into God's presence: *"Make a joyful shout to the Lord, all you lands."* The verb *joyful shout* includes a shout of triumph or a battle cry (see Ps. 98:4–6). Since God is great and greatly to be praised (Ps. 96:4), we are called to boisterous expression as we begin our worship. The whole world, *"all you lands,"* not just Israel, is to bring this shout before Him.

God looks upon the heart (1 Sam. 16:7). Behind the action of the joyful shout, there must be a proper attitude. Thus the psalmist calls us to *"serve the Lord with gladness"* ("rejoicing," v. 2). The verb *serve* means to minister. In worship, like the priests before the altar, we give ourselves to God. Similarly, Paul exhorts us to offer our bodies to the Lord as "living sacrifices," which is our "reasonable service" or ministry to Him (Rom. 12:1).

Next, our shout will turn to song: *"Come before His presence with singing."* Music is the form through which we are to express our gladness. Many people whistle or hum when they are happy. Our song is not to create our gladness but to express it.

Why this worship? The psalmist answers this question in verse 3. First of all, *"Know that the Lord* [Yahweh], *He is God."* In this affirmation the renunciation of all other gods is also implied. For example, after Elijah defeats the prophets of Baal on Mount Carmel, all the people "fell on their faces; and they said, 'The Lord, He is God! The Lord, He is God!'" (1 Kings 18:39). Since God is God, He is to be praised for *who He is,* not simply for what He has done. He is God! That's enough.

Second, He is the Creator: *"It is He who has made us, and not we ourselves."* We are not autonomous. We are not self-sufficient. We are the creation and therefore dependent upon Him for everything.

Third, beyond creation stands redemption. Thus *"we are His people."* This, of course, referred first to Israel, who was called out of Egypt to be God's son (Hos. 11:1). Now, however, the nations are also included in this call given to us in Christ (Acts 2:39). Thus the Gentiles can join in confessing, *"We are . . . the sheep of His pasture."* The metaphor of sheep assumes that God is the shepherd (see Psalm 23). Therefore, Isaiah promises, "He will feed His flock like a shepherd; / He will gather the lambs with His arm, / And carry them in His bosom, / And gently lead those who are with young" (Isa. 40:11). This picture is now fulfilled in Jesus, who presents Himself as the Good Shepherd who lays down His life for the sheep (John 10:11).

No wonder that we are to come to God with holy hilarity. He is our Creator! He is our Redeemer! He has made His name known to us. Yahweh is God, and we belong to Him.

PRAISE IN GOD'S PALACE

100:4 Enter into His gates with thanksgiving,
     And into His courts with praise.
     Be thankful to Him, *and* bless His name.
   5 For the LORD *is* good;
     His mercy *is* everlasting,
     And His truth *endures* to all generations.

                                                 Ps. 100:4-5

The scene now shifts to the temple in Jerusalem. Here, God is enthroned as King, living in His palace like any other monarch (cf. Ps. 48:2–3). Filled with joy, the worshipers ascend the temple mount. As they go through the outer gates, they are exhorted: *"Enter into His gates with thanksgiving"* (v. 4). Once again, they come to God's house with an attitude of gratitude. Next, they move to the various interior courts, being exhorted to enter them *"with praise"* ("boasting"). All of this centers in Yahweh: *"Be thankful to Him, and bless His name."* As I suggested, here is the heart of our worship. Gratitude turns now to blessing. The object of our worship is the personal God who reveals His *"name,"* which includes His presence and His authority, to us. Moreover, as He gives us His name, so He calls us by name into a relationship with Himself (see Exodus 3). This is climaxed in the Incarnation. To bless God's name is to praise Him for who He is as He relates to us.

But why should we engage in such worship? The answer is given in verse 5. First, we are to praise God because He *"is good."* The goodness of God is seen in His moral character and in His benevolence toward us. Second, we are to praise God because His *"mercy is everlasting."* *Mercy* here means covenant-love. God has bound us to Himself in a covenant or compact that He will never revoke or abandon. This promise is fulfilled for us in Jesus who, according to Hebrews, made a new covenant giving us an "eternal inheritance" (Heb. 9:15). Third, we are to praise God because *"His truth* ['trustworthiness'] *endures to all generations."* God and His self-revelation can be counted on, not only by ourselves, but by all who will follow us in years to come.

This psalm calls us to praise God. He is our God. He is our Creator. He is our Shepherd-King. He is good. He keeps His covenant. He is trustworthy. In an attitude of gladness and in actions of shouting and singing, we are to come to Him. This is the worship that blesses God. In turn, this worship will bless us as well. As Carol Wimber says, "A result of our worshiping and blessing God is being blessed by Him. We don't worship God in order to get blessed, but we are blessed as we worship Him. He visits His people with manifestations of the Holy Spirit."

CHAPTER ONE HUNDRED ONE

The State of the Union

Psalm 101

Annually, the president of the United States brings his State of the Union address before a joint session of the Congress. Here the nation's leader outlines his domestic policies for the coming legislative year. At the same time, he also raises foreign policy issues and gives his vision for the future of America. This moment is not merely a time for partisan politics. It is a time for statesmanlike leadership. Stepping into the national spotlight, the president hopes to unite the will of the people and a majority in the House and Senate behind his plans.

Similarly, in this psalm, we have a State of the Union address by the king. His concern, however, is not with domestic policy or foreign relations. His concern is with the moral character of the nation. Since the king is called by God to uphold His law and execute justice, his readiness to do this must be made known. God's blessing upon Israel is contingent upon her moral obedience. In his farewell address, Moses promises, "Now it shall come to pass, if you diligently obey the voice of the Lord your God, to observe carefully all His commandments . . . that the Lord your God will set you high above all nations of the earth" (Deut. 28:1). At the same time, however, he warns, "But it shall come to pass, if you do not obey the voice of the Lord your God, to observe carefully all His commandments . . . that all these curses will come upon you" (Deut. 28:15). This is followed by a list of specific plagues. No wonder that the king must make his moral vows before God and the people. As he sings of mercy and justice, he promises to "behave wisely in a perfect way" (vv. 1–2). This means that he will look upon nothing evil and not know wickedness (vv. 3–4). Moreover, slanderers, the proud, the deceitful and liars will be judged. The faithful will dwell with the king. But the wicked and the evil doers will be cut off (vv. 5–8).

Psalm 101 is attributed to David. We accept the traditional authorship here. As we have suggested, its form is that of a series of vows where the king affirms his moral integrity and plans. The thought moves from his vow to obey (vv. 1–2) to his vow to judge (vv. 3–8).

VOW TO OBEY

101:1 I will sing of mercy and justice;
　　　To You, O LORD, I will sing praises.
　　2 I will behave wisely in a perfect way.
　　　Oh, when will You come to me?
　　　I will walk within my house with a perfect
　　　　heart.

Ps. 101:1–2

In verse 1 David announces his intention: "*I will sing of mercy* ["covenant-love"] *and justice* ["judgment"]." Thus what follows will be sung rather than spoken. The covenant themes of "mercy" and "justice" provide the foundation for the vows to come. They determine David's response toward the wicked and the faithful. Since "mercy" and "justice" come from God, David immediately adds, *"To You, O Lord, I will sing praises."* God is worshiped because He is the source and standard of all righteousness. Mercy and justice are both His gift and our calling.

Having announced his theme and having praised God, David vows his own moral obedience to the Lord. He promises: *"I will behave wisely in a perfect way"* (v. 2). The verb *behave wisely* can also mean "consider" or "teach." Thus as the king acts in a *"perfect way"* he also teaches the people. The *"perfect way"* here means a "blameless" or an "upright" way. David will walk with moral integrity.

Next, David turns to prayer: *"Oh, when will You come to me?"* As he comes to God, he asks God to come to him. Moral perfection does not guarantee God's presence. Based upon his resolve to be blameless, David invites the Lord to come. This prayer also suggests that apart from God's presence David will never live a blameless life. He prays elsewhere, "Create in me a clean heart, O God, / And renew a steadfast spirit within me. / Do not cast me away from Your presence, / And do not take Your Holy Spirit from me" (Ps. 51:10–11).

After this brief invocation, David reinforces his resolve to behave *"in a perfect way."* He continues, *"I will walk within my house with a perfect heart."* Here David's example is set in *"his house,"* the circle of his family or his court, namely, those who are closest to him. Accountability begins at home. A *"perfect heart"* determines a *"perfect way."* The *heart* includes mind and will; David's thoughts and behavior will reflect the law of Yahweh.

The mercy and justice of God, and the worship of God, lead David to moral resolve. Holiness belongs to God and comes from being in His presence. In the gospel, what God demands from us, He gives to us. Thus as our righteousness is Christ (1 Cor. 1:30), it is also His gift to give (Phil. 3:9). As we grow in the knowledge of Him and in our love for Him, the "fruits of righteousness" will appear in our lives (Phil. 1:9–11).

VOW TO JUDGE

> 101:3 I will set nothing wicked before my eyes;
> I hate the work of those who fall away;
> It shall not cling to me.

4 A perverse heart shall depart from me;
  I will not know wickedness.
5 Whoever secretly slanders his neighbor, Him I
    will destroy;
  The one who has a haughty look and a proud
    heart,
  Him I will not endure.
6 My eyes *shall be* on the faithful of the land,
  That they may dwell with me;
  He who walks in a perfect way,
  He shall serve me.
7 He who works deceit shall not dwell within
    my house;
  He who tells lies shall not continue in my
    presence.
8 Early I will destroy all the wicked of the land,
  That I may cut off all the evildoers from the
    city of the LORD.

Ps. 101:3–8

David now expresses his moral resolve in personal detail (vv. 3–4). His eyes will not see anything wicked, the work of the apostate will not claim him, and a perverse heart will depart from him. His moral integrity prepares him for his role as judge (vv. 5–8). This will result in justice against the wicked and in the vindication of the faithful.

In verse 3 David vows to see *"nothing wicked."* The word *wicked,* "Bêlī'al" in the Hebrew, means "without worth." Later, it becomes a name for Satan (2 Cor. 6:15). David vows to guard his eyes. What we see determines what we know and what we fantasize. Jesus says, "The lamp of the body is the eye. Therefore, when your eye is good, your whole body is full of light. But when your eye is bad, your body also is full of darkness" (Luke 11:34). In this pornographic generation we must take heed.

David hates *"the work of those who fall away"* ("turn aside," "apostasize"). Those who abandon the law abandon him. He resolves that their work *"shall not cling* ["cleave," "stick"] *to me."* Moreover, if someone comes with a *"perverse* ["twisted"] *heart* ["mind"],*"* David vows that he (and it) *"shall depart from me."* His "bottom line" is: *"I will not know wickedness."* The verb *know* means knowledge by experience. With this vow, David closes his eyes to evil and separates himself from its works and its workers. Thus he will "behave wisely in a perfect way" (v. 2).

Now David is ready to execute justice. He is a judge worthy of his calling. First, he promises to *"destroy"* ("cut off") the one who *"secretly slanders his neighbor"* (v. 5). This resolve enforces the ninth commandment: "You shall not bear false witness against your neighbor" (Exod. 20:16), and includes those who lie in a court of law. Second, he vows not to endure *"the one who has a haughty look* [literally, "the proud of eyes"] *and a proud heart."* David reflects the attitude of God who promises that "the haughtiness of men shall be brought low" (Isa. 2:17).

David resolves to see *"the faithful* ["trustworthy"] *of the land"* in verse 6. His eyes shall be upon them (contrast v. 3, "I will set nothing wicked before my eyes"). It is these "covenant keepers" who *"may dwell with me."* David will be built up in his obedience as he surrounds himself with those of like character. Thus, *"He who walks in a perfect* ["blameless," see v. 2] *way, / He shall serve* ["minister to"] *me."* David staffs his court with those who embrace his lifestyle. We are not only known by the company we keep; we are kept by that same company.

A good friend of mine who had achieved substantial wealth began to spend his time on the golf course with older, retired men. In conversation one day with Billy Graham, he described his present companions. Billy's response was abrupt. He counseled, "Get rid of those people." His reason was that my friend needed to be around energetic, goal-directed companions or he would go to seed. This advice changed his social circle and changed his life.

After affirming the faithful, David addresses the wicked and their disposition (vv. 7–8). First, *"He who works deceit* ["treachery"] *shall not dwell within my house."* There will be no Judas there. (Again, *house* may mean family or court; see v. 2.) Second, the liar *"shall not continue in my presence"* (literally, "shall not be established before my eyes"). Once he is exposed, he is gone.

From a base of personal integrity in his family and court, David will bring just judgment to Israel in verse 8. He vows: *"Early* [literally, "at the mornings," or "morning by morning," which may indicate the zeal of David, starting his day early, or the time for holding court] *I will destroy* ["cut off"] *all the wicked* ["criminals," "lawbreakers"] *of the land."* His reason is to purify God's people. Thus *"the evildoers"* ("workers of iniquity") will be *cut off from the city of the Lord* (Jerusalem).

As severe as this psalm sounds, it represents not only the ministry of David, but the ministry of Jesus. He too comes to "sing of mercy and justice." He too walks "in a perfect way." He too hates wickedness. He too humbles the proud, and He too will destroy the wicked from the city of the Lord. Thus we read of the New Jerusalem, "But there shall by no means enter it anything that defiles, or causes an abomination or a lie, but only those who are written in the Lamb's Book of Life" (Rev. 21:27).

At the same time, Jesus does not merely look for the "faithful of the land"; He creates the faithful. It is only by His grace that the just judgment that we deserve falls upon Him. Thus David's royal vow is upheld by Jesus and fulfilled by Him at the same time. As Paul writes, "[God] made Him who knew no sin to be sin for us, that we might become the righteousness of God in Him" (2 Cor. 5:21).

CHAPTER ONE HUNDRED TWO

Prayer in Pain

Psalm 102

Some years ago, C. S. Lewis wrote a book entitled *The Problem of Pain.* Indeed, pain is a problem. Often people object to the goodness of God because of it. While suffering as a result of moral failure can be understood, and while pain as a reaction to harm or threat can be welcomed, there is still a vast amount of human ill that lies beyond our comprehension. Recently, a television series documented the

Jewish Holocaust in Poland under the German occupation. As participants and observers were interviewed, we saw a monstrous evil, which had descended upon victim and victor alike.

How we deal with pain is as important as the pain itself. Do we run from it? Do we rationalize it? Do we live in denial of it? Do we become cynical because of it? Or in anger, do we sink into depression and sink all those who are around us as well?

Rich Buhler, a wise radio talk-show host, said to a caller recently that we only learn through pain. It is pain that causes us to change. Pain may take us to a doctor for help. Pain may send us back to school. Pain may force us to dissolve a destructive relationship. Pain may bring us to God.

In Psalm 102 we hear a man in pain. He wants an answer from God *now* (v. 2). His days vanish like smoke. His bones are burning; his heart is stricken. His appetite is gone. He groans and wastes away (vv. 3–5). Moreover, his enemies deride him (v. 8), and God's wrath is upon him (v. 10). He withers like grass (v. 11). His strength is weakened and his days shortened (v. 23). In this pain he calls out to God. While he passes away, God endures forever (v. 12). Moreover, God has mercy on Zion (v. 13), and, therefore, "He shall regard the prayer of the destitute" (v. 17). God hears the groaning of the prisoner and looses those appointed to death (v. 20). This then becomes the psalmist's prayer: "O my God, / Do not take me away in the midst of my days" (v. 24).

The author of this psalm is unknown. Commentators identify its form as a combination of a hymn and an individual lament. The call for God to have mercy on Zion (v. 13) and the promise that "the Lord shall build up Zion" (v. 16) places its composition in the time of the Babylonian conquest (see also the reference to Zion's stones and dust, v. 14, and the prisoner, v. 20). The thought moves from the psalmist's call to God's answer (vv. 1–2), to his condition (vv. 3–11), to God's character (vv. 12–17), to God's response (vv. 18–22) and concludes with the psalmist's response (vv. 23–28).

THE PSALMIST CALLS; GOD ANSWERS

102:1 Hear my prayer, O LORD,
And let my cry come to You.

2 Do not hide Your face from me in the day of
   my trouble;
  Incline Your ear to me;
  In the day that I call, answer me speedily.

                                         Ps. 102:1–2

Verse 1 opens with a call for Yahweh's attention: *"Hear my prayer,
O Lord"* (see Ps. 143:1; cf. Ps. 61:1). The psalmist continues, *"And let
my cry ["cry for help"] come to you."* This positive petition is immediately followed by a negative: *"Do not hide Your face from me in the day
of my trouble ["distress"]"* (v. 2). Since God turns from us in His anger
(see Ps. 13:1), the request for Him not to hide His face suggests that
He has already done this (see v. 10).

Again, the psalmist asks God to hear him: *"Incline ["bend," "turn"]
Your ear to me,"* and then calls for a quick response: *"answer me
speedily."*

From these opening verses, where the request for an answer is
labored, we have a sense of God's distance. Moreover, the psalmist
is in crisis; he needs help now.

THE PSALMIST'S CONDITION

102:3 For my days are consumed like smoke,
     And my bones are burned like a hearth.
  4 My heart is stricken and withered like grass,
     So that I forget to eat my bread.
  5 Because of the sound of my groaning
     My bones cling to my skin.
  6 I am like a pelican of the wilderness;
     I am like an owl of the desert.
  7 I lie awake,
     And am like a sparrow alone on the housetop.
  8 My enemies reproach me all day long;
     Those who deride me swear an oath against
       me.
  9 For I have eaten ashes like bread,
     And mingled my drink with weeping,
  10 Because of Your indignation and Your wrath;
     For You have lifted me up and cast me away.

> 11 My days *are* like a shadow that lengthens,
>   And I wither away like grass.
>
>   *Ps. 102:3–11*

We learn why the psalmist cries out to the Lord to hear and answer; his condition is critical.

First of all, his days *"are consumed like smoke"* (v. 3). In his pain they have no substance or meaning. Next, his *"bones* [frame?] *are burned like a hearth."* This may be a poetic description of a fever or a literal description of inflammation of the joints. Furthermore, his *"heart is stricken* ["smitten"] *and withered like grass"* (v. 4). The *"heart"* here is equivalent to the "self." The psalmist is dried up inside with a resulting loss of appetite: *"So that I forget to eat my bread."* This has led to a significant weight loss: *"Because of the sound of* [literally, "the voice of"] *my groaning* ["sighing"] / *My bones cling to my skin"* (v. 5).

This literal description of distress is expressed poetically in verses 6–7. First, the psalmist is *"like a pelican of the wilderness."* Since pelicans are coastal birds, he is like a fish out of water. Next, he is *"like an owl of the desert."* The owl is unclean (see Lev. 11:17) and therefore represents his loneliness and rejection. Finally, the psalmist lies *"awake"* (literally, "I watch," suggesting sleeplessness); he is *"like a sparrow alone on the housetop."*

In verses 8–11 the psalmist turns from his physical and emotional state to the other causes of his pain: his enemies and God's wrath. In such distress he is hounded by his foes. They *"reproach* ["taunt," "scorn"] *me all day long"* (continually) and they *"swear an oath against me"* (v. 8); that is, they place a curse upon him. They conclude that because of his pain he is cursed by God, and they join in that curse.

The psalmist agrees with his enemies. He has *"eaten ashes like bread,"* the ashes representing grief and loss (v. 9; see Esther 4:1ff.). He also weeps, mingling his tears with his drink. And what is the reason for this torment? *"Because of Your indignation and Your wrath"* (v. 10). He continues, *"For You have lifted me up and cast me away."* He has been thrown out, excommunicated (see vv. 6–7). Now he is at the sunset of his life. His days *"are like a shadow that lengthens"* (v. 11); he dries up *"like grass"* (see v. 4). The heat of God's wrath sucks him dry.

Behind the psalmist's pain is a theology that says that sin brings divine wrath. His sickness is the result (cf. John 9:2; James 5:16). The psalmist, however, never addresses his sin. He does not offer a prayer of confession. Rather he is simply aware of the results he is experiencing: personal pain, his enemies' rejection, and the sense of God's distance. Is the psalmist ignorant of his sin? Is he in denial? We cannot know. His distress is comprehensive and real. Even though he may not know its cause, he knows its solution and that is to turn to the living God.

GOD'S CHARACTER

102:12 But You, O LORD, shall endure forever,
> And the remembrance of Your name to all
> generations.
13 You will arise *and* have mercy on Zion;
> For the time to favor her,
> Yes, the set time, has come.
14 For Your servants take pleasure in her stones,
> And show favor to her dust.
15 So the nations shall fear the name of the LORD,
> And all the kings of the earth Your glory.
16 For the LORD shall build up Zion;
> He shall appear in His glory.
17 He shall regard the prayer of the destitute,
> And shall not despise their prayer.
18 This will be written for the generation to
> come,
> That a people yet to be created may praise the
> LORD.
19 For He looked down from the height of His
> sanctuary;
> From heaven the LORD viewed the earth,
20 To hear the groaning of the prisoner,
> To release those appointed to death,
21 To declare the name of the LORD in Zion,
> And His praise in Jerusalem,
22 When the peoples are gathered together,
> And the kingdoms, to serve the LORD.

Ps. 102:12-22

As we suggested above, the issue is not whether we shall have pain. The issue is what we shall do with it. Here, for the psalmist, pain becomes redemptive. He is not even put off by his perception of God's wrath. Beyond the "No" of that wrath is the "Yes" of God's grace (Karl Barth). Thus he cries out: *But you, O Lord* (v. 12).

The first thing that the psalmist now considers is the eternity of God; He *shall endure* [literally, "dwell"] *forever*" (see vv. 24, 26–27). Time and people pass. God remains. In calling upon God, he calls on the God who is "the Alpha and the Omega, the Beginning and the End . . . who is and who was and who is to come" (Rev. 1:8). Since God "endures forever," all future generations will also remember His name (v. 12).

Next, Yahweh will *arise* [from His throne, and go into action] *and have mercy* ["compassion"] *on Zion,*" His holy mountain in Jerusalem (v. 13; for Zion see Ps. 48:1–2). The time has now come for Him *to favor* ["be gracious to"] *her.*" It is likely that this thought denotes the passing of the judgment of the Exile (cf. Isa. 40:1). That this time of mercy is also a *set time*" suggests that in His gracious action God will be fulfilling His prophetic promises. Furthermore, Yahweh's mercy occurs in response to the love of Israel for Jerusalem. Even in her ruins, His *servants* [those who serve Him in worship] *take pleasure in her stones, / And show favor* ["grace"] *to her dust* (v. 14). As God shows the same favor by restoring Zion, *the nations*" shall *fear*" ("reverence") His name, and *the kings of the earth*" His *glory.*" This glory is the praise evoked by God when He intervenes to redeem His people.

The psalmist comes to a ringing conclusion in verse 16: *For the Lord shall build up Zion.*" As He does this, *He shall appear in His glory.*" The return of Israel will display God's *glory*" ("heaviness," the "heaviness" of a warrior praised for the spoils he brings home from battle). Furthermore, *He shall regard* ["turn to"] *the prayer of the destitute* [those praying for the return from Exile], / *And shall not despise their prayer*" (v. 17).

As God is to be remembered to all generations (v. 12), so now in being gracious to Zion *this will be written* ["recorded"] *for the generation to come,*" that it may *praise the Lord*" (v. 18).

The summary of the record is given in verses 19–22. First of all, God *looked down from the height of His sanctuary* ["holy place"]; / *From heaven the Lord viewed the earth*" (v. 19; cf. Exod. 2:23–25).

Second, as He looked, He heard *"the groaning of the prisoner"* (the captive in exile). He also looked in order that He might intervene, *"to loose* ["free"] *those appointed to death* [literally, "the sons of death"]*"* (v. 20). Third, as a result, His name will be declared *"in Zion, / And His praise in Jerusalem"* (v. 21). To bring His people home is to restore His name (presence and authority) and His worship. This is given an eschatological note in verse 22. As a result of God's action *"the peoples"* (races, tribes) and *"the kingdoms"* (authorities) will be gathered *"to serve* ["minister to"] *the Lord."* Isaiah promises, "Now it shall come to pass in the latter days / That the mountain of the Lord's house / Shall be established on the top of the mountains, / And shall be exalted above the hills; / And all nations shall flow to it" (Isa. 2:2).

Yahweh is the living God. He sees; He hears; He acts. Worship is the proper response to what He has done. But what does this have to do with the psalmist's pain? Perhaps he is among the prisoners waiting to go home to Jerusalem. Apart from this, however, it is clear that if God shows mercy to His people and restores the fortunes of Zion, then God may well show mercy to him. Likewise, we too should take heart. The same God will show mercy to us, and He has done so in His Son. Jesus is our "welcome home" from the heart of God.

THE PSALMIST'S RESPONSE

102:23 He weakened my strength in the way;
    He shortened my days.
  24 I said, "O my God,
    Do not take me away in the midst of my days;
    Your years *are* throughout all generations.
  25 Of old You laid the foundation of the earth,
    And the heavens *are* the work of Your hands.
  26 They will perish, but You will endure;
    Yes, they will all grow old like a garment;
    Like a cloak You will change them,
    And they will be changed.
  27 But You *are* the same,
    And Your years will have no end.
  28 The children of Your servants will continue,
    And their descendants will be established
      before You."

Ps. 102:23–28

The psalmist looks at himself first and returns to prayer (vv. 23–24). Then he looks at God who is eternal and concludes by extolling His greatness (vv. 25–28).

In verse 23 the psalmist restates his condition (cf. vv. 3–11). He has known God's wrath: *"He weakened* ["afflicted," "humbled"] *my strength in the way; / He shortened my days."* To have his strength weakened "in the way" means that he was struck down before he completed his destination. Death pressed in on him as his days were shortened.

At the same time, however, the psalmist prayed: *"I said, O my God, / Do not take me away in the midst* ["in half"] *of my days."* Up against death, he simply asks to be spared. This is the heart of his prayer and cry to God (vv. 1–2). Sometimes, the simple prayers are best. In pain and urgency, we get to the point quickly.

As the psalmist cries out in his mortality, he immediately thinks of God's eternity: *"Your years are throughout all generations"* (see v. 12). It is God who created the world: *"Of old You laid the foundation of the earth"* (v. 25). Moreover, *"the heavens are the work of Your hands"* (v. 25; see Gen. 1:1). This means, of course, that God preexisted His creation. The earth and the heavens are passing: *"They will perish, but You will endure* ["stand"]*"* (v. 26). Now, using a simile, the psalmist depicts them growing old *"like a garment."* Continuing the thought, they are *"like a cloak,"* which God will change. The creation is finite and transitory. It will both be destroyed and changed, or transformed. So we read in 2 Pet. 3:10, "But the day of the Lord will come as a thief in the night, in which the heavens will pass away with a great noise, and the elements will melt with fervent heat: both the earth and the works that are in it will be burned up." Peter concludes, "Nevertheless, we, according to His promise, look for a new heaven and a new earth in which righteousness dwells" (2 Pet. 3:13).

In the midst of decay, destruction, and transformation, the psalmist interjects an emphatic antithesis: *"But You are the same* [see v. 12], / *And Your years will have no end"* (v. 27). This also means that Yahweh will be the God of generations yet to come: *"The children of Your servants* [see v. 14] *will continue* [literally, "will dwell"], / *And their descendants* ["seed"] *will be established before You."* God will hold and keep His people that they may worship Him (see v. 18).

In conclusion we may ask, what does the psalmist learn in his pain? First, he learns to pray large prayers. Second, he becomes honest before God in his lament. Third, he meditates upon God's eternal nature and His mercy to Zion in confidence that Yahweh will restore His people. Fourth, this leads the psalmist to ask that wrath be lifted and life restored (v. 24). This psalm leaves us with two crucial questions. First, does our pain bring us to God or drive us from God? Second, if it brings us to God (as it should) what do we learn from Him?

CHAPTER ONE HUNDRED THREE

Mercy over All

Psalm 103

A friend of mine was battling with a serious drug problem. I agreed to help him get a job through some mutual acquaintances, and no sooner had he started to work than he relapsed and stayed up all night doing coke. Failing to make our breakfast date the next day, I found him drunk, trying to come down from his drug high with whiskey. Since he drove the company van he couldn't call in sick, so I drove both him and the van out to the plant where he worked. As we approached our destination, he was in a state of panic asking over and over, "What shall I say?" Finally, I responded, "Tell the truth."

As we went into the building, we were greeted by the woman who was his direct superior. She took one look at him and asked what was wrong. He replied, "I blew it and got stoned last night." Her response was simple, direct, and from God's heart. She put her arm around him and said, "We are a family here, and I am a recovering alcoholic. Go home and get some sleep and come back tomorrow." Finding that the owner was also in the office, I took my friend to see her. She, too, asked what was wrong. After he told her what had happened, she took his hand, prayed for him to have victory over his addiction, and then drove him home to sleep. What my friend expected was judgment. He planned to be fired. What he received, however, was mercy, and in this he experienced a parable of the gospel.

Psalm 103 is one of the high points in the Psalter, revealing the mercy of God. Here we are crowned with "tender mercies" (v. 4). Here God is identified as "merciful and gracious," "slow to anger, and abounding in mercy" (v. 8). Here God's mercy is described as so great "as the heavens are high above the earth" (v. 11). Here "the mercy of the Lord is from everlasting to everlasting" (v. 17). No wonder the psalmist addresses himself: "Bless the Lord, O my soul; / And all that is within me, bless His holy name" (v. 1).

Tradition ascribes this psalm to David. Most scholars reject this because of the close analogies in the text to Isaiah 40–66. At the same time, no one knew more of God's mercy than David (cf. Psalm 51), and we accept his authorship here. The form of Psalm 103 is that of a hymn or meditation since it contains no direct address to God. The thought moves from a call to worship the merciful God (vv. 1–5), to the triumph of God's mercy (vv. 6–10), to the greatness of God's mercy (vv. 11–14), to the eternity of God's mercy (vv. 15–18) and concludes with a call to worship the eternal King (vv. 19–22).

WORSHIP THE MERCIFUL GOD

103:1 Bless the LORD, O my soul;
    And all that is within me, *bless* His holy name!
2 Bless the LORD, O my soul,
    And forget not all His benefits:
3 Who forgives all your iniquities,
    Who heals all your diseases,
4 Who redeems your life from destruction,
    Who crowns you with lovingkindness and
        tender mercies,
5 Who satisfies your mouth with good *things*,
    So that your youth is renewed like the eagle's.
                    Ps. 103:1–5

Verse 1 shows, in Kierkegaard's phrase, the "self transcending itself" as David speaks to his soul: *"Bless the Lord, O my soul; / And all that is within me, bless His holy name."* What does it mean to bless God? Scharbert answers that the Hebrew verb (in the *piel*) "always means to express solemn words that show the appreciation, gratitude, respect, joint relationship, or good will of the speaker, thus promoting respect for the one being blessed. . . . When God is the object, *brk* . . . should always be rendered 'praise'" ("*brk*," in *Theological Dictionary of the Old Testament,* vol. 2). David's praise is given to *"the Lord,"* that is to Yahweh (God as personal) and to *"His holy name"* (God as transcendent presence and authority). As he blesses this God, he throws himself fully into his worship; he gives *"All that is within me."* His worship is a "living sacrifice" (Rom. 12:1).

The call to bless God is repeated in verse 2 with the added thought: *"And forget not all His benefits* ["dealings"]*."* Thus David gives all that is within himself to God and remembers all that God has done for him. Memory is always one of our best aids in worship.

God's benefits are elaborated upon in verses 3–5. God's first benefit is that He *"forgives all your iniquities* ["deviations from the norm," "guilt"]*"* (v. 3). Forgiveness is the foundation for fellowship. Thus the prophetic call is always to repent, and the gospel promises that confession of sin brings cleansing (1 John 1:9). The second benefit is that God *"heals all your diseases."* The link between forgiveness and healing is clear. In fact much of our physical and emotional illness is psychogenic, due to moral failure. The only relief is God's forgiveness, which will result in healing (so James 5:16). Notice also that healing is part of the blessing of salvation. Jesus proclaimed the Kingdom and cast out demons and healed diseases (see Matt. 4:23; Luke 6:17–19).

The third benefit from God is that He *"redeems* ["rescues"] *your life from destruction* [literally, "the pit"]*"* (v. 4). This may well be a consequence of God's healing. *"Destruction"* would be the pit of death (see Ps. 28:1). Ultimately, of course, God redeems us from eternal death. As Jesus promises: "I am the resurrection and the life. He who believes in Me, though he may die, he shall live. And whoever lives and believes in Me shall never die" (John 11:25–26).

The fourth benefit from God is that He *"crowns you with loving-kindness* ["covenant-love"] *and tender mercies* [plural intensive, "compassion"]." The symbol of being crowned suggests that our royal glory and authority are divine love and mercy. Thus Paul sees believers as reigning with Christ "that in the ages to come He might show the exceeding riches of His grace in His kindness toward us in Christ Jesus" (Eph. 2:7).

The fifth benefit is that God *"satisfies your mouth with good things"*; that is, physical strength and health are pleasurably restored and *"your youth is renewed like the eagle's."* So Isaiah promises, "But those who wait on the Lord / Shall renew their strength; / They shall mount up with wings like eagles" (Isa. 40:31).

No wonder, then, that David commands his soul to bless God. His benefits are full and satisfying, and they climax in the crown of God's "lovingkindness and tender mercies" (v. 4).

THE TRIUMPH OF GOD'S MERCY

103:6 The LORD executes righteousness
And justice for all who are oppressed.
7 He made known His ways to Moses,
His acts to the children of Israel.
8 The LORD *is* merciful and gracious,
Slow to anger, and abounding in mercy.
9 He will not always strive *with us,*
Nor will He keep *His anger* forever.
10 He has not dealt with us according to our sins,
Nor punished us according to our iniquities.
Ps. 103:6–10

Now David shows God's mercy for sinners. He begins with the fact that the Lord *"executes* [literally, *"works"*] *righteousness"*; that is, He manifests His faithfulness to His covenant and *"justice"* ("judgment") on behalf of *"all who are oppressed"* (v. 6). This is documented from the Exodus. *"He made known His ways* [character? plans?] *to Moses, / His acts to the children of Israel."* In His deliverance of His people from bondage, God shows His *"righteousness,"* and in His judgments on Pharaoh God shows His *"justice"* or judgment. Revelation is not merely in what God says; it is also in what God does. We see this supremely in Jesus Christ who comes to bear the word of God and perform the work of God. In a fellow pastor's phrase, He is the "Word-Worker."

Moreover, Yahweh is *merciful and gracious* (v. 8). In the Exodus He proclaims to Moses: "The Lord, the Lord God, merciful and gracious, long-suffering, and abounding in goodness and truth, keeping mercy for thousands, forgiving iniquity and transgression and sin" (Exod. 34:6–7). Moreover, He is *slow to anger.* His wrath is not easily provoked. He is *abounding in mercy* ("covenant-love"). Therefore, David concludes, *"He will not always strive* ["contend," as in a law court] *with us, / Nor will He keep* ["maintain"] *His anger forever"* (v. 9). There is a limit to God's wrath; it is temporal, not eternal. Furthermore, *"He has not dealt with us according to our sins,* [actions which miss the mark] */ Nor punished us according to our iniquities* ["crookedness," deviations from the path]." The point is that if God gave us what we deserved we would all perish. For example, in the Exodus, Israel along with Egypt should have lost her firstborn to the angel of death. But God provided a substitute in the Passover lamb. Therefore, He did not deal with His people according to their sins. By what right do we stand before God now? We have no inherent right. God provides that right for us, however, in Jesus, the "Lamb of God who takes away the sin of the world" (John 1:29). Again, God does not deal with us according to our sins. Indeed, God's mercy is triumphant. It "triumphs" over His wrath, and it triumphs over our sin. As Paul says, "But where sin abounded, grace abounded much more" (Rom. 5:20).

THE GREATNESS OF GOD'S MERCY

103:11 For as the heavens are high above the earth,
　　　So great is His mercy toward those who fear
　　　Him;
　　12 As far as the east is from the west,
　　　So far has He removed our transgressions from
　　　us.
　　13 As a father pities *his* children,
　　　So the LORD pities those who fear Him.
　　14 For He knows our frame;
　　　He remembers that we *are* dust.

Ps. 103:11–14

David now sketches the dimensions of God's mercy. First of all, *"as the heavens are high above the earth, / So great is His mercy* ["covenant-love"] *toward those who fear* [are in awe of] *Him"* (v. 11). God's mercy, therefore, towers over us. When we look into the clear blue sky or see the most distant star, we must remember that God's mercy is higher still. Notice also that God's mercy connects to our *"fear."* As we are humbled before Him in reverence and awe, He reaches out and touches us with His forgiveness and love.

Second, after describing the vertical dimension of God's mercy, David continues with the horizontal, *"As far as the east is from the west, / So far has He removed our transgressions* ["willful acts of rebellion"] *from us."* In this engaging comparison, David assures us that as east and west will always be opposite and separated, so too will we always be separated from our sins. Notice that this is God's act: *"He has removed"* them from us. This removal ultimately takes place in the cross. As Isaiah promised, this is what God has done: "And the Lord has laid on Him the iniquity of us all" (Isa. 53:6).

Finally, it is the divine *"pity"* ("compassion"), like a father to his children, that has bought this great mercy to *"those who fear Him"* (v. 13; for *fear*, see v. 11). Moreover, God's *"pity"* is toward us because He understands us, *"He knows our frame* ["form"]; */ He remembers that we are dust"* (v. 14). Thus He remembers how He has created us. So we read in Gen. 2:7: "And the Lord God formed man of the dust of the ground."

It is God's vast mercy, beyond all physical dimensions, that has taken away our sins. God looks at our frailty, our weaknesses, our struggles, and He has pity on us. In the Incarnation, God takes the next step. He becomes one with us and shares in our humanity. As Hebrews says, "For we do not have a High Priest who cannot sympathize with our weaknesses, but was in all points tempted as we are, yet without sin" (Heb. 4:15).

THE ETERNITY OF GOD'S MERCY

103:15 *As for* man, his days *are* like grass;
As a flower of the field, so he flourishes.
16 For the wind passes over it, and it is gone,
And its place remembers it no more.

17 But the mercy of the LORD *is* from everlasting
    to everlasting
   On those who fear Him,
   And His righteousness to children's children,
18 To such as keep His covenant,
   And to those who remember His
    commandments to do them.

Ps. 103:15–18

David continues to meditate upon our human weaknesses (see v. 14). Our days are like the grass (v. 15). We flourish *"as a flower of the field."* Then, the *"wind passes over it, and it is gone."* Moreover, it is forgotten: *"And its place remembers it no more"* (v. 16). Isaiah writes, "All flesh is grass, / And all its loveliness is like the flower of the field. / The grass withers, the flower fades, / Because the breath ['wind'] of the Lord blows upon it; / Surely the people are grass" (Isa. 40:6–7). This, indeed, is our human pathos. The Middle East is a great graveyard of ancient civilizations now ground into dust. Their monuments, buried in the sand, are silent testimony to the truth in these verses. We flourish for a season, and then, like the desert winds blowing across the fields, we are carried away, forgotten, and gone.

Nevertheless, there is another option. It is the God who remembers us (see v. 14). His *"mercy* ["covenant-love"] *is from everlasting to everlasting"* (v. 17). And this eternal mercy is *"on those who fear Him."* Moreover, *"His righteousness"* (see v. 6) is *"to children's children."* It courses down the generations. This mercy and righteousness are for those who *"keep His covenant / And to those who remember His commandments to do them"* (v. 18). The Lord in His mercy remembers those who remember Him. They believe in Him and obey Him. While they live in time they are grounded in eternity, knowing God's eternal mercy as their own.

WORSHIP THE ETERNAL KING

103:19 The LORD has established His throne in heaven,
       And His kingdom rules over all.
    20 Bless the LORD, you His angels,
       Who excel in strength, who do His word,
       Heeding the voice of His word.

21 Bless the LORD, all *you* His hosts,
   You ministers of His, who do His pleasure.
22 Bless the LORD, all His works,
   In all places of His dominion.
   Bless the LORD, O my soul!

Ps. 103:19–22

The God who keeps us is the God who transcends time and space. Thus David proclaims: *"The Lord has established His throne* [authority] *in heaven"* (v. 19; see Ps. 102:19). While we pass away, He does not. Moreover, *"His kingdom rules over all."* All are, therefore, under His sovereignty.

Since God is King (see Ps. 99:1), all must worship Him. Thus David concludes this meditation on God's mercy by calling upon all of creation to join in his praise. First, the heavenly angels, *"who excel in strength, who do His word, / Heeding the voice of His word,"* are to bless the Lord (v. 20). These mighty, supernatural beings surround God's throne and obey His bidding as His messengers (see Luke 1:11, 19; 2:9). Second, the hosts, the *"ministers of His, who do His pleasure,"* are to bless the Lord (v. 21). They are the angelic armies, which are a part of the celestial court (see Luke 2:13; Matt. 26:53). Third, all the rest of creation, *"all His works, / In all places of His dominion* ["realm"],*"* are to bless the Lord (v. 22). Finally, David joins the chorus, echoing verse 1, *"Bless the Lord, O my soul!"*

Psalm 103 displays the mercy of God. To our amazement, we do not get what we deserve. We deserve rejection; we get acceptance. We deserve wrath; we get mercy. We deserve hell; we get heaven. We deserve the devil; we get Jesus. As I mentioned in the introduction, my friend, high on drugs, deserved to get fired. Instead, he got a good night's sleep and a parable of the gospel. Indeed, God's mercy is over all.

God's Care for Creation

Psalm 104

With the rise of Enlightenment, philosophers supposed that nature ran itself by laws of cause and effect. A rational God had created a rational world to be understood by rational people. Everything in the closed system of the universe could be easily comprehended. It was as if God were a celestial clockmaker who had made the perfect timepiece, wound it up, and then stepped out to let it run. Any interference would upset or stop the clock. This philosophy, it was supposed, gave great glory to God. The perfection and order of all things mirrored His perfection and order. In fact, however, it made God irrelevant. He was reduced to a "first cause" and man was left, if not to run the show, then at least to understand the show by his autonomous reason. Thus, God had abdicated His authority, and man was in charge. To be sure, demons would rush into this moral and spiritual vacuum, as the Enlightenment gave way to bloody world wars beyond anyone's comprehension. Moreover, "gangster politicians" (Paul Johnson) would arise after the bright light of reason was overpowered by the dark side of life. Hitler and Stalin quickly stepped to center stage.

Today, scientists are more humble than the Enlightenment philosophers. They see an expanding universe that holds both order and indeterminacy in dynamic tension. It is just this indeterminacy that opens the door for a God who holds all things together in His governing, providential care. In fact, the God of the Bible shows His intensive care for this planet. This is the thesis of Psalm 104.

In this psalm the broad canvas of creation is surveyed. God is praised for His glory, revealed in the heavens. Everywhere His active presence is seen. The clouds are His chariot (v. 3), and His angels minister as flames of fire (v. 4). Moreover, God creates the earth

and its waters. He also gives them their proper boundaries (vv. 5–9).
He provides the earth's water supply (vv. 10–13), grows its vegetation, and arranges its hills (vv. 14–18). The seasons and the days are
ordered by Him (vv. 19–23); so also is the sea and its contents
(vv. 24–26). God is Lord over life and death, birth and renewal
(vv. 27–30). Everywhere His active presence is seen. This thesis is
well summed up in verse 27, where the psalmist asserts: "[the living
creatures] all wait for You." God is not an absent clockmaker. He is
the mainspring of all that He has made.

The author of this psalm is unknown. Commentators identify it as
a nature psalm, which doesn't tell us much. The style alternates between hymnic meditation and direct address to God in praise. The
psalm also reflects the themes of Genesis 1 and wisdom literature
(cf. Job) with its descriptions of nature. The thought moves from
blessing and extolling God's greatness (vv. 1–2), to the heavens (vv.
3–4), to the earth and the waters (vv. 5–9), to the springs and the
rain (vv. 10–13), to the vegetation and the hills (vv. 14–18), to the
seasons and the days (vv. 19–23), to the sea (vv. 24–26), to life and
death (vv. 27–30) and concludes with benedictions (vv. 31–32),
vows, and final praise (vv. 33–35).

BLESSING AND EXTOLLING
GOD'S GREATNESS

104:1 Bless the LORD, O my soul!
    O LORD my God, You are very great:
    You are clothed with honor and majesty,
  2 Who cover *Yourself* with light as *with* a
       garment,
    Who stretch out the heavens like a curtain.
Ps. 104:1–2

Verse 1 opens with the psalmist addressing himself: *"Bless the Lord,
O my soul!"* (cf. Ps. 103:1). To bless Yahweh is to bring praise to Him.
The highest act of the human spirit is offered to Him. This is the
purpose of our creation, and it is also the goal of redemption. As Jesus
says to the woman at the well: "But the hour is coming, and now is,

when the true worshipers will worship the Father in spirit and truth; for the Father is seeking such to worship Him" (John 4:23).

Having offered his praise, the psalmist turns to the glory of God: *"O Lord my God, You are very great."* Notice that this God is also personal. He is *"my God."* As a sign of His greatness, God is robed with kingly *"honor* ['splendor'] *and majesty."* (Ps. 21:5 describes the king blessed by God: "Honor and majesty You have placed upon him.") God is covered *"with light as with a garment"* (v. 2). Likewise, John tells us that "God is light and in Him is no darkness at all" (1 John 1:5). This light communicates His holiness and is self-revealing. Finally, God stretches *"out the heavens like a curtain."* With this thought we move from the Creator to the creation. The heavens are made by Him and controlled by Him (see Gen. 1:1). This clause also serves as a transition to the next section of the psalm.

THE HEAVENS

104:3 He lays the beams of His upper chambers in the
        waters,
      Who makes the clouds His chariot,
      Who walks on the wings of the wind,
    4 Who makes His angels spirits,
      His ministers a flame of fire.

Ps. 104:3–4

Now the psalmist details the heavens. *"The beams of His* [God's] *upper chambers"* are laid down *"in the waters"* (v. 3). These beams are the foundations which support God's palace. The noun *upper chamber* denotes a room on the roof. Such chambers were atop Solomon's temple (1 Chron. 28:11; 2 Chron. 3:9) and are appropriate for God's heavenly dwelling. The *"waters"* here are the waters above the firmament (Gen. 1:7). God is enthroned over them. Moreover, He *"makes* ['sets'] *the clouds"* as *"His chariot."* Jesus is taken up from the earth in a cloud (Acts 1:9) and will return "in the clouds with great power and glory" (Mark 13:26). God also *"walks on the wings of the wind"* (see Ps. 18:10 where He "flew upon the wings of the wind"). Both the clouds and the wind display God's sovereignty over nature and symbolize His transcendent glory. Furthermore, He creates and commands the angels. He makes them *"spirits* [or *"*winds"] / *His ministers* ["servants"] *a flame of fire"* (v. 4). Is it possible that these angelic presences account for the wind and fire on the Day of Pentecost? (See Acts 2:2–3.) Note also that verse 4 is quoted in Heb. 1:7 and is used to contrast the ministering angels with the enthroned Son of God.

God reigns as King above the heavens, commanding the clouds, the wind, and His ministering angels as He rules over the earth.

THE EARTH AND THE WATERS

104:5 *You who* laid the foundations of the earth,
So *that* it should not be moved forever,
6 You covered it with the deep as *with* a
garment;
The waters stood above the mountains.
7 At Your rebuke they fled;
At the voice of Your thunder they hastened
away.
8 They went up over the mountains;
They went down into the valleys,
To the place which You founded for them.
9 You have set a boundary that they may not
pass over,
That they may not return to cover the earth.
Ps. 104:5–9

The psalmist's thought moves to this planet. It is God who *"laid the foundations of the earth"* (v. 5; cf. Eph. 1:4). Thus in creation He secured the earth *"so that it should not be moved forever."* This does not mean that the earth is eternal. It does mean that it will not *"be moved"* ("totter," "slip," "fall") into chaos or autonomy, because God made it, upholds it, and will keep it always. In the fullness of God's Kingdom, the Bible sees not a destroyed earth but a renewed earth (see 2 Pet. 3:13).

God covered the earth *"with the deep,"* like a garment to be worn (v. 6; see Gen. 1:2). Thus *"the waters stood above the mountains."* They then receded; *"At your rebuke they fled"* (v. 7). Likewise, as God thundered (poetic for commanded) *"they hastened away"* (v. 7). The waters then flowed *"over the mountains"* (as the land appeared) and *"went down into the valleys,"* as streams coursing toward the sea (v. 8). The waters went *"to the place which you founded for them."* Here they are held within the bounds of the ocean that they may not *"return to cover the earth"* (v. 9). So we read in Gen. 1:9: "Then God said, 'Let the waters under the heavens be gathered together into one place, and let the dry land appear'; and it was so."

God not only creates the earth with its seas and continents; He also rules it. He commands the waters, and they flee (v. 7). He establishes a place for them (v. 8). He sets their boundary (v. 9). He is in charge.

THE SPRINGS AND THE RAIN

104:10 He sends the springs into the valleys;
They flow among the hills.
11 They give drink to every beast of the field;
The wild donkeys quench their thirst.
12 By them the birds of the heavens have their
home;
They sing among the branches.
13 He waters the hills from His upper chambers;
The earth is satisfied with the fruit of Your
works.

Ps. 104:10–13

Although the waters of the deep have gone to the oceans, God still provides the needed moisture for the earth. Thus *"He sends the springs into the valleys"* from the hills above (v. 10). These springs supply *"every beast of the field,"* here represented by *"wild donkeys"* who *"quench their thirst"* (v. 11). At the same time, they provide for the *"birds of the heavens"* (v. 12). In response, *"these birds sing* ["give voice"] *among the branches."*

Rainfall also accompanies the natural springs. In verse 13 God *"waters the hills from His upper chambers"* (see v. 3). Since He dwells above the watery firmament, He opens His windows and sends the showers. Likewise, in the flood "the windows of heaven were opened" (Gen. 7:11). As a result, *"the earth is satisfied* ["sated"] *with the fruit of Your* [God's] *works."* Again, we see God's active, providential care for His earth. As Jesus says, "He makes His sun rise on

the evil and on the good, and sends rain on the just and on the
unjust" (Matt. 5:45).

THE VEGETATION AND THE HILLS

104:14 He causes the grass to grow for the cattle,
      And vegetation for the service of man,
      That he may bring forth food from the earth,
   15 And wine *that* makes glad the heart of man,
      Oil to make *his* face shine,
      And bread *which* strengthens man's heart.
   16 The trees of the LORD are full *of sap,*
      The cedars of Lebanon which He planted,
   17 Where the birds make their nests;
      The stork has her home in the fir trees.
   18 The high hills *are* for the wild goats;
      The cliffs are a refuge for the rock badgers.

Ps. 104:14–18

With the earth watered, God *"causes the grass to grow for the
cattle, / And vegetation for the service of man"* (v. 14). The noun
vegetation means "herb." As Gen. 1:29 says, "See, I have given
you every herb that yields seed which is on the face of all the earth,
and every tree whose fruit yields seed; to you it shall be for food."

Now humankind is able to farm the land. God's purpose is *"that he
may bring forth food* [literally, "bread"] *from the earth."* This includes
the grape that produces *"wine,"* which *"makes glad the heart of man,"*
and *"oil"* from the olive tree, *"to make his face to shine"* (v. 15). This
oil protects and cleanses the skin. It is a sign of blessing: "You anoint
my head with oil" (Ps. 23:5). Finally, there is *"bread which strengthens*
["supports"] *man's heart."* These foods are the staples of life in Israel.

Beyond grass and food there are the trees. In verse 16 the NKJV
reads, *"The trees of the Lord are full of sap."* The Masoretic Text, however, has "the trees of the Lord will be satisfied," meaning that they
will be blessed. The trees are specifically named *"the cedars of
Lebanon which He planted."* Notice that it is Yahweh who puts these
trees in Lebanon. They provide habitation for the birds who nest
there (v. 17), again made specific by *"the stork* [who] *has her home in
the fir trees* [cypress?]." Beyond the vegetation there are the hills:

246

"The high hills are for the wild goats; / the cliffs are a refuge for the rock badgers" (v. 18).

In this passage God designs and controls the ecosystems of nature. Man and beast are fed from the earth. Trees provide for the birds, and hills and cliffs house appropriate animals. All of this again reveals the direct care of God Himself. He makes it all happen.

THE SEASONS AND THE DAYS

104:19 He appointed the moon for seasons;
   The sun knows its going down.
 20 You make darkness, and it is night,
   In which all the beasts of the forest creep
    about.
 21 The young lions roar after their prey,
   And seek their food from God.
 22 *When* the sun rises, they gather together
   And lie down in their dens.
 23 Man goes out to his work
   And to his labor until the evening.
         Ps. 104:19–23

It is God who *"appointed the moon for seasons* ['set times']*"* (v. 19). In Canaan the Hebrew year followed the West Semitic calendar with a year of twelve lunar months. The first day of each new month was considered holy. Thus the monthly "new moon" was associated with the weekly Sabbath (see Isa. 1:13; Col. 2:16). Unlike her neighbors, for Israel the moon is no god. It functions under Yahweh's rule.

Next, *"The sun knows its going down."* This happens by God's design: *"You make darkness, and it is night"* (see Gen. 1:4–5). Now *"all the beasts of the forest creep about"* (v. 20). This is made specific by the *"young lions who roar after their prey, / And seek their food from God"* (v. 21).

After the night passes, *"the sun arises,"* and the lions return to their dens *"and lie down"* to sleep (v. 22). It is man's turn to work now, and he does *"his labor* ['service'] *until the evening."* So God commands, *"Six days you shall labor"* (Exod. 20:9). In his work he reflects the creative work of God (cf. Gen. 2:2–3).

God commands the calendar. The seasons and the nights and days are His.

THE SEA

104:24 O LORD, how manifold are Your works!
        In wisdom You have made them all.
        The earth is full of Your possessions—
     25 This great and wide sea,
        In which *are* innumerable teeming things,
        Living things both small and great.
     26 There the ships sail about;
        There is that Leviathan
        Which You have made to play there.

                                    Ps. 104:24–26

In verse 24 the psalmist pauses to declare the greatness of creation: *"O Lord, how manifold are Your works!"* This reflects both what has preceded and what is yet to come. He continues, *"In wisdom You have made them all."* Prov. 3:19 reads, "The Lord by wisdom founded the earth; by understanding He established the heavens." God's wisdom is seen in the way in which all of creation works together under His sovereign will.

Since God is the Creator, the psalmist continues, *"The earth is full of Your possessions."* Paul speaks of Christ as the agent of creation and declares, "all things were created through Him and for Him" (Col. 1:16). Everything is under His copyright. Everything is stamped with His trademark. Everything is signed with His name (see Job 41:11).

The psalmist documents God's ownership in verse 25 by looking at *"this great and wide sea"* (the Mediterranean), filled with *"innumerable teeming things, / Living things both small and great."* "Ships sail" upon it (v. 26). And *"Leviathan,"* made by God, plays there. *Leviathan* may be a whale. In Job 41 he appears like a dragon. Those who hold to a young earth theory suggest he could be a dinosaur (Henry Morris).

LIFE AND DEATH

104:27 These all wait for You,
        That You may give *them* their food in due
          season.
     28 *What* You give them they gather in;

> You open Your hand, they are filled with
> good.
> 29 You hide Your face, they are troubled;
> You take away their breath, they die and
> return to their dust.
> 30 You send forth Your spirit, they are created;
> And You renew the face of the earth.
>
> *Ps. 104:27–30*

In verse 27 the psalmist continues, *"These all wait for You, / That You may give them their food in due season."* The *"these"* are all the types of life mentioned above. It is God who cares and provides for them all. In verse 28 they merely gather in what God gives them. There is no autonomy here: *"You open Your hand, they are filled with good."*

Likewise, if God brings pestilence or famine, if He hides His face (in His wrath, see Ps. 102:2), *"they are troubled* ['dismayed']*"* (v. 29). *"You take away* ['gather'] *their breath* ['spirit']*, they die and return to their dust"* (cf. Gen. 2:7; Job 34:15). Since it is God who takes life, death is not just a natural process or a privilege over which we have autonomous authority.

Moreover, God gives life: *"You send forth Your Spirit, they are created"* (v. 30; cf. Gen. 1:2). God also makes the world new again and again: *"And You renew the face of the earth."* He is active in its creation, preservation, and restoration.

BENEDICTIONS

> 104:31 May the glory of the LORD endure forever;
> May the LORD rejoice in His works.
> 32 He looks on the earth, and it trembles;
> He touches the hills, and they smoke.
>
> *Ps. 104:31–32*

The psalmist blesses God: *"May the glory of the Lord endure* ['be'] *forever."* This *"glory,"* which evokes praise, has been seen in all of His creative acts. He continues, *"May the Lord rejoice* ['take pleasure'] *in His works."* The creation is God's and it exists for Him. Thus Eric Liddle, the Scottish Olympic runner, gave as his motive for competition: "God has made me fast, and I run for His good pleasure."

God's joy is seen in His continuing command of the earth in verse 32. When He looks at it, *"it trembles"* (with an earthquake?). When He *"touches the hills, . . . they smoke* [volcanic eruption?].*"*

Vows to Praise

104:33 I will sing to the LORD as long as I live;
       I will sing praise to my God while I have my
          being.
   34 May my meditation be sweet to Him;
       I will be glad in the LORD.
   35 May sinners be consumed from the earth,
       And the wicked be no more.
       Bless the LORD, O my soul!
       Praise the LORD!

                                              Ps. 104:33–35

In verse 33 the psalmist vows to sing *"to the Lord"* as long as he lives. The thought reappears in synonymous parallelism (see *Introduction, Psalms 1–72,* Communicator's Commentary, Old Testament, no. 13, 20): *"I will sing to my God while I have my being."* As this whole psalm is written to be sung, this vow is being fulfilled.

The psalmist asks that his *"meditation be sweet to Him* [God]*"* (v. 34). This seems assured when he adds, *"I will be glad in the Lord."* Then he offers a ritual petition against evildoers: *"May sinners be consumed* ["come to an end"] *from the earth, / And the wicked* ["lawbreakers"] *be no more."* This is the only note on sin or rebellion in this psalm. The great description of God's intensive care for His creation concludes as it began: *"Bless the Lord, O my soul!"* This exhortation is then fulfilled: *"Praise the Lord!"*

As we saw in our introduction, the God of the Bible is active in His created world. He orders it all according to His will. He establishes the cycles of nature and provides for the needs of His creatures. Through nature God's glory is seen, and He rejoices in His works (v. 31). This evokes songs of praise. Our proper response to revelation is worship.

If our planet is to be salvaged from ecological disaster, we must return to this view of the world and its order as intimately known and cared for by God. Otherwise, He will surely hide His face from us, and in our trouble we will die and return to our dust (v. 29). If we don't accept His care, we will still need His care, for life here will be terminal.

CHAPTER ONE HUNDRED FIVE

Claim the Covenant!

Psalm 105

Memory is an important part of our political and social relationships. A shared past forges our future. We celebrate national holidays so that we can remember our moments of triumph and be bound together by them once again. For similar reasons we also remember birthdays and anniversaries. We look back to a key event in the past and emotionally return to it as we thumb through picture albums and reminisce with relatives and friends. Likewise, memory is an important component for our spiritual lives. Many of us have mountain peaks where, like Moses, we have seen the Lord "face to face," and we need to recall them.

At times my mind will go back to my conversion at fifteen years of age. I can still see the large camp meeting room where the evangelist, Jim Rayburn, who founded Young Life, spoke. I can hear the singing and feel the impact of Jim's message of the cross as it was driven down from my head to my heart. I can see myself standing before hundreds of fellow high school students to give my quivering confession of faith.

My memory shifts to a hillside in Glendale, California. I had climbed there often in my early years to pray. Now, as a college professor, I was waiting upon the Lord. Then, I felt the Holy Spirit coming upon me, wave after wave.

Likewise, Psalm 105 is filled with the memory of what God has done. We are reminded of His "deeds" (v. 1), His "wondrous works" (v. 2), His "marvelous works," and His "wonders" (v. 5). All of this is based upon His covenant, which He remembered forever (v. 8). Thus God protected the patriarchs in their wanderings (v. 14) and prepared to save Israel from famine through Joseph in Egypt (v. 17). Then He sent Moses to bring His people out of bondage (v. 26), revealing His judgments in the plagues (vv. 27–36). Thus Israel escaped "with silver and gold" (v. 37), and God provided for her in the wilderness wanderings (vv. 39–41). Why was this? It was because God "remembered His holy promise, / And Abraham His servant" (v. 42). Thus He gave His people their land. It is exactly this memory that fuels the fires of praise (vv. 1–3; 45).

The author of this psalm is anonymous. Its form is a hymn. Its content covers the history of Israel from Abraham to the conquest of Canaan. Filled with historical memory, it was probably used in the temple liturgy. Verses 1–15 are employed in 1 Chron. 16:8–22 as a part of the celebration following the arrival of the Ark of the Covenant in Jerusalem. This would make this psalm ancient, which is likely since its narrated history ends with Israel's entrance into the Holy Land. The thought moves from praising God for His promise (vv. 1–15), to His provision (vv. 16–25), to His judgment (vv. 26–36), to His redemption (vv. 37–41) and concludes with the affirmation that He keeps His promise (vv. 42–45).

PROMISE

105:1 Oh, give thanks to the LORD!
Call upon His name;
Make known His deeds among the peoples!
2 Sing to Him, sing psalms to Him;
Talk of all His wondrous works!
3 Glory in His holy name;
Let the hearts of those rejoice who seek the
LORD!
4 Seek the LORD and His strength;
Seek His face evermore!

5 Remember His marvelous works which He has
    done,
  His wonders, and the judgments of His mouth,
6 O seed of Abraham His servant,
  You children of Jacob, His chosen ones!
7 He *is* the LORD our God;
  His judgments *are* in all the earth.
8 He remembers His covenant forever,
  The word *which* He commanded, for a
    thousand generations,
9 *The covenant* which He made with Abraham,
  And His oath to Isaac,
10 And confirmed it to Jacob for a statute,
  To Israel *as* an everlasting covenant,
11 Saying, "To you I will give the land of Canaan
  As the allotment of your inheritance,"
12 When they were few in number,
  Indeed very few, and strangers in it.
13 When they went from one nation to another,
  From *one* kingdom to another people,
14 He permitted no one to do them wrong;
  Yes, He rebuked kings for their sakes,
15 *Saying,* "Do not touch My anointed ones,
  And do My prophets no harm."

Ps. 105:1–15

Verse 1 is a call to worship: *"Oh, give thanks to the Lord!"* God deserves this gratitude because He has done *"wondrous works"* (v. 2) and *"He has remembered His covenant forever"* (v. 8). The psalmist continues: *"Call upon His name."* This may mean calling *out* His name, or it may mean calling upon His name to answer our prayers. Speaking the name of God evokes His presence and His authority. Knowing His name also assumes that we have a personal relationship with Him (cf. Exod. 3:13–15). Now worship turns to witness: *"Make known His deeds among the peoples."* These deeds will be expounded throughout the rest of the psalm.

Verse 2 continues the worship/witness structure. Here we are exhorted to *"sing"* to Yahweh, *"sing psalms* ["sing with accompaniment"] *to Him."* Also we are called to *"talk of* [or "muse on"] *all His wondrous works* [that is, His supernatural interventions]." Miracles may embarrass us, but the Hebrews reveled in them.

In verse 3, we are to *"glory* ["boast"] *in His holy name,"* for in that name we have been redeemed. In Isaiah God reveals Himself as "the Redeemer of Israel" (Isa. 49:7). God's name is *"holy."* This means that it is separate and unique. God says, "I am Yahweh, and there is no other" (Isa. 45:18). The psalmist exhorts us: *"Let the hearts of those rejoice who seek* ["inquire for"] *the Lord."* To seek Him is an occasion for joy. The verb *seek* may be a technical term for seeking God in the temple. This exhortation continues in verse 4: *"Seek the Lord and His strength* ["might"]." Thus to know God is to know His power. Beyond His benefits, however, is the Lord Himself. The psalmist concludes, *"Seek His face evermore* ["continually"]."

As we pursue God, we are to remember what He has done. Much of this psalm is devoted to that memory. In verse 5 we are told to *"remember His marvelous works* ["mighty interventions," see v. 2] *which He has done, / His wonders."* These miracles refer especially to the Exodus. Moses sings, "Who is like You, O Lord . . . doing wonders? You stretched out Your right hand; the earth swallowed them" (that is, the Egyptians, Exod. 15:11–12). We are also to remember *"the judgments of His mouth."* This refers to God's words of doom delivered to Pharaoh (see, e.g., Exod. 11:1ff.).

At this point the psalmist shifts to his hearers, reminding them of their identity (v. 6). They are the *"seed of Abraham His* [God's] *servant."* Thus they inherit the covenant God made with him (see below). They are also *"children of Jacob* [Isaac's second son, see Gen. 25:26], / *His chosen ones!"* God says to Israel through Moses, "the Lord your God has chosen you to be a people for Himself, a special treasure above all the peoples on the face of the earth" (Deut. 7:6).

After telling God's people who they are, the psalmist reminds them of who God is in verses 7–12. First, *"He is the Lord our God"* (v. 7). He is Yahweh, the covenant God of Israel (Exod. 20:2). Second, *"His judgments* [see v. 5] *are in all the earth."* As we learn in verse 27, Moses and Aaron performed God's "wonders in the land of Ham" (Ham was the ancestor of Egypt; see Gen. 10:6—"Mizaim"). Third, God remembers *"His covenant forever"* (v. 8). For Him to remember His covenant means that He enforces it and is faithful to it (see Exod. 2:24–25). The *"covenant"* is defined as God's *"word which He commanded, for a thousand generations."* But what is its content?

Originally, as we have seen, the covenant was made with Abraham (v. 9; see Gen. 17:1ff.). In it God vowed to be Abraham's God and to give the Promised Land to him and to his descendants forever (see v. 8; Gen. 17:7–8). This covenant-treaty is modeled on the royal grant given by a king to his loyal subject for faithful service. Thus it is totally gracious and unconditional in its provisions.

Since God's covenant is *"forever"* (v. 8), it is reconfirmed to Abraham's son Isaac as an *"oath"* (v. 9; see Gen. 26:3–4). Then it extends to Isaac's son *"Jacob for a statute, / To Israel* [Jacob's new name given at the ford of Jabbok, Gen. 32:28] *as an everlasting covenant"* (v. 10). It was necessary for it to be confirmed to Jacob since the covenant now continues only through his line (see Rom. 9:10–13). From that point on it belongs to Israel, the nation coming from Jacob and bearing his new name.

God's covenant-promise is cited in verse 11, where the *"land of Canaan"* is designated as Israel's *"inheritance."* *"Canaan"* indicates the Syro-Palestinian coastland, especially Phoenicia proper (see Num. 13:29). The name was extended to cover the hinterland as well. This promise of the land was given *"when they* [the Patriarchs] *were but few in number"* and *"strangers"* ("sojourners") as well (v. 12). Thus they *"went from one nation to another"* (v. 13). At the same time, God protected them (v. 14); *"Yes, He reproved kings for their sakes."* This is seen in His punishing Pharaoh for taking Abram's wife Sarai into his household (Gen. 12:17). Furthermore, God did not allow harm to come to His *"anointed ones"* (anointed with the Holy Spirit; see Gen. 41:38), who were also His *"prophets"* (Gen. 20:7).

In verses 1–15 we are called to praise God because He has intervened on behalf of His people. We are to remember His mighty acts in response to His covenant with Abraham and his descendants. God promised them a land and protected them as they wandered. With that promise before them, they lived toward the future. They were also, however, anchored in the past. God had made a covenant, and they trusted Him to keep it.

We, too, live as they lived. God has given us a covenant in His Son. In His death and resurrection, He has intervened on our behalf. We, too, now live toward the future. Paul tells us that as we celebrate the Lord's Supper in remembrance of Him we proclaim His death until He comes (1 Cor. 11:26). But we are also anchored in the past. The one who will come has already come. In Christ we have the promise, not of Canaan, but of heaven, and we can trust God to keep both His promise and us.

PROVISION

105:16 Moreover He called for a famine in the land;
      He destroyed all the provision of bread.
  17 He sent a man before them—
      Joseph—*who* was sold as a slave.
  18 They hurt his feet with fetters,
      He was laid in irons.
  19 Until the time that his word came to pass,
      The word of the LORD tested him.
  20 The king sent and released him,
      The ruler of the people let him go free.
  21 He made him lord of his house,
      And ruler of all his possessions,
  22 To bind his princes at his pleasure,
      And teach his elders wisdom.
  23 Israel also came into Egypt,
      And Jacob dwelt in the land of Ham.
  24 He increased His people greatly,
      And made them stronger than their enemies.
  25 He turned their heart to hate His people,
      To deal craftily with His servants.
                   Ps. 105:16–25

The psalmist, in his recital of patriarchal history, now comes to a crisis. God *"called for a famine in the land; / He destroyed all the provision of bread"* (v. 16; see Gen. 41:5–57). At the same time, He provided for Jacob and his family by sending his son Joseph *"before them* [to Egypt] . . . *sold as a slave"* (v. 17; see Gen. 37:27, 36). After rejecting the advances of his master's wife, however, he ended up in prison. There *"they hurt his feet with fetters, / He was laid in irons"* (v. 18). But *"his word came to pass"* (either his own earlier dream, Gen. 37:5ff., or his interpretation of the butler's and the baker's dreams in prison, Gen. 40:5ff.), for *"the word of the Lord tested him"*; that is, God put him to the test. Thus after correctly interpreting Pharaoh's dream (Gen. 41:14ff.), he was released from prison (v. 20), and made *"lord of his* [Pharaoh's] *house, / And ruler of all his posses-sions"* (v. 21; see Gen. 41:37ff.). Now Joseph commanded Pharaoh's princes. He was able *"to bind"* ("imprison") them *"at his pleasure,"* and he taught *"his elders wisdom"* (v. 22; see Gen. 41:39–40, 44).

In this setting *"Israel also came into Egypt* [Gen. 46:6], / And Jacob *sojourned in the land of Ham"* (v. 23). There God did two things. The psalmist says in verse 24 that *"He increased His people greatly"* so that they were *"stronger than their enemies"* (see Exod. 1:7) and in verse 25 that He turned the hearts of Egypt *"to hate His people, / To deal craftily with His servants"* (cf. Exod. 1:10–11).

In all of this, God was sovereignly working toward one goal: the fulfillment of His covenant-promise to Abraham to give his seed the Promised Land. While the patriarchs were few in number (v. 12), they could have never taken the land by force. In Egypt, however, Israel grew great in number. This created an invasion force with which to enter the land (v. 24). The stage was set for God to intervene, release Israel from bondage, and fulfill His covenant by taking His people through the Jordan into Canaan.

JUDGMENT

105:26 He sent Moses His servant,
    And Aaron whom He had chosen.
27 They performed His signs among them,
    And wonders in the land of Ham.
28 He sent darkness, and made *it* dark;
    And they did not rebel against His word.
29 He turned their waters into blood,
    And killed their fish.
30 Their land abounded with frogs,
    Even in the chambers of their kings.
31 He spoke, and there came swarms of flies,
    And lice in all their territory.
32 He gave them hail for rain,
    And flaming fire in their land.
33 He struck their vines also, and their fig trees,
    And splintered the trees of their territory.
34 He spoke, and locusts came,
    Young locusts without number,
35 And ate up all the vegetation in their land,
    And devoured the fruit of their ground.
36 He also destroyed all the firstborn in their
        land,
    The first of all their strength.

Ps. 105:26–36

Now the psalmist focuses in on the events of the Exodus. Moses, called by God to bring Israel out of bondage, and Aaron, his brother (Exod. 4:14), are identified respectively as God's *"servant"* and the one *"whom He had chosen"* (v. 26). Under His sovereignty they did His will, *"performing His signs* [literally, *"the words (or matters) of His signs"]* . . . *and wonders* [*"miracles,"* see v. 5] *in the land of Ham"* (v. 27; see v. 23). God promised to Moses, "I will harden Pharaoh's heart, and multiply My signs and My wonders in the land of Egypt" (Exod. 7:3). The *"signs"* are actions or events that point beyond themselves, while the *"wonders"* are extraordinary, supernatural events that evoke awe (cf. Acts 2:43). These signs and wonders are enumerated in verses 28–36.

First, there is *"darkness"* (v. 28). In Exodus this is the ninth plague (Exod. 10:21ff.). Since the Egyptians worshiped the sun, this judgment displayed Yahweh's power over that god. The psalmist continues, *"And they did not rebel against His word."* This clause, however, would make more sense as a question, *"And did they not rebel against His word?"* Second, the *"waters"* are turned into *"blood"* and the *"fish"* die (v. 29; see Exod. 7:14–18). This is the first plague in Exodus. Third, the *"frogs"* are sent as the second plague (v. 30; see Exod. 8:2). Fourth, there are *"swarms of flies."* This is the fourth plague (v. 31; see Exod. 8:20ff.). Fifth, there are *"lice,"* which is actually the third plague (see Exod. 8:16). Sixth, *"hail"* fell accompanied by lightning, *"flaming fire"* (v. 32), which destroyed the *"vines, fig trees,"* and *"splintered the trees of their territory"* (v. 33). In Exodus this is the seventh plague (Exod. 9:13–25). Seventh, there are the *"locusts"* of the eighth plague (v. 34), who consume what is left after the hail (vv. 34–35; see Exod. 10:1ff.). Finally, there is the tenth plague, the death of *"all the firstborn in their land, / The first* [*"firstfruits"*] *of all their strength"* (v. 36; see Exod. 12:29–30). These are Yahweh's signs and wonders. They are "His deeds" which are to be made known "among the peoples" (v. 1). This exhortation to witness is actually carried out in verses 26–36. Indeed, the "marvelous works" and "the judgments of His mouth" are remembered (v. 5).

God gets glory over Pharaoh and releases Israel from bondage. Here is a people ready to receive the land promised so long ago to Abraham. Yahweh "has remembered His covenant forever" (v. 8).

REDEMPTION

105:37 He also brought them out with silver and
      gold,
    And *there was* none feeble among His tribes.
  38 Egypt was glad when they departed,
    For the fear of them had fallen upon them.
  39 He spread a cloud for a covering,
    And fire to give light in the night.
  40 *The people* asked, and He brought quail,
    And satisfied them with the bread of
      heaven.
  41 He opened the rock, and water gushed out;
    It ran in the dry places *like* a river.
                      Ps. 105:37–41

God now brings Israel out *"with silver and gold"* (v. 37). These were the most precious metals of antiquity. Taking their spoils, according to Exod. 12:36, Israel *"plundered the Egyptians."* Moreover, God's people are also healthy: *"And there was none feeble* ["stumbling"] *among His tribes."* Egypt is pictured as *"glad* ["exulting"] *when they departed"* (v. 38), because *"the fear of them had fallen upon them"* (see Exod. 12:29–33).

God leads His people with a *"cloud for a covering, / And a fire to give light in the night"* (v. 39). Thus they are able to travel without stopping (Exod. 13:21–22). In response to their requests, God gives His people *"quail"* (Num. 12:31), *"the bread of heaven"* ("manna," Exod. 16:4), and *"water"* from the rock (Exod. 17:6; vv. 40–41). Israel departs from Egypt rich, healthy, protected, and with full provision. God's people are ready for the Promised Land.

The issue of salvation is not only what we are saved *from* but also what we are saved *for*. Israel was saved *from* Egypt and the bondage of her demon-idols to be sure. But what was she saved *for?* Here we have some hints. In the Exodus she knew God's bounty. All of her physical needs were well provided for. Moreover, she knew God's presence in the cloud and fire. Likewise, in Christ we not only receive salvation from sin; we also receive the gift of His Spirit and the companionship of His people as we, like Israel, march toward our Canaan.

THE PROMISE KEPT

105:42 For He remembered His holy promise,
      And Abraham His servant.
   43 He brought out His people with joy,
      His chosen ones with gladness.
   44 He gave them the lands of the Gentiles,
      And they inherited the labor of the nations,
   45 That they might observe His statutes
      And keep His laws.
      Praise the LORD!

Ps. 105:42–45

Why did God keep the patriarchs in their wanderings, provide for Israel in the famine, and bring His people out of Egypt? The answer is that He made a covenant with Abraham (v. 9), and down through the generations *"He remembered His holy promise* [literally, "the word of His holiness"], / *And Abraham His servant"* (v. 42). God is true to what He says and true to the one to whom He says it. All of history finds its meaning as God pursues and fulfills His promise. What look like delays and defeats, such as the wandering of the patriarchs and Joseph in jail in Egypt, are not what they seem. God is still faithful to His *"holy promise,"* that promise which is "holy" or "sacred" because it comes from the holy God Himself. Through it, He is working out His will in His way according to His time.

In verse 43, when Israel left Egypt, God *"brought out His people with joy* ["exultation"], / *His chosen ones with gladness* ["a ringing cry"]." As Moses sings, "The Lord is my strength and my song, / And He has become my salvation; / He is my God, and I will praise Him; / My father's God, and I will exalt Him" (Exod. 15:2). God brought them to the Promised Land. *"He gave them the lands of the Gentiles* [Canaan, v. 11], / *And they inherited the labor of the nations."* Undeserved and unearned bounty and blessing were theirs. God's purpose in all of this was *"that they might observe* ["preserve," "protect"] *His statutes* / *And keep* ["obey"] *His laws* ["revelation"]." Thus salvation issues in obedience. As Paul writes, "For we are His workmanship, created in Christ Jesus for good works, which God prepared beforehand that we should walk in them" (Eph. 2:10). God calls us to Himself to make us like Himself. He has made us in His image and wants to restore that image in us.

Psalm 105, in one sense, is a brief course in history for God's people. Here Israel is called to recall the mighty acts of God. In this, she will know that God keeps His covenant. As He revealed Himself then, so will He reveal Himself now.

As suggested earlier, we too need to have touch with our spiritual memory. We need to embrace God's work revealed in history. We need also to embrace the consummation of that history given to us in the New Covenant in Jesus' blood. Moreover, we need to write our own personal history of the "signs and wonders" that God has performed in our lives. Only then will we praise Him as we ought, and only then will our worship and witness come from hearts made new.

CHAPTER ONE HUNDRED SIX

Depravity, Destruction, and Deliverance

Psalm 106

When the roof falls in, we check for termites. When our check bounces, we call the bank. But as long as everything seems in order we go on about our business. What is true for the world is also true for the church. It was only when Germany was abused by indulgences that Luther said, "No." It was only when the churches were closed to Wesley that he preached in the fields. It was only when the back of the bus became intolerable that Martin Luther King went to the streets.

Recently the roof fell in on Jim and Tammy Bakker, televangelists and founders of the PTL Club. By a series of revelations concerning sexual immorality and greed, the Bakkers were forced to abandon their extravagant ministry. As the dust began to settle, the whole world of televangelism was shaken. Jamie Buckingham, a charismatic leader, comments, "Across the years I have sensed this spirit of 'We can do it without God' taking control of many of the major ministries of America. To be sure, no one would dare say that on the air (the funds would immediately dry up), but off camera and in the top executive offices it is rampant." He then concludes, "I raise up enemies to bring things down," God said, "then I deal with the enemies." In short: God is purifying His church!

Similarly, God purified Israel in the Exile. With the temple burned, Jerusalem's walls torn down, and the cream of her leadership either slaughtered or deported, a hard look had to be taken at her history and what God was doing with her now. From the depths of exile, Psalm 106 is written. The purpose of the psalmist appears in verse 47: "Save us, O Lord our God, / And gather us from among the Gentiles." This cry for help comes at the end of a long recital of Israel's sins starting at the Red Sea (vv. 6–12), going then through the wilderness wanderings (vv. 13–33), and concluding with the conquest and the Exile (vv. 34–46). Again and again we are greeted by Israel's depravity and God's deliverance. While God acts on their behalf, the people rebel. The psalmist laments, "They soon forgot His works; / They did not wait for His counsel" (v. 13). Judgment is sure to follow. In sum, "Many times, He delivered them; / But they rebelled against Him by their counsel, / And were brought low for their iniquity" (v. 43). Nevertheless, God is merciful and remembers His covenant (v. 45). The call for salvation does not fall on deaf ears. The real cry of this psalm is for God to "do it again."

The author of Psalm 106 is unknown, although 1 Chron. 16:34–36 quotes verses 1 and 47–48 as a part of David's psalm upon bringing the Ark of the Covenant to Jerusalem. If this is correct, these verses are at least pre-Exilic. Its form is a personal lament (see vv. 4–5) on behalf of the people: "We have sinned with our fathers" (v. 6). "Save us" (v. 47). The thought moves from a call to worship (vv. 1–3), to a personal call for salvation (vv. 4–5), to a history of Israel's sin (vv. 6–46) and concludes with the people's call for salvation and praise to the Lord (vv. 47–48).

CALL TO WORSHIP

106:1 Praise the LORD!
    Oh, give thanks to the LORD, for *He is* good!
    For His mercy *endures* forever.
  2 Who can utter the mighty acts of the LORD?
    Who can declare all His praise?
  3 Blessed *are* those who keep justice,
    And he who does righteousness at all times!

Ps. 106:1-3

Verse 1 opens with a standard blessing: *"Praise the Lord!"* We transliterate this in English: Hallelujah! This is immediately followed by a call to worship: *"Oh, give thanks to the Lord, for He is good!"* God's goodness is His perfection in all His ways. *"His mercy* ["covenant-love"] *endures forever."* It is this covenant commitment from God that the psalmist counts on as he prays (see v. 45; Ps. 105:9). If he is quoting a Davidic tradition here (see above), his intention would be to remind God of David's faith and affirm it as his own.

The psalmist asks rhetorically, *"Who can utter the mighty acts of the Lord? / Or who can declare* [literally, "cause to hear"] *all His praise"* (v. 2)? The answer is, "No one." No one is worthy to witness to God's works or to worship Him rightly. This is especially true in light of the dark history to follow (vv. 6–43).

A blessing is given in verse 3: *"Blessed* ["happy"] *are those who keep justice,"* that is, who are just as God is just, and *"he who does righteousness,"* that is, he who obeys Torah, *"at all times"* (continually). By implication, if Israel had done this, she would never have gone into exile.

PERSONAL CALL FOR SALVATION

106:4 Remember me, O LORD, with the favor *You have*
    toward Your people.
    Oh, visit me with Your salvation,
  5 That I may see the benefit of Your chosen
    ones,
    That I may rejoice in the gladness of Your
    nation,
    That I may glory with Your inheritance.

Ps. 106:4-5

The psalmist pleads to Yahweh for himself: *"Remember me, O Lord, with the favor* ["acceptance"] *You have toward Your people,"* or literally, *"in the favor of your people"* (v. 4). This favor comes because God has bound Himself to them by the covenant. Mercy to Israel will bring mercy to the psalmist. Next, he prays, *"Oh, visit me with Your salvation* ["deliverance"]." The context of these pleas is the Exile from which the psalmist longs to be rescued (see v. 47). As God acts once again, he will *"see the benefit* ["good"] *of Your chosen ones"* (v. 5). (Note that Israel is God's people by His election and call; see Deut. 7:7–8.) Once this good is manifest by Israel's deliverance, the psalmist will *"rejoice in the gladness of Your nation."* Praise is always evoked by God's gracious action. Finally, the psalmist will *"glory* ["boast"] *with Your inheritance* [the nation; see Ps. 33:12]."

As the psalmist has called us to worship in verses 1–3, now he calls God to act on his and Israel's behalf in verses 4–5. The result will be joy and glory (boasting). Israel will be God's people of praise once again. After the darkness comes the light.

A History of Israel's Sin

106:6 We have sinned with our fathers,
    We have committed iniquity,
    We have done wickedly.
  7 Our fathers in Egypt did not understand Your
      wonders;
    They did not remember the multitude of Your
      mercies,
    But rebelled by the sea—the Red Sea.
  8 Nevertheless He saved them for His name's
      sake,
    That He might make His mighty power
      known.
  9 He rebuked the Red Sea also, and it dried up;
    So He led them through the depths,
    As through the wilderness.
 10 He saved them from the hand of him who
      hated *them,*
    And redeemed them from the hand of the
      enemy.

11 The waters covered their enemies;
   There was not one of them left.
12 Then they believed His words;
   They sang His praise.
13 They soon forgot His works;
   They did not wait for His counsel,
14 But lusted exceedingly in the wilderness,
   And tested God in the desert.
15 And He gave them their request,
   But sent leanness into their soul.
16 When they envied Moses in the camp,
   And Aaron the saint of the LORD,
17 The earth opened up and swallowed Dathan,
   And covered the faction of Abiram.
18 A fire was kindled in their company;
   The flame burned up the wicked.
19 They made a calf in Horeb,
   And worshiped the molded image.
20 Thus they changed their glory
   Into the image of an ox that eats grass.
21 They forgot God their Savior,
   Who had done great things in Egypt,
22 Wondrous works in the land of Ham,
   Awesome things by the Red Sea.
23 Therefore He said that He would destroy them,
   Had not Moses His chosen one stood before
       Him in the breach,
   To turn away His wrath, lest He destroy *them.*
24 Then they despised the pleasant land;
   They did not believe His word,
25 But complained in their tents,
   And did not heed the voice of the LORD.
26 Therefore He raised His hand *in an oath*
       against them,
   To overthrow them in the wilderness,
27 To overthrow their descendants among the
       nations,
   And to scatter them in the lands.
28 They joined themselves also to Baal of Peor,
   And ate sacrifices made to the dead.
29 Thus they provoked *Him* to anger with their
       deeds,

265

And the plague broke out among them.
30 Then Phinehas stood up and intervened,
And the plague was stopped.
31 And that was accounted to him for
righteousness
To all generations forevermore.
32 They angered *Him* also at the waters of strife,
So that it went ill with Moses on account of
them;
33 Because they rebelled against His Spirit,
So that he spoke rashly with his lips.
34 They did not destroy the peoples,
Concerning whom the LORD had commanded
them,
35 But they mingled with the Gentiles
And learned their works;
36 They served their idols,
Which became a snare to them.
37 They even sacrificed their sons
And their daughters to demons,
38 And shed innocent blood,
The blood of their sons and daughters,
Whom they sacrificed to the idols of Canaan;
And the land was polluted with blood.
39 Thus they were defiled by their own works,
And played the harlot by their own deeds.
40 Therefore the wrath of the LORD was kindled
against His people,
So that He abhorred His own inheritance.
41 And He gave them into the hand of the
Gentiles,
And those who hated them ruled over them.
42 Their enemies also oppressed them,
And they were brought into subjection under
their hand.
43 Many times He delivered them;
But they rebelled in their counsel,
And were brought low for their iniquity.
44 Nevertheless He regarded their affliction,
When He heard their cry;
45 And for their sake He remembered His
covenant,

> And relented according to the multitude of His
>   mercies.
> 46 He also made them to be pitied
> By all those who carried them away captive.
>
> *Ps. 106:6-46*

We turn now to the great heart of this psalm. Starting at the Red
Sea in the Exodus (vv. 6–12) and then moving through the wilderness wanderings (vv. 13–33), the psalmist shows the tiresome pattern of God's grace and Israel's sin. Once the land was occupied, the
pattern continued (vv. 34–39), and God's wrath could be the only
result (vv. 40–43). In the midst of the Exile, God hears the groans of
His people again (vv. 44–46).

The psalmist begins with a corporate confession of guilt in verse
6: *"We have sinned* ['missed the mark'] *with our fathers, / We have
committed iniquity* ['been perverse'], */ We have done wickedly* ['been
lawbreakers']*."* He confesses his solidarity with the past. By using
the plural, he also draws his generation into this mire of sin and
guilt. But what is the substance of this sin? In the narration that
follows, it will unfold.

The sins of the fathers (v. 6) are exposed, starting in verse 7.
To begin with, *"in Egypt"* they *"did not understand Your wonders*
['miraculous interventions']*."* If they had grasped the plagues, they
would have been humbled and repentant before Yahweh. Because
they suffered from spiritual amnesia, *"they did not remember the multitude of Your mercies* ['covenant-love' in the plural; thus 'acts of
love']*,"* including God's Passover protection from the death of the
firstborn (see Exodus 12). Instead, they *"rebelled by the sea—the Red
Sea."* (The name 'Red Sea' may mean 'the Sea of Reeds'; its exact
location is debated.) The psalmist recalls God's people's response
when Pharaoh pursued them with his chariots, horsemen, and army.
They cried out, "Because there were no graves in Egypt, have you
taken us to die in the wilderness? For it would have been better for
us to serve the Egyptians" (Exod. 14:11–12).

"Nevertheless, [God] *saved* ['delivered'] *them for His name's sake"*
and parted the sea (v. 8). In other words, God saved them to uphold
His reputation (see Exod. 14:18) and covenant-commitment, although they all deserved to die there. Thus He made *"His mighty
power known"* ('experienced'); for the Bible God is a God of power

(see Ps. 105:4). He is no absentee landlord or distant first cause. Neither can He be "demythologized" into simply giving us existential information about our own self-decisions.

God's power appears in verse 9. First, *"He rebuked the Red Sea also, and dried it up"* (Exod. 14:15–22). God speaks and it is done (compare Mark 4:39). Next, He led Israel *"through the depths, / As through the wilderness."* *"He saved* ["delivered"] *them from the hand* [authority] *of him who hated them* [Pharaoh], */ And redeemed* ["ransomed" by the cost of His power, (Leon Morris)] *them from the hand of the enemy"* (v. 10). Thus the Egyptians all drowned (v. 11). As Moses sang, "The depths have covered them; / They sank to the bottom like a stone" (Exod. 15:5). Israel then *"believed* ["trusted"] *His* [God's] *words"* and worshiped: *"They sang His praise"* (so Exodus 15). This was, however, short lived. It was an emotional response to rescue rather than a deep commitment to Yahweh. We learn that it is one thing to praise God for His benefits. It is quite another thing to praise God as God. Today, do we praise God for who He is, or merely for what He does for us?

The psalmist continues in verse 13, *"They soon forgot His works* [cf. v. 7]; */ They did not wait for His counsel* ["advice"]." Rather, they *"lusted exceedingly* [literally, "they desired a desire"] . . . / *And tested God."* They placed their demands upon Yahweh, rather than asking Him for His demands and direction. Exodus illustrates this point amply. So "the people murmured against Moses, saying, 'What shall we drink?'" (Exod. 15:24). Later they cried, "Oh, that we had died by the hand of the Lord in the land of Egypt. . . . For you have brought us out into this wilderness to kill this whole assembly with hunger" (Exod. 16:3). God, of course, provided for Israel: *"And He gave them their request"* (v. 15). At the same time, however, He *"sent leanness into their soul."* The noun *leanness* may indicate a "wasting disease" such as came after the provision of quail (Num. 11:33). It may also, however, indicate their spiritual poverty, which is a deeper judgment because of Israel's constant rebellion.

In verse 16 the next sorry event tells of Dathan and Abiram who shared in Korah's rebellion against Moses and Aaron (Num. 16:1ff.). Moses, of course, was God's spokesman and leader in the Exodus. Aaron was his brother (Exod. 4:14), *"the saint of the Lord,"* or better, "the holy one of Yahweh," as the High Priest of Israel (Exod. 39:30). This attack against them occurred because of envy. The rebel charged that Moses and Aaron exalted themselves "above the congregation of the Lord" (Num. 16:3). God, however, quickly ended this revolt by splitting the earth and swallowing up both them and their tents (v. 17; Num. 16:23–24, 31–33). Moreover, 250 of their followers, who brought censers with incense before the Lord, were consumed by fire (v. 18; Num. 16:35).

The greatest sin, however, is that of idolatry, the violation of the First Commandment (v. 19; see Exod. 20:3). This, of course, was practiced by Israel when the golden calf was worshiped *in Horeb"* (Sinai; see Exod. 19:20; cf. Deut. 5:2). There, when Moses was delayed on the mountain, the people convinced Aaron to make a molded calf of gold (Exod. 32:1ff.). The psalmist notes, *"Thus they changed their glory* [i.e., Yahweh; see Ps. 3:3; cf. Ps. 24:7–10] / *Into the image of an ox that eats grass"* (v. 20). This manufacture of an image, of course, violated the Second Commandment (Exod. 20:4–6). The symbolism of the calf is disputed, but it may represent one of the gods of Egypt.

Again, the psalmist charges Israel with spiritual amnesia: *"They forgot God their Savior"* (literally, "who saved them," v. 21; cf. v. 7). They forgot the God *"who had done great things in Egypt, / Wondrous works* ["miracles"] *in the land of Ham* [for Ham see Ps. 105:23], / *Awesome things* ["fearful things"] *by the Red Sea"* (v. 22; see vv. 9–11). God's response for this is to consume Israel (v. 23; Exod. 32:10). However, Moses interceded *"to turn away His wrath, lest He destroy them"* (Exod. 32:11–14).

In verses 24–27, we have Israel's refusal to obey God and take the Promised Land. *"They despised* ["rejected"] *the pleasant* ["desirable"] *land; / They did not believe His word"* (v. 24; see Num. 14:1ff.). God's people *"murmured in their tents, / And did not heed* ["hear"] *the voice of the Lord"* (v. 25). As a result of their refusal, God judged them (v. 26). As we read in Num. 14:26–29: "And the Lord spoke to Moses and Aaron, saying, 'How long shall I bear with this evil congregation who complain against Me? . . . Say to them . . . The carcasses of you who have complained against Me shall fall in this wilderness.'" This judgment, however, did not merely fall upon that generation. Similar unbelief later brought the Exile. *"Their descendants"* ("seed") were overthrown *"among the nations"* where they were scattered (v. 27; see the warning in Lev. 26:33).

In the continuing catalog of sin, the psalmist turns to Israel's idolatry when she joined herself to *"Baal* [a local Canaanite fertility god meaning "husband"] *of Peor* [a mountain in Moab], / *And ate sacrifices made to the dead* [metaphor for idols?]" (v. 28). In Num. 25:2–3 we read that Moabite harlots "invited the people to the sacrifice of their gods, and the people ate and bowed down to their gods. So Israel was joined to Baal of Peor, and the anger of the Lord was aroused against Israel." This resulted in God being provoked *"to anger with their deeds, / And the plague broke out among them"* (v. 29). *"Phinehas,"* however, Aaron's grandson, took a javelin and executed "the man of Israel and the woman" who were offenders. *"So the plague was stopped"* (v. 30; Num. 25:7–8). His deed *"was accounted* ["reckoned"] *to him for righteousness* [see Gen. 15:6] / *To all generations forevermore."* That is, he was pronounced righteous for his zeal for Yahweh down through the generations.

Next, God was angered *"at the waters of strife"* (Meribah, v. 32; see Num. 20:1ff.). There the people of Israel contended again with Moses, and he brought water out of the rock. However, the psalmist continues that *"it went ill with Moses on account of them."* Israel rebelled against God's *"Spirit* [or, perhaps Moses' spirit], / *So that he* [Moses] *spoke rashly with his lips"* (v. 33). Rather than giving glory to God, in his anger he cried, "Hear now, you rebels! Must we bring water for you out of this rock?" (Num. 20:10). Therefore, God judged him, "Because you did not believe Me, to hallow Me in the eyes of the children of Israel, therefore you shall not bring this congregation into the land which I have given them" (Num. 20:12).

This concludes the tragic history of Israel from the Red Sea to Meribah. The sins of the people include rebellion (v. 7), forgetfulness (v. 13), lust and testing God (v. 14), envy (v. 16), idolatry (v. 19), unbelief (v. 24), murmuring and disobedience (v. 25), idolatry again (v. 28), and strife and rebellion (vv. 32–33). Such a catalogue of sins anticipates Paul's lists in the New Testament (see Rom. 1:28–31; 1 Cor. 6:9–10; Gal. 5:19–21). Indeed, "there is none righteous, no, not one" (Rom. 3:10).

Verses 34–39 show a further corruption with the settlement of Canaan. Once she was in the land, Israel tolerated her pagan neighbors rather than annihilating them as God had commanded (v. 34; see Num. 33:53). Her wars of conquest were "Holy Wars," where the enemy was to be given to Yahweh and utterly destroyed (see Josh. 6:21). Israel, however, *"mingled with the Gentiles / And learned their works"* (v. 35). These works centered in idolatry, *"which became a snare to them"* (v. 36). Moreover, pagan worship included child sacrifice (see Lev. 18:21), made to *"demons"* who were masked behind the idols (see Deut. 32:17). Such corruption is only worthy of the devil and his minions. Thus *"innocent blood"* was shed, *"even the blood of their sons and daughters"* (v. 38). These were *"sacrificed to the idols of Canaan; / And the land was polluted* [made unclean] *with blood."* In verse 39 the psalmist concludes that *"they were defiled by their own works."* Sin always corrupts the sinner. For example, when Paul describes homosexual acts as a sign of God's wrath, he concludes that those who engage in them receive *"in themselves the penalty of their error which was due"* (Rom. 1:27). Moreover, they *"played the harlot by their own deeds."* This unfaithfulness to Yahweh is literal in pagan cultic sexual acts and metaphorical, since in going after other gods Israel broke her marriage covenant to Yahweh (Hos. 2:16–20).

God's response to this corruption is now expounded in verses 40–43. In a word, it is *"wrath"* (v. 40). This wrath *"was kindled* ["burned"] *against His people."* The word *"wrath,"* which at its root means *"snorting,"* suggests that God's anger breathed heavily against Israel. Thus *"He abhorred* ["regarded as an abomination"] *His own inheritance"* (see v. 5). This resulted in their rejection by Him. In verse 41 God *"gave them unto the hand* [power] *of the Gentiles."* This came for the Northern Kingdom in 721 B.C. when Assyria destroyed Samaria, and for the Southern Kingdom in 586 B.C. when Babylonia destroyed Judah. Thus *"those who hated them ruled over them."* It was as if they were back in Egypt all over again. Moreover, *"their enemies also oppressed them* [in slavery], / And they were brought into subjection* ["humbled"] *under their hand* [authority]" (v. 42).

With verse 43 the psalmist draws his conclusion to this sorry history. God was there again and again: *"Many times He delivered them."* We need only think back to the Red Sea, the provisions in the wilderness, and God staying His judgment at Horeb. Nevertheless, they turned to their own designs: *"they rebelled against Him by their counsel"* rather than waiting for His (see v. 13). Thus they received Yahweh's judgment: *"And were brought low for their iniquity* ["guilt"]." The Exile sealed their fate.

Judgment, however, in the Bible is not the last word. In verse 44 the light begins to shine again: *"Nevertheless He regarded* ["saw"] *their affliction, / When He heard their cry."* Similarly, Israel's cry in Egypt comes up to God, and He hears their groaning (Exod. 2:23–24). God *"for their sake . . . remembered His covenant"* (v. 45). Likewise, in Egypt "God remembered His covenant with Abraham, with Isaac, and with Jacob" (Exod. 3:24). (For the covenant, God's unconditional royal grant to Israel, see Ps. 105:8–11.) Next, God *"relented according to the multitude of His mercies* ["covenant-love"]." Furthermore, He changed the hearts of their oppressors: *"He also made them to be pitied* [literally, "He gave them to tender mercies"] / *By all those who carried them away captive."* This, of course, prepared for their return to Canaan.

In verses 44–46 God sees Israel's pain. He remembers His promise, which is unfailing. Since His mercy overshadows His judgment, He begins to move in the hearts of Israel's enemies. Indeed, verse 1 is right: "His mercy endures forever." Israel counted on that, and so does the church today. As Paul says, "the gifts and the calling of God are irrevocable" (Rom. 11:29).

THE PEOPLE'S CALL FOR SALVATION

106:47 Save us, O LORD our God,
And gather us from among the Gentiles,
To give thanks to Your holy name,
To triumph in Your praise.

Ps. 106:47

Israel, as with one voice, cries out to God: *"Save* ["deliver"] *us, O Lord our God."* The psalmist's prayer in verse 47 here becomes the people's prayer. If they are saved, he is saved. His destiny is welded to theirs. Salvation is physical, historical, and concrete. It means Israel's return to Canaan: *"And gather us from among the Gentiles."* Thus Isaiah commands, "Go forth from Babylon! / Flee from the Chaldeas! / With a voice of singing, / Declare, proclaim this, / Utter it even to the end of the earth; / Say, 'The Lord has redeemed / His servant Jacob!'" (Isa. 48:20).

The result of God's "mighty acts" (v. 2) will be worship: Israel will *"give thanks to Your holy* ["sacred"] *name."* She will *"triumph* ["boast"] *in Your praise."*

PRAISE TO THE LORD

106:48 Blessed *be* the LORD God of Israel
From everlasting to everlasting!
And let all the people say, "Amen!"
Praise the LORD!

Ps. 106:48

Since at this point Book Four of the Psalms comes to its close, this verse may be added to conclude this section rather than to conclude this psalm. Worship is to be offered continually to Yahweh: *"Blessed* ["praised"] *be the Lord God of Israel / From everlasting to everlasting!"* Next, the proper response is called for: *"And let all the people say, 'Amen'* ["true," "yes, indeed"]!" This is followed by a final hallelujah: *"Praise the Lord"* (see v. 1).

In Psalm 106 we see the continual sifting of God as He relates to His people. He does not condone or excuse their sin. His judgments are certain and sure. Yet, mercy triumphs over wrath as He proves faithful to His covenant. As the psalm closes, we are sure that God will come to Israel in Exile with His mercy and "do it again." Certainly, this psalm also forces the question: Will there always be this cycle of sin, judgment, and grace? Will the pattern ever break?

Certainly the history of the church mirrors the history of Israel in many respects. We too have fallen into sin and apostasy. We too have experienced the sifting of the Lord. We too need to cry out for His mercy. Nevertheless, will the pattern ever break? In Christ there is a triumphant, "Yes." In His cross, sin is dealt with "once for all" (Heb. 10:10). In His resurrection, death is dealt with "once for all" (1 Cor. 15:20). And by His Spirit, we are empowered and healed to live anew "once for all" (Rom. 8:13). Let us believe this, receive this, and claim our inheritance.

Riotous Renewal

Psalm 107

The church today is in desperate need of renewal. Secularism has gripped her vitals. The major denominations continue to experience an erosion of members and ministry. For example, in the last twenty-five years the Presbyterian Church in the U.S. has lost a third of its membership and half of its Sunday school enrollment. According to a major survey by the Princeton Religion Research Center reported in *The Unchurched American 1988,* 44 percent of all adults in the United States never attend church. Moreover, attendance among Canadians has fallen from 60 percent in 1957 to 32 percent in 1988. Statistics overseas are even more dismal. In 1979 it was estimated that only 9 percent of the population of England regularly attended church, with only 2 percent attending in large cities. This makes the urban areas effectively pagan.

What we need in this hour is for God to restore His church as the instrument of His kingdom to evangelize the so-called Christian West. We need a fresh outpouring of His Spirit with a clear call to repentance and godliness. We need God to bring us out of the bondage of our disobedience and restore us into the stream of His favor and blessing. We need God to lift His judgment from us for our worldliness and idols. What we need is riotous renewal.

In several periods of her history Israel too needed such a renewal. Certainly this was true when she labored under Pharaoh's taskmasters in Egypt. It was also true during the period of the Judges, when sin and disobedience led to punishing invasions by the pagan peoples who surrounded her. After the establishment of the monarchy, foreign alliances led to intermarriage with unbelievers and the setting up of their idols even in the temple itself. Such disobedience climaxed in 586 B.C. when God collapsed the walls of Jerusalem and carried

His people off into captivity in Babylon. Through all of this history of bondage, sin, and judgment, however, God remained faithful to His covenant promise to restore Israel to Himself and to bless her. Psalm 107 reflects this faithfulness, as God intervenes in the midst of judgment to bring Israel deliverance from exile, return to the land, and the reversal of her fortunes. As God worked with His ancient people, so He will work with us, and this psalm can become a gateway into the renewal and revival that we so desperately need in this hour. The themes here include the sense of calamity that has come upon God's people (vv. 4–5, 10–12, 17–18, 23–27), their cry for help and God's answer (vv. 6–7, 13–14, 19–20, 28–30), and a stylized refrain: "Oh, that men would give thanks to the Lord for His goodness, / And for His wonderful works to the children of men!" (vv. 8, 15, 21, 31).

Commentators have divided Psalm 107 into two sections: a thanksgiving (vv. 1–32) and a wisdom hymn (vv. 33–42). While there is a definite stylistic break at verse 33 and an appeal to the wise in verse 43: "Whoever is wise will observe these things . . . ," the unity of the psalm is assured by the major themes, which are sustained throughout. While the author is unknown, the context is post-Exilic (vv. 2–3) and the content celebrates God's intervention to redeem and restore the fortunes of His people. It is also influenced, as we have noted, by extensive wisdom themes. The thought moves from the call to worship (vv. 1–3) to deliverance (vv. 4–9), to salvation (vv. 10–16), to healing (vv. 17–22), to calm (vv. 23–32) and ends with renewal (vv. 33–42) and reflection (v. 43). This psalm begins Book Five of the Psalter (see *Introduction, Psalms 1–72,* Communicator's Commentary, Old Testament, no. 13, 20).

CALL TO WORSHIP

107:1 Oh, give thanks to the LORD, for *He is* good!
    For His mercy *endures* forever.
  2 Let the redeemed of the LORD say *so,*
    Whom He has redeemed from the hand of the
      enemy,
  3 And gathered out of the lands,
    From the east and from the west,
    From the north and from the south.

Ps. 107:1–3

Verse 1 tells us both what to do and why to do it, as we are called
to worship. The what is to *"give thanks to the Lord,"* and the why,
our motive, is His character: *"He is good"* and *"His mercy endures
forever."* It is the continuing mercy of God that has now tran-
scended His judgments, restoring Israel. As we pray for revival, we
too need to begin with this kind of worship, claiming the mercy of
God beyond our sin and the decay of the church. Revival will begin
with the restoration of a proper vision of who God is, His goodness, His moral perfection, and His mercy, which is extended toward us. As we trust that the Lord is merciful, we will experience
His mercy again.

As we often see in the Psalms, worship turns to witness in verse 2:
"Let the redeemed of the Lord say so." The word *redeemed* refers to
those who have been purchased from slavery. Normally a cost is involved in their redemption, and for the Old Testament this cost is the
mighty exertion of Yahweh Himself. Nehemiah refers to Israel as
*"Your servants and Your people, whom You have redeemed by Your
great power, and by Your strong hand"* (Neh. 1:10). In this psalm
redemption comes *"from the hand of the enemy."* Israel is snatched
from bondage and returned to her home. In verse 3 she is gathered
"out of the lands," and this gathering is comprehensive as she comes
from east, west, north, and south (or, according to the Hebrew text,
"from the sea [Mediterranean]").

In Christ, we too are redeemed from the "hand of the enemy." Our
enemy, however, is not Egypt or Babylon, our enemy is the devil
himself. Paul tells us that God "has delivered us from the power of
darkness and translated us into the kingdom of the Son of His love,
in whom we have redemption through His blood" (Col. 1:13–14).
Like Israel, the church also is gathered from throughout the whole
world, as it is God's intention to have representatives from every
tongue and tribe and nation before His throne (Rev. 7:9). No wonder
as the redeemed we are to "say so." We are to worship and witness to
the Lord who is good and whose mercy endures forever.

This call to "say so" is very personal to me. I was converted
through the ministry of Young Life, an evangelistic outreach to high
school students founded by Jim Rayburn. On the day in which I accepted Christ as my Savior, I found myself in what Jim called a "Say
So Meeting," gathered with hundreds of high school students who
one by one were witnessing to their new-found faith. Trembling, I

too joined them, standing to my feet, and sharing that I had just opened my heart to Jesus. Unknown to me then, the exhortation of verse 2 was fulfilled by me in that moment, and my life would never be the same.

DELIVERANCE

> 107:4 They wandered in the wilderness in a desolate
> way;
> They found no city to dwell in.
> 5 Hungry and thirsty,
> Their soul fainted in them.
> 6 Then they cried out to the LORD in their
> trouble,
> *And* He delivered them out of their distresses.
> 7 And He led them forth by the right way,
> That they might go to a city for a dwelling
> place.
> 8 Oh, that *men* would give thanks to the LORD
> *for* His goodness,
> And *for* His wonderful works to the children
> of men!
> 9 For He satisfies the longing soul,
> And fills the hungry soul with goodness.
>
> Ps. 107:4–9

Who are the redeemed of verse 2? In verses 4–5 we learn the answer. They are the exiles, those, like the generation of the Exodus, who *"wandered in the wilderness."* They were in a *"desolate* [desert] *way."* They were homeless: *"They found no city to dwell in"* (v. 4). Moreover, unlike Israel in the Exodus, they were *"hungry and thirsty."* This calamity, however, is not just physical: *"Their soul fainted in them."* Clearly they are under the judgment of God. The good news is that in adversity Israel came to know her need. Hungry, thirsty, and faint, she lived under no illusions. The modern church is still able to harbor her illusions because of her intellectual power, financial assets, tradition, and religiosity. We stand in the position of the church of Laodicea who receives this word from the reigning Lord, "You say, 'I am rich, have become wealthy, and have need of nothing'—and do

not know that you are wretched, miserable, poor, blind, and naked"
(Rev. 3:17). Nevertheless, Jesus warns us in order to restore us, "As
many as I love, I rebuke and chasten. Therefore be zealous and repent" (Rev. 3:19).

Lost in exile, Israel knows what to do. Rather than starting a new
program for renewal, or hiring an expert in church growth, in verses
6–7 she cries out to the Lord in her *"trouble"* ("bondage, restriction,"
v. 6). We learn that God brings adversity upon us in order to bring
us to Himself. He breaks us in order to make us into intercessors
before His throne. His judgment is not intended to make us more
self-reliant, but to make us reliant upon Him. Thus, the psalmist
continues, *"And He delivered them out of their distresses."* The verb
"delivered" can mean "to take the prey out of an animal's mouth."
God snatches Israel from her distresses as she calls to Him.

Such deliverance in verse 6 leads to God's continuing action in
verse 7. He takes them from the "desolate way" in verse 4 to the *"right
way."* Rather than no city to dwell in, they *"go to a city for habitation."*
In other words, God brings them home, home to His land, home to
Himself. As Isaiah promises, "And they [the nations] shall call them
[Israel] The Holy People, / The Redeemed of the Lord; / And you
shall be called Sought Out / A City Not Forsaken" (Isa. 62:12).

What is to be our response for such mercy? Verse 8 answers: *"Oh,
that men would give thanks to the Lord for His goodness* ["lovingkindness"] *and for His wonderful works* ["miracles, marvelous works"]."
These works refer to His direct, supernatural interventions in deliverance, leadership, and provision and are to evoke gratitude. This
gratitude becomes very personal in verse 9: *"For He satisfies the longing soul, / And fills the hungry soul with goodness."* The calamity of
verse 5 ("Hungry and thirsty, / Their soul fainted in them") is re-
versed. We need a city to dwell in, but more than that we need to
know the King of the city. As Augustine prays, "Thou hast made us
for Thyself, and our hearts are restless until they rest in Thee."

SALVATION

107:10 Those who sat in darkness and in the shadow
of death,
Bound in affliction and irons—

11 Because they rebelled against the words of
     God,
   And despised the counsel of the Most High,
12 Therefore He brought down their heart with
     labor;
   They fell down, and *there was* none to help.
13 Then they cried out to the LORD in their
     trouble,
   And He saved them out of their distresses.
14 He brought them out of darkness and the
     shadow of death,
   And broke their chains in pieces.
15 Oh, that *men* would give thanks to the LORD
     for His goodness,
   And *for* His wonderful works to the children
     of men!
16 For He has broken the gates of bronze,
   And cut the bars of iron in two.

Ps. 107:10–16

The psalmist returns to our calamitous condition. Not only are we exiles, wandering in the desert; we are also captives destined for death. Verses 10–12 spell this out. Those in exile are in *"darkness"* and the *"shadow of death"* (v. 10; see Ps. 23:4). This darkness denotes the absence of the God who is light. Moreover, where God is absent, death reigns (cf. Isa. 9:2). To compound the problem, the captives are also *"bound in affliction and irons."* When Jerusalem was destroyed by Nebuchadnezzar, her final king, Zedekiah was taken in bronze fetters to Babylon (Jer. 52:11). But why this judgment? The psalmist continues, *"Because they rebelled against the words of God, / And despised the counsel of the Most High"* (for this title see Ps. 47:2). Starting with Adam and Eve in the garden, sin always begins with the rejection of God's word. Our spiritual battles are launched in the mind. Believe God and live. Deny God and die. There are no alternatives. For us today, the loss of vitality in the modern church is a direct result of the loss of faith in the Bible as divine revelation and, as a result, the loss of faith in the God who reveals Himself there.

Judgment now falls upon unbelief (v. 12). The psalmist continues, *"He brought down their heart with labor,"* or, better, "He subdued their heart with travail (birth pangs)"—a spiritual heart attack. Next,

"They fell down [literally, *"stumbled"*], / *And there was none to help."*
Israel, therefore, is suffering and alone, abandoned. Where are her
"lovers," her idols now? Where are the nations who promised to help
her? All have fled and gone. Now, as in Egypt, she is ready for
Yahweh's intervention.

Verse 13 mirrors verse 6. The people cry *"out to the Lord in their
trouble."* C. S. Lewis remarks that God's great condescension toward
us is that He will allow Himself to be the God of our last resort.
When all else fails and we turn to Him, He is still there for us. The
psalmist continues, *"And He saved them out of their distresses."* God
delivers His people from their darkness, the shadow of death, and
breaks *"their chains in pieces"* (v. 14). His light dispels their darkness.
His life dispels their death. His power cuts their fetters. Liberated
from pagan night, they come out and they come home.

In this context, no wonder the psalmist cries out, *"Oh, that men
would give thanks to the Lord for His goodness, and for His wonderful
works"* (v. 15; cf. v. 8). These wonderful works are His miracles,
which flow because He is good, He is trustworthy, and He does not
go back on His covenant (treaty) promise to be faithful to His people. This hearty worship is based in God's breaking *"the gates of
bronze"* and cutting *"the bars of iron in two"* (v. 16) as Israel is released from her exile. It is worth noting that the Greek historian
Herodotus records that Babylon had one hundred gates of bronze in
her walls.

The ultimate fulfillment of this salvation is given to us in the Lord
Jesus Christ. He has come to defeat the devil and to liberate this
planet, which, since the Fall, has been under his bondage and control. It was for this reason that Satan could offer Jesus the kingdoms
of this world in the temptation. As John writes, "the whole world lies
under the sway of the wicked one" (1 John 5:19). Nevertheless, Jesus
is the Warrior-King who has come to bind the strong man (the devil)
and plunder his goods (Mark 3:27). No wonder an essential aspect of
His ministry is casting out demons (Mark 1:27). It is He who takes us
out of the devil's domain of death, breaks down the bronze gates of
hell, and cuts the bars of iron. Recently I have seen this clearly as
I have experienced people delivered from demons manifesting themselves in compulsive addictions and unbroken suicidal thoughts
through the power of the Holy Spirit and the mighty name of Jesus. If
the church is to be revived today, she will have to recover a biblical

perspective on who her enemy is and learn that her warfare, as Paul says, is not against flesh and blood but against these spiritual powers in the heavenly places (Eph. 6:12).

HEALING

107:17 Fools, because of their transgression,
     And because of their iniquities, were afflicted.
 18 Their soul abhorred all manner of food,
     And they drew near to the gates of death.
 19 Then they cried out to the LORD in their
        trouble,
     And He saved them out of their distresses.
 20 He sent His word and healed them,
     And delivered *them* from their destructions.
 21 Oh, that *men* would give thanks to the LORD
        for His goodness,
     And *for* His wonderful works to the children
        of men!
 22 Let them sacrifice the sacrifices of
        thanksgiving,
     And declare His works with rejoicing.
                                     Ps. 107:17–22

With God's judgment upon her, Israel experienced not only wandering in the wilderness and imprisonment; she also became ill. We all know how loss of home and loved ones will lead to dislocation and grief. If this grief is not healed, it can become a sickness unto death. Such a diagnosis is given in verses 17–18. The exiles are called *"fools."* Refusing the counsel of God's wisdom (see v. 11; cf. v. 43), they sinned and were judged (*"afflicted"*) for their *"transgression"* ("willful acts of rebellion") and their *"iniquities"* ("crookedness, going astray"). This judgment or affliction was experienced as a loss of appetite (*"Their soul abhorred all manner of food"*) and a sense of death (*"And they drew near to the gates of death,"* v. 18). The relationship between sin and sickness is clearly established. As we well know today, moral failure can have disastrous effects upon our physical health. Grief unhealed, leading to chronic depression, can result in death. In the exile, Israel's grief was not simply the loss of homeland

and family; her grief was the loss of God's presence because of her rebellion and sin. This is the greatest grief imagined.

Even in this dark hour, Israel cries out to the Lord (v. 19). Sin and abandonment do not keep her from calling out for help. The One who has judged her is the One who can heal her. Even from the cross, in His abandonment as the sin-bearer, Jesus prays, "My God, My God, why have You forsaken Me?" (Mark 15:34). So the psalmist reports, *"He saved them out of their distresses"* (cf. vv. 6 and 13). But how did this healing take place? *"He sent His word and healed them, / And delivered them from their destructions* [literally, "their pitfalls"]" (v. 20). We must remember that God's word is a creative, life-giving word. His word works. Jesus heals the sick by command, and we are commissioned to do the same. As the church is being renewed, we are not only recovering a sense of the spiritual warfare that we are in against the devil and his hosts; we are also recovering the reality that the healing ministry of Jesus is for us today. As He warns, however, those who are well don't need a doctor. We will only come to Jesus for healing when we as individuals and as a church recognize how sick we are. Then, we too will be delivered from our destructions.

What is to be our response to the healing power of God? Verse 21 reflects verses 8 and 15: *"Oh, that men would give thanks to the Lord for His goodness, / And for His wonderful works to the children of men!"* Such divine healing needs to lead to worship. I say "needs" because often I find that people who have been prayed for and dramatically healed do not necessarily praise God for what He has done. Selfish before their healing, they remain selfish after. This subnormal response is not to be ours. The psalmist continues that we are to *"sacrifice the sacrifices of thanksgiving* [originally communion sacrifices, which expressed gratitude for God's help], / *And declare His* [God's] *works with rejoicing."* For those of us who are healed today, our praise is our sacrifice. The last bloody sacrifice has been made by Jesus on the cross. Our sacrifice now is to be our bodies offered in worship (Rom. 12:1) and praise to God, which is the fruit of our lips (Heb. 13:15). As noted in verses 1–2, our worship is also for witness. We are to tell what God has done "with rejoicing." This joy expresses our gratitude for our healing. Joy is always a byproduct of revival and renewal in the church.

CALM

107:23 Those who go down to the sea in ships,
    Who do business on great waters,
 24 They see the works of the LORD,
    And His wonders in the deep.
 25 For He commands and raises the stormy wind,
    Which lifts up the waves of the sea.
 26 They mount up to the heavens,
    They go down again to the depths;
    Their soul melts because of trouble.
 27 They reel to and fro, and stagger like a
      drunken man,
    And are at their wits' end.
 28 Then they cry out to the LORD in their trouble,
    And He brings them out of their distresses.
 29 He calms the storm,
    So that its waves are still.
 30 Then they are glad because they are quiet;
    So He guides them to their desired haven.
 31 Oh, that *men* would give thanks to the LORD
      for His goodness,
    And *for* His wonderful works to the children
      of men!
 32 Let them exalt Him also in the assembly of the
      people,
    And praise Him in the company of the elders.
                    Ps. 107:23–32

The historical circumstances of the exile and the return have been addressed. God delivers, saves, and heals. At this point the psalmist turns to an extensive, poetic analogy of Israel's recent history, which is drawn from the experience of sailors. Like God's people, they too know calamity and divine intervention. The description of nature here suggests the influence of wisdom teaching, which is also reflected in the Book of Proverbs.

Verse 23 introduces the context for this meditation. It is structured around *"those who go down to the sea in ships."* They are not naval vessels, however. They are merchants, *"those who do business on great waters."* Such sailors see God's *"works"* and *"wonders"* ("miracles," deliverance? on the ocean, v. 24). These works are displayed as God sends a great wind *"which lifts up the waves of the sea"* (v. 25; notice that God, not Mother Nature, commands the waters). Like sailors on the Gulf during a hurricane, *"they mount up to the heavens, / They go down again to the depths."* Because of the storm *"their soul melts"* (v. 26). They are out of control in the storm, reeling *"to and fro . . . like a drunken man* [seasick], / *and are at their wits' end* [literally, *"all their wisdom will swallow itself up"]"* (v. 27). John Wesley experienced such a storm on his voyage to England after being an unsuccessful missionary in the Colonies. The storm brought him to fear for his life and, after seeing the faith of some Moravians on shipboard, it paved the way for his conversion when he returned to London. What we learn from the psalm at this point is that God can use both history (the Exile) and nature to bring us to the end of ourselves, and it is only then that we are ready for God.

Now, in verse 28 the sailors *"cry out to the Lord in their trouble."* Like Israel in the Exile, they too experience God's deliverance from *"their distresses."* Similar to Jesus on the Sea of Galilee, He *"calms the storm"* (literally, *"He sets the tempest to stillness,"* v. 29). Now the sailors experience a great quiet. God not only delivers them from their danger; He also guides them to a safe *"haven"* (literally, *"the city of their desire,"* v. 30).

The response to such rescue is to be like Israel returning from exile. Thus, the psalmist repeats his call: *"Oh, that men would give thanks to the Lord for His goodness, / And for His wonderful works to the children of men!"* (v. 31; cf. vv. 8, 15, 21). Like the exiles, the sailors are to enter into witness and worship. They are called upon to *"exalt Him also in the congregation of the people, / And praise Him in the company of the elders"* (v. 32). Their praise must be corporate and public for such rescue. Likewise, as God brings us through the storms of our present history and rescues His church from destruction, we are to publicly praise Him and exalt His name.

Renewal

107:33 He turns rivers into a wilderness,
      And the watersprings into dry ground;
  34 A fruitful land into barrenness,
      For the wickedness of those who dwell in it.

35 He turns a wilderness into pools of water,
   And dry land into watersprings.
36 There He makes the hungry dwell,
   That they may establish a city for a dwelling
      place,
37 And sow fields and plant vineyards,
   That they may yield a fruitful harvest.
38 He also blesses them, and they multiply
      greatly;
   And He does not let their cattle decrease.
39 When they are diminished and brought low
   Through oppression, affliction and sorrow,
40 He pours contempt on princes,
   And causes them to wander in the wilderness
      where there is no way;
41 Yet He sets the poor on high, far from
      affliction,
   And makes *their* families like a flock.
42 The righteous see *it* and rejoice,
   And all iniquity stops its mouth.

Ps. 107:33-42

The psalmist offers us a meditation upon the judgment and redemption of the Lord, which we have seen take place both in history
and in nature. The wicked experience His wrath (vv. 33–34). The
hungry, however, are restored and made fruitful (vv. 35–38). Princes
are judged, but the poor are exalted (vv. 39–42). Let us look at each of
these sections.

First of all, because of people's *"wickedness"* (v. 34) God ruins their
land in judgment. *"Rivers"* (continual, spring fed) become a *"wilderness"* ("desert"), and, in parallel, *"watersprings"* become *"dry ground"*
(v. 33). The end of the water supply results in a *"fruitful land"* becoming barren (literally, turned *"to saltness,"* v. 34). As we saw
above, Yahweh, rather than Baal or Mother Nature, commands the
weather map. As distant as this may be for us, the Bible holds that
He uses nature to accomplish His moral judgments. For example,
Elijah proclaims to wicked King Ahab, "As the Lord God of Israel
lives, before whom I stand, there shall not be dew nor rain these
years, except at my word" (1 Kings 17:1). Thus, for the psalmist,
morality affects both personal health and material prosperity (see

vv. 17–18). We may assert that the sins of the church have also produced barrenness—the absence of God's powerful Spirit and of the
life-giving washing of His Word (see John 15:3).

Second, the *"hungry"* (v. 36) and destitute are restored by the
mercy of God (vv. 35–38). Beyond (or after) His judgments, *"He turns
a wilderness into pools of water, / And dry land into watersprings"*
(v. 35). The returned exiles can dwell again in the land, establishing
"a city for habitation" (v. 36). Secure there, they are able to *"sow
fields," "plant vineyards,"* and take the time for a *"fruitful harvest"*
(v. 37). The command given in creation to be fruitful and multiply as
a sign of God's blessing is fulfilled (v. 38; see Gen. 1:28). Even the
cattle prosper under God's hand.

When we repent of our sins and return to the Lord today, we
are made secure and prosperous. As Jesus promises, *"Blessed are
those who hunger and thirst for righteousness, / For they shall be
filled"* (Matt. 5:6). Churches that are experiencing the blessing of
God are churches that have gone through a deep cleansing. Out of
this a fresh spiritual hunger has developed, which only God can
satisfy.

Third, God's people, although blessed by Him, are still subject to
"oppression, affliction ["evil"], *and sorrow,"* which will diminish them
and bring them low (v. 39). They are still engaged in warfare with
their world. Thus, while Jesus promises His disciples great abundance in this life, it will come with persecutions (Mark 10:30).
Nevertheless, God will act. He will pour *"contempt on princes"* and
cause them *"to wander in the wilderness,"* lost (*"where there is no way,"*
v. 40). The proud will be humbled and broken. As God promises
through Isaiah, *"For the day of the Lord of hosts / Shall come upon
everything proud and lofty, / Upon everything lifted up— / And it
shall be brought low"* (Isa. 2:12). At the same time, *"the poor"*
("needy") will be exalted, *"set on high* [like on a fortress rock or high
tower], *far from affliction."* They will multiply, growing *"families like
a flock"* (v. 41). The *"righteous"* (true Israel) will see the oppressors
judged and the poor vindicated and *"rejoice* ["take pleasure in,
exult"], */ And all iniquity"* is silenced; that is, it *"stops its mouth"* (v.
42). Even before the return of the Lord, we too can expect to see the
oppressors of God's people fall under His judgment and the poor
who trust in Him exalted. No wonder the gospel is spreading like
wildfire among the poor in the Third World today.

REFLECTION

107:43 Whoever *is* wise will observe these *things,*
       And they will understand the lovingkindness
       of the LORD.

Ps. 107:43

The final verse of this psalm is like a postscript. The *"wise"* will agree with its analysis. They are not like those who "rebelled against the words of God," despising His counsel (v. 11). They are not like the "fools" who were afflicted "because of their iniquities" (v. 17). Like the psalmist, they too *"observe these things."* Having done this, they *"understand the lovingkindness* ["covenant-love"] *of the Lord."* Knowing Israel's God, they know His ways, the ways of His covenant. They know that He judges sin and, at the same time, redeems the sinner. They know that when all other hope is gone, they can still hope in Yahweh. They know that He will restore their fortunes and return them to the land of promise. They know that He will rescue them from evil and judge their oppressors, and, knowing this, they are ready to worship the living God and witness to His mighty works. Why is this? Because they have experienced riotous revival. God has brought them home.

As Israel never lost hope in her exile, so must we never lose hope in the God who still performs miracles today. Regardless of how worldly and corrupt we may be, it is He who will restore and heal the church. When the storm rages, it is He who will lead us to a safe haven. It is He who will protect and vindicate the poor. It is He who will make our land fruitful again. As He sends forth His word and pours out His Spirit, riotous revival will be ours again.

A Combination of Psalms 57:7–11 and 60:5–12

Psalm 108

A CONTINUING TRADITION OF PRAISE AND INTERCESSION

108:1 O God, my heart is steadfast;
 I will sing and give praise, even with my
  glory.
 2 Awake, lute and harp!
 I will awaken the dawn.
 3 I will praise You, O LORD, among the peoples,
 And I will sing praises to You among the
  nations.
 4 For Your mercy *is* great above the heavens,
 And Your truth *reaches* to the clouds.
 5 Be exalted, O God, above the heavens,
 And Your glory above all the earth;
 6 That Your beloved may be delivered,
 Save *with* Your right hand, and hear me.
 7 God has spoken in His holiness:
 "I will rejoice;
 I will divide Shechem
 And measure out the Valley of Succoth.
 8 Gilead *is* Mine; Manasseh *is* Mine;
 Ephraim also *is* the helmet for My head;
 Judah *is* My lawgiver.
 9 Moab *is* My washpot;
 Over Edom I will cast My shoe;
 Over Philistia I will triumph."

10 Who will bring me *into* the strong city?
   Who will lead me to Edom?
11 *Is it* not *You,* O God, *who* cast us off?
   And *You,* O God, *who* did not go out with our
      armies?
12 Give us help from trouble,
   For the help of man is useless.
13 Through God we will do valiantly,
   For *it is* He *who* shall tread down our enemies.

                                        Ps. 108:1-13

Similar to Psalm 53, which is a variant on Psalm 14, here we have a combination of elements from two previous psalms. The first is from Ps. 53:7–11 and covers verses 1–6. The second is from Ps. 60:5–12 and covers verses 7–13. The reader is directed to our commentary on *Psalms 1–72* for the relevant exposition of these sections.

Of interest here is the wedding of these psalms and their repetition in the Word of God. We can learn from this that God does not share our values about the economy of language. He is quite happy to repeat Himself. This is evident in the Pentateuch as various laws are echoed more than once, in the history of Israel as we compare 1 and 2 Kings and 1 and 2 Chronicles, and in the Synoptic Gospels (Matthew, Mark, and Luke). As my former professor, W. D. Davies, notes, "It is a poor teacher who doesn't repeat himself." Moreover, the combination of these two psalms shows us that the Psalter is a living book that was used in the worship of Israel. Thus, it was appropriate to take sections of other psalms, much as we do in our church Scripture readings today, and knit them together for special liturgies or personal devotion. That this practice is allowed by God is witnessed to by the example of Psalm 108. Finally, the cry for deliverance in the first section (see v. 6) is answered by a divine oracle in the second section (starting in v. 7). God will redeem His people from defeat. His promise long ago is available again in new circumstances. Thus, the written word becomes the living word as it is repeated and applied to our lives today. This is the functional value of including these two psalm sections in the Psalter as they are combined for us in a new way here.

How to Pray When Falsely Accused

Psalm 109

This psalm shocks our liberal sensitivities, fashioned in an age of relativism. Its curses, its calls for punishment, the satisfaction that it seems to reflect over human suffering strikes us as vindictive and hard-hearted. Apart from the spirit of our age, well summed up by "live and let live," how can the calls for retribution here be squared with Jesus' demand that we love our enemies and pray for those who despitefully use us? This point is the deeper one. This psalm seems to contradict the whole gospel. Let me give just one example from the text: "Let his children be fatherless, / And his wife a widow" (v. 9). While all of us may harbor such anger at times, we would hardly dare to speak it.

At this point, let me make some preliminary observations before we turn to the text. First, the Old Testament is dominated by the reality that God is King, enthroned in glory, and as King He is also the just judge of all people. The word *just* is important here because God is absolutely holy. Israel was trained in her sense of justice by the justice of God Himself. The law was given as the instrument of that training. Since it not only reveals the will of God but also our own sin, as sinners we can only come into His presence by sacrifice. In light of the holiness of God, we can understand how a man, wronged by an intimate friend, would want God to execute judgment on his behalf. What the psalmist knew and expected was that since we are sinners, we deserve punishment for our sin. Now, in Christ we receive grace, but we must never forget that it is "amazing grace." Second, revelation is progressive. Certainly Israel knew the mercy of God. Nevertheless, under the law, she was continually confronted with His demand and her disobedience. She was not able to read the psalms as we do, in the light of Christ. Thus, to apply Jesus' call for us to love our enemies to a much earlier and incomplete time of revelation is irrelevant. We must also remember that in Christ the holiness of God was not overturned but fulfilled. Moreover, the justice of God was not set aside but satisfied on the cross. Third, the whole of the Bible agrees that if we reject God's mercy we will pay with our lives. Thus, even though Jesus prays for His enemies' forgiveness, there will be a time when He will execute flaming vengeance upon them (2 Thess. 1:8). The age of grace will end. With this in mind, we are ready to look at Psalm 109.

This psalm is written in the white heat of anger, and, as we know, anger is the flip side of love. The psalmist has been betrayed by the wicked and deceitful (v. 2). As he says, "In return for my love they are my accusers" (v. 4). This circle of accusation becomes focused on one person in the great central section (vv. 6–20). He is apparently the ringleader who "persecuted the poor and needy man" (v. 16). The nature of the accusation is not spelled out specifically, which allows Psalm 109 to be used by all who are falsely accused.

Most commentators identify this psalm as an individual lament. Tradition, which we accept, gives its authorship to David. There are many tumultuous circumstances in his life that could have produced it. The thought moves from a general call to judgment (vv. 1–5) to the spelling out of specific judgments in the form of curses (vv. 6–20), to a cry for deliverance (vv. 21–25), to a cry for vindication (vv. 26–29) and concludes with a vow to worship (vv. 30–31).

GENERAL CALL FOR JUDGMENT

> 109:1 Do not keep silent,
>   O God of my praise!
>   2 For the mouth of the wicked and the mouth of
>   the deceitful
>   Have opened against me;
>   They have spoken against me with a lying
>   tongue.
>   3 They have also surrounded me with words of
>   hatred,
>   And fought against me without a cause.

> 4 In return for my love they are my accusers,
>   But I *give myself to* prayer.
> 5 Thus they have rewarded me evil for good,
>   And hatred for my love.
>
> *Ps. 109:1–5*

Verse 1 calls upon God to speak: *"Do not keep silent, / O God of my praise!"* The Lord's breaking silence includes David's vindication before his enemies and their punishment by Him (see vv. 20–21). He is identified here as the One whom David worships, the God of his praise, his "hallelujah." The reasons for divine intervention are given in verses 2–5. A circle of opposition, engaging in deceit and accusation, is exposed. Those who attack him are *"wicked"* ("criminals, lawbreakers"). Their attacks at this point are verbal rather than physical. They have opened their deceitful mouths, as he says, speaking *"against me* [literally, "with me," to my face?] *with a lying tongue"* (v. 2). These false accusations contain *"words of hatred,"* which surround him like a street gang. They are groundless, however, as he says, they *"fought against me without a cause"* (v. 3). David exposes the depths of his anger, which, as we noted, is the flip side of love: *"In return for my love they are my accusers"* (v. 4). No wonder he is so hurt and angry.

His response at this point is crucial. Rather than plotting against them, he turns to prayer. It is God who will vindicate him as He deals with those who *"have rewarded me evil* [literally, "set evil upon me"] *for good, / And hatred for my love."* The noun *evil* means "misery" or "distress," and this psalm is its exposition. What we have here is a general call for judgment. David asks God to take care of those who have betrayed his love. His hurt is honest, his anger clear. As we would say today, "David is in touch with his emotions." He is not dealing by denial; he is straightforward and up-front. This alone is therapeutic. Moreover, he takes his case to God, expecting God to act. Since He knows his heart, David must be direct with Him. At the same time, the truth of this attack and his suffering is seen in his willingness to come directly to the divine Judge Himself. Here he will rest his case and await the results, since he is not locked into a world-view that denies the supernatural.

One of the things I have learned over the years is that, like David, as much as I want people to like me, I will have enemies. In certain instances, I had to turn to prayer and leave my case with God Himself. He is the only One who can vindicate us and He will take care of us and our situations as He wills. Our hearts may cry for justice, but only God can bring it. He may demand mercy from our hearts, and, again, only He can give it.

SPECIFIC JUDGMENTS SPELLED OUT

109:6 Set a wicked man over him,
    And let an accuser stand at his right hand.
  7 When he is judged, let him be found guilty,
    And let his prayer become sin.
  8 Let his days be few,
    And let another take his office.
  9 Let his children be fatherless,
    And his wife a widow.
 10 Let his children continually be vagabonds, and
      beg;
    Let them seek *their bread* also from their
      desolate places.
 11 Let the creditor seize all that he has,
    And let strangers plunder his labor.
 12 Let there be none to extend mercy to him,
    Nor let there be any to favor his fatherless
      children.
 13 Let his posterity be cut off,
    And in the generation following let their name
      be blotted out.
 14 Let the iniquity of his fathers be remembered
      before the Lord,
    And let not the sin of his mother be blotted
      out.
 15 Let them be continually before the Lord,
    That He may cut off the memory of them from
      the earth;
 16 Because he did not remember to show mercy,
    But persecuted the poor and needy man,
    That he might even slay the broken in heart.
 17 As he loved cursing, so let it come to him;
    As he did not delight in blessing, so let it be
      far from him.

18 As he clothed himself with cursing as with his
   garment,
   So let it enter his body like water,
   And like oil into his bones.
19 Let it be to him like the garment which covers
   him,
   And for a belt with which he girds himself
   continually.
20 *Let* this *be* the LORD's reward to my accusers,
   And to those who speak evil against my
   person.

Ps. 109:6–20

David now engages in a long list of curses, which spell out what he
would like God to do in bringing His judgment upon the apparent
ringleader of the opposition. David is at his vindictive best. Indeed
this man might receive an "eye for an eye." An avalanche of evil is to
come upon him *"because he did not remember to show mercy, / But
persecuted the poor and needy man, / That he might even slay the broken
in heart"* (v. 16). The formula is simple: no mercy *from* his enemy, no
mercy *for* his enemy. As we noted in our introduction, this attitude is
morally correct; our whole system of criminal justice is built upon it.
Only in Jesus do we see mercy triumph over the merciless. What
then are these judgments to be?

In verse 6 David asks for a *"wicked man"* to be set over his enemy
(as judge). Since his enemy is wicked (v. 2), he deserves the same.
Also an *"accuser"* ("adversary") is to be at the judge's *"right hand."* His
sentence in the case is guaranteed to be *"guilty."* His enemy's protest
of innocence to God will be exposed for what it is: *"And let his prayer
become sin"* (missing the mark of God's will, v. 7).

As a result of this judgment, David continues, *"Let his days be few"*
(v. 8). Such public disgrace may well kill him with a deep depression. Next, *"And let another take his office."* Apparently this enemy
comes from the officials of Israel. There is intrigue at the center of
the court. Public disgrace is also to lead to private despair. Thus,
with his untimely death, *"Let his children be fatherless, / And his wife
a widow"* (v. 9). The loss of the "breadwinner" leads to the next curse:
"Let his children continually be vagabonds, and beg." They will proceed
from a ruined house, that is, *"their desolate places"* (v. 10). The destruction of his household is completed as the creditor seizes *"all that*

he has," plundering his labor (v. 11). Since he has not extended mercy (see v. 16), *"Let there be none to extend mercy to him,"* or to his children (v. 12). Verse 13 expresses the ultimate disaster that is to befall him, the end of his family line. Since there was nothing more precious to the ancient Hebrew than generations to come, David cries, *"Let his posterity be cut off, / And in the generation following let their name be blotted out"* (v. 13). Judgment is to fall upon this traitor and upon his family. We can sum up the curses simply, "Death to them all!"

Such disastrous judgment is pronounced even upon the man's predecessors: *"Let the iniquity of his fathers be remembered before the Lord."* Although they are deceased, they are still accessible to God's judgment in eternity. His mother, too, is to receive no forgiveness (v. 14). When David says, *"Let them be continually before the Lord,"* he is asking that their sins be always before Him. God's judgment will follow: *"That He may cut off the memory of them from the earth"* (v. 15). We can sum up the thought this way: Remembered by God, forgotten by men.

But why all of this evil? David gives the ground for such severe judgment in verse 16. His enemy forgot to *"show* [or, *"do"*] *mercy* ["covenant-love"] but, rather, *"persecuted the poor and needy man"* (David himself). His vindictiveness was such *"that he might even slay the broken in heart."* When David was down, he kicked him below the belt. When wounded, he wounded him again. The remembrance of this injustice triggers a new set of curses, which follow in verses 17-20.

The basic thought, as we have seen, is an "eye for an eye." In other words, "God, give him what he deserves." So David cries, *"As he loved cursing, so let it come to him."* Likewise, since *"he did not delight in blessing, so let it be far from him"* (v. 17). The theme of cursing continues in verses 18-19. It is as if David is saying, "My enemy loved curses, so I am giving them to him. Since he cursed me, I am returning the favor." Thus, he says, *"As he clothed himself with cursing as with his garment,"* that is, since cursing was his style, his image, *"So let it enter his body like water, / And like oil into his bones"* (v. 18). These curses are to be as elemental as water is to our physical life, and as "special" as oil is when rubbed upon our bodies. Moreover, these curses are to be *"like the garment which covers him, / And for a belt with which he girds himself continually"* (v. 19). All of

David's curses, starting in verse 6, are to hound him and determine his life.

Unlike the curses of the ancient world, which (like those of modern witches) carried demonic power in themselves, David's curses can only reflect God's just judgments. Thus, David concludes, addressing the whole circle of deceit rather than just the ringleader, *"Let this be the Lord's reward to my accusers, / And to those who speak evil against my person* ["life," "soul"]" (v. 20). But it is not enough for David's enemies to be judged. David needs God's help for himself, and to this he turns.

CRY FOR DELIVERANCE

109:21 But You, O GOD the Lord,
        Deal with me for Your name's sake;
        Because Your mercy *is* good, deliver me.
    22 For I *am* poor and needy,
        And my heart is wounded within me.
    23 I am gone like a shadow when it lengthens;
        I am shaken off like a locust.
    24 My knees are weak through fasting,
        And my flesh is feeble from lack of fatness.
    25 I also have become a reproach to them;
        When they look at me, they shake their heads.
                                    Ps. 109:21–25

Under the burden of rejection, David needs God's deliverance. His insides hurt. People have made him into a reproach. In this context he solemnly prays, *"But You, O God the Lord."* Turning from his enemies, he asks God to *"deal with me* [literally, "work with me"] *for Your name's sake,"* that is, for His own purpose and glory. Having not received mercy from people, David asks for mercy from God. This *"mercy"* is an expression of divine goodness; therefore, he concludes, *"deliver me"* ("snatch me from my enemies' mouth," v. 21).

David offers the reason for his plea. He is *"poor and needy,"* and his *"heart is wounded"* (literally, "pierced," v. 22; cf. v. 16). His life is passing; it vanishes like a *"shadow"* lengthening at sunset. He is shaken off, rejected, set aside, like someone would shake off a bug (*"locust,"* v. 23). The physical impact of this calamity is extensive. He wastes away; his knees are *"weak through fasting"* (v. 24, probably involuntary, but perhaps also a religious act in preparation for God's answer; compare 2 Sam. 12:16 where David fasted for the life of his son born of Bathsheba). This fast is of long duration: *"my flesh is feeble from lack of fatness"* (v. 24). His accusers, however, are unimpressed. He is a reproach to them, and he adds, *"When they look at me, they shake their heads"* (v. 25) in disdain (see Ps. 22:7–8). No wonder he needs deliverance.

Those of us who have experienced similar attacks can identify with David. A wounded heart bleeds. Rejection breeds depression; the appetite flees. Former friends are cut off; the satisfaction of their presence and love is lost. Public humiliation results in people's avoidance. Social leprosy is the result. Having gone through this, we can all identify with David's hurt and pain. In our longing for justice we can also identify with his curses. At the same time, because of Christ, there is another word beyond justice and revenge. Only when we have felt David's pain, however, can we honestly deal with that word.

CRY FOR VINDICATION

> 109:26 Help me, O LORD my God!
>   Oh, save me according to Your mercy,
> 27 That they may know that this *is* Your hand—
>   *That* You, LORD, have done it!
> 28 Let them curse, but You bless;
>   When they arise, let them be ashamed,
>   But let Your servant rejoice.
> 29 Let my accusers be clothed with shame,
>   And let them cover themselves with their own
>   disgrace as with a mantle.
>
> *Ps. 109:26–29*

David again calls upon God to act. As we have noted above, the fact that he does not take justice into his own hands is crucial. If he is wrong in his understanding of the situation, God will reveal that. He certainly believes that he is right and is willing to entrust the outcome to the only just Judge there is. In verse 26 he cries out, addressing God as he did in verse 21, with solemn fullness: *"Help me, O Lord my God!"* He desires salvation or deliverance *"according to Your mercy* ["covenant-love"]*."* Even though his enemies are unmerciful (v. 16), God remains merciful. As He intervenes, David's enemies will know *"that this is Your hand— / That You, Lord, have done it!"* (v. 27). The hand represents power (cf. Exod. 15:6). As God judges his enemies, so He will also exalt David. They may curse him, but God will bless him. When they arise (to come against him as an enemy), they will be defeated: *"let them be ashamed."* In this, David, as God's servant (the subject of His Kingdom), will rejoice (v. 28). David's curses, which were to be their garment (v. 19), are now fulfilled by their own shame and disgrace (v. 29).

When we are hurt, can we entrust our lives and our case to God? David did. Only God can execute justice. We must wait for Him to act, and He will.

Vow to Worship

109:30 I will greatly praise the LORD with my mouth;
　　　 Yes, I will praise Him among the multitude.
　31 For He shall stand at the right hand of the
　　　　poor,
　　　 To save *him* from those who condemn him.
　　　　　　　　　　　　　　　　Ps. 109:30–31

David concludes with a confession of faith, confident that God will act and vindicate him. With formulas which are traditional, he promises to *"greatly praise the Lord."* He will not be guilty of thin or cheap worship. This praise will also be public; all will know what Yahweh has done: *"Yes, I will praise Him among the multitude"* (v. 30). The basis for his boisterous worship and witness is given in verse 31. God stands at the *"right hand of the poor"* man. He is his advocate and defense (cf. v. 6). He saves *"him from those who condemn him."*

I am the first to admit that the righteous are not always vindicated in this life. At the same time, God will often intervene directly on their behalf. When He doesn't it is because of a greater purpose. Thus, Jesus was left to die on the cross, and in that abandonment He saved us from our sins. There will be a final day of vindication, however. On that day perfect justice will be done by the perfect Judge. In the meantime, we can see hints of that day as God rights moral wrongs even in this world. With a high sense of justice and a deep hurt, David cries out for God to destroy those who have betrayed him. As we have noted, there is another word that he does not know here. It is Jesus' word of forgiveness. When we pray this psalm in our hurt, we need to be as honest as David. We too have his full capacity to curse our enemies. Nevertheless, since we are also sinners and stand under the judgment of God, we need to know the final word—the word of the gospel. Psalm 109 will keep us honest when we are hurt. But in Christ we cannot stay here. It drives us toward the New Testament, where the Savior stands to forgive us as His enemies and to summon us into a similar life of forgiveness (see Luke 6:27–36; 23:34).

CHAPTER ONE HUNDRED TEN

Whose Son Is the Messiah?

Psalm 110

There are some psalms that are frankly messianic and prophetic. Any attempt to interpret them otherwise is futile and confusing. There is no doubt that modern scholars have problems with this assertion. This is because they share in the secularism and antisupernatural bias of our age. Throughout most of the history of Israel and the church, however, this has not been so. It was only during the period of the Enlightenment that rationalism became king, locking God out of His universe in favor of immanent laws of nature, which were claimed to control all things within a chain of cause and effect. This chain could be readily understood by unaided human intellect.

Behind this assumption was a not-so-veiled attack upon God's sovereign reign over His universe. Man was to be the new lord. By his scientific tools he would claim control over all reality. Nevertheless, the predictive element of Scripture cannot be so easily dispensed with. The New Testament rings with it. Again and again the Old Testament is cited as prophesying the things that come to pass with Jesus' appearance. The test for a word from God is that it comes true in its time. Otherwise it is a presumptive word (Deut. 18:21–22). More than once, the New Testament uses Psalm 110 as that predictive word now fulfilled.

In the Gospels Jesus raises the crucial question of His identity. He asks the Pharisees what they think about the Messiah, "Whose Son is He?" (Matt. 22:42). They reply that He is the son of David. Jesus challenges their answer by reminding them that David (under divine inspiration) called the Messiah "Lord" in Ps. 110:1. How could he do this if he was only his son? No father would so address his offspring. Jesus leaves them with a question: "If David then calls Him 'Lord,' how is He his Son?" In other words, the Messiah must be more than the son of David, He must be the Son of God. Later, on the Day of Pentecost, as Peter preaches, he cites the same text to prove that Jesus has been exalted to the position of authority, to the right hand of God (Acts 2:33–35). The Book of Hebrews also uses this text to prove that Jesus is greater than any angel because He alone reigns in heaven (Heb. 1:13). Later Hebrews also makes reference from the same psalm to Melchizedek and applies this to Christ (Heb. 5:6). What God promised in the Old Testament concerning His Son has been fulfilled in the New Testament. It is that simple. As we come to Psalm 110, then, we must accept it as predictive or violate both the world-view and the specific usage of Scripture. As we do this, the text will open up for us.

Most commentators take this psalm to be a liturgical piece that was employed during the enthronement of the king. Their exegesis is strained, however, and filled with conjecture because they miss or downplay the prophetic element. They have no way to really understand how Israel's king reigns at God's right hand (v. 1). They also cannot account for him being called "a priest forever / According to the order of Melchizedek" (v. 4). It is enough simply to say that God revealed this prophetic psalm to prepare for the coming of the Messiah. Tradition gives it to David. Clearly Jesus held this view

(Matt. 22:43). Its content consists of divine words (prophetic oracles) and their application. The thought runs from the Messiah as Lord and King (vv. 1–2) to the Messiah as Warrior-Priest (vv. 3–4) and concludes with His judgment of the nations (vv. 5–7).

LORD AND KING

110:1 The LORD said to my Lord,
　　　"Sit at My right hand,
　　　Till I make Your enemies Your footstool."
　　2 The LORD shall send the rod of Your strength
　　　out of Zion.
　　　Rule in the midst of Your enemies!

Ps. 110:1–2

Verse 1 opens with the majestic announcement that Yahweh has spoken to *my Lord.* Here is the divine address to the Son of God. He is invited to sit at His right hand: *"Till I make Your enemies Your footstool."* Clearly this is a prophetic invitation to reign, which is fulfilled when Jesus conquers sin, Satan, and death and is then exalted into heaven. There He assumes the position of authority at God's right hand. Jesus identifies Himself as coming from heaven "sitting at the right hand of the Power [God]" (Matt. 26:64). Echoing this Paul tells the Ephesians that Christ is seated at God's "right hand in the heavenly places" (Eph. 1:20) and that all things have been put under His feet (Eph. 1:22). His exaltation and reign are in effect until all of His enemies have been conquered. The victory is symbolized as they become like the footstool of His throne. Under His feet, they submit and are humiliated. Thus, this heavenly reign goes on right now as the Kingdom of God is extending throughout the earth, overcoming Satan's kingdom of evil, until all things are subject to the Son of God.

Enthroned in glory, Yahweh sends *"the rod of Your strength out of Zion."* This is the rod or scepter of the Son's power as a great military commander. We read in Ps. 2:9: "You [the Messiah] shall break them [the nations] with a rod of iron." That this power goes from Mount Zion [Jerusalem] is seen as Jesus is raised from the dead there, and as His gospel goes forth to the nations from there. Furthermore, when the exalted Lord returns in glory, He will reign from Jerusalem and subject all things to Himself.

The command is given: *"Rule in the midst of Your enemies!"* This word from God is the marching order for the church. Jesus is to rule over all things, since all authority has been given to Him (Matt. 28:18). His real enemies are not just the pagan nations, but the demonic hordes, including Satan himself, which are to be subdued in His name. We learn from verses 1–2 that Jesus reigns as Lord and that Jesus rules. This is the word of God given long before His coming. It has been fulfilled in His ministry as He inaugurated the Kingdom of God and in His exaltation to the right hand of the Father. When we evangelize in His name, and pray in His name, and cast out demons in His name, and heal in His name, His reign is being extended, not in the safe realms of heaven, but in the midst of His enemies, here on the battleground of earth.

WARRIOR-PRIEST

110:3 Your people *shall be* volunteers
In the day of Your power;
In the beauties of holiness, from the womb of
the morning,
You have the dew of Your youth.
4 The LORD has sworn
And will not relent,
"You *are* a priest forever
According to the order of Melchizedek."
Ps. 110:3–4

The warfare theme continues in verse 3. As the Messiah extends God's reign throughout the earth, His *"people"* (subjects? army? hosts?) will be *"volunteers,"* or literally, "willing offerings." They will gladly submit to His reign. This will take place *"in the day of Your power,"* which refers to the time period in which the Messiah sits at the right hand of the Father (see v. 1). The *"day of power"* would cover this present age of grace between the first and second comings of Christ. Moreover, the Messiah's people serve Him in *"the beauties* ["majesties"] *of holiness."* They are a separated people, holy unto the Lord. Peter exhorts us, "but as He who called you is holy, you also be holy in all your conduct, because it is written, 'Be holy, for I am holy'" (1 Pet. 1:15–16). Notice that holiness is not some grim legalism. It is beautiful. It is the restoration of God's creation before the Fall. It is our conformation to His very character. It is being remade in the image of Christ (2 Cor. 3:18).

The next line of verse 3, *"from the womb of the morning* ["dawn"]*,"* could refer to the people of the Messiah who come forth fresh as in a new day. However, it may also be the beginning of a new sentence. This would mean that it refers to the Messiah and is parallel to the next line: *"You have the dew of Your youth."* The thought would then be that the reigning King is fresh like the morning, having the "dew" of His youth, that is, having the vitality of His youth. He is the Warrior-King, commanding His holy people with fresh, youthful strength as He retakes the earth from Satan's grip.

God speaks again to His Son, the reigning messianic King, in verse 4. He gives an oath which is fixed and permanent: *"The Lord has sworn / And will not relent."* Here is what He proclaims: *"'You are a priest forever / According to the order of Melchizedek.'"* As we learn from Gen. 14:18ff., Melchizedek was the priest-king of the old Jebusite city of Jerusalem. His name means "the king of righteousness." As a priest, Abraham paid tithes to him after a battle victory. Psalm 110 takes up his priesthood and applies it to the Messiah. This is later used extensively by the Book of Hebrews to contrast Christ's heavenly priesthood, which is a whole new, eternal order separate from that of the Old Testament priesthood coming from Aaron (see Heb. 5:6–11; 7:1–28). The point of this text is that the King is also Priest and that His priesthood is forever. He not only reigns, He also represents us to God, making eternal intercession for us. Thus, Hebrews unites Christ's being seated at the right hand of God with His priestly role: "Now this is the main point of the things we are saying: We have such a High Priest, who is seated at the right hand of the throne of the Majesty in the heavens, a Minister of the sanctuary and of the tabernacle which the Lord erected and not man" (Heb. 8:1–2). There is no way that verse 4 can be understood apart from its messianic fulfillment in the New Testament.

THE JUDGMENT OF THE NATIONS

110:5 The Lord *is* at Your right hand;
He shall execute kings in the day of His wrath.

> 6 He shall judge among the nations,
>   He shall fill *the places* with dead bodies,
>   He shall execute the heads of many countries.
> 7 He shall drink of the brook by the wayside;
>   Therefore He shall lift up the head.
>
> *Ps. 110:5–7*

This psalm concludes with a prophetic vision of the end, *"the day of His* [God's] *wrath"* (v. 5). This refers to the final battle which the Messiah will lead against the kings of this planet who, according to the New Testament, are under the rule of Satan and his earthly representative, Antichrist (see 2 Thess. 2:1–12; Revelation 13). When the Warrior-King comes from heaven, He will come with the very power of God because: *"The Lord is at Your right hand."* As John tells us, "Now I saw heaven opened, and behold, a white horse. And He who sat on him was called Faithful and True, and in righteousness He judges and makes war. . . . Now out of His mouth goes a sharp sword, that with it He should strike the nations. And He Himself will rule them with a rod of iron. He Himself treads the winepress of the fierceness and wrath of Almighty God" (Rev. 19:11–15). Bringing His judgment, He will *"execute* ["shatter"] *kings."* As John tells us, "And I saw the beast [Antichrist], the kings of the earth, and their armies, gathered together to make war against Him who sat on the horse and against His army" (Rev. 19:19). Destroying their power, *"He shall judge among the nations"* (v. 6). In His wrath corpses will fill the earth, and the heads of state will be put on the block. Again, as John tells us, after the beast and false prophet are thrown into the lake of fire, "the rest were killed with the sword which proceeded from the mouth of Him who sat on the horse. And all the birds were filled with their flesh" (Rev. 19:21).

The Son, who is the reigning King and eternal Priest, celebrates His victory in verse 7. In poetic picture *"He shall drink of the brook by the wayside."* The battle is won. Rest and refreshment are His. As David says of the Good Shepherd, "He leads me beside the still waters. / He restores my soul" (Ps. 23:2–3). In victory, finally, *"He shall lift up the head."* He is triumphant. As David prays, "But You, O Lord, are a shield for me / My glory and the One who lifts up my head" (Ps. 3:3). Indeed, the kingdoms of this world shall become the kingdoms of our Lord and of His Christ, and He shall reign forever and ever (Rev. 11:15).

In the midst of the Psalter stands this prophetic word of God, the promise of the establishment of the Messiah's rule over the nations and the final triumph of His Kingdom. It is this hope that kept Israel facing the future with faith. It is this hope that began its fulfillment on a starlit night in Bethlehem. It is this hope that will take us through the trials and sufferings of our present life, as we look to our reigning, priestly King who will return in glory. All other hopes pale before Him.

CHAPTER ONE HUNDRED ELEVEN

The Works of the Lord

Psalm 111

The word of God and the works of God must go together. In the modern church, we have tended to separate them to our peril. In evangelical circles there is a proper stress on the Word. We love the Bible. We honor it as divine revelation. At the same time, we have tended to neglect the works of God. This is not to say that we have done nothing about our faith. To the contrary, since the beginning of the "Billy Graham Era," we have supported education, published scholarly works, sent missionaries, engaged in programs of evangelism, planted churches, and even recovered a concern for the poor. Nevertheless, because of our antisupernatural environment, we have tended to reduce God's works to our efforts of obedience and to see the vast arena of nature and history as secular, unrelated to His goodness and grace. The challenge before us is to repent of our worldly mind-set and to reintegrate ourselves into a biblical world-view. We need to recapture a comprehensive picture of reality as God has revealed it to us. We need to open ourselves up to His mighty works. Psalm 111 can be our guide.

The theme of this psalm is clear: it centers upon the works of God.

"The works of the Lord are great" (v. 2).
"His work is honorable and glorious" (v. 3).
"He has made His wonderful works to be remembered" (v. 4).
"He has declared to His people the power of His works" (v. 6).
"The works of His hands are verity and justice" (v. 7).

For the psalmist, these works are seen as a consequence of the covenant. "He will ever be mindful of His covenant" (v. 5). "He has commanded His covenant forever" (v. 9). This covenant with Abraham is God's unconditional treaty, based upon grace alone, through which He, as the sovereign King, grants the promise of a land and a great nation to come. Moreover, all of the nations of the earth will also be blessed through this one man (Gen. 12:1–3). Since God has established His covenant with His people, He works His works in their midst.

Commentators see this psalm as a hymn of praise or thanksgiving. No human author is identified. The thought moves from a call to worship (v. 1) to God's works in our provision (vv. 2–6), to God's works in revelation and redemption (vv. 7–9) and offers a comprehensive conclusion centering on fearing, obeying, and praising God (v. 10).

CALL TO WORSHIP

111:1 Praise the LORD!
I will praise the LORD with *my* whole heart,
In the assembly of the upright and *in* the
congregation.
Ps. 111:1

Verse 1 opens with a simple imperative: *"Praise the Lord!"* The Hebrew transliterates into English as "Hallelujah." This is *what* we are to do; we are to praise God as we worship Him. But *how* are we to do it? The psalmist answers directly and personally: *"I will praise the Lord with my whole heart."* He models enthusiastic, uninhibited thanks. To illustrate this we can turn to Psalm 100: "Make a joyful shout to the Lord, all you lands! / Serve the Lord with gladness; / Come before Him with singing" (Ps. 100:1–2). Such worship fulfills the first commandment, to love God with all our heart (Deut. 6:5). But *where* are we to engage in such worship? The answer is: *"In the assembly of the upright* ['straight, just'] *and in the congregation* ['assembly of God's people']." This praise is to be corporate and public, when the righteous of Israel gather. We need continually to test our public worship in the church today by the word of God. This verse is a good standard. Are we praising God with our whole heart? When we worship do we "go for it"? Do we long to worship with God's people? Or is Sunday a chore, a duty only? If so, we are subbiblical at the heart of what God has called us to do.

GOD'S WORKS: PROVISION

111:2 The works of the LORD *are* great,
    Studied by all who have pleasure in them.
3 His work *is* honorable and glorious,
    And His righteousness endures forever.
4 He has made His wonderful works to be
    remembered;
    The LORD *is* gracious and full of compassion.
5 He has given food to those who fear Him;
    He will ever be mindful of His covenant.
6 He has declared to His people the power of
    His works,
    In giving them the heritage of the nations.
Ps. 111:2–6

The basic theme of the psalm, identified earlier, is introduced: *"The works of the Lord are great, / Studied* ['sought out'] *by all who have pleasure in them"* (v. 2). These works are more clearly defined in verse 3. God's *"work"* ('extraordinary, marvelous work,' 'miracle') is *"honorable and glorious,"* or, literally, "Glory (splendor) and majesty (is) His wonderful work." In God's acts, His might is revealed. The revelation of His power in the Exodus would make an appropriate commentary on this theme. Moreover, *"His righteousness endures* ['is standing'] *forever."* Faithful to His covenant, God executes His justice on behalf of His people. By bringing Israel out of Egypt His righteousness was seen. And, because God is not fickle, we can count on His righteousness. It goes on forever.

In verse 4, the psalmist explains that God has acted, in part, so that we will remember what He has done: *"He has made His wonderful works* ["miracles"] *to be remembered."* In the Exodus, when God passes over the houses of Israel in the last plague (the death of the firstborn) and institutes the feast of Passover, it is not only for the sake of His people, but also for the sake of generations yet to come (Exod. 12:24–28). They are to remember that they also were redeemed that night. Thus, His actions reveal His character: *"The Lord is gracious and full of compassion* [plural intensive]." I cannot stress enough here that the works of God reveal the attributes of God. Too often we suppose that we simply know God in His Word. While this is true, it is also an abstraction, unless it leads us to know Him in His works. These works (miracles) do not simply document or prove revelation; they are revelation. If I am drowning, I do not need to know that someone on the shore loves me; I need to be pulled out of the water. When I realize that I am lost in sin and under Satan's power, I need rescue, I need the work of God in my life. The remembrance of His past works will open me up to His present works. As I see what He has done for others, I will begin to believe that He can do the same for me. I will begin to believe that He is gracious and full of compassion, that is, that He is ready to do His *"wonderful works"* in me!

The psalmist turns to a specific work of God in verse 5: *"He has given food to those who fear Him; / He will ever be mindful of His covenant."* This divine provision is not just the annual harvest. It does not merely represent God's general providence. We know this because the psalmist has previously used the word "miracles" to define God's works. Quite certainly he is thinking here of the manna from heaven and the quail that fed Israel in the wilderness (see Exodus 16; Num. 11:31ff.). The feeding of Israel is also linked to the covenant. In this supernatural supply, He proved that He remembered His covenant-treaty with His people, to be their God and to care for them in time of trouble.

But God not only cared for Israel in the wilderness; He also brought her into the Promised Land. As verse 6 states, *"the power of His works"* is declared as God gives His people *"the heritage of the nations."* Food and land document His mighty deeds as He keeps His covenant.

While we remember with gratitude what God did in the Exodus, we also remember what He has done for us in sending His Son to earth. We have a greater exodus from Satan's dominion and the penalty and power of sin. Again, we know God not just in His conceptual revelation in the Bible, but in His interventions in history. But this knowledge will avail us nothing, unless we also experience His interventions in our personal lives. The day when I accepted Christ into my heart was the day that God's provision and attributes became a reality to me. Apart from this all is still "head knowledge." Unfortunately, many born-again Christians can date their conversion, but can see little of God's continuing works in their lives. Israel knew that she had come out of Egypt, but she also knew God's direct care for her as she journeyed, and then entered into the land under His mighty hand. Certainly the psalmist knows this personal, direct action of God in his life as he vows to praise God with his whole heart (v. 1).

GOD'S WORK: REVELATION AND REDEMPTION

111:7 The works of His hands *are* verity and justice;
All His precepts *are* sure.
8 They stand fast forever and ever,
And are done in truth and uprightness.
9 He has sent redemption to His people;
He has commanded His covenant forever:
Holy and awesome *is* His name.

Ps. 111:7–9

Once again the theme of this psalm is addressed in verse 9: *"The works of His hands are verity and justice* [literally, "truth and judgment"]." God's judgment, for example, is seen when He drives the pagan nations out of the Promised Land. Another work is seen when He gives Israel the law on Sinai. Thus, *"All His precepts* [this word is found only in the Psalter and is identified with the law in Ps. 119:4] *are sure* ["steadfast"]." The work of God and the word of God go together; they are one. For God's word is a powerful, life-giving word. Since, as the mighty King, He speaks it from His throne, it goes into action. It accomplishes the purpose for which He gives it (Isa. 55:11).

God's word is trustworthy; it will stand and endure. As the psalmist continues, *"They* [His precepts] *stand fast* ["are established, enacted"] *forever and ever"* (v. 8). Moreover, they are *"done* [made] *in truth and uprightness."* As we stand upon them, they will stand up. Jesus said, "Heaven and earth will pass away, but My words will by no means pass away" (Matt. 24:35). When everything else goes, they last.

God's mighty works are not only seen in revelation; they are also seen in redemption. As the psalmist recalls in verse 9: *"He has sent redemption* [or "ransom"] *to His people; / He has commanded His covenant forever."* To be redeemed means to be bought out of slavery. Israel experienced this in the Exodus. As Moses sings after passing through the Red Sea: "You in Your mercy have led forth / The people whom You have redeemed; / You have guided them in Your strength" (Exod. 15:13). God's work of redemption proves that He keeps His covenant-treaty with His people. He has commanded it forever. In His word and work He shows Himself. As verse 9 concludes: *"Holy and awesome is His name."* God's name is holy, separate, unique, above all other names. God's name is also awesome; it evokes terror from His enemies and wonder from His friends. All of this is revealed in the mighty works of Yahweh. No wonder Isaiah cries out before Him, "Woe is me" (Isa. 6:5). This is the God who puts us on our faces.

CONCLUSION

111:10 The fear of the LORD *is* the beginning of
wisdom;
A good understanding have all those who do
His commandments.
His praise endures forever.
Ps. 111:10

Finally, the psalmist sums up what our response to the living God is to be. Giving up our foolishness, we are to become wise by fearing Him. This is the beginning of wisdom (see Prov. 1:7). Proper fear or awe will issue in our obedience to what He says. This will give us a *good understanding.* All is climaxed in our worship of Him, which will go on for all eternity: *"His praise endures* ["is standing"] *forever."* Such is the value of knowing the God who works, and who reveals Himself by what He does. We worship no dead idol. We worship the mighty King. We worship the God who saves, delivers, heals, provides, rescues, conquers, and reigns. We worship the God whose word works in our lives. Amen!

CHAPTER ONE HUNDRED TWELVE

God's Blessing upon the Righteous

Psalm 112

Why serve God? I have often been asked this question. Since the 1960s, there has been an abandonment of Christian values and traditional morality in this country. For example, a majority of Roman Catholics use birth-control devices, which is contrary to the teaching of their church. How can the pope's authority be held absolute in light of such mass disobedience? Many seek abortions (over one million each year) to dispense with unwanted pregnancies. They claim the right to their own bodies, never suspecting that their unborn children have rights too, regardless of how they were conceived. That abortion is murder is denied by most. Homosexuals have also come out of the closet in order to demand their rights and receive full acceptance within our culture. As they continue to practice and affirm their lifestyle, they advocate that the church ordain them into its clergy and provide some sort of a marriage service for their commitments to each other. The 1980s have presented us with the Age of Greed. Yuppies demand the symbols of success in order to satisfy their lusts and shore up their egos. We have lived through a period of unrestrained borrowing and corruption. "Buy now and pay later" is our theme. In the meantime the poor continue to suffer as we glut ourselves with gaudy things. We not only consume these things; we also consume each other. Relationships become as dispensable as a Styrofoam cup. Divorce and extramarital affairs are the order of the day. At the same time, in deep pain, we have become a culture of addicts. Legal and illegal drugs anesthetize our true emotions as we go up or down with caffeine, nicotine, alcohol, tranquilizers, and a host of "street drugs." Many ask again, "Why serve God?" Won't He take away my fun? Put me into a moral straightjacket? Make me seem odd to my friends? Does He really offer me a satisfying life?

Psalm 112 boldly answers our question. It states, "Blessed is the man who fears the Lord, / Who delights greatly in His commandments" (v. 1). This psalm doesn't simply state its thesis. It documents it with a description of the righteous person who gives his life to God. The ancient Hebrews were pragmatists. They didn't shy away from the consequences of living a godly life. They were able to ask, "What's in it for me?" This psalm offers the answer. Those who worship the Lord and walk in His ways will have mighty descendants and wealth; they will live in the light, be honest in business, and be secure when evil news comes or enemies attack. They will care for the poor, and their righteousness will endure forever. As a footnote to this, the psalm concludes that the wicked will see the life of the righteous, be grieved, melt away, and perish. These are the concrete results of knowing God and receiving His blessing.

Commentators identify this psalm as a wisdom poem. Many connect it to Psalm 111, suggesting that it is a commentary on its concluding verse, "The fear of the Lord is the beginning of wisdom; / A good understanding have all those who do His commandments" (Ps. 111:10). Its date and author are unknown. The thought moves from the call to worship and blessing (v. 1) to the rewards of that blessing (vv. 2–9) and ends with a footnote about the wicked (v. 10).

CALL TO WORSHIP AND BLESSING

112:1 Praise the LORD!
Blessed is the man *who* fears the LORD,
Who delights greatly in His commandments.
Ps. 112:1

Verse 1 opens (as does v. 1 of the previous psalm) with a call to
worship: *"Praise the Lord!"* This liturgical formula tells us *what* we are
to do as it brings us into the presence of God and prepares us for the
meditation that follows. Next, we are told *who* is to worship. Thus,
the foundational assertion is made: *"Blessed is the man who fears
the Lord."* The blessing of God is His grace and bounty, which come
upon us for our happiness (see Ps. 1:1). The happy man is the one
who bows before God in fear (awe) and who then rises to serve Him
from the heart as he *"delights* [the verb means "to be mindful of,
attentive to, keep, have pleasure in"] *greatly in His commandments."*
Here is the summary of how to live: know God and obey God. Jesus
puts it more deeply, "If you love Me, keep My commandments" (John
14:15). Life is not to be found in the adventure of illicit sex or in a
condo and a BMW. Neither is it to be found in a drug high; it is to be
found in knowing and loving God and doing His will in this world.
Having said this, we are ready for the pragmatic question: "So
what?" "What is the value of a godly or righteous life?"

THE REWARDS OF GOD'S BLESSING

112:2 His descendants will be mighty on earth;
The generation of the upright will be blessed.
3 Wealth and riches *will be* in his house,
And his righteousness endures forever.
4 Unto the upright there arises light in the
darkness;
He is gracious, and full of compassion, and
righteous.
5 A good man deals graciously and lends;
He will guide his affairs with discretion.
6 Surely he will never be shaken;
The righteous will be in everlasting
remembrance.

> 7 He will not be afraid of evil tidings;
>   His heart is steadfast, trusting in the LORD.
> 8 His heart *is* established;
>   He will not be afraid,
>   Until he sees *his desire* upon his enemies.
> 9 He has dispersed abroad,
>   He has given to the poor;
>   His righteousness endures forever;
>   His horn will be exalted with honor.
>
> *Ps. 112:2–9*

The answer to the issue of benefits is given in verses 2–9. Throughout this section it is the righteous who are being described (vv. 2, 3, 4, 6, 9). They are the ones who fear God and delight in His commandments. What then does God promise for a godly life?

First, in verse 2, the righteous person's *"descendants"* ("seed") will be *"mighty on earth."* The word "mighty" is used of a "mighty man," a man of valor and substance. These descendants will overcome their enemies (see v. 8). As we might render this in our context today, they will be able to do spiritual battle over the forces of evil and prevail (cf. Eph. 6:10ff.). In Christ we know that our enemies have been defeated and that "we are more than conquerors through Him who loved us" (Rom. 8:37). Thus, *"the generation* [or family] *of the upright* ["straight, just"] *will be blessed* ["happy"]." The godly person not only benefits himself but also his family. As he is blessed, they are blessed. As he models a just life, they learn that life from him. As he is no longer a channel for sin and corruption to flow into his household, they receive the benefits. No one lives to himself or dies to himself (Rom. 14:7).

Second, in verse 3, *"wealth and riches will be in his house."* Material bounty is a sign of divine blessing. Since God is King over His Kingdom, He wants His subjects to prosper. Rather than justify our greed, however, the psalmist affirms God as Creator and the blessings of His creation, which He desires to bring upon us. We are blessed by fearing Him (v. 1)—not by our money in the bank. Nevertheless, the fear of God will lead to the bounty of His Kingdom. This is why Jesus healed people and delivered them from demons. He came to restore God's fallen creation to its original, perfect order, and He wants to continue to grant us this blessing today. Earthly riches, however, are passing. Thus, the psalmist adds that the godly person's *"righteousness endures* ["is standing"] *forever."* We need to know that material things are a benefit of fearing God, and keep our eyes upon that which is eternal.

Third, *"Unto the upright there arises light in the darkness"* (v. 4). This light is the very light of God. As Isaiah promises, "The people who walked in darkness / Have seen a great light" (Isa. 9:2). This light is the coming of the Messiah (Isa. 9:6–7). John tells us that "God is light and in Him is no darkness at all" (1 John 1:5). It is to the upright that the light of God comes. They are not overcome by the darkness of this fallen, pagan world. We take the second half of verse 4 to apply to God rather than to the upright. This means that we have a description of the divine light as it shines here: *"He is gracious, and full of compassion* ["merciful"], *and righteous."* The light shines God's grace upon us, showing us His heart as compassionate and, at the same time, reaffirming that His character is righteous. This is the light that dispels the darkness of our confusion and illusions about God. Divine mercy welcomes us as sinners, and divine righteousness changes us into the very character of God Himself.

Fourth, the righteous person will reflect God's presence in everyday life. He deals *"graciously and lends,"* and *"guides* ["nourishes"] *his affairs with discretion* ["right judgment," *mišpot*]." Freed from materialism, and blessed with the bounty of God, he will open his heart to the less fortunate and needy. God's graciousness (v. 4) will be reflected in his graciousness. As Jesus says, "Give to everyone who asks of you" (Luke 6:30). At the same time, in all of his affairs he will use discretion, namely judgment based upon God's justice. Material blessing and business dealings come from God's hand and are to reflect His character. We cannot pray to heaven on Sunday and live like hell the rest of the week. There is to be no sacred/secular dichotomy in our lives. God wants His blessing to reign over us in all that we do.

Fifth, the righteous man will be secure; *"he will never be shaken"* ("moved," v. 6). He will always be before God, *"in everlasting remembrance."* Because of this, bad news will not bring fear, because his *"heart is steadfast, trusting* ["secure, unconcerned"] *in the Lord"* (v. 7). Because *"His heart is established* ["resting, supported"]; / *He will not be afraid, / Until he sees his desire upon his enemies"* (v. 8). His opponents will be overcome. When our heart is with the Lord, neither bad news nor bad people can get to us. Notice that the psalmist doesn't promise that our lives will be free of trouble; what he does promise is that the God who holds us will resolve all things.

Sixth, the righteous person cares for the poor just as God does (v. 9). Thus, *"He has dispersed abroad* [literally, "He has scattered," like a farmer sowing seed], / *He has given to the poor."* When Paul is affirmed in his apostleship by Peter, James, and John, he is only told to remember the poor, and he adds, "[This was] the very thing which I also was eager to do" (Gal. 2:10).

As a result of all of this, the psalmist concludes: *"His righteousness endures* ["stands"] *forever; / His horn* [strength] *will be exalted with honor* ["glory"]." The godly man who worships the Lord and obeys His commandments (v. 1) will stand before Him and be lifted up by Him. He will be vindicated by God and blessed throughout all eternity.

A FOOTNOTE FOR THE WICKED

112:10 The wicked will see *it* and be grieved;
He will gnash his teeth and melt away;
The desire of the wicked shall perish.
Ps. 112:10

Part of the satisfaction of the godly is to be vindicated not only before God but also before his enemies. Such vindication serves as a moral and a warning. Thus, the wicked will see the blessing upon the righteous *"and be grieved."* In anger (and perhaps pain) *"he will gnash his teeth and melt away."* Such an end is also reflected in Psalm 1 where the wicked are like the chaff that blows away (Ps. 1:4). Finally, his *"desire"* perishes. Indeed, in this postscript the promise in verse 8 that the righteous will see "his desire upon his enemies" is fulfilled. This final verse shows us our alternatives. There are only two ways; one goes to heaven, the other to hell. In this world we can live only two lives, either that of the godly or that of the wicked. In light of the end, since "the desire of the wicked shall perish," is not the choice clear? Isn't the reason to serve God, rather than this decaying culture and its lusts, clear?

The What and Why of Worship

Psalm 113

The renewal of worship in the church is one of the great, current facts. By this I don't mean the so-called liturgical renewal. While this movement has been in gear for some time now, its force is spent. Born of the cultural crisis of the 1960s, in which traditional worship seemed so archaic and irrelevant, and fed by such events as the Second Vatican Council, which changed the Latin Mass into the vernacular and fostered informality in the church, this renewal was one based in a liberalizing theology with a resulting change in language and theater. It was not a dynamic change caused by the renewing power of the Holy Spirit. It was a change on the outside rather than on the inside. That it did not accomplish what its proponents claimed is apparent in the continuing slide in membership and strength of the very denominations that experienced such liturgical innovations. The renewal in worship that I mean and have experienced has come from other quarters. Its center was first in the Jesus movement, that revival at the end of the 1960s that brought so many from the counterculture into the church. As these "flower children" came to Christ, they brought their culture with them. They too, along with the liturgical renewal movement, were responding to cultural change. Their response, however, was not calculated to gain relevancy; it was simply the expression of their culture, and it was coming from their souls. Since this new worship was inaugurated in the context of revival, it stuck. Essential to its heart was the recovery of biblical praise. As I mentioned in the introduction to my first volume on the Psalms, I attended Calvary Chapel in Costa Mesa, California, and heard people sing the psalms using their open Bibles as the lyric sheet. As these new converts were being delivered from the power of the devil, expressed in the drug culture, the violence of the streets, and all kinds of personal brokenness, they were rejoicing before God with open hearts. This spiritual renewal has continued in force in the Vineyard Movement, which grew out of the older Calvary Chapels. Probably the most important characteristic of its worship, which has impacted the larger church, is the insistence that worship be directed to God Himself, rather than to the congregation. For example, the chorus "He Is Lord" becomes real worship with the change to the second person singular pronoun, "*You* are Lord." Before we are ready to worship, however, we must know the God to whom we are to direct our praise. This is clearly revealed in Psalm 113.

In our text, we are called to direct our praise to the Lord and are then greeted by an extensive exhortation as to who is to praise Him. After this, the *basis* for such praise is given as we are told about the God who is to be praised. Such a description becomes a powerful motivational force for us to fulfill the call to worship in verses 1–3. As we focus upon God's greatness, His condescension toward us, and His exaltation of the poor, the needy, and the barren in verses 4–9, we will want to praise Him all the more. Our careful study of this psalm will enhance our praise. We will come into the presence of the God who really is.

Commentators traditionally have identified Psalm 113 as a part of the Hallel (praise) psalms, which include Psalms 113–118 and 120–136. These texts were employed in the great annual festivals of Israel. Also Psalms 113–118 were sung at home during the Passover meal. The date and author of Psalm 113 are unknown. Its thought moves from the call of worship, *who* is to respond (vv. 1–3), to the motivation for worship, *why* we are to respond (vv. 4–9).

CALL TO WORSHIP: WHO?

113:1 Praise the LORD!
    Praise, O servants of the LORD,
    Praise the name of the LORD!
   2 Blessed be the name of the LORD
    From this time forth and forevermore!

>   3 From the rising of the sun to its going down
>   The LORD's name *is* to be praised.
>
>   *Ps. 113:1-3*

Verse 1 opens, as did Psalms 111 and 112, with the explosive ex-hortation: *"Praise the Lord!"* With repetition for emphasis, those who are to enter into this worship are now identified: *"Praise, O servants of the Lord."* These servants are the people of Israel who have been redeemed by Yahweh in order to subject themselves to Him as their mighty King. Their (and our) basic service is the service of worship before His throne. As God says in the Exodus, "And you shall be to Me a Kingdom of priests and a holy nation" (Exod. 19:6). Israel's worship and now ours is summed up by the book of He-brews: "Therefore by Him [Christ] let us continually offer the sacri-fice of praise to God, that is, the fruit of our lips, giving thanks to His name" (Heb. 13:15). For emphasis, the exhortation is repeated: *"Praise the name of the Lord!"* (v. 2). God's name reveals His person. As He tells Moses at the burning bush, He is the eternal, personal God, "I am Who I am" (Exod. 3:14). Where His name is spoken in faith, relationship is established. Where His name is spoken in faith, His power and presence are manifested. No wonder we are to praise His name.

Moreover, praise is always in season. We are to praise God *"from this time forth and forevermore!"* As we praise Him from our hearts we are engaging in that which lasts through eternity. The Revelation is laced with pictures of the redeemed in heaven worshiping and praising God before His throne. Not only is God to be praised con-tinually; He is also to be praised *"from the rising of the sun to its going down"* (v. 3). The whole earth, as far as the eye can see, from the east to the west, is to be caught up in praise. Indeed, the world has been created to praise Him.

I know the delight and joy of praising God in spiritual worship. Burdens are lifted as we lift our hearts to Him. All cares seem to melt away. At the same time, I must confess that I do not continually praise God and that much of the planet is filled with bitterness and the silence of despair rather than song. These facts are calls to per-sonal repentance and world evangelization. As Paul says, when the world comes to Christ, "grace, having spread through the many, [causes] thanksgiving to abound to the glory of God" (2 Cor. 4:15). These verses also inform our vision of the future. The day will come when God will be praised continually and when this worship will encompass all of the universe. As Paul again says, "at the name of Jesus every knee should bow, of those in heaven, and of those on earth, and those under the earth, and that every tongue should confess that Jesus Christ is Lord, to the glory of God the Father" (Phil. 2:10–11).

MOTIVATION FOR WORSHIP: WHY?

> 113:4 The LORD *is* high above all nations,
>   His glory above the heavens.
>   5 Who *is* like the LORD our God,
>   Who dwells on high,
>   6 Who humbles Himself to behold
>   *The things that are* in the heavens and in the
>   earth?
>   7 He raises the poor out of the dust,
>   *And* lifts the needy out of the ash heap,
>   8 That He may seat *him* with princes—
>   With the princes of His people.
>   9 He grants the barren woman a home,
>   Like a joyful mother of children.
>   Praise the LORD!
>
> *Ps. 113:4–9*

We are to praise God, first of all, because He is exalted above all that we know. He transcends all of the pomp and pride of humankind. He is greater than a thousand nuclear blasts. He makes the strutting of dictators as nothing. The nations may roar, but God is not impressed or worried: *"The Lord is high above all nations."* As Isaiah says, "All flesh is grass" (Isa. 40:6) and "the nations are as a drop in a bucket" (Isa. 40:15). God is even higher than the heavens; *"His glory* ["heaviness," like spoils from battle that evoke praise] *above"* them (v. 4). Thus, Solomon asks as he dedicates the Jerusalem temple: "But will God indeed dwell on the earth? Behold, heaven and the heaven of heavens cannot contain You" (1 Kings 8:27). In other words, this great God alone is worthy of our worship.

Second, we are to worship God, not only because of His transcendence, but also because of His uniqueness. The psalmist asks, *"Who is like the Lord our God, / Who dwells on high"* (or literally, "Who makes [Himself] high to dwell")? The answer is, "No one." God is God. He is incomparable. He judges all and is judged by no one. At the same time, He also *"humbles Himself to behold / The things that are in the heavens and in the earth."* He is the God of great condescension and love toward us. In His majesty He is not aloof from our problems. He orders the stars in their courses and provides the bread on our tables. He also makes Himself known to us. Calvin says that He leans over our crib and lisps His word to us as a mother does to her newborn child. What a paradox! The one God, exalted and humbled. The mighty King, caring about our little lives. These thoughts prepare us for the New Testament. In Jesus Christ we see the consummation of the God who, although exalted, humbles Himself. As the Christmas hymn puts it, "Veiled in flesh the Godhead see, / Hail incarnate deity." This God deserves our wondering worship.

Third, the God who humbles Himself cares for the humble. He not only beholds the things of earth, as we have seen, He intervenes in them. Thus, *"He raises the poor out of the dust, / And lifts the needy out of the ash heap"* (v. 7). The ash heap is like the garbage dump in Tiajuana, Mexico, where the poorest of the poor live. But God is there to rescue them. When Jesus begins His public ministry in Luke's Gospel He cites a text from Isaiah, "The Spirit of the Lord is upon Me, / Because He has anointed Me to preach the gospel to the poor" and then asserts, "Today this Scripture is fulfilled in your hearing" (Luke 4:18–21). In Jesus God's concern for the poor is consummated. His goal in rescuing them is to exalt them: *"That He may seat him* [the poor and needy] *with princes— / With the princes of the people"* (v. 8). No wonder the New Testament announces that we are joint heirs with Christ and that we shall reign with Him (Rom. 8:17). God also cares about the *"barren woman"* who is a reproach (compare Luke 1:25). She will have a home *"like a joyful mother of children"* (or, literally, "[be] a glad mother of sons," v. 9). Her womb will be fruitful. While God brings down the proud, He exalts the humble. We are to praise Him for His mighty deeds.

True worship, the praise of God, is based upon His character. He is the transcendent King who reigns far above the heavens. He also humbles Himself to care about the things of this earth. He delivers the poor and exalts them. He makes fruitful the barren womb and removes reproach. No wonder His praise should be eternal (v. 2). No wonder His praise should be comprehensive, from the rising of the sun to its setting (v. 3). No wonder we are to *"Praise the Lord"* (v. 9). Here is true renewal in worship.

CHAPTER ONE HUNDRED FOURTEEN

What Makes God's People Special?

Psalm 114

Often I have wondered, "Is there anything special about the church?" So much of her history is mixed, to say the least. We may mention to a seeker the hospitals, schools, orphanages, and other host of good works that have covered the planet in the name of Christ, only to be reminded about the Inquisition and the Crusades. Are church buildings with their esthetic power her special gift? Hardly. Temples and mosques also command our admiration or even affection. Is it the quality of her relational life? Oh, that that were so. Unfortunately, we find the same hypocrisy and lack of caring among church people as we do in the world. Then perhaps it is her theology or her liturgy? While these may be special in the sense of being unique, they are not the secret to her life. There can be only one answer, and it is the answer of this psalm: It is the presence of God that makes us special in this world.

By sheer grace, Abraham was bound into a covenant-treaty with Yahweh and granted His presence. This covenant was based upon

God's call to this one man. Abraham merely believed the word that
came to him, and the relationship was sealed. Although generations
later Abraham's offspring found themselves in slavery, God remembered His covenant-promise to be their God and delivered them
from Pharaoh. But what was God's purpose in rescuing His people?
The answer is both simple and profound: He brought them out of
Egypt in order to dwell in their midst (v. 2). This is why the earth
trembled and the sea parted before them—God was there (vv. 3–8).
The earth will tremble and the sea will part before us for exactly the
same reason.

Commentators usually call this psalm a hymn, but it could just as
well be called a meditation. Like Psalm 113 it was used historically
in the Passover festival. Its date and author are unknown. The
thought moves from God indwelling Israel (vv. 1–2) to the response
of the earth to Israel (vv. 3–6) and concludes with God's presence as
the reason for that response (vv. 7–8).

GOD INDWELLS ISRAEL

114:1 When Israel went out of Egypt,
　　　The house of Jacob from a people of strange
　　　　language,
　　2 Judah became His sanctuary,
　　　And Israel His dominion.

Ps. 114:1–2

Verse 1 begins with the mighty event of the Exodus, which is the
setting for the psalm: *"When Israel went out of Egypt, / The house
of Jacob from a people of strange language* [literally, "speaking
strangely"]." The *"house of Jacob"* is a synonym for Israel, since the
twelve tribes came from Jacob's twelve sons. The result of Israel's
going out of Egypt is that *"Judah* [a single tribe here representing
the whole and parallel to Israel] *became His* [God's] *sanctuary* ["holy
place"], / *And Israel His dominion."* Here we are at the heart of
Israel's faith. God redeemed His people in order that He might
dwell with them, that they might be holy as He is holy. Moses tells
God, "If Your Presence does not go with us, do not bring us up
from here. For how then will it be known that Your people and I

have found grace in Your sight, except You go with us? So we shall be separate, Your people and I, from all the people who are upon the face of the earth" (Exod. 33:15–16). Along with God's presence, Israel is unique because she is His "dominion" or kingdom. God is King, and the chosen people are His subjects where His rule and reign will be displayed. God will both dwell and rule in the midst of His people. What was true then is also true now. As the church, we are to be known not for impressive buildings or "relevant" programs or profound theology, we are to be known as the people in whom God is present and over whom He reigns. This is why Jesus proclaimed the Kingdom of God and called His hearers to enter that Kingdom. He came to establish the rule of God in our midst as He brought the presence of God to us.

NATURE'S RESPONSE TO ISRAEL

114:3 The sea saw *it* and fled;
     Jordan turned back.
  4 The mountains skipped like rams,
     The little hills like lambs.
  5 What ails you, O sea, that you fled?
     O Jordan, *that you* turned back?
  6 O mountains, *that* you skipped like rams?
     O little hills, like lambs?

Ps. 114:3–6

The psalmist now describes Israel's journey from Egypt to the Promised Land by recalling what nature did before God's people. First of all, *"the sea saw it and fled."* This clearly refers to the parting of the Red Sea (or, Sea of Reeds) when Israel passed through on dry ground and Pharaoh's pursuing chariots were submerged (see Exodus 14). Next, *"Jordan turned back"* (v. 3). Here the psalmist recalls the parting of the Jordan River before Israel when she actually entered the land under Joshua (see Joshua 3). Then, *"the mountains skipped like rams, / The little hills like lambs"* (v. 4). While some take this to refer to the earth quaking at the giving of the law at Sinai, in the sequence it could also refer to the conquest of the Promised Land which included military campaigns through the hill country. As we see from verse 5, the skipping of the mountains and hills is not in joy but in fear. Thus, the psalmist asks, *"What ails you, O sea, that you fled? / O Jordan, that you turned back? / O mountains that you skipped like rams?"* These questions are answered in verses 7–8.

GOD'S PRESENCE IS THE REASON
FOR THE RESPONSE

114:7 Tremble, O earth, at the presence of the Lord,
    At the presence of the God of Jacob,
  8 Who turned the rock *into* a pool of water,
    The flint into a fountain of waters.

Ps. 114:7–8

Yahweh, making Judah "His sanctuary, / And Israel His dominion" (v. 2), causes the uproar of nature. Here is naked power. Here is the Creator who is Lord of His creation acting on behalf of His people. Thus, the imperative in verse 7 is also descriptive of what actually happened in the Exodus: *"Tremble* ["be pained"], *O earth, at the presence of the Lord / At the presence of the God of Jacob."* The earth responds to Yahweh as He makes it a vehicle of His mighty acts. When God comes, things happen. One further example beyond the sea parting and the mountains shaking is offered in verse 8: Our God is the God *"who turned the rock into a pool of water, / The flint into a fountain of waters."* As Moses commands water from the rock, God answers and Israel's thirst is quenched (Exod. 17:1–7). This proves that Yahweh is in her midst (Exod. 17:7).

I asked earlier, "What makes the church special?" The answer is clearly given in the psalm: it is the presence of the living God in her midst. When Jesus entered into His messianic ministry, demons were cast out and the sick were healed. In this, God's powerful presence and dominion were manifested. Where the church is coming alive today, similar things are happening because the same God is there.

For example, I had the privilege of leading a healing conference at my former home church last winter. As we prayed for several hundred people, we saw the power of God come. Some slipped to the floor, overcome by His Spirit. Others stood transfixed. Some were delivered from demons. By their body language they were witnessing to the fact that the living God who commands the physical realm was in our midst. After that conference many would never be the same again. They would know from experience what the psalmist meant when he said, "Tremble, O earth, at the presence of the Lord" (v. 7).

CHAPTER ONE HUNDRED FIFTEEN

What to Say When Unbelievers Scoff

Psalm 115

What can we say when God seems to be absent or silent or both? What happens when, in the midst of suffering and tragedy, God doesn't act according to our expectations? What do we have to say to people when we have assured them that God is real and that He will provide for us, and then the evidence doesn't seem to back up our claim? What do we have to say to the scoffers?

The context of Psalm 115 seems to be exactly this situation. The Gentiles are asking in contempt: "So where is their God?" (v. 2). The assurance that the Lord has remembered His people and that He *will* bless them assumes that His blessing is not being experienced (vv. 12–13). While it is clear that God is in heaven (vv. 3, 16), what is He doing on earth (v. 16)? The psalmist lives now in the silence, but it will not always be so. Thus, he prays in hope. God will give glory to His name (v. 1). Since He is sovereign in heaven (v. 3), He is not like the idols who can do nothing (vv. 4–7). He is Israel's help and shield (vv. 9–11). He remembers His people (v. 12), and His blessing will come to "those who fear the Lord, / Both great and small" (v. 13). They will be fruitful again (vv. 14–15). While the dead do not praise God, Israel does, "From this time forth and forevermore" (v. 18).

Commentators note the mixed literary forms in this psalm. It contains elements of both a lament and a hymn and appears to have been used liturgically in public prayer. Its date and author are unknown. The thought moves from a prayer for God's glory to confound the Gentiles (vv. 1–2) to a confession that God is God and the idols are nothing (vv. 3–8), to a call to trust in the Lord (vv. 9–11), to a confession of confidence that God will bless His people again (vv. 12–13), to a blessing that God may grant Israel increase (vv. 14–15) and concludes with the people's response in blessing and praising the Lord (vv. 16–18).

PRAYER: MAY YOUR GLORY CONFOUND THE GENTILES

115:1 Not unto us, O LORD, not unto us,
But to Your name give glory,
Because of Your mercy,
Because of Your truth.
2 Why should the Gentiles say,
"So where *is* their God?"

Ps. 115:1–2

Verses 1–2 are determined by the Gentiles' scoffing. They ask, *"'So where is their God?'"* Whatever devastation has come upon Israel, it appears that God is absent or indifferent to the whole affair. People today look at the horror of the holocaust, the genocide of Cambodia, the famine in sub-Sahara Africa, the grinding poverty of the Third World, the bleeding of Northern Ireland and ask the same question. If, as Christians claim, there is a loving God in the universe, where is He? In light of this question, the psalmist prays in verse 1: *"Not unto us, O Lord, not unto us* [the repetition is for emphasis], / *But to Your name give glory."* If God will appear and act, He will vindicate Himself. It is His name that will be praised and honored (given glory, the praise that comes when troops return from battle heavy with spoils) rather than mocked and despised. No wonder Jesus teaches us to pray, "Thy kingdom come. Thy will be done on earth as it is in heaven." Ultimately, it is for His sake rather than ours that we long to see God act.

The psalmist calls upon God to vindicate His name because of His character, *"Your mercy* ["covenant-love"] . . . *Your truth* ["faithfulness, trustworthiness"]." He expects God to keep His covenant and be true to His promises to His people as He delivers them from the mocking Gentiles. We must remember that prior to Christ's return, God does not promise to resolve all of the evils of this world. We are a part of a fallen creation, and the devil is still our active enemy. Nevertheless, God does determine to bless His people, those who believe in Him, and bring them through. This is because it is His very nature to be faithful to His covenant.

CONFESSION: YOU ARE GOD;
THEIR IDOLS ARE NOTHING

115:3 But our God *is* in heaven;
   He does whatever He pleases.
  4 Their idols *are* silver and gold,
   The work of men's hands.
  5 They have mouths, but they do not speak;
   Eyes they have, but they do not see;
  6 They have ears, but they do not hear;
   Noses they have, but they do not smell;
  7 They have hands, but they do not handle;
   Feet they have, but they do not walk;
   Nor do they mutter through their throat.
  8 Those who make them are like them;
   So *is* everyone who trusts in them.
          Ps. 115:3–8

In the midst of God's apparent inactivity, the psalmist reveals His invisible, heavenly reign. He is *"in heaven; / He does whatever He pleases."* In His sovereignty He is not accountable to us; we are accountable to Him. Instead of Yahweh, the mocking Gentiles (see v. 2) worship the idols of earth, the gods of this world. While they certainly can be seen, they do nothing, they are vain, empty. They are made of precious metals, *"silver and gold."* Rather than making humankind, they are made by man, *"the work of men's hands"* (v. 4). Having mouths, they cannot speak. Having eyes, they cannot see (v. 5). Having ears, they cannot hear. Having noses, they cannot smell (v. 6). Their hands do not handle, and their feet do not walk. *"Nor do they mutter* ["meditate"; see Ps. 1:2] *through their throat"* (v. 7). All of this can be contrasted with Yahweh who speaks (Gen. 1:3), sees (Gen. 6:8), hears (Ps. 27:7), smells (Gen. 8:21), and handles and walks (Exod. 15:6; Gen. 3:8).

This section closes with a profound truth: *"Those who make them are like them; / So is everyone who trusts in them"* (v. 8). We become like that which we worship. Empty idols make empty people. As Paul tells the Romans, "Professing to be wise, they [the Gentiles] became fools, and changed the glory of the incorruptible God into an image made like corruptible man. . . . Therefore God also gave them up to uncleanness, in the lusts of their hearts, to dishonor their bodies among themselves" (Rom. 1:22–24). Worship lust and become lusty. Worship pride and become prideful. Worship God and become godly.

CALL TO TRUST IN THE LORD

115:9 O Israel, trust in the LORD;
     He *is* their help and their shield.
  10 O house of Aaron, trust in the LORD;
     He *is* their help and their shield.
  11 You who fear the LORD, trust in the LORD;
     He *is* their help and their shield.

Ps. 115:9–11

In contrast to the mocking Gentiles, Israel is God's people. They are called to *"trust* ["feel secure," "be unconcerned"] *in the Lord."* This call is given three times for emphasis (vv. 9, 10, 11). At the same time, the threefold promise is also given: *"He is their help and their shield"* (vv. 9, 10, 11). The *"shield"* denotes a small, round, defensive piece of armor made of metal or wood and carried in battle. God's people are addressed as *"Israel"* (the whole nation), the *"house of Aaron"* (the priests, see Numbers 3), and *"You who fear the Lord,"* which refers especially to the pious and perhaps to Gentile converts (see Acts 13:16). All the people of God are to trust Him and rely upon Him as the one who will help them and protect them in battle, especially in the battle against the pagan nations and their idols.

We too must trust God as we war against the idols of earth. There is a spiritual battle raging whether we know it or like it or not. As with Israel of old, God will be our help and shield. Paul tells the Corinthians, "For though we walk in the flesh, we do not war according to the flesh. For the weapons of our warfare are not carnal but mighty in God for pulling down strongholds, casting down arguments and every high thing that exalts itself against the knowledge of God, bringing every thought into captivity to the obedience of Christ" (2 Cor. 10:3–5).

CONFIDENCE: GOD WILL BLESS US AGAIN

115:12 The LORD has been mindful of *us;*
       He will bless us;
       He will bless the house of Israel;
       He will bless the house of Aaron.
   13 He will bless those who fear the LORD,
       Both small and great.

Ps. 115:12–13

God's blessing is now promised to the three categories of Israel mentioned in verses 9–11, *"the house of Israel," "the house of Aaron,"* and *"those who fear the Lord, / Both small and great."* Despite appearances, God has not forgotten His people (v. 12). He has been *"mindful of us,"* and His ultimate purpose (based upon His covenant) is to bless. He promises Abraham, "I will make you a great nation; / I will bless you and make your name great; / And you shall be a blessing" (Gen. 12:2). This promise is not just for Israel as He adds that in Abraham "all the families of the earth shall be blessed" (Gen. 12:3). As we have seen, this blessing stands in the future. Despite God's silence and the Gentile's derision, God will be true to His promise and therefore true to Himself. Likewise, when all seems dark for us, we have the commitment that God has made to us in His Son. He will bless us. Jesus will return and resolve all things in Himself. It is this "blessed hope" that has held the church through the most severe persecution. God's blessing is also not simply for a certain class of people: it is for *small and great* (v. 13). All who trust in Him are included.

CONTENT: MAY GOD GIVE US INCREASE

115:14 May the LORD give you increase more and
more,
You and your children.
15 *May* you *be* blessed by the LORD,
Who made heaven and earth.

Ps. 115:14–15

Now the psalmist turns from his confidence in God's blessing to the content of that blessing. In this he takes us back to Genesis 1. After we were created in the image of God, a special command was given: "Then God blessed them and God said to them, 'Be fruitful and multiply; fill the earth'" (Gen. 1:28). As Karl Barth notes, our sexuality is separated from our being made in the divine image. God is no fertility cult. At the same time, our sexuality is a part of His good creation. It comes with His blessing. So the psalmist restates this blessing in verses 14–15: "May the Lord give you increase more and more, / You and your children. May you be blessed by the Lord." After destruction comes reconstruction. After death comes life. When God's blessing returns we are fruitful again. All of this comes from the Creator *who made heaven and earth.* Likewise, in Christ we are called to be fruitful. Jesus tells the disciples before the cross that He has chosen them to go and bear fruit, "and that your fruit should remain, that whatever you ask the Father in My name He may give you" (John 15:16). Fruitfulness has been transposed from the physical realm to the spiritual realm. As we pray, God will bless us with His answers, and we will see the fruit of those answers and rejoice.

This whole area of intercessory prayer is the cutting edge of my present relationship with the Lord. God wants to take me deeper into Himself. He wants me to know more of His supernatural power in my life. He wants me to enjoy a more intimate relationship with

Himself. As I pray and He answers, the fruit appears. He is the living realization of His renewed blessing upon me. Out of this blessing, like the psalmist, let us bless one another.

RESPONSE: BLESS AND PRAISE
THE LORD

115:16 The heaven, *even* the heavens, *are* the LORD's;
But the earth He has given to the children of men.
17 The dead do not praise the LORD,
Nor any who go down into silence.
18 But we will bless the LORD
From this time forth and forevermore.
Praise the LORD!

Ps. 115:16–18

The contrast between heaven and earth, which has been implied in verse 3, is clearly stated in verse 16: *"The heaven, even the heavens, are the Lord's; / But the earth He has given to the children of men."* Heaven is God's natural dwelling. In the creation He delegated His authority on earth to us (Gen. 1:28ff.). And what is our responsibility here? Many biblical answers could be given to this question. At this point, however, the psalmist goes right to the heart of the matter. On earth we are to *"bless the Lord / From this time forth and forevermore. / Praise the Lord!"* (v. 18). This privilege and responsibility of worship is contrasted with the *"dead"* in verse 17. They do not praise the Lord. They simply *"go down into silence"* (cf. Ps. 6:5). Since revelation is progressive, the full understanding of eternity had not yet been given. Thus the psalmist views the grave as silence. This is only partially true. What we know in Christ is that the dead who are under God's judgment do not praise Him. However, at the point of death the redeemed are ushered into the presence of the Lord, where they join the holy angels in worship before God's throne (see Rev. 5:8–14).

Since it is God's promise to bless us (vv. 12–13), we will respond by blessing Him (v. 18). Our praise will be perpetual and continual. The God who has acted will act again. When the scoffers scoff, we are to remember that we worship the invisible, eternal God who is

332

sovereign over all (v. 3). At the same time, He is filled with mercy and truth (v. 1). He has established His covenant, and He will keep it. The God who blessed us in creation will bless us in redemption, and our increase will have no end (v. 14). In light of this, let the worship begin (v. 18).

CHAPTER ONE HUNDRED SIXTEEN

When Death Doesn't Get through the Door

Psalm 116

I know many people who have had serious brushes with death. With some it has come in an automobile accident. Recently, dear friends were driving to northern California for Thanksgiving. Suddenly, on the freeway, five cars ahead, a tire blew. There was no time for reaction. Like billiard balls the cars behind plowed into each other. My friends totaled their vehicle. Their daughter, sleeping in the back, was knocked unconscious as the glass and steel crashed in upon them. It was a moment of truth, which came unexpectedly. Other people in my life have experienced similar brushes with death, with frightening chest pains and numbness in their arms, followed by a rush to the emergency room with the dreaded heart attack. My father-in-law and brother-in-law both received the grim word one day: cancer. So it goes. We all could offer our own examples. Such crises evoke primitive fears in all of us. They also take us in a fresh way to God.

Death and deliverance are the themes of Psalm 116. The writer tells us in verse 3 that "the pains of death encompassed me." In this he found "trouble and sorrow." He confesses that he was "brought low" in verse 6. Crying out to God, he was delivered from death and his tears were dried (v. 8). As a result of his healing, he has a new spiritual life: worship and witness are now his (vv. 12–19). Like so many others, he has received life out of death. This is central to the gospel and finds its ultimate fulfillment in Jesus Himself.

Commentators note the mixed style of this psalm, which uses complaint and petition, along with thanksgiving. This suggests that the prayer was not a literary work, but a personal devotion that later took written form. The continual use of the first person singular pronoun reinforces this suspicion. Its author and date are unknown. The thought moves from the thesis "why I pray" (vv. 1–2) to "my condition; my response" (vv. 3–4), to the God who hears (vv. 5–7), to the God who acts (vv. 8–11), to "my resolve" (vv. 12–15) and concludes with "my commitment" (vv. 16–19).

WHY I PRAY

> 116:1 I love the LORD, because He has heard
>   My voice *and* my supplications.
>   2 Because He has inclined His ear to me,
>   Therefore I will call *upon Him* as long as I live.
>   *Ps. 116:1–2*

Verse 1 explains why the psalmist prays: *"I love the Lord, because He has heard / My voice and my supplications* ["requests for favor or grace"]*."* The simple expression of love for God is rare in the Old Testament, although it is the fulfillment of the greatest commandment, to love God with all that we are (Deut. 6:5). This love arises because God hears our prayers. He is the living God, intimately concerned with the crises of our lives. The verb *hear* also includes the meaning "answer." The psalmist has cried out to the Lord, and He has intervened. Death has come knocking, but has not gained access.

Such an answer to prayer leads to a personal vow in verse 2: *"I will call upon Him as long as I live."* The dramatic healing that the psalmist has received encourages him to pray continually. This divine intervention results in his commitment to a lifestyle of devotion, which causes him to become accountable to the community (vv. 14, 18–19). His is no foxhole, private faith. When we experience God's work in our lives, we must relate it to the body of believers, lest it become only an isolated memory of a moment of grace. The psalmist's vow to prayer is predicated upon God's *ear* being turned toward him. When God turns away from us, we experience His judgment. When He turns toward us, we experience His grace.

My Condition: My Response

116:3 The pains of death surrounded me,
    And the pangs of Sheol laid hold of me;
    I found trouble and sorrow.
   4 Then I called upon the name of the LORD:
    "O LORD, I implore You, deliver my soul!"

Ps. 116:3–4

The crisis that has evoked such prayer is now identified. Death has come knocking: *"The pains of death* [literally, "the cords of death"] *encompassed me, / And the pangs* ["straits"] *of Sheol* [the abode of the dead, Hades] *laid hold of me."* As a result, the psalmist found *"trouble* ["bondage, restriction"] *and sorrow"* (v. 3). His response is neither denial nor rationalization. He confronts the truth of his situation, and his emotions are appropriate. In touch with his crisis, he turns to God. The vehicle of this is prayer: *"Then I called upon the name of the Lord."* Here he identifies the one to whom he turns with His personal name, Yahweh (*"Lord"*), and gives us the summary of his prayer, *"O Lord* ["Yahweh"], *I implore You, deliver my soul* ["life"]!" (v. 4). He is direct and to the point. In his pain the psalmist is focused; he knows what he wants and asks for it.

The God Who Hears

116:5 Gracious *is* the LORD, and righteous;
    Yes, our God *is* merciful.

> 6 The LORD preserves the simple;
> I was brought low, and He saved me.
> 7 Return to your rest, O my soul,
> For the LORD has dealt bountifully with you.
> > *Ps. 116:5–7*

The psalmist describes the God to whom he prays: *"Gracious is the Lord and righteous; / Yes, our God is merciful"* (v. 5). Here is the God of the covenant. He redeems His people. He upholds them because He is true to Himself, and His promises stand. All of this we now find in Christ. He is *"full of grace"* (John 1:14). And He is our *"righteousness"* (1 Cor. 1:30). Since this is His character, the psalmist continues, *"The Lord preserves the simple"* ("foolish," here "helpless"?), and adds his own confession, *"I was brought low, and He saved* ["delivered"] *me"* (v. 6). Divine help comes in the context of human pain. The question is not if we will have crises. The question is how we will respond to them. We can live in denial. We can rationalize our situation, or we can medicate ourselves against the reality. The psalmist's response, however, is to face it squarely and then turn to the only one who can help him, the living God. We too must make the same response.

With his prayer answered, he addresses himself: *"Return to your rest* [plural of fullness], *O my soul."* We are the only beings who can transcend ourselves. Conscious of our own existence, we can reflect upon who we are, address ourselves, and enter into the inner dialogue that is displayed here. Death came knocking but did not gain access. God intervened and delivered the psalmist. Rest is now his reward. The reason that his soul is now at peace is that *"the Lord has dealt bountifully with you"* (literally, "has rewarded upon you," v. 7).

THE GOD WHO ACTS

> 116:8 For You have delivered my soul from death,
> My eyes from tears,
> *And* my feet from falling.
> 9 I will walk before the LORD
> In the land of the living.

10 I believed, therefore I spoke,
   "I am greatly afflicted."
11 I said in my haste,
   "All men *are* liars."

Ps. 116:8–11

What God has done in answering the psalmist's cry is made clear. He has delivered him *"from death."* His pain is gone, as his eyes are free *"from tears"* and his *"feet from falling"* (into the grave? v. 8). He knows God as the God of the supernatural. He is no distant Creator who has wound up the universe and then left it to others. He is no God of nature who is locked out of our lives by a closed universe. He is no mystical blur, aloof from our physical pain, who calls us into an undifferentiated spirituality. He is the living God, Creator, Preserver, and Redeemer. When we cry to Him, He answers. When we are in pain, He knows and cares. His arm is not shortened that He cannot save. The psalmist has been healed and delivered by God according to his own confession (see v. 6). Since his falling feet have been caught, he now vows: *"I will walk before the Lord / In the land of the living"* (v. 9). Here, again, is no foxhole faith. The psalmist will live his new life before God as a witness to His grace. As he continues, *"I believed, therefore I spoke, / I am greatly afflicted* [or, "I have been humbled greatly"]." He has no reason to hide his witness from others. The point is not his pride; the point is God's good work in him. At the same time, he has experienced disappointment from others. Thus he continues, *"I said in my haste* [my knee-jerk reaction], *'All men are liars.'"* Such a response was hasty because he should have known from the start that men could not help him. Like all the rest of us, when death knocks, his case is only for God Himself, and it is God who has delivered him (see v. 8).

MY RESOLVE

116:12 What shall I render to the LORD
    For all His benefits toward me?
  13 I will take up the cup of salvation,
    And call upon the name of the LORD.

14 I will pay my vows to the LORD
Now in the presence of all His people.
15 Precious in the sight of the LORD
Is the death of His saints.

Ps. 116:12–15

In the context of his dramatic deliverance from death, the psalmist asks what he can give to the Lord in return *"for all His benefits"* ("bounty," v. 12). First, he will take up the *"cup of salvation"* (a drink offering, Num. 28:7). Second, he will *"call upon the name of the Lord"* in praise and worship (v. 13; cf. vv. 4, 17). Third, he will pay his *"vows to the Lord"* (a votive sacrifice, which he has promised to offer) as a witness *"in the presence of all His people"* (v. 14; repeated in v. 18). These responses are legislated in the Old Testament and are appropriate to what God has done for him (cf. Mark 1:44). In response to our salvation, we are to offer our bodies as living sacrifices to the Lord in worship (Rom. 12:1).

A footnote is offered in verse 15: *"Precious* ["costly"] *in the sight of the Lord / Is the death of His saints."* God heals them and delivers them so that they may continue to worship and serve Him on earth.

MY COMMITMENT

116:16 O LORD, truly I *am* Your servant;
I *am* Your servant, the son of Your
maidservant;
You have loosed my bonds.
17 I will offer to You the sacrifice of
thanksgiving.
And will call upon the name of the LORD.
18 I will pay my vows to the LORD
Now in the presence of all His people,
19 In the courts of the LORD's house,
In the midst of you, O Jerusalem.
Praise the LORD!

Ps. 116:16–19

Building on his resolve in verses 12–15, the psalmist offers himself anew as God's *"servant"* or slave. God is King; he is His subject.

This reality is the foundation of Israel's covenant relationship with Yahweh. The psalmist's submission is also a part of his heritage; he was born from a mother who was *"Your maidservant."* To be submitted to God is to be free from all other bondages: *"You have loosed my bonds"* (v. 16). The specific reference may be to the bonds of death (see v. 3). As a result, the psalmist will offer to God the *"sacrifice of thanksgiving"* and, as noted before, call upon His *"name"* in worship (see vv. 4, 13). Next, he promises again to pay his vows publicly, *"in the presence of all His* [Yahweh's] *people"* (v. 18; cf. v. 14). This will take place in the temple, *"in the courts of the Lord's house, / In the midst of you, O Jerusalem"* (v. 19). Worship becomes witness. God has delivered him from death, and everybody will know it. No wonder the psalm concludes *"Praise the Lord!"* For such a mighty act, God's people will join in giving glory to His name.

A close friend of mine has been institutionalized in the California mental health system for many years. Six months ago he became a Christian. As a result he has experienced incredible healing, including deliverance from demonic oppression. Now he has been freed from conservatorship, the legal control by the state over his life. He is living with Christian friends and has found a job. When the conservatorship ended, we gathered a group of friends to celebrate what God had done in his life. As he shared his testimony, there was not a dry eye in the room. Indeed, God had literally brought him back from death's door. His witness to his healing evoked our praise to God. As one friend who had known him in his old life said, "If I ever doubt God's power to heal, I only have to remember Joe." Praise the Lord!

Praise for the Instant Generation

Psalm 117

It is good to know that God does not require long prayers. The issue is not the length or the words, but the intention of our hearts. For this reason, Jesus warned us about elaborate praying, thinking that we are heard for our many words (Matt. 6:7). Perhaps this shortest of all the psalms was included to make this point. Brief praise is enough when it expresses where we are with the Lord. At the same time, the specialness of this prayer is that it is focused on the Gentiles (v. 1). They too are upon God's heart. They too are to know Him. He is the Creator of all, and He will become the Redeemer of all. Israel does not have a corner upon Him. Her call is to be a light to the Gentiles.

Commentators see this psalm as a hymn of praise. Its date and author are unknown. The thought moves from a missionary call for the Gentiles to be included in the worship of Yahweh (v. 1) to the basis for this worship, which is found in His character (v. 2).

CALL TO WORSHIP

117:1 Praise the LORD, all you Gentiles!
     Laud Him, all you peoples!
  2 For His merciful kindness is great toward us,
     And the truth of the LORD *endures* forever.
     Praise the LORD!

Ps. 117:1–2

Verse 1 states the thesis of the psalm. It is a call for the Gentiles to worship Yahweh: *"Oh, praise the Lord, all you Gentiles! / Laud Him, all you peoples!"* Such a call clearly relates to the promise in Isaiah that "all nations" will flow to "the mountain of the Lord's house" in the latter days (Isa. 2:2). God will be God over all people. The fulfillment of this promise now stands in the Great Commission. Jesus commands the apostles to make disciples out of all the nations (Matt. 28:18–20). Although much of the church today may be indifferent to this order, it has not been rescinded. God wants those from every tongue and tribe and nation before His throne. Our refusal to send missionaries or go ourselves is simply a sign of our disobedience. Only as we evangelize the world can we pray this psalm with integrity. Here is a short prayer for a missionary heart.

The Gentiles are to worship God (as is Israel) because of His character (v. 2). *"His merciful kindness* ["covenant-love"] *is great toward us* [or, "strong upon us"], */ And the truth of the Lord endures forever."* God's covenant is not merely for Israel. Thus, Jesus dies for the whole world (John 3:16), enacting the final covenant in His blood so that all people may have access to God. This covenant stands because the *"truth"* or *"trustworthiness"* of Yahweh stands *"forever."* We can count on this because we can count on Him. No wonder we are exhorted: *"Praise the Lord!"*

Mercy! Mercy! Mercy!

Psalm 118

Israel as a nation often was at war with her neighbors. She was born in battle as God delivered her in the Exodus. She secured her land in battle through the conquest. She retained her land by fighting battle after battle once she settled there. Many of her great leaders, such as Joshua, Saul, and David, were generals. Her historical books recount her conflicts. The psalms often mirror these bloody events as well. In a sense, much of the Old Testament is forged in war. Israel's history, however, is not just a drama of political and military events. Since all of the nations of the ancient world were theocracies, they found their origins in either Yahweh or in a hierarchy of pagan deities. Thus, behind the drama of their battles is the cosmic battle between God and Satan (and his demons who, according to the Old Testament, stand behind the idols of the surrounding nations). Warfare includes spiritual struggle. This supernatural part of the conflict is with us to this day.

Every Christian is called to battle. No longer are we to take up arms in the name of the Lord. Our calling is to battle against the devil and his demonic hosts. As Paul reminds us, we war not against flesh and blood, but against spiritual hierarchies of evil in the heavenly places (Eph. 6:12ff.). Thus, the psalms that were born in battle (such as Psalm 118) are not just for ancient warriors; they are for us as well. We too need to know the mercy of the Lord toward us as we face our enemies (vv. 2–4). We too need to destroy "in the name of the Lord" the evil forces that would engulf us (vv. 10–12). We too need to know God's "right hand" of power (vv. 15–16). As we experience this, we will join the psalmist in vital worship to the living

342

God (vv. 19–29). The victory that He gives us will evoke our praise and joy (vv. 24, 28). Indeed, we shall know His mercy, which "endures forever" (v. 2).

Commentators identify this psalm as a liturgy of thanksgiving. Its author and date are unknown. According to Jewish tradition, it was used during the Feast of Tabernacles. Its literary structure includes hymnic elements (vv. 1–4) and personal and corporate responses (vv. 5ff). Two major contexts, that of battle (vv. 5–18) and that of the temple (vv. 19–29), also determine the content. The thought moves from the call to worship (v. 1) to a confessional response of God's mercy (vv. 2–4), to mercy in distress (vv. 5–9), to mercy in battle (vv. 10–18) and concludes with public praise for God's mercy (vv. 19–29).

CALL TO WORSHIP

118:1 Oh, give thanks to the LORD, for *He is* good!
For His mercy *endures* forever.

Ps. 118:1

Verse 1 opens with the call "*Oh, give thanks to the Lord, for He is good!*" This exhortation tells us what to do ("give thanks") and why to do it ("for He [the Lord] is good"). The second clause of the verse can also be rendered, "for it (giving thanks) is good." The clear focus of our thanksgiving and this psalm appears in the words "*Because His mercy* ["covenant-love," "grace"] *endures forever.*" This mercy is seen in the salvation that God accomplishes (vv. 5, 21) as He fulfills His covenant (treaty) commitment to Israel. This commitment is not fickle; it "*endures forever.*" To be merciful is the nature of God. In the verses that follow we shall see an exposition of this mercy or covenant-faithfulness. The final verse (29) repeats the first verse, reinforcing and sealing mercy as its theme. And what a great theme it is. We are sinners. We deserve the judgment of God. We have our enemies who are out to destroy us, but God is merciful, and this mercy has now been given to us in His Son and the authority of His name. In this we stand.

CONFESSIONAL RESPONSE

> 118:2 Let Israel now say,
> "His mercy *endures* forever."
> 3 Let the house of Aaron now say,
> "His mercy *endures* forever."
> 4 Let those who fear the LORD now say,
> "His mercy *endures* forever."
>
> *Ps. 118:2–4*

The exhortation continues with a call for response by *"Israel"* (v. 2), the *"house of Aaron"* (the priests, v. 3), and *"those who fear the Lord"* (either the pious at the temple or the proselytes, v. 4). The threefold response suggests that this psalm was liturgically employed in public worship. It is as if all the people of God say *"amen"* to the witness of the psalmist, which will follow (vv. 5ff.). At the same time, the writer could simply be employing a liturgical refrain from public worship in his personal prayer, much as we may quote a Scripture passage in our own private devotions.

What then are the people of God to say? They are all to reflect the final sentence of verse 1 as they make their three-fold response: *"His [God's] mercy endures forever."* Yes, God will be true to His character. Yes, God will keep His word. Yes, God will follow through on His covenant. Yes, when all else fails, we can trust God. We can trust Him now. We can trust Him forever.

MERCY IN DISTRESS

> 118:5 I called on the LORD in distress;
> The LORD answered me *and set me* in a broad
> place.
> 6 The LORD *is* on my side;
> I will not fear.
> What can man do to me?
> 7 The LORD is for me among those who help me;
> Therefore I shall see *my desire* on those who
> hate me.
> 8 *It is* better to trust in the LORD
> Than to put confidence in man.

9 *It is* better to trust in the LORD
Than to put confidence in princes.

Ps. 118:5–9

Where do we see God's mercy? Where do we see Him come through for us? And how can we receive His help? The psalmist begins his answer by relating, *"I called on the Lord in distress* ['restriction, trouble']." It is when we are in touch with our need, our *"distress,"* that we see the mercy of God. Moreover, we receive that mercy when we pray. As we call to the Lord, He acts. Thus, the psalmist continues, *"The Lord answered me and set me in a broad place"* (v. 5). This is salvation, to be taken from a place of constriction and to be set in a roomy, open, free place. I have often heard people say that when they came to Christ they felt as if an emotional or even physical burden had been lifted. It is as if a great pressure on them had been removed. Moreover, I know many other believers who have been delivered from demonic influences in their lives after their initial conversion. This is the broad place of God's freedom in which He wants us to dwell.

God's answer to prayer in verse 5 leads to a renewal of His presence in verse 6. As the psalmist continues, *"The Lord is on my side* [literally, "Yahweh is for me"], / *I will not fear."* This fearlessness is a result of God's awesome power and the security of knowing that He is here. A small child, afraid of the dark, finds those fears vanish when his parents come into the room in response to his call. There is great security in holding our father's hand. As Paul reminds Timothy, God has not given us a spirit [demon] of fear, but a Spirit [the Holy Spirit] of power, love, and self-control (2 Tim. 1:7). Thus, the psalmist asks, *"What can man do to me?"* The answer implied is, "Nothing." Man is no match for God. No wonder the martyrs went into the arena singing. As Isaiah says, "Sever yourselves from such a man, / Whose breath is in his nostrils; / For of what account is he?" (Isa. 2:22).

Not only does God answer our prayers and grant us His presence; He also gives us His help (v. 7). Thus, the psalmist confesses, *"The Lord is for me among those who help me* [or "as my Helper"]." With this, his enemies are defeated: *"Therefore I shall see my desire on those who hate me."* The literal rendering of the text is more accurate: "Therefore I shall see on those who hate me"; that is, "I shall look (in victory) on those who hate me."

345

With this we are ready for the conclusion that is repeated twice in verses 8–9: *"It is better* ["good"] *to trust in the Lord / Than to put confidence* ["feel secure"] *in man"* (v. 8). The repetition reveals synthetic parallelism (see *Introduction, Psalms 1–72,* Communicator's Commentary, Old Testament, no. 13, 20) in verse 9 with the added thought that it is better to trust in the Lord than *"princes."* Neither the people nor their leaders are any substitute for trusting the living God. When are we going to learn this in the church? When are we going to take our eyes off famous pastors or TV evangelists or great theologians and put them on God Himself?

How hard it is to learn the lesson of verses 8–9. We would think that as God answers our prayers, grants us His presence and helps us, we would no longer trust people to do that which only God can do for us. But, sadly, I have had to learn this truth again and again, and my education is not over yet. I am easily let down and have been maliciously hurt by people. God has come through regularly for me, yet my trust wavers. It is easy to become dependent upon that which we can see, and in our need for security we often mistake dependency for love. Let us pray that God will write verses 8–9 on our hearts: "It is better to trust in the Lord."

MERCY IN BATTLE

118:10 All nations surrounded me,
    But in the name of the LORD I will destroy
    them.
11 They surrounded me,
    Yes, they surrounded me;
    But in the name of the LORD I will destroy
    them.
12 They surrounded me like bees;
    They were quenched like a fire of thorns;
    For in the name of the LORD I will destroy
    them.
13 You pushed me violently, that I might fall,
    But the LORD helped me.
14 The LORD *is* my strength and song,
    And He has become my salvation.
15 The voice of rejoicing and salvation

Is in the tents of the righteous;
The right hand of the LORD does valiantly.
16 The right hand of the LORD is exalted;
The right hand of the LORD does valiantly.
17 I shall not die, but live,
And declare the works of the LORD.
18 The LORD has chastened me severely,
But He has not given me over to death.

Ps. 118:10–18

The distress in verse 5 is not directly identified. Now, however, we see that the psalmist is surrounded by nations who clearly have approached to attack him, but he vows to destroy them (vv. 10–12). Though they push him violently, God saves him (vv. 13–14). The repetition of the word *surrounded* four times in three verses (10–13) suggests the urgency of the hour. The nations are like bees swarming for the sting; they are like a *"fire of thorns,"* which is quickly quenched (v. 12). In this crisis the psalmist comes against them confessing three times, *"But in the name of the Lord I will destroy them"* (vv. 10, 11, 12). The key to His victory is "the name of the Lord." It is in Yahweh's authority, presence, and power, represented by His name, that he is victorious. He does not come against his enemies in his own name (that would be presumption) or in the name of the state (that would be idolatry) but in the name of the one, true God.

The verb *destroy* used in verses 10, 11, and 12 means literally "to cut off" or "to circumcise." It may be that we should render it as "circumcise" here. The nations then would surround the psalmist like a foreskin. They are, however, cut away as they are defeated in battle, and Israel is united to Yahweh again.

In verse 13 the enemy nations are personified as one individual: "You pushed me violently [or literally, "thrusting, you thrust me"], *that I might fall."* This attack, however, is thwarted: *"But the Lord helped me"* (see v. 7). God's aid leads to the confession in verse 14: *"The Lord is my strength and song* ["psalm"], / *And He has become my salvation* ["deliverance"]." Out of His great resources and our responding worship in song, God acts. He intervenes and delivers Israel from the nations surrounding her, just as He delivers us from our foes as well.

One of the more controversial areas of Christian ministry today has to do with delivering people from demons. As we mentioned in the introduction, we are called to spiritual warfare. The fact that Jesus and the apostles cast demons out of people suggests that this is also to be a part of our ministry today. The demons did not depart the planet after the first century. In a recent book, C. Fred Dickason, professor of theology at Moody Bible Institute, shows that deliverance from demons is a continuing ministry of the church (in *Demon Possession and the Christian*). I have now had several experiences of praying for people who are demon-possessed. I have actually seen demons depart when ordered to do so in the name of Jesus. Through such ministry I have seen years of compulsive sin, such as drug addiction, broken in a moment. Thus, I confess with the psalmist that, although surrounded by evil forces, "in the name of the Lord I will destroy them."

As a result of Yahweh's salvation, Israel, encamped for battle, praises Him. Thus verse 15 continues, *"The voice of rejoicing* ["shouting, a ringing cry"—of victory] *and salvation / Is in the tents of the righteous."* The remainder of verse 15 and all of verse 16 may be the citation of that voice. If so the warriors cry: *"The right hand of the Lord does valiantly* [or "is doing with might," i.e., is performing a mighty victory], / *The right hand of the Lord is exalted* [perhaps as a sign of triumph, like "thumbs up"], / *The right hand of the Lord does valiantly."* God's right hand is the hand of power (see Exod. 15:6). Thus Israel celebrates God's defeat of her enemies by His intervention as her Warrior-King, who has bared His hand of power.

Now the psalmist confesses: *"I shall not die, but live"* (v. 17). The battle is won; he is saved. As a result he will witness to what God has done by declaring *"the works of the Lord."* He is prepared to give the glory to Yahweh for what has happened. He continues, *"The Lord has chastened me severely."* The psalmist has been broken. He is humbled; the victory is God's not his. At the same time, in his humiliation God *"has not given me over to death"* (v. 18). As Paul puts it, "We are hard pressed on every side, yet not crushed; we are perplexed, but not in despair, persecuted, but not forsaken; struck down but not destroyed" (2 Cor. 4:8–9). In all of this the apostle, like the psalmist, learns to rely upon the Lord. This is God's mercy: the mercy of His victorious "right hand," and the even deeper mercy of our humiliation and brokenness before Him. In our spiritual warfare we are brought to the end of ourselves and learn that the victory and the glory go to the reigning Lord alone.

PUBLIC PRAISE FOR GOD'S MERCY

118:19 Open to me the gates of righteousness;
       I will go through them,
       And I will praise the LORD.
  20 This is the gate of the LORD,
       Through which the righteous shall enter.
  21 I will praise You,
       For You have answered me,
       And have become my salvation.
  22 The stone *which* the builders rejected
       Has become the chief cornerstone.
  23 This was the LORD's doing;
       It *is* marvelous in our eyes.
  24 This *is* the day the LORD has made;
       We will rejoice and be glad in it.
  25 Save now, I pray, O LORD;
       O LORD, I pray, send now prosperity.
  26 Blessed *is* he who comes in the name of the
       LORD!
       We have blessed you from the house of the
       LORD.
  27 God *is* the LORD,
       And He has given us light;
       Bind the sacrifice with cords to the horns of
       the altar.
  28 You *are* my God, and I will praise You;
       You are my God, I will exalt You.
  29 Oh, give thanks to the LORD, for *He is* good!
       For His mercy *endures* forever.

Ps. 118:19–29

Victorious in battle through the mighty hand of Yahweh, the army returns to Jerusalem. Thus the psalmist calls: *"Open up to me the gates of righteousness; / I will go through them, / And I will praise the Lord"* (v. 19). His destination is the temple. The *"gates of righteousness"* are probably the temple gates, and as he enters them he is filled with praise to Yahweh. Moreover, he identifies the gate as *"the gate of the Lord"* and encourages the army to follow him into the temple by declaring that through this gate *"the righteous shall enter"* (v. 20; cf. v. 15, "the tents of righteousness"). Next, the psalmist vows in prayer (direct address to Yahweh): *"I will praise You"* (v. 21). Again, this worship is in response to what God has done: *"For You have answered* [or *"heard"*; see v. 5] *me, / And have become my salvation"* (v. 21; see v. 14).

God always brings life out of death. Thus the psalmist continues, *"The stone which the builders rejected / Has become the chief cornerstone"* (v. 22). In the context of entering into the temple with its great stones, this picture is apt. The immediate context reveals that this rejected stone refers to the psalmist and the army of Israel who were hard pressed in battle. God always calls the foolish things to confound the wise, and in our weakness, He makes us strong. At the same time, this verse is prophetic. It is not just fulfilled in the history of Israel or in a particular battle in which God intervenes; it is fulfilled in the Lord Jesus Christ. He is the rejected stone, and it is He who is now the *"chief cornerstone."* He holds up the whole temple of God, the living temple which is built upon Jesus Himself (see Eph. 2:20–22; Mark 12:10; Acts 4:11; 1 Pet. 2:7).

The exaltation of the stone that man has rejected is God's work. Thus the psalmist continues: *"This was the Lord's doing; / It is marvelous* [*"extraordinary"*] *in our eyes"* (v. 23). Such a mighty act of God evokes worship: *"This* [the day of deliverance] *is the day which the Lord has made; / We will rejoice and be glad in it"* (v. 24). When we see God intervene and deliver people from bondage and death, the response of our hearts is praise and joy. Our worship today becomes vital and real as we see God act to deliver us from our enemies as well.

As he worships, the psalmist engages in intercession, blessing, and sacrifice and vows his praises to God (vv. 25–29). First, he asks Yahweh for salvation and prosperity: *"Save now, I pray, O Lord; / O Lord, I pray, send now prosperity"* (v. 25). These ejaculatory requests express the heart of Israel's faith. God delivers His people from their enemies in order to bless them with His bounty. Israel was redeemed from Egypt not to live in the wilderness but to enter the Promised Land. As we pray for people to be delivered from demonic power, we must also pray for them to be filled with God's Spirit and blessing. Otherwise the spiritual vacuum created will attract a worse corruption (see Matt. 12:43ff.).

Second, in verse 26, the psalmist gives a blessing to *"he who comes in the name of the Lord!"* This blessing originally may have been pronounced upon the psalmist himself by the priests, especially if he is the king returning from battle. To come in the Lord's name, as we have seen, is to come in His authority and power (see vv. 10–12). The New Testament interprets this verse as messianic. It is Jesus who comes to us in God's name and who rolls back the kingdom of darkness (see Mark 11:9). As the deliverer comes, Israel responds from the temple: *"We have blessed you from the house of the Lord."* This blessing may also have been given by the priests in its original context.

Third, the direction is given concerning sacrifice in verse 27. It begins with the confession *"God is the Lord"* (literally, "God is Yahweh") and continues *"He has given us light."* This is the light of His revelation. The imperative follows: *"Bind the sacrifice with cords to the horns of the altar."* These horns are the projections at each of the altar's four corners and represent God's power. The idea of binding the sacrifice to them is unique here in the Old Testament.

Fourth, the psalmist vows his praises to God. Thus he confesses, *"You are my God"* (v. 28). Because of this, he continues *"and I will praise You."* Again, in a parallel clause he states, *"You are my God, I will exalt you."* Intercession, blessing, and sacrifice all are consummated in praise. God delivers us from our enemies in order that we might worship Him, honor Him, and delight in Him. Since He is the mighty King, He alone deserves our submission, and He alone should receive our glory.

This psalm concludes as it begins (v. 29; cf. v. 1). We are called to give thanks to the Lord *"for He is good!"* His goodness is seen in His *"mercy,"* which *"endures forever."* This mercy is the theme throughout. Divine mercy is seen as God answers our distress (v. 5), granting us His presence (v. 6), destroying our enemies (vv. 10–12), helping us (v. 13), and becoming our salvation (v. 14). By this we know that God is good. Satan and his demonic hosts must flee before His mighty name. No wonder we are to respond in worship; God's mercy endures forever! The final victory is His!

The Word of God

Psalm 119

Psalm 119 is an extended meditation upon the revelation ("law," *Torah*) of God. It is by far the longest psalm in the Bible. In it we find classic verses that stand alone when lifted from their context, such as "How can a young man cleanse his way? / By taking heed according to Your word" (v. 9), and "Your word I have hidden in my heart, / That I might not sin against You" (v. 11). And again, "Forever, O Lord, / Your word is settled in heaven" (v. 89); "Your word is a lamp to my feet / And a light to my path" (v. 105). The psalmist makes clear that our knowledge of God and our ability to live in this world is based upon divine revelation. The wonderful truth is that God has spoken, and we have a trustworthy record of His speech in His word.

While Psalm 119 stresses the objective nature of revelation, it never sees that revealed word as standing between us and God. Thus the psalmist affirms the instrumental use of Scripture. God's word is His instrument to bring us into a living union with Himself. Since this is true, we are not to worship revelation (or the Bible); rather we are to worship the God who reveals Himself in the Bible. While this psalm teaches a high view of revelation, it is never at the expense of living before God. For example, in verse 2 the psalmist says, "Blessed are those who keep His testimonies, / Who seek Him [rather than them] with the whole heart!" Again the psalmist confesses, "With my whole heart I have sought You" (not just the Bible, v. 10).

As we have asserted, there is an objective, revealed guide to understanding who God is and how we are to live. For this reason, again and again in the psalm we find the phrase "according to Your word." Go back to verse 9. Here the question is asked, "How can a young man cleanse his way?" The answer is given, "By taking heed according to Your word." In the word of God, the standard is given by which we can know the will of God. We are not left to wallow in our own subjectivity.

Psalm 119 teaches that the living God is the God who speaks. He stands behind His written word. Since it is God who has revealed Himself there, this word is true. As we have seen, it is settled in heaven (v. 89); it comes with eternal and divine authority. Moreover, since the word of God is revelation, God must prepare our hearts to receive it. The psalmist does not rely upon his unaided reason in order to understand God's word; the God who speaks must illumine our hearts so that we can hear His speech. Thus the psalmist prays, "Open my eyes, that I may see / Wondrous things from Your law" (v. 18). Again, "Teach me, O Lord, the way of Your statutes" (v. 33).

God must not only reveal His will to us; He must direct us in that will. Thus the psalmist asks, "Make me walk in the path of Your commandments" (v. 35). Because of our weakness and sin he prays, "Revive me in Your righteousness" (v. 40; see v. 25). Furthermore, we face opposition from the world as we choose a godly walk. For this reason, the psalmist accepts the comfort of God's word in his affliction (v. 50) and, at the same time, prays for God to judge those who persecute him (v. 84).

As the psalmist lives according to the word of God, there is great reward. He is blessed (v. 1). He is cleansed (v. 9). He is guarded from sin (v. 11). His soul is satisfied (v. 20). He is revived (v. 25; see v. 154). He is strengthened (v. 28). His heart is enlarged (v. 32). Salvation comes to him (v. 41). He has answers for his enemies (v. 42). He walks at liberty (v. 45). His witness is certain (v. 46). He is comforted and given life (v. 50; see vv. 93–94). He receives mercy (v. 58). He is dealt with well (v. 65). Affliction is turned to good (v. 71). He has hope (v. 74; see vv. 114–116, 147). He is not ashamed (v. 80). He is wise (v. 98). He knows more than his teachers and the ancients (vv. 99–100). He is restrained from evil (v. 101). His path is lit (v. 105; see v. 130). He fears God's judgments (v. 120). His eyes fail from seeking God's word (v. 123). He pants for God's commandments (v. 131). He weeps for those who disobey God's law (v. 136). He is consumed by zeal (v. 139). He knows the truth (v. 160). His heart is in awe (v. 161). He is filled with praise (v. 164). No wonder those are blessed "who walk in the law of the Lord!" (v. 1).

Commentators point out that this psalm is organized according to the structure of twenty-two strophes. Each strophe has eight verses, and the whole psalm forms an acrostic poem since the strophes are arranged in the sequence and number of the Hebrew alphabet. In literary form the psalm is a hymn, containing blessings, laments, thanksgivings, etc. Its author is unknown. But he is engaged in a real battle with his enemies (see vv. 98, 139, 157). They include the princes of Israel (vv. 23, 161), who reproach him (vv. 22, 39, 42) as they persecute him (vv. 84, 86, 157–58). They are proud (vv. 51, 69, 78, 85, 122) and wicked (vv. 53, 95, 110, 115, 119, 150). Moreover, they are double-minded (v. 113), regard God's law as empty (v. 126), and are treacherous (v. 158). In opposition to them, the psalmist stands on the word of God and prays for the work of God in salvation ("deliverance," see vv. 81, 94, 170).

The psalmist is also engaged in a battle with himself. Thus he has shame (v. 6), is in danger of wandering (v. 10), and is vulnerable to sin (v. 11). His soul clings to the dust (v. 25); he has heaviness (v. 28), is vulnerable to lying (v. 29) and covetousness (v. 36), and has gone astray (vv. 67, 176). His soul faints (v. 81), he cries for help (v. 147), and he needs deliverance. The continual repetition throughout the psalm only serves to underscore its great themes.

The thought moves from the word of God blesses us (vv. 1–8) to the word of God cleanses us (vv. 9–16), to the word of God reveals wondrous things (vv. 17–24), to the word of God revives us (vv. 25–32), to the word of God teaches us (vv. 33–40), to the word of God saves us (vv. 41–48), to the word of God gives us hope (vv. 49–56), to the word of God reveals mercy (vv. 57–64), to the word of God in affliction (vv. 65–72), to the word of God in comfort (vv. 73–80), to the word of God in persecution (vv. 81–88), to the word of God is eternal (vv. 89–96), to the word of God gives us wisdom (vv. 97–104), to the word of God is light (vv. 105–12), to the word of God brings us godly fear (vv. 113–20), to the word of God is vindicated (vv. 121–28), to the word of God gives us light (vv. 129–36), to the word of God is righteous (vv. 137–44), to the word of God is to be obeyed (vv. 145–52), to the word of God revives us (vv. 153–60), to the word of God brings awe (vv. 161–68) and concludes with the word of God as our delight (vv. 169–76).

THE WORD OF GOD BLESSES US

119:1 Blessed *are* the undefiled in the way,
Who walk in the law of the LORD!
2 Blessed *are* those who keep His testimonies,
Who seek Him with the whole heart!
3 They also do no iniquity;
They walk in His ways.
4 You have commanded *us*
To keep Your precepts diligently.
5 Oh, that my ways were directed
To keep Your statutes!
6 Then I would not be ashamed,
When I look into all Your commandments.
7 I will praise You with uprightness of heart,
When I learn Your righteous judgments.
8 I will keep Your statutes;
Oh, do not forsake me utterly!

Ps. 119:1-8

Verse 1 begins as does Psalm 1, with the pronouncement of a blessing: *"Blessed* ["happy," plural of fullness] *are the undefiled* ["upright"] *in the way, / Who walk in the law of the Lord!"* By this the psalmist means blessed are the moral. Blessed are the obedient. Blessed are those who walk through life submitted to God's revelation (see Deuteronomy 28). As we noted in our introduction, this blessing does not come upon us because of grim duty or because of legalistic, external performance. Thus the psalmist immediately adds, *"Blessed are those who keep* [or "preserve"] *His testimonies, / Who seek Him with the whole heart!"* The word *testimonies* is derived from a legal term meaning "witness." Here it refers to God's legislation given in the covenant law. Blessing comes with a combination of external obedience and internal affection. We not only seek God's will; we seek God Himself with all that we are, our *"whole heart."* Thus the Great Commandment calls us: *"You shall love the Lord your God with all your heart, with all your soul, and with all your might"* (Deut. 6:5).

A benefit of seeking God is found in verse 3: *"They also do no iniquity* ["injustice"]; / *They walk in His ways."* Sin will be banished from

355

our lives. This whole-hearted seeking after God is itself grounded in revelation: *"You have commanded us / To keep* ["preserve, protect"] *Your precepts diligently."* Note that the psalmist addresses God directly in prayer as he affirms the divine will. The word *diligently* means "greatly." We are to go after God's word without reserve. Since this is God's will, the psalmist immediately turns to intercession for himself: *"Oh, that my ways were directed / To keep* ["preserve, protect"] *Your statutes!"* (v. 5). God must give him the desire for obedience. He will pray later, "Incline my heart to Your testimonies" (v. 36).

What would be the result of such obedience? The psalmist concludes, *"Then I would not be ashamed, / When I look into all Your commandments"* ("decrees," v. 6). Calvin teaches us that the law of God is like a mirror. When we look in a mirror, we see ourselves as we really are. The law shows us our sin when we are disobedient. This is meant to lead us not to despair but to repentance. The law is ultimately designed to drive us to Christ and His salvation. At the same time, when we do the will of God our shame is lifted. The law no longer condemns. Conscience no longer accuses. Rather than being captured in shame, we are ready for worship. The psalmist continues, *"I will praise You with uprightness of heart, / When I learn Your righteous judgments"* (v. 7). Instruction in God's word is the proper preparation for His praise. Such worship also includes a vow: *"I will keep Your statutes"* (v. 8; see v. 5). But vows are only kept by grace. Thus this strophe concludes: *"Oh, do not forsake me utterly!"*

How does the word of God bless us? It keeps us undefiled in our walk as we seek Him with our heart (vv. 1–2). It guards us from iniquity (v. 3). It defends us from shame (v. 6). Moreover, it leads us to praise and worship as God fulfills His word in us (vv. 7–8).

THE WORD OF GOD CLEANSES US

119:9 How can a young man cleanse his way?
By taking heed according to Your word.
　10 With my whole heart I have sought You;
Oh, let me not wander from Your
commandments!

11 Your word I have hidden in my heart,
   That I might not sin against You.
12 Blessed *are* You, O LORD!
   Teach me Your statutes.
13 With my lips I have declared
   All the judgments of Your mouth.
14 I have rejoiced in the way of Your testimonies,
   As *much as* in all riches.
15 I will meditate on Your precepts,
   And contemplate Your ways.
16 I will delight myself in Your statutes;
   I will not forget Your word.

                                   Ps. 119:9–16

As the second strophe begins, the classic question is raised in verse 9: *"How can a young man cleanse his way?"* The question is classic because it is the great issue of the Bible. How can a sinner stand in the presence of a holy God? The cleansing of our way implies that we have fallen. How can we be washed and restored? The reference to youth reminds us of the Book of Proverbs (cf. Prov. 1:4, 8, 10, 15, etc.). The answer to the question is as follows: *"By taking heed according to Your word."* This taking heed includes two things. First, the word of God cleanses us as it separates us from this world and all of its uncleanness. Thus Jesus tells His disciples, *"*You are already clean because of the word which I have spoken to you*"* (John 15:3). But, second, the word of God also cleanses us as it directs us in the paths of righteousness. It not only separates us from the world; it also separates us to God. The word works to bring us into the will of God.

Next, the psalmist confesses: *"With my whole heart I have sought You"* (v. 10; see v. 2). Because of his singleness of purpose, his *"whole heart,"* he can then continue, *"Oh, let me not wander from Your commandments."* God not only reveals His will to us; He keeps us in that will. We must note again that the psalmist is not a legalist. He has no illusions that He can do God's will in his own strength. He is entirely dependent upon the God who calls him to keep him. This divine keeping is a matter of the heart. Thus he continues in verse 11, *"Your word I have hidden ['laid up'] in my heart, / That I might not sin against You."* As the word is memorized and internalized, it becomes directive for our lives. No wonder Jesus tells us that if we

357

"abide" ("continue, remain") in His word, then we are His disciples (John 8:31). His word will determine our walk.

As a new Christian I was encouraged to memorize Scripture. Introduced to the Topical Memory System of the Navigators, I amassed several score of verses on salvation, prayer, the Christian life, etc. Often during my high school lunch hour I would slip away to a quiet place for review. This investment was for a lifetime. Again and again in preaching and counseling, these verses have come back to me. How grateful I am that as a young believer I was introduced to hiding God's word in my heart.

With a sense of joy, the psalmist crys out in verse 12: *"Blessed are You O Lord!"* In the immediate context, this blessing God has to do with his cleansed way and his not sinning (vv. 9–11). In light of a life of victory over sin, he continues, *"Teach me Your statutes"* (v. 12). God will be his rabbi. As John promises us, "you have an anointing from the Holy One, and you know all things" (1 John 2:20). Such teaching then leads to confession and meditation in verses 13–16.

The psalmist offers his witness: *"With my lips* [vocally] *I have declared / All the judgments of Your mouth"* (v. 13). Notice here his high view of inspiration. The law of God comes from His mouth. It is literally His word. This confession also brings him *"joy in the way of Your testimonies."* God's way encompasses His mighty acts and His revealed will. The joy that the psalmist has in all riches, he now has in revelation (v. 14). With such a high value in God's word, his vow is not unexpected: *"I will meditate on Your precepts, / And contemplate Your ways* [literally, "look at Your paths"]" (v. 15). Such meditation is heart felt. Thus he continues, *"I will delight myself in Your statutes."* This positive promise is followed by a negative in parallel: *"I will not forget Your word"* (v. 16). This forgetting is more than memory lapse; it is abandoning and turning from what God has said.

In this strophe the word of God cleanses us from sin, claiming us from the world. Jesus prays, "Sanctify them by Your truth. Your word is truth" (John 17:17). The word of God also keeps us from sin. Jesus promises, "If you abide in My word, you are My disciples indeed." He adds, "And you shall know the truth, and the truth shall make you free" (John 8:31–32). This freedom He defines as freedom from the bondage of sin (John 8:34). Such is the cleansing power of the word of God.

THE WORD OF GOD REVEALS
WONDROUS THINGS

119:17 Deal bountifully with Your servant,
      That I may live and keep Your word.
  18 Open my eyes, that I may see
      Wondrous things from Your law.
  19 I *am* a stranger in the earth;
      Do not hide Your commandments from me.
  20 My soul breaks with longing
      For Your judgments at all times.
  21 You rebuke the proud—the cursed,
      Who stray from Your commandments.
  22 Remove from me reproach and contempt,
      For I have kept Your testimonies.
  23 Princes also sit *and* speak against me,
      But Your servant meditates on Your statutes.
  24 Your testimonies also *are* my delight
      And my counselors.

Ps. 119:17–24

God's blessing comes upon us in order that we may know Him and obey Him in this world. In order to do this, however, He must open us up and show us His *wondrous things* (v. 18). Apart from this, in the words of Bob Dylan, "I'm a little too blind to see." This strophe shows us the God who intervenes in our lives through His word.

The psalmist begins this section by praying, *"Deal bountifully with* ["reward"] *Your servant, / That I may live and keep Your word"* (v. 17). Since God is King, he is submitted to Him as His servant or slave. The divine bounty which he receives sustains his life, which, in turn, allows him to obey God. But how can he understand this word? The answer is: Only by divine illumination. Thus he continues, *"Open my eyes, that I may see / Wondrous things* ["miracles, mighty acts"] *from Your law"* (v. 18). These wondrous things would include God's signs and wonders against Egypt in the Exodus and His supernatural provision through the wilderness march. These mighty acts, however, can only be rightly understood as the manifestations of God's kingdom power as He opens our eyes. Apart from this we will view them as random upheavals of nature, or mythological stories, or a morality play, rather than as the judgments of Yahweh as He redeems His people from bondage and reveals His law to them. No wonder Paul says that spiritual things must be spiritually discerned (1 Cor. 2:11ff.).

Apart from needing such discernment, another reason that the psalmist must ask God to open his eyes is that he is *a stranger* ['sojourner'] *in the earth*" (v. 19). Apart from divine illumination by the Creator, he will not understand the world that he is passing through. So he pleads, *"Do not hide Your commandments from me."* This need to know is intensely personal as he confesses in verse 20, *"My soul breaks* ['shatters'] *with longing / For Your judgments at all times* [continually]." Having renounced the world, as a sojourner and a servant of Yahweh, he can only be satisfied by the word of God.

At the same time, God's servant is viewed as a fanatic, as narrow-minded and dogmatic. Thus he asks Him to *"rebuke the proud,"* those *"who stray from Your commandments"* (v. 21). These unbelievers cover him with *"reproach and contempt,"* as he says, *"For I have kept Your testimonies"* (v. 22). His enemies also include *"princes"* who *"sit and speak against me"* (v. 23). The word *princes* can include the heads of families or tribes or soldiers and officials of the court. Thus, the psalmist is experiencing general rejection. It is an evil time. Nevertheless, he is God's *"servant,"* who *"meditates on Your statutes."* Having lost his human counselors, God's testimonies become, as he says, *"my delight / And my counselors"* (v. 24). They are the weapons of his warfare.

In the darkness of our world, God shines His light. He opens our eyes so that we can see His wonders (v. 18). Since we are strangers here, it is He who reveals His commandments to us (v. 19). In this our longing for His word is satisfied (v. 20), and His word becomes our counselor (v. 24). Not human reason or inspiration but divine revelation satisfies our souls (v. 20). It is the word of God that reveals wondrous things.

THE WORD OF GOD REVIVES US

119:25 My soul clings to the dust;
    Revive me according to Your word.
  26 I have declared my ways, and You answered me;
    Teach me Your statutes.

27 Make me understand the way of Your
        precepts;
   So shall I meditate on Your wonderful works.
28 My soul melts from heaviness;
   Strengthen me according to Your word.
29 Remove from me the way of lying,
   And grant me Your law graciously.
30 I have chosen the way of truth;
   Your judgments I have laid *before me.*
31 I cling to Your testimonies;
   O LORD, do not put me to shame!
32 I will run the course of Your commandments,
   For You shall enlarge my heart.

Ps. 119:25-32

This strophe is structured by verses 25 and 28. They reveal the psalmist's condition. In verse 25 his *"soul clings to the dust"* and in verse 28 it *"melts from heaviness."* Thus he prays for revival in verse 25 and strength in verse 28, *"according to Your word."*

Revival comes when we reach the end of our own resources, repent, and call upon God to intervene. The psalmist is clearly in this condition. He is humbled and broken. His soul, clinging *"to the dust"* in verse 25, suggests that he is near death (see Ps. 104:29). What then can he do? The answer is, "Nothing." Thus, he prays, *"Revive me according to Your word."* This prayer for revival is based upon God's word, God's promise to give life. This revival will also be biblical; it will be consistent with God's word. True revival in the history of the church is always *"according to Your word."*

The psalmist continues that he has made himself known to God: *"I have declared my ways."* The content of this declaration is left open. It could well include his confession of sin and repentance. As a result, *"You answered me."* Now his heart is ready. Thus he prays *"Teach me Your statutes"* (v. 26) and adds *"Make me understand the way of Your precepts"* (v. 27). God is the instructor. The psalmist is the submissive student. His responsibility is to continually expose himself to God's word: *"So shall I meditate on Your wonderful works* ('miraculous acts')."

As we have seen, verse 28 reflects verse 25. In verse 28 the psalmist's soul *"melts* ['drops'] *from heaviness."* The picture suggests grief and depression. As a result he prays, *"Strengthen me* ["set me up"] *according to Your word.*" The next verse suggests the reason for his pain: "*Remove me from the way of lying*" (v. 29). This way may be the way of enemies who have done him in (those who reject God's law; see v. 21), or it may be the way of falsehood in which he has been trapped. To lose touch with God is to lose touch with reality. It is to move from life to death. Thus he asks "*grant me Your law graciously.*" The word of God will restore him to truth. As Jesus says to the Father, "Your word is truth" (John 17:17). No wonder the psalmist continues "*I have chosen the way of truth* ["faithfulness"]; / *Your judgments I have laid before me*" (v. 30). The word of God will restore him. It is the light that dispels the darkness (see v. 130). Upon God's word he will stand: "*I cling* ["cleave"] *to Your testimonies.*" At the same time, he prays that God will come through for him: "*O Lord, do not put me to shame!*" This is always the risk of faith. When I preach the gospel and call people to Christ, will anyone respond? When I pray for the sick, will anyone be healed? Will God show up? Will God act? If we are to walk on the water, we must step out of the boat. This fear turns to faith as the psalmist concludes: "*I will run in the way of Your commandments* [that is, in obedience to You], / *For You shall enlarge my heart*" (v. 32). The word *heart* can also be rendered "mind" or "understanding." As the psalmist absorbs God's word and obeys it, both his comprehension and experience of divine truth and trustworthiness grow.

This is the way to revival. Out of our brokenness, out of our weakness, we cry out to God and He answers, according to His word. He comes to revive us. He comes to strengthen us. He places us in the path of truth. To stand upon His word and do it is the solid foundation for our lives (cf. Matt. 7:24). In our weakness, we find His strength (2 Cor. 12:9). This should give us hope. God will come and give us life once again.

THE WORD OF GOD TEACHES US

119:33 Teach me, O LORD, the way of Your statutes,
And I shall keep it *to* the end.
34 Give me understanding, and I shall keep Your law;
Indeed, I shall observe it with *my* whole heart.

35 Make me walk in the path of Your
    commandments,
    For I delight in it.
36 Incline my heart to Your testimonies,
    And not to covetousness.
37 Turn away my eyes from looking at worthless
    things,
    And revive me in Your way.
38 Establish Your word to Your servant,
    Who *is devoted* to fearing You.
39 Turn away my reproach which I dread,
    For Your judgments *are* good.
40 Behold, I long for Your precepts;
    Revive me in Your righteousness.

Ps. 119:33–40

The theme of revival is sustained in this strophe (see vv. 37, 40; cf. v. 25). As the psalmist is restored to life by the power of God, he must grow in that life. Therefore, he continues to pray, asking that the God who has revived him now teach him. He asks, *"Teach me, O Lord, the way of Your statutes, / And I shall keep it to the end"* (v. 33). Beyond dramatic encounters with God is the life of discipleship. Isaiah suggests that the goal of renewal is not merely to rise up on wings as eagles or to run without weariness. The real goal is to walk and not faint (Isa. 40:31). This walking is the road to maturity. I recall Chuck Smith saying, "I don't care how high you jump; I care how well you walk when you come down." There is a valid point to this observation, although the high jump (if it is really God) will sustain you in your walk. After our hearts are forgiven and refreshed by the Spirit of God, we need God to teach us. Thus the psalmist continues: *Give me understanding, and I shall keep Your law* (v. 34). It is one thing to be taught and another to understand the teaching. A good coach begins to teach his team with basic plays and drills. So with God. He shows us the basics, and we must start there. It is His responsibility to grant not only content but also understanding. As we ask for it and obey what He shows us, our knowledge will grow through a lifetime. The psalmist's obedience is no mere legalism. He vows: *"Indeed, I shall observe it* [Your law] *with my whole heart."*

While the psalmist's desire is to give himself wholly to God, at the same time, he continues to know his own weaknesses. Thus he doesn't trust his commitments; he trusts the God to whom he is committed. This explains his next request: *"Make me walk in the path of Your commandments"* (v. 35). However much he may want to please God, God must give him the strength to do it. Paul says that God has made us obedient from the heart (Rom. 6:17). Only He can give us both the motivation and the energy to follow Him. The psalmist adds: *"For I delight in it* [the path of Your commandments]." The change is real; it comes from his heart.

As God continues to teach him in a life of discipleship, he also knows that his heart must be renewed again and again. We cannot live on yesterday's manna. We cannot draw on the currency of past spiritual experiences in order to substitute for a vital walk today. The psalmist prays: *"Incline my heart to Your testimonies."* God must continue to deal with him. The threat of a hard heart is always a real possibility. One source for this is *"covetousness"* (v. 36). It is the desire for things rather than for God. It is the worship of the creation rather than the Creator (Rom. 1:25). Paul calls it idolatry (Eph. 5:5). To underscore his request, the psalmist prays, *"Turn away my eyes from looking at worthless things* ["vanity," idols?], / *And revive me in Your way"* (v. 37). He refers to what John calls the "lust of the eyes" (1 John 2:16). God does not just remove us from the "passing show," however, He grants us His way and renews us to walk in it. The life of discipleship is not a list of denials or negatives; it is the positive joy of knowing God and serving Him. Next, the psalmist asks to be established in God's word, defining himself as God's *"servant, / Who is devoted to fearing You"* (v. 38). As we have seen, to call himself God's servant means that God is King. The psalmist's fear of God is the expression of holy awe before His majesty.

As the psalmist desires a life of discipleship, he also prays to be delivered from his enemies: *"Turn away my reproach which I dread."* This is the reproach of those who do not follow God's law (compare v. 21). Thus he adds, *"For Your judgments are good"* (v. 39). He longs for God's *"precepts"* and concludes this strophe by returning to the theme of renewal: *"Revive me* ["keep me alive"] *in Your righteousness"* (v. 40). The intention of this petition is either "Since You are righteous, be true to Yourself and revive me" or "Revive me through the instrument of Your righteousness." We really don't need to choose between these meanings. Both are true. God is righteous, and as we turn to Him He will make us alive. At the same time, His righteousness convicts us of sin, brings us to repentance, and (now in Christ) restores us into a vital fellowship with Himself. God teaches us as He gives us His word and leads us in His way, and also as He continually addresses our hearts and brings us back to our first love of Him.

THE WORD OF GOD SAVES US

119:41 Let Your mercies come also to me, O LORD—
    Your salvation according to Your word.
42 So shall I have an answer for him who
    reproaches me,
    For I trust in Your word.
43 And take not the word of truth utterly out of
    my mouth,
    For I have hoped in Your ordinances.
44 So shall I keep Your law continually,
    Forever and ever.
45 And I will walk at liberty,
    For I seek Your precepts.
46 I will speak of Your testimonies also before
    kings,
    And will not be ashamed.
47 And I will delight myself in Your
    commandments,
    Which I love.
48 My hands also I will lift up to Your
    commandments,
    Which I love,
    And I will meditate on Your statutes.
                        Ps. 119:41–48

The psalmist's prayer for salvation or deliverance stands in the context of the one who reproaches him (v. 42). This reproach is a personal attack because of his heart for God and His word. Moreover, he is in danger of being ashamed of his faith, evidently struggling with the rejection that he may receive as he stands up for it (v. 46). With these very human struggles, the psalmist turns to God.

Verse 41 begins, *"Let Your mercies* ["covenant-love," in the plural for fullness] *come also to me, O Lord."* The consequence of this will be *"salvation"* or *"deliverance."* And it will be *"according to Your word,"* according to the promise that God has already made to His people. For example, when Israel was in bondage in Egypt, she cried out to Yahweh. He heard her prayers and remembered His covenant with Abraham (Exod. 2:24). Based upon this promise of faithfulness, He acted. Likewise, when we need God's help, we can be sure of His answer because He has promised to be our God, to hear and help us, and that promise has been sealed in His Son.

As God answers the psalmist's cry for salvation, he will have an answer *"for him who reproaches me"* (v. 42). The answer will be God's action on his behalf. He is confident that God will act, as he says, *"For I trust in Your word."* As we know the promises of God in His word, we can pray and believe in boldness. The word becomes a weapon in our warfare.

The rest of this strophe (vv. 43–48) is a meditation upon the importance and value of God's word. The psalmist confesses the trustworthiness of that word as he asks, *"And take* ["snatch," like prey] *not the word of truth utterly out of my mouth, / For I have hoped in Your ordinances* ["judgments"]*"* (v. 43). God is sovereign. He gives His word, and He withholds His word. His silence is a sign of judgment. In asking that God not remove His word, the psalmist is asking that His mercy and truth continue to be with him as a sign of divine favor. This will sustain his hope as he continues to trust the promises of God. As God gives him His word, he vows: *"So shall I keep* [that is, "obey"] *Your law continually, / Forever and ever"* (v. 44). God's word is not given merely for our information. God's word is given for our obedience. This will be the theme of the psalmist's life. Is it ours?

Such a life may appear to us as bondage, but the psalmist continues, *"And I will walk at liberty* ["in a broad place"] */ For I seek Your precepts"* (v. 45). This is the liberty of a man delivered from his enemies (v. 42). This is the liberty of a man who knows the truth (v. 43). This is the liberty of a child of God who knows who he is and where he is going. Out of this strong sense of identity, the psalmist vows his witness in verse 46: *"I will speak of Your testimonies also before kings, / And I will not be ashamed."* Whether he has access to royalty is uncertain. It is certain that he is ready to confess God's truth in the highest courts of human power and not be ashamed. Here is a free person indeed.

Boldness in witness comes from a joy and a security in God's word. The psalmist (who is free from the bondage of man) continues, *"And I will delight myself in Your commandments, / Which I love."* Truth has moved from head to heart. When we love God's word in our hearts, we will delight in telling others about it. As Dale Brunner says, "That which goes deepest to the heart goes widest to the world." The psalmist adds, *"My hands also I will lift up to Your commandments, / Which I love"* (v. 48). This is a physical posture for prayer, representing his devotion to God's word (cf. 1 Kings 8:54). He not only devotes himself to that revelation by his commitment; he also devotes himself by his actions. He concludes, *"And I will meditate on Your statutes."* The word of God will be in his mouth (v. 43), it will determine his walk (v. 45), it will be the substance of his witness (v. 46), it will be his delight, his love (v. 47), and the content of his meditation (v. 48). All of this is a result of God's salvation in his life *"according to Your word"* (v. 41). What would the strength of the church be today, if born-again Christians made a similar response to the gift of salvation, which they have received in Christ?

THE WORD OF GOD GIVES US HOPE

119:49 Remember the word to Your servant,
　　　Upon which You have caused me to hope.
　50 This *is* my comfort in my affliction,
　　　For Your word has given me life.
　51 The proud have me in great decision,
　　　Yet I do not turn aside from Your law.
　52 I remembered Your judgments of old, O LORD,
　　　And have comforted myself.
　53 Indignation has taken hold of me
　　　Because of the wicked, who forsake Your law.
　54 Your statutes have been my songs
　　　In the house of my pilgrimage.

55 I remember Your name in the night, O LORD,
   And I keep Your law.
56 This has become mine,
   Because I kept Your precepts.

Ps. 119:49–56

Hope shines brightest in the darkness. In this strophe the psalmist experiences both realities. He is afflicted (v. 50). He is derided by the proud (v. 51). He is indignant over the wicked (v. 53). Nevertheless, he has hope (v. 49). He is comforted and has been given life (v. 50). The statutes of God have been his songs (v. 54). Anchored in God's word, he is unmoved and confident as he faces adversity.

Verse 49 begins as the psalmist calls upon God to remember His word or promise, which He has given him and which is the source of his hope. This word is *"the word to Your servant."* It is the word of the divine King, which He has given to His subject, His slave. It is the word of the covenant, which He has made with Israel and which is the foundation of her hope in this world. Because God promises to be true to His people, the psalmist asserts, *"This is my comfort in my affliction, / For Your word has given me life* [or, "kept me alive"]" (v. 50). The affliction that he is experiencing becomes clearer in verse 51: *"The proud have me in great derision* [or "have scorned me much"]." These "proud" are those who refuse to submit to God's word. They presume to be autonomous, independent of such authority or need. Thus they are defined in verse 21 as those who "stray from Your commandments." They castigate the psalmist for the foolishness of trusting in God's word. Nevertheless, he asserts, *"I do not turn aside from Your law."* In fact, he remembers *"Your judgments of old"* and takes his comfort here (v. 52). These *"judgments"* or "ordinances" probably include the whole history of God's dealings with Israel as recorded in the Pentateuch. The thought of God's mighty acts, steel him for the suffering and rejection that he endures. When we are in the battle for faith, we need to remember what God has done for us. As Bob Munger puts it, "Don't doubt in the darkness what God has revealed in the light."

As the psalmist renews his strength by remembering what God has done, he becomes angry at those who reject His word. *"Indignation* ["horror"] *has taken hold of me / Because of the wicked, who forsake Your law"* (v. 53). The *"wicked"* are enemies of God, guilty of rebelling against Him (see Ps. 1:1). Their wickedness is defined in abandoning God's revelation. As a result of his righteous indignation, the psalmist expresses his own attitude toward God's word: *"Your statutes have been my songs* ['psalms'] / *In the house of my pilgrimage"* (v. 54). While the wicked deny God's word, the psalmist sings it. The *"house of my pilgrimage"* may refer to the temple where he would sing his psalms or to this world, which he is passing through. The psalmist also thinks of God at night remembering His *"name"* (v. 55). His re-membering the name of God would imply actually praying to Him and meditating upon Him. The name of God communicates His be-ing, His character, His power, and His presence. Meditation then turns to vigilance: *"And I keep* ['preserve, protect'] *Your law."* He now concludes in verse 56: *"This* [vigilance] *has become mine, / Because I kept Your precepts."*

In this strophe the psalmist overcomes his affliction (caused by his enemies) by remembering God's word. Through this word he receives comfort and life (v. 50). His sorrow turns to song (vv. 53-54) as he remembers what God has done for him (vv. 54-55). Here is the basis of his hope (v. 49). God will be true to His covenant. What He has done, He will do again.

THE WORD OF GOD REVEALS MERCY

119:57 *You are* my portion, O LORD;
    I have said that I would keep Your words.
  58 I entreated Your favor with *my* whole heart;
    Be merciful to me according to Your word.
  59 I thought about my ways,
    And turned my feet to Your testimonies.
  60 I made haste, and did not delay
    To keep Your commandments.
  61 The cords of the wicked have bound me,
    But I have not forgotten Your law.
  62 At midnight I will rise to give thanks to You,
    Because of Your righteous judgments.
  63 I *am* a companion of all who fear You,
    And of those who keep Your precepts.
  64 The earth, O LORD, is full of Your mercy;
    Teach me Your statutes.

Ps. 119:57-64

The theme of this strophe appears in its final verse: *"The earth, O Lord, is full of Your mercy"* (v. 64). For this reason the psalmist can pray, *"Be merciful to me according to Your word"* (v. 58). But why does he need mercy? There is a two-fold answer. First, his own ways, living for himself, have clearly been unsuccessful (v. 59). Second, he has been attacked by the wicked (v. 61). For personal and circumstantial reasons, he cries out for the mercy of God.

Verse 57 opens with the confession that God is the psalmist's *portion*. Originally portion referred to that part of the Promised Land that was given to each tribe. The Levites received no land because, as priests, God Himself was to be their portion (Deut. 10:9). As the psalmist's portion, Yahweh is his inheritance, his security and provision. Because of this, he continues, *"I have said that I would keep* ["preserve, protect"] *Your words."* He will guard and be faithful to what God has said.

The psalmist turns to the issue on his heart in verse 58: *"I entreated Your favor with my whole heart,"* or literally, "I entreated Your face with all my heart." For God to turn His face toward him means that He bestows favor upon him. He continues, *"Be merciful to me according to Your word."* The confidence that we have in the mercy of God is not some sentimental hope. It is our confidence in God's word, His revelation that He is merciful, and God's work, the exercise of that mercy in His redemptive acts. The need for mercy is seen in verse 59 because the psalmist has considered his *"ways."* Whatever the specifics may be, he is not happy about what he sees. His ways have not been God's ways (cf. Isa. 55:8). Thus he quickly adds, *"And* [I] *turned my feet to Your testimonies."* Notice that he turns his feet rather than merely his mind. God's truth is truth to be done. God's ways are to be walked in. Obedience is the psalmist's preoccupation. He continues, *"I made haste, and did not delay* [added for emphasis] / *To keep Your commandments"* (v. 60). The urgency reflects the intention of his heart and the pressure of his circumstances.

In verse 61 the psalmist reveals that he has not only strayed from God's ways, but he has also been caught by the wicked: *"The cords of the wicked* ["criminals, lawbreakers"] *have bound me."* They have set a trap for him like hunters snare a wild animal. He, however, is steadfast: *"But I have not forgotten Your law."* He worships Yahweh at midnight, *"Because of Your righteous judgments"* (v. 62). Furthermore, he stands with believers, *"all who fear* [are in awe of] *You / And . . . who keep Your precepts"* (v. 63).

The psalmist ends this strophe with his thesis: *"The earth, O Lord, is full of Your mercy* ["covenant-love"]*"* (v. 64). Everywhere he looks, he sees the signs of God's commitment to the earth, His covenant-treaty to be Israel's King which brings His mercy upon His people. It is upon this basis that he has previously prayed, "Be merciful to me according to Your word" (v. 58). Since God is faithful to him, he will be faithful to God. With his way restored and his enemies defeated, he will be a pupil in the divine school. Thus he concludes, *"Teach me Your statutes."*

THE WORD OF GOD IN AFFLICTION

119:65 You have dealt well with Your servant,
      O LORD, according to Your word.
  66 Teach me good judgment and knowledge,
      For I believe Your commandments.
  67 Before I was afflicted I went astray,
      But now I keep Your word.
  68 You *are* good, and do good;
      Teach me Your statutes.
  69 The proud have forged a lie against me,
      But I will keep Your precepts with *my* whole
         heart.
  70 Their heart is as fat as grease,
      But I delight in Your law.
  71 *It is* good for me that I have been afflicted,
      That I may learn Your statutes.
  72 The law of Your mouth *is* better to me
      Than thousands of *coins of* gold and silver.
                          Ps. 119:65-72

As we noted in our introduction, this psalm comes out of the context of warfare. The psalmist is attacked by *"the proud"* (v. 69; cf. vv. 21, 51). He has experienced much affliction (vv. 67, 71). At the same time, his faith is forged in the fire. Thus he begins this strophe with the observation: *"You have dealt well* [or, "Good you have done"] *with Your servant* [a slave bound into the covenant with Yahweh as King] / *O Lord, according to Your word"* (v. 65). Based upon God's goodness toward him, he prays, *"Teach me good judgment* ['discernment'] *and knowledge* [more than concepts, knowledge that is gained by experience] / *For I believe* ['trust in, rely upon'] *Your commandments"* (v. 66). Such discernment and knowledge will come from God's word as it is applied to the psalmist's life. He is ready to learn from the Lord because formerly he went astray. Then affliction came (v. 67). In adversity he was caught up short and brought back to God.

We can easily identify with the psalmist. How often I meet people who have come to Christ in affliction. When life presses in upon them, they learn that they do not have the answers, that they have made wrong choices, and that they are ready for outside help. No wonder the first step in recovery for Alcoholics Anonymous is the admission that we are powerless over our lives. We have come to the end of our ropes. Part of God's goodness (v. 65) has been to allow affliction to come into the psalmist's life. In the resulting change he admits: *"But now I keep* ['guard'] *Your word"* (v. 67). For emphasis, and with a grateful sense of the sovereign hand of God upon him, he repeats in verse 68: *"You are good, and do good"* (compare v. 65). As a result he prays: *"Teach me Your statutes."* Broken by affliction, he is ready to be taught.

The psalmist still lives in conflict. So he continues in verse 69: *"The proud have forged a lie against me."* Apparently they are angry at his newfound faithfulness to God. Nevertheless, he vows: *"I will keep Your precepts with my whole heart."* He has put his hand to the plow. There is no turning back. Knowing God's truth also makes him wise about those who oppose him. Thus he observes, *"Their heart is as fat as grease."* Fat hearts are dulled to God's truth (compare Isa. 6:10). But in contrast to them, he confesses, *"I delight in Your law"* (v. 70).

As the psalmist looks back upon his pain he concludes, *"It is good for me that I have been afflicted, / That I may learn Your statutes"* (v. 71). Often we understand God's goodness toward us as we see the results that come from our adversity. God has used adversity to bring the psalmist back to Himself. Now he is a learner once again. Thus he concludes, *"The law of Your mouth is better to me / Than thousands of shekels of gold and silver"* (v. 72). Now he has his values straight. His treasure is in heaven. He is committed to that which lasts. As with the prodigal son in the far country, affliction has done its good work and the psalmist has come home to the Father's house.

THE WORD OF GOD IN COMFORT

119:73 Your hands have made me and fashioned me;
Give me understanding, that I may learn Your
commandments.
74 Those who fear You will be glad when they
see me,
Because I have hoped in Your word.
75 I know, O LORD, that Your judgments *are* right,
And *that* in faithfulness You have afflicted me.
76 Let, I pray, Your merciful kindness be for my
comfort,
According to Your word to Your servant.
77 Let Your tender mercies come to me, that I
may live;
For Your law *is* my delight.
78 Let the proud be ashamed,
For they treated me wrongfully with
falsehood;
But I will meditate on Your precepts.
79 Let those who fear You turn to me,
Those who know Your testimonies.
80 Let my heart be blameless regarding Your
statutes,
That I may not be ashamed.

Ps. 119:73–80

The theme of affliction from the previous strophe continues (v. 75). The proud who treat the psalmist badly also reappear (v. 78). But he knows that God is in control. It is He who has used the affliction to bring the psalmist back to Himself (v. 75). Now, experiencing God's mercy, he is comforted (v. 76).

Verse 73 opens with the confession that God is the Creator. It is His hands that have *"made"* and *"fashioned"* the psalmist. He has been molded like the potter molds his clay (cf. Jer. 1:5; see Gen. 2:7). But since the Fall it is not enough for us to have been created by God. We must also be remade by Him. Thus the psalmist prays: *"Give me*

understanding, that I may learn Your commandments." Instructed by
God, he will be a blessing to fellow believers; when God blesses us
He also blesses others through us. Thus the psalmist notes, *"Those
who fear* [are in awe of] *You will be glad when they see me, / Because I
have hoped in Your word"* (v. 74). His hope will encourage them to
hope also. His witness will lift their spirits.

The psalmist turns to his affliction in verse 75. Although he has
been in pain, he never doubted the justice of God. Thus he confesses: *"I know, O Lord, that Your judgments are right."* Whatever has
come to him, he deserved it. If we were all sent to hell, God would
still be just. Since we are sinners, the amazing thing is not that some
are lost; the amazing thing is that any are saved. The psalmist continues, *"in faithfulness You have afflicted me."* As we saw in the previous strophe, the psalmist had gone astray before God's punishment
came. This affliction, however, is redemptive. It has brought him
back to faith. Thus the tone changes abruptly in verse 76: *"Let, I
pray, Your merciful kindness* ["covenant-love"] *be for my comfort, / According to Your word to Your servant* [submitted to God as King]." Embraced by God again, he knows His mercy, forgiveness, and peace,
which all come from living in His Kingdom under His covenant. He,
however, wants more. Therefore he prays, *"Let Your tender mercies*
[plural intensive] *come to me, that I may live"* (v. 77). And where are
they to be found? In the word of God. As he adds, *"For Your law is
my delight."*

In verse 78 the psalmist turns to the proud with a curse: *"Let the
proud be ashamed."* The proud are those who have not lived under
the authority of God's word. The basis for this curse is given: *"For
they treated me wrongfully* ["perverted me"] *with falsehood."* Their lies
led him astray. Now, however, he is back. So he adds, *"But I will
meditate upon Your precepts."* Next, he calls out for those who fear
God (see v. 74), namely, *"those who know Your testimonies,"* to turn to
Him. Here the God-fearers are defined. They are people of God's
word. They are the ones that he now wants to be in his company.
Finally, he asks for himself, *"Let my heart be blameless regarding Your
statutes."* And what is his motive for this pure heart? He adds, *"That
I may not be ashamed"* (like the proud in v. 78). And what is that
shame? The ultimate shame would be being found out by God Himself—the shame of being a hypocrite and being exposed as one
on the day of judgment. The comfort of this verse, however, is that

God will answer his prayer. He and He alone will establish our hearts blameless. But how can we know this? Because He has already done so by establishing us in the righteousness of Christ (Rom. 3:21–22). In Him God's sentence on the final day has already been pronounced over us. And it is, "No condemnation" (Rom. 8:1). Here is comfort indeed!

THE WORD OF GOD IN PERSECUTION

119:81 My soul faints for Your salvation,
      But I hope in Your word.
  82 My eyes fail *from searching* Your word,
      Saying, "When will You comfort me?"
  83 For I have become like a wineskin in smoke,
      Yet I do not forget Your statutes.
  84 How many *are* the days of Your servant?
      When will You execute judgment on those who
        persecute me?
  85 The proud have dug pits for me,
      Which *is* not according to Your law.
  86 All Your commandments *are* faithful;
      They persecute me wrongfully;
      Help me!
  87 They almost made an end of me on earth,
      But I did not forsake Your precepts.
  88 Revive me according to Your lovingkindness,
      So that I may keep the testimony of Your
        mouth.

Ps. 119:81–88

In this strophe the psalmist is in anguish. His soul faints (v. 81), his eyes fail as he looks for comfort (v. 82), he is persecuted (v. 84), the proud have set their traps for him (v. 85), he is attacked wrongfully (v. 86), and he almost dies (v. 87). Yet, he continues to seek God's word and prays for revival, as he says, *"So that I may keep the testimony of Your mouth"* (v. 88).

Verse 81 opens with the theme of suffering and the longing for divine intervention. The psalmist reveals, *"My soul faints* ["has been consumed"] *for Your salvation."* The hour is urgent. The crisis is clear. The need is great. He is, however, not in despair, as he says, *"But I hope in Your word."* When God seems absent and the darkness stalks us, we still have the light of His promises to us. The psalmist's anguish is well represented in verse 82. In his pain, he continually searches the word of God. His eyes even now fail or grow dim from his study. This is no academic exercise. As he reads he cries, *"When will You comfort me?"* Now using a simile, the psalmist describes himself as a *"wineskin in smoke"* (v. 83). This means that he is shriveled up like a wineskin in a smoky room or in the fire. He is cracked and dry. Nevertheless, he stands upon God's word in his distress: *"Yet I do not forget Your statutes."* In the pain God's promises are there.

With the shortness of his life before him, the psalmist now asks, *"How many are the days of Your servant* [the one submitted to the covenant-God as a slave]" (v. 84)? The implied answer is, "Not many." Time is running out (cf. v. 87). With the sands of the hourglass near exhaustion, he prays, *"When will You execute judgment on those who persecute me?"* The psalmist's pain comes from relentless attacks. His enemies are like hunters who have dug their pits for him, to catch him like prey (v. 85). But their attacks are not the execution of divine justice. Their illegal actions are not *"according to Your law."* God's word is *"faithful"* ("trustworthy, true"). In light of this standard, the psalmist concludes, *"They persecute me wrongfully."* His prayer is simple, *"Help me!"* (v. 86). Note that the psalmist does not take matters into his own hands. He presents his case to God and expects His intervention. Like Jesus on the cross, he trusts Him in his hour of agony.

Verse 87 shows us that the situation is critical. It is a matter of life or death. He says, *"They almost made an end of me on earth."* Under such severe stress, however, he remained true to God's word: *"But I did not forsake Your precepts."* The final verse of this strophe of pain gives us the basis for his prayer: *"Revive me according to Your lovingkindness* ["covenant-love"]." Notice that the psalmist at this point does not say "according to Your word." Certainly he could use this phrase. His ultimate trust, however, is not in revelation, but in the God who reveals Himself. Thus he appeals to the covenant promise of Yahweh. God will come through for him because as King He has bound Himself to His people Israel. As He revives him and restores him, he promises to *"keep* ["guard"] *the testimony of Your mouth."* Like Bunyan's Pilgrim, he will be valiant for God's word in this world.

Christians of every age have found comfort in the Scriptures when under persecution. I remember a missionary to Korea, Harold Vokel, recounting his work among prisoners of war during the conflict there. He saw thousands of these young men come to Christ. As they were discipled in the internment camps, one book of the Bible drew them without fail. It was the Book of Revelation, which some memorized in its entirety. Why so? This book is for the suffering church. In the midst of war and loss, its pages gave them comfort and hope. The final victory belonged to the Lamb who became a Lion. As these prisoners fainted for God's salvation, they continued to hope in His word (v. 81).

THE WORD OF GOD IS ETERNAL

119:89 Forever, O LORD,
     Your word is settled in heaven.
  90 Your faithfulness *endures* to all generations;
     You established the earth, and it abides.
  91 They continue this day according to Your
       ordinances,
     For all *are* Your servants.
  92 Unless Your law *had been* my delight,
     I would then have perished in my affliction.
  93 I will never forget Your precepts,
     For by them You have given me life.
  94 I *am* Yours, save me;
     For I have sought Your precepts.
  95 The wicked wait for me to destroy me,
     But I will consider Your testimonies.
  96 I have seen the consummation of all
       perfection,
     But Your commandment *is* exceedingly broad.
                  Ps. 119:89–96

The context of the previous strophe continues. The psalmist is suffering affliction (v. 92); the wicked seek to destroy him (v. 95). Nevertheless, he is held by the word of God.

As the battles of life rage, the psalmist has one confidence: *"Forever, O Lord, / Your word is settled* ['standing'] *in heaven"* (v. 89). Life on this planet is filled with relativities. The one thing of which we can be certain is change. Beyond earth, however, is heaven. Beyond time is eternity. Beyond change is the changeless promise of God. Thus the psalmist turns to God's word and finds the mark of heaven upon it. It is the one absolute for his life. It is settled in heaven because God Himself has given it to us and it will be fulfilled by Him. As the psalmist continues, *"Your faithfulness endures to all generations"* (v. 90). Out of His faithfulness God will perform His word in His season. So He promises that as the rain waters the earth and produces fruit, "So shall My word be that goes forth from My mouth; / It shall not return to Me void, / But it shall accomplish what I please, / And it shall prosper in the thing for which I sent it" (Isa. 55:11).

While the earth is in constant flux, nevertheless, there is a stability to it. The rising of the sun day by day speaks of the faithfulness of God. In His providence He cares for us. Thus the psalmist continues, *"You established the earth, and it abides, / They* [heaven and earth?] *continue this day according to Your ordinances, / For all are Your servants"* (vv. 90–91). Even the elements serve the God who rules them and witness to His faithfulness. As the angels and the hosts of God's heavenly army are to bless Him, so "all His works, / In all places of His dominion" are also to join in that blessing (Ps. 104:22).

The faithfulness of God is not only reflected by His upholding creation; it is supremely seen in His word. As the psalmist confesses, *"Unless Your law had been my delight, / I would then have perished in my affliction"* (v. 92). As we learn and trust the word of God, we are prepared to withstand whatever pain may come our way. In His word God shows us the secret of suffering. He shows us Satan as our true enemy. He shows us what sin has done to ravish His earth. He shows us that He is not distant from our sorrow, but in His Son He is a participant in it. He also shows us how suffering can become redemptive, and He gives us hope that He will come and save us and heal us from evil. Therefore, the psalmist continues, *"I will never forget Your precepts, / For by them You have given me life"* (v. 93). God's word is creative. As He speaks, creation comes into being (Gen. 1:1ff.). As He speaks, salvation is accomplished. As Paul says, the word of the cross, to those who are being saved, is the power of God (1 Cor. 1:18).

The word of God leads the psalmist to God Himself. So, having said that His precepts have given him life, he immediately adds: *"I am Yours, save me"* (v. 94), after which the basis for his cry is offered: *"For I have sought Your precepts."* By this he does not mean that he has earned God's help. That help is guaranteed by the unconditional covenant that He established with His people. It does mean that he is diligent in seeking the God who saves. As he seeks God's precepts, he learns again and again of His gracious promise of salvation.

The cry for salvation can be seen in its proper context as the psalmist reveals, *"The wicked wait for me to destroy me"* (v. 95). Nevertheless, he continues to hope in God's word. Despite the persecution, he vows *"But I will consider Your testimonies"* and adds, in verse 96, *"I have seen the consummation of all perfection* [or, better, "I have seen the end to all (earthly) perfection"], / *But, Your commandment is exceedingly broad* ["wide, unlimited"]." Even the most nearly perfect things in this world come to an end. Only God and His word are "exceedingly broad," that is, unlimited and endless. Indeed, *"Your word is settled in heaven"* (v. 89). As Jesus says, "Heaven and earth will pass away, but My words will by no means pass away" (Matt. 24:35). When we are engaged with God's word, we are engaged with that which lasts forever.

THE WORD OF GOD GIVES US WISDOM

119:97 Oh, how I love Your law!
    It *is* my meditation all the day.
  98 You, through Your commandments, make me
    wiser than my enemies;
    For they *are* ever with me.
  99 I have more understanding than all my
    teachers,
    For Your testimonies *are* my meditation.
 100 I understand more than the ancients,
    Because I keep Your precepts.
 101 I have restrained my feet from every evil
    way,
    That I may keep Your word.
 102 I have not departed from Your judgments,
    For You Yourself have taught me.
 103 How sweet are Your words to my taste,
    Sweeter than honey to my mouth!
 104 Through Your precepts I get understanding;
    Therefore I hate every false way.
                    Ps. 119:97-104

A friend of mine who has been a drug addict for several years recently became clean and sober. As he began his recovery, he told me that the issue for him was not merely ceasing his drug abuse; the real issue was learning how to live. This is our issue too. It is the issue of life on this planet. How shall we live? Where is the guide to life? Every new car comes with an owner's manual. But where is the owner's manual for us? The psalmist answers in this strophe that it is the word of God.

Verse 97 begins with the ejaculation: *"Oh, how I love Your law!"* The following sentence proves that he is telling the truth: *"It is my meditation all the day."* But why is he so preoccupied with God's word? Why does he fill his mind with it rather than with the newspaper, junk novels, or MTV? The answer is that through it he has become wise. The word of God is teaching him how to live. It is his owner's manual.

The importance of the Scriptures is documented by the psalmist. God's commandments make him *"wiser than my enemies."* He is never distracted or seduced by their lies, *"For they* [the commandments] *are ever with me"* (v. 98). Moreover, he even has *"more understanding"* than all of his teachers. Why is this so? *"For Your testimonies are my meditation"* (v. 99). Human thoughts, however brilliant, come and go. When they are based upon God's word, they may even be trustworthy and true. Nevertheless, by learning to use the Bible for ourselves, we can have more understanding than our teachers because we have gone to the source of their wisdom. The psalmist claims that he even understands *"more than the ancients* ["old men"]." He goes behind his teachers to those who have the wisdom of a lifetime. Not even they can compete with God's word, however. He transcends them, *"Because I keep Your precepts"* (v. 100).

What, however, is the practical value of knowing the word of God? Verse 101 answers that the psalmist has restrained his feet from *"every evil way, / That I may keep Your word."* God's word is the guide for his life. It is the owner's manual that shows him where to walk. It keeps him from evil, and, by implication, directs him in righteousness. He has not departed from *"Your judgments"* because he has been taught by God Himself: *"For You Yourself have taught me"* (v. 102). These judgments reveal God's justice and order life according to His will. Is the will of God burdensome to the psalmist? Hardly. He now confesses: *"How sweet are Your words to my taste, / Sweeter than honey to my mouth!"* (v. 103). As he takes in the word of God, it is a pleasure. There is a delight in knowing that we have a sure guide to life. There is a relief in knowing that we are not left to wander alone. The psalmist concludes, *"Through Your precepts I get understanding; / Therefore I hate every false way"* (v. 104). The antithetical structure of revelation (see our comments on Psalm 1) shows him what is true and what is false. This understanding engendered by God's word leads him not to tolerate falsehood (as in our relativistic world today where all is gray). He hates those false ways that lead to death. This is not arrogance. This is honesty, born from a man who has learned from the owner's manual how to live.

THE WORD OF GOD IS LIGHT

119:105 Your word *is* a lamp to my feet
  And a light to my path.
106 I have sworn and confirmed
  That I will keep Your righteous judgments.
107 I am afflicted very much;
  Revive me, O LORD, according to Your word.
108 Accept, I pray, the freewill offerings of my
   mouth, O LORD,
  And teach me Your judgments.
109 My life *is* continually in my hand,
  Yet I do not forget Your law.
110 The wicked have laid a snare for me,
  Yet I have not strayed from Your precepts.
111 Your testimonies I have taken as a heritage
   forever,
  For they *are* the rejoicing of my heart.
112 I have inclined my heart to perform Your
   statutes
  Forever, to the very end.
         Ps. 119:105-12

The themes of affliction and persecution reappear (see vv. 107, 110; cf. vv. 81-88). This world is a battleground. No wonder Paul exhorts us to put on our spiritual armor and to take up the "sword of the Spirit," which is the word of God (Eph. 6:17). It is by this word that we will conquer.

In verse 105 the psalmist confesses: *"Your word is a lamp to my feet / And a light to my path."* I recall years ago the great Christian educator, Henrietta Mears citing this verse and illustrating it from her experience at Forest Home, the camp that she founded in the San Bernardino Mountains in Southern California. There in the woods at night it is difficult to see anything. Even if we have a flashlight, we may not see the whole trail, but we see where we are to place our next step. Likewise, God's word lights our path as we walk through the darkness of this world one step at a time.

With this light before him the psalmist confesses: *"I have sworn and confirmed / That I will keep Your righteous judgments"* (v. 106). His language is legal and emphatic. He will uphold the law of God as it applies to the situations of this life. His ethics are absolute rather than relative. They are not determined by the particular context within which he finds himself. At the same time, such a stance provokes persecution. Thus he continues, *"I am afflicted very much,"* and requests *"Revive me, O Lord, according to Your word"* (v. 107; cf. v. 25). As God renews his spirit, he promises *"the freewill offerings of my mouth"* (v. 108). These are his praises for relief. They are what the Book of Hebrews calls the "sacrifice of praise," which is "the fruit of our lips" (Heb. 13:15). With an open heart to God he asks, *"And teach me Your judgments."* Worship makes us receptive to the word of God. After we have opened our hearts to Him in praise we are ready to receive what He has for us. The psalmist laments that his life is *"continually in my hand,"* that is, that it is continually at risk (see Job 12:10, "[The Lord] in whose hand is the life of every living being"). Yet, he adds, *"I do not forget Your law"* (v. 109). In fact, this law sustains him through the fears and trials of this life. In verse 110 he reveals that the *"wicked"* seek to trap him like a wild bird, laying *"a snare for me."* Nevertheless, he remains faithful to God's word as he confesses: *"Yet I have not strayed* ["wandered"] *from Your precepts."*

Regardless of the suffering and persecution of this life, the psalmist finds confidence in God's word. It alone endures. He asserts, *"Your testimonies I have taken as a heritage* [literally, "I have inherited Your testimonies"] *forever."* The word of God becomes his Promised Land. In God's testimonies he finds *"the rejoicing of my heart"* (v. 111). There is no legalism here. He adds, *"I have inclined my heart to perform Your statutes / Forever, to the very end"* (v. 112). As God knows his heart, so God knows what is upon his heart, and it is to obey His will forever.

The word of God is our light. In it we come to know God. In it we come to know His will for us. Through it we have strength to stand against our enemies and endure persecution in this life. This is our eternal heritage. The book is open. It is before us. We must not miss it.

THE WORD OF GOD BRINGS US GODLY FEAR

119:113 I hate the double-minded,
    But I love Your law.
  114 You *are* my hiding place and my shield;
    I hope in Your word.
  115 Depart from me, you evildoers,
    For I will keep the commandments of my
      God!
  116 Uphold me according to Your word, that I
      may live;
    And do not let me be ashamed of my hope.
  117 Hold me up, and I shall be safe,
    And I shall observe Your statutes continually.
  118 You reject all those who stray from Your
      statutes,
    For their deceit *is* falsehood.
  119 You put away all the wicked of the earth *like*
      dross;
    Therefore I love Your testimonies.
  120 My flesh trembles for fear of You,
    And I am afraid of Your judgments.
                      Ps. 119:113–20

At this point the psalmist reflects upon those who reject God's word. They are double-minded (v. 113), evildoers (v. 115), strayers, deceitful (v. 118). Their judgment is certain: *"You put away all the wicked of the earth like dross"* (v. 119). No wonder he feels a righteous fear before God (v. 120). In this age of sentimentalism and vague spirituality, we need to share his sense of awe and reverence.

The psalmist announces in verse 113: *"I hate the double-minded, /
But I love Your law."* The double-minded falter between two opinions.
They are more concerned with popularity than with truth. As James
says, the double-minded man is "unstable in all his ways" (James 1:8).
In opposition to this vacillation, the psalmist loves God's law, which
is straightforward, trustworthy, and absolute. The word of God leads
him to the God of the word as he confesses: *"You are my hiding place
and my shield"* (see Ps. 28:7). With these metaphors, he shows us that
God is his protection and his protector. Like a deep cave, he hides in
the Almighty. Like a shield in battle, while God covers him, no enemy can dent him. Thus, he concludes, *"I hope in Your word"* (v. 114).
The reason for this is simple: there God is revealed as the One who
will take care of him.

With divine boldness, the psalmist commands, *"Depart from me,
you evildoers."* He has no time for those rebelling against the word of
God. If we are known by the company we keep, evildoers are not to
be a part of his company. Thus he confesses: *"For I will keep* ["preserve"] *the commandments of my God!"* (v. 115). Based upon this decision, he prays, *"Uphold me according to Your word, that I may live."* It
is important to note that God not only gives us His word; He also
gives us the strength to obey it. Life is to be found here, in fellowship with Him and in obedience to Him. The psalmist adds the appeal, *"And do not let me be ashamed of my hope"* (v. 116). Shame
would come if God did not come through for him.

In a similar appeal to verse 116, the psalmist prays: *"Hold me up,
and I shall be safe"* (or, "saved"). As God lifts him to Himself, he will
find safety or deliverance (from the evildoers, see v. 115). As a result, he vows: *"And I shall observe* [or, "I will look in"] *Your statutes
continually"* (v. 117). His life will be devoted to the word of God.

The alternative to this godly life is given in verses 118–19. The
psalmist begins: *"You reject all those who stray from Your statutes."* God
is holy, and He calls us to a life of holiness. Thus He says to Israel,
"And you shall be to Me a kingdom of priests and a holy nation"
(Exod. 19:6). God rejects strayers because *"their deceit is falsehood"*
(v. 118). No liar can stand before the God who is true (see Rev. 21:8).
The destiny of these deceivers is clear: *"You put away all the wicked of
the earth like dross."* *Dross* is that which is burned out of metal when it
is refined in the fire (cf. 1 Cor. 3:11–15). The psalmist confesses:

"Therefore I love Your testimonies" (v. 119). This is in his self-interest. By loving God's word, he will not be among the wicked who will be consumed. Furthermore, as God destroys the wicked, He Himself will be vindicated and His word will be shown to be true.

In light of the judgment to come, and in light of God's character, which stands behind it, the psalmist concludes: *"My flesh* ["humanity"] *trembles for fear of You, / And I am afraid of Your judgment"* (v. 120). Here is godly fear. It is evoked because of the greatness of God and the certainty of His judgments against all the double-minded and evildoers. As He reveals Himself we must fall on our faces before Him. Thus Isaiah cried out, "Woe is me" when he saw the holiness of God in the temple (Isa. 6:5). While this is an important word, which will save us from a false hope or naive sentimentality, it is not the last word. John writes centuries later that fear has to do with punishment, and when Jesus comes with His perfect love and fills us with His Spirit, that love casts out fear. Now we can stand before God in assurance, because we stand in Christ (1 John 4:17–18).

The Word of God Is Vindicated

119:121 I have done justice and righteousness;
  Do not leave me to my oppressors.
 122 Be surety for Your servant for good;
  Do not let the proud oppress me.
 123 My eyes fail *from seeking* Your salvation
  And Your righteous word.
 124 Deal with Your servant according to Your
   mercy,
  And teach me Your statutes.
 125 I *am* Your servant;
  Give me understanding,
  That I may know Your testimonies.
 126 *It is* time for *You* to act, O LORD,
  For they have regarded Your law as void.
 127 Therefore I love Your commandments
  More than gold, yes, than fine gold!
 128 Therefore all *Your* precepts *concerning* all
   things

> I consider *to be* right;
> I hate every false way.

Ps. 119:121–28

The thesis of this strophe appears in the final verse: *"I consider* [Your precepts] *to be right; / I hate every false way"* (v. 128). Its context is the oppressors of verse 121 and the proud of verse 122, who regard God's word as empty or void (v. 126). Contrary to their opposition and denial, however, the word of God stands as true. It is for this reason that God must intervene against them, showing Himself to be the living God.

Verse 121 opens with the psalmist's confession: *"I have done justice and righteousness."* In other words, he has obeyed the law of God; he has been faithful to the covenant. Therefore, he can ask boldly, *"Do not leave me to my oppressors."* He goes on in verse 122 to describe himself as God's *"servant,"* which, as we have seen, means that God is King and that he is submitted to Him. In asking Him to be *"surety"* for him *"for good,"* he uses a legal term that means that he wants God to take the responsibility for his debt. In other words, he asks God to stand up for him and to stand in on his behalf. He then repeats the petition of the previous verse: *"Do not let the proud oppress me."*

The desperation and determination of the psalmist is expressed in verse 123 as he relates: *"My eyes fail from seeking Your salvation / And Your righteous word"* (cf. v. 82). He presents himself as continually devoted to Scripture, reading until his eyesight grows dim. God's *"righteous word"* will not merely give him comfort; it will come against his oppressors. He asks that the Lord give him *"mercy"* ("covenant-love"), identifying himself as His covenant *"servant,"* adding, *"And teach me Your statutes"* (v. 124). It is out of that covenant bond so clearly revealed in Scripture that the psalmist expects God to act upon his behalf. No wonder he asks Him to be his teacher. He adds in verse 125: *"I am Your servant, / Give me understanding."* It is not enough to know the content of God's word; we must also ask Him to illumine it for us.

The previous verses, with their confessions of righteousness and reminders of the covenant, all lead up to the psalmist's request given in verse 126: *"It is time for You to act, O Lord, / For they have regarded Your law as void."* *They* refers, of course, to the oppressors and the

386

proud (vv. 121–22). These evildoers have rejected God's law; they pronounce it as empty. The call is for Yahweh to vindicate His person and His word by bringing judgment upon them. Notice that the psalmist does not view God as distant or unable to act. His word has not been separated from His work as it has in much modern church-life. There is no bibliolatry here. Neither is there any bias in favor of dispensational theology, which relegates God's signs and wonders to a past age, or bias against the supernatural.

Having asked God to act according to His word, the psalmist contrasts himself with his oppressors by vowing: *"Therefore, I love Your commandments."* They are more precious to him than *"gold,"* or even *"fine gold,"* that which has been refined in the fire (v. 127). Having said this, the psalmist concludes that all of God's precepts are *"right,"* adding, *"I hate every false way"* (v. 128). The *"false way"* is the way of the proud, who in their rebellion and self-sufficiency regard God's law as void (v. 126).

Fundamental to this strophe is the understanding that the God who speaks in His word is also the God who acts. As the truth of His word is maligned, He will intervene. As the psalmist says, *"It is time for You to act, O Lord, / For they have regarded Your law as void"* (v. 126). Isn't there something in us, as we see the blatant materialism of our world, filled with oppression and injustice toward the poor, that cries out? Do we not wish for divine power to be released as we see a compromised and impotent church living in denial of spiritual power? If so, this strophe is for us.

THE WORD OF GOD GIVES US LIGHT

119:129 Your testimonies are wonderful;
   Therefore my soul keeps them.
  130 The entrance of Your words gives light;
    It gives understanding to the simple.
  131 I opened my mouth and panted,
    For I longed for Your commandments.
  132 Look upon me and be merciful to me,
    As Your custom *is* toward those who love
     Your name.
  133 Direct my steps by Your word,
    And let no iniquity have dominion over me.

134 Redeem me from the oppression of man,
   That I may keep Your precepts.
135 Make Your face shine upon Your servant,
   And teach me Your statutes.
136 Rivers of water run down from my eyes,
   Because *men* do not keep Your law.

                                          Ps. 119:129–36

In this strophe the psalmist continues to know the power of evil, which tries to subvert him from the living God. He prays, therefore, against iniquity and oppression (vv. 133–34). He weeps over those in rebellion against God's word (v. 136). In the midst of the darkness, however, there is the light, which shines from divine revelation (v. 130).

The psalmist opens this strophe with the confession that God's *"testimonies are wonderful"* (v. 129); that is, they evoke a sense of awe and wonder because of the God who acts through them. With the sense of God's power before him, he continues, *"Therefore my soul keeps* ["has preserved"] *them."* This sense of power from the word of God becomes specific in the next verse. The psalmist observes, *"The entrance* ["the opening (to me)"] *of Your words gives light."* This explosion of light in our minds is an awesome reality. Often in reading the Scriptures I have received dramatic illumination. We realize that there is a power here beyond our unaided reason. J. B. Phillips recounts that when he first began to translate Paul's letters into modern English, his experience was like that of rewiring an old house with the electricity still left on. The psalmist concludes, *"It gives understanding to the simple"* (v. 130). The simple are not dumb. They have simply reached the end of themselves and recognized that, in order to know God, God must speak to them and make Himself known.

On the receiving end of revelation, the psalmist admits, *"I opened my mouth and panted, / For I longed for Your commandments"* (v. 131). He portrays himself as a thirsty animal, dying for water in the desert. As God feeds us from His word, He also increases our thirst after Him. He both fills us and leaves us unsatisfied at the same time. With his need pressing, the psalmist prays for God to see him; God's face turned toward him is a sign of His favor. Thus he adds, and *"be merciful to me"* (v. 132). Only divine mercy will satisfy the longing of his soul. He reminds God that such mercy is His *"custom . . . toward those who love Your name"* (v. 132). To love God's name is to love Him as a person and to enter into relationship with Him.

Mercy leads to obedience. As the psalmist prays, *"Direct my steps by Your word* [or, "establish my steps in Your word"], / *And let no iniquity* [straying from God's path] *have dominion over me"* (v. 133). He will be controlled by God rather than by sin or the devil. He adds, *"Redeem* ("ransom") *me from the oppression of man."* Like Israel in Egypt, he will be bought out of man's bondage by God's outstretched arm of power (Exod. 15:12-13). The result will be obedience: *"That I may keep Your precepts"* (v. 134).

The psalmist asks for a full, open relationship with God as he prays, *"Make Your face to shine upon Your servant."* This request recalls the benediction of Aaron and his sons: "The Lord bless you and keep you; / The Lord make His face shine upon you, / And be gracious to you; / The Lord lift up His countenance upon you, / And give you peace" (Num. 25:24-26). As God reveals His face to the psalmist, so He instructs him: *"And teach me Your statutes"* (v. 135). This longing reminds him of those who reject God's word. Thus he adds (and concludes): *"Rivers of water run down from my eyes, / Because men do not keep Your law"* (v. 136). Our blindness makes him weep.

God's word gives light. It is aggressive. It dispels the darkness. Moreover, it comes from the God who makes His face to shine upon us. In this, it is the very reflection of the countenance of God Himself. We should join the psalmist in weeping for those who prefer to stay in the darkness.

THE WORD OF GOD IS RIGHTEOUS

119:137 Righteous *are* You, O LORD,
    And upright *are* Your judgments.
    138 Your testimonies, *which* You have
        commanded,
        Are righteous and very faithful.
    139 My zeal has consumed me,
        Because my enemies have forgotten Your
        words.

140 Your word *is* very pure;
     Therefore Your servant loves it.
141 I *am* small and despised,
     Yet I do not forget Your precepts.
142 Your righteousness *is* an everlasting
          righteousness,
     And Your law *is* truth.
143 Trouble and anguish have overtaken me,
     Yet Your commandments *are* my delights.
144 The righteousness of Your testimonies *is*
          everlasting;
     Give me understanding, and I shall live.
                                         Ps. 119:137–44

The word of God reflects the character of God. Therefore, since God is *"righteous"* (true to His covenant relationship), His *"judgments"* must be *"upright"* ("straight, just," v. 137). His revelation cannot be less than Himself. To underscore the point, the psalmist continues: *"Your testimonies, which You have commanded, / Are righteous and very faithful* ["trustworthy"]" (v. 138). When he thinks of his *"enemies"* ("distressers"), however, he is *"consumed"* by his *"zeal"* ("abandoned devotion [toward God's revelation]"), because they have *"forgotten Your words"* (v. 139). How could they do this? Do they not know what God's word is?

Now the psalmist meditates: *"Your word is very pure"* (like refined metal; compare v. 127). Because of this, as a *"servant"* of the covenant God, he *"loves it"* (v. 140). The purity of the word reflects the purity of its author. He now continues that although he is *"small and despised"* by men, insignificant and rejected, he does not capitulate to their pressures. He confesses: *"Yet I do not forget Your precepts"* (v. 141). And why is this? The psalmist responds, *"Your righteousness is an everlasting righteousness."* By implication, why surrender to that which is passing away? God's righteousness, His salvation and peace, lasts forever. Pursue that which endures. Moreover, *"Your law is truth* ["trustworthy"]" (v. 142). When all else fails, he can count on it. The Hebrew idea of truth is not merely that it is reasonable, but that it will hold us up when we lean our weight upon it. Despite his warfare in this world, where *"trouble* ["bondage, restriction"] *and anguish have overtaken me,"* God's commandments *"are my delights"* (v. 143). Now, to complete this meditation upon God's word, the psalmist adds, *"The righteousness of Your testimonies is everlasting; / Give me understanding and I shall live"* (v. 144). God's word is eternal, since He is its source. But if we are to understand it, He must open it to us. The psalmist shows us how to ask for understanding. As we receive it, we live. The ultimate fulfillment of this prayer is in Christ, where through His Spirit He convicts us of sin, regenerates us by His Spirit, and brings us into life (see John 3:1–16).

This strophe is bound together by the theme of righteousness, which means that God is true to His covenant with His people. He will save them, judge them, bless them, and give them peace. Since God Himself is righteous (v. 137), His righteousness is eternal (v. 142). Therefore, His testimonies are righteous (v. 138) and as eternal as He is (v. 144). Life comes in understanding this. Life comes in submitting to the covenant God. All else is a sham and fleeting.

THE WORD OF GOD IS TO
BE OBEYED

119:145 I cry out with *my* whole heart;
    Hear me, O LORD!
    I will keep Your statutes.
146 I cry out to You;
    Save me, and I will keep Your testimonies.
147 I rise before the dawning of the morning,
    And cry for help;
    I hope in Your word.
148 My eyes are awake through the *night*
        watches,
    That I may meditate on Your word.
149 Hear my voice according to Your
        lovingkindness;
    O LORD, revive me according to Your justice.
150 They draw near who follow after wickedness;
    They are far from Your law.
151 You *are* near, O LORD,
    And all Your commandments *are* truth.
152 Concerning Your testimonies,
    I have known of old that You have founded
        them forever.

Ps. 119:145–52

In this strophe the psalmist is clearly in trouble. He stresses that he cries out to God three times (see vv. 145–47). He is in need of help. Those who follow wickedness draw near (v. 150). At the same time, God is near (v. 151). Thus his cry is heard. As he asks God to save him, he also vows that he will keep or obey His word. As Jesus says, "If you love Me, keep My commandments" (John 14:15).

Strong emotion comes through in the opening of this strophe: *"I cry out with my whole heart; / Hear me, O Lord!"* This cry is heartfelt. The word *hear* can also be rendered "answer." The psalmist wants God to respond to his plea. The vow then follows: *"I will keep* ["preserve"] *Your statutes"* (v. 145). In the following verse he repeats, *"I cry out to You."* The answer that he wants from God is divine intervention: *"Save me, and I will keep Your testimonies"* (v. 146). His vow is parallel to the previous verse; he will obey God.

The intensity of the psalmist's cry is revealed in verse 147. He rises while it is still dark, as he says, *"and* [I] *cry for help."* The help that he needs is divine deliverance. The basis of his prayer is God's revelation: *"I hope in Your word."* His hope is based upon the covenant commitment that Yahweh has made to save His people. No wonder the psalmist cries to God before the dawn; he has already been awake *"through the night watches"* (which were divided into several time periods; see Judg. 7:19), meditating *on Your word"* (v. 148).

The psalmist asks God to answer his cry in verse 149. The basis for this is not his midnight devotions, however. As noted above, he is no legalist. The basis is God's covenant with Israel: *"Hear my voice according to Your lovingkindness* ["covenant-love"]; / *O Lord, revive me according to Your justice."* The reason for his urgency appears when he explains that those *"draw near who follow after wickedness,"* who are *"far from Your law"* (v. 150). At the same time, the psalmist confesses *"You are near, O Lord."* It is God's nearness that enables us to overcome the nearness of those who disobey His word. While the psalmist counts on God's presence, he also counts on the authority of His law. Thus he adds: *"And all Your commandments are truth* ["trustworthy"]" (v. 151). Too often the church has settled for a false dichotomy. Either we have welcomed a Bible that is true but feared the vital presence of God in our midst, or we have gone after an experience of God and abandoned the normative standard of objective revelation. As the Reformers taught, the two must be held together, and this is exactly what the psalmist does here.

This strophe concludes with a confession: *"Concerning Your testimonies, / I have known of old* [that is, "for a long time"] *that You have founded them forever"* (v. 152). God's word is established in heaven (v. 89). As Isaiah says, "The grass withers, the flower fades, / But the word of our God stands forever" (Isa. 40:8). No wonder the psalmist promises to keep God's statutes and testimonies (vv. 145–46). In doing so, he is following that which endures into eternity.

THE WORD OF GOD REVIVES US

119:153 Consider my affliction and deliver me,
　　　　For I do not forget Your law.
　154 Plead my cause and redeem me;
　　　　Revive me according to Your word.
　155 Salvation *is* far from the wicked,
　　　　For they do not seek Your statutes.
　156 Great *are* Your tender mercies, O LORD;
　　　　Revive me according to Your judgments.
　157 Many *are* my persecutors and my enemies,
　　　　Yet I do not turn from Your testimonies.
　158 I see the treacherous, and am disgusted,
　　　　Because they do not keep Your word.
　159 Consider how I love Your precepts;
　　　　Revive me, O LORD, according to Your
　　　　　　lovingkindness.
　160 The entirety of Your word *is* truth,
　　　　And every one of Your righteous judgments
　　　　　　endures forever.

Ps. 119:153–60

The theme of revival has already appeared substantially in verses 25–32. It also recurs throughout Psalm 119 (see, e.g., vv. 107, 149). The prayer for revival is voiced in this strophe in verses 154, 156, and 159. The psalmist suffers affliction (v. 153). He is dogged by the wicked (v. 155), persecutors, enemies (v. 157), and treacherous people (v. 158). In the crisis he needs God to step in and reawaken him.

Verse 153 opens with the plea that God will see the psalmist's *"affliction"* and *"deliver"* him. He is bold to ask this, as he says, *"For I do not forget Your law."* It is the law of God that assures him God is his deliverer. It is also his obedience to that law that indicates he takes God's covenant seriously. The psalmist asks God to be his advocate, to plead his cause (v. 154). This will happen, not only as he is justified before his enemies, but also as God redeems him from the bondage of his affliction. He adds: *"Revive me according to Your word."* The word *revive* means to keep alive or to make alive. It assumes that the psalmist has been alive before; now God will make him alive again.

The psalmist distances himself from the *"wicked."* Salvation, he asserts, is far from them, *"For they do not seek Your statutes"* (v. 155). In their disobedience, they stand under the just judgment of God. Nevertheless, the psalmist confesses: *"Great are Your tender mercies, O Lord."* Based upon God's covenant commitment to him, he continues, *"Revive me* ["give me life"] *according to Your judgments"* (v. 156). Again, the psalmist's mind moves to the crisis surrounding him: *"Many are my persecutors and my enemies* ["distressers"]." They, however, cannot influence him. As he says, *"Yet I do not turn from Your testimonies"* (v. 157). It is these very testimonies that have given him a true knowledge of God and a true moral sense. Thus he adds, *"I see the treacherous* ["offenders"], *and am disgusted* ["grieved"], / *Because they do not keep Your word"* (v. 158).

The psalmist is not like these evil and disobedient people. Thus he is bold to pray, *"Consider how I love Your precepts."* He asks God to revive him, *"according to Your lovingkindness* ["covenant-love"]" (v. 159). Once again, his confidence in God's new work in his life is not based upon his obedience to God but upon God's faithfulness to His covenant. Whenever God acts afresh in our lives, it is by His grace. In fact, the irony of revival is that it usually comes in the darkest hour. For example, when the Evangelical Awakening in England struck in the eighteenth century, the church was dissipated with deism and the country with gin. Then, because of the prayers of a few, God moved, and the course of history was changed through the preaching of George Whitfield and John Wesley. It is God's *"lovingkindness"* that will change us again.

The psalmist concludes with a key to revival in verse 160: *"The entirety of Your word is truth, / And every one of Your righteous judgments endures forever."* A half-hearted faith and a half-hearted preaching will never bring revival. We must believe the totality of God's revelation, which is both true and eternal. Because of destructive criticism, the Bible has been shredded for most Christians today. Weak in authority, the church endures with a weak faith. Billy Graham struggled with the question of biblical authority before his career-changing Los Angeles crusade years ago. Finally, he got down on his knees, spread the Bible before him, and prayed, "Lord, I take this book as Your inspired word by faith." From that prayer, he arose with a new sense of power and became the most famous evangelist of our generation. Such renewed commitment today will bring renewed faith and spark the revival for which we pray.

THE WORD OF GOD BRINGS AWE

119:161 Princes persecute me without a cause,
But my heart stands in awe of Your word.
162 I rejoice at Your word
As one who finds great treasure.
163 I hate and abhor lying,
But I love Your law.
164 Seven times a day I praise You,
Because of Your righteous judgments.
165 Great peace have those who love Your law,
And nothing causes them to stumble.
166 LORD, I hope for Your salvation,
And I do Your commandments.
167 My soul keeps Your testimonies,
And I love them exceedingly.
168 I keep Your precepts and Your testimonies,
For all my ways *are* before You.
Ps. 119:161–68

Who calls the shots? For the psalmist it is not the rulers of this world. Their persecution does not humble him. God's word alone does that. As he says in verse 161, *"Princes persecute me without a cause, / But my heart stands in awe* ["dread"] *of Your word."* This dread is because of the great and mighty God who speaks it. It is also because of the absolute demand that it makes upon us and the day of judgment to which it points. There is a great secret here that we should not miss. Since the psalmist is in awe of God, he is not in awe of anyone else. This is our true freedom in this world. Luther puts it this way,

> Let goods and kindred go. This mortal life also;
> The body they may kill: God's truth abideth
>   still;
> His Kingdom is forever.

In this freedom the psalmist confesses, *"I rejoice at Your word / As one who finds great treasure* [or, "much spoil"]*"* (v. 162). He expresses the joy of a warrior returning with booty from battle when he opens God's word. Many times I have had a similar joy as I have heard the Lord speak to me there. A part of his joy is that in the word of God he finds the truth. Thus he continues, *"I hate and abhor lying, / But I love Your law"* (v. 163). This love comes because God is reality and He makes us real. Such love leads to worship: *"Seven times a day I praise You."* Seven here is probably to be taken as the number of perfection (God created the world in seven days, and it was perfect). We can paraphrase this thought, *"*Perfectly or fully I praise You.*"* And why such an outpouring of devotion? He continues, *"Because of Your righteous judgments* [or, "the judgments of Your righteousness"]*"* (v. 164). Moreover, since he loves God's law he finds *"great peace"* ("wholeness"), and there is nothing to stumble over (v. 165). When God's word comes, sin must depart. As the old saying goes, "Sin will keep you from God's word, or God's word will keep you from sin."

The psalmist expresses his hope for *"Your salvation"* ("deliverance"). Since this is future, it refers to the final salvation of the end. In the meantime, he adds, *"And I do Your commandments"* (v. 166). This comes from his heart: *"My soul keeps* ["preserves, protects"] *Your testimonies, / And I love them exceedingly"* (v. 167). With repetition for emphasis, he continues, *"I keep Your precepts and Your testimonies."* But what is the motive for such obedience? He concludes, *"For all my ways are before You"* (v. 168). In other words, God sees him and knows his walk, the way in which he goes.

In sum, the word of God brings the psalmist awe. It is like great treasure or booty to him (v. 162). It contains righteous judgments (v. 164). Loving it brings great peace (v. 165). As the day of salvation draws near, all of the psalmist's ways stand before his Judge. This is enough for awe indeed.

THE WORD OF GOD IS OUR DELIGHT

119:169 Let my cry come before You, O LORD;
   Give me understanding according to Your
    word.
 170 Let my supplication come before You;
   Deliver me according to Your word.
 171 My lips shall utter praise,
   For You teach me Your statutes.
 172 My tongue shall speak of Your word,
   For all Your commandments *are*
    righteousness.
 173 Let Your hand become my help,
   For I have chosen Your precepts.
 174 I long for Your salvation, O LORD,
   And Your law *is* my delight.
 175 Let my soul live, and it shall praise You;
   And let Your judgments help me.
 176 I have gone astray like a lost sheep;
   Seek Your servant,
   For I do not forget Your commandments.
          Ps. 119:169–76

The final strophe, in a sense, sums up the whole psalm. It is a meditation upon the word of God, and it comes from one who knows what it is like to go astray and be brought back home again (v. 176). Verse 169 expresses the psalmist's longing: *"Let my cry come before You, O Lord."* And what is it that he prays for? *"Give me understanding according to Your word."* This illumination is God's alone to give. How often have we comprehended the historical and even theological substance of the Bible but missed the spiritual point, the real understanding. This comes from God's Spirit as He ministers to us.

The psalmist continues his petition or *"supplication"* as he prays, *"Deliver* ['rescue," like taking prey out of an animal's mouth] *me according to Your word"* (v. 170). In the larger context of the psalm we know that the author faces many enemies, the proud, the oppressors, who would do him in. As God intervenes and instructs him by His actions, he promises, *"My lips shall utter praise."* The basis for this is: *"For You teach me Your statutes"* (v. 171). Such instruction results in witness: *"My tongue shall speak of Your word, / For all Your commandments are righteousness"* (v. 172). The content of that witness concerns the righteous laws of God.

The psalmist asks that God's *"hand become my help."* His hand represents His power (see Exod. 15:6). Here is a call for divine intervention. The basis for this is that the psalmist has *"chosen Your precepts"* (v. 173). Knowing them, he knows that God is a God of action. Honoring His word is also a sign of faithfulness to His covenant. The psalmist adds, *"I long for Your salvation, O Lord."* This would include deliverance from his enemies (see v. 170). Now he reveals, *"And Your law is my delight"* (intensive plural). As God intervenes in his life he will worship Him. Thus he prays, *"Let my soul live, and it shall praise You."* But he also needs to know how to live: *"And let Your judgments help me"* (v. 175). This help includes giving him guidance as he walks through this life. He then confesses *"I have gone astray like a lost sheep,"* but he needs God to find him: *"Seek your servant."* Why should God go looking for him? Because he is a member of the covenant people: *"For I do not forget Your commandments"* (v. 176). Certainly this final claim is true. It is documented by the whole of Psalm 119.

Throughout this extensive prayer-meditation, we have seen that the word, the testimonies, the statutes, the precepts, the commandments, and the law of God have been the psalmist's preoccupation. From the eternal self-revelation of the living God he has received truth, salvation, righteousness, justice, and peace. These are all words of the covenant. They express the gifts that Yahweh, King of Israel, has bestowed upon His people. Through them they are made secure, shown how to walk, defended from their enemies, and prepared for life eternal. The importance of God's word cannot be stressed enough. It reveals the very nature of God as the God who speaks. Through His word He is shown to be personal and to desire a personal relationship with us as He addresses us. By His word we can know Him substantially. By His word we can also know His will for our lives; we can learn how to live.

And how are we to receive His word? There is only one answer. With humility. We are not to be among the proud who declare their independence from God. They believe their own words to be the final authority. They refuse to accept the divine word from the outside. Their end, however, is destruction. But the person who comes to know the God who speaks will live forever. His life will be established because it is not built upon human opinion, but upon divine revelation. As Psalm 119 says, "Forever, O Lord, / Your word is settled in heaven" (v. 89).

CHAPTER ONE HUNDRED TWENTY

How to Deal with Liars

Psalm 120

Psychologists have recently made addiction a major focus of their interest. It is becoming clear that we not only live in a drug- and alcohol-oriented society; we also live in an addictive society. In other words, the problem is not just with substance abuse; it is with the whole culture that creates the context for that abuse and supports it. One of the major characteristics of the addict is dishonesty. For example, the addict will deny that he or she has a problem with alcohol or drugs. Such deception allows the addiction to continue, and it creates confusion, a smoke screen to hide behind, allowing the addict to maintain the illusion of control. Lying is a major tool that perpetuates the addict and the addictive society. We can see this in the political realm. Politicians constantly use double-talk and innuendo in order to maintain their power. Rarely do they speak honestly and directly. This perpetuates the environment of addiction because people hear what they want to hear rather than what is really going on. Little by little, deception removes us from reality.

The issue of dishonesty is the issue of this psalm. The author is faced with "lying lips" and "a deceitful tongue" (v. 2). Rather than perpetuating it, enjoying it, participating in it, however, he asks God to deliver him from it. In other words, what he wants is reality. The psalmist does not want confusion, which allows others to maintain control, to continue. In this context he asks God to intervene.

Commentators identify Psalm 120 as a psalm of thanksgiving. This is based on viewing verse 1 as an answer to prayer. At the same time, it may also be a lament, especially if the psalmist is still waiting for God to act. The meaning of the subtitle in the text, A Song of Ascents, which stands before each of Psalms 120–36 is unknown to us. It suggests a stylistic or liturgical or historical reference, which has now been lost. The thought moves from the cry for help (vv. 1–2) to the content of the answer (vv. 3–4) and concludes with a woe or lament (vv. 5–7).

CRY FOR HELP

120:1 In my distress I cried to the LORD,
     And He heard me.
   2 Deliver my soul, O LORD, from lying lips
     And from a deceitful tongue.
                                        Ps. 120:1–2

Verse 1 sets the context. The psalmist is in *"distress"* ("to be bound, restricted, troubled"). This crisis clearly relates to those who are deceiving him in the next verse. The answer to his condition is prayer. Thus he relates, *"I cried to the Lord."* His cry does not go unanswered, as he adds, *"And He heard me."* Whenever we face adversity we also face options. We can worry. We can complain. We can seek to manipulate our situation. Or we can pray. The psalmist's distress works well for him. It drives him to his knees. Here is the beginning of the real answer. But what is the content of his prayer?

The psalmist cries out to God: *"Deliver my soul, O Lord, from lying lips / And from a deceitful tongue* [or, "a tongue of guile"]." The word *deliver* originally indicated taking prey out of an animal's mouth.

Here it means: "snatch or tear away, remove." His *"soul"* is himself, that is, "me." He wants to be delivered from liars, those who mask their true intentions by deceit. Being with other addicts who are in denial helps to prevent an addict from changing. The road to recovery in an addictive society is to change friends—to be delivered from those who practice deception. When this happens, the fog lifts. If we are to recover from our addictions, we must both face them and live in reality. The secret of Alcoholics Anonymous is that it brings addicts into the light. I recall visiting my first AA meeting and hearing everyone introduce themselves: "Hi, I'm John. I'm an alcoholic." Here is facing reality. At the time I wondered what it would be like for us in the church to follow a similar pattern: "Hi, I'm John. I'm a sinner." We must notice that as the psalmist prays for deliverance, he asks God to do what he cannot do. In an addictive society, only God can set us free as we pray and experience reality with Him.

THE CONTENT OF THE ANSWER

> 120:3 What shall be given to you,
>   Or what shall be done to you,
>   You false tongue?
>   4 Sharp arrows of the warrior,
>   With coals of the broom tree!
>
> *Ps. 120:3-4*

I take these next two verses as an oracle from God. Here is His answer to the psalmist's cry. God speaks prophetically to the liars. He asks, *"What shall be given to you, / Or what shall be done to you* [or, "added to you"], / *You false tongue?"* (v. 3). With this word He gains their attention. He also prepares them for His answer, and it is a harsh one. The liar, represented by the *"false tongue"* will receive *"the sharp arrows of the warrior* ["mighty man"]," and the *"coals of the broom tree"* (v. 4). *"The warrior"* refers to God Himself as He answers the psalmist's request. He will bring His arrows down upon the liar. This may well mean physical destruction, especially as the liar himself seeks war (see v. 7). Moreover, he will be burned with the fiery coals of the *"broom tree,"* a twelve-foot tree that provided good wood for fuel and coal. Such a fire could burn down the gates of the liar's city.

God announces His judgment upon the liar. He will destroy those who deceive. Their punishment lies in His hands, not in ours, but He will expose them and remove them in His time. Indeed, our sins will find us out; they will come back down upon our heads (cf. Ps. 3:10). When we are caught in a web of deceit, we need to pray for God to break it. We need to ask Him to remove the confusion and assume His control. We need to call for His arrows and coals. His justice is sure. No liar will enter His Kingdom (see Rev. 21:8).

WOE

120:5 Woe is me, that I dwell in Meshech,
      That I dwell among the tents of Kedar!
   6 My soul has dwelt too long
      With one who hates peace.
   7 I *am for* peace;
      But when I speak, they *are* for war.

                                              Ps. 120:5–7

After the psalmist records God's oracle, he expresses his own lament. If we are to be a part of the solution to deception, we have to be honest about our own feelings and express them. He lets us know more of the circumstances within which he has prayed for God to act. To begin with, he is exiled from home; he sojourns in *"Meshech"* and dwells among the *"tents of Kedar"* (v. 5). Since Meshech is in the north, near the Black Sea, and Kedar is in the Arabian desert, these references are probably not literal locations. The psalmist uses them symbolically in order to express his alienation. He is separated from God's land and God's people. No wonder he lives among liars; he lives in this fallen world. As he says in verse 6: *"My soul has dwelt too long / With one who hates peace."* A corrupted environment will corrupt us. Living with addictive people can make us addicts. It is a bad infection. Nevertheless, the psalmist has not capitulated to those around him. Thus his prayer for deliverance (v. 2). As he says, *"I am for peace."* However, he continues, *"when I speak, they are for war"* (v. 7). Obviously he doesn't belong. He is in a different world. Their world is one of deception and war. His is one of truth and peace. No wonder he prays for deliverance. What he hears is that God will take care of the liars. Judgment belongs to Him alone (see Rom. 12:19).

This is the way out of the deception and confusion of an addictive society. First, we need to be honest about ourselves. We need to know who we are. We need to be for truth and peace. Second, we need to see the addiction for what it is. Third, we need to guard ourselves against being corrupted by that environment. Fourth, we need to confess with AA that we need a 'Higher Power' to rely on. Our higher power is in the living God, and as we pray He will act. God's intervention will be our deliverance. Anything else is dysfunctional.

CHAPTER ONE HUNDRED TWENTY-ONE

When the Going Gets Tough

Psalm 121

All of us know the lonely hours when the lights go off after the business of the day is ended. These moments can be healing if they lead us to thought and prayer. One of the things we need to discover is that it is good to be alone. We should also know that God is there in the quiet. He is there when life is fragile. The ground can quake (v. 3). Nature itself can become a threat (v. 6). Evil stalks us (v. 7), and death stands before us. The road to freedom, however, is not to deny the ultimate threat of death, but to come to know the God who has conquered death. This thought takes us to Psalm 121.

The classic beauty of this psalm is haunting. It speaks of nature, time, eternity, and the God who is there through it all. Commentators identify Psalm 121 as a meditation, which results from the question raised in verse 1. Its date and author are unknown. The thought moves from the admission of need for help (vv. 1–2) to the nature of that help (vv. 3–8).

NEED FOR HELP

121:1 I will lift up my eyes to the hills—
From whence comes my help?
2 My help *comes* from the LORD,
Who made heaven and earth.

Ps. 121:1–2

Verse 1 asks a timeless, personal question with poetic power: *"I will lift up my eyes to the hills— / From whence comes my help?"* The hills or *"mountains"* could be the hills of Jerusalem where Yahweh dwells in His temple. They could also represent other mountains of God such as Sinai and Carmel, where He has come down and made His presence known. Lifting up our eyes also suggests the transcendence of God. We are of the earth and must look up to heaven. We need help far beyond our own limited resources and our human answers. Modern man has been infected with the myth of autonomy, the myth of self-sufficiency. He has been told to be the captain of his own fate, the commander of his own destiny. Yet a simple virus can fell him. The road to recovery from such illusions is one word: *"Help."* It is the admission that I have to ask someone for something beyond myself.

Verse 2 is the answer to the cry of verse 1: *"My help comes from the Lord* [Yahweh], */ Who made heaven and earth."* Now our eyes are not only lifted up to the hills; they are lifted up to the Creator of the hills. They are lifted up to the God who stands before, outside, and within His creation. They are lifted up to the God who commanded the gaseous stars into space. They are lifted up to the God who placed our planet into orbit around the sun. They are lifted up to the God who orders our geological and historical life. They are lifted up to the God who made heaven, the angels and all their hosts, and the earth, the world, and all that dwell within it. Here, from the eternal, living God is help indeed.

THE NATURE OF HELP

121:3 He will not allow your foot to be moved;
     He who keeps you will not slumber.
    4 Behold, He who keeps Israel
     Shall neither slumber nor sleep.
    5 The LORD *is* your keeper;
     The LORD *is* your shade at your right hand.
    6 The sun shall not strike you by day,
     Nor the moon by night.
    7 The LORD shall preserve you from all evil;
     He shall preserve your soul.
    8 The LORD shall preserve your going out and
       your coming in
     From this time forth, and even forevermore.
Ps. 121:3-8

The style changes from personal address (vv. 1–2) to a reflection upon the God who is our help. Verses 3–4 carry the first theme: He keeps us. Verses 5–6 carry the second theme: He protects us. And verses 7–8 carry the third theme: He preserves us.

In verses 3–4 God is our keeper. As the psalmist promises, *"He will not allow your foot to be moved."* God is the firm foundation for our lives. He is the rock of our salvation. He is our security. Those of us who live in California have few illusions about terra firma. The earth moves often and without warning. A recent example of this upheaval was a devastating quake in Armenia, which took over 50,000 lives. The only way in which our foot cannot be moved is for it to be standing upon the solid ground of God Himself. When we are anchored in eternity, we can deal with time. When we are united to the one who moves all things, we ourselves cannot be moved.

We are on solid ground because God *keeps* ("guards, protects") us, and He *"will not slumber."* Verse 4 underscores this great truth: *"Behold, He who keeps Israel / Shall neither slumber nor sleep."* God is always awake. We can pray to Him at midnight, and He hears and answers. Moreover, God is always faithful to His covenant with His people. He puts a special mantle of protection around us. He *"keeps Israel,"* His chosen one. People age, grow weary, become exhausted, and die. God neither slumbers nor sleeps. He knows our every moment. His eye is upon us. He walks in our way.

In verses 5–6 the psalmist offers an expansion of the thought in verse 3 that God keeps us. We are kept in His protective hand. Thus verse 5 opens with the confession: *"The Lord is your keeper."* But what does that mean? The psalmist continues that He will be *"your shade at your right hand."* To be shaded by God is to be protected from whatever may harm us. He casts His shadow over us. He stands between us and the sun's deadly ultraviolet rays. As the psalmist promises: *"The sun shall not strike you by day."* We are not only faced with the threat of the day, however. There is also danger at night. We can become moonstruck. God will also be our guardian then: *"the moon* [shall not strike you] *by night."* No evil will befall us when we are shadowed by God.

Does this mean that no adversity can come to the Christian? Does this mean that we should enjoy perfect health and wealth? If we were to take these verses out of their context, we might reach that conclusion. The fact is, however, that the psalmist has already seen his need for help in verse 1. He knows difficulty, and in it he cries out for God to intervene. God does not promise that we will never have problems; He does promise to be with us in our problems, and He assures us that nothing can touch our souls and separate us from His love (Rom. 8:37–39). Moreover, since God guards us, we know that our eternal destiny is held securely in His hand. All must pass before Him before it comes to us. When He allows it to come to us, it is for our ultimate good.

Verses 7–8 show us that God does not merely protect us from physical evil; He also protects us from personal evil: *"The Lord shall preserve you from all evil."* But what does this mean? No sickness? No sorrow? No suffering? The psalmist replies, *"He shall preserve your soul"* (v. 7). No sin, no attack from the devil, no evil can take us away from Him. His love is constant. His presence is unfailing. He guards us to eternity. Thus He keeps us as we go out and come in (v. 8). Every departure and arrival (the danger of change) is monitored by Him. But how long will this be? The psalmist answers, *"From this time forth, and even forevermore."* Starting now and throughout eternity. This is the help we need, and this is the help we get.

For myself I must add that this psalm is true. From the day of my conversion, which now was long ago, to the present, through years of intellectual pursuit, through three pastorates, through sixteen years of marriage, through college and seminary teaching, through relational crises, through being fired from a job, through profound emotional stress, through death and grief, the Lord has preserved my going out and my coming in, and He will keep on doing it right into eternity.

CHAPTER ONE HUNDRED TWENTY-TWO

The Joy of Jerusalem

Psalm 122

Once Jerusalem was captured by David and made the capital of Israel, she became the focus of the political and religious life of God's people. Every true Jew longed to be in Jerusalem. The rabbis described the city as "the navel of the universe." Remarkable after three thousand years is the role Jerusalem still plays in the history of the world. It is the Holy City for both Christians and Jews today. It is the second most holy place for Muslims. Thus racial, religious, and political tempers run high in dealing with this city. It was the goal of diaspora Jews. It was the goal of the Crusades. Before Muhammad ever prayed toward Mecca, he prayed toward Jerusalem. What happens to Jerusalem has the potential to ignite a world war.

Psalm 122 tells us the secret of the Holy City. God dwells there in His temple (v. 9). Thus the psalmist has joy with Jerusalem as his destination (v. 1). There the tribes of Israel give thanks to God (v. 4). There Israel's moral and legal life is resolved (v. 5). No wonder the psalmist prays for the peace and prosperity of this city (vv. 6–9).

Commentators describe this psalm as a song that includes testimony (v. 1), meditation (vv. 3–5), and exhortation (v. 6). It may well have been used in one of the annual festivals to Jerusalem. While it is ascribed to David, this seems to be a later addition, since the temple was not built until after his death (cf. vv. 1 and 9). The thought moves from the release of joy (vv. 1–2) to the reason for joy (vv. 3–5) and concludes with the response to joy (vv. 6–9).

THE RELEASE OF JOY

122:1 I was glad when they said to me,
    "Let us go into the house of the LORD."
   2 Our feet have been standing
    Within your gates, O Jerusalem!
   3 Jerusalem is built
    As a city that is compact together,
   4 Where the tribes go up,
    The tribes of the LORD,
    To the Testimony of Israel,
    To give thanks to the name of the LORD.
   5 For thrones are set there for judgment,
    The thrones of the house of David.

Ps. 122:1–5

The psalmist is delighted when he hears the call: *"'Let us go into the house of the Lord'"* (v. 1). This invitation may be from the priests, welcoming the pilgrims who have come up to Jerusalem into the temple. His response is that he is *"glad"* ("takes pleasure in, exalts"). Verse 2 shows us that he has already arrived in the Holy City as he recounts: *"Our feet have been standing / Within your gates, O Jerusalem."* He has come for one reason, to enter the house of the Lord and worship Him. Responding with joy to the call, he is ready to move into the presence of God.

Where does his joy come from? The answer is given in verses 3–4. First of all, the psalmist admires the city itself. It is built *"compact together."* That is, it is a walled city, well defended and protected. As Ps. 48:12 says, "Walk about Zion, / And go all around her. Count her towers; / Mark well her bulwarks" (Ps. 48:12–13). This suggests a city of power and strength, and it is a joy to know it. Second, Jerusalem is the focus of Israel's life. It is where the *"tribes go up, / The tribes of the Lord."* Thus it provides for their unity. When the times of pilgrimage come, they assemble and renew the covenant. Here they are refreshed in worship. Here the law of God is taught. Here they are reminded once again that they are God's people. Here they celebrate His mighty acts. No wonder there is such joy in pilgrimage. Third, they go *to the Testimony of Israel.* The NKJV capitalizes *testimony* as a symbol for God, taking it in parallel with *"the name of the Lord"* in the next clause. This, however, would be peculiar. It is better to take *testimony* as referring to the tribes: "[They are] a testimony to Israel," as they come for the festival. Fourth, the purpose of their coming is *"to give thanks to the name of the Lord"* (v. 4). They come to worship Yahweh and experience His presence and power. Here their joy is released before Him. Fifth, they come for judgment. Jerusalem is the seat of the monarchy, the *"thrones of the house of David,"* which are *"set for judgment"* (v. 5). The disputes of individuals and of the tribes will be settled there. Such resolutions also produce joy.

The psalmist experiences the joy of Jerusalem's power, delight in the presence of the other tribes coming together, ecstatic worship, and the execution of justice. We can gain some hint of what he felt even as we see pilgrims make their way to Rome or Mecca today. Greater still is our joy when we come together in the presence of the Lord and in our love for each other to worship Him, and to receive His strength and kingdom order for our lives.

THE RESPONSE OF JOY

122:6 Pray for the peace of Jerusalem:
    "May they prosper who love you.
  7 Peace be within your walls,
    Prosperity within your palaces."
  8 For the sake of my brethren and companions,
    I will now say, "Peace *be* within you."
  9 Because of the house of the LORD our God
    I will seek your good.

Ps. 122:6–9

Because of all that Jerusalem means as God's city, the psalmist exhorts us: *"Pray for the peace of Jerusalem." Peace* here means security, well-being. A double blessing follows. First, a blessing is pronounced upon those who live in or long for Jerusalem: *"'May they prosper ['be secure"] who love you'"* (v. 6). Next, the city is blessed: *"'Peace be within your walls, / Prosperity ['security"] within your palaces'"* ["courts"] (v. 7). The psalmist places all of Jerusalem under the blessing of God. He pronounces this blessing not only for himself, but also for the sake of *"my brethren [blood family] and companions ["neighbors," fellow Hebrews].*" He sums up and gives the final, simple blessing: *"I will now say, 'Peace be within you'"* (v. 8). Jerusalem is to be secure under the security of God.

Why this blessing? Why should we pray for the peace of Jerusalem? The answer is given in verse 9: *"Because of the house of the Lord our God / I will seek your good."* Notice that the psalmist does not pray for Jerusalem because it is a great city, a center of political and military might. He does not pray for Jerusalem because the king dwells there. He prays for the city because God's house, His palace or temple, is there. God dwells in the Most Holy Place in the temple, and here Israel comes to worship Him. Here the priests offer sacrifices before Him to atone for the sins of the people. Here the prayers of Israel rise as incense before His throne. The strength of Jerusalem is the strength of Yahweh her God.

Today Solomon's temple lies in ruins, buried under the Dome of the Rock, the great Muslim mosque, which dominates the Old City. Today the Jews weep over their sins at the Wailing Wall, the last remaining remnant of the Second Temple. Today Jerusalem knows little peace as Christian sects haggle over the shrines there, and Arab and Jew are at each other's throats. In light of this, three things must be said. First, Jesus foretold the destruction of Jerusalem because she rejected her Messiah (Mark 13:1ff.). This took place under the Roman general Titus in A.D. 70. Since that hour, Jerusalem has known no peace, and the presence of God in the temple has only been a distant memory. Second, all Christians today, indwelt by God's Spirit, are the temple of God (1 Cor 6:19). God now chooses to live in us. Together we are also being built up into a living temple in the Lord (Eph. 2:19–22). Third, when this age is complete, the New Jerusalem will be revealed as the restored center of the presence and worship of God (Rev. 21:2). This city is the church made glorious by His unfailing presence in the perfection of the new creation. As we pray for the peace of Jerusalem today, we pray for the peace of God's church and we pray for the prosperity which is to come when Jesus returns and establishes His reign on this planet. The redeemed will then stand before Him with shining faces reflecting His very glory.

CHAPTER ONE HUNDRED TWENTY-THREE

Waiting for God's Mercy

Psalm 123

Much of our life is lived in between the times, between God's promise and His fulfillment. This is structurally so because we live between the first and second comings of our Lord Jesus Christ. Having the promise of the consummation of all things, we await its fulfillment. At the same time, there is a realized aspect to that promise, since He has already come two thousand years ago. Thus the Kingdom which He preached is both come and coming, and where we see demons cast out today and the sick healed, we see that the mercy of God, His Kingdom, is in our midst (Luke 17:21). Nevertheless, we are waiting for the end of this age, and as we do, our faith is tested as it grows.

Psalm 123 is a cry for mercy. The very fact that the psalmist is asking for it means that he has not presently experienced it. At the same time, he expects God to deliver, and thus he prays. Hounded by those who treat him (and Israel?) with contempt (v. 3) and by the scorn of the proud (v. 4), he casts himself before the Lord. Only God can lift this oppression from him. From this brief prayer we can learn how to pray between the times.

Commentators see this prayer as an individual lament that becomes corporate in verse 2. The author and date are unknown. The thought moves from our position before God (vv. 1–2) to our prayer to God (vv. 3–4).

OUR POSITION

123:1 Unto You I lift up my eyes,
       O You who dwell in the heavens.
    2 Behold, as the eyes of the servants *look* to the
          hand of their masters,
       As the eyes of a maid to the hand of her
          mistress,
       So our eyes *look* to the LORD our God,
       Until He has mercy on us.

Ps. 123:1–2

Verse 1 reveals the God to whom we pray. He is the transcendent Lord, the ruler of all things, the King of glory (Ps. 24:7). Thus the psalmist lifts his eyes *up* to Him. Not only does this tell us that God is above and over us, it also suggests that the psalmist is downcast. The next phrase defines God in His majesty: "*O You who dwell* [or, "sit (on Your throne)"] *in the heavens* [plural of fullness]." We are to worship Him because He is greater than we are; He is above us. We also come to Him because, as the exalted Lord, He has the resources to meet our needs.

When adversity strikes, we will discover our real view of God. If He is merely a first cause, now aloof or distant, or a mystical fluff unrelated to our sufferings, we will not turn to Him, expecting His intervention in our lives. If, because of our antisupernatural bias, we have locked Him out of His universe, then certainly we will not expect Him to act, nor will we ask Him to do so. This explains why so many people do not experience more of God's healing or His power in their lives. They simply don't believe enough to ask Him for it. For example, for years I did not pray for the sick because I did not believe that God healed the sick. It was that simple. Here, however, the psalmist believes in a majestic God and turns to Him in His need.

Verse 2 changes from the singular to the plural. The reason for this may be that now all of Israel is drawn into the prayer. Perhaps the proud of verse 4 represent a foreign nation that is threatening her. The thought is simple: God's people are before Him as petitioners in the same way as a slave comes before his or her master. This is to be taken as literally true. When God established His covenant with Israel, He became her King and she became His subject. Thus she is His slave, bought out of bondage by Him, and called to serve Him in this world. Prayer then is looking to Yahweh "*as the eyes of servants look to the hand of their masters.*" Moreover, women are not excluded from these petitions; they pray "*as the eyes of a maid [look] to the hand of her mistress.*" With these similes before us, the point is made: "*So our eyes look to the Lord our God, / Until He has mercy on us.*" Note that this prayer is continual; it goes up until the mercy comes down. We are to pray in faith, expecting God to act, and, like Jacob, not let Him go until He blesses us. Note also that the psalmist expects the mercy of God. This is based upon the covenant-treaty that He has made with His people Israel.

This is our position before God. We are petitioners coming into the presence of the Great King. We come based upon His covenant-commitment to us, expecting His mercy and remaining there before Him until we receive it.

OUR PRAYER

123:3 Have mercy on us, O LORD, have mercy on us!
    For we are exceedingly filled with contempt.
  4 Our soul is exceedingly filled
    With the scorn of those who are at ease,
    With the contempt of the proud.
                                        Ps. 123:3–4

The actual cry for mercy is given in verse 3. Here is the model for our prayer when we come before the mighty God: "*Have mercy on us, O Lord, have mercy on us!*" In this the psalmist is simple and direct. The repetition is for emphasis; it expresses the crisis nature of his need. It also suggests that he will stay before the throne of God until he gets what he requests.

The psalmist, like a good lawyer coming before a judge, gives the basis or reason for his petition: "*For we are exceedingly filled* ["satiated"] *with contempt."* The nature of this contempt receives some elaboration in verse 4 as the psalmist continues: *"Our soul is exceedingly filled* ["satiated"] *with the scorn* ["mocking"] *of those who are at ease, / With the contempt of the proud." "Those who are at ease"* can represent the wealthy, those who do not have to work. *"The proud"* are the self-sufficient, those who do not humble themselves and bow before Yahweh. This contempt and scorn of the proud is enough; as we might say colloquially, "We have had it up to here!" Now, it is up to God to act. The psalmist will wait for His mercy. We may well assume that His mercy will humble the proud and their contempt and mockery will be gone.

What can we learn here? First, in our distress we are to humble ourselves before God and petition Him rather than taking matters into our own hands. He may well be using this adversity in order to renew our prayer life and make us more dependent upon Him. Second, we are to trust Him as the source of mercy. His heart is open to us. Third, we are to believe that God can and will act, and we are to pray until He does. Since we live between the times, we do not have it all now. At the same time, since Jesus has inaugurated His Kingdom and it is now operating in our midst, we can come boldly to God, expecting Him to show His hand on our behalf.

CHAPTER ONE HUNDRED TWENTY-FOUR

Gratitude for God's Mercy

Psalm 124

It is an exciting thing to experience God as the living God. Too often we are so caught up in the routine of life, even church life, that we miss the drama of calling out to Him and knowing that He hears and answers us. Biblical life, however, is intensely personal. God has opened Himself up to His people, and they now enjoy a living relationship with Him. Since He is their King, He intervenes upon their behalf with mighty acts of deliverance. He does not abandon them to the grinding laws of nature or to their foes. He is the God who is with us and for us. If, in Dietrich Bonhoeffer's phrase, Jesus is the "man for others," in a deeper sense, He is also the God for others; He is on our side when we submit ourselves to His side, and He will prove this to us as we call upon His name.

Thematically, if not historically, Psalms 123 and 124 go together. The former prayer is for God to act. The latter prayer is Israel's response to His action. The psalmist tells us that men rose up against her with fury. Nevertheless, God was for His people, and He has delivered them (v. 7). As a result, He is to be blessed by Israel, and as we experience His deliverance we will join in that blessing (v. 6).

Commentators take this psalm as a prayer of corporate thanksgiving. The liturgical elements are clear in verses 1-2. Tradition gives its authorship to David. The thought moves from what might have happened (vv. 1-5) to what did happen (vv. 6-8).

WHAT MIGHT HAVE HAPPENED

124:1 'If it had not been the LORD who was on our
        side,'
    Let Israel now say—
   2 'If it had not been the LORD who was on our
        side,
    When men rose up against us,
   3 Then they would have swallowed us alive,
    When their wrath was kindled against us;
   4 Then the waters would have overwhelmed us,
    The stream would have gone over our soul;
   5 Then the swollen waters
    Would have gone over our soul.'
                                    Ps. 124:1-5

Verse 1 opens with the conditional clause: "*If it had not been the Lord who was on our side* [literally, "for us"].'" It is possible that this

415

sentence is being spoken in the temple where the people have gathered for worship. This would explain the imperative that follows, *"Let Israel now say,"* and then the repetition of the first clause as their response: *"'If it had not been the Lord who was on our side.'"* The consequences of God not being with His people are made clear by a series of striking pictures in verses 2–7.

The need for God's presence is practically caused by the *"'men* ["man," *ādām,* collective noun] [who] *rose up against us'"* (v. 2). In the crisis, the psalmist continues, *"'they would have swallowed us alive* [like prey in an animal's mouth]'"* (see v. 6), because *"'their wrath was kindled* [literally, "being in wrath, their anger was"] *against us'"* (v. 3). The cause of this wrath and the uprising against Israel are not specific. Since God's deliverance is being celebrated in the temple by all the people, however, this must reflect a national emergency. As the psalmist continues, the crisis is described as a great flood in verse 4: *"'Then the waters would have overwhelmed* ["overflowed," like a river breaking over its banks] *us.'"* The threat was lethal: *"'The stream would have gone over our soul.'"* This uprising was a threat to life itself. The thought is repeated in verse 5 for emphasis: *"'Then the swollen* [literally, "proud," that is, inflated] *waters / Would have gone over our soul.'"*

All of this describes what would have happened if God had not been on Israel's side. She would have been devoured. She would have been drowned. She would have vanished. Her existence in this world is determined, not by her economic and political strength, but by the God who called her into being and whom she worships. We today must learn the same lesson. We smugly assume that the existence of the church and its ministry depends upon us. This is true in appeals for funds and in recruiting workers. We hear that if we don't give, the gospel won't go out. We hear that if we don't work, the job will not be accomplished. This simply is not true. God is not dependent upon us to accomplish His purposes. He is not sitting in heaven, biting His nails, wondering if we will give and go. If we do not praise Him, the rocks will cry out. The ministry is not ours; it is His. It is not accomplished by human effort, but by divine effort in and through us. As a friend of mine once said, the church is always one generation from extinction, and if the Lord is not on our side we will be devoured and drowned. But the good news is that He is for us and that nothing can separate us from His love (Rom. 8:39).

WHAT DID HAPPEN

124:6 Blessed *be* the LORD,
    Who has not given us *as* prey to their teeth.
  7 Our soul has escaped as a bird from the snare
      of the fowlers;
    The snare is broken, and we have escaped.
  8 Our help *is* in the name of the LORD,
    Who made heaven and earth.

Ps. 124:6-8

The psalmist turns to blessing Yahweh who has delivered His people. He leads us in the cry: *"Blessed be the Lord."* But who is the God whom we bless? He is the One *"who has not given us as prey to their* [our enemies'] *teeth"* (v. 6; see v. 3). He has not allowed them to devour us. We have escaped the trap set for us *"as a bird* [escapes] *from the snare of the fowlers"* (v. 7). Whether the snare has been broken by God or by Israel is irrelevant. The point is that Yahweh is on our side, and it is only because of this that we are free (v. 1). The psalmist concludes with the confession: *"Our help is in the name* ["presence and power"] *of the Lord, / Who made heaven and earth"* (v. 8). This is our God. Our Helper is our Creator. He who made all things intervenes to save us.

As we suggested in our introduction, there is a thematic connection between this psalm and the previous one. There the psalmist cries for mercy and waits. Here the psalmist (and Israel) have received mercy and bless the Merciful. What could have happened didn't happen. God stepped in and all was changed. My fear that God will not come through for me has been a major inhibition in my Christian life. It has kept me from preaching evangelistic sermons and calling people forward for fear that no one would come. It has kept me from going and laying hands on the sick and praying for them for fear that they would not be healed. What I have been learning in dealing with this fear is exactly what the psalmist confesses here: "If it had not been the Lord who was on our side. . . ." The

answer to wild animals and floods is not to be locked in fear;
the answer is to have faith in the living God. He is the Creator, and
our help is in His name.

CHAPTER ONE HUNDRED TWENTY-FIVE

Clearing the Moral Air

Psalm 125

We live in a world of great insecurity. Old absolutes have collapsed. Our mind-set today is that all is relative. As Allan Bloom
notes in *The Closing of the American Mind,* when you look into
the mind of a relativist, you discover that nothing is there. An "open
mind" is an empty mind. This attitude makes us vulnerable to anything and everything. With no standards by which to judge, we are
easily prey to evil, and, alas, evil is close at hand. How can we recover from this madness? The answer lies in rediscovering the God
who is true and beginning to see the world again through His eyes.
Now evil will be seen as evil, and good will be seen as good. At last,
we will have standards by which to discriminate again and to understand the real battle that is raging.

As Psalm 125 shows us, there is a "scepter of wickedness," there is
a kingdom of evil, which seeks to dominate us (v. 3), and there are
"workers of iniquity," which threaten to take us away (v. 5). In opposition to this stands the Lord who will hold us (v. 2) and the way of
righteousness in which we must walk (v. 4). To know this is to know
God's peace (v. 5).

Commentators see this psalm as a national lament or a prayer of
trust. Its author and date are unknown. The thought moves from a

confession (vv. 1–2) to an expression of confidence (v. 3) and concludes with a call for God's goodness and judgment (vv. 4–5).

CONFESSION

125:1 Those who trust in the LORD
     Are like Mount Zion,
     Which cannot be moved, *but* abides forever.
   2 As the mountains surround Jerusalem,
     So the LORD surrounds His people
     From this time forth and forever.

Ps. 125:1–2

Verse 1 announces that *"those who trust* ["feel secure"] *in the Lord /
Are like Mount Zion."* This is the mountain upon which Jerusalem is
built (see Ps. 48:2). Like it, they *"cannot be moved"*; they abide
"forever." They endure as God Himself endures. The fulfillment of
this promise is found not in Palestine but in the New Jerusalem, the
heavenly city of God's people to which we are destined (Rev. 21:2).
There we will live for all eternity.

As we have seen, those who trust in the Lord are unmovable because of the God in whom they trust. Thus the psalmist continues,
"As the mountains surround Jerusalem, / So the Lord surrounds His people." We are held by God as Zion is held by the higher range around
it. As we read these lines, we may suspect that the author writes
from Jerusalem itself and reflects on these truths as he surveys the
landscape. Thus he sees that God's faithfulness endures. He surrounds us *"from this time forth and forever"* (v. 2). By this we see that
we can clear the moral air and recover a proper sense of absolutes
when we commit ourselves to the true God and become secure in
Him. Thus our minds will be renewed, and He will give us perspective upon this world.

CONFIDENCE

125:3 For the scepter of wickedness shall not rest
     On the land allotted to the righteous,

> Lest the righteous reach out their hands to
>   iniquity.
>
>   *Ps. 125:3*

God's protection over us is seen as the psalmist announces that *"the scepter of wickedness shall not rest / On the land allotted* [literally, "the lot," the share of land given] *to the righteous."* The scepter is a weapon used in battle that came to represent the sovereignty of the king who carried it. This *"scepter of wickedness"* denotes evil dominion. The promise is that it shall not fall upon Israel, "the land allotted to the righteous," because, if it does, God's people will *"reach out their hands to iniquity"* (v. 3). In other words, they will be like the ruler who rules them. If they are ruled by God, they will be like Him, and if they are ruled by the devil (or by the pagan empires dominated by his demon-idols, see Deut. 32:17), they will be like him. Here we see that God makes us like Him, in order that we may represent Him in this world.

We must now understand this *"scepter of wickedness,"* not as Egypt or Assyria, but as Satan and his evil kingdom. Here is the source of our moral confusion today. As Paul tells the Colossians, we have been delivered from that kingdom in order to live under the rule of God's Son (Col. 1:13). Here we are protected from iniquity. Here we walk and live in the light (1 John 1:7). Here things become clear again as the fog lifts.

CALL FOR GOD'S GOODNESS
AND JUDGMENT

> 125:4 Do good, O LORD, to *those who are* good,
>   And to *those who are* upright in their hearts.
>   5 As for such as turn aside to their crooked
>   ways,
>   The LORD shall lead them away
>   With the workers of iniquity.
>   Peace *be* upon Israel!
>
>   *Ps. 125:4–5*

Based upon the assurance of God's surrounding protection (v. 2) and His desire for us to be righteous (v. 3), the psalmist now prays:

"Do good, O Lord, to those who are good." The good trust in the Lord (v. 1). They are not good in their own strength. Their goodness comes by being in relationship with the God who is good. Their goodness is also not by external performance; it comes from *"those who are upright* ["straightforward, just"] *in their hearts"* (v. 4). They are the pure in heart who Jesus says will see God (Matt. 5:8). As we know in light of the cross, they are those who have been cleansed by the blood of Jesus shed there for them. They (and we) will blessed in increasing measure by God doing good to them.

At the same time, in the light of God's revelation, we can know evil. Thus the psalmist addresses those who *"turn aside to their crooked ways."* They will receive not God's goodness but His judgment: *"The Lord shall lead them away / With the workers of iniquity* [those who have strayed from the straight path]." They may think that they are free, on their own, by straying from God's way, but He is still sovereign. He will *"lead them away"* with all who do evil as they go to face Him.

Things are now clear in a confusing age. It is really simple. We are to trust in the Lord. As we do so, we will be firm and secure (v. 1) because God will keep us (v. 2). We will not be under the kingdom of darkness with its moral confusion and compromise (v. 3), but we will be under the Kingdom of God, receiving His goodness (v. 4). Those who turn from this will be led into judgment by the God who is still sovereign (v. 5). When we know these things, we will be centered upon the truth and serene. The psalmist rightly concludes: *"Peace be upon Israel!"*

CHAPTER ONE HUNDRED TWENTY-SIX

Homecoming!

Psalm 126

In memory's eye I can see the joy on the prisoners' faces as they were released by the Allied armies at the close of World War II. After years of internment, after daily inspections, bad food, boards for bunks in steamy, overcrowded dorms, after interrogation, intimidation, and genuine fear of torture, disease, and even death, suddenly the guards and their dogs were gone. The watchtowers stood deserted, and the hated gates made of barbed wire yawned open. Freedom beckoned these men, and their memories of home lured them into reality once again. In their shock and surprise, there was still a joy unspeakable as the tanks rolled in and the Nazis faded away, sneaking into the night.

Israel too experienced her internment. Assyria carried the Northern Kingdom into exile in 721 B.C., and Babylon did the same to the Southern Kingdom in 687 B.C. Now far from home, these exiles died, assimilated into the native populations, or sustained their Jewish identity and prayed to see Jerusalem once again. A remnant was rewarded for this longing. They began the return to Palestine when the Persians conquered once-great Babylon, now abandoned in the dust (see Ezra 1–6). Psalm 126 captures much of the exiles' feelings, as it witnesses to God's mighty work.

Commentators see this psalm as a national lament. Its author is unknown and its date is after the beginnings of the return (starting in 538 B.C.). The thought moves from the joy of coming home (vv. 1–3) to a prayer for return and concludes with an oracle of return (vv. 5–6).

422

THE JOY OF COMING HOME

126:1 When the LORD brought back the captivity of
     Zion,
    We were like those who dream.
  2 Then our mouth was filled with laughter,
    And our tongue with singing.
    Then they said among the nations,
    "The LORD has done great things for them."
  3 The LORD has done great things for us,
    And we are glad.

Ps. 126:1-3

Verse 1 sets the stage for what follows. The psalmist begins by describing what God did and how the exiles felt: *"When the Lord brought back* ["in the returning of"] *the captivity of Zion, / We were like those who dream."* Note that it is Yahweh, not Cyrus or some other king, who releases Israel. She is in exile under His judgment. Only He can set her free. As Isaiah says, Cyrus, king of Persia, is His anointed (Isa. 45:1). Whether he knows it or not Cyrus must do Yahweh's will. The God of history runs history. Zion, the mountain upon which Jerusalem stands, represents Israel. The dream state of the exiles probably refers to their shock and their unbelief at what was happening. "Is this real?" they asked, in a daze. Internment makes people pliable for their masters. It can break the will. Freedom, when it comes, can evoke unbelief.

However, in verse 2, the reality of release breaks in, and the exiles laugh and sing. This is the expression of their joy. The gates are open; the bars are shattered. Their captors lie slaughtered, and the road opens before them, calling them home. I have seen people released from prison, experiencing a similar joy. A friend of mine in his early thirties has spent the last twelve years in the penitentiary, three of them in solitary confinement. Recently he became a Christian, and now he is on parole. The great event of freedom for him was not when the prison gates opened; it was when God opened the prison of his heart. Then, like the exiles homeward bound, his mouth was *"filled with laughter,"* and his *"tongue with singing."*

God's work of redemption for Israel also evokes a response *"among the nations."* They react to her release by admitting that this is God and say: *"'The Lord has done great things for them.'"* By this act Yahweh frees His people and obtains glory for Himself. The exiles echo this witness in verse 3 by saying, *"The Lord has done great things for us, / And we are glad* ["exult"]*."*

A Prayer for Return

126:4 Bring back our captivity, O LORD,
         As the streams in the South.

Ps. 126:4

This verse may describe the exiles praying as the news of their release reaches them. They may also be praying for those left in exile, asking God fully to restore their fortunes. They petition for their *"captivity"* to be brought back (cf. v. 1), *"As the streams in the South"* (*Negev,* the southern part of Judah). The streams pictured are the wadis, which turn into flash floods when fed by cloudbursts. They can sweep everything before their torrents. Thus in the return, the exiles want to sweep all enemies and opposition before them.

The Oracle of Return

126:5 Those who sow in tears
          Shall reap in joy.
       6 He who continually goes forth weeping,
          Bearing seed for sowing,
          Shall doubtless come again with rejoicing,
          Bringing his sheaves *with him.*

Ps. 126:5–6

We take these next two verses as God's direct address to Israel. He now speaks prophetically in answer to the petition in verse 4. God promises that those who have sown in tears will *"reap in joy* ["shouting"]*"* (v. 5). In the fertility cults around Israel, sowing was associated with death. Thus the weeping during sowing was a ritual act identifying with the death of the cult god. While God's people rejected this "theology," the idea of sowing and death was in common currency. As Jesus much later says, "unless a grain of wheat falls into the ground and dies, it remains alone" (John 12:24). Thus Israel was sown in the exile of death. This is a sign of judgment. Nevertheless, because of this sowing, this death, there is now a harvest. The time has come to *"reap in joy."* Jesus promises that the wheat that has died in the ground "produces much grain" (John 12:24).

The contrast between sowing and reaping is strengthened in verse 6. The one who goes into the field *"continually"* (literally, "Walking, he who walks") with tears, will certainly return with the joy of the harvest, *"Bringing his sheaves with him."* There will be great bounty as a result of his sowing. Indeed, God promises Israel will come home in blessing and joy. The time of mourning and death will be passed. The great chapters of Isaiah 40–66 provide an extensive commentary upon this truth. In Isaiah God speaks pardon to His people (Isa. 40:1ff.). He promises that they will be freed from exile. Moreover, He promises that their return to the Promised Land will be filled with joy (Isa. 61:3–7).

Often in traditional preaching, this oracle in verses 5–6 has been taken as a missionary text, proposing that the seed to be sown in suffering is the word of God, and that a great harvest will result. The context, however, does not support this application. It is Israel that is sown in death in the exile, and as we die to ourselves at the cross, we are also sown in death with Jesus. Nevertheless, there is a promise here. Joy will come. After death there is resurrection. The grain of wheat that dies rises up again to bear a great harvest. Israel came home and was the people out of which the Messiah came to be the Savior of the world. Here is the ultimate homecoming—to come home to the Father's house, set free, not from Babylon but from Satan, sin, and death. Thus will our mouths be filled with laughter and song for eternity.

God's Energy or Our Vanity

Psalm 127

One of the tensions in Christian theology has been whether to stress the sovereign grace of God or human responsibility. Some have feared that if we stress His grace, we will cut the moral nerve. People will become presumptive. They will claim that all is of grace and sink into apathy. Thus we are told that we should pray as if God does everything and work as if we do everything. Such a resolution to the problem may be clever, but it is unsatisfying and unbiblical, to say the least. Better to magnify God than ourselves. Better to stress His grace than our works. Why is this so? For no other reason than it is true. We can see this in creation, for even the breath that we breathe comes from His hand. Moreover, we can see this in redemption, because unless God not only saves us but also keeps us moment by moment we will remain in bondage to sin and the devil.

Psalm 127 provides a commentary upon the thesis that all comes from God's hand. The house will only be built if He builds it. The city will only be guarded if He guards it (v. 1). It is vain for us to labor for the "bread of sorrows," on our own, when God grows the food and gives rest to His beloved (v. 2). One of the greatest examples of this comes in the bearing of children. What do we do to create them? They are simply a gift of God, a happy reward from the Creator (vv. 3–5).

Commentators view this psalm as a wisdom poem. Solomon is its traditional author. The thought starts with God building and guarding His people (vv. 1–2) and concludes with the certainty that His reward comes with children (vv. 3–5).

GOD BUILDS AND GUARDS HIS PEOPLE

127:1 Unless the LORD builds the house,
　　　They labor in vain who build it;
　　　Unless the LORD guards the city,
　　　The watchman stays awake in vain.
　　2 *It is* vain for you to rise up early,
　　　To sit up late,
　　　To eat the bread of sorrows;
　　　For so He gives His beloved sleep.
　　　　　　　　　　　　　　　　Ps. 127:1-2

Verse 1 opens with the observation that *"unless the Lord builds the house, / They labor in vain who build it."* The building of a house can refer to the actual construction of a dwelling, or the creation of a family (see Deut. 25:9), or both. The point is that God must do it. He must inspire and empower the construction. Otherwise, all human plans and effort are vain. If Solomon is thinking here of building a family, the meaning is even clearer. Who today believes that he or she can be a proper husband or wife and parent children effectively? In our frustration, we have to admit that these responsibilities are beyond us. We must not abandon our duty, however, but surrender it to the only one who can bear it, the living God. As we pray over our task, God will do it. He will give us wisdom for our roles. He will guard our spouses and our children. He will be with them when we are not. He will be their ultimate parent, and He will rear them Himself.

I have dealt with many alcoholic families. One of the symptoms of this disease is dependency. Within dysfunctional families, one member may become dependent upon the drug, while the rest become dependent upon perpetuating the alcoholic's behavior (codependents). The road to healing involves the surrender of this dependency. The rest of the family must give up trying to control the alcoholic's behavior. The ability to make this surrender is often found when the truth of this verse comes home: the Lord must build our house. We can't do it anymore.

Then again: *"Unless the Lord guards the city, / The watchman stays awake in vain"* (v. 1). Not only can we not control or build our families; neither can we protect our cities. The watchman may stand on the walls all night, scanning the horizon for invaders, but he cannot control their approach in the darkness. They may have already infiltrated the walls. They may hide in their Trojan horse. They may be tunneling under the defenses, unseen. If this was true in the ancient world, how much more is it true today. We have now created the Stealth bomber in order to be invisible to Soviet radar. The Lord continually guards the city. It will stand or fall only as He desires.

Based upon God's sovereignty and our need of Him, Solomon points out the futility of being anxious about our lives. He describes the vanity of working night and day in order to earn *the bread of sorrow*. In an agricultural world, it is God who grows the harvest, just as He builds the house and guards the city. Rather than being anxious about provision, as His beloved we are to rest: *"For so He gives His beloved sleep"* (v. 2). Life is His creation, and life is His provision. Jesus teaches that we are not to be anxious about what we shall eat or what we shall wear, but we are to seek first God's Kingdom and His righteousness, and then our other needs will be met as well (Matt. 6:33).

HIS REWARD COMES

127:3 Behold, children *are* a heritage from the LORD,
         The fruit of the womb *is* a reward.
    4 Like arrows in the hand of a warrior,
         So *are* the children of one's youth.
    5 Happy *is* the man who has his quiver full of
            them;
         They shall not be ashamed,
         But shall speak with their enemies in the gate.
                                              Ps. 127:3–5

If God is the author and sustainer of our life, if He provides all good things for us, then He certainly will give us children (v. 3). Who can create his own progeny? As Solomon asserts, *"Behold, children* [literally, "sons"] *are a heritage from the Lord."* To extend our name and our blood into the next generation is a part of God's blessing and promise to us (Gen. 1:28). Moreover, a fruitful womb *"is His reward."* With poetic power Solomon likens *"children of one's youth"* to the *"arrows in the hand of a warrior"* (v. 4). They serve to protect the family. Like physical arms, they give their father a sense of security. Therefore, *"Happy"* ("Blessed," plural of fullness) is the man who has many, *"a quiver full."* Solomon concludes, in verse 5 that the sons will have such strength in numbers that they will be able to confront their enemies at the gate, where justice is dispensed. Moreover, they will prevail without shame. Here, indeed is great reward from the God who provides all things for us.

In light of Psalm 127 we have a choice to make. We can either rely on our vanity or upon God's energy. We can either fool ourselves into believing that we can control things, or we can surrender our false sense of control to the living God. Here is the promise: if we make the surrender, God will build our house, God will guard our city, God will provide for our needs, and God will reward us with fruitfulness to the next generation. Is there really any choice to make? As we give up control, we will become emotionally and mentally healthy, to say nothing about having God's true perspective on our lives.

CHAPTER ONE HUNDRED TWENTY-EIGHT

The Blessing of a Healthy Fear of God

Psalm 128

The idea of fearing God has vanished from our world-view. We suppose that it is left over from the Middle Ages. Some Christians have taught the monstrous opinion that the God of the Old Testament is a God of wrath and that the God of the New Testament is a God of love. Not only does this destroy the very idea of the covenant, which is based on grace, but it casts a dark shadow upon Judaism and the whole foundation for the Christian faith. This opinion also fails before the facts. Jesus often warned of God's judgment that is to come. He prophesied the destruction of the temple as a sign of the end (Mark 13:1ff.). The rest of the New Testament joins Him in witnessing to God's wrath as well as to His grace. In fact, we only can understand this grace in light of His wrath. We need to learn to fear God. Such a disposition is not only biblical; it is also healthy. It is healthy to fear the judge who can sentence us to prison. It is healthy to fear the soldier who can invade our territory and plunder our goods. It is healthy to fear God who can send us to hell.

Psalm 128 calls the person who fears God "blessed." In fact, fear of Him is the secret to a happy and fulfilling life (vv. 2–4). The word of blessing is put into action as verses 5–6 reveal the blessing actually given.

Commentators describe this psalm as a wisdom psalm. Its date and authorship are unknown. The thought moves from the blessing announced (v. 1) to the blessing described (vv. 2–4) and concludes with the blessing pronounced (vv. 5–6).

BLESSING ANNOUNCED

128:1 Blessed *is* every one who fears the LORD,
Who walks in His ways.

Ps. 128:1

In verse 1 the blessing of God is announced for *"every one who fears the Lord."* The word *"blessed"* is written in the plural, denoting a sense of fullness. It means "happy," giving us "well-being." Marcus Barth proposes that it could be rendered "Congratulations," since it comes with the good news of God's favor upon us. Those who are blessed are those who fear God. This fear means a sense of awe and reverence before His majesty. It presupposes that He is the sovereign King, reigning in glory, who holds all of the issues of our lives in His hands. We are to have wonder before His glory and also fear before

His holiness and justice. His mighty works, the signs and wonders that He performs, also evoke this sense of awe. When He unleashes His power, we stagger in fear before Him. On Sinai He veils Himself in smoke and fire and warns that anyone who touches His mountain will die (Exod. 19:12). This should strike fear in us. God is unapproachable in His purity; He is a consuming fire. Thus when Isaiah sees Him in the temple, he cries out "Woe!" (Isa. 6:5). In our churches today we need to recapture this sense of the fear of God.

Amazing as it may seem, those who fear God are happy. In light of what we have just said, we would expect that they would be cursed. To the contrary, they are happy because they have bowed before the Creator who is also their Redeemer. They have acknowledged Him to be God, and, having made that submission, they now belong to the covenant, know Him, and worship Him. They are blessed in this relationship. The psalmist gives evidence that this surrender is real in the next clause: "[Blessed is every one] *who walks in His ways,*" that is, who obeys Him, who does what He says. It is a happy thing to be humbled before God and to be lifted up to serve Him in this world.

BLESSING DESCRIBED

128:2 When you eat the labor of your hands,
  You *shall be* happy, and *it shall be* well with
   you.
 3 Your wife *shall be* like a fruitful vine
  In the very heart of your house,
  Your children like olive plants
  All around your table.
 4 Behold, thus shall the man be blessed
  Who fears the LORD.

Ps. 128:2-4

What does it mean to be blessed by God? First, the psalmist promises that the results of our work will be enjoyed. Rather than losing the labor of our hands to pestilence or invading armies, we will be able to eat it in peace. As he says, *"You shall be happy* [or, "O your blessings"], *and it shall be well with you"* (v. 2). The word *well* denotes a sense of completion according to God's purpose. For this reason, God calls each day of creation "good" or "fulfilled" as it is completed by Him (Gen. 1:10). In considering God's blessing, the picture that comes to my mind is the Norman Rockwell painting of a family gathered for Thanksgiving dinner. The great turkey is presented before the three generations seated around the bountiful table. All faces smile with a sense of well-being. The family members enjoy the labor of their hands.

Second, the psalmist promises to the husband that his wife will be *"like a fruitful vine / In the very heart* ["innermost part," that is, in her special room or place] *of your house."* To be fruitful means, of course, that she shall have many children. We learn from the story of Abraham and Sarah about the curse of being childless (Gen. 16:2–5). A closed womb is considered to be a sign of God's judgment. A fruitful womb means blessing, because it fulfills the command in creation when God blessed us and said, "Be fruitful and multiply" (Gen. 1:28). Notice that monogamy is also assumed here.

Third, the blessed man will have *"children* ["sons"] *like olive plants* [or, "shoots," the plural suggests many] / *All around your table"* (v. 3). Many children are also a blessing. They provide emotional satisfaction and safety for the family (see Ps. 127:4), but they also provide labor and the transmission of the bloodline. The conclusion is now given in verse 4: *"Behold, thus shall the man be blessed / Who fears the Lord."* It is important to see here the affirmation of creation: work, marriage, sexuality, and family. None of this is related to the Fall. It is only corrupted when sin enters into the world. God's covenant with Israel, however, restores His reign over her and with that comes the renewal of creation and its blessings. In the New Covenant in Christ, we also find creation restored. Thus the New Testament affirms the very same blessing of God upon us in work, marriage, sexuality, and family (see, e.g., Ephesians 4–5).

BLESSING PRONOUNCED

128:5 The LORD bless you out of Zion,
     And may you see the good of Jerusalem
     All the days of your life.
  6 Yes, may you see your children's children.
     Peace *be* upon Israel!

                         Ps. 128:5–6

Having announced the blessing and having described the blessing, the psalmist doesn't leave us. He actually pronounces the blessing upon God's people. Thus he says, *"The Lord bless you out of Zion."* Blessing is God's to bestow. A fruitful life comes from Him. It comes from Zion, the mountain of God where His house or temple is located (see Pss. 2:6; 48:2).

The blessing of the individual, however, is also dependent upon the blessing of the nation. As the psalmist continues, *"And may you see the good of Jerusalem / All the days of your life"* (v. 5). Finally, the blessing is not only for us, it is also for our inheritance. Thus it concludes: *"Yes, may you see your children's children* [your grand-children]." In seeing the generations continue, they will carry the blessing and we also will be blessed. This blessing is concluded by a postscript: *"Peace* ["wholeness"] *be upon Israel!"*

It is important to remember in verses 5–6 that there is power in the pronouncement of the blessing. These are not just empty words. They come with divine authority, and they accomplish the work of blessing. We learn that it is not enough to announce the blessing and to describe the blessing; we must also pronounce it, set it free to happen as we speak it in faith. In the evangelical church, we are good at announcing and describing but poor in pronouncing. We easily preach the gospel without calling people to come forward and receive Christ. We might even risk saying that God heals people today, but we refuse to pray for the sick. We learn in this psalm however, that word and work must go together. If people are to be blessed, we must bless them. As the word is pronounced in the power of God's Spirit, it does its work. And as we see it work we will have a healthy fear of God. We will be in awe of His authority and might as He moves in our midst, and in surrender and obedience we will be blessed by Him.

A Curse upon Our Enemies

Psalm 129

The idea of putting a curse on someone seems foreign to our modern sensitivities. In most times and cultures, however, curses with magical powers have been a part of life. In fact, today most people curse with regularity as an expression of their anger. As they pronounce divine condemnation upon things or people, for example, when hitting their finger with a hammer or when being cut off in traffic, they are mindless of what they are really saying. If confronted with the content of their invectives, they would be shocked at consigning a bad driver to the flames of hell. There was a time, however, when curses were taken seriously. When they are pronounced with supernatural power, or superior authority, they should still be taken seriously today. If not, sickness and even death may be the result.

In the ancient world curses were used to bring destruction upon foes. In Deuteronomy, Moses warns Israel that if she is disobedient to the covenant made at Sinai, the curses of God will come upon her bringing disaster. Thus he says, "'But it shall come to pass, if you do not obey the voice of the Lord your God, to observe carefully all His commandments and His statutes which I command you today, that all these curses will come upon you and overtake you: Cursed shall you be in the city, and cursed shall you be in the country.'" (Deut. 28:15–16). Divine or devilish curses are not playthings.

Psalm 129 recounts the sufferings of Israel (vv. 1–4). The psalmist follows with curses against her enemies. Those who hate Zion will be shamed (v. 5). They will be fruitless and wither (vv. 6–7), and they will not be blessed with the blessing of the Lord (vv. 8). As much as this may bother us, it is a fundamental reality. We are either blessed by God, or we are cursed by God. As Augustine says, we are either under His grace or under His wrath. There is no third alternative, much as the modern mind looks for one (see exposition of Psalm 1).

Commentators identify two forms within this psalm. Verses 1–4 are a collective thanksgiving, and verses 5–8 are a curse, which may come from a divine oracle of judgment. The date and author are unknown. The thought moves from the confession, Israel's affliction and God's intervention (vv. 1–4), to the curse (vv. 5–8).

CONFESSION: AFFLICTION AND INTERVENTION

129:1 "Many a time they have afflicted me from my
         youth,"
     Let Israel now say—
   2 "Many a time they have afflicted me from my
         youth;
     Yet they have not prevailed against me.
   3 The plowers plowed on my back;
     They made their furrows long."
   4 The LORD *is* righteous;
     He has cut in pieces the cords of the wicked.

Ps. 129:1–4

Verse 1 opens with, *"'Many a time they have afflicted me from my youth,'"* which is followed by an invitation for Israel to join in liturgically, *"Let Israel now say—."* The response that she is to make (which is an echo of the opening clause in v. 1) is provided in verse 2: *"'Many a time they have afflicted me from my youth.'"* The structure suggests that this psalm was used in the temple where Israel would be the whole people gathered in worship. The prepositional phrase *"from my youth"* often is applied to the Exodus events that brought God's people into being as a nation (cf. Hos. 11:1). The point is simple: from her beginning on, Israel has always suffered in this world. Verse 2 points out that although this is true, *"Yet they have not prevailed against me."* The personal pronoun is to be taken collectively; *me* represents the whole nation. Through it all Israel has stood.

A striking metaphor is employed in verse 3 in order to picture the persecution she has received: *"'The plowers plowed on my back; / They made the furrows long.'"* This probably represents the punishing cuts made by a whip; Israel has been lashed by her enemies (cf. Exod. 5:14). Moreover, the wounds are long. It is a severe testing.

Even so, Yahweh never abandoned His people. Again and again, He intervened upon their behalf. Thus verse 4 confesses: *"The Lord is righteous; / He has cut in pieces* ["cut asunder"] *the cords of the wicked* ["criminals"]." The word *righteous* here means that God is true to His covenant with Israel. He is her mighty King who comes to rescue her from her tormentors. He breaks the cords that the wicked have used to bind her and sets her free.

Here is the double reality of Israel's life in this world. She is persecuted by her enemies and rescued by her God, who is faithful to His covenant-promise. A classic example of this is found in Exodus, where Israel is in bondage in Egypt. She cries out to the Lord, "So God heard their groaning, and God remembered His covenant with Abraham, with Isaac, and with Jacob. And God looked upon the children of Israel, and God acknowledged them" (Exod. 2:24–25). He is ready to call Moses and go into battle by besieging Pharaoh.

The confession of Israel's suffering and God's intervention in verses 1–4 provide the context for the curses to follow. These curses bear the powerful word of God, which does His work of judgment against His peoples' enemies.

CURSE

129:5 Let all those who hate Zion
　　　　Be put to shame and turned back.
　6 Let them be as the grass *on* the housetops,
　　　　Which withers before it grows up,
　7 With which the reaper does not fill his hand,
　　　　Nor he who binds sheaves, his arms.
　8 Neither let those who pass by them say,
　　　　"The blessing of the LORD *be* upon you;
　　　　We bless you in the name of the LORD!"
　　　　　　　　　　　　　　　　　Ps. 129:5–8

What follows Israel's confession are actually three curses (vv. 5, 6, 8). While the speaker is not identified, it may be God or the psalmist speaking in His name. The first appears in verse 5: *"Let all those who*

hate Zion / Be put to shame and turned back ["driven backward"]."
Zion, the mountain upon which Jerusalem was built, symbolizes
God's people. Those who hate her are to be shamed by defeat in
battle and turned back like a retreating army. As a result, Israel will
be victorious.

The second curse appears in verses 6–7: *"Let them be as the grass on
the housetops, / Which withers before it grows up"* (v. 6). The flat roofs
in ancient Israel were constructed of beams covered with branches.
They were then topped off with a layer of clay. When it rained, grass
easily grew from the clay, only to wither in the beating sun. In this
curse, the enemies of Israel are to be like that grass, quickly scorched.
Moreover, in verse 7 these enemies are not to be fruitful, as would
be the harvest where the *reaper* fills his hand with the stalks as he
cuts them and then makes sheaves of the corn.

In the third curse in verse 8, these enemies are to remain un-
blessed. As the psalmist writes, *"Neither let those who pass by them
say, / 'The blessing of the Lord be upon you; / We bless you in the name*
[presence, authority] *of the Lord.'"* This reference to the blessing
would refer to Israel as she passes by the territory of her enemies.
Since they are under the curse of God's judgment, His people must
not bless them in a neighborly way.

In sum, those who afflict God's people will receive a threefold
curse. In the first, those who hate Zion are put to flight in battle. In
the second, they are to be fruitless at home, and, in the third, they
are held under the curse; no one is to bless them in God's name.

God delivers His people from their oppressors (vv. 1–4). But as
Israel is liberated, her enemies are cursed (vv. 5–8). As I pointed out
in the introduction, though it is hard for us to accept this, we have
no options. Those who trust God are blessed; those who deny God
are cursed. As God says in His call of Abraham, "I will bless those
who bless you, / And I will curse him who curses you" (Gen. 12:3).
You can be one or the other and that's that. This is the root structure
and thinking of biblical faith.

When Guilt Overwhelms Us

Psalm 130

We are socialized by good doses of guilt. Our behavior is controlled by the fear of it. When we fail to meet set standards, we feel the weight of it. While much of this is simply cultural, there is a deeper guilt still, the sense that we have failed to live up to all that we were designed to be and to become. This is existential guilt, which resides at the core of our being. In the words of Paul Tournier, this is "guilt before God."

How do we deal with guilt? One way is by denial. We simply refuse to admit its existence. Another way is through rationalization. We admit that we are guilty, but we immediately blunt the edge of our confession by pointing out all of the extenuating circumstances that have conspired to make us this way. If we can't blame our parents or our teachers, we blame the government or our genes. Another way to deal with guilt is by relativization. We simply point out that everyone else is thinking or doing exactly what we are, and that we aren't so bad. When we find worse examples than ourselves, it makes us look better. By this we also take the spotlight off ourselves and put it on someone else, much to our relief. There is another way to deal with guilt, however, and this way gets to its root. This is by admission, confession, and forgiveness. The advantage of this way is that we don't have to carry the guilt anymore. Since this way is healing, it is God's way, and Psalm 130 witnesses to it. Before God we can not only be relieved of the guilt of our behavior; we can also be relieved of the guilt of our fallen existence. This is freedom indeed!

The psalmist cries out in pain and urgency to God for forgiveness (vv. 1–4). He is in the position of waiting for God to act (vv. 5–6). As he waits, he hopes in what He has promised. For he knows God as the merciful Redeemer who will "redeem Israel / From all his iniquities" (v. 8).

Commentators identify this psalm as an individual lament. Its date and authorship are unknown. The thought moves from a cry to God from the depths (vv. 1–2) to a confession of forgiveness (vv. 3–4) to waiting for the Lord (vv. 5–6) and concludes with a call for hope (vv. 7–8).

CRY FROM THE DEPTHS

130:1 Out of the depths I have cried to You, O LORD;
   2 Lord, hear my voice!
     Let Your ears be attentive
     To the voice of my supplications.

                 Ps. 130:1–2

In verse 1 we see the psalmist's inner anguish as he reveals: *"Out of the depths I have cried out to You, O Lord."* The *depths* in Hebrew refers to the depths of the sea, the watery chaos of life. In Psalm 69 the depths symbolize both danger and David's response to it: "Save me, O God! / For the waters have come up to my neck. I sink in deep mire, / Where there is no standing; / I have come into deep waters ['the depths of waters'], / Where the floods overflow me. I am weary with my crying" (Ps. 69:1–3). These depths represent the general travail that the psalmist is feeling, including the iniquities that he will address in verse 3.

The urgency of the psalmist's situation is dramatically felt as he elaborates on his cry to God in verse 2: *"Lord, hear my voice! / Let Your ears be attentive / To the voice of my supplications* ['requests for favor or grace']." The repetition underscores his crisis. For God to hear his voice means that He is turned toward him with favor (contrast Ps. 10:11). Where do we turn when we are in the depths? We can seek to medicate the pain through drugs or alcohol. We can surrender to the pain and sink into the darkness of depression, or we can cry out to God. This, the psalmist does.

CONFESSION OF FORGIVENESS

130:3 If You, LORD, should mark iniquities,
     O Lord, who could stand?

4 But *there is* forgiveness with You,
That You may be feared.

Ps. 130:3–4

Because God's heart is open to him with mercy and love, the psalmist knows that his cry is not in vain. As he thinks about God and his sin, there are two alternatives. The first is that God will note every sin that we commit and hold us accountable. The second is that God, knowing our sin, will accept responsibility for it and forgive us. The psalmist reflects: *"If You, Lord, should mark* ["keep," that is, keep account of] *iniquities* [deviations from God's path], / *O Lord, who could stand?"* (v. 3). If, as the Pharisees thought, God has a great ledger upon which He writes our credits and debits, our account would be so lopsided that we would fall before His justice. The guilt would be so heavy that our punishment would be certain. The other alternative, however, is the true one: *"But there is forgiveness with You."* Here is the gospel. We are in the depths. Our guilt is before us. We cry to God, and He hears us and comes, not with judgment but with forgiveness. This we know supremely in the face of Jesus Christ. It was He who stood before the woman taken in the act of adultery and said, "He who is without sin among you, let him throw a stone at her first." The irony of this statement is that only Jesus Himself is qualified to stone her, since He is the sinless Son of God. Nevertheless, He forgives her, "Neither do I condemn you; go and sin no more" (John 8:11). Indeed, we are certain, as the psalmist says of Yahweh, "there is forgiveness with You." As a result of this divine mercy, he adds, *"That You may be feared"* (v. 4). When we truly understand God's forgiveness and the cost of it, in sending Christ to the cross, we are broken and humbled, as we bow in awe before God. There is no presumption here. There is no flippancy here. We deserve judgment; we receive mercy. Like the returning prodigal son, we are staggered by the Father who welcomes us home free (see Luke 15:11ff.).

WAITING FOR THE LORD

130:5 I wait for the LORD, my soul waits,
And in His word I do hope.

> 6 My soul *waits* for the Lord
> More than those who watch for the morning—
> Yes, *more than* those who watch for the
> morning.

Ps. 130:5–6

Now we learn the present position of the psalmist. As he is in the depths (v. 1), as he is crying to God (v. 2), as he knows that God is merciful (vv. 3–4), he waits. As he says (again, with repetition for emphasis), "*I wait for the Lord, my soul waits.*" But what is this waiting? It is sitting in the silence (Ps. 62:5). It is being before God in expectation and patience (Ps. 40:1). It is standing on the promises of "*His word*" in "*hope*" (v. 5). It is knowing that God will act, and waiting for Him to do so.

Again, as if to make the point crystal clear, the psalmist says, "*My soul waits for the Lord / More than those who watch for the morning* [from the city walls]— / *Yes,* [note the labored repetition] *more than those who watch for the morning*" (v. 6).

Our lives are busy. In this instant society, we know little of sustained meditation and prayer. We know less of just being before God with expectancy. One of the things that He is teaching me, however, is the value of waiting upon Him. In the quiet, as we quiet the chattering of our left brain with its linear thinking, we can hear His voice. Rather than stepping out on the theological truth of God's forgiveness, the psalmist waits to be forgiven. Thus, planted firmly upon the promises of God and hoping in Him, he waits for Him to speak and act in his life. He needs to know (experience) the reality of his guilt lifted, his sin forgiven, and he will not settle for less. No wonder our spiritual lives are so shallow; we refuse to wait upon the Lord. When we stop and rest before Him, however, He will act.

CALL FOR HOPE

> 130:7 O Israel, hope in the LORD;
> For with the LORD *there is* mercy,
> And with Him *is* abundant redemption.
> 8 And He shall redeem Israel
> From all his iniquities.

Ps. 130:7–8

The psalmist generalizes from his own experience. He addresses all of God's people: *"O Israel, hope in the Lord."* Could it be that he has been encountered by the living God between verses 6 and 7? Does this account for his call here? His imperative to hope in Yahweh is grounded in His character: *"For with the Lord there is mercy [ḥesed,* "covenant-love"], / *And with Him is abundant redemption"* (v. 7). God will be true to His commitment to His people; He will come through for them by delivering them from sin, guilt, and bondage. Since there is *"abundant redemption"* in Him, He will act: *"And He shall redeem Israel / From all his iniquities"* (v. 8). Who God is will determine what He does. At the same time, because of who He is, we are to expect Him to act. As the psalmist waits upon Him, He knows that he will experience God's forgiveness, His covenant-love, His redemptive power. Isn't that what millions of church people need today? They have heard about God, but they don't know God. They have heard that He is merciful, but they haven't received mercy. Thus they carry their guilt as best they can. Who can judge them for rationalizing it or repressing it when they don't know that they can release it to the merciful God? Rather than waiting upon Him and for Him, they labor alone. For them, this psalm has good news. God loves and God lifts our burden. We need not carry it any longer.

CHAPTER ONE HUNDRED THIRTY-ONE

How to Get Ready for God

Psalm 131

Richard J. Foster writes in his classic *Celebration of Discipline,* "Superficiality is the curse of our age. The doctrine of instant satisfaction is a primary spiritual problem. The desperate need to-day is not for a greater number of intelligent people, or gifted peo-ple, but for deep people. The classical Disciplines of the spiritual life call us to move beyond surface living into the depths. They invite us to explore the inner caverns of the spiritual realm. They urge us to be the answer to a hollow world. John Woolman coun-sels, 'It is good for thee to dwell deep, that thou mayest feel and understand the spirits of people'" (p. 1). What Foster calls the in-ward disciplines (such as meditation, prayer, fasting, and study) will show us how to dwell deep. This is what this brief psalm is all about. In verse 1 the psalmist describes himself, and, based upon this sober sense, offers his response in verse 2.

Commentators describe the form of this psalm as a psalm of trust. It is ascribed to David. The thought moves from who I am (v. 1) to what I do (v. 2) and ends with a conclusion for all Israel (v. 3).

Who I Am

131:1 Lord, my heart is not haughty,
Nor my eyes lofty.
Neither do I concern myself with great
matters,
Nor with things too profound for me.

Ps. 131:1

Verse 1 opens with David confessing his spiritual condition to God: *"Lord, my heart is not haughty, / Nor my eyes lofty."* He has not lifted himself up in his pride. Rather than looking above or over people, he looks at them or down in a sense of unworthiness. He is a finite man, and he knows it. He is a sinner and admits it. His heart is lowly. Before God he has a proper sense of proportion. He would admit with Isaiah that all flesh is grass (Isa. 40:6). He knows with James that life is a vapor (James 4:14). And, above all, he knows that God resists the proud and gives grace to the humble (James 4:6).

Because of this sense of himself, David goes on to admit: *"Neither do I concern myself with* [literally, "Neither have I walked in"] *great matters, / Nor with things too profound* ["wonderful, marvelous"] *for me."* These *"great matters"* and *"wonderful things"* are the schemes

443

and speculative plans of man. They come from his arrogance rather than from his humility. They are a sign of his rebellion against God rather than his submission to him. They are also a commentary upon the modern world with its Enlightenment base, which thinks that everything is possible for us. We can fly to the stars and control the destiny of nations. In our pride we suppose that nothing is impossible for us. Then the earthquake in Armenia hits and more than 50,000 people vanish from the planet. Then the AIDS virus strikes and stalks us. Yet, we refuse to be humbled. Not so with David. Before God he confesses, "Who I am."

WHAT I DO

131:2 Surely I have calmed and quieted my soul,
Like a weaned child with his mother;
Like a weaned child *is* my soul within me.
Ps. 131:2

With a humble, proper sense of ourselves, paradoxically, we are ready for God, we can go to the depths, and David tells us how to get there. Thus he says: *Surely I have calmed* ["set"] *and quieted my soul* ["self"]." Here we see, in Kierkegaard's phrase, the self transcending itself. We are not merely instinctual animals. We are conscious of ourselves. This allows us to calm and quiet ourselves before God, and this is exactly what David does. He now describes the sense that he has of himself: *"Like a weaned child with his mother, / Like a weaned child is my soul within me."* Here is contentment. David is not like a baby crying and harassing his mother for her milk. He is like an older child who knows rest and security in the presence of his mother. Thus his soul (self) is at rest.

Richard Foster writes in *Celebration of Discipline,* "In contemporary society our Adversary majors in three things: noise, hurry, and crowds. If he can keep us engaged in 'muchness' and 'manyness,' he will rest satisfied. Psychiatrist Carl Jung once remarked, 'Hurry is not *of* the Devil; it *is* the Devil'" (p. 15). How can we get ready for God when we are continually distracted? How can we wait for Him (see Ps. 130:5)? What we need to do is calm our souls. We need to find a quiet place and sit awhile. We need to get in touch with our

444

deeper selves and listen to our hearts. We need to take time alone, even if that is scary. Now we are receptive. Now we are listening. Now God can begin to speak to us.

CONCLUSION

131:3 O Israel, hope in the LORD
      From this time forth and forever.

Ps. 131:3

Based upon his own experience of a proper sense of himself and his quieted soul, David exhorts his people, Israel. He concludes that they should *"hope in the Lord."* This is the ultimate purpose of any spiritual discipline. We go to the depths to meet the God who is deeper still. This hope is not merely for a moment; it is to be *"from this time forth and forever* [that is, "continually"]." This hope is to be sustained until it turns to sight and is realized, "face to face" (1 Cor. 13:12). With such hope we can quiet ourselves and get ready for God.

CHAPTER ONE HUNDRED THIRTY-TWO

God's Rule and Realm

Psalm 132

The one, great, central theme of the Bible is that God is King. As King He is the ruler of all things, and as King He also has His realm, His Kingdom. As King He commands creation to come into being from His throne. As King He delegates to us His dominion, in order that we may exercise it over this planet in His name (Gen. 1:28). As King, when His Kingdom is rejected by Satan and his fellow angels, He comes to defeat this enemy and regain Paradise Lost. As King He establishes His covenant-treaty with Abraham, in order that He may bless the nations through him (Gen. 12:3). As King He also goes to war with Pharaoh to deliver His people from bondage (Exod. 3:1ff.). Later when He allows for the establishment of the human monarchy, He tells Samuel that Israel has rejected Him from being King over her, and He delegates His reign to a human king (1 Sam. 8:7). At the same time, in His love, God continues to dwell with His people. He calls Israel's King His son and grants His presence when the temple, His earthly palace, is dedicated by Solomon (1 Kings 8:10). Now it is through David and his heirs that God rules over His realm. At the same time, there is a tension. Who is King? Yahweh or David? This tension is resolved in the Incarnation when Jesus comes as both the eternal Son of God and the human son of David. In Christ, God reestablishes His direct reign over His people and also fulfills His promise to David that he would have an heir upon his throne forever (2 Sam. 7:13). What cannot be resolved in the Old Testament is resolved in the New. God reigns both directly as God and indirectly as man, in His Son, the God-man. This is the necessary background within which to understand the messianic Psalm 132.

God's realm (Zion) and His reign (through David) are the substance of Psalm 132, which commentators view as a composition for one of the great feasts in Jerusalem. Its royal and liturgical context is clear in verses 8–10, which appear in 2 Chron. 6:41–42 as the concluding part of Solomon's prayer when he dedicates the temple. The actual date and author are unknown. The thought moves from David's vow to find God's dwelling (vv. 1–5) to the fulfillment of that vow (vv. 6–9), to God's promise to David (vv. 10–12) and concludes with God's promises to Zion (vv. 13–18).

DAVID'S VOW TO FIND
GOD'S DWELLING

132:1 Lord, remember David
And all his afflictions;

2 How he swore to the LORD,
And vowed to the Mighty One of Jacob:
3 "Surely I will not go into the chamber of my
house,
Or go up to the comfort of my bed;
4 I will not give sleep to my eyes
Or slumber to my eyelids,
5 Until I find a place for the LORD,
A dwelling place for the Mighty One of Jacob."
Ps. 132:1–5

Verse 1 opens with the request that God remember *"David / And all his afflictions* [or, "all his being humbled"]." While the content of these afflictions could be his whole life, the reference is probably intended to be to his trials in taking Jerusalem and bringing the Ark of the Covenant (the portable box where God dwells; see Exodus 37) there (2 Samuel 5–6). God is asked to remember David's vow: *"How he swore to the Lord, / And vowed to the Mighty God of Jacob"* (literally, "the Mighty One of Jacob"; this is God's name to Jacob; see Gen. 49:24; v. 2).

The content of David's vow is given in verses 3–5. He promises, *"Surely I will not go into the chamber* [literally, "tent," probably his bedroom where he would have sexual intercourse] *of my house"* or the *"comfort of my bed"* (v. 3), or sleep (v. 4), *"Until I find a place for the Lord, / A dwelling place for the Mighty God of Jacob"* (v. 5). In other words, David will not rest until God rests. He must secure the site for God to dwell in, and he finds it in Jerusalem, where the presence of God will be manifested.

THE FULFILLMENT OF
DAVID'S VOW

132:6 Behold, we heard of it in Ephrathah;
We found it in the fields of the woods.
7 Let us go into His tabernacle;
Let us worship at His footstool.
8 Arise, O LORD, to Your resting place,
You and the ark of Your strength.
9 Let Your priests be clothed with righteousness,
And let Your saints shout for joy.

10 For Your servant David's sake,
Do not turn away the face of Your Anointed.

Ps. 132:6–10

The psalmist recounts in verse 6 that Israel heard of the Ark in *"Ephrathah,"* the hometown of Boaz, David's ancestor (Ruth 4:11), and that it was found *"in the fields of the woods"* (or, the fields of Jaar, Kirjath-Jearim, from where it was brought to Jerusalem, 1 Chron. 13:3ff.). Thus the pilgrims are summoned: *"Let us go into His tabernacle; Let us worship at His footstool"* (v. 7). The tabernacle would be the temple in Jerusalem. To *"worship"* there means literally to "bow down" before God's *"footstool,"* which stands before the throne upon which He reigns as King.

As God's people bow before Yahweh, the worshipers cry in verse 8: *"Arise, O Lord, to Your resting place, / You and the ark of Your strength* ["might"]." Often the power of God came through the ark, especially in battle (see 1 Samuel 5–6). The call for God to rise up reflects the ancient call for Him to stand up from His throne and to go into battle on behalf of His people. Here, however, God is to rise up (as the Ark, symbolizing His presence, was brought to Jerusalem) and go to His final dwelling place there. Appropriate to the awesome majesty of God, the priests who conduct worship before His altar are to *"be clothed with righteousness"* (they are to communicate God's faithfulness to His covenant-promise by their character), and His *"saints"* (the holy people of Israel) are to *"shout for joy"* ("give a ringing cry," v. 9).

Here is true worship. Here is the proper response to David's vow to find a dwelling place for the Lord (v. 5). We are called to enter that place, to bow before Him as King, and to worship Him there in all of His strength with the righteousness of His priests and the explosive joy of His people.

GOD'S PROMISE TO DAVID

132:11 The LORD has sworn *in* truth to David;
He will not turn from it:
"I will set upon your throne the fruit of your
body.

> 12 If your sons will keep My covenant
> And My testimony which I shall teach them,
> Their sons also shall sit upon your throne
>   forevermore."
>
> *Ps. 132:10–12*

Having established the permanent place for Yahweh, the psalmist, in interceding for King David, turns to the one who exercises His rule. He bases this intercession upon the covenant-promise that God gave to David: *"For Your servant David's sake"* (v. 10). Thus he asks, *"Do not turn away the face of Your anointed* [that is, the present, reigning king]." (For *anointed* see Ps. 2:2.) To turn the king's face away would be to reject him. The request for God's continued favor is based on the commitment that He made to David: "When your days are fulfilled and you rest with your fathers, I will set up your seed after you, who will come from your body, and I will establish his kingdom. He [Solomon] shall build a house for My name, and I will establish the throne of his kingdom forever. . . . But My mercy shall not depart from him. . . . And your house and your kingdom shall be established forever before you. Your throne shall be established forever" (2 Sam. 7:12–16). It is upon this promise that God is asked to sustain the monarchy. This is now reflected in verse 11, *"The Lord has sworn in truth to David; / He will not turn from it: 'I will set upon your throne the fruit of your body'* [that is, your blood heir]." The promise, however, is made conditional in verse 12: *"'If your sons will keep My covenant* ["treaty," here probably the Mosaic covenant] / *And My testimony* ["law"] *which I shall teach them, / Their sons also shall sit upon your throne forevermore.'"* We know from history that the covenant was broken and that the monarchy was destroyed. The unconditional promise given to David, however, was later fulfilled by Jesus Christ who, in His risen glory, now reigns at the right hand of God as the exalted messianic King forever (Eph. 1:20). Thus, He executes God's direct reign in His restored realm, not in geographical Zion but in the heavenly Jerusalem, the glorified church (Rev. 21:2).

GOD'S PROMISE TO ZION

> 132:13 For the LORD has chosen Zion;
> He has desired *it* for His dwelling place:

14 'This *is* My resting place forever;
   Here I will dwell, for I have desired it.
15 I will abundantly bless her provision;
   I will satisfy her poor with bread.
16 I will also clothe her priests with salvation,
   And her saints shall shout aloud for joy.
17 There I will make the horn of David grow;
   I will prepare a lamp for My Anointed.
18 His enemies I will clothe with shame,
   But upon Himself His crown shall flourish.'
                            Ps. 132:13–18

The final section of this psalm is largely a prophetic word or oracle from God concerning Jerusalem (vv. 14–18). It is introduced by the statement that Yahweh *"has chosen Zion* [the mountain upon which Jerusalem rests, Ps. 48:2]; / *He has desired it for His habitation"* (v. 13). Here is where He wants to dwell. Thus He says to Israel: *"'This is my resting place* [where His throne stands] *forever; / Here I will dwell, for I have desired it.'"* Since Jerusalem is Yahweh's abode, her larder will be well stocked as He promises to *"abundantly bless her provision,"* and *"satisfy her poor with bread"* (v. 15). Her priests will be clothed *"with salvation"* and her saints will *"shout aloud for joy"* (v. 16; cf. v. 9). Thus God will provide for the proper worship of Himself there. The monarchy will also prosper. He says, *"'I will make the horn* [symbolizing power] *of David grow.'"* He continues, *"'I will prepare a lamp for My Anointed'"* (the Messiah to come, v. 17), who will be victorious in battle.

With the first reading it is easy to take verses 13–18 as relating to historical Zion. If so, Israel would be led to assume that God would never forsake His city, that He would dwell there forever (v. 14) and that the Davidic dynasty will always grow and prosper. It is this attitude that the prophets attacked, especially Jeremiah. In fact, God removed His presence from Jerusalem (see Ezekiel 10) and destroyed the monarchy. How can we square these facts with these verses? The answer is that the whole passage is prophetic and messianic.

When God promises that He will dwell in Zion forever (v. 14), this is the heavenly city of the redeemed. As John shows in the Revelation: "And I heard a loud voice from heaven saying, 'Behold, the tabernacle of God is with men, and He will dwell with them, and they shall be His people, and God Himself will be with them and be their God'" (Rev. 21:3). He says of the New Jerusalem, "But I saw no temple in it, for the Lord God Almighty and the Lamb are its temple" (Rev. 21:22). The promise of abundant provision and the feeding of the poor in verse 15 is also a messianic theme. In Psalm 72, where the ideal King is portrayed, the poor receive justice and the land prospers (Ps. 72:4, 16). John also sees the heavenly Jerusalem receiving the tribute of the nations and the bounty of the tree of life (Rev. 21:26; 22:2). Furthermore, as in verse 16, the divine city is filled with the joyous worship of those who fall down before God's throne (Rev. 7:9–17). Since Jesus, the Son of God and the son of David, reigns as the Lamb of God, David's horn (power) grows and His crown (authority) flourishes (vv. 17–18; see Isa. 9:7; Rev. 21:22–23).

We now see clearly that what God did in establishing His rule by bringing the Ark to Jerusalem and enthroning David there as His king was to prepare Israel for the day that He would consummate that rule in His Son. We who know and love Him are His Zion, His holy city where He dwells through His Spirit. It is in our hearts that His rule is established as we bow before Him, and it is through our hearts that this rule will be extended to the world. Through us His enemies, Satan and his demons, will be clothed with shame, and *"His crown will flourish"* (v. 18).

CHAPTER ONE HUNDRED THIRTY-THREE

Dwelling in Unity

Psalm 133

The world is broken. Fences and walls are the symbols of our age. All of this is a consequence of the Fall. We now live separated from God and separated from each other. We not only have to think of the continuing conflict of the super powers, but of a thousand similar conflicts as well. Since the end of World War II, there have been 140 other wars on the planet, hardly a witness to the United Nations, or to a united earth.

The real scandal, however, is not the brokenness of the world but the brokenness of the church. The truth of this is not merely seen in the expanding number of denominations and independent congregations. The real truth of this is in the brokenness of relationships within those congregations. I recall Keith Miller telling of boldly hugging an elderly widow on the steps of a church one Sunday. With tears in her eyes she informed him that no one had touched her for twenty years. This is the real isolation. I have rarely been in a body of believers that has not been divided into factions. Issues of political control always raise their ugly heads when there is influence to be acquired. This is especially true when prominent people with economic influence control church boards. They are used to money talking in the business world, and they expect it to talk in the church. Unfortunately, too often the pastor also listens to its fleshly chatter. Years ago the great evangelist Dwight L. Moody preached a sermon in which he noted that Christians in his day wanted influence. Instead, Moody said, what they need is power, the power of the Holy Spirit. This is the power that we need to tear down the walls, freeing us to embrace each other once again. This is the power that we need, and it cannot be elected or bought or sold. In fact when one man tried to buy it long ago, the Apostle Peter replied (in the translation of J. B. Phillips), "To hell with you and your money" (see Acts 8:20).

The brief psalm before us is about unity among believers. Commentators identify it as a wisdom psalm. It is attributed to David. Its thought runs from a definition of unity (v. 1) to a description of unity (vv. 2–3).

WHAT UNITY IS

> 133:1 Behold, how good and how pleasant *it is*
> For brethren to dwell together in unity!
> *Ps. 133:1*

Verse 1 tells us *"how good and how pleasant"* unity is. The word *good* means fulfilling or perfect. *Pleasant* denotes our response to being together. It means "delightful, lovely, beautiful" and can be attributed to wealth, singing praises to Yahweh, keeping wise teachings, and our attitude toward physical beauty. Unity gives us a sense of completion and makes us happy. No wonder David says that it is good *for brethren to dwell together in unity!*" The idea of dwelling together should probably not be taken literally. It is doubtful that the psalmist is referring to a family living under one roof (but see Deut. 25:5). Especially in light of the next two verses, we take David to be addressing the value of spiritual unity for God's people.

Many Christians have been frustrated by the disunity of the church. They have spent sleepless nights because of unresolved conflicts. They have spent endless hours seeking to reconcile people. They have preached to congregations where, when certain subjects have been raised, they have seen the frowns of groups who don't go along with their theology. The issues have been avoided rather than confronted. Some Christians give money, letting the pastors know as the check is handed over that they expect favors and influence. And others have been hurt by gossip that has come in the form of prayer requests or "deep Christian concern."

At the same time, there are Christians who *do* worship together. Their fellowship is a joy for everyone, and that joy is rooted in a mutual commitment to working out difficulties and refining relationships. They know exactly what David meant here; indeed, it is good and pleasant for brethren to dwell together in unity.

What Unity Is Like

133:2 *It is* like the precious oil upon the head,
    Running down on the beard,
    The beard of Aaron,
    Running down on the edge of his garments.
3 *It is* like the dew of Hermon,
    Descending upon the mountains of Zion;
    For there the LORD commanded the blessing—
    Life forevermore.

                            Ps. 133:2-3

David describes the pleasantness of unity with two poetic images. The first is the anointing oil of the high priests, and the second is the dew of Mount Hermon. In verse 2 he tells us that being together *is like the precious oil upon the head, running down on the beard . . . of Aaron."* The word rendered *"precious"* here is actually "good." This good oil is probably scented oil used in anointing the high priests, represented by Aaron, the first high priest and brother of Moses (Exod. 4:14). Thus we read in Exod. 29:7 that after Aaron is ceremonially dressed, "you shall take the anointing oil, pour it on his head, and anoint him." This anointing, which followed a ritual bath, set him apart. There is reason to believe from the anointing of David with oil and the immediate coming of the Holy Spirit upon him, that the oil represented the blessing and presence of God's Spirit (compare 1 Sam. 16:13). This would also account for the singular description of the oil flowing down Aaron's beard and *"running down on the edge"* [literally, "mouth"] *of his garments."* Thus the unity of the brethren is like Aaron, covered with the oil of the Spirit. In the New Testament, the Holy Spirit is the Spirit of unity (Eph. 4:3). It is the Spirit who makes us one, leveling the walls that stand between us, as He authors God's new creation in us and anoints us with Himself (2 Cor. 1:21–22).

In verse 3, being together in unity is like the *"dew of* [Mount] *Hermon,"* the dew that descends *"upon the mountains of Zion."* Since Hermon is a high peak in Syria, its dew is heavy, and it is this heavy dew that also falls upon the mountains surrounding Jerusalem, situated on Mount Zion (Ps. 48:2). Since the dew comes from heaven, it too is an apt image for the blessing of God that creates unity. That this blessing is upon His mountain (Zion) is obvious in the conclusion of verse 3, as David says, *"For there* [on Zion] *the Lord commanded the blessing — / Life forevermore."*

Our unity comes from the Spirit of God flowing over us like oil, and the heavenly dew descending upon us, bringing God's blessing of life—eternal life, forever and ever. It is only God's Spirit and His promise of eternal life that will break down the sin in our hearts, crucifying our selfishness, making us one. As verse 1 says, "Behold, how good and pleasant it is." Now let's live in it!

How to Have a "Good Night"

Psalm 134

For many people the night is filled with fears. As the darkness falls, we sense things closing in upon us. Jesus says that men love darkness rather than light because their deeds are evil (John 3:19). Paul says that we are of the day; "We are not of the night nor of darkness." He then exhorts us, "Therefore let us not sleep, as others do, but let us watch and be sober. For those who sleep, sleep at night, and those who get drunk are drunk at night" (1 Thess. 5:5–7).

While Psalm 134 is addressed to God's servants in the temple who lead worship at night, it has an application to us. God is to be praised in the darkness. He is to be worshiped in the night watches. Since there is no night with Him, we are to be perpetually praising Him and presenting ourselves to Him. For this reason the priests ministered to Him at night in the temple, and the congregation joined them, especially during the festivals. We are to learn from them and continue that same ministry in our night watches. This will dispel the darkness and get us through the night as we live it in God's presence.

Commentators identify the form of this psalm as a combination of hymn (vv. 1–2) and blessing (v. 3). Its date and author are unknown. The thought moves from the call to bless God (v. 1) to how to bless God (v. 2) and concludes with the secret to our blessing (v. 3).

CALL TO BLESS GOD

134:1 Behold, bless the LORD,
    All *you* servants of the LORD,
    Who by night stand in the house of the LORD!
                    Ps. 134:1

Verse 1 tells us *what* God's *"servants"* are to do and *when* and *where* they are to do it. As to the what, they are to *"bless the Lord."* This means that they are to give their praise and exultation to Him. They are to load their happiness upon him. As to when, they are to bless Him *"by night,"* as they stand before Him in worship. As to where, they are to do this in the *"house of the Lord,"* namely in the temple in Jerusalem. But who are these servants? They may be the priests who serve before the altar, but they also can be the whole people of God who have been called into His Kingdom to be His subjects and to serve Him. For example, in the decalogue, the commandment against making graven images includes this prohibition, "you shall not bow down to them nor serve them. For I, the Lord your God, am a jealous God" (Exod. 20:5). Israel is to bow down only to Yahweh and serve Him.

How to Bless God

> 134:2 Lift up your hands *in* the sanctuary,
> And bless the LORD.
>
> *Ps. 134:2*

In this verse the question concerning how we are to bless God receives a simple answer: we are to *"lift up"* our *"hands in the sanctuary"* (literally, "holy place," which could mean "toward the holy of holies," where God Himself dwells behind the veil). Thus when Solomon dedicated the temple, he "stood before the altar of the Lord in the presence of all the congregation of Israel, and spread out his hands toward heaven" and prayed (1 Kings 8:22). The idea of lifting up our hands in this text communicates lifting them up in blessing as the priests do when they pronounce a benediction over the people. Thus the next phrase tells us that as we lift them we are to *"bless the Lord."* Here we learn that our worship is to be not only verbal but visual also. In other words, our body language is important. As the church is being renewed in worship today, there is increasing freedom for physical expression, which is appropriate to the situation. Thus raising our hands as we bless God is not only biblical; it is also edifying as we find our whole selves participating in our worship.

THE SECRET TO OUR BLESSING

134:3 The LORD who made heaven and earth
Bless you from Zion!

Ps. 134:3

We can bless God and worship Him in the night watches for one reason alone: He blesses us. The secret to our worship is that God is the initiator. He calls us; He saves us; He sanctifies us; and He will glorify us in His presence (Rom. 8:29–30). Thus as we proposed in the introduction to the first volume of this commentary, the real secret to our worship is that God initiates it, and He fulfills it as well. In His Son, who is our Mediator, He worships through us (Bonhoeffer). Thus this psalm ends, not with our blessing God, but with Him blessing us: *"The Lord who made heaven and earth / Bless you from Zion!"* The one who blesses us is our Creator. He holds all power in His hands. Moreover, He is also our Redeemer; He blesses us from Zion, the holy hill upon which His temple stands. Here sacrifices are made to atone for our sins, and, ultimately, here Jesus died as the Lamb of God who takes away the sin of the world (John 1:29). As God blesses us, we are able to bless Him in response.

When the darkness presses in, when the shadows fall, when the enemy attacks, we have one great opportunity and one great recourse: we are to bless God. Worship is the delight of our soul, and it is also the strongest weapon of our warfare. It is the way to have a "good night"!

Know the God You Worship

Psalm 135

The true worship of God must come from a true knowledge of God. We are so slovenly in our worship, because we are so slovenly in our thinking. If we were to have an audience with Queen Elizabeth, we would gather all the information that we could on the proper way to meet her. We would practice our introduction and know whether to curtsy or bow. We would also be told to never touch the queen. When the day arrived, we would dress our best, giving attention to every detail. We would want to arrive in good time, rather than rushing in at the last minute. Why are we so careless in our approach to God? The answer is that we know little of the God into whose presence we come. Ignorant of His majesty and power, mindless of His splendor and grace, we stumble into His presence in order to mumble through a few rote prayers and weakly join in a hymn or two while we check out the audience and see who is there. If what I have just said has any application to you or to your church, then the psalm before us will be of help.

The author calls us to praise God (v. 1) and tells us about the God whom we are praising. He is good (v. 3); He has chosen us (v. 4); He is the Lord of creation (vv. 5–7), and whatever He pleases, He does (v. 6). Moreover, He revealed His majesty and grace in redeeming Israel from Egypt. There He displayed His "signs and wonders" (v. 9). He also defeated many peoples as He conquered the Holy Land. His name is eternal, and He will judge us (vv. 13–14). The idols who oppose Him, however, are nothing (vv. 15–18). Since God is everything, we are to bless and praise Him (vv. 18–21).

Commentators describe Psalm 135 as a liturgical hymn. Its author and date are unknown. The thought moves from a call to worship (vv. 1–4) to God's sovereignty over creation (vv. 5–7), to His sovereignty over judgment and redemption (vv. 8–12), to the greatness of His name (vv. 13–14), to the nothingness of the idols (vv. 15–18) and concludes with blessing God (vv. 19–21).

CALL TO WORSHIP

135:1 Praise the LORD!
      Praise the name of the LORD;
      Praise *Him,* O you servants of the LORD!
  2 You who stand in the house of the LORD,
      In the courts of the house of our God,
  3 Praise the LORD, for the LORD *is* good;
      Sing praises to His name, for *it is* pleasant.
  4 For the LORD has chosen Jacob for Himself,
      Israel for His special treasure.

                                    Ps. 135:1–4

We are called to worship in verse 1: *"Praise the Lord [Hallĕlu-Yâh (weh); literally, 'Hallelujah']!"* Our praise is to be directed to His *name.* His name reveals His personhood, His identity. When we call upon it in faith, He releases His presence and power. But who is to worship Him? The psalmist answers: *"Praise Him, O you servants of the Lord!"* These servants are those who have submitted to Him as King. They are His subjects, now a part of His covenant-treaty, bound to His rule and living in His realm. As His servants, they also *"stand in the house of the Lord, / In the courts of the house of our God"* (v. 2). God's house is His palace or temple, where He dwells. It is there that we go to meet Him and to offer our devotion to Him.

As we enter into the presence of God, we are again exhorted to praise Him (v. 3) with the added incentive *"for the Lord is good."* The goodness of God means His moral purity, His purposeful will, which brings all things to completion, and His trustworthiness because He keeps His covenant with us. Therefore, we are exhorted: *"Sing praises to His name, for it* [His name] *is pleasant* ["delightful, lovely"]." His worshipers love His name because it evokes His person and all that He has done for us.

We do not worship God because we are especially spiritually insightful or open hearted to Him. We worship Him because He has taken the initiative with us. He has broken our bonds and called us into life. As John says, "We love Him because He first loved us" (1 John 4:19). Thus the psalmist continues, *"For the Lord has chosen Jacob for Himself, / Israel for His special treasure* ["possession, property"]" (v. 4). *"Jacob,"* the father of the twelve tribes, is synonymous with *"Israel."* The word *treasure* here means "possession" or "property." Thus God says in the Exodus, "you shall be a special treasure to Me above all people" (Exod. 19:5).

It would be fair to say that God called Israel for the very purpose of worshiping Him. This is true for us as well. God wants us to know Him so that we will praise and glorify His name. Our identity is found in whom we worship. This worship is also not just our individual devotion; it is the public praise of our hearts (see v. 2).

GOD IS SOVEREIGN OVER CREATION

135:5 For I know that the LORD *is* great,
And our Lord *is* above all gods.
6 Whatever the LORD pleases He does,
In heaven and in earth,
In the seas and in all deep places.
7 He causes the vapors to ascend from the ends
of the earth;
He makes lightning for the rain;
He brings the wind out of His treasuries.
Ps. 135:5–7

Now the psalmist confesses the greatness of God. He knows this personally: *"For I know* [by experience] *that the Lord is great."* The proof of this is that He is *"above all gods"* (v. 5). Later we will find out that all the gods are idols and therefore nothing (vv. 15–18). Here, however, he simply makes the point of God's supreme authority. Not only is He above all other gods; He is also sovereignly free (v. 6). The theater of His activity is also universal: *"In heaven and in earth, / In the seas and in all deep places* [that is, underground water sources]" (v. 6). He commands nature. It is He who causes the vapors to rise *"from the ends of the earth."* He makes the lightning that accompanies the rain, and *"brings the wind out of His treasuries* ["storehouses"]" (v. 7). Moses promises that among God's blessings upon His people for their obedience, "The Lord will open to you His good treasure, the heavens, to give the rain to your land in its season, and to bless all the work of your hand" (Deut. 28:12).

God is great. He is above all and over all, as He, rather than the Baals of the fertility cults, creates and commands nature. This knowledge of Him is enough to put us on our faces in worship. There is, however, more to come.

GOD IS SOVEREIGN OVER
JUDGMENT AND REDEMPTION

135:8 He destroyed the firstborn of Egypt,
　　　Both of man and beast.
　9 He sent signs and wonders into the midst of
　　　you, O Egypt,
　　　Upon Pharaoh and all his servants.
　10 He defeated many nations
　　　And slew mighty kings—
　11 Sihon king of the Amorites,
　　　Og king of Bashan,
　　　And all the kingdoms of Canaan—
　12 And gave their land *as* a heritage,
　　　A heritage to Israel His people.

Ps. 135:8–12

　　The greatness of God (v. 5) is seen by His mighty acts in history. In the final plague, as Israel languished in Egypt, God killed the firstborn, *"both of man and beast"* (see Exodus 11–12; v. 8) and delivered His people as a result. Thus God *"sent signs and wonders into the midst of you, O Egypt, / Upon Pharaoh and all his servants"* (v. 9). These *"signs"* are events that point to the power of God and the *"wonders"* are miracles that evoke our amazement (see Exod. 7:3). God's power is seen as He fought for Israel in bringing her into the Promised Land. To do this, *"He defeated many nations,"* slaying their kings (v. 10). First among the dead were *"Sihon king of the Amorites"* (Num. 21:21–32) and *"Og king of Bashan"* (Num. 21:33–35). Then the inhabitants of the land itself were destroyed, *"all the kingdoms of Canaan"* (v. 11). Once the land was cleared, God gave it as *"a heritage to Israel His people"* (v. 12). We see His mighty acts of judgment as He delivers Israel from Egypt, destroying her enemies, and bringing her into the land that He had promised her. If creation doesn't bring us to worship Him, certainly His judgments will humble and break us before Him. They will also cause us to praise Him, for He is our Redeemer.

GOD'S NAME IS GREAT

135:13 Your name, O LORD, *endures* forever,
      Your fame, O LORD, throughout all
        generations.
   14 For the LORD will judge His people,
      And He will have compassion on His servants.
                      Ps. 135:13–14

In light of creation and history, the psalmist addresses God directly, saying that His name *"endures forever."* This simply means that our God is the eternal God. His name represents His personhood and His character, which will not pass away. Furthermore, God's *"fame"* ("remembrance") is passed down *"throughout all generations"* (v. 13). As the account of His mighty works is extolled, He will be glorified by His people again and again.

Verse 14 returns to the third person singular by offering a direct quote from Deut. 32:36. The greatness of God's name and fame is sealed by this confessional statement: God *"will judge His people, / And He will have compassion on His servants."* As judge He will order their affairs and establish justice among them. At the same time, He will bring His compassion to those who have submitted to Him as King, His servants who have been bound to Him in the covenant. No wonder the name of God is to be praised (v. 1); it is lovely (v. 3). When we say "Yahweh" we speak of (and to) the God who creates and commands all things, redeems us, judges us, and has compassion upon us. Indeed, what a lovely name.

THE IDOLS ARE NOTHING

135:15 The idols of the nations *are* silver and gold,
      The work of men's hands.
   16 They have mouths, but they do not speak;
      Eyes they have, but they do not see;

17 They have ears, but they do not hear;
   Nor is there *any* breath in their mouths.
18 Those who make them are like them;
   So is everyone who trusts in them.
>   *Ps. 135:15–18*

The description of the idols here is a revised edition of Ps. 115:4–8. The substance of the two passages is the same. As in the use of Deut. 32:26 in verse 14, we have the psalmist incorporating elements of previous tradition in his work. Whether he is quoting the other psalm or using oral tradition or a liturgical piece from public worship, we cannot say. We do see that such tradition in Israel is living, used here much as a preacher might cite Scripture texts in a sermon.

While the substance of these verses has already been discussed in Psalm 115, we may say, in sum, that the idols (in contrast to Yahweh) are simply a human creation (v. 15), unable to speak, see, hear, or breathe (vv. 16–17). Moreover, those who make them and trust in them become like them (v. 18). By implication, those who trust in Yahweh, who speaks, sees, hears, and breathes, will become like Him. God is to be praised.

BLESS THE LORD

135:19 Bless the LORD, O house of Israel!
       Bless the LORD, O house of Aaron!
   20 Bless the LORD, O house of Levi!
       You who fear the LORD, bless the LORD!
   21 Blessed be the LORD out of Zion,
       Who dwells in Jerusalem!
       Praise the LORD!
>   *Ps. 135:19–21*

In the introduction, I stated that the true worship of God depends upon the true knowledge of God. We have received a substantial dose of knowledge. Our God is great; He is above all gods (v. 5). Throughout the text we have seen the exposition of that greatness. When we consider the folly of worshiping idols, the living God is exalted all the more.

This psalm concludes with a call for us to bless the Lord. The *"house of Israel,"* the whole nation, is to join in this blessing. Likewise, the *"house of Aaron,"* the priesthood, is to bless Yahweh (see Exodus 29; v. 19). Also the *"house of Levi,"* which assisted Aaron and the priests (see Num. 3:5ff.), is to bless Him. Added to these groupings are *"You who fear the Lord."* While this could mean the proselytes, it also may designate the pious, the lowly. They too are to *"bless the Lord"* (v. 20).

Having summoned all Israel to join in blessing God, the actual pronouncement is given: *"Blessed be the Lord out of Zion* [the mountain upon which Jerusalem was built, Ps. 48:2], / *Who dwells in Jerusalem!"* An epilogue concludes the psalm, repeating verse 1: *"Praise the Lord!"* Since we know the God whom we are to worship, verse 21 engages us in the act of worship. It is as if the psalmist says, "We have discussed what we are to do; now let's do it, let's bless Him!"

CHAPTER ONE HUNDRED THIRTY-SIX

Blest Be the Tie That Binds

Psalm 136

One unique aspect of God's self-revelation in the Old Testament is that He is the God of the covenant. He establishes His covenant first with Abraham, as He binds him to Himself, and then renews it with the rest of the patriarchs. But what is a covenant? The Abrahamic covenant (in contrast to the Mosaic covenant) is a treaty, which is modeled upon compacts made between kings and favored retainers.

Thus the covenant with Abraham is similar to the royal grants given by Hittite kings, in which the monarch gives a city or a tract of land to a general or an administrator who has served him well. The grant is unconditional, gracious, and perpetual. It comes from a greater (king) to a lesser (his subject) and is imposed upon him as an offer that he cannot refuse. This becomes the basis of their relationship, and the king promises to defend his covenant-commitment forever. When God promises Abraham that he will become a great nation and have his own land, the basis of this promise is the covenant-treaty that He makes with him (see Gen. 15:1ff.).

God's covenant with His people follows them down through the generations. It guarantees that He will be gracious toward them. Based upon His unconditional commitment, they continue to live in this world, even to this very day. The presupposition behind the covenant is that God is King and that Israel is His subject people. They have surrendered to Him and now worship Him and serve Him. At the same time, because of His covenant promise, He continues to be faithful. He may judge Israel for her disobedience, but He never destroys her. He also judges her enemies, and promises a day when He will write a new covenant on her heart (Jer. 31:31ff.). This is the foundation for the coming of Jesus into the world. He enacts a New Covenant in His blood and opens up a new and living way to God, incorporating the Gentile nations into the salvation that God first granted to Israel. All of this is a necessary foundation for our understanding of Psalm 136, which is raised in praise to the God of the covenant and to that covenant, which are the blessed "tie that binds."

Throughout this psalm God is to be praised "for His mercy endures forever." This theme is repeated twenty-six times in twenty-six verses. The word rendered "mercy" means "covenant-love" (ḥesed). This psalm celebrates the covenant-faithfulness and the covenant-mercy of Yahweh toward His people. Faithfulness and mercy are seen both in creation (vv. 4–9) and in redemption (vv. 10–25), which are exposited through the great events of the Exodus that form a confessional-historical liturgy. All of this is narrated for one ultimate reason, in order that we may join in praising and worshiping the one, true, living God who is (vv. 1–3, 26).

Commentators describe Psalm 136 as a liturgy of thanksgiving. The refrain that repeats itself throughout may have been recited or sung by the worshiping congregation or choir. The author and date are unknown. The thought moves from a call to worship (vv. 1–3) to the praise of the Covenant-God who created all things (vv. 4–9), to the praise of the Covenant-God who redeemed His people from Egypt and gave them the Promised Land (vv. 10–25) and concludes with a repetition of the call to worship in verse 1 (v. 26).

CALL TO WORSHIP

136:1 Oh, give thanks to the LORD, for *He is* good!
  For His mercy *endures* forever.
 2 Oh, give thanks to the God of gods!
  For His mercy *endures* forever.
 3 Oh, give thanks to the Lord of lords!
  For His mercy *endures* forever:

Ps. 136:1–3

Verses 1–3 give us a threefold call to worship. Here we are exhorted: *"Oh, give thanks to the Lord"* (v. 1); *"Oh, give thanks to the God of gods"* (v. 2); *"Oh, give thanks to the Lord of lords!"* (v. 3). In this exhortation we learn that we are to worship the Lord, that is, Yahweh, the personal God of Israel (see Exod. 3:14). He is also *"the God of gods"*; there are no other gods before Him (Exod. 20:3). He is also *"the Lord of lords"*; there is no other dominion or authority above Him. In the fullness of God's revelation in His Son, we still have this rigorous monotheism. As Paul says, "we know that an idol is nothing in the world, and that there is no other God but one. For even if there are so-called gods, whether in heaven or on earth (as there are many gods and many lords), yet for us there is only one God, the Father, of whom are all things, and we for Him; and one Lord Jesus Christ, through whom are all things, and through whom we live" (1 Cor. 8:4–6).

But why are we to worship this God? The answer is not merely because He exists. We are to worship Him because He has revealed Himself to us as worthy of our worship. He is *"good"* (v. 1); that is, He is perfect and brings all things to His perfection. But this is not the bottom line. Even more than His goodness is His *"mercy,"* His covenant-love, which *"endures forever."* He is the God who commits Himself unconditionally to His people and never abandons that commitment. We change, the world changes; God endures forever and His love never fails toward us. No wonder that we are to worship this God. But how are we to understand His mercy? The answer is given by surveying God's power in creation. In the created world where we live, God commits Himself to us.

THE PRAISE OF THE COVENANT GOD WHO CREATES ALL THINGS

136:4 To Him who alone does great wonders,
For His mercy *endures* forever;
5 To Him who by wisdom made the heavens,
For His mercy *endures* forever;
6 To Him who laid out the earth above the
waters,
For His mercy *endures* forever;
7 To Him who made great lights,
For His mercy *endures* forever—
8 The sun to rule by day,
For His mercy *endures* forever;
9 The moon and stars to rule by night,
For His mercy *endures* forever.

Ps. 136:4–9

It is of utmost importance for the Bible that the God of Redemption is also the God of Creation. It is from His throne that He brings all things into being. As He creates us, He addresses His court, which consists of the holy angels gathered before Him. This explains why He says in the plural, "Let us make man in our image" (Gen. 1:27). Since He is the Creator, when He redeems us He is not redeeming us from creation; He is redeeming us as His (fallen) creation. This is the context within which to understand verses 4–9.

The psalmist calls upon us to give thanks (v. 3) to God, "*To Him who alone does great wonders*" (v. 4). These "*wonders*" or "*miracles*" are usually related to His mighty acts of redemption. Here, however, they are applied to His acts of creation. He is the God who "*by wisdom made the heavens*" (v. 5). As Proverbs tells us, "The Lord by wisdom founded the earth; / By understanding He established the heavens" (Prov. 3:19). What this means is that He has a divine plan in creation, which comes through His wisdom. Wisdom is personified here, which points us to the full revelation of the New Testament, where God creates through the instrument of His eternal Word (John 1:3) or wisdom (1 Cor. 1:30). He also *laid out* ["spread out by beating," like a thin layer of metal] *the earth above the waters,"* which lie below its surface (v. 6). He *"made great lights"* (v. 7), *"the sun to rule by day"* (v. 8) and *"the moon and stars to rule by night"* (v. 9; see Gen. 1:14–18).

In the creation God shows us His power, His order, and His sovereign plan for this world. It is also upheld by Him; it is a sign of His mercy, His covenant-love. As we meditate upon each facet of His works, we are to remember that all of this comes from the covenant God by reciting, *"For His mercy endures forever"* (vv. 4, 5, 6, 7, 8, 9).

The Praise of the Covenant God
Who Redeems Us

136:10 To Him who struck Egypt in their firstborn,
　　　　For His mercy *endures* forever;
　11 And brought out Israel from among them,
　　　　For His mercy *endures* forever;
　12 With a strong hand, and with an outstretched
　　　　arm,
　　　　For His mercy *endures* forever;
　13 To Him who divided the Red Sea in two,
　　　　For His mercy *endures* forever;
　14 And made Israel pass through the midst of it,
　　　　For His mercy *endures* forever;
　15 But overthrew Pharaoh and his army in the
　　　　Red Sea,
　　　　For His mercy *endures* forever;
　16 To Him who led His people through the
　　　　wilderness,
　　　　For His mercy *endures* forever;
　17 To Him who struck down great kings,
　　　　For His mercy *endures* forever;
　18 And slew famous kings,
　　　　For His mercy *endures* forever—

19 Sihon king of the Amorites,
> For His mercy *endures* forever;
20 And Og king of Bashan,
> For His mercy *endures* forever—
21 And gave their land as a heritage,
> For His mercy *endures* forever;
22 A heritage to Israel His servant,
> For His mercy *endures* forever.
23 Who remembered us in our lowly state,
> For His mercy *endures* forever;
24 And rescued us from our enemies,
> For His mercy *endures* forever;
25 Who gives food to all flesh,
> For His mercy *endures* forever.

Ps. 136:10–25

Beyond Creation stands the Fall. Sin, Satan, and death are our lot in this world. Nevertheless, God intervenes to bring us back to Himself, and this appears for Israel in the great events of the Exodus. Thus we are to give thanks to Him who *"struck Egypt in their first-born"* (v. 10; see Exod. 12:29–30). In this final plague, when all of the firstborn of Egypt died on the night of Passover, Israel was redeemed from bondage and liberated to worship God alone and serve Him, rather than serving the idolator, and presumptuous god-king, Pharaoh. We are to give thanks to Him who *"brought out Israel from among them"* (the Egyptians, v. 11), *"with a strong hand* [great power, Exod. 15:6], *and with an outstretched arm"* (v. 12). The Creator is also the Warrior-King who leads His people to victory in battle. We are to praise *"Him who divided the Red Sea in two"* (v. 13) *"and made Israel pass through the midst of it"* (v. 14), and who then closed the sea back up, as He *"overthrew* [literally, "shook off"] *Pharaoh and his army"* (v. 15; see Exod. 14:21–31). Our God is a God of redemption and judgment. As He executes His wrath upon our enemies, He is faithful to His covenant to deliver us and keep us.

We are to praise God for His guidance and provision. We thank Him *"who led His people through the wilderness"* (v. 16), and *"who struck down great"* and *"famous kings"* (vv. 17–18), *"Sihon king of the Amorites,"* and *"Og king of Bashan"* (vv. 19–20; see Ps. 135:11). Their lands He gave to *"Israel His servant"* ("slave" submitted to Yahweh as Master), as a *"heritage"* ("inheritance") when she prepared to enter the

Promised Land (vv. 21–22). As in the meditation on creation, as each of these points is made, we are to remember them individually and collectively and recite, *"His mercy* [covenant-love] *endures forever"* (vv. 10, 11, 12, 13, 14, 15, 16, 17, 18, 19, 20, 21, 22). Through this liturgical response, the point of God's faithfulness to His covenant is punched home.

In Christ, we have much to add to this litany of praise. We can add that God has sent His Son, "For His mercy endures forever," to redeem us from our sins, "For His mercy endures forever," so that we can live with Him in heaven, "For His mercy endures forever." With this, the revelation of God's covenant-faithfulness is complete. This is the "tie that binds" for eternity.

Verses 23–25 sum up the God of the covenant. We give thanks to Him *"who remembered us in our lowly state* [bondage in Egypt? v. 10f.] (v. 23), *who rescued us from our enemies"* (v. 24), and *"who gives food to all flesh"* (v. 25), that is, who providentially sustains His whole creation. He is the God who also remembers *us* in the lowly estate of our sin. He also sends us a Savior, who rescues us from our enemies: Satan and death. He feeds us with Himself unto life eternal (John 6). Indeed, we can join heartily in the refrain: "For His mercy endures forever."

CALL TO WORSHIP

136:26 Oh, give thanks to the God of heaven!
For His mercy *endures* forever.

Ps. 136:26

Verse 26 repeats verses 1–3, the extended call to worship with which this psalm opens. We are to praise the *"God of heaven."* As we have seen, He is the personal God, Yahweh (v. 1). He is the supreme God, "God of gods" (v. 2). He is the God over all authority, "Lord of lords" (v. 3), and He is the *"God of heaven,"* the transcendent, exalted, eternal God. Our thanks to this God, Creator, and Redeemer is appropriate. He keeps His covenant because of His covenant-love; "His mercy endures forever."

No Song in Exile

Psalm 137

The spirituals of Black music have tremendous power born of suffering. This appears clearly in gospel music, which sings of the glory of heaven and contrasts it with the hell of earth. The longing for freedom, ultimately, is the longing to go home to the Lord. A more secular form of the Black experience of suffering and slavery is the blues. In it there is a soulful anguish, usually on a more personal theme, such as "My man left me." Songs of hope and songs of suffering are appropriate in their context. It is inappropriate, however, to sing songs of joy and triumph in the midst of loss and sorrow. For this reason, Israel was unable to sing the songs of Zion in exile. The praises of Yahweh intended for entering the temple could not be sung when it stood in ruins. The delights in Jerusalem could not be sung when Jerusalem had been burned to the ground. Songs of home did not fit in a foreign land. Instead, songs like Psalm 137 could be sung, songs of lament, songs of loss, vows for the future, and calling down of curses upon those who had destroyed God's holy places and exiled His holy people.

This psalm opens "by the rivers of Babylon" (v. 1). There, the author and the other exiles are asked to sing a song of Zion (v. 3). There is, however, no song of Jerusalem to be sung (vv. 4–5). Instead, the psalmist calls upon God to remember Edom in judgment for demanding the razing of the Holy City and pronounces a blessing upon the destroyer of Babylon who brought Israel into captivity (vv. 7–9).

Commentators identify Psalm 137 as a combination of a lament and a psalm of cursing. While its author is unknown, a plausible suggestion has been made that he was one of the temple singers who

was carried off to Babylon when the city fell in 586 B.C. This psalm
would have been written before the temple was rebuilt in 515 B.C.
The thought moves from the affirmation "We wept" (vv. 1–3) to "We
will not forget Jerusalem" (vv. 4–6) and concludes with blessings on
those who punish her destroyer (vv. 7–9).

WE WEPT

137:1 By the rivers of Babylon,
     There we sat down, yea, we wept
     When we remembered Zion.
  2 We hung our harps
     Upon the willows in the midst of it.
  3 For there those who carried us away captive
       asked of us a song,
     And those who plundered us *requested* mirth,
     Saying, "Sing us *one* of the songs of Zion!"
                             Ps. 137:1–3

Verse 1 sets the scene: *"By the rivers of Babylon, / There we sat down,
yea, we wept."* The *"rivers"* referred to here are probably the great
irrigation channels fed by the Euphrates, which watered the fertile
plains surrounding the city. Jewish exile settlements were located
there, for example by the Chebar (Exod. 1:1). The captives lament
because they have *"remembered Zion"* (the mountain upon which
Jerusalem was built, see Ps. 48:2). Clearly their minds went back to
her former magnificence and her present destruction. There is to be
no music in exile. The psalmist continues: *"We hung our harps* ["lyres,"
instruments of three to twelve strings] / *Upon the willows in the midst
of it"* (v. 2). The harps are hung up both because of the sadness
the exiles experience and out of loyalty to Jerusalem (see v. 4). Their
captives, however, demand a *"song"* (literally, "the words of a song").
The psalmist adds: *"And those who plundered us required of us mirth*
["gladness, exultation"], / *Saying, 'Sing us one of the songs of Zion!'"*
(v. 3). The singers, however, are weeping (v. 1). There will be no
cultural event in Babylon, no folk festival of old Hebrew tunes. In
exile there is no song.

WE WILL NOT FORGET JERUSALEM

137:4 How shall we sing the LORD's song
     In a foreign land?
   5 If I forget you, O Jerusalem,
     Let my right hand forget *its skill!*
   6 If I do not remember you,
     Let my tongue cling to the roof of my mouth—
     If I do not exalt Jerusalem
     Above my chief joy.

Ps. 137:4-6

The rhetorical question is asked in verse 4: *"How shall we sing the Lord's song in a foreign ["strange"] land?"* The implied answer is, "We can't." Perhaps we could sing, "Swing Low, Sweet Chariot" or some blues number, but the songs of Zion, the *"Lord's song"* cannot be sung there. These songs are not for performance. They are not entertainment. Therefore, they cannot be sung out of context. Songs of Zion must be sung in Zion. Songs of worship must be presented to the living God, not to pagan princes. At the heart of this lies a critical theological point: songs of praise must be presented to the One worthy of our praise. Otherwise, they are perverted by their very presentation.

For example, I heard a great Christmas program broadcast by noted musicians. While it was technically flawless, it was flat. They clearly did not know the one about whom they sang. They presented their music to the audience rather than to the Lord. In contrast to this, I have a treasured broadcast of Christmas music by the great Black opera singer Jessye Norman. The setting of the concert is a medieval cathedral in England, with a professional backdrop of choirs and symphony orchestra. Ms. Norman glows with an inner light. She presents her music to Jesus Christ, not to her audience. Her eyes often soar upward, beyond the vaults of the ceiling. Traditional carols ring with truth as she offers them heavenward. It is clear. She sings the songs of Zion in Zion, and the angels sing with her.

In verses 5–6, the psalmist puts curses on his own head. *"If I forget you, O Jerusalem, / Let my right hand forget her skill"* (v. 5). Regardless of the present state of Jerusalem, he refuses to forget that she is God's city, where His temple and name dwell. The sanctity of the city was a passion for the pious Jew. Blood would be shed if she were dese-crated, as the Romans were later to learn, much to their dismay. Again the psalmist curses, *"Let my tongue cling to the roof of my mouth— / If I do not exalt Jerusalem / Above my chief joy"* (v. 6). Thus he seeks the exaltation of the Holy City above all else. If the psalmist doesn't use his tongue to sing praises to Zion, he may as well be struck dumb. What other ultimate use is there for our voices, if not to praise God and worship him? There is a conviction in these simple thoughts. We exalt the rich and famous. We exalt rock stars, movie stars, and fast-lane tycoons. We use our voices to express our joy over many idle things. How does our devotion to the living God measure up to the simple thoughts in these verses? How willing would we be (seriously) to be maimed or silenced if we did not praise God above all our other joys?

BLESSINGS ON THOSE WHO PUNISH
JERUSALEM'S DESTROYERS

137:7 Remember, O LORD, against the sons of Edom
The day of Jerusalem,
Who said, "Raze *it*, raze *it*,
To its very foundation!"
8 O daughter of Babylon, who are to be
destroyed,
Happy the one who repays you as you have
served us!
9 Happy the one who takes and dashes
Your little ones against the rock!

Ps. 137:7–9

The psalmist "remembers" Zion (v. 1). Conversely, he refuses to "forget" Jerusalem (v. 5), and, therefore, "remembers" her (v. 6). Now he prays, *"Remember, O Lord, against the sons of Edom"* (v. 7). These sons were the descendants of Esau, the brother of Jacob, and there-fore closely related to the Jews (see Gen. 25:25–26). In remembering them, he wants God to remember them in judgment for their siding against Jerusalem in the day of her destruction. They cried, *"'Raze it* [literally, "Make it bare"], *raze it, / To its very foundation!'"* Now God will take vengeance upon them for their vengeance upon Jerusalem (see Ezek. 25:12–14).

The real culprit, however, is Babylon. Because of her pride in destroying God's city, she is *"to be destroyed."* This verse (8) and the following one could be taken as a divine oracle. They may also simply be the psalmist's conclusion, especially if the dashing of children offends us. Either way, he is certain of Babylon's fall. In judgment God will often use a pagan nation to punish Israel for her sins. However, the pagan nation does not escape His judgment in return. So here Babylonia's avenger is blessed: *"Happy* ['Blessed," plural of fullness] *shall he be who repays you* [Babylon] *as you have served* ['rewarded'] *us!"* In other words, "Blessed is he who gives you what you deserve." In a violent metaphor, *"Happy shall he be who takes and dashes / Your little ones against the rock"* (v. 9). That is, "Blessed is he who cuts off your next generation," who engages in a war of annihilation. With this, the psalm abruptly ends.

Rather than singing the song of Zion in exile, the psalmist (whether still there or now having returned to Jerusalem in verses 5–6) curses himself if he should forget God's city and blesses the one who will destroy Babylon. Having experienced God's judgment by the Exile, he knows the sorrow and the songs of slavery. He knows the blues. There will be no joyful singing in Babylon. This is reserved for the presence of God.

We too are exiles in a foreign land, knowing that our citizenship is in heaven (Phil. 3:20). Nevertheless, because our Savior has come, we have a taste of home. Because His Kingdom has broken in upon us, we can sing the songs of Zion here. We no longer have to journey to Jerusalem to find God's temple. Jerusalem has come to us, as God's Spirit has been poured into our hearts. Even by the rivers of Babylon, or New York or Paris, we can sing the Lord's song and exalt Jerusalem above our chief joy (v. 6).

Why Worship?

Psalm 138

What will get us to show up for the public worship of God? There are many answers to this question. As Professor C. Peter Wagner of Fuller Theological Seminary points out, there are churches that present themselves as teaching centers where we come to learn. Everybody in attendance has an open Bible. There are also churches that present themselves as social centers, engaged in the crises of our time. These congregations are issue-oriented and pride themselves as being on the cutting edge. Then there are churches designed strictly for inspiration; they are sort of spiritual shopping centers for all our needs. Their pastors smile a lot and are upbeat, with how-to sermons. Other churches flourish ministering to the "rock" generation, with an informal, contemporary format in worship.

Some people show up at these churches in order to engage in public worship out of a sense of history or tradition. In parts of the world, church attendance is still an expected ritual. Others worship publicly in order to assuage guilt or to satisfy family expectations. Some even go to church in order to gain favor with God, as if He is impressed with our attendance. Then there are those who attend because of a pastor's pressure, or for business contacts or a Friday-night date. Some even appear occasionally with a vague feeling that it is good for them. Others come out of desperation, sincerely looking for God. Then there are those who worship out of disciplined discipleship. They are present, not so much to get, as to give. They hunger to give themselves to God in praise and to give themselves to each other in love and ministry. Some today even anticipate that when they attend worship, God may speak directly to them or release the gifts of His Spirit within them for ministry in the moment

476

(see 1 Corinthians 12). These more charismatically oriented churches appear vital to some and chaotic to others. But why should we engage in public worship, really?

Psalm 138 addresses the issue of motives in worship. For the psalmist, worship begins with the character of God. He is to be worshiped for who He is: for His covenant-love and His truth (v. 2). But how is this to be known? The answer is that God Himself speaks and acts when we call upon Him. God has "magnified" His words (v. 2) and answered prayer (v. 3). He has had regard for the lowly (v. 6), bringing revival (v. 7). He acts against the psalmist's enemies (v. 7), saving him by the works of His hands (v. 8). In sum, God is to be worshiped because of His word (He reveals Himself) and His work (He acts upon our behalf). These two facts should bring us to our knees in submission and to our feet in praise.

Commentators describe Psalm 138 as an individual psalm of thanksgiving. While tradition gives it to David as the author, its language seems at points to be close to Isaiah 40ff. The thought moves from a confession of personal praise (vv. 1-3) to a vision of universal praise (vv. 4-6) and ends with confidence in divine protection (vv. 7-8).

PERSONAL PRAISE

> 138:1 I will praise You with my whole heart;
>   Before the gods I will sing praises to You.
>   2 I will worship toward Your holy temple,
>   And praise Your name
>   For Your lovingkindness and Your truth;
>   For You have magnified Your word above all
>   Your name.
>   3 In the day when I cried out, You answered me,
>   *And* made me bold *with* strength in my soul.
>   Ps. 138:1-3

The psalmist begins verse 1 confessing that he will *"praise"* God, as he says, *"with my whole heart."* This includes both his mental and emotional capacities. Thus he will fulfill the Great Commandment to love God with all that he is (see Deut. 6:4–5). He will sing praises to Yahweh *"before the gods."* The *"gods"* (*ʾĕlōhîm*) can best be understood as "heavenly beings." The Septuagint rightly translates "angels." They make up the divine court gathered around Yahweh who is King (cf. Ps. 103:20–21). At the same time, the psalmist doesn't simply worship toward heaven and the heavenly host; he also worships facing the Jerusalem temple, or in the temple facing the holy of holies, because there is where the presence and the name of God dwell on earth (v. 2; cf. Dan. 6:10). Thus God is to be worshiped as both the transcendent and the immanent King. We now know Him as the God who reigns in glory and who also comes to us in humility and in our humanity in His Son, the ultimate expression of His immanence.

Having told us what he does in worship in verses 1–2a, the psalmist tells us his motives in verses 2b–3. He praises God for His *"lovingkindness"* ("covenant-love," "mercy," see Psalm 136), and His *"truth"* ("trustworthiness"). The psalmist continues: *"For You have magnified Your word above all Your name."* He probably means by this that God's present revelation surpasses that which we have known of Him in the past and therefore that which we have associated with His name. To put it colloquially, "You have outdone Yourself." This magnifying of His word is seen in verse 3 in answered prayer: *"In the day when I cried out, / You answered me, / And made me bold* ["set me up"] *with strength in my soul."* There is nothing which will expand our understanding of God and give us spiritual vitality like answered prayer. Why then do we not experience more answers? It is simple. Because we don't pray. As James says, "You do not have because you do not ask" (James 4:2).

UNIVERSAL PRAISE

> 138:4 All the kings of the earth shall praise You, O
> LORD,
>   When they hear the words of Your mouth.
>   5 Yes, they shall sing of the ways of the LORD,
>   For great *is* the glory of the LORD.
>   6 Though the LORD *is* on high,
>   Yet He regards the lowly;
>   But the proud He knows from afar.
> *Ps. 138:4–6*

The psalmist shows us his eschatological vision. He sees the universal praise of God, from the greatest, *"all the kings of the earth"* (v. 4), to the least, *"the lowly"* (v. 6). The kings will *"praise You, O Lord, / When they hear the words of Your mouth"* (v. 4). As they submit to Yahweh and His words, so also their kingdoms will join in. As Isaiah says, all the nations will flow to Zion (Isa. 2:2). Once God's Son rules there, He will have the nations as His inheritance (Ps. 2:8). Their kings and judges are now exhorted: "Serve the Lord with fear, / And rejoice with trembling. / Kiss the Son, lest He be angry, / And you perish in the way" (Ps. 2:11–12).

Not only will the kings praise God for His word, they will also *"sing of the ways of the Lord"* (v. 5). The reason for this is that the *"glory of the Lord"* is *"great."* His glory, however, is not merely seen as kings worship Him. Although He is *"on high,"* at the same time, *"He regards the lowly."* He incorporates them into His kingdom, because, in their brokenness, they are closer to Him than the *"proud"* who *"He knows from afar"* (v. 6), that is, to whom He is distant. Here is the universality of our God. He is great enough for kings and lowly enough for the poor and abased. He is the mighty Warrior who comes with His arm ruling for Him, but He is also the tender shepherd, carrying His little lambs in His bosom (Isa. 40:10–11). When God acts, all the nations and their peoples, from the greatest to the least, will join in the psalmist's personal worship expounded in verses 1–3.

DIVINE PROTECTION

138:7 Though I walk in the midst of trouble, You will
        revive me;
      You will stretch out Your hand
      Against the wrath of my enemies,
      And Your right hand will save me.
    8 The LORD will perfect *that which* concerns me;
      Your mercy, O LORD, *endures* forever;
      Do not forsake the works of Your hands.
                                        Ps. 138:7-8

The psalmist moves from His worship of God for His word (v. 2) to the worship of God for His works. First, God revives him, or makes him alive, *"in the midst of trouble* ["distress"]." Second, He stretches His *"hand"* out *"against the wrath"* of his *"enemies,"* and His *"right hand"* (His power and authority, see Exod. 15:6) saves or delivers him (v. 7). Third, God perfects or completes *"that which concerns"* him, as His *"mercy* ["covenant-love"; see v. 2] *endures forever."* A final plea concludes the psalm: *"Do not forsake the works of Your hands"* (v. 8). This is probably a reference to Israel as God's creation.

God is to be worshiped because He renews us and delivers us in the midst of our troubles from our enemies. He also completes His work in us, because He is true to His covenant-love, which lasts for all eternity. What should draw us into public worship? Why should we praise God with our whole heart (v. 1) before His angels and in His temple? The answer is clear. God is God. He keeps His covenant. His word is magnified as He answers our prayers. All the nations will worship Him. In the meantime, He works on our behalf. He delivers us from our enemies and completes His work in us. As Paul tells the Philippians: "being confident of this very thing, that He who has begun a good work in you will complete it until the day of Jesus Christ" (Phil. 1:6). Here is answer enough to the question: "Why worship?"

CHAPTER ONE HUNDRED THIRTY-NINE

God's Intimacy with Us

Psalm 139

It is clear today that many people suffer from a lack of intimate relationships. Our technological society has made it possible for us to live in one city, work in another, and relate to people in another. This has led to a significant breakdown in community. At the same time, we function in a highly competitive society. We tend to look upon people as combatants rather than as companions. We constantly judge how we are measuring up and find little freedom to share our struggles and our weaknesses with each other for fear that they will be used against us. In this decade, style has replaced substance as our preoccupation. We are excessively concerned about the image that we project to people, because we are uncertain that there is anything behind it. People also tend to become means to our ends, rather than ends in themselves. We all know how it feels to be used, stepped on, and stepped over. At the bottom of all of this is a spiritual sickness. Our lack of intimacy with each other comes from our lack of intimacy with God. The recovery of intimacy starts with allowing God to become intimate with us. This is what He desires, and He will do it if we will let Him.

Psalm 139 is compelling in its descriptions of how close God wants to be to us. He is not satisfied to be simply the reigning King, exalted in heaven, enthroned before a sea of angels. He desires to have a personal relationship with us on the deepest level. He searches and knows us (v. 1); His eye is always upon us (vv. 2–3). He hears all that we say (v. 4), and His hand is upon us (v. 5). All of this staggers the psalmist (v. 6). Moreover, God's presence is always there, in heaven or hell, in darkness or in light (vv. 7–12). But why is it that God knows us so intimately? The answer is that He has created us (vv. 13–16). He knows us the way a painter knows his picture, or a sculptor knows his statue. As a result of all of this, God's thoughts are precious to the psalmist (v. 17–18), and he hates those whom God hates (vv. 19–22). He concludes with an invitation for God to search him, try him, know him, and lead him "in the way everlasting" (vv. 23–24).

Commentators describe this psalm as a psalm of personal thanksgiving. Its authorship is ascribed to David. The thought moves from his being seen by God (vv. 1–6) to his being pursued by God (vv. 7–12), to his being fashioned by God (vv. 13–16), to his loving God's thoughts (vv. 17–18), to his hating God's enemies (vv. 19–22) and concludes with an invitation to intimacy (vv. 23–24).

SEEN BY GOD

139:1 O Lord, You have searched me and known *me*.
  2 You know my sitting down and my rising up;
     You understand my thought afar off.
  3 You comprehend my path and my lying down,
     And are acquainted with all my ways.
  4 For *there is* not a word on my tongue,
     But behold, O LORD, You know it altogether.
  5 You have hedged me behind and before,
     And laid Your hand upon me.
  6 *Such* knowledge *is* too wonderful for me;
     It is high, I cannot *attain* it.

Ps. 139:1–6

In verse 1 David establishes his thesis: *"O Lord, You have searched* ["examined"] *me and known me."* God is like a doctor giving us a physical. He is like a psychiatrist exploring our inner depths. He is like an intimate friend who probes us until we reveal all. As a result, He knows us. This is not just analytical knowledge; this is relational knowledge, that which is gained from intimacy. Verse 2 elaborates on this thesis. God knows when we sit down and when we rise up. Even though He is the exalted Lord, He understands our thoughts *"from afar off."* Note that He doesn't merely know what we think; He *understands* what we think. He knows the hidden motives and agendas that stand behind our thought processes. Moreover, David continues, *"You comprehend* [literally, "winnow," "sift"] *my path and my lying down."* God's eye follows our course through the day and is upon us when we retire. The psalmist concludes: *"And* [You] *are acquainted with all my ways"* (v. 3). He knows what we think about people. He knows our motives as we talk with them and make promises to them. He knows the path we take through the day, each pause, each detour.

God knows every word on David's tongue; He knows it *"altogether"* (v. 4). If no thought escapes Him (v. 2), then certainly no word escapes Him either. All of our communication is monitored by Him, and He clearly knows us better than we know ourselves. I cannot help but speculate how my own thoughts and words would change if I really believed this, or, better, experienced this, knowing the active presence of God in my life moment by moment. As Paul says, his goal is to bring every thought into captivity "to the obedience of Christ" (2 Cor. 10:5). Can we desire less?

God not only knows our speech; He also protects us from all harm. As David confesses: *"You have hedged* ["bound," "enclosed"] *me behind and before, / And laid Your hand upon me"* (v. 5). Like a human father, God goes before us and behind us, as His hand guides us. He is not only distant in glory; He is present in care and concern. Now staggered by the overwhelming sense of God as God, David concludes that all of this is *"too wonderful* ["marvelous," "miraculous"] *for me; / It is high, I cannot attain it"* (v. 6). Indeed, he cannot and would not apart from divine revelation.

PURSUED BY GOD

139:7 Where can I go from Your Spirit?
       Or where can I flee from Your presence?
    8 If I ascend into heaven, You *are* there;
       If I make my bed in hell, behold, You *are there.*
    9 *If* I take the wings of the morning,
       And dwell in the uttermost parts of the sea,
   10 Even there Your hand shall lead me,
       And Your right hand shall hold me.
   11 If I say, "Surely the darkness shall fall on me,"
       Even the night shall be light about me;
   12 Indeed, the darkness shall not hide from You,
       But the night shines as the day;
       The darkness and the light *are* both alike *to You.*
                                              Ps. 139:7–12

While David's first response to the presence of God in his life is wonder (v. 6), his next response seems to be flight (v. 7). It is as if he wants to run away from the intimacy that God wants with him. But, he cannot do it. Thus he asks rhetorically: *"Where can I go from Your Spirit?"* The answer is "Nowhere" (cf. Rom. 8:38–39). Again, he asks: *"Or where can I flee from Your presence* [literally, "face"]?" Again, the answer is, "Nowhere." If David goes up into heaven, God is there. If he goes down into *"hell"* (*Sheol*, the abode of the dead), he says, *"behold, You are there"* (v. 8). God commands His whole creation; there is no corner in which He is absent, either in life or in death.

After having lived the early part of my Christian life in the western United States, I remember taking the plane to New York for college. It was my first time that far away from parents and home. When I stepped off the aircraft at La Guardia Airport, I remember praying and feeling the presence of God. I thought to myself, "He is here just as in California." Indeed, like David, I have never been able to escape Him.

David continues that if he takes the *"wings of the morning"* (literally, "the dawn," the east), and dwells *"in the uttermost parts* [or *"end"*] *of the sea* [the far west]," it makes no difference. He continues, *"Even there Your hand shall lead me, / And Your right hand* [Your power, Exod. 15:6] *shall hold me"* (v. 10). He is guided and protected, held by God, wherever he goes. If he cannot escape geographically, perhaps he can try to hide in the darkness. This doesn't work either. He says, *"Even the night shall be light about me"* (v. 11). As if to underscore this thought, he adds, *"Indeed, the darkness shall not hide from You, / But the night shines as the day."* Both darkness and light are the same to God (v. 12). He made them (Gen. 1:4–5); He commands them. There is no escape in them.

Once we are known by God we cannot flee His presence. He is everywhere, and He will personally pursue us, wherever we go. We will run into Him at every turn. We cannot escape Him in the darkness, even the darkness of our own souls. He is a jealous lover, and His love will not be denied.

FASHIONED BY GOD

139:13 For You formed my inward parts;
      You covered me in my mother's womb.
   14 I will praise You, for I am fearfully *and*
        wonderfully made;
      Marvelous are Your works,
      And *that* my soul knows very well.
   15 My frame was not hidden from You,
      When I was made in secret,
      And skillfully wrought in the lowest parts of
        the earth.
   16 Your eyes saw my substance, being yet
        unformed.

And in Your book they all were written,
The days fashioned for me,
When *as yet there were* none of them.

Ps. 139:13-16

How can it be that God knows our very thoughts as well as our words? Is it because there is a divine bugging device in our brains? To be sure, part of the answer is in divine omniscience. Another part of the answer, however, is that God has made us, and He knows how we work. David confesses: *"You have formed* ["created"] *my inward parts* ["reins," the seat of conscience]." Moreover, *"You have covered me in my mother's womb"* (v. 13). The verb rendered *"covered"* is better taken as "woven together," like a cloth on a loom. The wonder of his own creation brings David to conclude: *"I will praise You, for I am fearfully and wonderfully* ["marvelously"] *made."* Who has not had a sense of awe in considering how the human brain works or how the immune system attacks infection. The scientific study of the human body can only underscore David's conclusion a thousandfold. He adds: *"Marvelous are Your works, / And that my soul knows very well"* (v. 14). He gives his own witness to the reality; it is as if he says, "Amen," to God's great works. Notice that David does not assume a position of objectivity as he views himself. He is in constant devotion and praise to God for His creation as he moves from description to worship.

In verse 15 David continues: *"My frame* ["bone"] *was not hidden from You, / When I was made in secret* [that is, in the womb, unobserved]." God saw and knew what his structure was to be. He continues that he was *"skillfully wrought* ["embroidered," like a color- ful piece of cloth] *in the lowest parts of the earth* [in parallel to "in secret" above, another metaphor for the womb]." What is hidden to us, however, is not hidden to God. He is the Creator. Thus *"Your eyes saw my substance* ["embryo"], *being yet unformed."* There could be no stronger statement concerning the sanctity and dignity of the un- born child than is given in this verse and its context. Like Jeremiah, we are known to God before He forms us in the womb (Jer. 1:5). This is a foundational text for anti-abortion forces, who defend the rights of the unborn child.

Not only does God know us in the womb; He also knows us be- yond the womb. He knows our whole life. David continues that God writes all of our days which He has *"fashioned"* ("formed," "devised")

for us in His book. This is no journal or court record made moment
by moment. These days are fashioned *"when as yet there were none of
them"* (v. 16). God is sovereign. He not only sees the end from the
beginning; He molds it. Our own freedom and the workings of
the devil are always secondary to the reign of God over our lives.
God is not caught by surprise, and His will *will* be done.

I LOVE YOUR THOUGHTS

139:17 How precious also are Your thoughts to me, O
       God!
       How great is the sum of them!
    18 *If* I should count them, they would be more in
       number than the sand;
       When I awake, I am still with You.
                                        Ps. 139:17–18

David lyrically expresses his wonder at all that God has revealed.
He confesses that His thoughts are *"precious"; "How great is the sum of
them!"* (v. 17). The context for this remark is the preceding verses. As
David has surveyed God's knowledge of him, His presence with him,
and His creation of Him, he has seen much of the greatness of God's
thoughts. Indeed, there is a divine order to life. God does not merely
create us and then let us go. He rules over His creation, and He rules
over us. His thoughts toward us moment by moment are overwhelming. David says that they outnumber the sand itself. While billions of
prayers may ascend to God each day, untold billions of messages
come from Him to us, as He answers our prayers and intimately
guides us through each moment. David concludes, *"When I awake, I
am still with You"* (v. 18). He may have lost consciousness of God in
sleep, but God never lost consciousness of him. No wonder David
loves His thoughts, which come to him like the rays of the sun.

I HATE YOUR ENEMIES

139:19 Oh, that You would slay the wicked, O God!
       Depart from me, therefore, you bloodthirsty
       men.

20 For they speak against You wickedly;
   Your enemies take *Your name* in vain.
21 Do I not hate them, O LORD, who hate You?
   And do I not loathe those who rise up against
      You?
22 I hate them with perfect hatred;
   I count them my enemies.

Ps. 139:19–22

Verse 19 marks an abrupt transition. David turns from the greatness of God's thoughts to the vileness of His enemies. With a longing
for justice, he cries out for God to *"slay the wicked"* ("criminals").
He commands: *"Depart from me, therefore, you bloodthirsty men"*
(literally, "you men of blood," that is, "murderers"). The reason for
David's moral indignation is that these evil people *"speak against You
wickedly; / Your enemies take Your name in vain"* (v. 20). Thus his concern is for God's honor. His commitment is clear; he hates those who
hate God and loathes (or is grieved with) those who rebel against
Him (v. 21). His hatred, his moral outrage is complete: *"I hate them
with perfect hatred."* Since they have rejected God, David rejects them
(v. 22).

David's strong reaction is not against "sinners." He is not a self-
righteous judge who will not stain himself with this world. His
reaction is against those who revile God's name, who are His enemies (v. 20). It is those who hate God and rise up against Him that
incur his wrath. And why is this so? Because the God who is so
exquisitely described in verses 1–18 deserves our praise and worship. To withhold this is to deserve both human and divine wrath.

INVITATION TO INTIMACY

139:23 Search me, O God, and know my heart;
       Try me, and know my anxieties;
    24 And see if *there is any* wicked way in me,
       And lead me in the way everlasting.

Ps. 139:23–24

Having judged God's enemies, David is quite willing to place himself under the same judgment—to have the Lord turn the spotlight on

his inner being. Thus he prays: *"Search* ["examine"] *me, O God, and know my heart."* In inviting God to become intimate with him, he is only responding to the reality that God has already searched him and known him (see v. 1). When we submit to God's work in our lives, we grant Him permission to do that which He has already purposed. Our dignity is not in overturning His sovereignty, but in freely submitting to it. As God knows David, David will know himself. But his goal is not merely self-knowledge; his goal is righteousness. Thus he continues: *"Try me, and know my anxieties* ["misgivings"]*"* (v. 23). He wants God to search out his cares, those things that would challenge his faith and lead him into sin. He continues, *"And see if there is any wicked way* ["painful, grieving way"] *in me."* Have his cares led to sin? Is there something he doesn't know about that needs to be changed in him? David does not only want to know his deviations, however. If they are there, he wants to be corrected and restored: *"And lead me in the way everlasting"* (v. 24). Having come from God, he wants to go to God. The way everlasting is the way home to the Father's heart.

This is the intimacy that God wants to have with us. He formed us in the womb. He knows our frame. He sees our embryo. He fashions our days. He knows our thoughts. He hears our words. He knows when we sit down and when we stand up. He protects us. His hand is upon us. He who inhabits all things is near to us. We cannot escape His presence. In the light He sees us. In the dark He sees us. We are the continual object of His thoughts. He searches us. He changes us. Here is true intimacy, and if we can allow God to become intimate with us, we can establish a growing intimacy with each other. Secure in His presence and His love, we can risk opening up. We can even risk rejection, because we are held in His hand (v. 10).

Prayer for Deliverance

Psalm 140

Throughout the Old Testament we find records of warfare. In one sense the history of Israel is a history of her battles. These altercations are not only on a national scale, such as in the Exodus; they are also very personal. Again and again we see lying, deception, plots, and counterplots. The court history of David is filled with such intrigue. The Old Testament is not distant from our own experience. We too live in the midst of warfare. With the nuclear standoff, we have been spared another world war, but we have been a party to many smaller conflicts. Some, such as Korea and Vietnam, have left many of our own people dead or wounded.

Beside national and international issues, however, are the personal conflicts that we find ourselves engaged in regularly. Human relationships are fragile. They tend to break down, because of overt sin, but also because of failures to communicate, fears, the projection of our own issues onto other people—the list goes on and on. It is in this context that Psalm 140 leaves the world of ancient Israel and enters our world. We too have our battles.

This psalm centers in conflict. Evil, violent men are attacking (vv. 1, 4). They make evil plans and plot war (v. 2). They also have poison tongues (v. 3). They are proud; they set traps (v. 5). A battle looms (v. 7). The psalmist therefore pronounces judgment upon them in a series of curses (vv. 9–11). He is confident that the Lord will maintain the cause of the afflicted, the poor, and the upright (vv. 12–13).

Commentators identify this psalm as a personal lament. Authorship is given to David. The thought moves from petitions (vv. 1–5) to a confession of faith and intercession (vv. 6–8), to curses (vv. 9–11) and concludes with a personal confession (vv. 12–13).

PETITIONS

140:1 Deliver me, O LORD, from evil men;
  Preserve me from violent men,

 2 Who plan evil things in *their* hearts;
  They continually gather together *for* war.

 3 They sharpen their tongues like a serpent;
  The poison of asps *is* under their lips. Selah

 4 Keep me, O LORD, from the hands of the
   wicked;
  Preserve me from violent men,
  Who have purposed to make my steps
   stumble.

 5 The proud have hidden a snare for me, and
   cords;
  They have spread a net by the wayside;
  They have set traps for me. Selah

           Ps. 140:1–5

Verse 1 begins a series of petitions as David deals with his enemies. Structurally, verses 1–3 and 4–5 are parallel to each other. Each section begins with a prayer for deliverance, which is followed by a description of the wicked. David opens this psalm praying: *"Deliver me, O Lord, from evil* ["bad," "malignant"] *men,"* adding the request that God will *"preserve"* him from *"violent men."* But who are these people? Verses 2–3 answer this question.

First of all, they *"plan* ["devise"] *evil things in their hearts."* Their evil is premeditated. In whatever is left of our humanistic optimism, we still have trouble admitting that there are people who are not merely maladjusted or sick, but morally evil. Even after Hitler and Stalin we tend to deny this. Nevertheless, I have seen it in the faces of drug dealers in the seaside town of La Jolla, California where I live. I know of people who would kill to punish for a bad drug debt. I know of people who prey upon small children, seeking to entice them into addiction and even prostitution. This is evil, and they are evil.

David experiences this premeditated evil from those who *"continually gather together for war"* (v. 2). In the context of his descriptions here and the history of his own life, we may assume that this means civil war. There are those who plot against his reign, and in so doing they are plotting against God's anointed. Initially they are engaged in a war of words. Thus in verse 3: *"They sharpen their tongues like a serpent; / The poison* ["wrath"] *of asps* [probably the Egyptian cobra] *is under their lips."* Culturally, the serpent is seen as wise and crafty. He has a sharp tongue for intrigue, making him an apt instrument for Adam's and Eve's temptation in Genesis 3. At the same time, his bite can be deadly, as it certainly is in the case of these plotters. The description of depravity here is later used by Paul as a generalization to document the sinfulness of the whole race (Rom. 3:13). We all must admit that the same potential for sin lurks in us as in these depraved men. We all have a little Adolf Hitler inside of us wishing to get out and rule our world. We all have wild animals within (caged for the most part); only occasionally do they break loose in fits of rage or hatred.

David asks again: *"Keep me, O Lord, from the hands* [power] *of the wicked* ["lawbreakers"]." He adds the same parallel member as in verse 1: *"Preserve me from violent men"* (v. 4). Who are these men? They are the ones who plan to make him *"stumble"* (literally, "to thrust down my steps"). They are the *"proud"* (often used to describe those who rebel against God's law and go their own way; see Ps. 119:122), who want him to fly into their *"snare"* ("bird trap") like a wild bird. They want their net to fall upon him. They want him to fall into their *"traps"* (literally, a bait or lure in a fowler's net, v. 5). In other words, their plotting (v. 2) and their verbal assaults (v. 3) have gone into action. An ambush has been set for David.

CONFESSION AND INTERCESSION

140:6 I said to the LORD: "You *are* my God;
    Hear the voice of my supplications, O LORD.
  7 O GOD the Lord, the strength of my salvation,
    You have covered my head in the day of
       battle.
  8 Do not grant, O LORD, the desires of the
       wicked;
    Do not further his *wicked* scheme,
    Lest they be exalted.   Selah

                      Ps. 140:6-8

David's response to assault is prayer. As he turns to God, he makes his confession: *"You are my God . . . O God the Lord* [Yahweh], *the strength of my salvation* ["deliverance," or "my strong deliverer"], / *You have covered my head in the day of battle'"* (vv. 6–7). God is his protection, his helmet. Because of who God is, David asks Him to hear his *"supplications"* ("requests for favor or grace," v. 6). Their content is given in verse 8.

David asks that the desires of the wicked not be granted, that the *"wicked scheme"* not succeed, as he says, *"Lest they be exalted."* David comes against his enemies in prayer; they will be defeated by Yahweh Himself. It is God who will confuse their plans. It is God who will keep them from winning and exalting themselves. I believe this is the test of faith. Do we really believe in the justice of our cause, and are we willing to allow God to act on our behalf, or, do we have to take matters into our own hands? Can we trust Him to vindicate His work and to vindicate us? If not, then we will try to work it out for ourselves and, may I add, fail.

CURSES

> 140:9 *"As for* the head of those who surround me,
>   Let the evil of their lips cover them;
>   10 Let burning coals fall upon them;
>   Let them be cast into the fire,
>   Into deep pits, that they rise not up again.
>   11 Let not a slanderer be established in the earth;
>   Let evil hunt the violent man to overthrow
>   *him."*
>
> Ps. 140:9–11

David pronounces curses upon his enemies. He wants God to bring down judgment upon their *"head"*; he wants them to get a taste of their own medicine. This includes *"the evil* ["grievousness"] *of their lips"* (see v. 3) coming back upon them to *"cover them"* (v. 9). Moreover, he calls down *"burning coals"* to fall upon them and asks God to *"Let them be cast into the fire,"* the fire of judgment. Since his enemies sought to trap him like a wild bird, he consigns them to fall into a trap from which they will never be free (v. 10). David also desires justice to prevail, as he says, *"Let not a slanderer* [literally, "the man of (false) tongue] *be established in the earth"* (v. 11). Rather than evil being used against David, *"evil"* (see v. 1) will *"hunt the violent* [see v. 4] *man to overthrow him"* (v. 11). All of these curses will be the answer to his prayer in verses 6–8. They are not consequences of a bad temper. They are consequences of facing real evil and of wanting God's righteousness to be vindicated on this planet. We can only join David in these prayers if we have his heart. At the same time, the reality of God's judgment is not the last word in this world. However much we may be morally incensed against evil people, Jesus calls upon us to love our enemies and to forgive them. When we know the depths of evil, and experience our own moral revulsion, we will be ready for the gospel. The final word in this world is the message that while we were yet sinners Christ died for us (Rom. 5:8).

CONFESSION

140:12 I know that the LORD will maintain
        The cause of the afflicted,
        And justice for the poor.
   13 Surely the righteous shall give thanks to Your
           name;
        The upright shall dwell in Your presence.
                                        Ps. 140:12-13

David confesses God's heart for the lowly and downcast. God goes into battle (v. 7) for their sake. Thus David is certain (*"I know"*) that Yahweh will *"maintain / The cause of the afflicted, / And justice for the poor"* (v. 12). Jesus promises, "Blessed are you poor, / For yours is the Kingdom of God" (Luke 6:20). As God defends them, the *"righteous,"* those who belong to the covenant, will give *"thanks to Your name,"* and the *"upright"* will live (*"dwell"*) before God, in His *"presence"* (*"face"*). It is God who will resolve our battle with evil in this world; He will deliver us. We cannot and must not deliver ourselves. Justice is in His hands. He will defeat our enemies. His ultimate victory is in His Son at the cross, where sin, Satan, and death were done in. He will defend the poor and needy, and those who know Him and love Him will live with Him forever.

Praying against the Deeds of the Wicked

Psalm 141

Evil strikes a chord in our hearts. If it did not have a landing place there, temptation would be a nonissue. We would have no moral dilemmas to face. One of the consequences of the gift of freedom is that we can violate this gift. When we have a real choice to make, we can choose evil. Even the greatest saint has the potential of being the greatest sinner. The godly person recognizes this. The closer we draw to God, the more we become aware of our own mixed motives and the potential residing within us to do evil.

This psalm is realistic about the infection that evil can bring. If we traffic with it, it may well traffic with us. Thus the psalmist prays for God to guard his mouth and his lips and turn his heart from "any evil thing." He asks for protection against the allure of the "delicacies" of men who work iniquity (v. 4). Recognizing his own vulnerability, he asks for the reproof of the righteous (v. 5) and God's judgment upon the wicked (v. 5c–6). At the same time, the psalmist vows to keep his eyes on God and asks to be delivered from the snares that the evil have laid for him (vv. 8–10).

Commentators identify this psalm as an individual lament. Its authorship is traditionally given to David. The thought moves from a prayer for protection (vv. 1–4) to self-curses (v. 5) and concludes with intercession against the wicked (vv. 5c–10).

PRAYER FOR PROTECTION

141:1 Lord, I cry out to You;
　　　Make haste to me!

Give ear to my voice when I cry out to You.

2 Let my prayer be set before You *as* incense,
The lifting up of my hands *as* the evening
sacrifice.

3 Set a guard, O LORD, over my mouth;
Keep watch over the door of my lips.

4 Do not incline my heart to any evil thing,
To practice wicked works
With men who work iniquity;
And do not let me eat of their delicacies.

Ps. 141:1-4

Verse 1 opens with David's prayer: *"Lord, I cry out to You."* He calls
out for Him to come, asking for a sense of His presence. For emphasis
(and with a sense of urgency) he adds, *"Give ear to my voice when I cry
out to You."* For God to give him His ear is for Him to hear his intercession. As David prays elsewhere: *"*I have called upon You, for You
will hear me, O God; / Incline Your ear to me, and hear my speech*"
(Ps. 17:6). Now he asks that his prayer may be as *"incense"* ascending
from the altar (Exod. 35:15). He asks that the lifting up of his hands
before God (cf. Ps. 134:2) be received *"as the* [regular] *evening sacrifice"* (not in place of it, v. 2; see 1 Kings 18:29). His prayer is an act of
worship.

The content of David's prayer is given in verses 3-4. He asks first
for God to place a *"guard"* over his mouth, and adds in parallel: *"Keep
watch over the door of my lips"* (v. 3). His desire is that no evil word
passes from him. Behind guarding our mouths, however, is the issue
of our hearts. When that is solved, our speech will no longer trouble
us. As Jesus says, *"*There is nothing that enters a man from outside
which can defile him . . . What comes out of a man, that defiles a
man. For from within, out of the heart of men, proceed evil thoughts,
adulteries, fornications, murders, thefts, covetousness, wickedness,
deceit, lewdness, an evil eye, blasphemy, pride, foolishness. All
these evil things come from within and defile a man'" (Mark 7:15,
20-23). Thus David immediately adds, *"Do not incline my heart to any
evil thing, / To practice wicked works* ["criminal acts"] / *With men who
work iniquity* ["stray from the straight path"]." Knowing his potential
for evil, he continues: *"And do not let me eat of their delicacies"* (v. 4;
cf. Dan. 1:8). He knows that his heart can be turned toward evil and
prays against that real temptation. He knows that the table of men

who work iniquity has an attraction to him, and he prays that the Lord will arm him in the fight against temptation. Spiritual battles must be fought spiritually, and for this reason he prays. After Paul exhorts us to put on our spiritual armor in order to stand against the devil, he tells us to pray without ceasing (Eph. 6:18). We move forward in this war on our knees.

SELF-CURSES

> 141:5 Let the righteous strike me;
> *It shall be* a kindness.
> And let him rebuke me;
> *It shall be* as excellent oil;
> Let my head not refuse it.
>
> *Ps. 141:5a–b*

David's prayer for protection is followed by curses that he makes against himself if he should sin. These underscore the seriousness of his prayer. He begins: *"Let the righteous strike me; / It shall be a kindness."* Perhaps this blow will bring him back to reality, a physical "wake-up call." He continues: *"And let him rebuke ["reprove"] me; / It shall be as excellent oil* [literally, "oil of the head"]." That is, fine oil. He adds, *"Let my head not refuse it."* That which may hurt (a reproof) is actually a blessing, and David asks to welcome it as he would anointing oil. We are now certain that he does not want to traffic with "wicked works" or "men who work iniquity" (v. 4). If he does, he will bring these curses upon himself. He wants his sin to be interrupted as he himself is exposed to the light.

INTERCESSION AGAINST THE WICKED

> 141:5 For still my prayer *is* against the deeds of the
> wicked.
> 6 Their judges are overthrown by the sides of
> the cliff,
> And they hear my words, for they are sweet.
> 7 Our bones are scattered at the mouth of the
> grave,

As when one plows and breaks up the earth.
8 But my eyes *are* upon You, O GOD the Lord;
   In You I take refuge;
   Do not leave my soul destitute.
9 Keep me from the snares they have laid for
      me,
   And from the traps of the workers of iniquity.
10 Let the wicked fall into their own nets,
   While I escape safely.

Ps. 141:5c–10

After David has prayed for himself, to be protected in his heart from evil, and cursed himself if he falls, he prays against evildoers. He says, *"For still my prayer is against the deeds of the wicked* [literally, *"their evils"]"* (v. 5c). In verse 6 he says, *"Their judges are overthrown by the sides of the cliff."* The Hebrew can be taken temporally, that is, "When their judges." Thus David says that when the leaders (judges) of the wicked are judged, *"they hear my words, for they are sweet."* His words, which are true, will be accepted when they face reality. Nevertheless, David still suffers. Thus in verse 7 his bones are like those *"scattered at the mouth of the grave"* (or *sheol*, "the abode of the dead") when a plow cuts up the earth over an old burial site. For this reason he cries out to God, seeking refuge in the hour of trial (v. 8). He asks God not to let him down: *"Do not leave my soul destitute* ["bare"]." Next, David prays for protection. He asks God to keep him from *"the snares* [literally, "the hands of the snare"] *which they* [the evil people] *have laid for me"* (cf. Ps. 140:5). These are the *"traps of the workers of iniquity"* (v. 9), who want to net him like a wild bird.

David concludes this psalm with a curse on the evildoers: *"Let the wicked fall into their own nets"* (cf. Ps. 9:16). And he adds, *"While I escape safely* [or, "pass by"]" (v. 10). Since he has prayed against the evil and since he has asked for his own protection, he is confident that God will answer. The temptations of those who work iniquity will not overwhelm him; he will escape, while they fall into their own traps, and he will walk on in the will of God.

Only recently have I begun to pray actively for God's protection against my enemies because only recently have I seen clearly that I am engaged in hand-to-hand combat with Satan and his demonic hosts. This puts my life at risk. There are casualties in spiritual warfare. At the same time, Jesus is greater than the devil and has defeated him at the cross. Therefore, I pray for His protection over myself, my wife, our house, our automobiles, our pets, our larger family, our relationships, and the totality of our lives in His name and by His blood. In prayer I find security as I walk with Him through this life.

CHAPTER ONE HUNDRED FORTY-TWO

Abandoned by All but God

Psalm 142

One of the most primitive experiences we have as small children is that of abandonment. Psychologists tell us that a baby feels this loss when his mother leaves the room. As she returns time after time, confidence is built that her leaving is not an ultimate loss, a death experience. Some children, however, do experience leaving as loss. This oftentimes has to do with the withholding of love, which far transcends physical absence. On the other hand, the value of being left physically (not emotionally) is that we can begin to believe that we can function on our own. Those who do not achieve this become obsessively dependent and fearful. A friend of mine was raised in a large family, the sixth child in line. Since he often wandered off alone, more than once he was forgotten as the family car pulled away from a vacation spot. In his adult years he still has fears of abandonment and has a hard time sleeping alone. The ultimate fear behind the fear of being left has nothing to do with people. It is the fear of our own mortality, the fear of death. In conquering this fear, we must replace our need of people and the emotional security of relating to them with a solid trust in God. He promises to never leave us, and He alone can back up that promise.

There is a stark loneliness in Psalm 142. The author complains: "there is no one who acknowledges me; / Refuge has failed me; / No one cares for my soul" (v. 4). With a sense of being overwhelmed (v. 3), he prays, bringing his complaint and trouble to the Lord (vv. 1–2). Why does he do this? Because God still knows his path (v. 3). Even though he has persecutors (v. 6) and his soul is in prison (v. 7), he knows that God can set him free. God is his refuge and portion (v. 5), and he will praise Him again (v. 7). There is light beyond the darkness. This is his answer to abandonment.

Commentators identify this psalm as an individual lament. Its authorship is given to David. The thought moves from his complaint (vv. 1–2) to his abandonment (vv. 3–4) and concludes with God's faithfulness (vv. 5–7).

COMPLAINT

142:1 I cry out to the LORD with my voice;
    With my voice to the LORD I make my
        supplication.
 2 I pour out my complaint before Him;
    I declare before Him my trouble.

Ps. 142:1-2

David cries out to God in verse 1. This is no silent prayer; he cries out, as he says, *"with my voice."* He clearly wants to get God's attention. I have seen people pray in crisis. I have heard them shout to God without liturgical language. In their pain they are raw and direct, reflecting many of the psalms. Emphatically, David adds: *"With my voice to the Lord I make my supplication"* (that is, "request for favor"). In verse 2 he continues: *"I pour out my complaint before Him,"* adding that this "complaint" presents his *"trouble"* ("pressure").

Clearly David is in pain. The good news is that he prays in his pain. He knows who he can go to. He knows God; he has walked with Him. In the crisis it is natural to turn to Him. The relationship we cultivate with Him day by day will become clear when we are faced with our crises, when we are abandoned, when we face the ultimate loss of death itself.

ABANDONED

142:3 When my spirit was overwhelmed within me,
    Then You knew my path.
    In the way in which I walk
    They have secretly set a snare for me.
  4 Look on *my* right hand and see,
    For *there is* no one who acknowledges me;
    Refuge has failed me;
    No one cares for my soul.

Ps. 142:3–4

We find out clearly why David is crying out to God. First, he tells us that his *"spirit was overwhelmed"* within him. Nevertheless, God knew it: *"Then You knew my path."* Thus God knew that David's enemies had *"secretly set a snare"* (as for a wild bird) for him (v. 3). The nature of this ambush is left open, but we know that he has been abandoned. As he says, *"Look on my right hand and see, / For there is no one who acknowledges me."* His right side, the place of power and authority, is empty. He adds, *"Refuge* ['flight," "place of escape'] *has failed me* [literally, "Refuge perished"]; / *No one cares for my soul."* He is alone and can't run anymore. Help has vanished.

Within all of this gloom, there is, however, a glimmer of light. It appears in verse 3 when David admits: *"You knew my path."* Regardless of how difficult the way, God knows. In Christ we have even a deeper truth than David could have known. God not only knows our way of sorrows; He has trod it. Therefore, we have a High Priest interceding for us who understands our pain, who has shared our loneliness, and who has experienced our rejection. We are to come boldly to Him *"that we may obtain mercy and find grace to help in time of need"* (Heb. 4:16).

GOD'S FAITHFULNESS

142:5 I cried out to You, O LORD:
    I said, "You *are* my refuge,
    My portion in the land of the living.
  6 Attend to my cry,
    For I am brought very low;
    Deliver me from my persecutors,

For they are stronger than I.
7 Bring my soul out of prison,
  That I may praise Your name;
  The righteous shall surround me,
  For You shall deal bountifully with me."

Ps. 142:5-7

With all human resources exhausted, David remembers: *"I cried out to You, O Lord"* (see vv. 1–2). Why does he call upon Yahweh? The answer follows: David told Him, *"'You are my refuge* ['shelter'].'" When no one else is there to protect him, when there is no place else to flee, God is there for him. God is his secure hiding place. He is also his *"portion in the land of the living"* (v. 5). The word *portion* can refer to a tract of land, booty from a battle, and the part of the sacrifice reserved for the priests before the altar. Thus God can be called the portion or possession of His servants. He alone satisfies them and meets their needs. As Psalm 73 puts it: "God is the strength of my heart and my portion forever" (Ps. 73:26). Based upon this confession of faith, David asks God to hear him and attend to him, *"For I am brought very low."* He prays for God to deliver him *"from my persecutors* ['pursuers']." He needs divine help, *"For they are stronger than I"* (v. 6). Moreover, he needs to be released from *"prison."* This represents the bondage of both the attack that he is experiencing and the overwhelming feelings that accompany it (see v. 3).

As a result of divine deliverance, David promises to praise God's *"name"* (which communicates His personhood and presence). His loneliness will be broken as the *"righteous,"* those who keep God's covenant, surround him. He concludes, *"'For You shall deal bountifully with me'"* (v. 7). Here is the resolution for David's experience of abandonment. God is still there for him, and because this is true, he believes that others will be there for him again also.

David's secret can be ours. We can overcome our own fears of abandonment, and the ultimate fear of death, as we cry out to the living God. He will be our refuge when all others fail (v. 5). But more than a place to hide, God will also be our *"portion,"* that is, He will be the satisfaction of our lives. I can believe this theologically. However, repeatedly in my life, like David, I have had to lose the little refuges I cherished most in order to know that God is still my ever-present refuge.

Big Prayer: Answer Me, Deliver Me, Revive Me

Psalm 143

The size of our prayers will depend upon the size of our God. I have often heard people say that they don't want to bother God with the little things of their lives. I suppose that means that they won't bother Him with most things in their lives, since life is largely made up of little things. The question isn't really whether God is too big and too busy to hear of their aches and pains; the real question is whether He cares at all, and if He does whether He will do anything about it. Since He is a loving Father, nothing is too incidental for Him.

Once again the psalmist is in crisis. He is persecuted, crushed, in death's darkness, overwhelmed, and distressed (vv. 3–4). He is thirsty for God (v. 6). His spirit fails (v. 7). Hounded by enemies, he needs deliverance (v. 9). His soul is in trouble and afflicted (vv. 11–12). In the context of all of this catastrophe, how should he pray? The answer is that since he has a big God, he prays big prayers. He is no stoic simply asking for the strength to endure. He is a biblical man. He wants God to act on his behalf. He wants answers (v. 7). He wants deliverance (v. 9). He wants revival (v. 11). He wants God to bring his soul out of trouble and destroy his enemies (vv. 11–12).

Commentators view this psalm as a personal lament. Tradition gives its authorship to David. The thought moves from a cry to God (vv. 1–2) to reflection on present loss and personal response (vv. 3–6) and concludes with a series of petitions for God to answer (vv. 7–8), for God to deliver (vv. 9–10), and for God to revive (vv. 11–12).

CRY TO GOD

143:1 Hear my prayer, O LORD,
       Give ear to my supplications!
       In Your faithfulness answer me,
       And in Your righteousness.
   2 Do not enter into judgment with Your servant,
       For in Your sight no one living is righteous.

Ps. 143:1–2

Verse 1 opens with a request: *"Hear my prayer, O Lord, / Give ear to my supplications* [request for mercy]!" David, however, does not merely want the satisfaction of knowing that almighty God has heard his prayer; he wants Him to act. Thus he continues, *"In Your faithfulness answer me / And in your righteousness."* God has made a covenant-treaty with His people. He will be faithful to it. His *"righteousness"* is seen as He upholds it. It is upon this basis, it is upon what He has done in binding Israel to Himself, that David can expect Him to hear and answer his petitions. It is for this reason that he continues, *"Do not enter into judgment with Your servant, / For in Your sight no one living is righteous"* (v. 2). Thus it is not by his works, by his merit, that he expects God to answer. If justice were the basis of their relationship, he would only be condemned, since no one is righteous before God. The basis for his prayers, however, is God's faithfulness and righteousness, and David counts on that as he prays.

This psalm opens with a strong gospel statement. Like David, it is not because of our works of righteousness that we can come to God. It is only on the basis of His mercy made known to us in Christ. We are righteous before God in the righteousness of His Son. This is His gift to us. This is the New Covenant in His blood, which cleanses us and makes us whole. When we pray to God in the name of His Son, we are claiming that covenant as the basis for His hearing and answering our prayers.

PRESENT LOSS AND PERSONAL RESPONSE

143:3 For the enemy has persecuted my soul;
       He has crushed my life to the ground;

503

He has made me dwell in darkness,
Like those who have long been dead.
4 Therefore my spirit is overwhelmed within
    me;
My heart within me is distressed.
5 I remember the days of old;
I meditate on all Your works;
I muse on the work of Your hands.
6 I spread out my hands to You;
My soul *longs* for You like a thirsty
    land.   Selah

Ps. 143:3–6

David recounts his present circumstances, and they are grim. He is under attack: *"The enemy has persecuted* ["pursued"] *my soul"* (see v. 9). The assault has been successful: *"He has crushed my life to the ground."* As a result, David feels like a dead man. He has been made to *"dwell in darkness* ["dark places," the darkness of the tomb], / *Like those who have long been dead* [or, "like the dead of old"]" (v. 3). As a result he suffers a deep depression: *"my spirit is overwhelmed within me; / My heart within me is distressed* ["desolate"]" (v. 4). He is broken as a total man, *"soul"* ("self"), *"spirit"* (animating breath of life), and *"heart"* (including mental faculties). What can he do? His response is given in verses 5–6.

First, David gets in touch with his memory, his past. He says, *"I remember the days of old; / I meditate on all Your works; / I muse on* [or, "study"] *the work of Your hands"* (v. 5). For meditation as audible recitation see our comments on Ps. 1:2. The object of David's thought and study is what Yahweh has done in history. He basks in the record of His mighty works in creation and redemption. Psalms such as 106 and 107 would be examples of such musing. Memory builds faith. As we see what God has done, our hearts cry out, "Do it again!"

Second, David turns naturally to prayer in verse 6: *"I spread out my hands to You."* Praying with his hands outstretched places him in the position of a supplicant coming with requests to a mighty king. This is the basic prayer posture of Israel (see Exod. 9:29; 1 Kings 8:22, 54; Ezra 9:5). The longing of his heart, however, is not just for relief from his distress. His longing is for God Himself: *"My soul longs for You like a thirsty land* [longs for water]." Here is the beginning of recovery from the assaults he has received. It is recovery in his prayer closet.

PETITION FOR GOD TO ANSWER

143:7 Answer me speedily, O LORD;
    My spirit fails!
    Do not hide Your face from me,
    Lest I be like those who go down into the pit.
   8 Cause me to hear Your lovingkindness in the
      morning,
    For in You do I trust;
    Cause me to know the way in which I should
      walk,
    For I lift up my soul to You.

Ps. 143:7–8

As David comes to the Lord in prayer, his major concern is to get some answers, as we noted above, not just to be granted endurance. In light of his present crisis, he needs them now: *"Answer me speedily, O Lord."* He needs to know that God is there for him, since his *"spirit fails!"* (cf. v. 4). If God turns from him, hiding His face from him, he will be like a dead man, *"like those who go down into the pit"* (v. 7). What he wants to hear is the affirmation of God's *"lovingkindness* ["covenant-love"] *in the morning."* *"The morning"* represents the passing of his darkness (v. 3), the rising of the sun of faith. He believes that he will hear this, *"For in You do I trust* ["feel secure"]" (v. 8). Along with this assurance, David also needs to know what to do, how to deal with his crisis. He needs direction. Thus he continues, *"Cause me to know the way in which I should walk, / For I lift my soul to You."* It is out of this surrender, lifting his soul in worship, that he will know God's way. Now, having let go of himself, his plans, his self-will, he can begin to receive the answers he so deeply desires (see v. 7).

PETITION FOR GOD TO DELIVER

143:9 Deliver me, O LORD, from my enemies;
    In You I take shelter.

10 Teach me to do Your will,
   For You *are* my God;
   Your Spirit *is* good.
   Lead me in the land of uprightness.

Ps. 143:9–10

One of the big answers to prayer that David needs is deliverance from his enemies, and in verse 9 he asks for it. In God Himself, his crushed life will be restored; the darkness will be dispelled (v. 3). His depression will be broken (v. 4), and he will be secure, as he confesses, *"In You I take shelter"* ('I conceal myself"). David's faith is no foxhole religion, however. He immediately adds that as God rescues him he also wants Him to become his teacher. He wants to do God's will because God is God: *"For You are my God."* Doing His will is simply a proper act of submission. Moreover, His *"Spirit is good. /* [Therefore] *Lead me in the land of uprightness,"* or better, because His "good Spirit will lead me in the land of uprightness" (or, "on level ground," v. 10). Once he makes his surrender, the Holy Spirit will command his life and lead him in God's perfect way. The *"land of uprightness"* is the level, smooth, easy way of God's will (cf. Isa. 40:4).

PETITION FOR GOD TO REVIVE

143:11 Revive me, O LORD, for Your name's sake!
    For Your righteousness' sake bring my soul out
       of trouble.
  12 In Your mercy cut off my enemies,
    And destroy all those who afflict my soul;
    For I *am* Your servant.

Ps. 143:11–12

David's next big prayer is for revival. He has been near death (v. 3). Now he asks for God to make him alive again: *"Revive me, O Lord, for Your name's sake!"* It is not for his sake but for God's sake, for God's glory, that he asks for this new work. As God says through Ezekiel when He promises to renew Israel, "I do not do this for your sake, O house of Israel, but for My holy name's sake. . . . And I will sanctify My great name, which has been profaned among the nations" (Ezek.

36:22–23). David asks for his soul to be brought out of trouble *"for Your righteousness' sake"* (v. 11). As God rescues him, He will vindicate His faithfulness to His covenant and thus prove Himself righteous.

David returns to the pressing issue of his enemies, asking that in God's *"mercy"* ("covenant-love," see v. 8) they be *"cut off"* (destroyed). He adds that this will be the end to *"all of those who afflict my soul."* In conclusion he expects God to act, *"For I am Your servant"* (v. 12). That is, he is enslaved to the mighty King who has redeemed Israel and bound her into a covenant with Himself.

David has a big God and therefore prays big prayers. He expects divine intervention against his enemies. He expects God to rescue him and revive him and restore him to His will. As we learn to pray like David, we will receive answers like him as well. But for this to happen, we will have to reacquaint ourselves with the God of the Bible who is the one, true, living God in our midst and fall down before Him.

CHAPTER ONE HUNDRED FORTY-FOUR

Battle and Blessing

Psalm 144

The battle cries of the Bible still bother most of us. We tend to be embarrassed by the onslaught of fire, smoke, and bloodshed. While admitting that Israel as a nation had to have her armies and go to war, we see this as a passing political reality, rather than a divine disposition. The so-called holy wars of the Old Testament, where

God commands His armies into battle and fights for them, even, at times, providing their strategy for victory, are viewed by modern scholars as a rationalization or justification for political reality, rather than as real acts of God. Before dismissing all of this so easily, however, we need to take a deeper look at it.

For the Bible the whole universe is at war. This war rages between God and His angelic hosts on one side and the devil and his demons on the other. It explains the entrance of sin into the world, and the continuing power and influence of pagan religion. Behind the idols stand demonic powers that determine their influence. Thus when Israel as a nation goes into battle against her neighbors, she is engaged not only in a military struggle but in a spiritual struggle as well. Yahweh, the God of Israel, is fighting against the false gods through her.

At the same time, God is King over His people, and one of His covenant-treaty responsibilities is to defend them from their enemies. No wonder that He not only goes to battle for Israel, but also uses His angelic powers and even nature itself (which is under His command) to fight for her. All of this is not remote for us as God's church today. We continue the spiritual struggle against Satan and his demons. The weapons of our warfare are spiritual now, but they are still weapons. Paul tells us that we battle against demonic powers in the universe that control men and nations, and exhorts us to put on the whole armor of God in order to stand against them. The biblical call to battle is not just for bloody Israel. The biblical call to battle is for the church as well. This makes Psalm 144 ring with relevance for us.

The psalmist is facing an invasion of foreign troops, who speak vain words and whose right hand (the hand of power) is a "right hand of falsehood" (vv. 8, 11). This falsehood stems from the worship of idols. It is against this enemy that he asks God to arm him for battle (v. 1). At the same time, he wants God to bring nature to bear on the advancing hosts by raining lightning from heaven like fiery arrows (v. 6). As God wins the battle, Israel will dwell in safety and her land will be fruitful again (vv. 12–14). The manifestation of God's Kingdom in her midst will show that the people who know God as Lord are happy (v. 15).

Commentators identify this psalm as a royal complaint of mixed form. Its author is David, and the setting is that of a foreign invasion (see vv. 7–8; 11). Its companion psalm is Ps. 18. The thought moves from a blessing (vv. 1–2) to the question, "Why me?" (vv. 3–4), to the call of battle (vv. 5–8), to praise to the Deliverer (vv. 9–10) and concludes with a prayer for deliverance (vv. 11–15).

BLESSING

144:1 Blessed *be* the LORD my Rock,
    Who trains my hands for war,
    And my fingers for battle—
  2 My lovingkindness and my fortress,
    My high tower and my deliverer,
    My shield and *the One* in whom I take refuge,
    Who subdues my people under me.

Ps. 144:1-2

In verse 1 David blesses God, whom he calls *"my Rock,"* his fortress and his defense. This title is commonly given to Yahweh in the psalms. For example, in Ps. 71:3 we read, "Be my strong habitation," which is literally translated, "Be to me for a Rock of dwelling" (see also Ps. 18:2). Such a rock provides a strategic defensive position. That David is thinking in battle images is made immediately clear. He continues: "[my Rock] *who trains* ['who is teaching'] *my hands for war,* / *And my fingers for battle*" (see Ps. 18:34). God makes him a soldier, giving him the skill and discipline he needs. In verse 2 he describes God as *"My lovingkindness* ['covenant-love,' or 'loyal help'] *and my fortress,* / *My high tower and deliverer,* / *My shield* [a small, circular, defensive shield] *and the One in whom I take refuge"* (cf. Ps. 18:2). God is the one who upholds the covenant (making Him liable to fight for Israel as her divine King). He is also David's *"fortress"* and *"high tower,"* which are both defensive positions of strength and security. Yahweh is his protection and covering. He also gives him security at home, for He is the one *"who subdues my people under me"* (see Ps. 18:47), establishing his reign over them (see 2 Sam. 5:1–5). No wonder that David blesses God. He has prepared him for battle, and He will take him through, surrounding him and protecting him with Himself.

WHY ME?

144:3 LORD, what *is* man, that You take knowledge of
          him?
        Or the son of man, that You are mindful of
          him?
    4 Man is like a breath;
        His days *are* like a passing shadow.
                                                    Ps. 144:3–4

David has meditated upon the security he finds in God as he faces
the battle lying ahead. At the same time, the fact that God is so faithful and personal to him is a bit overwhelming. So he asks: *"Lord,
what is man that You take knowledge of* [or, "have known"] *him? / Or
the son of man, that you are mindful of him?"* (v. 3; cf. Ps. 8:4). That
God would bind Himself to David, that God would care about his
battles and prepare him for them, staggers him. Out of this comes
the universal question: "Why would God bother?" Especially since
"man is like a breath ["vapor"]; / *His days are like a passing shadow"*
(cf. James 4:14).

These questions are allowed to stand without answer. It is important to have them before us. God does love us, and He does equip us
for battle (especially our spiritual battles today). Nevertheless, we
must not take this for granted. We need to maintain a sense of wonder and worship before Him. He is eternal; we are temporal. He
stands; we pass away (but continue to stand in Him). "Why me?" The
only answer is grace.

CALL TO BATTLE

144:5 Bow down Your heavens, O LORD, and come
          down;
        Touch the mountains, and they shall smoke.
    6 Flash forth lightning and scatter them;
        Shoot out Your arrows and destroy them.
    7 Stretch out Your hand from above;
        Rescue me and deliver me out of great waters,
        From the hand of foreigners,
    8 Whose mouth speaks lying words,

> And whose right hand *is* a right hand of
> falsehood.
>
> *Ps. 144:5–8*

Knowing that God has equipped him for battle (vv. 1–2), and knowing his own unworthiness (vv. 3–4), David calls upon God to act, asking that the Lord of nature use nature as a weapon against the enemy. He wants God to show His hand as He did in the Exodus. There He commanded locust hordes, hail, darkness, mighty winds, and other natural forces to humble Pharaoh. So here he prays: *"Bow down* ['stretch apart'] *Your heavens, O Lord, and come down"* (cf. Exod. 19:11). He is asking God to descend as He did at Sinai. Thus he continues, *"Touch the mountains, and they shall smoke"* (v. 5, see Exod. 19:18). Here is theophany, the awesome, numinous manifestation of the holy God. Specifically, David prays that God will send lightning bolts against his enemies like arrows *"and destroy them"* (v. 6; see Ps. 18:14). Moreover, David prays for his own rescue as God stretches out His hand from above (cf. Exod. 15:6) and delivers him *"out of great waters* [see Ps. 18:16–17], / *From the hand* [that is, power] *of foreigners"* (v. 7). The *"great waters"* represent the invading armies; they also suggest the watery chaos of the underworld in ancient mythology. Furthermore, these *"foreigners"* are known, not for their cultural or racial differences, but for their *"vain words"* and their bogus authority represented by a *"right hand of falsehood"* (v. 8). In other words, since they worship idols, they are vain and their power is vain. They share in the illusions of this fallen world, which is under the domination of the evil one—the one whom Jesus calls a liar from the beginning and the father of lies (John 8:44). As God comes against David's enemies, He also comes against the idols who control them and keep them in confusion and deception. Victory over them will in turn be a victory for the truth.

PRAISE TO THE DELIVERER

> 144:9 I will sing a new song to You, O God;
> On a harp of ten strings I will sing praises to
> You,
> 10 *The One* who gives salvation to kings,

> Who delivers David His servant
> From the deadly sword.
>
> *Ps. 144:9–10*

Anticipating a great victory, David vows to sing *"a new song to You, O God."* This new song will be the celebration of His triumph. David will accompany himself on a *"harp of ten strings"* (cf. Ps. 33:2–3). Thus, he says, *"I will sing praises to You"* (v. 9). The content of his song is given in verse 10. He will praise Yahweh as *"the One who gives salvation to kings,"* *salvation* here means *"deliverance"*—from his enemies. Specifically, He delivers *"David His servant* (under the covenant the king is Yahweh's slave) / *From the deadly* [literally, "evil"] *sword."*

God's interventions in our lives are for the purpose of our praising Him. In His Son He has stepped into history in order to deliver us, not from a foreign enemy, but from Satan himself. This is the final, great deliverance, and it evokes in us a new song, a song of salvation to the Lamb who was slain (Rev. 5:9ff.).

PRAYER FOR DELIVERANCE

> 144:11 Rescue me and deliver me from the hand of
>   foreigners,
>   Whose mouth speaks lying words,
>   And whose right hand *is* a right hand of
>   falsehood—
> 12 That our sons *may be* as plants grown up in
>   their youth;
>   *That* our daughters *may be* as pillars,
>   Sculptured in palace style;
> 13 *That* our barns *may be* full,
>   Supplying all kinds of produce;
>   *That* our sheep may bring forth thousands
>   And ten thousands in our fields;
> 14 *That* our oxen *may be* well-laden;
>   *That there be* no breaking in or going out;
>   *That there be* no outcry in our streets.
> 15 Happy *are* the people who are in such a state;
>   Happy *are* the people whose God *is* the LORD!
>
> *Ps. 144:11–15*

The petition for rescue from the hand of foreigners and their vanity in verses 7c–8 (with the exception of the prepositional phrase "out of great waters") is repeated in verse 11. Next, the results of this rescue are dramatically and ideally sketched. First, the nation's sons will mature, "*as plants grown up in their youth,*" rather than being cut down. Second, the nation's daughters will be "*as pillars, / Sculptured in palace style*" (v. 12). This image suggests their strength and beauty. Third, in great bounty, which is a sign of God's blessing, the nation's barns will be full from a harvest of all kinds of produce, her sheep will multiply thousands and ten thousands (v. 13), and her oxen will be well-laden (loaded with goods, verse 14a). Fourth, there will be "*no breaking in* ["breach" in the city walls] *or going out,*" that is, to exile. Fifth, there will be "*no outcry* [in distress or grief] *in our streets*" (v. 14). In other words, God's Kingdom and His peace will rule. This picture offers an ideal state; that is, it is eschatological. It shows us what God's people will be like when their final deliverance has been achieved. It gives us a sense of heaven on earth (cf. Psalm 72).

In light of the above, David rightly concludes: "*Happy* ["Blessed"] *are the people who are in such a state; / Happy are the people whose God is the Lord!*" (v. 15). Why is this so? Because the God of Israel is the God of battle. He is the Warrior-King of the covenant-treaty who instructs His soldiers in warfare and then leads them into battle with His mighty signs and wonders. In this He defeats the foreigners who serve the vain idols and bring lies and pollution to the land, restoring His perfect reign there, bringing bounty and peace to His people.

As suggested in the introduction, we too are in a battle whether we like it or not. It is a spiritual battle for our minds: the truth of God versus the lies of the devil; the life of God versus the death of the evil one. God wants to train and arm us spiritually for this battle. He gives us spiritual armor to wear for the fight (Eph. 6:11ff.). He also promises to intervene on our behalf through the power of His Spirit and His holy warrior angels. By the authority of His word, the lies of Satan will be exposed, and the idols of the nations will be seen as vain. The outcome of this battle for planet earth will be praise for the victory, which God has already won in His Son and which will be consummated upon His return. In this praise we will sing a new song. Then the redeemed will experience all the the blessings and bounty of heaven and earth made new, and we will say, "*Happy are*

the people who are in such a state; / Happy are the people whose God
is the Lord!"

CHAPTER ONE HUNDRED FORTY-FIVE

Praising God the King

Psalm 145

In her book, *The Lives of the Kings and Queens of England*, the
editor, Antonia Fraser, writes, "it will be obvious to all but the most
dedicated supporters of the Marxist theory of history that the per-
sonalities and peculiar characteristics of various sovereigns played
at least some part in the shaping of events" (p. 11). If this is true in
British history, how much more is it true in biblical history? Here
the "personality and peculiar characteristics of Yahweh" determine
the life of Israel.

For the Bible, the central reality is that God is King over all of His
creation. He reigns in glory surrounded by a great multitude of
angels who worship Him, serve Him, and do His bidding throughout the universe (see Dan. 7:9–10). Moreover, God created this
planet to be an arena for His purposes. In order to accomplish this,
He gave us dominion over the earth so that we might exercise His
delegated authority here (Gen. 1:28). With the Fall, however, Satan
stole that dominion, and the battle on earth ever since has centered
in God's recovering His rightful rule. To do this He first called
Abraham to become the instrument of His Kingdom in this world.
Through His covenant-treaty with him, God promises to bless him,
give him a land as his own possession, make a great nation of him,

and bless all the nations of the earth through him (see Gen. 12–15). For the New Testament, this blessing is fulfilled with the salvation given to the Gentiles, which is sealed by the power of the Holy Spirit (see Gal. 3:6ff.). Throughout all of her history, God is King over Israel His people. But how do we approach the King? How do we relate to Him? What do we do before Him? Psalm 145 answers these questions.

This psalm is a commitment to praise. The psalmist will extol God as King (v. 1). And why is this? It is because, "Great is the Lord and greatly to be praised" (v. 3). The generations will also engage in this praise (v. 4), which includes declaring the mighty acts of God. All of God's works will praise Him, and His saints will join in too (v. 10). They shall talk of the glory of God's Kingdom and His mighty power (v. 11). God upholds His people and provides for them (vv. 14–16). He is righteous and gracious (v. 17). No wonder the psalmist will "speak the praise of the Lord, / And all flesh shall bless His holy name / Forever and ever" (v. 21).

Commentators identify this psalm as an imperatival type of hymn. It is written in an acrostic form, which follows the letters of the Hebrew alphabet. Tradition gives its authorship to David. The thought moves from a commitment to praise (vv. 1–3) to the generations praise You (vv. 4–9), to Your works praise You (vv. 10–13), to You uphold those who fall (vv. 14–16, to You are righteous to all who call upon You (vv. 17–21).

COMMITMENT TO PRAISE

> 145:1 I will extol You, my God, O King;
>   And I will bless Your name forever and ever.
>   2 Every day I will bless You,
>   And I will praise Your name forever and ever.
>   3 Great *is* the Lord, and greatly to be praised;
>   And His greatness *is* unsearchable.
>
> Ps. 145:1-3

Verse 1 opens with David's resolve to praise God: *"I will extol* ["exalt," "raise up"] *You, my God, O King* [literally, "the King," He is the only ultimate King there is]; */ And I will bless Your name forever and* *ever.*" The Hebrew word for *bless* here may share a common root with kneel. Thus to bless God would be also to submit to Him. His name communicates His person, and calling upon it actualizes His presence. For this reason David blesses His name continually ("*forever and ever*"). By this he lives in His real presence. Verse 2 elaborates on this thought as David vows: "*Every day I will bless You, / And I will praise Your name forever and ever.*" His worship will be disciplined day by day. The repetition of his vow to praise God's name continually gives added emphasis to his thought. In verse 3 David tells us why he praises God so diligently: "*Great is the Lord, and greatly to be praised*" (for God as great see Pss. 48:1; 86:10; 99:2; 135:5). But how are we to understand this greatness? We can't. David adds, "*And His greatness is unsearchable.*" God is infinite; we are finite. God is eternal; we are temporal. God is holy; we are sinners. Indeed, for us, "*His greatness is unsearchable.*" We will only know Him as He chooses to make Himself known to us (Calvin). It is God's very greatness, however, that evokes such praise from David, and as we grasp this, we too will join in the worship.

THE GENERATIONS PRAISE YOU

145:4 One generation shall praise Your works to
        another,
     And shall declare Your mighty acts.
   5 I will meditate on the glorious splendor of
        Your majesty,
     And on Your wondrous works.
   6 *Men* shall speak of the might of Your awesome
        acts,
     And I will declare Your greatness.
   7 They shall utter the memory of Your great
        goodness,
     And shall sing of Your righteousness.
   8 The LORD *is* gracious and full of compassion,
     Slow to anger and great in mercy.
   9 The LORD *is* good to all,
     And His tender mercies *are* over all His works.
                                        Ps. 145:4–9

David does not praise Yahweh as an isolated, existential man. He joins past worshipers and shares the responsibility of bringing up the next generation to know God and to submit to Him. Thus he asserts: *"One generation shall praise Your works to another, / And shall declare Your mighty acts"* (v. 4). The fact that this psalm stands before us witnesses to his executing this responsibility and to the continuing responsibility which we share with him. Notice also the relationship between worship and witness. Our worship is to be public. As we praise God for who He is and for what He has done, this worship becomes witness to those gathered with us. They are then also encouraged to join in praising God as their faith is strengthened.

The proper praise of God comes from the proper knowledge of God. It is not conjured up out of some emotional blood bath. Thus in verse 5 David vows: *"I will meditate on the glorious splendor of Your majesty, / And on Your wondrous ["miraculous"] works."* He will consider both who God is in His person and what He has done in His mighty miracles. Out of this meditation men will speak, and he will speak. The witness will be both corporate and personal. As he says, *"Men shall speak of the might of Your awesome acts* [or, "terrible acts"], */ And I will declare Your greatness"* (v. 6). This witness will come from remembering God's *"great goodness,"* His perfection, and it will result in singing (or shouting for joy) of God's *"righteousness,"* that is, His faithfulness to His covenant (v. 7).

Having told us what he will do, in praise, witness, meditation, and shouting for joy, David now tells us why he will do it. All of this worship is based upon who God is: *"The Lord is gracious ["merciful"] and full of compassion."* He is also *"slow to anger and great in mercy* ["covenant-love"]" (v. 8). In an overload of synonyms, David tells us of the loving heart of God. This is the reason for His mighty acts (vv. 4, 6). Out of His love He redeems His people, saving them from their enemies, healing their diseases, and blessing them with His bounty. Thus David continues, *"The Lord is good to all,"* and His goodness is seen as *"His tender mercies ["love," "compassion"] are over all His works"* (v. 9). It is out of love that He created us, and it is out of love that He has come to redeem us. We must tell the generations yet to come of this mighty God and King. There is no greater need that we all have than to be loved, and the deepest expression of this is to be loved by the one, true God.

YOUR WORKS PRAISE YOU

145:10 All Your works shall praise You, O LORD,
And Your saints shall bless You.
 11 They shall speak of the glory of Your kingdom,
And talk of Your power,
 12 To make known to the sons of men His mighty
acts,
And the glorious majesty of His kingdom.
 13 Your kingdom *is* an everlasting kingdom,
And Your dominion *endures* throughout all
generations.

Ps. 145:10–13

Not only do David and the generations following him praise God, but all of God's works have been made to praise Him as well (v. 10). By their very existence they give Him glory, and as we see them, we join in their praise. We see the majesty of nature, a plunging waterfall, a brilliant sunset, or God's works in history, the triumph of redemption in the Exodus or the resurrection of Jesus from the dead, and praise wells up inside us. David adds: *"And Your saints* [those who belong to the covenant] *shall bless You."* They will also talk together, first of the *"glory"* of God's *"kingdom,"* the majesty of His rule and reign, and, second, of His *"power"* ("might," v. 11). This will turn to witness, as they *"make known to the sons of men* [ordinary people] *His mighty acts, / And the glorious majesty of His kingdom"* (v. 12). This majesty appears in the purity and holiness of God and in His power and awesome might, which evoke fear of Him and submission to Him. Moreover, His Kingdom-reign is *"everlasting."* His *"dominion"* (authority, rule) endures *"throughout all generations"* (v. 13; cf. v. 4). Yahweh reigns in *"glorious majesty,"* and we bless and praise Him for it. Our proper worship is to bow before Him and to lavish our love and praise upon Him, for He is the mighty King, the great, eternal God.

YOU UPHOLD THOSE WHO FALL

145:14 The LORD upholds all who fall,
And raises up all *who are* bowed down.

15 The eyes of all look expectantly to You,
And You give them their food in due season.
16 You open Your hand
And satisfy the desire of every living thing.

Ps. 145:14–16

God's Kingdom may be filled with glory, but He is also compassionate and merciful, as we have seen (vv. 8–9). Thus when we fall He lifts us up. As David says, *"The Lord upholds* [or *"supports"*] *all who fall."* When our sins overwhelm us, when Satan seeks to carry us away, when our enemies oppress us, God is there as our support. He doesn't promise to keep us *from* evil days; He promises to keep us *in* evil days. He also *"raises up all those who are bowed down"* (v. 14). There is no burden too heavy that He will not bear. As Peter says, *"*casting all your care upon Him, for He cares for you" (1 Pet. 5:7).

God also feeds all who look expectantly to Him, like a mother bird at the nest, giving *"them their food in due season"* (v. 15). David continues, *"You open Your hand / And satisfy the desire of every living thing"* (v. 16; cf. Ps. 104:27–28). It is God who has created the food chain. When His Kingdom-reign operates, all are cared for. Likewise, we may add, when His reign is rejected, the earth is ravished and we move to the edge of ecological catastrophe.

YOU ARE RIGHTEOUS TO ALL WHO
CALL UPON YOU

145:17 The LORD *is* righteous in all His ways,
Gracious in all His works.
18 The LORD *is* near to all who call upon Him,
To all who call upon Him in truth.
19 He will fulfill the desire of those who fear
Him;
He also will hear their cry and save them.
20 The LORD preserves all who love Him,
But all the wicked He will destroy.
21 My mouth shall speak the praise of the LORD,
And all flesh shall bless His holy name
Forever and ever.

Ps. 145:17–21

David confesses that Yahweh is *"righteous in all His ways."* As God deals with us, He is true to Himself and true to His covenant-treaty with us. The way He walks is trustworthy. He is also *"gracious* ["kind," "keeping covenant"] *in all His works"* (v. 17). Because of this we can trust His actions toward us. He is not fickle or capricious. While He is enthroned in glory as the mighty King (v. 1), He is also *"near to all who call upon Him . . . in truth"* (v. 18). To call in truth here means to call "faithfully," standing on His covenant promise as we pray. These prayers will be answered. *"The desires of those who fear* [have awe toward] *Him"* will be fulfilled, and, as their cry is heard, they will be saved (v. 19).

David concludes that *"the Lord preserves* ["keeps"] *all who love Him."* Note here they do not only believe in Him; they also love Him, they devote their hearts to Him with affection and abandon. The *"wicked"* ("criminals"), however, are not so. *"He will destroy"* them (v. 20; cf. Ps. 1:4–6). In light of this fact of judgment, David vows *"to speak* [out loud] *the praise of the Lord."* Moreover, *"all flesh"* (humankind) will join in blessing His *"holy* ["separated," from all profanity] *name / Forever and ever"* (v. 21). The universal praise of Yahweh is the goal toward which all of creation now moves.

We have an awesome picture of God as King (v. 1) and His eternal Kingdom-reign (v. 13). In light of His glory (v. 11), His majesty (v. 12), His unsearchable greatness (v. 3), His mighty acts (vv. 4, 5, 6, 10, 12, 17), His righteousness (v. 7), His compassion (vv. 8–9), and His power (v. 11), He deserves the praise and worship of His whole creation (v. 21). We are to bless Him daily (v. 2). Our worship is not to merely be a Sunday affair. We are to give time and energy each day to being alone with Him, reading His word, bowing in prayer, and rising in praise. Furthermore, we are to remind each other of how great He is (vv. 4, 6, 11) and call upon Him (v. 18). He is honored when we trust Him. He is honored when we give Him the opportunity to vindicate Himself and so prove to be God. In this way we praise Him as King and live vitally in His Kingdom.

Where to Get a Good Return on Your Investment

Psalm 146

One of the best-selling popular journals today is *Money* magazine. The point of its various articles and departments is simple: it is a guide to making more money. It tells you which stocks are hot, how to avoid taxes legally, which banks are granting the highest returns on their money market accounts, and how to save money as you spend it on a host of luxury items. *Money Magazine* also profiles prudent investors and suggests ways to join the ranks of the affluent. It is a magazine of the decade, a decade of greed. People, however, have always been concerned about their investments. Our economy is powered on the amassing and expenditure of capital. The possibility of an inside tip has always allured us. The problem with all of this, however, is that when we deal with money we are dealing with that which passes away. The real investment is for eternity rather than for time. This is the investment with the big payoff, and this is the subject of Psalm 146.

The psalmist begins by praising God. He then warns against trusting in men (v. 3). The problem is simply their mortality. When a man dies his spirit departs, he returns to the earth, and his plans perish (v. 4). What good are all of his investments to him now? Where are all those things which he cherished? The blessed person is the one who has God for help. That one's hope is in Him (v. 5). God is the Creator and the Redeemer (vv. 6–9). Over against our human mortality stands this truth: "The Lord shall reign forever." Here is where we can stand. Our sure investment is in Him.

Commentators identify Psalm 146 as a congregational hymn. Its date and author are unknown. The thought moves from a call to praise God (vv. 1–2) to a warning against praising men (vv. 3–4), to a blessing upon those who trust in God as their Creator and Redeemer (vv. 5–9) and concludes with the confession that God reigns (v. 10).

PRAISE GOD

146:1 Praise the LORD!
   Praise the LORD, O my soul!
  2 While I live I will praise the LORD;
    I will sing praises to my God while I have my
     being.
               Ps. 146:1–2

Verse 1 opens with the imperative: *"Praise the Lord!"* In the plural, this is addressed to the readers or the congregation. It is immediately followed by the personal imperative, which the psalmist addresses to himself: *"Praise the Lord, O my soul!"* We can learn from this that we need to exhort ourselves to actively engage in worshiping God. The psalmist vows that as long as he lives (literally, "in my life"), *"I will praise the Lord."* Such praise will be his theme. Thus he adds, *"I will sing praise to my God while I have my being"* (v. 2; compare Ps. 104:33). Notice that praise is to be sung. It is a dynamic expression of joy.

DO NOT PRAISE MEN

146:3 Do not put your trust in princes,
   Nor in a son of man, in whom *there is* no help.
  4 His spirit departs, he returns to his earth;
   In that very day his plans perish.
               Ps. 146:3–4

We are faced with only two alternatives in life, either to trust men (including ourselves) or to trust God. Most people, when they are really honest, admit that they spend most of their time trusting men. They trust politicians to run the country. They trust news commentators to tell them what's going on in the world. They trust professors to educate them. They trust doctors to diagnose them, and they trust pastors and priests to care for their souls. Here is where we make our investments. We put our faith, time, money, and energy into what people say. Most of us would admit that we do not really pray over decisions. We do not expect God to run our lives day to day. Nevertheless, the psalmist clearly tells us that we are foolish to continue this. He writes, *"Do not put your trust in princes, / Nor in a son of man* [a *"man,"* see Ps. 8:4], *in whom there is no help* [literally, *"salvation"]"* (v. 3). As we look to men, even great spiritual leaders, we need to ask one question: "Can this person save me?" This question places even kings and presidents in perspective.

Now we are told why we should make no ultimate investment in a man. First, *"his spirit departs."* The life can be crushed out of him. Mortality is his lot. Thus, *"he returns to his earth."* The idea of "his earth" designates the earth from which he was created (see Gen. 2:7). He is dust. Would you trust dust with your destiny? Second, when he dies, *"in that very day his plans* [or *"thoughts"*] *perish"* (v. 4). What good are his schemes now? What benefit are his investments to him? When he is taken, all is taken from him. Why then would we trust man? Why would we praise him? There is a far better alternative; that is to trust God. To this we turn.

TRUST IN GOD AS CREATOR
AND REDEEMER

146:5 Happy *is he* who *has* the God of Jacob for his
          help,
       Whose hope *is* in the LORD his God,
   6 Who made heaven and earth,
       The sea, and all that *is* in them;
       Who keeps truth forever,
   7 Who executes justice for the oppressed,
       Who gives food to the hungry.
       The LORD gives freedom to the prisoners.
   8 The LORD opens *the eyes of* the blind;
       The LORD raises those who are bowed down;
       The LORD loves the righteous.
   9 The LORD watches over the strangers;
       He relieves the fatherless and widow;

But the way of the wicked He turns upside
down.

Ps. 146:5–9

The psalmist pronounces a blessing upon the one *"who has the God of Jacob for his help."* He calls him *"Happy"* or *"Blessed."* *"The God of Jacob"* is not only a title for Yahweh, it also brings to our minds all that God did to help this patriarch, making him wealthy, blessing him after breaking him through a night of wrestling with an angel, giving him twelve sons who became the fathers for the twelve tribes of Israel, rescuing him from famine, and restoring his lost son Joseph to him (see Gen. 25:26ff.). The inference is that as God did with Jacob so will He do with us. Thus, the man is blessed *"whose hope is in the Lord his God"* (v. 5). Why is this so? First, because He is the Creator; He made *"heaven and earth, / The sea, and all that is in them."* In hoping in Him, we are hoping in the God who is eternal, who stands outside of His creation, who is not bound by it, and who is sovereign over it. He is not like man who is passing away (see v. 4). Second, He is forever trustworthy (v. 6). Third, He *"executes justice for the oppressed"*; He takes up their cause, He defends them and vindicates them (see Psalm 72). Fourth, He feeds *"the hungry."* Fifth, He *"gives freedom to the prisoners"* (v. 7; see Isa. 40:1–2; 61:1). He brings the captives home from exile. He sets at liberty those who are dominated by the devil. Sixth, He *"opens the eyes of the blind."* He heals their physical eyes and their spiritual eyes. Seventh, He *"raises those who are bowed down,"* those who are burdened and heavy-laden. Eighth, He *"loves the righteous,"* those who keep His covenant. Ninth, He *"watches over the strangers* ["sojourners," non-Jews] . . . [and] *relieves* ["lifts up"] *the fatherless and widow."* He cares for the poor and dispossessed. He cares for those who have lost all other support and care in this world. At the same time, He also comes against the wicked: *"But the way of the wicked* ["lawbreaker"] *He turns upside down* ["bends," that is "frustrates"]" (v. 9).

Now it is clear. The reasons for our investing ourselves in God and His plans for us are abundant. Moreover, we see the fulfillment of what is described here in the ministry of Jesus Christ. He executes God's justice, feeds the hungry, sets the captives free, opens blind eyes, lifts up the burdened, and cares for the rejected and outcast (see Luke 4:18–19; 7:20–23), and we are to do the same in His name (that is, His authority, see Luke 9:1–2; 10:9).

GOD REIGNS

146:10 The LORD shall reign forever—
        Your God, O Zion, to all generations.
        Praise the LORD!

                                                    Ps. 146:10

This psalm opens with the call: *"Praise the Lord!"* It also closes with the same call. Here is our sure investment for life. Here is an investment with an eternal return. Here is an investment that will not pass away. As the psalmist says: *"The Lord shall reign forever."* When we put our faith, our love, our time, and our energy into serving Him, we are not only preparing for eternity; we are experiencing some of eternity right now. Since God will reign forever, He is also Zion's God *"to all generations."* The eternal God encompasses all of Israel's history. He stands over each epoch. He also embraces all of the history of spiritual Israel, the church now made one in Christ. We join with the psalmist, responding to his call: *"Praise the Lord!"*

CHAPTER ONE HUNDRED FORTY-SEVEN

One of a Kind

Psalm 147

Claims for uniqueness attract us. We enjoy viewing masterpieces in museums, in part, because they stand alone. We collect antiques because they have no seconds. Auctions draw the world's wealthy in the hopes of purchasing something "one of a kind." Films are marketed as "unforgettable," so special that they will leave an indelible impression. Actors and athletes are sold to us in the same way. To see them perform, we are told, will be an unrepeatable experience. So it goes. We are all on the hunt for something that will not only be unique, but something that will tell us that we are unique as well. On the dark side, this hunt draws many into street drugs and takes them down the path of addiction. In truth, the only really unique experience we will ever have is the experience of the living God. To know Him is unique because He is "one of a kind," and He has made us in the same way. No two thumbprints are alike; God has put His special signature on us all. Regardless of how the humanists enjoy proving that all religions are the same in their several disguises, this simply is not true. We are unique, and God is unique. The psalm before us witnesses to that fact.

Psalm 147 reveals the specialness of the living God. He has made Himself known uniquely to Israel, and as verse 20 proclaims, "He has not dealt thus with any nation; / And as for His judgments, they have not known them." All that is said of Yahweh in this psalm proclaims Him as "one of a kind." He builds up Jerusalem, He regathers the exiles, He heals the broken, He commands creation, He lifts up the humble, and He humbles the proud (vv. 2–6). He provides for the earth and feeds the animals (vv. 8–9). He protects Jerusalem, blesses her children, and grants her peace and bounty (vv. 13–14). He commands nature by His word (vv. 15–18) and gives that word to His special people (vv. 19–20). There is no God like Yahweh, and He alone deserves our praise.

Commentators identify this psalm as a hymn. Its date and author are unknown, although it is probably post-Exilic (see v. 2), composed after the rebuilding of Jerusalem (v. 13). The thought moves from a call to worship (v. 1) to the God whom we worship (vv. 2–6), to our response in song (vv. 7–11) and concludes with our response in praise (vv. 12–20).

CALL TO WORSHIP

147:1 Praise the LORD!
For *it is* good to sing praises to our God;
For *it is* pleasant, *and* praise is beautiful.
Ps. 147:1

Verse 1 opens with the call for us to *"Praise the Lord!"* We are to do so *"For it is good to sing praises to our God."* That is, it is *"good"* or *"fulfilling"* for us to praise Him. Praise here is to be sung. It comes with joy, and with full melodic range and expression. As the psalmist says, *"For it is pleasant, and praise is beautiful."* He may be implying the use of human voices as well as the use of instruments in bringing praise to the Lord (see Psalm 150). To be caught up in a congregation of worshipers, to express our full human capacity to praise God, and to be in the midst of those doing the same is to experience some of God's beauty. To release our joy before Him is a pleasure, which is His gift to us. Moreover, to know His Spirit in our midst, directing this worship, is to receive a divine ecstasy.

THE GOD WHOM WE WORSHIP

147:2 The LORD builds up Jerusalem;
  He gathers together the outcasts of Israel.
 3 He heals the brokenhearted
  And binds up their wounds.
 4 He counts the number of the stars;
  He calls them all by name.
 5 Great *is* our Lord, and mighty in power;
  His understanding *is* infinite.
 6 The LORD lifts up the humble;
  He casts the wicked down to the ground.
             Ps. 147:2–6

The implied question is, "Who is this God to whom we bring our praise?" First, He is the one who *"builds up Jerusalem"* and *"gathers together the outcasts of Israel"* (v. 2). This suggests that the psalmist lives in the time of the rebuilding of the ruined city, when the exiles of 586 B.C. began to come home from Babylon (see Ezra and Nehemiah). Today we also live in a time when God is rebuilding His church, after the inroads of rationalism, secular humanism, and legalism have brought her to the edge of ruin, and after His judgment has been set against her (cf. Revelation 2–3). As the church is renewed, God is also gathering His elect from all the nations of earth.

Second, *"He heals the brokenhearted / And binds up their wounds* [or, *"sorrows," "pain"*]*"* (v. 3). God not only rebuilds His city and brings

His people into it; He also heals them. Their hearts have been broken by the Exile, which is a consequence of their idolatry and His judgment. That grief, however, is over, and they are coming home. As they return, they are healed spiritually and physically. According to Isaiah, this becomes the work of the Suffering Servant of the Lord, as he prophesies of Him, "He has sent me to heal the brokenhearted, / To proclaim liberty to the captives" (Isa. 61:1). This prophecy is fulfilled in the New Testament by Jesus (Luke 4:18) and is a key to His healing ministry.

Third, this God whom we are to praise also creates and commands nature: *"He counts the number of the stars; / He calls them all by name."* It is Yahweh, not some Babylonian astrologer, who controls the heavens and names them (in order to have authority over them). By inference, He also is sovereign over the demons that now control the stars as dark "principalities and powers" (see Eph. 6:12).

All of this witnesses to the affirmation given in verse 5. Yahweh is *"great,"* and *"mighty in power"* (or, "of much strength"). Moreover, He weds His power to His wisdom for *"His understanding is infinite"* (literally, "to His understanding there is not numbering"). The surprising wisdom of God is illustrated in verse 6. He lifts up the *"humble,"* and casts down the *"wicked* ["lawbreakers"] . . . *to the ground."* The ultimate expression of this is in Christ. In order to exalt the humble, God humbles Himself in His Son. In His rejection, the wicked who crucify Him are themselves destroyed.

OUR RESPONSE IN SONG

147:7 Sing to the LORD with thanksgiving;
Sing praises on the harp to our God,
8 Who covers the heavens with clouds,
Who prepares rain for the earth,
Who makes grass to grow on the mountains.
9 He gives to the beast its food,
And to the young ravens that cry.
10 He does not delight in the strength of the horse;
He takes no pleasure in the legs of a man.
11 The LORD takes pleasure in those who fear Him,
In those who hope in His mercy.

Ps. 147:7–11

In light of verse 1, it is no surprise that we are called to sing. With an expanding knowledge of the greatness of God (vv. 2–6), we are ready to lift our voices to Him. Thus we are exhorted: *"Sing to the Lord with thanksgiving."* This is the expression of our gratitude, for we are among the exiles brought home, and we have experienced the healing of our God. More specifically, we are directed to *"Sing praises on the harp* [or *"lyre,"* a stringed instrument with a gourdlike chamber] *to our God"* (v. 7).

As if to reinforce our desire to sing, the psalmist tells us that this God *"covers the heavens with clouds,"* bringing rain to earth, and then *"makes grass to grow on the mountains"* (v. 8). Thus both animals and birds are fed by Him (not by some fertility cult, or *"Mother Nature"*). *"*[God] *gives to the beast its food, / And to the young ravens that cry"* (v. 9). Furthermore, our God is unimpressed with *"the strength of the horse"* or the *"legs of a man"* (v. 10). He does not delight in the power of this world. He is not breathless watching the Olympics or Monday Night Football. His delight is in *"those who fear Him, / In those who hope in His mercy* [*"covenant-love"*]*"* (v. 11). God loves those who love Him. His joy is in those who are humble enough to bow to Him (v. 6) and who hope in His faithfulness to His covenant rather than in their own plans and power. These are the ones who are on His heart.

Our Response in Praise

147:12 Praise the LORD, O Jerusalem!
    Praise your God, O Zion!
   13 For He has strengthened the bars of your
      gates;
    He has blessed your children within you.
   14 He makes peace *in* your borders,
    And fills you with the finest wheat.
   15 He sends out His command *to the* earth;
    His word runs very swiftly.
   16 He gives snow like wool;
    He scatters the frost like ashes;
   17 He casts out His hail like morsels;
    Who can stand before His cold?

> 18 He sends out His word and melts them;
>   He causes His wind to blow, *and* the waters
>   flow.
> 19 He declares His word to Jacob,
>   His statutes and His judgments to Israel.
> 20 He has not dealt thus with any nation;
>   And *as for His* judgments, they have not
>   known them.
>   Praise the LORD!
>
> *Ps. 147:12–20*

As in verse 7, we are exhorted to worship. All of God's people are to join in: *"Praise the Lord, O Jerusalem! / Praise your God, O Zion* [the mountain upon which Jerusalem stands]!" (v. 12). But why this outbreak of joy? First, God *"has strengthened the bars of your gates."* He makes the city secure. He defends her with reinforcing steel. Second, He blesses *"your children within you"* (v. 13). His blessing would include growing numbers and well-being. Third, Jerusalem knows *peace* along her borders and is filled with *"the finest wheat* [literally, *"fat wheat"]"* (v. 14). Thus it is a time of idyllic, messianic blessing and bounty.

God also commands nature (see vv. 8–9). He controls the seasons as He speaks His word from His throne. When He says it, it is done. Thus *"His word runs very swiftly"* (v. 15). *"Snow like wool"* comes at His command. When winter passes, *"He scatters the frost like ashes"* (v. 16). Hail also falls *"like morsels"* (manna from heaven?) when He speaks. The psalmist asks rhetorically, *"Who can stand before His cold?"* (v. 17). The answer, of course, is, "No one." He commands again and melts the hail; *"He causes His wind to blow, and the waters flow"* (v. 18). With poetic power the psalmist shows us the greatness of our God and His authoritative word. With spiritual eyes we see both creation and redemption as His gifts to us.

In verses 19–20 the psalmist concludes by focusing on the word of God, which He *"declares . . . to Jacob"* (Israel as a spiritual entity, see our comments on Ps. 20:1), and on His *statutes* and *judgments* (or, "ordinances"), which He gives to Israel. Here is God's uniqueness, and here is Israel's uniqueness. He gives His special revelation to His special people. They receive His spoken word and His legislation, His laws which direct their life. Because Yahweh is "one of a kind," *"He has not dealt thus with any nation; / And as for His judgments* ["ordinances"], *they have not known them."* But Israel knows. She knows God, and she knows His will for her in this world. As the new Israel after the spirit, we too know Him in His Son, and we know His will for us in this world. This makes her, and us, unique. As the psalmist concludes, *"Praise the Lord!"*

CHAPTER ONE HUNDRED FORTY-EIGHT

Total Worship

Psalm 148

The goal of all of creation is to join in the worship of the one, true living God. All things are moving toward that eternal destiny. Paul tells us that there will be a day when every knee will bow and every tongue confess that "Jesus is Lord" to the glory of God the Father (Phil. 2:5–11). The great, heavenly visions of The Revelation show us the saints gathered before God's throne offering their praises to Him. This fulfillment of their salvation, as they worship the God who is both Creator and Redeemer, will also include the creation of a new heaven and a new earth. They will both be united again, as they were before Satan's revolt and our earthly fall, in the praise of God.

Psalm 148 anticipates the great, eschatological consummation of all things. It reveals heaven and earth joined together in worship. Verses 1–6 call for the heavens to praise the Lord. Verses 7–12 call for nature and the nations to praise the Lord. All things are to join in this praise, especially His chosen people (vv. 13–14).

531

Commentators identify this psalm as a hymn. Its date and author are unknown. The thought moves from the call to heaven to worship (vv. 1–6) to the call to earth to worship (vv. 7–12) and concludes with all things worshiping, especially Israel (vv. 13–14).

CALL TO HEAVEN TO WORSHIP

148:1 Praise the LORD!
    Praise the LORD from the heavens;
    Praise Him in the heights!
   2 Praise Him, all His angels;
    Praise Him, all His hosts!
   3 Praise Him, sun and moon;
    Praise Him, all you stars of light!
   4 Praise Him, you heavens of heavens,
    And you waters above the heavens!
   5 Let them praise the name of the LORD,
    For He commanded and they were created.
   6 He also established them forever and ever;
    He made a decree which shall not pass away.
                                     Ps. 148:1–6

Verse 1 opens with the familiar exhortation in the plural: *"Praise the Lord!"* This sets the theme of the psalm. This praise is to come *"from the heavens."* It is transcendent; it is to come *"from the heights!"* It ascends from above and can be glimpsed on earth as, "The heavens declare the glory of God" (Ps. 19:1). The great angelic hosts gathered before God's throne are also to join in: *"Praise Him, all His angels; / Praise Him, all His hosts!"* These *"hosts"* are the angelic armies of the Lord (cf. Ps. 103:20–21). The celestial beings are also to join in this worship: *"Praise Him, sun and moon; / Praise Him, all you stars of light!"* (v. 3). As they shine in the heavens, they give their Creator glory. Moreover, the highest heavens *"And you waters above the heavens"* (see Gen. 1:7, the heavenly ocean above the firmament) are to praise God (v. 4). Implied in verse 4 are the gradations in the heavenly realms. This is supported by Paul's reference to the "third heaven" (2 Cor. 12:2).

Why is there to be this outburst of praise? All the heavens and all the angels are to worship God because *"He commanded and they*

532

were created" (v. 5). They owe their existence to Him. Furthermore, they were created for His pleasure and for His glory. They find their destiny then in praising their Creator. They have been *"established . . . forever and ever"* (permanently). God not only creates them; He also upholds them, and *"He has made a decree* [or, *"gave their boundaries"] which shall not pass away"* (v. 6). He orders their order. Yahweh, rather than laws of physics, determines their destiny, and they are held in His hand. No wonder that they are to praise Him.

CALL TO EARTH TO WORSHIP

148:7 Praise the LORD from the earth,
    You great sea creatures and all the depths;
  8 Fire and hail, snow and clouds;
    Stormy wind, fulfilling His word;
  9 Mountains and all hills;
    Fruitful trees and all cedars;
  10 Beasts and all cattle;
    Creeping things and flying fowl;
  11 Kings of the earth and all peoples;
    Princes and all judges of the earth;
  12 Both young men and maidens;
    Old men and children.

Ps. 148:7-12

The earth is to join heaven in worshiping Yahweh. Thus the psalmist exhorts us: *"Praise the Lord from the earth"* (compare v. 1). But who here is to participate in this? First, the *"great sea creatures and all the depths"* (v. 7). These creatures could include extinct sea monsters as well as marine mammals and all the depths of the oceans, which once covered the planet (see Gen. 1:2). Next, the elements are to join in praising God: fire, water *("hail, snow and clouds"),* and stormy wind. As they do so they will fulfill *"His word,"* His call to worship (v. 8). Then, the earth itself is to join the chorus: the *"mountains,"* all the *"hills,"* the fruit trees, and all the *"cedars"* (of Lebanon?). All that lives upon the land is to praise Him. This includes *"beasts and all cattle* [that is, wild and domesticated animals]; / *Creeping things and flying fowl* [snakes, insects, and birds]" (v. 10). Finally, humankind is to join the choir of praise: *kings* with their kingdoms, their subjects, *"princes"* and *"judges,"* *"young men"* and women, the elderly and *"children"* (vv. 11–12); all are to worship their Creator. This is the goal of our creation. Here is the restoration of Eden. Here is the renewed earth. Here is a planet without ecological disaster or political bondage. Here is a planet where sin, Satan, and death are no more. Here is a planet where God's Kingdom is consummated and His praise flows up to Him in harmony and unity.

ALL THINGS ARE TO PRAISE HIM

148:13 Let them praise the name of the LORD,
       For His name alone is exalted;
       His glory *is* above the earth and heaven.
    14 And He has exalted the horn of His people,
       The praise of all His saints—
       Of the children of Israel,
       A people near to Him.
       Praise the LORD!

Ps. 148:13–14

This vision of praise is concluded with a universal exhortation in verse 13a and the reasons for that exhortation in verses 13b–14. The psalmist calls: *"Let them praise the name of the Lord."* We take the *"them"* to refer to all those who have been exhorted to worship throughout the previous verses. Notice that their worship is to be personal and directed. They are to praise *"the name"* of Yahweh. But why this praise? Because He is the only God. He alone deserves our worship: *"For His name alone is exalted; His glory* [or, *"honor"*] *is above the earth and heaven"* (v. 13). Nothing else can compete with Him. He stands alone. He is unique (see Ps. 147:20), and all things, by definition, are under Him. But we are not only to worship Yahweh because He is our Creator; He is also our Redeemer. Thus *"He has exalted the horn* [power] *of His people, / The praise of all His saints"*; that is, *"[He is] the praise of all His saints."* These saints are *"the children of Israel, / A people near to Him"* (v. 14). The word *saint* denotes one who belongs to God's covenant. We too are included through the New Covenant established in the blood of His Son. Thus in this final verse we learn that, while God is to be praised for His majesty in creation, He is also to be praised for His love. He is exalted, and He has exalted a people to worship Him out of gratitude because they are "near to Him," they are His. "But now in Christ Jesus you who once were far off have been made near by the blood of Christ" (Eph. 2:13). As the psalmist concludes, *"Praise the Lord!"*

CHAPTER ONE HUNDRED FORTY-NINE

A New Song

Psalm 149

There are different songs for different occasions. When we are lonely, we sing the blues. When we want to have fun, we "rock out." When we are sentimental, we want to hear old favorites. When we are patriotic, we want marching bands with colors flying. Sometimes an event calls for new music. It has been customary to compose a new symphony for each coronation of a British monarch. In this psalm there is a call for such a new song. We may well suspect that as God does a new work, we will sing about it in a new way.

Psalm 149 is filled with exhortation to praise Yahweh and to sing to Him (v. 1). Worship is to be celebrated because He is the mighty King (v. 2). This praise is to include dancing, timbrel, and harp (v. 3). He is being praised in this way because He brings salvation (v. 4). Thus His saints are to sing to Him and execute His judgment upon His enemies (vv. 5-9). In all of this God is to be praised.

Commentators identify this psalm as a hymn of victory. Its date and author are unknown. The thought moves from a call to worship

(v. 1) to general hows and whys of worship (vv. 2–4) and concludes with more specific hows and whys of worship (vv. 5–9).

CALL TO WORSHIP

> 149:1 Praise the LORD!
> Sing to the LORD a new song,
> *And* His praise in the assembly of saints.
> *Ps. 149:1*

Verse 1 begins with the plural, liturgical exhortation for us to *"Praise the Lord!"* This praise includes singing to Him a *"new song."* Moreover, our worship is to be corporate and public: we are to praise Him in *"the congregation of saints"* (those who belong to the covenant). This *"new song,"* which represents a new work of God, is for all of His people. His new work has to do with them.

GENERAL HOWS AND WHYS
OF WORSHIP

> 149:2 Let Israel rejoice in their Maker;
> Let the children of Zion be joyful in their King.
> 3 Let them praise His name with the dance;
> Let them sing praises to Him with the timbrel
> and harp.
> 4 For the LORD takes pleasure in His people;
> He will beautify the humble with salvation.
> *Ps. 149:2–4*

How are we to worship? God's people are to *"rejoice* ["be glad"] *in their Maker;"* the *"children of Zion* [the mountain upon which Jerusalem was built, see Ps. 48:2]" are to be *"joyful in their King"* (v. 2). Therefore, they are to come before Him with delight and praise worthy of His majesty. This means that they are to *"praise His name* [Yahweh] *with the dance,"* and sing songs to Him accompanied with *"timbrel* [a popular woman's instrument used in dancing] *and harp* [or, "lyre"]" (v. 3). This festive music is the way to worship a mighty ruler. It also releases the full physical and emotional energy that He has given us.

Why are we to worship God in song and dance? The answer is profound: He likes it. Thus the psalmist continues, *"For the Lord takes pleasure in His people."* He is like a great King, smiling down upon their praise and worship. In one pastor's words God finds our worship irresistible. He comes to bless us as we bless Him. Moreover, as we praise Him, *"He will beautify* ["adorn"] *the humble with salvation* [or, "victory"]*"* (v. 4). Our worship becomes a weapon for the warfare God calls us to in this world (see vv. 6b–9). I have often seen the Lord come and minister to people as we worship. When the presence of God is manifest, demons flee and salvation comes. Dear friends of mine walked into a church where the worship was intense and the Spirit of God clearly active. Not being Christians, they returned for a year before they accepted Christ, because, in their words, "God was in that place."

SPECIFIC HOWS AND WHYS
OF WORSHIP

149:5 Let the saints be joyful in glory;
    Let them sing aloud on their beds.
  6 *Let* the high praises of God *be* in their mouth,
    And a two-edged sword in their hand,
  7 To execute vengeance on the nations,
    And punishments on the peoples;
  8 To bind their kings with chains,
    And their nobles with fetters of iron;
  9 To execute on them the written judgment—
    This honor have all His saints.
    Praise the LORD!

Ps. 149:5–9

The exhortation to worship continues. The *"saints,"* those who are set apart by the covenant, are to be *"joyful in glory"* (that is, in the presence of God's glory), and *"sing aloud* [or, "shout with joy"] *on their beds"* (v. 5). This could mean that they are to worship privately as well as publicly and also continually, that is, when they recline.

Their beds could also be prayer rugs, such as are used by Muslims today.

Worship, however, is not escape. Worship, the sense of the "new song" (v. 1), is a preparation for battle. Thus the saints are to lift the "high praises of God" and, at the same time, have a "two-edged sword" [literally, "a sword of mouths," a devouring sword?) in their hand" (v. 6). They worship in order to receive the power to "execute vengeance on the nations, / And punishments [literally, "rebukes"] on the peoples" (v. 7). The saints become the instruments of divine judgment. As a result, the pagan kings will be bound in "chains, / And their nobles with fetters of iron" (v. 8). This is no nationalistic war of aggression. The saints merely execute what God has decreed in advance with His "written judgment" (see Rev. 20:12). This is their "honor" (v. 9). Thus, the psalmist concludes, "Praise the Lord!"

Verses 6–9 are to be taken prophetically and eschatologically. The worshiping saints enter into battle against the forces of evil. In Christ we understand those forces to be, not simply pagan rulers, but the powers and structures of evil that lie behind them. We come against their idols and the demons that they mask (see Deut. 32:16–17). Our sword in this age is not a physical weapon, but the "sword of the Spirit," which is the word of God (Eph. 6:17). As we take authority over the evil spirits, we bind them and cast them out in the name of Jesus (see Acts 16:18). This psalm also points to the final battle that the exalted Christ will fight against Antichrist and the massed forces of evil on this planet (see Rev. 19:11–21). When evil is finally defeated, the new song of victory will be sung in the New Jerusalem, which will come down from heaven (see Rev. 21:1ff.). It is appropriate as the Psalter draws to a close that we should have this psalm point us to the consummation of all things, our redemption, which draws nigh.

Praise the Lord!

Psalm 150

The final shout of the Psalter is the imperative to "Praise the Lord!" Throughout this vast body of literature, we have been called to do this again and again. Our study of the psalms would be a futile exercise if we failed to hear and heed this exhortation. The greatest truth of God is that He is worthy of our worship, and the deepest truth about ourselves is that we have been created to worship Him. When we actually do this, we find the real and eternal end or *telos* of our existence. Why is it that so many people are hard, cold, loveless, fearful, introverted, sad, scared, empty, angry, violent, cunning, self-centered, self-consumed? The answer, bottom line, is that they have never really worshiped God. They have never bowed to Him, submitted to Him, seen Him in His glory and love, and risen up to praise Him, to make joyful noises and shouts before Him. They have never known this release, or if they have known it for a moment, they have refused to stay there, wedded to worship, dwelling in the presence and receiving the power of almighty God granted to us through His Son in His Spirit.

As the end of this age draws near, the issues will become increasingly clear. The battle lines will be drawn. We will either worship the living God, or we will worship the devil with all his masks and disguises. But how shall we worship? Where will we learn to worship Him? The first answer is biblical. The psalms will teach us and reform our worship, if we will hear them. They will lead us to God-centered worship, rather than to man-centered aesthetics or theatrics. They will teach us that worship is surrender to the great King who reigns, and we will make that surrender. They will show us how to praise Him, recounting His character and His works, which make

Him worthy of our praise and evoke our joy. We will also learn to wait upon Him, to sit in the silence, to listen for His voice. We will grow in the expectancy that we will hear His living word addressed to us. We will also learn to petition Him as our King, and expect to receive His answers and see Him prove that He is the living God who is active in our midst once again. We will expect to see His salvation, healing, deliverance, peace, and comfort as we hear His word and see His work. All of this will result in greater and greater surges of praise ascending to His throne, until that day when we are caught up to be with Him forever.

Psalm 150 ends the Psalter with a call to praise. The word *praise* is repeated thirteen times in six verses. This psalm is a little introduction to and summary of what real worship is: expressing joyful delight in the presence of God.

Commentators identify this psalm as a hymn. Its author and date are unknown; it is timeless. The thought moves from what to do before God and where to do it (v. 1) to why to do it (v. 2) and concludes with how to do it (vv. 3–6).

WHAT AND WHERE?

> 150:1 Praise the LORD!
> Praise God in His sanctuary;
> Praise Him in His mighty firmament!
>
> *Ps. 150:1*

Verse 1 opens with the common exhortation: *"Praise the Lord!"* Written in the plural, it is addressed to all of us. It answers the question of *what* we are to do when we come into the presence of the mighty King. We are to come offering Him our cries and shouts of glory to His name. We are to come expressing our love, our delight, our adoration to Him. But where are we to do this?

First, we are to praise God *"in His sanctuary."* This, of course, is His temple or palace in Jerusalem. The Jews went up to Jerusalem to worship the Lord down through the generations as long as the temple stood. With the coming of Jesus, however, the veil of the temple, which separated the people from the holy presence of God, was removed, and the temple itself was later destroyed in judgment. Now we worship God through the temple of the risen body of Jesus Himself (John 2:13ff.), and as believers, we are all incorporated into that body. Also our individual bodies (in reflection of His) have become little temples where God chooses to dwell in His Spirit (1 Cor. 6:19). Thus today, as we gather in corporate worship, we are the living temple of God, and we are the body of Christ in ministry together.

We are also to worship God *in His mighty firmament!* He is to be worshiped across the vast expanse of heaven. Heaven and earth are to join together and become one in praising Him (see Psalm 148).

WHY?

150:2 Praise Him for His mighty acts;
      Praise Him according to His excellent
        greatness!

Ps. 150:2

What is our motive to be as we come into the presence of the Lord to praise Him? First, we are to *praise Him for His mighty acts.* To do this we must remember the great things He has done in creation and in history, for His acts reveal His character. Through them we learn of the majesty of the Creator. Through them we learn of His awesome righteousness and justice as He pounds Egypt with plagues and tears down the walls of Jerusalem. And through them we learn of His love and mercy, His covenant-treaty with us, which expresses His faithfulness toward us and which consummates in the New Covenant in His Son's blood.

We must also remember His mighty acts in our own lives. He provides for us day by day. He enters our lives through His Spirit. He answers our prayers. He delivers us from our enemies. He heals our diseases. He unites us to each other in love. He matures us in His word, and He remains faithful toward us. Indeed, *"Praise Him for His mighty acts."*

We are also to *praise Him for His excellent greatness* [literally, "the multitude of His greatness]!" God is great, He is full of *"greatness."* No one is greater than He. We praise Him for who He is, not only for what He has done. He is the mighty King. He is the eternal God. He is the source of all things; all things come from Him and return to Him.

He is filled with holiness, justice, trustworthiness, and covenant-love. He is the alpha and the omega. He is the beginning and the end. Worship this great God. Our motives for praise are twofold. We praise God for what He has done, and we praise Him for who He is. But how are we to praise His name?

How?

150:3 Praise Him with the sound of the trumpet;
Praise Him with the lute and harp!
4 Praise Him with the timbrel and dance;
Praise Him with stringed instruments and
flutes!
5 Praise Him with loud cymbals;
Praise Him with clashing cymbals!
6 Let everything that has breath praise the
LORD.
Praise the LORD!

Ps. 150:3–6

The psalmist offers us the means of our praise. In doing this he describes the ancient musical instruments of Israel. God is to be praised with the *"sound of the trumpet"* (the ram's horn, used for signaling), the *"lute"* (a several-stringed instrument with a sound chamber), the *"harp,"* the *"timbrel"* (a woman's instrument used in dance), *"stringed instruments," "flutes," "loud cymbals,"* and *"clashing cymbals"* (types of percussion instruments). God is to be praised by a symphony of sound (vv. 3–5). Today we could legitimately add our own musical instruments to the list. There has been some controversy over introducing more than the organ into public worship, or even—in some cases—introducing the organ itself. This, however, is a matter of culture and taste rather than spirituality. Everything that evokes praise or expresses praise is a legitimate instrument of praise and therefore relevant for the culture and the people using it. An important step today in bringing the next generation into the church has been the introduction of guitars, electronic instruments, and drums into current praise. The issue is not what instruments we use; the issue is why we use them and how we use them.

Our voices lifted in praise are to be accompanied by instruments of praise. Moreover, we are also to *"dance"* (v. 4). In the liturgical renewal movement, sacred dance has been welcomed in experimental worship. This is not to be despised. The freedom to express ourselves physically in worship is important, whether through dance, raised hands, or kneeling benches. The real issues are whether such dance comes from the heart, is Spirit-led (rather than for show), and is appropriate to the gathering. Furthermore, is it presented as an offering to almighty God? I recall a young man from a former congregation. During the extended worship of the evening service, when the praise songs became instruments of joy and clapping, he would begin to dance at the side of the sanctuary, where few noticed him. He danced with joy, like a child, before the Lord. As I watched him I thought two things. The first was that I was glad that there was a church where he could express himself in this way. The second was that his heavenly Father must have delighted in this expression of himself before His throne.

As this psalm and the Psalter concludes, there is a final exhortation, which refers us back to verse 1: *"Let everything that has breath praise the Lord."* The animals have breath; they are to praise the Lord. The birds have breath; they are to praise the Lord. Humans have breath; they are to praise the Lord. This is the purpose of breath—the spirit (*rûaḥ*) which God breathed into us (Gen. 2:7). We are to breathe it back to Him in praise as we offer the essence of our life up to Him. Indeed, as the psalm ends, *"Praise the Lord!"*